For Reference

Not to be taken from this room

Date: 7/8/13

REF 917.303 HIS 2013
Historic documents.

Historic Documents of 2011

Historic Documents of 2011

Heather Kerrigan, Editor

Includes Cumulative Index, 2007–2011

Los Angeles | London | New Delhi
Singapore | Washington DC

Los Angeles | London | New Delhi
Singapore | Washington DC

FOR INFORMATION:

SAGE Publications, Inc.
2455 Teller Road
Thousand Oaks, California 91320
E-mail: order@sagepub.com

SAGE Publications Ltd.
1 Oliver's Yard
55 City Road
London EC1Y 1SP
United Kingdom

SAGE Publications India Pvt. Ltd.
B 1/I 1 Mohan Cooperative Industrial Area
Mathura Road, New Delhi 110 044
India

SAGE Publications Asia-Pacific Pte. Ltd.
3 Church Street
#10-04 Samsung Hub
Singapore 049483

Developmental Editor: Andrew Boney
Managing Editor: Heather Kerrigan
Contributors: Brian Beary, Anastazia
Clouting, Hilary Ewing,
Linda Fecteau, Melissa
Feinberg, Heather Kerrigan,
Michael D. Mosettig
Editorial Intern: Josh Benjamin
Production Editor: Brittany Bauhaus
Copy Editors: Taryn Bigelow, Alan J. Cook
Typesetter: C&M Digitals (P) Ltd.
Proofreader: Theresa Kay
Indexer: Enid L. Zafran

Printed in the United States of America

A catalog record of this book is available from the Library of Congress.

9781452225364

This book is printed on acid-free paper.

SFI® Certified Sourcing
www.sfiprogram.org
SFI-00453

12 13 14 15 16 10 9 8 7 6 5 4 3 2 1

Contents

JANUARY

FEBRUARY

MARCH

APRIL

MAY

JUNE

JULY

AUGUST

SEPTEMBER

OCTOBER

NOVEMBER

DECEMBER

Thematic Table of Contents

GOVERNMENT AND POLITICS

HEALTH AND SOCIAL SERVICES

INTERNATIONAL AFFAIRS

Africa

INTERNATIONAL AFFAIRS
Asia

INTERNATIONAL AFFAIRS
Europe

INTERNATIONAL AFFAIRS
Latin America and the Caribbean

INTERNATIONAL AFFAIRS
Middle East

INTERNATIONAL AFFAIRS
Russia and Former Soviet Republics

INTERNATIONAL AFFAIRS
Global Issues

NATIONAL SECURITY AND TERRORISM

RIGHTS, RESPONSIBILITIES, AND JUSTICE

List of Document Sources

CONGRESS

EXECUTIVE DEPARTMENTS, AGENCIES, AND COMMISSIONS

INTERNATIONAL GOVERNMENTAL ORGANIZATIONS

JUDICIARY

NONGOVERNMENTAL ORGANIZATIONS

NON–U.S. GOVERNMENTS

U.S. STATE AND LOCAL GOVERNMENTS

WHITE HOUSE AND THE PRESIDENT

Preface

Major political upheavals across North Africa and the Middle East, a devastating earthquake and tsunami in Japan, contentious debates on the American deficit and economy, the killing of Osama bin Laden, continuing economic crisis in the European Union, and significant Supreme Court rulings on the First Amendment, class action suits, prison overcrowding, and climate change are just a few of the topics of national and international significance chosen for discussion in *Historic Documents of 2011*. This edition marks the fortieth volume of a CQ Press project that began with *Historic Documents of 1972*. This series allows students, librarians, journalists, scholars, and others to research and understand the most important domestic and foreign issues and events of the year through primary source documents. To aid research, many of the lengthy documents written for specialized audiences have been excerpted to highlight the most important sections. The official statements, news conferences, speeches, special studies, and court decisions presented here should be of lasting public and academic interest.

Historic Documents of 2011 opens with an "Overview of 2011," a sweeping narrative of the key events and issues of the year that provides context for the documents that follow. The balance of the book is organized chronologically, with each article comprising an introduction entitled "Document in Context" and one or more related documents on a specific event, issue, or topic. Often an event is not limited to a particular day. Consequently, readers will find that some events include multiple documents that may span several months. Their placement in the book corresponds to the date of the first document included for that event. The event introductions provide context and an account of further developments during the year. A thematic table of contents (p. xvii) and a list of documents organized by source (p. xxi) follow the standard table of contents and assist readers in locating events and documents.

As events, issues, and consequences become more complex and far reaching, these introductions and documents yield important information and deepen understanding about the world's increasing interconnectedness. As memories of current events fade, these selections will continue to further understanding of the events and issues that have shaped the lives of people around the world.

How to Use This Book

Each of the 70 entries in this edition consists of two parts: a comprehensive introduction followed by one or more primary source documents. The articles are arranged in chronological order by month. Articles with multiple documents are placed according to the date of the first document. There are several ways to find events and documents of interest:

By date: If the approximate date of an event or document is known, browse through the titles for that month in the table of contents. Alternatively, browse the monthly tables of contents that appear at the beginning of each month's articles.

By theme: To find a particular topic or subject area, browse the thematic table of contents.

By document type or source: To find a particular type of document or document source, such as the White House or Congress, review the list of document sources.

By index: The five-year index allows researchers to locate references to specific events or documents as well as entries on the same or related subjects. The index in this volume covers the years 2007–2011. An online edition of this volume, as well as an archive going back to 1972, is available and offers advanced search and browse functionality.

Each article begins with a section entitled "Document in Context." This feature provides historical and intellectual context for the documents that follow. Documents are reproduced with the original spelling, capitalization, and punctuation of the original or official copy. Ellipsis points indicate textual omissions (unless they were present in the documents themselves indicating pauses in speech), and brackets are used for editorial insertions within documents for text clarification. The excerpting of Supreme Court opinions has been done somewhat differently from other documents. In-text references and citations to laws and other cases have been removed when not part of a sentence to improve the readability of opinions. In those documents, readers will only find ellipses used when sections of narrative text have been removed.

Full citations appear at the end of each document. If a document is not available on the Internet, this too is noted. For further reading on a particular topic, consult the "Other Historic Documents of Interest" section at the end of each article. These boxes provide cross-references for related articles in this edition of *Historic Documents* as well as in previous editions. References to articles from past volumes include the year and page number for easy retrieval.

Overview of 2011

The year 2011 was characterized by continuing global economic distress, historic civil unrest in the Middle East, and domestic policy struggles in the U.S. When President Barack Obama took the podium for his January 2011 State of the Union address, he made clear that the year would be dominated more by political bickering than substantial work on the issues plaguing the nation, including continued unemployment, a slow-growing economy, and rising debt, by making few new spending and program proposals. With Republicans gaining control in the U.S. House of Representatives, and narrowing the Democratic majority in the Senate in the 2010 midterm elections, passage of any bill required extensive political negotiations. This was evident as Republicans and Democrats in the House and Senate nearly failed to reach a compromise on the FY2012 budget, which would have led to a government shutdown, and came close to failing to reach an agreement on raising the debt ceiling before the United States defaulted. Both chambers failed to reach a consensus on how to handle U.S. debt while also encouraging economic growth and job creation, and it is likely that most difficult decisions will be left until after the 2012 presidential and Congressional elections.

Internationally, 2011 brought the overthrow of autocratic rulers and hints of reform in the Middle East, and continued financial hardship, especially in Europe. The Arab Spring dominated headlines with anti-government demonstrations that took place across Africa and the Middle East calling for economic equality, the end of corruption in government, and political reform. Demonstrations took place in Tunisia, Bahrain, Egypt, Jordan, Syria, Yemen, and Libya, with minor uprisings occurring in a number of other nations. By the end of 2011, the movements brought down the leaders of Egypt, Tunisia, and Libya. In Europe, the focus was on Greece's continued financial distress and its impact on the overall stability of the monetary union. EU leaders were forced to extend another bailout to the country and subsequently agreed to a Fiscal Treaty that would require all nations to cap their debt or risk hefty fines.

GLOBAL ECONOMICS

Although the global economic downturn continued to slow in 2011, no nation had completely recovered. In the United States, January 2011 opened with bright economic news of decreasing unemployment and rising payrolls, but quickly turned into a rollercoaster ride as the stock market experienced drastic rises and falls and consumer confidence continued to waver. The U.S. Census Bureau reported that the nation's poverty rate hit its highest level in seventeen years in 2010, with poverty rising across all sectors of the American population. A supplemental poverty report released by the bureau in November, which took into account social service benefits, medical care expenses, and payroll taxes, and also accounted for the cost of living in different parts of the country and whether a person rents or owns a home, found 49.1 million Americans living in poverty, making the economic landscape in the United States worse than the official measure had shown. Both reports found evidence that government investments made to expand unemployment insurance, food stamps, and other welfare benefit programs had a significant impact on a number of Americans.

Two reports released in 2011 established the cause of the financial collapse of 2007–2009. The Financial Crisis Inquiry Commission released the first official government review of the crisis, and found that it was caused by widespread financial regulation failure, too many risky business practices at financial firms, excessive borrowing, little preparation or knowledge on how to deal with a financial crisis, and a lack of ethics and accountability. According to the report, the financial sector and government watchdogs ignored warning signs of an impending fiscal crisis, and placed too much faith in financial markets to correct themselves. The Senate Permanent Subcommittee on Investigations released its own report that described reckless business practices that led to the financial crisis and were ignored by banks and federal regulators. Both reports expressed concern that without significant changes in government oversight and corporate responsibility, a repeat financial crisis could occur.

Anger over the lack of accountability in the financial sector and growing gap between the rich and poor manifested itself in the fall of 2011 in the Occupy Wall Street protests that began in New York City and spread across the country and around the world. The protesters, who set up camps where they lived for months, called themselves "the 99 percent," harkening to a federal report showing a concentration of America's wealth among the top one percent of income earners. The protesters decried corporate greed and social inequality and made demands ranging from the wealthy paying their fair share of taxes to banks being held accountable for their role in the financial crisis to more government intervention to aid the jobless.

In Europe, one year after austerity measures and bailouts drew public ire, leaders were again faced with growing debt. Greece was the year's biggest challenge, and it was put to European leaders to find a way to save the nation from default and financial collapse, and in turn protect the monetary union from significant damage. In July, EU member nations agreed to restructure Greece's debts by lowering interest rates and giving the nation more time to pay back what it had borrowed. Although the July agreement gave an initial boost to the Greek economy, as the year went on, the country's debts continued piling up and the government collapsed as citizens took to the streets protesting the spending cuts made to public programs.

In December, EU leaders met again to not only decide how to handle the situation in Greece but also to formulate a Fiscal Compact that would help avoid future financial crises. The Fiscal Compact, agreed to by most member nations, included a stipulation that EU governments keep structural deficits below 0.5 percent of gross domestic product (GDP), with an automatic fine levied for any government exceeding the 3 percent deficit limit. It additionally created a $930 billion bailout fund for future financial distress. The United Kingdom did not agree to the Fiscal Compact, fearing further infringement on its sovereignty by the European Union, and the Czech Republic also declined to be party to the deal.

DOMESTIC AFFAIRS

The large number of Republican victories at the state level during the 2010 midterm elections brought a number of fiscally conservative leaders to office. With state revenue still well below its 2008 peak, when governors delivered their State of the State addresses in early 2011, few ambitious agendas were announced; the focus instead was on continuing to cut back. Constitutional requirements for states to balance their budgets forced difficult financial decisions on state leaders. Many chose to make significant spending cuts in education, health care, unemployment compensation, and services for the elderly and disabled. Some states coupled these cutbacks with tax hikes.

The difficult economic decisions pitted a number of governors and legislators against each other and the public. Minnesota's governor and legislature could not reach a consensus on how to close the state's $5 billion budget gap in the biennial budget, leading to a two-week shutdown of state government in July. In Wisconsin, newly elected Governor Scott Walker, a Republican, proposed a budget bill for 2011 that required additional contributions from state employees to their pensions and health care plans and included provisions that would restrict collective bargaining rights. Unions and Democratic politicians from across the country called the move an assault on public employee rights, and Wisconsin's Democratic state senators fled to Illinois to prevent Republicans from having a quorum for a vote on the bill. Republican lawmakers worked around the need for a quorum by stripping all spending provisions from the budget bill and instead voted to pass a revised version that kept the collective bargaining restrictions intact. The union fight in Wisconsin prompted nine recall elections for members of the state Assembly and Senate. A recall election for Governor Walker was set for June 5, 2012.

It was against this politically charged backdrop that the 2012 Republican presidential primary race got underway. From early 2011, a large pool of contenders jockeyed for front-runner status and the right to take on President Obama in the November 2012 general election. Hot-button issues for the candidates included creating jobs, rebuilding the U.S. economy, and social issues like abortion and gay marriage. It was not until December that the field narrowed to the four most likely candidates: former Pennsylvania Senator Rick Santorum, former Massachusetts Governor Mitt Romney, former Speaker of the House Newt Gingrich, and Texas Representative Ron Paul.

In the White House, the president grappled with the ongoing impact of the wars in Iraq and Afghanistan. More than eight years after it began, the war in Iraq came to an end just before Christmas when the last group of 50,000 soldiers departed the country. A small contingent of 200 service members remained in Iraq to protect the U.S. embassy in Baghdad. With the U.S. troop presence ended, the question became what role America would continue to play in the country.

September 2011 marked the ten-year anniversary of American troop presence in Afghanistan, and public opinion of the war reached its lowest level. Throughout the year, the United States and its coalition partners began making plans for an accelerated troop withdrawal to begin in 2011 and conclude by 2014. As the international community debated the best methods and timeline for a troop withdrawal, the Taliban was making a slow comeback and it was readily apparent that Afghanistan was still struggling to take control of its own security and did not yet have the governance structures in place to ensure the democratic reforms the international community hoped to see. By the end of 2011, 10,000 U.S. troops had left Afghanistan.

After nearly ten years of unsuccessful attempts to locate and capture the man considered responsible for planning the September 11 attacks on the United States, in the early morning hours of May 1, a Navy SEAL team raided the Pakistan compound of Osama bin Laden, killing the al Qaeda leader. The location of bin Laden's compound in Pakistan raised questions about whether Pakistan had been supporting the terrorist leader while he was in hiding, and left open the question of the ongoing relationship between the United States and Pakistan.

CONGRESSIONAL ACTION

As Republicans and Democrats squabbled on the House and Senate floor over national debt and spending, political leaders and the public were reexamining civil discourse in the United States. The impact of inflammatory language used by politicians and opinion leaders, and the anti-government sentiment gripping the country was brought to the forefront on January 8, 2011, when an assassination attempt was made on Rep. Gabrielle Giffords, D-Ariz., as she spoke with constituents. Six people were killed in the incident and Giffords was shot in the head. Despite having a bullet penetrate her brain, Giffords made a recovery that doctors consistently referred to as miraculous, but resigned her seat in Congress in January 2012.

Despite being partway through the fiscal year, early 2011 was dominated by a deadlock on the fiscal year 2011 federal budget. Thus far, the government had been kept operational by a series of temporary spending measures. In mid-February, the House of Representatives passed a budget that included $61 billion in spending cuts, but the Senate, backed by President Obama, refused to vote on the bill. April 8 marked the deadline for the FY2011 budget or another continuing resolution to be passed, and in the weeks leading up to this deadline protracted negotiations took place at the White House between members of both parties. Just hours before the deadline, both the House and Senate agreed to a budget that would cut $38.5 billion in spending, the largest non-defense cut in U.S. history.

On May 16, the United States officially reached its debt ceiling, the cap that limits the amount of money the government can borrow. The secretary of the treasury, Timothy Geithner, said that he would be able to stop the government from defaulting until at least August 2, but both he and the president encouraged Congress to act quickly to raise the debt ceiling. Republicans and Democrats argued not only over whether it would be prudent to raise the debt ceiling in the current economic environment, but also over what impact a default would have. With the clock ticking on the August 2 deadline, leaders from both parties met at the White House, where on July 31, they reached a bipartisan agreement to raise the debt ceiling while making $2.4 trillion in spending cuts over the next decade. Despite the agreement, on August 5, credit rating agency Standard & Poor's downgraded the U.S. rating to AA+, one notch below the highest possible score. The downgrade was mostly symbolic, but the agency announced that if the United States did not take additional steps to deal with its ever-growing deficit, another downgrade was possible.

As part of the debt ceiling agreement, the House and Senate formed a congressional super committee, formally known as the Joint Select Committee on Deficit Reduction, tasked with finding $1.2 trillion of the $2.4 trillion in cuts. If the group failed to make recommendations for cuts, or if Congress failed to pass the recommendations, $1.2 trillion in automatic cuts would be made in January 2013 to military spending, education, transportation, and Medicare payments. Republicans and Democrats on the twelve-member committee made numerous proposals on how to make the necessary cuts, but in the end could not reach an agreement that made Republicans, who wanted to avoid tax cuts, and Democrats, who wanted to preserve entitlement spending, happy. On November 21, the committee announced that after three months of work, it had failed to reach a consensus, thus triggering the automatic future cuts.

In late 2011, a heated debate took place in the House and Senate over the extension of payroll tax cuts first established in 2010 that were set to expire in March 2012. The battle hinged on how to pay for continuing the extension. Democrats proposed raising taxes on high-income earners, which Republicans opposed. Unable to reach an agreement by the end of December to extend the tax cuts for a full year, the House and Senate agreed to a two-month extension that would give them time when they returned from recess in January to continue debating the measure. It was not until February 17, 2012, when the House and Senate agreed to extend the tax cut that impacted 160 million mostly middle-class Americans. In the compromise bill, cuts were made to federal health care programs and government pensions to help cover spending increases, new limits were put on unemployment compensation, and cuts were made to preventative health care spending mandated by the Affordable Care Act of 2010.

SUPREME COURT DECISIONS

In 2011, the U.S. Supreme Court handed down a number of important decisions on topics ranging from First Amendment rights and methods to curb illegal immigration to pharmaceuticals and greenhouse gas emissions. The Court heard two major First Amendment cases during the year. The first, *Snyder v. Phelps,* dealt with the small Westboro Baptist Church that actively protests the funerals of soldiers killed in action with picket signs bearing messages such as "Thank God for Dead Soldiers" and "God Hates Fags." The case against the church was brought by the father of fallen soldier Matthew Snyder who claimed he had been emotionally harmed by seeing these protesters near his son's funeral. In an 8–1 decision, the Court ruled that the First Amendment of the Constitution protected the right of the Westboro Baptist Church to picket the Snyder's funeral. Writing for the majority, Chief Justice John Roberts made clear that the First Amendment cannot be used to punish a speaker for pain inflicted by the speech, and that "the government may not prohibit the expression of an idea simply because society finds the idea itself offensive or disagreeable." Following the ruling, the Westboro Baptist Church promised to continue picketing military funerals at an increased rate.

Another First Amendment case that drew public attention was that of *Brown v. Entertainment Merchants Association* in which the Court ruled 7–2 on June 27, 2011, to overturn a California law that prohibited violent video games from being sold or rented to children. Four different opinions were issued with the ruling, highlighting the difficulty justices had in reaching a conclusion in a case that pits constitutional principles that are hundreds of years old against the newer technology of video gaming.

Congressional inaction on stronger immigration laws has prompted a number of states to take action to curb the influx of illegal Hispanic immigrants. In 2011, an Arizona statute with this aim landed on the Court's docket. In *Chamber of Commerce v. Whiting,* the Court reviewed a state law that allowed for the revocation of business licenses from companies found to knowingly hire illegal immigrants. The federal government asserted that it held the upper hand in illegal immigration enforcement, and that its own laws preempt state regulation. On May 26, 2011, a divided Court ruled 5–3 that federal law does not prohibit Arizona from invoking its business license statute. The minority expressed concern that the Court was overstepping the authority given to states by Congress and was setting up an environment ripe for discrimination against people of Hispanic origin. Because federal immigration authority has typically superseded state law, the Court's ruling may open up a loophole and allow for the creation and enforcement of fifty state immigration policies.

On June 20, 2011, the Supreme Court ruled on a class action case against the nation's largest retailer, Wal-Mart. The case was brought by 1.5 million current and former female employees of the company who claimed that they had been discriminated against in wage and promotion decisions. In a 5–4 decision in *Wal-Mart Stores, Inc. v. Dukes*, the Court did not rule on whether discrimination had taken place, but instead determined that the case could not proceed as a class action lawsuit because the parties to the case did not have enough in common to meet the class action threshold. The decision is expected to make it more difficult for employees of any company to prove commonality for a class action case.

The Court also took up the issue of greenhouse gas emissions. On June 20, 2011, the Court ruled unanimously in *American Electric Power Co. v. Connecticut* to block a lawsuit brought by six states, New York City, and three private land trusts claiming that the millions of tons of carbon dioxide released into the atmosphere each year by four power companies and the Tennessee Valley Authority were dangerous and contributed to global warming. Those bringing the suit wanted the Court to put a cap on the carbon dioxide emissions of these companies. Instead, the Court found that it is the role of the Environmental Protection Agency (EPA) to regulate greenhouse gases through the Clean Air Act, and outside of ensuring that the EPA fulfills what is required of it under the Clean Air Act, the Court cannot regulate greenhouse gases.

On June 23, 2011, the Supreme Court ruled for the third time in as many years on federal preemption in state medical labeling lawsuits. In the case of *Pliva v. Mensing*, the Court ruled 5–4 that generic drug companies cannot be sued in state courts for failing to provide labeling that adequately describes side effects because they are bound by Food and Drug Administration (FDA) regulations that require them to use the same label as their brand name counterpart. With the Court's ruling, those harmed by generic drugs now have no judicial recourse through state court, and drug manufacturers will be able to avoid some liability for injury caused by their products.

Foreign Affairs

Internationally, 2011 brought new governments, renewed hope for government reform, and continuing global tensions with nuclear nations. Nigeria, Russia, and the Democratic Republic of the Congo (DRC) all held significant elections in 2011. In Nigeria, where the government shifted from military to democratic rule in 1999, religious and regional divides have continued to spread because of government corruption and competition for natural resource wealth. In 2011, Nigerian President Goodluck Jonathan, a Christian, broke with a tradition that had helped keep religious tension at bay by announcing that he would seek a second term rather than allowing a Muslim president to take office and continue the Muslim-Christian presidential rotation that had been in place since 1999. Jonathan was reelected in April and was met with rioting and escalating violence.

In the DRC, President Joseph Kabila announced in January that he had revised the constitution to elect the president in one round of voting rather than through a runoff system in which one candidate must receive at least 50 percent of the vote. His opponents saw it as a move to ensure a Kabila victory in the 2011 presidential election. Kabila's election campaign was fraught with violence and allegations that his security forces had detained and shot voters who protested the Kabila regime. Despite voting irregularities exposed by international election observers, Kabila was declared the victor on December 9, 2011. Kabila's reelection raised questions about his administration's ability to effectively govern a starkly divided nation.

In Russia, where prime minister and former president Vladimir Putin has dominated the political scene, 2011 brought an unexpected challenge. Putin's party, United Russia, was expected to handily win the December election for the lower house of parliament, the

State Duma, where it held a more than two-thirds majority. However, growing distrust of the party and continued economic hardship, led voters to deal United Russia a significant blow, taking away its opposition-proof majority. Following the election, tens of thousands protested in Russian cities, motivated by allegations of vote fraud during the December 4 Duma vote. The protesters demanded new Duma elections, investigations into election fraud, a more open and transparent political system, and the release of prisoners arrested for protesting. The Duma election and subsequent protests had little impact on Putin, who was elected to a third non-consecutive term as president in March 2012.

The year brought a renewed sense of hope for citizens in Saudi Arabia and South Sudan. South Sudan gained independence from Sudan on July 9, 2011, after fifty-six years of armed struggle. A Comprehensive Peace Agreement from 2005 paved the way for the southern third of Sudan to cede. The agreement allowed for a referendum on separation that was passed by more than 98 percent of voters in January 2011. The new nation, which is led by the Sudanese People's Liberation Movement and President Salva Kiir, will provide new opportunities to investors—the nation holds 75 percent of the former Sudan's oil reserves and is located on abundant land ripe for crop production.

In September 2011, historic changes came to Saudi Arabia when King Abdullah announced that women would be given the right to participate in elections and government in the coming years. The move, provoked by political uprisings in other Arab nations in 2011, was a small step toward greater freedom for females in the kingdom, where their rights remain severely restricted.

International tension over nuclear capabilities in North Korea and Iran dominated headlines once again in 2011. In November, the United Nations's International Atomic Energy Agency (IAEA) released a report on nuclear activity in Iran. The report provided evidence that the nation was not following through on its obligations under the Nuclear Non-Proliferation Treaty (NPT) and was instead continuing its bomb-making program. The report gave no evidence that a nuclear weapon had been completed, but did indicate that weapons research and possible uranium acquisition was ongoing. Although Iran has long claimed that its nuclear program is purely for peaceful, civilian means, the IAEA was unable to confirm that there was no military aim of the program. Iran called the IAEA report "unbalanced, unprofessional," and motivated by political pressure from the United States in an effort to give Israel a case for a preemptive military strike against Iran.

Questions about the ongoing nuclear program in North Korea reached a peak on December 19, 2011, when it was announced that the nation's leader, Kim Jong-il, had died of a heart attack. Following Kim's death, his son, the young and untested Kim Jong-un assumed power, but a full transition is expected to take months or years. The new Kim is expected to rule North Korea in a similar fashion to his father, which leaves in doubt whether the six-party nuclear effort to disarm North Korea will move forward. After Kim's death, it was anticipated that tension would rise between North and South Korea, and there was some expectation that the North might attempt to militarily provoke the South to stave off questions of who is truly in charge in the communist state.

ARAB SPRING

Anti-government demonstrations spread across Africa and the Middle East in 2011, with protesters seeking regime change, democratic reforms, and economic equality. What became known as Arab Spring began in December 2010 in Tunisia when citizens turned to social media and took to the streets of the capital, determined to take down the government of President Zine al-Abidine Ben Ali, who they blamed for economic inequality. Ben Ali responded by firing his government and promising not to run for reelection in 2014. When his promises did not placate the demonstrators, Ben Ali declared a state of emergency. On January 14, the president made the surprising announcement that he would temporarily step down from his post. He subsequently fled the country, ending his twenty-three year reign.

Jordanians took to the streets in January protesting rising unemployment and high food and fuel prices. Unlike their counterparts in other Arab Spring nations, the protesters in Jordan were not attempting to topple King Abdullah II's monarchy, but instead sought government reforms that would take away some of the king's power and place it in the hands of a democratically elected body. The protests were largely peaceful, and resulted in few deaths. King Abdullah II responded to the demonstrations by naming a new cabinet and prime minister and promising future electoral reform, but offered little indication of when this might take place.

The pro-democracy movement in Yemen spanned 2011 and went into 2012, as protesters sought to remove President Ali Abdullah Saleh from power. During the demonstrations, Saleh wavered between promising to accept a number of international power transfer deals that were offered and using force against protesters. In November, Saleh consented to an agreement forged by the Gulf Cooperation Council to cede power to his vice president. In signing the agreement, Saleh avoided any future prosecution arising from his treatment of protesters, a point of contention among many anti-government demonstrators. It was not until February 25, 2012, when Saleh formally handed power over to his vice president.

In late January 2011, pro-democracy protesters took to Cairo, Egypt's Tahrir Square to protest the autocratic reign of President Hosni Mubarak. Nearly one million Egyptians participated in the protests, speaking out against government corruption, torture, and unemployment. On February 11, 2011, after weeks of refusing to give up power, Mubarak resigned his position, handing power to the nation's military. Citizen jubilation quickly turned to disdain for the new military regime after its leaders announced that they would remain in control of the nation's government, even after presidential and parliamentary elections took place.

In early 2011, protesters in Syria banded together to speak out against the policies of President Bashar al-Assad, specifically those involving unlawful torture and detention. Protesters called for Assad and his security forces to end one-party rule that had led to widespread corruption. Assad responded with violent crackdowns, allowing force to be used against the protesters, which resulted in the death of at least 3,500 and countless arrests. In response to Assad's crackdown, the protesters turned their demands to the president's removal from office. In response, Assad made a number of promises to reform his government and increase transparency, only to continue the violent crackdowns. In early 2012, the United Nations helped to broker a ceasefire with Assad, which was set to take effect on April 10.

In Bahrain, King Hamad bin Isa Al Khalifa was forced to face Shiite unrest that had been brewing against the Sunni leadership since 2009. In February and March 2011, protesters came to Bahrain's capital, frustrated by housing, education, and employment discrimination against the Shiite majority population. The protesters demanded a constitutional monarchy, an elected government, and the end of gerrymandering that kept Shiites out of government power. The king violently cracked down on protesters under the guise of emergency law. The three-month state of emergency was lifted on June 1, 2011, and by November, still facing unrest despite a heavy police presence, the king established a commission to investigate possible human rights violations during the spring. The commission found evidence of government involvement in many deaths, illegal detentions, and unlawful torture. King Hamad responded by promising to work with his government to institute reforms that he said would help avoid future unrest.

Arab Spring reached Libya in February as protesters called for the overthrow of Col. Muammar el-Qaddafi's four-decade regime. Throughout the spring and summer, Qaddafi defiantly remained in his position while subsequently authorizing his security forces to use any tactic necessary to stop the demonstrations. The anti-government protesters formed armed rebel groups that clashed with Qaddafi forces for control of major cities up and down the coast. Starting in March, UN and North Atlantic Treaty Organization (NATO) member states provided airstrikes in support of the rebel movement aiming to protect civilians from Qaddafi's security forces. The international aid coupled with rebel advances led to the overthrow of Qaddafi and his government in August. On October 20, Qaddafi was killed by his detractors.

—Heather Kerrigan

January

Congressional Response to the Attempted Assassination of Rep. Gabrielle Giffords

JANUARY 8 AND 12, 2011

On January 8, 2011, a local tragedy in Tucson, Arizona, captured the attention of the nation when a gunman opened fire at a constituent event hosted by Rep. Gabrielle Giffords, D-Ariz. In what officials later determined was an assassination attempt, six people were killed and fourteen wounded in the incident. Rep. Giffords herself was shot in the head. The shooting prompted political leaders and ordinary citizens alike to reexamine the state of civil discourse in the United States.

AN ATTEMPTED ASSASSINATION

On the morning of January 8, 2011, Giffords arrived at a Safeway grocery store in Tucson for her "Congress on Your Corner" event, an opportunity for constituents to meet her and share their concerns. Just a few days earlier, Giffords was sworn in for her third term in the House of Representatives since first winning election in 2006. In March 2010, Giffords attracted attention when the windows of her district office in Tucson were broken in an act of vandalism motivated by her support for the passage of health care reform legislation.

On the day of the shootings, Giffords had just begun to meet with local citizens when, shortly after 10:00 a.m. (MST), a man walked past the line of people waiting to see her, pulled out a gun, and shot her in the head before opening fire on the rest of the crowd. There was no security present at the event, and the gunman shot nineteen other individuals before being subdued by several of those in the crowd. Bystander Patricia Maisch grabbed the shooter's second magazine of ammunition as he fumbled to reload his gun, while former military pilot Bill Badger, who was wounded in the attack, forced the shooter to the ground and held him there with the help of Roger Salzgeber and Joseph Zamudio.

Five of the wounded victims sustained fatal injuries and died at the scene: John Roll, chief judge for the U.S. District Court for Arizona and a friend of Giffords's; Dorothy Morris; Phyllis Schneck; Dorwan Stoddard; and Gabriel Zimmerman, Giffords's director of community outreach. Nine-year-old Christina Taylor Green died later at a hospital.

Among the remaining wounded, Giffords was in the most critical condition. The shooter's bullet entered one side of her head and exited out the other after passing through her brain. In a move later credited with helping to save Giffords's life, intern Daniel Hernandez used smocks from the grocery store as a bandage, applying pressure to Giffords's wound to try to stop the bleeding. Giffords was taken to University Medical Center in Tucson and underwent emergency brain surgery immediately after the incident. Doctors removed nearly half of her skull to prevent further damage due to brain swelling and placed Giffords in a medically induced coma. Dr. Peter Rhee, director of the hospital's trauma and critical care unit, later said he was optimistic about her recovery, although he expected it would take months for her to regain her ability to move and speak.

Meanwhile, initial reports of the incident began appearing on local and national media outlets, but many were flawed. National Public Radio (NPR) incorrectly reported during its 2:00 p.m. (EST) newscast that Giffords had been killed. Within half an hour, cable networks were running the same story, with CBS News following shortly thereafter. Around 3:00 p.m., Darci Slaten, a spokesperson for University Medical Center, told CNN she could confirm that Giffords had been shot in the head but was alive and in surgery. Giffords's husband, National Aeronautics and Space Administration (NASA) astronaut Mark Kelly, heard the reports of his wife's death as he made his way from his home in Houston to Tucson, as did Giffords's mother and stepchildren. It was not until he reached one of Giffords's staff members that he learned the reports were false. NPR apologized to the family for their error, but continued to claim their information had come from two different governmental sources, including a contact in the Pima County Sheriff's Office.

THE NATION REACTS

The tragedy in Tucson captured the attention of Americans across the country and drew reactions of sadness and disbelief from leaders in Washington. "An attack on one who serves is an attack on all who serve," said House Speaker John Boehner, R-Ohio. "Acts and threats of violence against public officials have no place in our society. . . . This is a sad day for our country," he continued. Sen. John McCain, R-Ariz., issued a strongly worded statement condemning the actions of the shooter. "I am horrified by the violent attack on Representative Gabrielle Giffords and many other innocent people by a wicked person who has no sense of justice or compassion. . . . Whoever did this, whatever their reason, they are a disgrace to Arizona, this country and the human race," McCain said. President Barack Obama acknowledged that Giffords was "as tough as they come" and promised that "we're going to get to the bottom of this, and we're going to get through this."

Federal Bureau of Investigation (FBI) Director Robert Mueller traveled to Arizona to begin an investigation of the incident, while U.S. Capitol Police launched their own investigation and concluded there was no evidence to suggest a broader threat to federal officials. Capitol Police cautioned all lawmakers to "take reasonable and prudent precautions regarding their personal security," and urged them to contact local police in their respective districts to register their home and office addresses to further enhance their safety. Capitol Police Chief Phillip Morse, FBI officials, and other congressional security staff held a conference call with members of Congress, their staff, and spouses the day following the shooting to discuss their personal safety and security matters. During the call, Speaker Boehner asked House Sergeant at Arms Wilson Livingood, along with Capitol Police and the FBI, to conduct "an in-depth security overview" of the security of members of Congress, and arranged for the same officials to brief congressional staff in district offices around the country on advisable security measures. Several members of Congress began calling for increased security measures at home and in the Capitol Building. Rep. Jesse Jackson, Jr., D-Ill., urged his colleagues to approve an increased House budget that would allow for augmented security measures, including the installation of surveillance cameras in district offices, while Rep. Dan Burton, R-Ind., called for the installation of a security shield around the viewing gallery overlooking the House floor. Yet others denied that increased protection was necessary and argued that it would hamper the country's tradition of accessibility to lawmakers. Furthermore, the House seemed unlikely to approve funding for increased personal security measures. As of 2011, congressional security policy remains unchanged.

In addition to heightening security concerns, the Tucson incident focused the country's attention on the heated political rhetoric that had become a key element of civil discourse in the United States since the introduction of health care reform legislation in 2009. Many questioned whether the inflammatory language, antigovernment sentiment, and implicit instigations to violence used by various opinion leaders and on prominent display during nationwide health care–focused town halls and Tea Party rallies were in fact leading to real-life violence. Giffords had previously pointed to former Alaska governor Sarah Palin's use of crosshair graphics on a map of the United States on her Political Action Committee's (PAC) website to denote vulnerable Democratic House districts as a troubling use of violent imagery in political debate. The PAC removed the map from its site shortly after the shooting. The Arizona Tea Party was also quick to distance itself from the attack. "I want to strongly, strongly say we absolutely do not advocate violence," said DeAnn Hatch, cofounder of the Tucson Tea Party.

The Republican leadership in the House postponed all legislation scheduled for consideration on the floor the week of the shooting, but did pass a resolution on January 12 condemning the attack and offering condolences to the families and friends of the victims. The resolution also reaffirmed the House's "belief in a democracy in which all can participate and in which intimidation and threats of violence cannot silence the voices of any Americans."

SHOOTER IDENTIFIED

Officials identified twenty-two-year-old Jared Lee Loughner as the alleged shooter in the Tucson incident. Authorities initially suspected Loughner had been aided by an accomplice, but determined the man in question was a taxi driver who had merely brought him to Giffords's event. Loughner was taken into FBI custody on January 8, but refused to cooperate with authorities and invoked his Fifth Amendment rights. Officials later seized evidence from Loughner's home indicating the shooting was a preplanned assassination attempt and confirming Giffords as the target. He was charged with five federal counts the following day, including first-degree murder and attempted assassination of a member of Congress. Loughner would ultimately face forty-nine separate charges once state-level charges were filed.

Loughner had previously been suspended from Tucson's Pima Community College in September 2010 after five instances of classroom or library disruptions in which campus police were called. School officials said Loughner could only be readmitted if he received psychological counseling. In the months preceding the shooting, Loughner created a series of Internet postings, including at least one showing a gun, and several videos. Reuters described his work as "a rambling Internet manifesto" that accused the U.S. government of brainwashing and mind control, and called for the establishment of a new currency. Friends described a "twisted" sense of humor and an obsession for conspiracy theories, and Loughner had several run-ins with local law enforcement related to possession of drug paraphernalia.

Following a preliminary hearing in January, U.S. District Judge Larry Burns ruled on May 25 that Loughner was not fit to stand trial based on two court-ordered mental evaluations that diagnosed Loughner with paranoid schizophrenia and concluded that he would be unable to assist in his own defense. Instead, he was taken into custody of the U.S. attorney general and hospitalized at a Springfield, Missouri, facility for further evaluation and treatment. At Loughner's second court date on September 28, Judge Burns ruled Loughner could be made mentally fit to stand trial, claiming that "measurable progress has been made" in restoring him to the point where he could partake in his defense. Burns also ruled that facility officials could continue forcibly medicating Loughner with psychotropic drugs and extended his detention for a further four months.

Loughner's mental illness and ability to legally acquire a gun at a local Sportsman's Warehouse served to reignite the debate surrounding gun control issues. Several legislators raised the possibility of reinstating a federal ban on high-capacity magazines, like the one purchased by Loughner, which enable shooters to fire more than thirty bullets in a matter of seconds without having to reload. Others noted that mental illness by itself is not a disqualification for purchasing firearms under Arizona or federal law, and questioned whether additional measures might be necessary to prevent another incident similar to the Tucson shooting.

A REMARKABLE RECOVERY

Throughout the spring and summer of 2011, Giffords's doctors continually marveled at the speed of her recovery. On January 12, Giffords opened her eyes for the first time, was able to move her legs and hands shortly thereafter, and was able to stand without assistance eleven days after the shooting. On January 26, Giffords was transferred to the Institute for Rehabilitation and Research at Houston's Memorial Hermann Hospital (TIRR Memorial Hermann), a rehabilitation facility specializing in brain injuries. She was able to attend the launch of the Space Shuttle *Endeavour* in May, a mission led by her husband. Giffords was discharged from TIRR Memorial Hermann on June 15 in what the hospital described as a "major milestone." Giffords continued to receive outpatient care at the Houston home owned by her husband, and conducted daily physical therapy sessions focused on simple activities such as sitting up, walking, getting dressed, and bathing. By November, Giffords was once again able to talk and smile, and helped serve Thanksgiving dinner to airmen and retirees at the Davis-Monthan Air Force Base in Tucson.

—Linda Fecteau

Following is a statement from Rep. Gabriel Giffords's office in regard to the shooting in Tucson, Arizona, released on January 8, 2011; the full text of House Resolution 32, engrossed in the House on January 12, 2011, recognizing the victims and condemning the actions of the Tucson attack; and three statements delivered on the House floor on January 12, 2011, by representatives John Boehner, Nancy Pelosi, and Ed Pastor, in regard to the Tucson shooting.

Statement From the Office of Rep. Gabrielle Giffords, D-Ariz., on the Tucson Shooting

January 8, 2011

An unthinkable tragedy occurred at our Congress on Your Corner event today in Tucson. Our community has lost beloved friends and colleagues, and many more are injured. Our hearts and prayers go out to all of them and to those who are suffering the loss of treasured friends and family members.

Congresswoman Giffords is dedicated to serving the people of Southern Arizona. It was in this spirit that our office organized today's event. We will make further statements as details become available. We offer thanks to the law enforcement, first responders, and medical personnel who work to save lives and mend the injured.

SOURCE: Office of Democratic Whip Steny Hoyer. "A Statement From U.S. Representative Gabrielle Giffords' Chief of Staff, Pia Carusone." January 8, 2011. http://www.democraticwhip.gov/issues/tragedy-tucson-arizona.

House Resolution 32 on the Tucson, Arizona, Shooting

January 12, 2011

Whereas on January 8, 2011, an armed gunman opened fire at a 'Congress on your Corner' event hosted by Representative Gabrielle Giffords in Tucson, Arizona, killing 6 and wounding at least 14 others;

Whereas Christina Taylor Green, Dorothy Morris, John Roll, Phyllis Schneck, Dorwan Stoddard, and Gabriel Zimmerman lost their lives in this attack;

Whereas Christina Taylor Green, the 9-year-old daughter of John and Roxanna Green, was born on September 11, 2001, and was a third grader with an avid interest in government who was recently elected to the student council at Mesa Verde Elementary School;

Whereas Dorothy Morris, who was 76 years old, attended the January 8 event with George, her husband of over 50 years with whom she had 2 daughters, and who was also critically injured as he tried to shield her from the shooting;

Whereas John Roll, a Pennsylvania native who was 63 years old, began his professional career as a bailiff in 1972, was appointed to the Federal bench in 1991, and became chief judge for the District of Arizona in 2006, and was a devoted husband to his wife Maureen, father to his 3 sons, and grandfather to his 5 grandchildren;

Whereas Phyllis Schneck, a proud mother of 3, grandmother of 7, and great-grand-mother from New Jersey, was spending the winter in Arizona, and was a 79-year-old church volunteer and New York Giants fan;

Whereas Dorwan Stoddard, a 76-year-old retired construction worker and volunteer at the Mountain Avenue Church of Christ, is credited with shielding his wife Mavy, a longtime friend whom he married while they were in their 60s, who was also injured in the shooting;

Whereas Gabriel Matthew Zimmerman, who was 30 years old and engaged to be married, served as Director of Community Outreach to Representative Gabrielle Giffords, and was a social worker before serving with Representative Giffords;

Whereas Representative Gabrielle Giffords was a target of this attack, and remains in critical condition at an Arizona hospital;

Whereas 13 others were also wounded in the shooting, including Ron Barber and Pamela Simon, both staffers to Representative Giffords; and

Whereas several individuals, including Patricia Maisch, Army Col. Bill Badger (Retired), who was also wounded in the shooting, Roger Sulzgeber, Joseph Zimudio, and Daniel Hernandez, Jr., helped apprehend the gunman and assist the injured, thereby risking their lives for the safety of others, and should be commended for their bravery: Now, therefore, be it

Resolved, That the House of Representatives—

(1) condemns in the strongest possible terms the horrific attack which occurred at the 'Congress on your Corner' event hosted by Representative Gabrielle Giffords in Tucson, Arizona, on January 8, 2011;

(2) offers its heartfelt condolences to the families, friends, and loved ones of those who were killed in that attack;

(3) expresses its hope for the rapid and complete recovery of those wounded in the shooting;

(4) honors the memory of Christina Taylor Green, Dorothy Morris, John Roll, Phyllis Schneck, Dorwan Stoddard, and Gabriel Zimmerman;

(5) applauds the bravery and quick thinking exhibited by those individuals who prevented the gunman from potentially taking more lives and helped to save those who had been wounded;

(6) recognizes the service of the first responders who raced to the scene and the health care professionals who tended to the victims once they reached the hospital, whose service and skill saved lives;

(7) reaffirms the bedrock principle of American democracy and representative government, which is memorialized in the First Amendment of the Constitution and which Representative Gabrielle Giffords herself read in the Hall of the House of Representatives on January 6, 2011, of 'the right of the people peaceably to assemble, and to petition the Government for a redress of grievances';

(8) stands firm in its belief in a democracy in which all can participate and in which intimidation and threats of violence cannot silence the voices of any American;

(9) honors the service and leadership of Representative Gabrielle Giffords, a distinguished member of this House, as she courageously fights to recover; and

(10) when adjourning today, shall do so out of respect to the victims of this attack.

SOURCE: U.S. House of Representatives. "Expressing the Sense of the House of Representatives With Respect to the Tragic Shooting in Tucson, Arizona, on January 8, 2011." *Congressional Record* 2011, H. Res. 32. January 12, 2011. http://www.gpo.gov/fdsys/pkg/BILLS-112hres32eh/pdf/BILLS-112hres32eh.pdf.

DOCUMENT

Rep. John Boehner, R-Ohio, on the Shooting in Tucson, Arizona

January 12, 2011

Madam Speaker and my colleagues, today we are called here to mourn. An unspeakable act of violence has taken six innocent lives, and left several more—including our colleague, GABRIELLE GIFFORDS—battling for theirs. These are difficult hours for our country.

Among the fallen is Gabe Zimmerman, a member of Congresswoman GIFFORDS' staff—a public servant of the highest caliber—one of our own. Even in our shock, we are composed and determined to fulfill our calling to represent our constituents. This is the great cause for which Gabe gave his life.

Like us, Gabe swore an oath to uphold and defend the Constitution. At the time of the attack, he was engaged in the most simple and direct of democratic rituals: listening to the people, listening to his neighbors.

The brutality that shattered Saturday morning's calm was devastating, but brief. Bravery and quick thinking prevented a larger massacre, turning innocent bystanders into heroes.

The service and skill of first responders and medical professionals saved lives. Law enforcement officials are working to ensure swift justice. Look to Tucson right now, and you will be reminded that America's most plentiful source of wealth and strength is her people.

We are so thankful GABBY is still with us. We are so thankful that two of her staffers who were also wounded—Ron Barber and Pam Simon—are still with us as well.

In her stead, GABBY's staff has pressed on, opening for business Monday morning right on schedule. The men and women who faithfully serve the people of Arizona's 8th Congressional District have signaled that no act—no matter how heinous—will stop us from doing our duty and being among the people we serve.

To all of the dedicated professionals that we rely on to make this institution work, to each of you: thank you for what you do. And to GABBY's staff—and their families: please know that our hearts and prayers go out to each of you.

This body has yet to fully register the magnitude of this tragedy. We feel a litany of unwanted emotions no resolution could possibly capture.

We know that we gather here without distinction of party. The needs of this institution have always risen above partisanship. And what this institution needs right now is strength— holy, uplifting strength. The strength to grieve with the families of the fallen, to pray for the wounded, and to chart a way forward, no matter how painful and difficult it may be.

Today it is not ceremony, but tragedy that stirs us to renew our commitment to faithfully fulfill our oath of office. Let us not let this inhuman act frighten us into doing otherwise.

The free exchange of ideas is the lifeblood of our democracy, as prescribed by the First Amendment, that beacon of free expression Congresswoman GIFFORDS recited in this well just days ago.

These rights have not been handed down by dictate; they have been preserved and protected through generations of hard sacrifice and commitment. We will continue that unfinished work.

We will do it for Christina Taylor Green, Dorothy Morris, Phyllis Schneck, and Dorwan Stoddard, ordinary citizens who died participating in their democracy. And we will do it for Judge John Roll. And we will do it for Gabe Zimmerman. And we will do it for—and God willing, with—GABRIELLE GIFFORDS.

Our hearts are broken, but our spirit is not. This is a time for the House to lock arms in prayer for those fallen and the wounded, and in resolve to carry on the dialogue of democracy.

We may not yet have all the answers, but we already have the answer that matters most: that we are Americans, and together we will make it through this difficult period. We will have the last word.

God bless this House. God bless this Congress. And God bless America.

SOURCE: Rep. John Boehner. "Expressing Sense of House Regarding Arizona Shooting." *Congressional Record* 2011, 157 pt. H144-H145. http://www.gpo.gov/fdsys/pkg/CREC-2011-01-12/pdf/CREC-2011-01-12-pt1-PgH144.pdf.

Rep. Nancy Pelosi, D-Calif., Responds to the Tragedy in Arizona

January 12, 2011

Madam Speaker, I thank the gentleman for yielding, and extend my condolences to him, Mr. PASTOR, the senior member of the Arizona delegation, and to all of the members of the Arizona delegation.

Madam Speaker, I am saddened, greatly saddened, to join the Speaker of the House, Mr. BOEHNER, in coming together in sadness today to share our prayers and indeed our hopes for those who have lost so much because of the tragedy in Arizona involving our colleague, Congresswoman GABBY GIFFORDS, her staff, and innocent bystanders.

Words are inadequate at a time like this, but I hope it is a comfort to those who have lost loved ones or who were injured on Saturday that so many people mourn the losses but also pray for the survivors and care for them at this very difficult time.

I think the resolution in its description of what happened and the context with which it happened is an excellent resolution; and I hope people will read it, pray over it, and be grateful that we have this opportunity to comment on it.

Today, we will say many prayers for our country and for the victims of this horrific event. We think of our colleague, Congresswoman GABBY GIFFORDS, fighting to recover, and the 14 others who were injured and remember the six who were killed. Their names are mentioned, and they are described in the resolution. The Speaker has mentioned their names, but I think acknowledging them bears repetition.

[The following page has been omitted and contains a description of the victims.]

Those heroes at the scene were joined by first responders from county and municipalities, arriving just 3 minutes after the first 911 call, which performed excellently, and in doing so, saved lives. We also pay tribute to the skilled professionals at Arizona's University Medical Center, whose role is ongoing in healing the victims of this tragedy. Tonight, the University of Arizona community joins with Tucson, the State of Arizona and, indeed, the entire Nation to acknowledge together Saturday's tragedy. Appropriately, this remembrance is called "Together we thrive: Tucson and America."

"Together we thrive: Tucson and America" will be an opportunity to grieve, and it will be a demonstration of our strength: a strength in community—a strength in community that was demonstrated last Saturday, a strength in community there that is ongoing. Tucson demonstrated its strength on Saturday when the city was full of heroes—ordinary citizens, victims, first responders—coming together in the spirit of community.

Madam Speaker, our colleague Congresswoman GIFFORDS was the primary target of this cowardly act; and as she recovers, we honor her as a brilliant and courageous Member of Congress. She has brought to Congress an invigoration—the thinking of a new generation of national leaders. As a businesswoman and State legislator, she came to Congress full of ideas, and we will long continue to be blessed by them. I look forward to when she is present with us on the floor. She has spoken out courageously and led boldly when the times have demanded it.

It is especially tragic that those who lost their lives and those who were wounded had come together, as the resolution presents, to participate in an activity that reflects the best of our democratic tradition—a Representative of the people, of GABBY GIFFORDS and her staff hearing directly from the men and women she represents.

American democracy is founded on our commitment to a contest of ideas, not violence. Political disagreement and dissent must never violate our Nation's values, as expressed in the Constitution, of free expression, speech and peaceful assembly. GABBY spoke to that right here from the floor last week.

In this hour of anguish, we seek a renewed commitment to hope, to civility, to peace among the American people. In many of our churches, we sing on Sunday and on other days of the week: let there be peace on Earth, and let it begin, not just with us but with me—with each of us, within each of us. In speaking as one House today, coming together in peace, we offer our thoughts and support, our prayers for the health of our colleague, Congresswoman GABRIELLE GIFFORDS, and for all of the injured. We share the stories of the heroes of this tragedy and mourn those who perished. Let their actions and their memories are a blessing to our country.

We don't know why God saw this to be necessary, but let this be something that we cherish as an opportunity as we mourn the heartbreaking horror of it all. This resolution is a fitting tribute. It is a great resolution. Please read it again and again. Carry those names in your heart. Remember each of these people because, again, a tragic accident took lives and wounded people in the free expression of ideas. May this resolution remind us of the urgent need to uphold our democratic values, to treat one another with courtesy and with respect, and to act as Congresswoman GIFFORDS has always done and always will do—in a manner that reflects the best of American leadership. As our thoughts and prayers go out to the families of all who were affected, I want to call special attention to Commander, Navy Captain Mark Kelly, GABBY's husband, who has been a source of strength to all of us in this difficult time. We pray for him. We thank him for his and GABBY's service to our country. God truly blessed America with their leadership, with their service, and with their love for each other.

Source: Rep. Nancy Pelosi. "Expressing Sense of House Regarding Arizona Shooting." *Congressional Record* 2011, 157 pt. H145-H146. http://www.gpo.gov/fdsys/pkg/CREC-2011-01-12/pdf/CREC-2011-01-12-pt1-PgH144.pdf.

Rep. Ed Pastor, D-Ariz., on the January 8 Tucson Shooting

January 12, 2011

I also join my colleague from Arizona, JEFF FLAKE, in thanking the leadership in bringing this resolution here this morning. I also want to recognize that Representative GIFFORDS' staff is in the gallery with us this morning. So we want to wish them the best.

Madam Speaker, it is with great sadness I rise today to pay tribute to six innocent and precious Arizonans who, while participating in a public event designated to strengthen our democracy, so tragically lost their lives in a senseless act of violence last Saturday. I also want to pay tribute to those 14 Arizonans, including our dedicated and beloved colleague, and my personal friend, GABBY GIFFORDS, who were wounded.

These Americans, all dedicated to freedom and all loving their country so much that they chose to use their Saturday morning to participate in a public event to make their government better, are recovering at different paces and with unique and different needs. The city of Tucson, Pima County, and the entire State of Arizona stand poised to assist and welcome these brave heroes back to our communities once they have recovered.

GABBY continues to fight, literally fight, every minute for her life. And we are all reaching toward our God in prayer, contemplation, and silent whispers in our unified effort to bring about her quick recovery and return to us here in this House of Representatives.

[The following page has been omitted and contains a description of the victims.]

Again, I am encouraged by the reports concerning all the wounded. These individuals are the perfect example of the strength of Arizonans and all Americans. They will recover, we pray, and they will not shy from continuing to serve their community.

This is most true for GABBY. GABBY is a special person among us here in Congress. We all know that. We all love her pragmatism, her bipartisanship, her willingness to learn, her dedication to give, her compassion for her job and for each of us, and her spirit to continue striving to make the Eighth Congressional District of Arizona and America a better place to live and work.

Hopefully, it won't be much longer until we see her here, her smiling face with us again, doing what she loves, and working hard for the people of our country.

Our prayers go to GABBY, all the victims, and the families of the deceased. I reserve the balance of my time.

SOURCE: Rep. Ed Pastor. "Expressing Sense of House Regarding Arizona Shooting." *Congressional Record* 2011, 157 pt. H147-H148. http://www.gpo.gov/fdsys/pkg/CREC-2011-01-12/pdf/CREC-2011-01-12-pt1-PgH144.pdf.

OTHER HISTORIC DOCUMENTS OF INTEREST

FROM THIS VOLUME

FROM PREVIOUS *HISTORIC DOCUMENTS*

Deepwater Horizon Oil Spill Report Released

JANUARY 11, 2011

On April 20, 2010, the largest oil spill in U.S. history took place following the explosion and sinking of British Petroleum's (BP) oil well, Deepwater Horizon, which was drilling in the Macondo well off the coast of Louisiana. Eleven crew members were killed in the explosion, and more than 200 million gallons of oil spilled into the Gulf, impacting wildlife, tourism, and the coastal economy. At the request of President Barack Obama, a committee was established to investigate the cause of the spill and make recommendations to avoid future disasters. The committee released its report on January 11, 2011, faulting government regulators and the oil industry for systemic failures that could have been avoided. In response, the Obama administration worked with regulators to institute stricter enforcement of offshore drilling before deepwater oil exploration would be allowed to continue.

Obama Issues a Challenge

On May 22, 2010, President Barack Obama announced the creation of the National Commission on the BP Deepwater Horizon Oil Spill and Offshore Drilling. The team, made up of seven members appointed by the president, was tasked with analyzing what went wrong and providing possible solutions to avoid future disasters. The commission, cochaired by former senator Bob Graham of Florida and William Reilly, who served as head of the Environmental Protection Agency (EPA) after the *Exxon Valdez* spill, looked into the well and its operating conditions, how the explosion and spill happened, and how the industry and government responded. Without subpoena powers, access to a number of critical items such as the well's failed blowout preventer, and working on a tight deadline of six months, the commission was faced with a number of challenges.

During its six-month investigation, the commission reviewed thousands of pages of documents, interviewed hundreds of witnesses, and spent time hearing testimony from the Coast Guard, BP officials, local officials, scientists, environmental experts, members of the public, and those who were heavily affected by the disaster. In the first two days of hearings in New Orleans in 2010, Graham said, "The people of America are deeply moved by the scale of these tragedies and the courage demonstrated by the people of this community. We are proud of the tradition you continue." Reilly continued, "That's why we came here as we begin our investigation, by hearing from the people of the region, the people most affected, what they think, what you think, needs to be done." During the hearings, Reilly drew on his experience after the *Exxon Valdez* spill, coming down hard on BP officials with pointed lines of questioning. From Gulf Coast businesses, the commission heard testimony from those that had not yet reopened following the spill, and didn't know if they would be able to. "Due to this unnatural—unnatural—catastrophe in our waters, P&J may forever be extinct," said Sal Sunseri, the co-owner of P&J Oysters.

Final Report

A preliminary report of the commission's findings was released in October 2010, and was highly critical of the Obama administration's response to the spill. Four working papers released as part of the preliminary report indicated that the administration was confused about the rate of the spill, which affected how quickly it had responded. "The government appears to have taken an overly casual approach to the calculation and release of the 5,000 bbls/day estimate—which, as the only official estimate for most of May, took on great importance," the preliminary report said. "Putting aside the question of whether the public had a right to know the worst-case discharge figures, disclosure of those estimates, and explanation of their role in guiding the government effort, may have improved public confidence in the response," reads one of the working papers. The preliminary report and working papers further indicated that the White House proved to be either not completely forthcoming with information or not fully understanding of the situation at hand. According to the preliminary report and working papers, the administration relied on an overly optimistic estimate of the severity of the spill, believing that BP would be able to quickly contain and clean up the oil. The report cited an incident in which Carol M. Browner, director of the White House Office on Energy and Climate Change Policy, incorrectly said a report indicated that three quarters of the spill had already been cleaned up, while National Oceanic and Atmospheric Administration (NOAA) data indicated that number was closer to 50 percent. In another example of the administration's flawed response, the preliminary report said the Office of Management and Budget (OMB) delayed a worst-case scenario report by government scientists pertaining to the spill.

The White House quickly responded to the preliminary report, stating that confusion over the spill rate did nothing to impede the response to the spill. The effort "was full force and immediate, and the response focused on state and local plans and evolved when needed," said NOAA head Jane Lubchenco and OMB acting director Jeffrey Zients. Responding to accusations that the OMB report had been delayed to cover up the worst-case scenario, OMB spokesperson Kenneth Baer responded that the report had been delayed because revisions, which had nothing to do with the rate of the spill, were required. "The issue was the modeling, the science and the assumptions they were using to come up with their analysis. Not public relations or presentation," he said. "We offered NOAA suggestions of ways to improve their analysis, and they happily accepted it."

When the final 380-page report was released on January 11, 2011, it placed most of the blame for the spill on BP, Transocean, and Halliburton, the well's lessee, owner, and subcontractor, respectively. The report blamed the companies for poor cementing in the well and a lack of checks in place to ensure that this work had been completed properly. "Whether purposeful or not, many of the decisions that BP, Halliburton, and Transocean made that increased the risk of the Macondo blow-out clearly saved those companies significant time (and money)," the report reads. "BP did not have adequate controls in place to ensure that key decisions in the months leading up to the blowout were safe or sound from an engineering perspective." The report additionally concluded that, without significant government regulatory reforms and reforms in the oil industry, it should be expected that a similar spill could occur again. "If dramatic steps are not taken," said Graham, "I'm afraid at some point in the coming years another failure will occur, and we will wonder why did the Congress, why did the administration, why did the industry allow this to happen again."

In multiple instances the report noted that no one company or federal body could be blamed for the entire failure of the blowout preventer on the Deepwater Horizon rig. Government oversight officials needed to take as much responsibility as the companies involved in management. Part of the failure of the government, according to the report, involved underfunding the Minerals Management Service, which is tasked with overseeing offshore drilling to ensure that disasters do not take place. Further failure lies with both the government and the oil industry, which were unprepared to deal with a blowout and respond to a spill of this magnitude. However, the report found that although it will take decades to assess the impact of the spill, and although the economic impact on Gulf Coast states has already been severe, the spill and its impact could have been much worse.

The report left three questions unanswered. Without access to the blowout preventer, the commission was unable to make a determination of why that preventer failed and why workers did not respond more quickly to indications that gas was rising in the well. The report also made no mention of whether the executives at BP, Halliburton, and Transocean would be held responsible and liable for the effects of the spill.

RECOMMENDATIONS AND INDUSTRY RESPONSE

In the final report, the commission made recommendations it hoped could help prevent future oil spills. The commission called on Congress to approve new regulations and spending for offshore oil drilling regulation, and asked the oil industry to support these new regulations, which would make government oversight more predictable and their own businesses safer. President Obama commented that he was working to incorporate new regulatory changes, but that anything that would require additional spending would be hard to pass through Congress. "In keeping with the series of recommendations included in the commission report, our administration has already taken important steps to implement aggressive new reforms for the offshore oil and gas industry," said the president's then–press secretary Robert Gibbs. Members of Congress, specifically those leading environmental and natural resources committees, promised to review the report and introduce legislation as necessary.

A number of the recommendations from the final report involved additional investment in research and regulations. For example, the committee called for the creation of an environmental science office within the Interior Department that would have environmental protection review responsibilities. Additionally, the committee called for an in-house government expert on well containment and blowout, regulations based on risk, and the creation of an institute to help change the culture of safety for the oil and gas industry. These new regulations would require the oil industry to demonstrate how new procedures would mitigate risk. To support this effort, the committee suggested the creation of an industry-financed safety board and monitoring office within the Department of the Interior that would not be answerable to the Secretary.

In response to the recommendations the larger oil industry expressed the belief that if a company already has a good safety record, it should not be subjected to new regulations that could be costly and drive up energy prices. BP responded that the committee's report had generally the same findings of its own internal report, and that it planned to work with federal regulators to determine how best to use the lesson of Deepwater Horizon to avoid future spills. All of the companies named in the report are still subject to a Justice Department civil and criminal investigation as well as litigation brought by families of those killed and injured in the explosion, along with those whose businesses were damaged or lost because of the spill.

Deepwater Drilling Resumes

Even given the report's findings that there was a systemic failure of the oil industry that led to the Deepwater Horizon spill, no recommendations were made to end offshore drilling. The government had suspended offshore Gulf drilling in water deeper than 500 feet in June 2010 until the spill and its causes could be further investigated. In February 2011, drilling resumed in the deep water of the Gulf of Mexico, with Noble Energy becoming the first company to receive approval from the Interior Department for new drilling. Noble contracted with Helix Well Containment Group, which said that its containment technology could cap a blowout and handle a spill of 69,000 gallons of oil per day, approximately the amount that leaked from the Macondo well. The inclusion of the Helix technology enabled Noble's proposal to meet the new, more stringent government drilling standards, and the company was given a permit to drill at a depth of 6,500 feet off the coast of Louisiana.

The government gave no timetable for approval of other new permits, saying that each would be reviewed on a case-by-case basis, and that the rapid approval that had occurred before Deepwater Horizon would no longer be commonplace. Members of Congress complained about the new process for permit approval, saying that the slow pace would harm domestic energy development and lead to higher oil prices.

Eighteen months after the spill, BP was given approval to drill in up to 6,000 feet 200 miles off the Louisiana coast. U.S. officials, in defending the approval, said that BP was compliant with new heightened standards imposed for offshore drilling and that BP had placed additional requirements on itself internally.

—Heather Kerrigan

Following is the executive summary of the report issued to the president on January 11, 2011, in regard to the Deepwater Horizon Gulf oil spill, written by the National Commission on the BP Deepwater Horizon Oil Spill and Offshore Drilling.

National Commission Releases Report on Deepwater Horizon Oil Spill

DOCUMENT

January 11, 2011

[The dedication, acknowledgments, table of contents, and all footnotes have been omitted.]

Foreword

The explosion that tore through the *Deepwater Horizon* drilling rig last April 20, as the rig's crew completed drilling the exploratory Macondo well deep under the waters of the Gulf of Mexico, began a human, economic, and environmental disaster.

Eleven crew members died, and others were seriously injured, as fire engulfed and ultimately destroyed the rig. And, although the nation would not know the full scope of the disaster for weeks, the first of more than four million barrels of oil began gushing uncontrolled into the Gulf—threatening livelihoods, precious habitats, and even a unique way of life. A treasured American landscape, already battered and degraded from years of mismanagement, faced yet another blow as the oil spread and washed ashore. Five years after Hurricane Katrina, the nation was again transfixed, seemingly helpless, as this new tragedy unfolded in the Gulf. The costs from this one industrial accident are not yet fully counted, but it is already clear that the impacts on the region's natural systems and people were enormous, and that economic losses total tens of billions of dollars.

On May 22, 2010, President Barack Obama announced the creation of the National Commission on the BP Deepwater Horizon Oil Spill and Offshore Drilling: an independent, nonpartisan entity, directed to provide a thorough analysis and impartial judgment. The President charged the Commission to determine the causes of the disaster, and to improve the country's ability to respond to spills, and to recommend reforms to make offshore energy production safer. And the President said we were to follow the facts wherever they led.

This report is the result of an intense six-month effort to fulfill the President's charge.

From the outset, the Commissioners have been determined to learn the essential lessons so expensively revealed in the tragic loss of life at the *Deepwater Horizon* and the severe damages that ensued. The Commission's aim has been to provide the President, policymakers, industry, and the American people a clear, accessible, accurate, and fair account of the largest oil spill in U.S history: the context for the well itself, how the explosion and spill happened, and how industry and government scrambled to respond to an unprecedented emergency. This was our first obligation: determine what happened, why it happened, and explain it to Americans everywhere.

As a result of our investigation, we conclude:

- The explosive loss of the Macondo well could have been prevented.
- The immediate causes of the Macondo well blowout can be traced to a series of identifiable mistakes made by BP, Halliburton, and Transocean that reveal such systematic failures in risk management that they place in doubt the safety culture of the entire industry.
- Deepwater energy exploration and production, particularly at the frontiers of experience, involve risks for which neither industry nor government has been adequately prepared, but for which they can and must be prepared in the future.
- To assure human safety and environmental protection, regulatory oversight of leasing, energy exploration, and production require reforms even beyond those significant reforms already initiated since the *Deepwater Horizon* disaster. Fundamental reform will be needed in both the structure of those in charge of regulatory oversight and their internal decision making process to ensure their political autonomy, technical expertise, and their full consideration of environmental protection concerns.
- Because regulatory oversight alone will not be sufficient to ensure adequate safety, the oil and gas industry will need to take its own, unilateral steps to increase dramatically safety throughout the industry, including self-policing mechanisms that supplement governmental enforcement.
- The technology, laws and regulations, and practices for containing, responding to, and cleaning up spills lag behind the real risks associated with deepwater drilling into large, high-pressure reservoirs of oil and gas located far offshore and thousands of feet below the ocean's surface. Government must close the existing gap and industry must support rather than resist that effort.

- Scientific understanding of environmental conditions in sensitive environments in deep Gulf waters, along the region's coastal habitats, and in areas proposed for more drilling, such as the Arctic, is inadequate. The same is true of the human and natural impacts of oil spills.

We reach these conclusions, and make necessary recommendations, in a constructive spirit: we aim to promote changes that will make American offshore energy exploration and production far safer, today and in the future.

More broadly, the disaster in the Gulf undermined public faith in the energy industry, government regulators, and even our own capability as a nation to respond to crises. It is our hope that a thorough and rigorous accounting, along with focused suggestions for reform, can begin the process of restoring confidence. There is much at stake, not only for the people directly affected in the Gulf region, but for the American people at large. The tremendous resources that exist within our outer continental shelf belong to the nation as a whole. The federal government's authority over the shelf is accordingly plenary, based on its power as both the owner of the resources and in its regulatory capacity as sovereign to protect public health, safety, and welfare. To be allowed to drill on the outer continental shelf is a privilege to be earned, not a private right to be exercised.

"Complex Systems Almost Always Fail in Complex Ways"

As the Board that investigated the loss of the *Columbia* space shuttle noted, "complex systems almost always fail in complex ways." Though it is tempting to single out one crucial misstep or point the finger at one bad actor as the cause of the *Deepwater Horizon* explosion, any such explanation provides a dangerously incomplete picture of what happened—encouraging the very kind of complacency that led to the accident in the first place. Consistent with the President's request, this report takes an expansive view.

Why was a corporation drilling for oil in mile-deep water 49 miles off the Louisiana coast? To begin, Americans today consume vast amounts of petroleum products—some 18.7 million barrels per day—to fuel our economy. Unlike many other oil-producing countries, the United States relies on private industry—not a state-owned or -controlled enterprise—to supply oil, natural gas, and indeed all of our energy resources. This basic trait of our private-enterprise system has major implications for how the U.S. government oversees and regulates offshore drilling. It also has advantages in fostering a vigorous and competitive industry, which has led worldwide in advancing the technology of finding and extracting oil and gas.

Even as land-based oil production extended as far as the northern Alaska frontier, the oil and gas industry began to move offshore. The industry first moved into shallow water and eventually into deepwater, where technological advances have opened up vast new reserves of oil and gas in remote areas—in recent decades, much deeper under the water's surface and farther offshore than ever before. The *Deepwater Horizon* was drilling the Macondo well under 5,000 feet of Gulf water, and then over 13,000 feet under the sea floor to the hydrocarbon reservoir below. It is a complex, even dazzling, enterprise. The remarkable advances that have propelled the move to deepwater drilling merit comparison with exploring outer space. The Commission is respectful and admiring of the industry's technological capability.

But drilling in deepwater brings new risks, not yet completely addressed by the reviews of where it is safe to drill, what could go wrong, and how to respond if something does go awry. The drilling rigs themselves bristle with potentially dangerous machinery. The deep-water environment is cold, dark, distant, and under high pressures—and the oil and gas reservoirs, when found, exist at even higher pressures (thousands of pounds per square inch), compounding the risks if a well gets out of control. The *Deepwater Horizon* and Macondo well vividly illustrated all of those very real risks. When a failure happens at such depths, regaining control is a formidable engineering challenge—and the costs of failure, we now know, can be catastrophically high.

In the years before the Macondo blowout, neither industry nor government ade-quately addressed these risks. Investments in safety, containment, and response equip-ment and practices failed to keep pace with the rapid move into deepwater drilling. Absent major crises, and given the remarkable financial returns available from deepwater reserves, the business culture succumbed to a false sense of security. The *Deepwater Horizon* disas-ter exhibits the costs of a culture of complacency.

The Commission examined in great detail what went wrong on the rig itself. Our investigative staff uncovered a wealth of specific information that greatly enhances our understanding of the factors that led to the explosion. The separately published report of the chief counsel (a summary of the findings is presented in Chapter 4) offers the fullest account yet of what happened on the rig and why. There are recurring themes of missed warning signals, failure to share information, and a general lack of appreciation for the risks involved. In the view of the Commission, these findings highlight the importance of organizational culture and a consistent commitment to safety by industry, from the high-est management levels on down.

But that complacency affected government as well as industry. The Commission has documented the weaknesses and the inadequacies of the federal regulation and oversight, and made important recommendations for changes in legal authority, regulations, invest-ments in expertise, and management.

The Commission also looked at the effectiveness of the response to the spill. There were remarkable instances of dedication and heroism by individuals involved in the rescue and cleanup. Much was done well—and thanks to a combination of good luck and hard work, the worst-case scenarios did not all come to pass. But it is impossible to argue that the industry or the country was prepared for a disaster of the magnitude of the *Deepwater Horizon* oil spill. Twenty years after the *Exxon Valdez* spill in Alaska, the same blunt response technologies—booms, dispersants, and skimmers—were used, to limited effect. On-the-ground shortcomings in the joint public-private response to an overwhelming spill like that resulting from the blowout of the Macondo well are now evident, and demand public and private investment. So do the weaknesses in local, state, and federal coordination revealed by the emergency. Both government and industry failed to antici-pate and prevent this catastrophe, and failed again to be prepared to respond to it.

If we are to make future deepwater drilling safer and more environmentally respon-sible, we will need to address all these deficiencies together; a piecemeal approach will surely leave us vulnerable to future crises in the communities and natural environments most exposed to offshore energy exploration and production.

THE DEEPWATER DRILLING PROSPECT

The damage from the spill and the impact on the people of the Gulf has guided our work from the very beginning. Our first action as a Commission was to visit the Gulf region, to learn directly from those most affected. We heard deeply moving accounts from oystermen witnessing multi-generation family businesses slipping away, fishermen and tourism proprietors bearing the brunt of an ill-founded stigma affecting everything related to the Gulf, and oil-rig workers dealing with mounting bills and threatened home foreclosures, their means of support temporarily derailed by a blanket drilling moratorium, shutting down all deepwater drilling rigs, including those not implicated in the BP spill.

Indeed, the centrality of oil and gas exploration to the Gulf economy is not widely appreciated by many Americans, who enjoy the benefits of the energy essential to their transportation, but bear none of the direct risks of its production. Within the Gulf region, however, the role of the energy industry is well understood and accepted. The notion of clashing interests—of energy extraction versus a natural-resource economy with bountiful fisheries and tourist amenities—misses the extent to which the energy industry is woven into the fabric of the Gulf culture and economy, providing thousands of jobs and essential public revenues. Any discussion of the future of offshore drilling cannot ignore these economic realities.

But those benefits have imposed their costs. The bayous and wetlands of Louisiana have for decades suffered from destructive alteration to accommodate oil exploration. The Gulf ecosystem, a unique American asset, is likely to continue silently washing away unless decisive action is taken to start the work of creating a sustainably healthy and productive landscape. No one should be deluded that restoration on the scale required will occur quickly or cheaply. Indeed, the experience in restoring other large, sensitive regions—the Chesapeake Bay, the Everglades, the Great Lakes—indicates that progress will require coordinated federal and state actions, a dedicated funding source, long-term monitoring, and a vocal and engaged citizenry, supported by robust non-governmental groups, scientific research, and more.

We advocate beginning such an effort, seriously and soon, as a suitable response to the damage and disruption caused by the *Deepwater Horizon* emergency. It is a fair recognition not only of the costs that energy exploitation in the Gulf has, for decades, imposed on the landscape and habitats—and the other economic activities they support—but also of the certainty that Americans will continue to develop the region's offshore energy resources.

For the simple fact is that the bulk of our newly discovered petroleum reserves, and the best prospects for future discoveries, lie not on land, but under water. To date, we have made the decision as a nation to exploit the Gulf's offshore energy resources—ruling much of the Florida, Atlantic, and Pacific coasts out of bounds for drilling. The choice of how aggressively to exploit these resources, wherever they may be found, has profound implications for the future of U.S. energy policy, for our need to understand and assure the integrity of fragile environmental resources, and for the way Americans think about our economy and our security. Although much work is being done to improve the fuel efficiency of vehicles and to develop alternative fuels, we cannot realistically walk away from these offshore oil resources in the near future. So we must be much better prepared to exploit such resources with far greater care.

THE COMMISSION AND ITS WORK

While we took a broad view of the spill, it could not be exhaustive. There is still much we do not know—for instance, the blowout preventer, the last line of defense against loss of well control, is still being analyzed; and the *Deepwater Horizon* itself, after its explosive destruction, remained out of reach during our investigation. The understandable, immediate need to provide answers and concrete suggestions trumped the benefits of a longer, more comprehensive investigation. And as we know from other spills, their environmental consequences play out over decades—and often in unexpected ways. Instead, the Commission focused on areas we thought most likely to inform practical recommendations. Those recommendations are presented in the spirit of transforming America into the global leader for safe and effective offshore drilling operations. Just as this Commission learned from the experiences of other nations in developing our recommendations, the lessons learned from the Deepwater Horizon disaster are not confined to our own government and industry, but relevant to rest of the world.

We wish we could say that our recommendations make a recurrence of a disaster like the Macondo blowout impossible. We do not have that power. No one can eliminate all risks associated with deepwater exploration. But when exploration occurs, particularly in sensitive environments like the Gulf of Mexico or the Arctic, the country has an obligation to make responsible decisions regarding the benefits and risks.

The report is divided into three sections.

Chapters 1 through 3 describe the events of April 20th on the *Deepwater Horizon*, and, more important, the events leading up to it in the preceding decades—especially how the dramatic expansion of deepwater drilling in the Gulf was not met by regulatory oversight capable of ensuring the safety of those drilling operations.

Chapters 4 through 7 lay out the results of our investigation in detail, highlighting the crucial issues we believe must inform policy going forward: the specific engineering and operating choices made in drilling the Macondo well, the attempts to contain and respond to the oil spill, and the impacts of the spill on the region's natural resources, economy, and people—in the context of the progressive degradation of the Mississippi Delta environment.

Chapters 8 through 10 present our recommendations for reforms in business practices, regulatory oversight, and broader policy concerns. We recognize that the improvements we advocate all come with costs and all will take time to implement. But inaction, as we are deeply aware, runs the risk of real costs, too: in more lost lives, in broad damage to the regional economy and its long-term viability, and in further tens of billions of dollars of avoidable clean-up costs. Indeed, if the clear challenges are not addressed and another disaster happens, the entire offshore energy enterprise is threatened—and with it, the nation's economy and security. We suggest a better option: build from this tragedy in a way that makes the Gulf more resilient, the country's energy supplies more secure, our workers safer, and our cherished natural resources better protected.

Our Thanks and Dedication

We thank President Obama for this opportunity to learn thoroughly about the crisis, and to share our findings with the American public. We deeply appreciate the effort people in the affected Gulf regions made to tell us about their experiences, and the time and preparation witnesses before the Commission dedicated to their presentations. We have come to respect the seriousness with which our fellow Commissioners assumed our joint responsibilities, and their diverse expertise and perspectives that helped make its work thorough and productive. On their behalf, we wish to recognize the extraordinary work the Commission's staff—scientists, lawyers, engineers, policy analysts, and more—performed, under demanding deadlines, to make our inquiries broad, deep, and effective; and we especially highlight the leadership contributions of Richard Lazarus, executive director, and Fred Bartlit, chief counsel. Together, they have fulfilled an extraordinary public service.

Finally, to the American people, we reiterate that extracting the energy resources to fuel our cars, heat and light our homes, and power our businesses can be a dangerous enterprise. Our national reliance on fossil fuels is likely to continue for some time—and all of us reap benefits from the risks taken by the men and women working in energy exploration. We owe it to them to ensure that their working environment is as safe as possible. We dedicate this effort to the 11 of our fellow citizens who lost their lives in the *Deepwater Horizon* explosion. . . .

[The remaining ten chapters, endnotes, appendices, and index have been omitted.]

Source: National Commission on the BP Deepwater Horizon Oil Spill and Offshore Drilling. "Deep Water: The Gulf Oil Disaster and the Future of Offshore Drilling." January 11, 2011. http://www.oilspill commission.gov/sites/default/files/documents/DEEPWATER_ReporttothePresident_FINAL.pdf.

OTHER HISTORIC DOCUMENTS OF INTEREST

FROM THIS VOLUME

- Natural Gas Drilling, p. 210

FROM PREVIOUS *HISTORIC DOCUMENTS*

- Deepwater Horizon Explosion and Oil Spill, *2010*, p. 183
- Congressional Debate on the Ban on Offshore Drilling, *2008*, p. 411

Arab Spring: Tunisian President Zine al-Abidine Ben Ali Resigns

JANUARY 14, 15, AND 27 AND FEBRUARY 27, 2011

After localized demonstrations against Tunisia's government failed to direct public attention to economic inequality, citizens turned to social media and took to the streets of the capital, Tunis, determined to take down the government of President Zine al-Abidine Ben Ali. Their call for equality didn't end at economics—protesters also wanted the implementation of democratic reforms that would make the nation's government more inclusive of all sectors of Tunisia's population. By toppling Ben Ali's regime and bringing about democratic elections, Tunisia became a force that set in motion the later events of the Arab Spring, the term used to describe the revolutionary protests and demonstrations spanning from December 2010 through 2011, across the Middle East.

DEMONSTRATIONS TARGET PRESIDENT BEN ALI

Tunisia, considered to be one of the more liberal Arab states, erupted in protests in December 2010 when Mohamed Bouazizi, a fruit vendor, set himself on fire to protest his lack of economic opportunity. Smaller protests had occurred in mid-2010 that led to clashes with police, but the demonstrations never spread beyond the small villages in which they started. The difference in December was how those in Bouazizi's hometown of Sidi Bouzid worked to get news out about Bouazizi's demonstration and how social media was used to spread a message of economic inequality within and beyond Tunisia's borders. As demonstrations began in rural areas of Tunisia, the government forced Internet and power outages to stop the spread of information. Bloggers were arrested and YouTube videos were hacked and removed. Tunisia already had a long history of stringent controls on the Internet, but President Zine al-Abidine Ben Ali's government took matters one step further. In 2011, however, the protesters prevailed and used social media to organize demonstrations and spread the message of the uprising around the world.

Demonstrations soon moved to the capital of Tunis, and the uprising became known as the Jasmine Revolution. Undeterred by Ben Ali's crackdown, protesters united through the use of social media and protested high unemployment and food prices. A large number of educated but jobless college graduates joined the protest, taking the government by surprise. Economic growth, while slow, had been recently steady, allowing some Tunisians to turn a blind eye to government and police corruption and restrictions on their rights. As the protests took over the capital, Ben Ali first made an attempt to stop the demonstrations by promising elections. He then fired his interior minister and released those who had already been imprisoned during the demonstrations. The president called for the formation of a special committee to look into government corruption and promised to create 300,000 jobs, cut food prices, allow freedom of the press and Internet, and increase democratic freedoms and participation. Following his promises, the president dismissed his government and stated, contrary to earlier reports, that he would not change the constitution to allow himself to run for president again in 2014.

The promises of Ben Ali did little to placate the protesters. Demonstrators aimed a lot of anger at the president and his family for their lavish lifestyles in the face of continuing economic hardship for his countrymen. A WikiLeaks document from the American ambassador in Tunisia on a dinner at the home of Ben Ali's son-in-law said that the beach-front house was decorated with Roman artifacts, that food had been flown in from France, and that a pet tiger was being kept in a cage.

With no end of the demonstrations in sight, Ben Ali declared a state of emergency. Police forces fired on demonstrators, and the president backed the action, calling the protesters terrorists. According to a United Nations report, approximately 219 were killed in the violence. Tunisia's government reported that 78 had been killed. On January 14, Ben Ali made the surprising announcement that he would temporarily step down. He subsequently fled the country for Saudi Arabia, ending his twenty-three years in power.

Transitional Government Takes Control

Following his resignation, Tunisian authorities issued an international arrest warrant for Ben Ali. Eighteen charges were filed against him, including voluntary manslaughter and drug trafficking. It was expected that eventually forty-four charges would be brought against the president, his family, and former ministers. Following his resignation, thirty-three members of Ben Ali's family were arrested on suspicion of plundering Tunisia's resources.

As the search for Ben Ali continued, a new unity government was formed and sworn in, with all political parties being allowed back into the country, including those that had been banned by the former president. The day after the government was formed on January 17, the interim president, Foued Mebazaa, who had formerly served in Ben Ali's government as parliamentary speaker, and Prime Minister Mohamed Ghannouchi, who had held the position since 1999, quit Ben Ali's Constitutional Democratic Rally (RCD) party. Their decision followed the resignation of three ministers from the opposition General Union of Tunisian Workers protesting the involvement of the RCD in the new government. Although Mebazaa and Ghannouchi left the RCD to "split the state from the party," there were still those in the government and public who saw too much of Ben Ali's influence in the new government. The nominee for health minister refused to take his seat because of disagreement with RCD involvement.

Ghannouchi defended allowing RCD members to retain their seats, regardless of whether they formally defected from the party. "We have tried to put together a mix that takes into account the different forces in the country to create the conditions to be able to start reforms," Ghannouchi said. With his government set up, Ghannouchi made large promises to the public, calling for the release of those imprisoned for speaking out against the former government and for complete media freedom. "We are committed to intensifying our efforts to reestablish calm and peace in the hearts of all Tunisians. Our priority is security, as well as political and economic reform."

In late January, as protests over RCD involvement in the unity government continued, Ghannouchi replaced twelve cabinet ministers and renewed his vow that the current government was strictly transitional and meant to put the country on the path to democracy. The ministers of defense, interior, and finance, all of whom had worked under Ben Ali, were replaced. The foreign minister resigned as well. Ghannouchi promised to quit "in the shortest possible time frame" and pledged to hold elections for a permanent government within six months.

In February, Ghannouchi resigned his position after additional protests over his ties to the former regime. He was replaced by a former foreign minister, Beji Caid Essebsi, who was chosen because he had always worked to change government from the inside as part of Ben Ali's regime. Daily protests followed the prime minister's resignation. In September, Essebsi announced a security crackdown that banned meetings that were thought to be in direct conflict with the government and gave the security forces the ability to place anyone under house arrest.

OCTOBER ELECTIONS

Originally scheduled for July 24, parliamentary elections were delayed because of voter registration issues for many Tunisians. The delay also gave political parties formed during the January demonstrations additional time to campaign to compete with Ennahda, the party with the greatest amount of support in Tunisia, which had been banned under Ben Ali's rule. The low voter registration rate, with only 55 percent of those eligible registering before the October election, led to a government decision that even those who had not registered would be allowed to vote as long as they provided an identification card at the polling location.

In the buildup to the October elections, the High Independent Authority for the Elections (ISIE) banned all "comments and journalistic analyses directly or indirectly related to the elections" due to a "lack of a legal framework regulating the running of opinion polls of a political nature," but some newspapers did continue running election-related commentary. On September 12 all political advertisements were banned.

The ISIE was put in charge of formal election monitoring and worked with other local groups to ensure peaceful elections. International observers came from the European Union and the United States, including representatives from the Carter Center and the International Republican Institute. These two U.S. groups sparked controversy as to whether they should be involved after overseeing elections in Iraq and Afghanistan that were considered to have irregularities. The two groups were, in the end, allowed to assist in overseeing the election. More than 5,000 observers, approximately one fifth of whom were from international organizations, oversaw the October elections.

On October 23, the first general election to be held during Arab Spring took place in Tunisia, with millions turning out to choose the 217 members of the Constituent Assembly. One hundred ninety nine of the seats would be voted on in twenty-seven constituencies inside of Tunisia, while the remaining eighteen seats were left for Tunisians abroad in six constituencies. Representation would be proportional, with half of the candidates on each party list required to be women. The Assembly will subsequently be charged with drafting a constitution and choosing a transitional government until future elections to create a permanent government can be held. The Assembly was given one year to draft a constitution. The current constitution that will be replaced was adopted in 1959 and places most of the power in the hands of the president, which allowed Ben Ali to establish one-party rule.

Two major parties ran in the election to challenge Ennahda. The Progressive Democratic Party (PDP) is a well-established, secular party that was banned under the former president. It is led by Ahmed Najib Chebbi, who was chosen by Ghannouchi to join the unity government as regional development minister. The PDP considers itself a social democratic party. The second challenger was the Democratic Forum for Labor and Liberties, a party increasing in popularity and made up of social democrats who value transparency in government.

Turnout for the October vote was well above expected, with Tunisians coming to the polls focused on the economy, jobs, and ending government corruption. When the votes were counted, Ennahda won a 41 percent plurality, and will now be expected to work to reassure secular Tunisians that it will not try to impose Muslim code on the nation. Ennahda stated its desire to establish a pluralistic democracy, possibly using Turkey as a model.

—Heather Kerrigan

Following is a statement by Prime Minister Mohamed Ghannouchi, on January 14, 2011, announcing his taking the position of interim president; a statement on January 15, 2011, announcing the choosing of an interim president; a statement on January 27, 2011, announcing the members of the unity government; and a statement on February 27, 2011, on the appointment of a new prime minister.

DOCUMENT *Interim President of Tunisia Named*

January 14, 2011

By virtue of provisions of Article 56 of the Constitution which stipulates that, in case of his temporary inability, the President of the Republic could decree to delegate his powers to the Prime Minister.

By virtue of the decree signed by the Head of State, on January 14, 2011, Mr. Mohamed Ghannouchi has taken over as President of the Republic.

Mr. Mohamed Ghannouchi, with attendance of Messrs. Foued Mebazaa, Speaker of the Chamber of Deputies, and Abdallah Kallel, Speaker of the Chamber of Advisers, made a statement.

Here is this statement:

"In the Name of God, the Merciful, the Compassionate.

Fellow citizens,

By virtue of the provisions of Article 56 of the Constitution which stipulates that, in case of his temporary inability, the President of the Republic could decree to delegate his functions to the Prime Minister.

Given the President of the Republic's inability to exercise his duties, I, starting from now, have taken over the position of President of the Republic.

I call on all sons and daughters of Tunisia, from all political and intellectual stripes, and all categories and regions, to show their patriotic sense and their unity to help the homeland, so dear to us all, overcome this difficult stage and restore its security and stability.

I pledge myself, during this period of my duties, to respect the Constitution and implement, with rigor, the political, economic and social reforms that have been announced, in consultation with all national sides, political parties, national organizations and components of civil society.

May God lead us to success."

SOURCE: Republic of Tunisia. Prime Ministry Portal. "Mr. Mohamed Ghannouchi Announces Taking Over as Interim President of Republic." January 14, 2011. http://www.pm.gov.tn/pm/actualites/actualite .php?id=1898&lang=en.

New Interim President Chosen in Tunisia

January 15, 2011

Under the provisions of Article 57 of the Constitution and following the statement published by the Constitutional Council, on Saturday, January 15, 2011, on the announcement of the final vacancy for the post of the Presidency of the Republic, and since the constitutional requirements are met for the Speaker of the Chamber of Deputies to take over immediately the duties of acting President of the Republic, Mr. Foued Mebazaa assumed, today, the duties of the Presidency of the Republic for a period ranging between 45 days at least and 60 days at most, during which there will be election of a new President of the Republic for a five-year term.

Pursuant to the above-mentioned article, the person holding the office of acting President of the Republic can not bid for the Presidency of the Republic.

Mr. Foued Mebazaa, invested as acting President of the Republic, was sworn in before members of the Chamber of Deputies' and Chamber of Advisers' bureaus who met jointly on Saturday afternoon in Bardo Palace.

Mr. Foued Mebazaa, then, delivered the following address:

Fellow Citizens,

Sons and daughters of the valiant people of Tunisia, at this delicate juncture in the history of our beloved country, I invite you all, as well as all active forces, political parties, national organisations and various components of the civil society, to prioritise the higher interest of the homeland and support the Army and national security forces to establish security, preserve the private and public property and restore calm and serenity among citizens, in different regions, which is likely to meet all appropriate conditions to start a new stage that meets the ambitions and aspirations of the people for an advanced political life consecrating democracy, pluralism and effective participation of all sons of Tunisia, with neither exception nor exclusion, as part of a process of reconstruction.

Regarding the Government, and referring to the Constitutional Council, in accordance with paragraph 3 of Article 72 of the Constitution, on the functioning of the Constitutional Council;

Considering the provisions of articles 50 and 57 of the Constitution;

Given that the duties of the government ended, following its dissolution;

Given that the Prime Minister has been asked to propose members of the Government;

Given that the date of the announcement of the vacancy for the post of the President of the Republic, and considering that the other members of the Government have not yet been appointed, the government is thus not formed, which makes inapplicable provisions of paragraph 4 of Article 57, concerning the government;

Given that the functioning of the Constitutional public powers and the continuity of the State require the appointment of the government, in line with the spirit of the Constitution and its different provisions;

Given that the higher interest of the country requires the formation of a Government of national unity;

We ask Mr. Mohamed Ghannouchi, Prime Minister, to propose the members of this government, under article 50 of the Constitution."

SOURCE: Republic of Tunisia. Prime Ministry Portal. "Mr. Foued Mebazaa Sworn In." January 15, 2011. http://www.pm.gov.tn/pm/actualites/actualite.php?id=1912&lang=en.

Tunisian Transitional Unity Government Announced

DOCUMENT

January 27, 2011

Prime Minister Mohamed Ghannouchi announced, on Thursday January 27, 2011 evening, in an address broadcast live on national television, the new make-up of the National Unity Government (NUG) which he argued was the fruit of deep and intense consultations carried out among all national political sides and various components of civil society, and which resulted in a broad consensus on the new line-up of the NUG.

After reading out the full make-up of the Government, the Prime Minister pointed out that it comes out from the reshuffle that nine members have kept their ministerial portfolios and twelve members have been replaced, asserting that determination was strong that the chosen ministers be competent, experienced and able to take up the challenges and win the bets posed to the country.

He said that the announced government is a transition, an interim, government whose mission consists in helping the country achieve democratic transition and combine the required conditions for holding the next presidential election, which will offer the country the opportunity to voice its will freely and all guarantees so that this electoral event reflects the Tunisian people's determination.

Mr. Ghannouchi pointed out that the Government pledges itself that the coming election, by means of the chosen directions, take place under the oversight of an independent commission and with the attendance of international observers, so that voting be transparent and credible.

The Prime Minister underlined that the main mission of the interim government is to carry out the needed reforms, on the basis of participation of all sides of the political and civil landscape and competences in the Higher Political Reform Commission's works.

He added that the purpose consists in managing to introduce major and quality reforms which would touch on the different laws regulating public life, notably the Press Code, the Electoral Code, Fight Against Terrorism Act and the law on political parties, in such a way as to achieve review of all those anti-democratic pieces of legislation and broaden the scope and guarantees of freedom and pluralism.

The Prime Minister pointed out that, as part of the intense consultations on the formation of the new government, the different visions and stands had been listened to, and known national potentialities had been called on because of their credibility, experience, scientific ability and radiance, both on the national and international scales.

Mr. Ghannouchi extended, in this connection, consideration to all personalities and competences who responded favourably to the homeland's call and accepted to be member of the government, in spite of their international commitments, driven as they are by the sole purpose to serve Tunisia and promote the Nation.

Given the profound awareness of the hard and delicate situation the country is going through, the Prime Minister emphasised that the duty dictates to join all efforts and pour all energies in saving the country and ensuring return to normalcy under the shortest terms, in such a manner as to face up to the fall-out of the recent events and restore normal pace at all levels of activity, notably through resumption by Tunisia's children—pupils and students—of their courses, underlining that Government is in the service of all Tunisians, men and women, as well as the interest of the motherland.

He stressed the vital part falling on the three recently formed national commissions which have already, he specified, started operating, as they are the essential foundation on which rests the introduction of radical and deep reforms that would help the country enter a new stage, one during which liberties and democracy would be strengthened and guarantees to Human Rights would be entrenched.

The Prime Minister highlighted, in this regard, that the crucial mission entrusted, in particular, to the Higher Political Reform Commission which includes all sensitivities of the national scene, all parties, recognised or not, civil society organisations and skills, which would certainly help that conclusions coming out from its works be the crowning stage of all Tunisian men and women's consensus, at this decisive stage in the country's progress.

Mr. Mohamed Ghannouchi said that logic requires, at present, to be sincere with the Tunisians by telling them the truth about the delicate nature of the situation, that there are innumerable hardships in several fields and that the circumstances dictate their return to work and perseverance, pointing out that the whole world is watching the Tunisian people's revolution, also expressing esteem and consideration to them and wishing to see the Tunisians devote themselves to work and take up the posed challenges.

He said that Tunisia and its people have now an appointment with History and they are called upon, at all levels, to discharge their missions, as dictated on them by faithfulness to the martyrs of the motherland, in the first place of whom late Mohamed Bouazizi, which would hoist Tunisia, whose children aspire to build it up into a model for a people who practices its sovereignty, in liberty and democracy.

SOURCE: Republic of Tunisia. Prime Ministry Portal. "New Government, Fruit of National Consensus and Will to Achieve Democratic Transition." January 27, 2011. http://www.pm.gov.tn/pm/actualites/actualite.php?id=2066&lang=en.

DOCUMENT

Tunisian Interim President Appoints New Prime Minister

February 27, 2011

Interim President Foued Mebazaa addressed the Tunisian people on Sunday evening, announcing his decision to appoint Mr. Beji Caid Essebsi, as Prime Minister following the resignation of Mr. Mohamed Ghannouchi.

He said he was surprised by the resignation of Mr. Ghannouchi, adding that he had accepted his resignation upon his insistence and determination to do so.

The Interim President expressed his thanks to Mr. Ghannouchi for all the efforts he had exerted and for his devotion to serve Tunisia in this delicate situation facing the country.

Given his attachment to the interests of Tunisia and to guarantee the continuity of the State, with all its institutions, he said that he had asked Mr. Beji Caid Essebsi to hold the post of Prime Minister, a responsibility which he has accepted, stressing the patriotism and loyalty of the new prime minister.

Mr. Foued Mebazaa also said he will address the Tunisian people in a few days to present to them the roadmap for the next stage, in light of the proposals to be submitted by the higher committee for the achievement of the objectives of the Revolution and political reform.

He extended, in conclusion, his thanks and consideration to all those who have made efforts so that Tunisia remains always trustworthy, urging all sides to show calm and objectivity and strive to overcome the state of disorder witnessed by the country.

SOURCE: Republic of Tunisia. Prime Ministry Portal. "Interim President Appoints Mr. Beji Caid Essebsi as Prime Minister." February 27, 2011. http://www.pm.gov.tn/pm/actualites/actualite.php?id=2783&lang=en.

OTHER HISTORIC DOCUMENTS OF INTEREST

FROM THIS VOLUME

FROM PREVIOUS *HISTORIC DOCUMENTS*

FCC Approves NBC-Comcast Merger

On January 18, 2011, the Federal Communications Commission approved the merger of the nation's largest cable network operator, Comcast, with NBC Universal, creating the nation's newest media conglomerate. Comcast's goal in seeking Federal Communications Commission (FCC) approval for the merger was to control more video content and distribution, add on-demand content, and provide this new content to paid television subscribers. In seeking approval of the merger, Comcast promised that it would use its new market position not to subvert its competitors but to increase the universal around-the-clock availability of innovative content.

Media Merger Announced

On December 3, 2009, Comcast announced that it had reached an agreement with General Electric (GE) to acquire a majority share of its subsidiary NBC Universal. The initial terms of the agreement took nine months to develop, mainly because Comcast sought to contribute as little monetarily to the merger as possible, while also working on provisions to avoid any potential antitrust issues when the merger went before the Department of Justice (DOJ) for approval. The final hurdle to overcome in finalizing the merger was Comcast's buyout of Vivendi, which owned a 20 percent stake in NBC. The French media company was originally opposed to the deal; however, it eventually agreed to accept approximately $5.8 billion from GE for its share. In the final agreement, Comcast paid GE $6.5 billion in cash and GE retained 49 percent ownership of the new company. The total merger was valued at around $30 billion between Comcast's already booming cable service, its own cable channels, and NBC's assets.

In announcing the agreement with GE, Comcast Chief Executive Officer Brian Roberts called the deal "a perfect fit for Comcast and will allow us to become a leader in the development and distribution of multiplatform 'anytime, anywhere' media that American consumers are demanding." In the short term, few changes would be made at NBC, with no large-scale layoffs announced and the current head of the company, Jeff Zucker, retaining his job.

NBC was not Comcast's first attempt at a major merger. In 2004, Comcast offered to purchase the Walt Disney Company, an unsolicited attempt that ultimately failed. To keep competition to a minimum during the NBC merger negotiations, Comcast signed an agreement with GE in September, when details of the merger first leaked, to prohibit any additional bidders from entering the negotiations. Comcast's behavior in 2004, and the closure of the merger to other bidders, drew the attention of members of Congress, who promised to investigate the full details of the merger to ensure that it was carried out fairly and in a way that would not harm the American consumer. Of greatest concern was keeping prices affordable and preventing Comcast from using NBC to dominate the video marketplace on both the content and distribution sides.

Roberts made clear that he expected the approval process for the merger to be lengthy, but insisted that it was not the intention of Comcast to block content or significantly hike its prices. However, he acknowledged that the business model of NBC, which has long run in fourth place to the three other major networks, is threatened today by consumers seeking on-demand content on the Internet. The merger would present Comcast an opportunity, he said, to move toward more innovative distribution of online content.

The Congressional Research Service (CRS) released a report in February 2010 on the potential effects of the merger on the video marketplace. It concluded, however, that because this market is currently developing and changing rapidly, there is too much uncertainty for a clear assessment of the merger's impact. According to the report, two possible scenarios of the outcome of the merger include new media regulations and policies on all television, cable, and Internet providers, or an inability on the part of Comcast to capitalize on its market dominance because of conflicting incentives across the media marketplace.

APPROVAL CONDITIONS

On January 18, 2011, the FCC approved the merger to allow Comcast to combine its cable networks with NBC's assets to form NBCUniversal Media, LLC. Draft approval of the merger came in December 2010. Although the FCC noted five areas of concern with the merger, in the end, the FCC reported, the merger was deemed to be in the public interest. "After a thorough review, we have adopted strong and fair merger conditions to ensure this transaction serves the public interest," said FCC chair Julius Genachowski. The conditions set forth by the FCC "include carefully considered steps to ensure that competition drives innovation in the emerging online video marketplace," Genachowski said, responding to earlier concern that Comcast would now dominate online video creation and delivery. "Our approval is also structured to spur broadband adoption among underserved communities; to increase broadband access to schools and libraries; and to increase news coverage, children's television, and Spanish-language programming," the chair said. It is not uncommon for the FCC to impose conditions of approval for media mergers, though the Comcast conditions would remain in place for up to seven years, longer than has been required in the past. The 4–1 FCC approval vote featured a lone dissenter, Michael Copps, a Democratic member of the FCC who expressed concern that the merger would limit communications choices while raising costs for consumers. "At the end of the day, the public interest requires more—much more—than it is receiving," Copps said.

In order to gain FCC approval, Comcast was required to agree to all of the provisions of the merger, which included working to increase competition in the video marketplace. The FCC expressed concern that the merger could create risks "to the development of innovative online video distribution services." To alleviate this concern, Comcast agreed to abide by a stipulation requiring it to distribute certain content via the Internet if a competitor did as well. For example, if one network was distributing a reality television program to Apple TV, NBC would be required to do the same. Comcast also entered into a voluntary agreement with civil rights groups to designate certain channels for minority-owned and -produced content. The voluntary agreement was fundamental in getting Democratic Commissioner Mignon Clyburn's support. "After considering these additional voluntary commitments from the applicants, I determined that their resolve to improve diversity of viewpoint and programming is credible and they deserve discretion in taking steps they feel are necessary to make additional tangible improvements in those areas," Clyburn said. Comcast also agreed to abide by the FCC's net neutrality rules adopted in December 2010 that would prevent it from slowing down or blocking traffic in favor of its own content. The cable giant would still be allowed to use reasonable network management techniques.

Should Comcast not follow through on any of the provisions of the merger, the FCC can fine or take its broadcast license away. This type of punishment is rare, however, and Comcast would be given the opportunity to take the FCC to court as it did in 2008 when it was accused of violating net neutrality regulations. Comcast ultimately came out victorious in the case.

Comcast made a further concession to the DOJ, which investigated any potential violation of antitrust laws. Before approving the merger, the DOJ required NBC to give up its management stake in Hulu, a video sharing sited owned jointly by News Corp., NBC Universal, and Disney. "Without such a remedy, Comcast could, through its seats on Hulu's board of directors, interfere with the management of Hulu, and, in particular, the development of products that compete with Comcast's video service," the department said in a news release. "The conditions imposed will maintain an open and fair marketplace while at the same time allow the innovative aspects of the transaction to go forward," said Assistant Attorney General Christine Varney. Although forced to give up its board seat, Comcast was allowed to maintain its financial interest in Hulu. The Department of Justice said its approval was gained after also ensuring that Comcast would not retaliate against programmers and partners who did not give in to certain Comcast business demands.

MERGER COMPLETION

The Comcast-NBC merger was completed on January 28, 2011. Comcast now owns 51 percent of the shares of the $30 billion media empire. The thirteen months of work to complete the merger created a new company that includes NBC broadcast stations and cable channels such as Bravo, USA, CNBC, and MSNBC; Universal Studios; theme parks; and Comcast's cable channels, including regional sports networks, E!, Golf Channel, and Versus.

Even before the merger, Comcast was already a large company, with 23 million cable subscribers and 17 million Internet subscribers. Comcast CEO Roberts said the merger creates "the ideal entertainment and distribution company." Comcast further promised to continue to work toward anywhere, anytime access to its content.

OPPOSITION

Dissent to the merger was primarily on the grounds that it would give one company the ability to both create and distribute content. FCC Commissioner Copps said the merger was placing too much power in the hands of one company. "The Comcast-NBCU joint venture opens the door to the cable-ization of the open Internet. The potential for walled gardens, toll booths, content prioritization, access fees to reach end users, and a stake in the heart of independent content production is now very real," he said. To stop Comcast from abusing this power, the FCC already has rules in place, called *program access rules*, that require Comcast to provide its content to competitors at a fair rate. There was additional concern that Comcast would limit access to other networks, but the FCC rules ensure that it does not.

Sen. Al Franken, D-Minn., an ardent opponent of the merger, said "The FCC's action today is a tremendous disappointment. The commission is supposed to protect the public interest, not corporate interests. But what we see today is an effort by the FCC to appease the very companies it's charged with regulating." By approving the merger, Franken said the FCC gave too much control over content that reaches millions of Americans to one company. He anticipated that the merger would lead to higher cable and Internet prices and a decline in variety of content choices available to consumers. Franken vowed to continue to oppose any similar mergers that might arise in the future.

Media watchdogs expressed similar outrage. Josh Silver, president of Free Press, a nonprofit group dedicated to media reform, said, "This deal will give Comcast unprecedented control over both media content and the physical network that delivers it. The FCC has opened Pandora's Box, and we can soon expect a whole new swarm of mega-mergers that will have dire consequences for media and the Internet."

—Heather Kerrigan

Following is a press release issued by the Federal Communications Commission (FCC) on January 18, 2011, announcing the approval of the Comcast-NBCU merger, and a statement by FCC Commissioner Michael Copps on January 18, 2011, in opposition to the merger.

DOCUMENT

FCC Approves Comcast-NBCU Merger

January 18, 2011

Today, the Federal Communications Commission grants—with conditions and enforceable commitments—approval of the assignment and transfer of control of broadcast, satellite, and other radio licenses from General Electric Company (GE) to Comcast Corporation. The approval will allow GE and Comcast to create a joint venture involving NBC Universal, Inc. (NBCU) and Comcast. An Order further explaining the Commission's reasoning and the conditions and commitments will be issued shortly.

The Commission's decision is based on a thorough review of the record, which includes extensive data and voluntary commitments from the applicants, as well as thousands of comments from interested parties and public input received at a public forum held in Chicago. Based on this review, the Commission has determined that granting the application, with certain conditions and contingent upon enforceable commitments, is in the public interest.

As part of the merger, Comcast-NBCU will be required to take affirmative steps to foster competition in the video marketplace. In addition, Comcast-NBCU will increase local news coverage to viewers; expand children's programming; enhance the diversity of programming available to Spanish-speaking viewers; offer broadband services to low-income Americans at reduced monthly prices; and provide high-speed broadband to schools, libraries and underserved communities, among other public benefits.

More specifically, the conditions imposed by the Commission address potential harms posed by the combination of Comcast, the nation's largest cable operator and Internet service provider, and NBCU, which owns and develops some of the most valuable television and film content. These targeted conditions and commitments, which generally will remain in effect for seven years, include:

- *Ensuring Reasonable Access to Comcast-NBCU Programming for Multichannel Distribution.* Building on successful requirements adopted in prior, similar transactions, the Commission is establishing for rival multichannel video programming distributors (MVPDs) an improved commercial arbitration process for resolving disputes about prices, terms, and conditions for licensing Comcast-NBCU's video programming. The Commission is also requiring Comcast-NBCU to make available through this process its cable channels in addition to broadcast and regional sports network programming.
- *Protecting the Development of Online Competition.* Recognizing the risks this transaction could present to the development of innovative online video distribution services, the Commission has adopted conditions designed to guarantee *bona fide* online distributors the ability to obtain Comcast-NBCU programming in appropriate circumstances. These conditions respond directly to the concerns voiced by participants in the proceeding—including consumer advocates, online video distributors (OVDs), and MVPDs —while respecting the legitimate business interests of the Applicants to protect the value of their content. Among other things, the Commission requires that Comcast and/or Comcast-NBCU:
  - o Provides to all MVPDs, at fair market value and non-discriminatory prices, terms, and conditions, any affiliated content that Comcast makes available online to its own subscribers or to other MVPD subscribers.
  - o Offers its video programming to legitimate OVDs on the same terms and conditions that would be available to an MVPD.
  - o Makes comparable programming available on economically comparable prices, terms, and conditions to an OVD that has entered into an arrangement to distribute programming from one or more of Comcast-NBCU's peers.
  - o Offers standalone broadband Internet access services at reasonable prices and of sufficient bandwidth so that customers can access online video services without the need to purchase a cable television subscription from Comcast.
  - o Does not enter into agreements to unreasonably restrict online distribution of its own video programming or programming of other providers.
  - o Does not disadvantage rival online video distribution through its broadband Internet access services and/or set-top boxes.
  - o Does not exercise corporate control over or unreasonably withhold programming from Hulu.
- *Access to Comcast's Distribution Systems.* In light of the significant additional video programming Comcast will control after the merger with NBCU—programming that may compete with third-party programming Comcast currently carries or otherwise would carry on its MVPD service—the Commission requires that Comcast not discriminate in video programming distribution on the basis of affiliation or

nonaffiliation with Comcast-NBCU. Moreover, if Comcast "neighborhoods" its news (including business news) channels, it must include all unaffiliated news (or business news) channels in that neighborhood. The Commission also adopts as a condition of the transaction Comcast's voluntary commitment to provide 10 new independent channels within eight years on its digital tier.

- *Protecting Diversity, Localism, Broadcast and Other Public Interest Concerns.* The Commission is also imposing conditions and accepting voluntary commitments concerning a numbers of other public interest issues, including diversity, localism, and broadcasting, among others. For example, to protect the integrity of over-the-air broadcasting, network-affiliate relations, and fair and equitable retransmission consent negotiations with the joint venture, the Commission adopts a series of conditions that were independently negotiated between the Applicants and various network affiliates.

The Applicants have also made a number of additional voluntary commitments, many of which the Commission has adopted as conditions to the transaction's approval. Most of these commitments are geared towards enhancing the public interest as a result of the joint venture. These commitments include:

- *Broadband Adoption and Deployment.* Comcast will make available to approximately 2.5 million low income households: (i) high-speed Internet access service for less than $10 per month; (ii) personal computers, netbooks, or other computer equipment at a purchase price below $150; and (iii) an array of digital literacy education opportunities. Comcast will also expand its existing broadband networks to reach approximately 400,000 additional homes, provide broadband Internet access service in six additional rural communities, and provide free video and high-speed Internet service to 600 new anchor institutions, such as schools and libraries, in underserved, low-income areas.
- *Localism.* To further broadcast localism, Comcast-NBCU will maintain at least the current level of news and information programming on NBC's and Telemundo's owned-and-operated ("O&O") broadcast stations, and in some cases expand news and other local content. NBC and Telemundo O&O stations also will provide thousands of additional hours of local news and information programming to their viewers, and some of its NBC stations will enter into cooperative arrangements with locally focused nonprofit news organizations. Additional free, on-demand local programming will be made available as well.
- *Children's Programming.* Comcast-NBCU will increase the availability of children's programming on its NBC and Telemundo broadcast stations, and add at least 1,500 more choices to Comcast's on-demand offerings for children. It will provide additional on-screen ratings information for original entertainment programming on the Comcast-NBCU broadcast and cable television channels and improved parental controls. Comcast-NBCU also will restrict interactive advertising aimed at children 12 years old and younger and provide public service announcements addressing children's issues.
- *Programming Diversity.* Building on Comcast's voluntary commitments in this area, we require Comcast-NBCU to increase programming diversity by expanding its over-the- air programming to the Spanish language-speaking community,

and by making NBCU's Spanish-language broadcast programming available via Comcast's on demand and online platforms. As noted above, Comcast also will add at least 10 new independent channels to its cable offerings.

- *Public, Educational, and Governmental ("PEG") Programming.* Comcast will safeguard the continued accessibility and signal quality of PEG channels on its cable television systems and introduce new on demand and online platforms for PEG content.

Action by the Commission January 18, 2011 by: Memorandum Opinion and Order (FCC 11-4).

Chairman Genachowski and Commissioner Clyburn, with Commissioners McDowell and Baker concurring, and Commissioner Copps dissenting. Chairman Genachowski and Commissioners Clyburn and Copps each issuing a separate statement, with Commissioners McDowell and Baker issuing a joint statement.

MB Docket No. 10-56

SOURCE: Federal Communications Commission. "FCC Grants Approval of Comcast-NBCU Transaction." January 18, 2011. http://transition.fcc.gov/Daily_Releases/Daily_Business/2011/db0118/DOC-304134A1 .pdf.

FCC Commissioner Copps Issues Dissent on Comcast-NBCU Merger

January 18, 2011

Re: *Applications of Comcast Corporation, General Electric Company and NBC Universal, Inc. For Consent to Assign Licenses and Transfer Control of Licensees,* MB Docket 10-56

Comcast's acquisition of NBC Universal is a transaction like no other that has come before this Commission—ever. It reaches into virtually every corner of our media and digital landscapes and will affect every citizen in the land. It is new media as well as old; it is news and information as well as sports and entertainment; it is distribution as well as content. And it confers too much power in one company's hands.

For any transaction that comes before this Commission, our statutory obligation is to weigh the promised benefits against the potential harms so as to determine whether the public interest is being served. There are many potential harms attending this transaction—even the majority recognizes them. But all the majority's efforts—diligent though they were—to ameliorate these harms cannot mask the truth that this Comcast-NBCU joint venture grievously fails the public interest. I searched in vain for the benefits. I could find little more than such touted gains as "the elimination of double marginalization." Pardon me, but a deal of this size should be expected to yield more than the limited benefits cited. I understand that economies and efficiencies could accrue to the combined Comcast-NBCU venture, but look a little further into the decision and you will find that any such savings will not necessarily be passed on to consumers. When they tell you that at the outset, don't look for lower cable or Internet access bills. As companies combine and consolidate, consumers have seen their cable bills out-strip the Consumer Price Index by orders of magnitude.

Many of the new commitments that have been added aim no higher than maintaining the status quo. The status quo is not serving the public interest.

It is also claimed that the duration of the commitments made by Comcast-NBCU are longer than any that have been attached to previously-approved mergers. That may be true—but it is also true that power is patient and that big businesses can bide their time when they have to in order to reap the fullest harvest.

While approval of this transaction was from its announcement the steepest of climbs for me, given my long-standing opposition to the outrageous media consolidation this country has experienced over the past few decades, I did meet with stakeholders on all sides to make sure I understood their perspectives on the matter. And I worked to develop ideas to minimize the harms and to advance at least some positive public interest benefits. I know my colleagues worked assiduously on this proceeding, too. Commissioner Clyburn, for example, worked successfully to achieve commitments from Comcast-NBCU to improve diversity, expand broadband deployment in unserved areas and increase broadband adoption by low-income households. The Chairman and his team, led by John Flynn, and many, many other members of the FCC team put more effort into this transaction than I have seen put into any transaction during my nearly ten years here at the Commission. I also salute the unprecedented cooperation between the agency and the Department of Justice.

But at the end of the day, the public interest requires more—much more—than it is receiving. The Comcast-NBCU joint venture opens the door to the cable-ization of the open Internet. The potential for walled gardens, toll booths, content prioritization, access fees to reach end users, and a stake in the heart of independent content production is now very real.

As for the future of America's news and journalism, I see nothing in this deal to address the fundamental damage that has been inflicted by years of outrageous consolidation and newsroom cuts. Investigative journalism is not even a shell of its former self. All of this means it's more difficult for citizens to hold the powerful accountable. It means thousands of stories go unwritten. It means we never hear about untold instances of business corruption, political graft and other chicanery; it also means we don't hear enough about all the good things taking place in our country every day. The slight tip of the hat that the applicants have made toward some very limited support of local media projects does not even begin to address the core of the problem. Given that this merger will make the joint venture a steward of the public's airwaves as a broadcast licensee, I asked for a major commitment of its resources to beef up the news operation at NBC. That request was not taken seriously. Increasing the quantity of news by adding hours of programming is no substitute for improving the quality of news by devoting the necessary resources. Make no mistake: what is at stake here is the infrastructure for our national conversation—the very lifeblood of American democracy. We should be moving in precisely the opposite direction of what this Commission approves today.

There are many other facets of the joint venture that trouble me. I worry, for example, about the future of our public broadcast stations. Comcast-NBCU has committed to carry the signals of any of those stations that agree to relinquish the spectrum they are presently using. Will public television no longer be available to over-the-air viewers? And, what happens when the duration of this commitment has run its course? Might the public station be dropped to make room for yet more infotainment programming? In too many communities, the public television station is the last locally owned and operated media outlet left. Public television is miles ahead of everyone else in making productive, public interest use of the digital multi-cast spectrum licensed to it. Why in the world would we gamble with its future?

While the item before the Commission improves measurably on the program access, program carriage and online video provisions originally offered by the applicants, I believe loopholes remain that will allow Comcast-NBCU to unduly pressure both distributors, especially small cable companies, and content producers who sit across the table from the newly-consolidated company during high-stakes business negotiations for programming and carriage. Even when negotiations are successful between the companies, consumers can still expect to see high prices get passed along to them, as Comcast-NBCU remains free to bundle less popular programming with must-have marquee programming. Given the market power that Comcast-NBCU will have at the close of this deal over both programming content and the means of distribution, consumers should be rightfully worried.

In sum, this is simply too much, too big, too powerful, too lacking in benefits for American consumers and citizens. I have respect for the business acumen of the applicants, and have no doubts that they will strive to make Comcast-NBCU a financial success. But simply blessing business deals is not the FCC's statutorily-mandated job. Our job is to determine whether the record here demonstrates that this new media giant will serve the public interest. While I welcome the improvements made to the original terms, at the end of the day this transaction is a huge boost for media industry (and digital industry) consolidation. It puts new media on a road traditional media should never have taken. It further erodes diversity, localism and competition—the three essential pillars of the public interest standard mandated by law. I would be true to neither the statute nor to everything I have fought for here at the Commission over the past decade if I did not dissent from what I consider to be a damaging and potentially dangerous deal.

SOURCE: Federal Communications Commission. Commissioner Michael J. Copps. "Dissenting Statement of Commissioner Michael J. Copps." January 18, 2011. http://hraunfoss.fcc.gov/edocs_public/attachmatch/FCC-11-4A3.pdf.

OTHER HISTORIC DOCUMENTS OF INTEREST

FROM PREVIOUS HISTORIC DOCUMENTS

Lebanon Forms New Government

JANUARY 20, MARCH 29, JUNE 13, AND AUGUST 17, 2011

Following months of political deadlock, on January 12, 2011, Lebanon's unity government collapsed after eleven cabinet ministers representing Hezbollah and its allies resigned in opposition to the government's continuing support of a UN-backed tribunal investigating the murder of the former prime minister Rafiq Hariri. Hezbollah's exit ignited debate about whether the nation would devolve into violence not seen since the end of its civil war in 1990 or the political stalemate would continue. The country's delicate power balance, established in 2009, required the appointment of a new prime minister upon Hezbollah's exit, and left Prime Minister Saad Hariri as caretaker of the remainder of the government until the president named his replacement. In the end, it was Hezbollah that gained the upper hand, being named, along with its allies, to sixteen of thirty seats in the new cabinet, sparking international concern about the growing influence of Syria and Iran, allies of Hezbollah, in the nation.

Hezbollah's Exit

On January 12, 2011, the most powerful political force in Lebanon, Hezbollah, and its allies withdrew from the Lebanese government cabinet, signaling an end to the national unity government first formed in 2009. Given the volatility of Lebanese politics, little had been done for months preceding the resignations because the government remained deadlocked. The decision of eleven ministers to resign came after talks between Saudi Arabia and Syria, which were intended to mediate tensions in Lebanon between the various political factions, ended without resolution. The work by these two nations had been seen as the best attempt to date to bring an end to sectarian political struggles. Upon resigning, Hezbollah leaders called for the creation of a new government.

Because Syria backs Hezbollah, an agreement to ease the tension would have most likely distanced Lebanon from the UN-backed tribunal's investigation into the 2005 death of former Prime Minister Rafiq Hariri, who resigned from office in 2004. The tribunal was established in 2009 to determine responsibility for the bombing that killed the former prime minister and twenty-one others. Initially, the United Nations was expected to indict Syrian leaders, which led to Syria's withdrawal of its troops that had been stationed in Lebanon since 1976. As the investigation continued, it became clearer that members of Hezbollah were more likely the targets of the UN investigation.

Support for the tribunal in Lebanon came primarily from Saad Hariri and his allies. Hezbollah accused the tribunal of using flawed evidence and false witnesses to build a case. Hezbollah leader Sayyed Hassan Nasrallah called the tribunal a "U.S.-Israeli project."

Hezbollah had previously threatened to take action if the United Nations indicted any of its members in the murder of the former prime minister, though it did not indicate that resignations were possible. It was widely expected that when the United Nations released the findings of its tribunal in mid-2011, the Lebanese government would collapse, but few expected Hezbollah to leave the government as early as January.

At the time of the resignation, Prime Minister Saad Hariri was meeting with President Barack Obama at the White House. Hezbollah had hoped to have all eleven ministers resign shortly before the Obama meeting, which they thought would cause embarrassment for Hariri, who, without all the seats in his cabinet filled, would be little more than a caretaker prime minister.

Following Hezbollah's exit from the government, President Michel Suleiman named Hariri caretaker prime minister, and was constitutionally required to consult parliament on who the new prime minister would be, though the constitution dictated that the position be filled by a Sunni Muslim. With waning popularity, Hariri had few options following Hezbollah's withdrawal. Hariri had indicated that he would be willing to compromise with the leaders of Hezbollah to form a new unity government, but made it clear that he would not turn his back on the UN-backed tribunal. "There's no way to compromise on the issue of the court and justice," Hariri said in a statement released by Boutros Harb, a Lebanese minister. In response, Hezbollah seemingly ignored Lebanon's ties to the UN tribunal, saying "We don't want any escalation. We are committed to the constitution. We don't know what commitment the others are talking about," said Hezbollah allied official and health minister Mohamad Jawad Khalifeh.

Speculation flew about whether the new uncertainty caused by the Hezbollah withdrawal would spark renewed violence or prolong the existing political stalemate. Forming a new government had proved difficult for Lebanon in the past. Following the 2009 election, it took five months for the government to come together. The difficulty stems from the diversity of groups in Lebanon who must each be given a proportionate amount of power, creating a delicate power sharing agreement that ensures deal making between the Christian, Sunni, Shiite, and Druze communities is necessary and never-ending.

RECENT HISTORY OF CONFLICT

The January collapse of the Lebanese government instigated by Hezbollah's withdrawal is part of a long history of conflict between Hezbollah and other Lebanese government and military elements. A fifteen-year civil war (1975–1990) was followed by relative peace until 2005, when former Prime Minister Rafiq Hariri, the father of Saad Hariri, was killed by a bomb that hit his motorcade. The Syrians were held responsible for the bombing, and anti-Syrian protests, dubbed the Cedar Revolution, swept across the country. The revolution drove a number of Syrian troops, who had first entered Lebanon in 1976 to help stop the civil war, out of the country.

Following the Cedar Revolution, Lebanon's government became entrenched in a political stalemate until the current government was formed with the aim of keeping sectarian violence at bay. Since the end of the civil war in 1990, the Lebanese government has attempted to limit Hezbollah's military capacity, which sparked intermittent violence in the streets of Beirut. The sporadic violence lasted only until a new government was created early in 2009. A power-sharing agreement was reached in November following five months of deadlock. The new government required the president to be a Maronite Christian, the prime minister a Sunni Muslim, and the speaker of Parliament a Shia Muslim. Each faith represented in the three most powerful positions makes up approximately one third of Lebanon's population of four million. The national unity government gave fifteen ministerial positions to Hariri's bloc, ten to Hezbollah, and five to those nominated by the Lebanese president. The unity government was set up in this fashion so that no group would be able to hold a majority of the power. Even in the new unity government, Hezbollah's power has continued to grow, in part because of the alliances it has formed with Christian military leaders.

Hezbollah Returns to Take Power

Two weeks after Hezbollah's January 12 withdrawal from the government, a new prime minister was named to replace Hariri. Najib Mikati, a political independent and telecommunications billionaire, took the position. Mikati is unpopular in the Sunni community because of his close ties to Syria and what are viewed as past betrayals of Sunnis.

It took almost five months for Mikati to name his cabinet and form a government. The March 8 coalition, which draws its name from a March 8, 2005, demonstration in response to the Cedar Revolution and is made up of various Lebanese political parties including Hezbollah and its allies, had asked for two thirds of the seats, but it was Mikati's desire to keep one third plus one of the seats for his own party and allies to assure a constitutional veto. Further delays were caused by the Arab Spring uprising in Syria. Mikati was accused of taking too long to act as he waited to see how the situation in Syria would conclude. To move the formation of the government along, parliament offered one Shiite seat to the Sunnis.

In June Mikati named a new cabinet, which was dominated by Hezbollah and its allies who received sixteen of the thirty cabinet seats. For the first time since the civil war, there were more Sunnis than Shiites in the cabinet. After naming his cabinet, Mikati asked the Lebanese people to give the new government a chance to prove itself. "Do not judge intentions and people, but rather actions," he said. "The government is committed to maintaining strong, brotherly ties which bind Lebanon to all Arab countries without exception. . . . Let us go to work immediately according to the principles . . . [of] defending Lebanon's sovereignty and its independence and liberating land that remains under the occupation of the Israeli enemy." The new government opened the possibility of further influence by Syria and Iran in the country, both of which back Hezbollah. Syria in particular has been accused by international analysts of attempting to work with Hezbollah to subvert the power of any coalition government in Lebanon so as to stave off another possible prodemocracy movement.

Although Mikati had shown strong ties to Hezbollah by granting that party a majority in the cabinet, he did not bend to their desire to abandon the UN tribunal. Instead, Mikati announced that Lebanon would continue paying its 49 percent share for the tribunal expenses and would accept its ruling. In November, Mikati circumvented Hezbollah's power and sent Lebanon's tribunal payment. Hezbollah had threatened to veto the payment, and Mikati subsequently threatened to resign his post if the payment was not made. To avoid another government collapse, Mikati funneled the money through Lebanon's Higher Relief Committee, a move that did not require the approval of his cabinet.

Findings of the United Nations Tribunal

In July, the UN-backed tribunal issued the names of four men accused of the bombing that killed the former prime minister: Salim Jamil Ayyash, Mustafa Amine Badreddine, Hussein Hassan Oneissi, and Assad Hassan Sabra. All four men are Lebanese. Arrest warrants were issued on July 8. The full indictment, unsealed on August 17, listed the charges against the four men as conspiracy to commit a terrorist act. When the full indictment was unveiled, Antonio Cassese, the president of the tribunal, urged the four accused men to turn themselves in. The Lebanese government, which is required to arrest those indicted by the tribunal, announced that it had been unable to arrest or serve the indictment. As of the end of 2011, arrests of the four men had yet to take place, and it is unlikely, under the majority Hezbollah government, that they will occur.

International Influence in Lebanon

One of the key difficulties in governing Lebanon is the international influence from a variety of global players. The United States backed Saad Hariri's government and considers Hezbollah a terrorist organization. Since 2006, Lebanon's army has received $720 million in aid from the United States, which hoped the money would be used to help fight Hezbollah and remove Syrian and Iranian influence on Lebanon's government. Following the collapse of Hariri's government, the White House issued a statement further defining its view of Hezbollah's involvement in the government, stating, "The efforts by the Hezbollah-led coalition to collapse the Lebanese government only demonstrate their own fear and determination to block the government's ability to conduct its business and advance the aspirations of all of the Lebanese people." The question that now faces the United States is whether it will continue to send funds to Lebanon with what it sees as a terrorist organization largely in control. "For years, members of Congress warned that it was unwise to fund a Lebanese government in which Hezbollah participated. It was clear that Hezbollah's influence was growing and that the executive branch had no long-term strategy to deal with that reality and no contingency plan to stop U.S. aid from falling into the wrong hands," said Rep. Ileana Ros-Lehtinen, R-Fla., the chair of the House Foreign Affairs Committee.

On the other hand, Syria and Iran do support Hezbollah. Syria benefits from Mikati's new government, at least until the spring 2013 parliamentary elections. However, as politics continue to devolve in Syria, ramifications in Lebanon could include the fall of the new government. The two nations have long-standing political, economic, and social ties, with Syria holding a position of power in the relationship. If Syrian President Bashar al-Assad's regime were to fall, civil war could break out and spill over the porous border into Lebanon. This would pit Mikati against Hezbollah and its allies in his cabinet. The Hezbollah organization controls strategic weapons in Syria, and Syria in turn provides the group with additional arms and military training. Therefore, Hezbollah has a vested interest in stopping any prodemocracy movement in Syria. Mikati's government, however, has assumed a position of non-interference in Syria. The tension could cause a rift in Lebanon's government, with Hezbollah attempting to maintain its standing in the region by leaving the government or subverting Mikati's power some other way.

Challenges Ahead

Challenges remain for Mikati's new government. Most importantly, he must preserve it until the 2013 parliamentary elections. Since 2006, Lebanon's economy has been in recovery, with the banking, real estate, and tourism sectors continuing to grow. Continuing instability in the government, however, could curtail this economic growth and cause Lebanon's current $50 billion public debt to grow even further. With this staggering debt, spending on infrastructure and job growth has been neglected, with underutilized energy resources and outdated telecommunications systems as the consequence.

—Heather Kerrigan

Following is a press release issued by the United Nations on January 20, 2011, expressing hope for the formation of a new government in Lebanon; a press conference held on March 29, 2011, by the UN envoy to Lebanon on the continuing battle to form a government; a press release from the United Nations on June 13, 2011, commending Lebanon on the formation of its new government; and a press release from the United Nations on August 17, 2011, upon the unsealing of the indictment in the UN-backed tribunal to investigate the murder of Lebanon's former prime minister Rafiq Hariri.

UN and Lebanese Prime Minister Meet to Discuss New Government

January 20, 2011

Restoring political stability and achieving a new Lebanese government is possible if all parties are willing to cooperate towards that end, a top United Nations envoy said today following a meeting with the caretaker Prime Minister, Saad Hariri.

The meeting between Michael Williams and Mr. Hariri comes just over a week after the collapse of the government of national unity, resulting from the resignation of 11 cabinet ministers from Hizbollah and allied groups due to differences over the UN-backed tribunal set up to try suspects in the 2005 assassination of Mr. Hariri's father and former prime minister, Rafik Hariri.

Mr. Williams and the Prime Minister discussed the various international initiatives, most recently by Turkey and Qatar, and the prospect for achieving a new government and political stability in Lebanon.

"I believe that that is possible, provided that there is goodwill and cooperation of all political parties in working for justice as well as stability," said Mr. Williams, who serves as the UN Special Coordinator for Lebanon.

He also underlined the need for calm and order during the current period despite the political divisions in the country.

On Monday, the Prosecutor of the Special Tribunal for Lebanon, Daniel Bellemare, submitted the first indictment and supporting materials to the court, which is based in the Netherlands. The contents of the indictment remain confidential at this stage and need to be reviewed by the Pre-Trial Judge.

The Tribunal was set up following a probe by the International Independent Investigation Commission after an earlier UN mission found that Lebanon's own inquiry into the massive car bombing that killed Mr. Hariri and 22 others was seriously flawed, and that Syria was primarily responsible for the political tensions that preceded the attack.

UN officials, including Secretary-General Ban Ki-moon, have repeatedly stressed that the Tribunal is an independent body whose work should not be linked with any political debate.

SOURCE: United Nations. UN News Centre. "UN Envoy and Lebanese Prime Minister Discuss Prospects for New Government." January 20, 2011. http://www.un.org/apps/news/story.asp?NewsID=37328&Cr=leban&Cr1=.

DOCUMENT   *UN Press Conference on Lebanon*

March 29, 2011

With no real movement towards forming a Government in Lebanon following the collapse nearly three months ago of Saad Hariri's administration, United Nations envoy Michael Williams today called for an end to the political polarization in the Middle Eastern country so that both the security and development priorities of the people could be met.

"We look forward to the early formation of a Government that can address the priorities of the Lebanese people," said Mr. Williams, Special Coordinator for Lebanon, during a Headquarters press conference immediately following his briefing to the Security Council on the situation in that country and on implementation of resolution 1701 (2006), which ended the 2006 war in Lebanon between Israel and Hizbullah.

Before updating the press on his talks with the Council, he first expressed concern over the apparent abduction of seven Estonian cyclists in the Bekaa Valley late last week. "It has now been several days since their disappearance and I would like to take this opportunity to appeal for their immediate release from whoever is holding [them]," he said, adding that no purpose was served by their continued detention and he hoped the matter could be resolved soon.

Returning to the matter at hand, he said "enormous shifts and upheavals" were under way in the Middle East, and everywhere demands were being made for representative Governments. At the same time, the situation in Lebanon remained high on the Council's agenda while efforts continued in that country to form a new Government under the leadership of Prime Minister–designate Najib Mikati.

In his meetings over the past several months with Mr. Mikati and others, he had made it clear that the United Nations expected that any new Government would continue to respect its international obligations, especially those derived from 1701. He had been reassured by statements from Lebanese officials to that effect.

"On the Blue line itself, the cessation of hostilities continues to hold, and I am confident that this will remain the case in the coming period," he said, adding that he had also expressed his satisfaction to the Council that the Tripartite Mechanism, led by the United Nations Interim Force in Lebanon (UNIFIL), was continuing its important work. "This is really quite a remarkable group," he added, paying tribute to the commitment of UNIFIL, the Lebanese army and the Israel Defense Forces (IDF) to that important mechanism.

Continuing, he said, however, that all stakeholders seemed to feel the need to see more progress towards full implementation of resolution 1701, and he had reiterated in the Security Council his call on Israel to halt the "almost daily incursions of Lebanese airspace" and to withdraw from the northern part of the village of Ghajar. "In this regard, we have had ongoing discussions with senior Lebanese and Israeli officials, and I hope that following the formation of a new Government in Lebanon, that we can proceed with this issue and see the withdrawal of the Israeli army from this pocket of Lebanese territory," he said.

Mr. Williams said he had also told the Council that, inevitably, political polarization in Lebanon had affected implementation of the resolution. He had expressed regret that, for example, the national dialogue had been in abeyance for some time now and had not met since early November. He hoped that under the auspices of President [Michel] Suleiman that the dialogue's participants could meet again after the new Government was formed.

"I feel [the national dialogue] plays an important part in addressing differences and tensions," he said, adding in particular, that its role was vital to make progress on the development of a national defence strategy that would address arms outside the control of the State.

He said he had also expressed the hope in the Council that a new Government, once formed, would reinvigorate its engagement to improve its management and control of the country's borders. During the Council's consultations, Lebanon's representative, a non-permanent member of the 15-nation body, had raised the issue of maritime borders and the exploration and exploitation of natural resources.

Lebanon had approached the United Nations for assistance with the delimitation of its maritime boundaries, he noted. Inevitably, such a request required a decision by both Lebanon and Israel. Israeli authorities had expressed to him that Israel did not envisage a role for the United Nations in that regard. Nevertheless, they were anxious to avoid another area of conflict, and, as that was the case, the United Nations would continue to consider ways to keep the issue from becoming a source of friction. "That is the last thing we need," he added.

Taking a question on weapons smuggling to Syria, Mr. Williams said that the Secretary-General had made several statements during the past week expressing his concern, above all, about the loss of life there in the wake on ongoing anti-Government protests. He believed the Secretary-General had also spoken to Syrian President Bashar al-Assad to underline that concern. What was happening in Syria could not be seen in isolation "from this extraordinary wave of revolt that has swept from the Maghreb to the Gulf, encompassing so many countries," said Mr. Williams.

In all cases, sadly, there had been "some loss of life," he said, adding his hope that that would cease to continue, especially in Syria, which was Lebanon's immediate neighbour. He had seen press reports of arms smuggling from Lebanon, but had no knowledge of those activities. At the same time, he added later that "there are far too many weapons in Lebanon," particularly those not in Government hands.

To another question, he said events under way in North Africa and the Middle East could affect Lebanon both positively and negatively, but, overall, he believed that in the longer run, the fallout would be positive, both for Lebanon and throughout the region.

Connecting countries as far afield as Tunisia in the West and Bahrain in the East were popular protests affecting republics as well as kingdoms; countries that were pro-Western and those that might be seen as "more radical," he said. The events were based on demands for dignity and more representative forms of Government, and as that was the case, there might be positive ripple effects in Lebanon, which had a long tradition of more openness and freedom of the press than many of its neighbours.

However, there was always the possibility of increased tensions and violence, including sectarian violence, but he hoped that would not be the case.

Regarding the direct impact of the events in Syria on Lebanon, especially, said one correspondent, "since it's no secret that Syria has a lot of leverage in Lebanese politics," Mr. Williams reiterated his concern at the slow progress towards forming a new Lebanese Government. Indeed, Saad al-Hariri's Government had fallen in January, and there had been basically no movement since then.

He hoped that delay would not be much longer "but clearly there are difficulties." Recent talks between Syrian and Lebanese officials had been characterized by the view that it was in everyone's interest that a sound Lebanese Government was formed as quickly as possible. Yet, as the events in Syria were escalating, there might be further delays on the Lebanese side, he added.

To a query regarding the work and impact of the Special Tribunal set up to prosecute persons for the death of former Lebanese Prime Minister Rafiq Hariri, he recalled that, at the beginning of the year, the Prosecutor had passed the dossier to the pre-trial judge. At that time, it had been estimated that indictments would be handed down in six to eight weeks. But he believed that some of the indictments were being amended, and it was now being suggested that the delay could take up to a few months.

On the impact of the Tribunal's activities, he acknowledged that the body's work had contributed to political polarization in Lebanon, with some parties supporting it whole-heartedly and others expressing deep scepticism. Personally, he believed "the more clarity, the better," although he understood that "in some countries, legal issues had a tendency to drag out," as seen with the investigations and trials regarding crimes committed during the Balkan wars of the 1990s.

"Can Lebanon survive without a Government? Yes," he continued, noting that there was a caretaker Government in place and that Ministers were in their offices and ministries were functioning "and functioning rather well." Yet, extraordinary events were sweeping the region, which could have an impact on Lebanon. He very much hoped that, in the near-term, Prime Minister–designate Mikati, whom the United Nations fully supported, would be successful in his endeavours.

To a question regarding a rumoured visit by Security Council members to the region, he said he believed it had perhaps been decades since such a mission had been carried out in Lebanon. Meanwhile, the mechanism of Council missions "is tried and tested" and had been very successful in Sudan and other places in Africa, as well as in Afghanistan.

Perhaps, given the nature of recent events in the region, "there is a greater purpose" to such a visit to Lebanon by the Council, he said, adding that "timing would be everything," as always in such cases. Moreover, in the background was the stalled Israeli-Palestinian peace process. If the current round of face-to-face negotiations—on hold since early September 2010—was to restart, gain momentum and then take hold, that would certainly do much to raise the hope of bolstering stability in the wider region. The same held true regarding both Israel and Lebanon fulfilling their obligations under resolution 1701.

On the situation in Nahr al-Bared camp for Palestinian refugees, he said that despite worrying dismal conditions overall, he could report from a visit to the camp last November that real progress had been made towards reconstruction in the wake of fighting that had taken place in the area in 2007. At the same time, he "bitterly regretted" the pace of refugee returns. That process had been stalled by "many delays," but lack of funding was a major hurdle. There was a compelling humanitarian imperative for the situation in Nahr al-Bared and other Palestinian camps to be addressed. As such, he appealed to the Council, to countries in the West, "and especially those in the Arab world to do more."

"There needs to be greater will to take this process forward." He reiterated his overall concern about the situation in the camps, especially recent demonstrations against the United Nations Relief and Works Agency for Palestine Refugees in the Near East (UNRWA) and other agencies working to help the refugees.

SOURCE: United Nations. "Press Conference by United Nations Special Coordinator for Lebanon." March 29, 2011. http://www.un.org/News/briefings/docs/2011/110329_Lebanon.doc.htm.

DOCUMENT   *New Government Formed in Lebanon*

June 13, 2011

Secretary-General Ban Ki-moon today welcomed the formation of a new Government after nearly five months of disagreement between the country's various political groups, saying the move was an important step towards establishing a functional administration.

"The Secretary-General believes that the formation today of a new cabinet in Lebanon, following months of consultations under the auspices of President Michel Sleiman and Prime Minister Najib Mikati, is an important step toward establishing a functional, executive Government in Lebanon," said a statement issued by his spokesperson.

Mr. Ban said he hoped the new Government will enable Lebanon to address the economic, political and security challenges facing the country and underlined the importance for Lebanese leaders to maintain a spirit of national dialogue and cooperation.

"The Secretary-General looks forward to the finalization, as soon as possible, of the new Government's platform. He expects the Government of Lebanon to reiterate its commitment to the full implementation of Security Council resolution 1701 and to all of Lebanon's international obligations," the statement added.

The terms of Security Council resolution 1701 ended a month-long war between Israel and Hizbollah in 2006. It also calls for respect for the Blue Line separating Israel and Lebanon, the disarming of all militias in Lebanon, and an end to arms smuggling in the area.

Earlier, the UN Special Coordinator for Lebanon, Michael Williams, congratulated Mr. Mikati and expressed hope that the new administration will tackle Lebanon's many challenges. He said the new Government will "enable the country to address the manifold challenges facing the country, whether economic, political or security."

Mr. Mikati's nomination followed the collapse of the government led by Saad Hariri after 11 Hizbollah and allied ministers resigned, reportedly over its refusal to cease cooperation with the UN-backed court investigating the 2005 assassination of Mr. Hariri's father Rafiq and 22 others, amid reports that the tribunal was about to indict Hizbollah members for the murders.

SOURCE: United Nations. UN News Centre. "UN Chief Welcomes Formation of New Government in Lebanon." June 13, 2011. http://www.un.org/apps/news/story.asp?NewsID=38704&Cr=lebanon&Cr1=.

DOCUMENT *UN Tribunal Releases Indictments*

August 17, 2011

A judge in the United Nations–backed tribunal set up to try suspects in the 2005 assassination of former Lebanese prime minister Rafiq Hariri today ordered the unsealing of the full indictment that spells out prosecutors' case against four men accused of carrying out the crime.

In his ruling confirming the indictment, a pre-trial judge of the Special Tribunal for Lebanon (STL), Daniel Fransen, found that there was sufficient evidence to proceed to trial, where prosecutors will then have to prove that the accused are guilty beyond reasonable doubt.

"The pre-trial judge found that the indictment meets the requirements with regard to the specific facts and grounds as required under international case law, the statute and the rules (of procedure and evidence)," Mr. Fransen's decision states.

Last month, the tribunal released the identities of the four men accused of the crime, which was committed on 14 February 2005.

The four accused are Salim Jamil Ayyash, Mustafa Amine Badreddine, Hussein Hassan Oneissi and Assad Hassan Sabra. All Lebanese, they are charged over the massive car bombing in central Beirut that killed Mr. Hariri and 21 others. International arrest warrants were issued on 8 July.

In his decision today, Mr. Fransen explained why, until now, the indictment was confidential, saying the intention was to "ensure the integrity of the judicial procedure and, in particular, ensure that the search and, where appropriate, apprehension of the accused are carried out effectively."

Some parts of the judge's decision and small sections of the indictment remain confidential. They relate to issues that could affect the ongoing prosecution investigation, as well as the privacy and security of victims and witnesses.

Welcoming the judge's decision, Prosecutor Daniel A. Bellemare said "this unsealing of the indictment answers many questions about the 14 February 2005 attack. The full story will however only unfold in the courtroom, where an open, public, fair and transparent trial will render a final verdict."

According to the indictment, Mr. Hariri left his Beirut residence on the morning of his killing to attend a session of Lebanon's Parliament. The team of suspected assassins positioned themselves in several locations to track and observe Mr. Hariri's convoy, as they had done on previous days.

After leaving Parliament and then visiting a nearby café, Mr. Hariri headed back to his residence. As the convoy passed the St Georges Hotel about 12:55 p.m., a male suicide bomber detonated a large quantity of explosives concealed in the cargo area of a strategically placed Mitsubishi Canter van.

Shortly after the explosion, Mr. Oneissi and Mr. Sabra are accused of calling media outlets to give information on where to find a videotape that had been placed on a tree in a Beirut square.

In the video, later broadcast on television, a man named Ahmad Abu Adass falsely claimed to be the suicide bomber on behalf of a fictitious fundamentalist group using the name "Victory and Jihad in Greater Syria."

The indictment charges all four men with conspiracy to commit a terrorist act. Mr. Ayyash and Mr. Badreddine are also charged with committing a terrorist act by means of an explosive device, intentional homicide with premeditation, and attempted intentional homicide.

Mr. Oneissi and Mr. Sabra also face charges of being accomplices in the crimes. All charges in the indictment are crimes under Lebanese criminal law.

According to the indictment, Mr. Badreddine was the overall controller of the attack. Mr. Ayyash coordinated the team that was responsible for the actual perpetration of the attack. Mr. Oneissi and Mr. Sabra, along with others, were conspirators and allegedly prepared and delivered the video, which sought to blame the wrong people, in order to shield the conspirators.

Last week, the President of the tribunal, Antonio Cassese, issued an open letter urging the accused to present themselves before the court, after the Lebanese authorities notified him that that they have been unable to personally serve the accused with the indictment or arrest them.

Mr. Cassese advised the accused through the letter that they could appear before the tribunal in person or by video-link. "At the very least, it is extremely important for you to appoint legal counsel and to instruct them," he said in the letter in which he also detailed their rights under the tribunal's rules of procedure and evidence.

"The march to justice is inexorable, and one way or another we will end up with a trial," Mr. Cassese wrote. "I therefore strongly appeal to the accused to take advantage of the broad legal possibilities offered by our Rules of Procedure and Evidence, thereby contributing to the establishment of truth and the conduct of fair proceedings."

The tribunal is an independent court created at the request of the Lebanese Government, with a mandate issued by the Security Council. It is based in The Hague in the Netherlands.

SOURCE: United Nations. UN News Centre. "UN-Backed Tribunal Unseals Full Indictment Against Accused in Hariri Murder Case." August 17, 2011. http://www.un.org/apps/news/story.asp?NewsID=3 9318&Cr=Lebanon&Cr1=.

OTHER HISTORIC DOCUMENTS OF INTEREST

FROM THIS VOLUME

FROM PREVIOUS *HISTORIC DOCUMENTS*

State of the Union Address and Republican Response

In his second official State of the Union address, which came on the heels of an emotionally charged speech delivered in Tucson, Arizona, the site of a shooting that left Rep. Gabrielle Giffords, D-Ariz., fighting for life and six dead, President Barack Obama took a tack similar to that used in earlier speeches, calling on Democrats and Republicans to come together to solve the biggest problems facing the nation. Members of Congress sat side by side, regardless of their political party, to signal a move toward more civil political discourse in the wake of the Tucson shooting. Taking note of this, Obama said, "What comes of this moment will be determined not by whether we can sit together tonight, but whether we can work together tomorrow."

His speech was dominated by domestic policy, in particular his blueprint for continuing U.S. global economic dominance, dubbed "Winning the Future." In his one-hour speech, Obama made few new spending or policy proposals, shedding light on the new reality of a divided Congress. His 2010 State of the Union had been delivered after a series of major legislative victories for Democrats, but in 2011 the president knew he was facing more serious challenges to achieving legislative success in Congress. He recognized this, saying, "Reforming our schools, changing the way we use energy, reducing our deficit—none of this is easy." He continued, "And it will be harder because we will argue about everything. The costs. The details. The letter of every law . . . as contentious and frustrating and messy as our democracy can sometimes be, I know there isn't a person here who would trade places with any other nation on earth."

Obama called on the members of Congress gathered in the House chamber to work and struggle together in the days ahead to continue the nation's economic reemergence and ensure future growth in a number of areas to keep America a powerhouse on the global stage. "Sustaining the American Dream has never been about standing pat," the president said. "It has required each generation to sacrifice, and struggle, and meet the demands of a new age. And now it's our turn," he said.

WINNING THE FUTURE

A key component of Obama's 2011 State of the Union was "Winning the Future," a blueprint for ensuring continued U.S. economic dominance on the world stage. Winning the future, according to the president, included spending on education, high-speed rail, clean energy technology, and high-speed Internet—all aimed at competing in the global marketplace, specifically with the emerging powers of China and India. "We need to out-innovate, out-educate, and out-build the rest of the world," Obama said. "We have to make America the best place on Earth to do business. We need to take responsibility for our deficit and reform government. That's how our people will prosper." Furthermore, Obama added, "We can't win the future with a government of the past."

A major component of winning the future in Obama's 2011 address was education. Improving education policy and preparing students to compete in the global market-place, Obama said, was "our generation's Sputnik moment." Obama made clear that cutting investments in education might seem like good economic policy at first, but it would not get the nation far in the long term. Obama called for the addition of 100,000 science and technology teachers during the next ten years. The president had first announced this proposal in September 2010, reflecting a similar goal proposed by his predecessor, George W. Bush, during his 2006 State of the Union address. Obama asked, to applause from both Republicans and Democrats, that the country "reward good teachers and stop making excuses for bad ones." He also called for 2010's Race to the Top competition for federal education funding to be used as a model for the replacement of No Child Left Behind.

Obama highlighted the importance of postsecondary education in winning the future, calling on Congress to make college more affordable to more Americans. This included asking for the American Opportunity Tax Credit to be made permanent, which would give students up to $10,000 for four years of higher education, and also highlighting the provision included in the 2010 Affordable Care Act that would elimi-nate private lenders as intermediaries in federally subsidized student loans. Savings from this change could be reinvested in the Pell Grant, the president stated. He also asked Congress to take on immigration reform with an eye toward higher education, to help high-performing students who came to the United States illegally as children work toward citizenship. "Let's stop expelling talented, responsible young people who could be staffing our research labs, or starting a new business, who could be further enriching this nation," the president said.

Debt and Deficit

Although the issues of the U.S. debt and deficit played a major role in the Republican takeover of the House in the 2010 elections, Obama did not spend a significant amount of time covering these topics during his State of the Union address. He did, however, make two significant concessions to Republicans, promising to veto any bill containing earmarks and to fix what some considered a burdensome health care tax provision. The 1099 tax-reporting rule, as it became known, was repealed in April; it ended the require-ment that companies report all financial interaction with other businesses that totals more than $600 per year and raised the amount of tax credit overpayment subject to repayment under the health insurance exchange created by the health care law.

Leaving out any mention of the December recommendations by the bipartisan fiscal commission to bring the government's deficit under control, Obama proposed only a few budget-cutting measures. The first was a continued call for a five-year freeze on some domestic spending, which he said could reduce the deficit by more than $400 billion during the next ten years. He also announced his support for $78 billion in Pentagon budget cuts over the next five years. It was then–Secretary of Defense Robert Gates who proposed the cuts to his agency's budget in early January. Obama took the opportunity of his address before a joint session to reiterate Gates's support for the cuts, speaking directly to members of the Republican Party who thought that $78 billion would cut the defense budget too far.

Economic Growth and Jobs

In discussing the importance of creating American jobs and growing the economy, Obama pointed to Speaker John Boehner, R-Ohio, "someone who began by sweeping the floors of his father's Cincinnati bar." Describing his rise to Speaker of the U.S. House of Representatives, Obama said it made it clear that the United States is "a country where anything is possible." But he reminded listeners of the difficult challenges the nation finds itself facing to create jobs that are able to compete in the global economy. "The world has changed," the president said. "The competition for jobs is real. But this shouldn't discourage us. It should challenge us. Remember—for all the hits we've taken these last few years, for all the naysayers predicting our decline, America still has the largest, most prosperous economy in the world." The president went on to describe the success of American businesses and entrepreneurs, and the importance of maintaining the quality of colleges and universities to produce a high-quality labor force.

In previous speeches, Obama had focused on the role former-President George W. Bush's administration played in creating the economic issues that plagued the nation. In his January 26 address, Obama changed his tone, instead looking to the positive rather than placing blame, and indicating that the nation is emerging from its economic crisis. "Two years after the worst recession most of us have ever known, the stock market has come roaring back," he said. "Corporate profits are up. The economy is growing again."

Foreign Affairs

For the third year in a row, foreign affairs took a backseat to domestic issues in Obama's address before a joint session of Congress. Although the speech coincided with the prodemocracy events of the Arab Spring taking place in the Middle East, Obama made little reference to their importance. He made only one statement of support for the demonstrators, specifically those in Tunisia who had overthrown the authoritarian president's regime. "The United States of America stands with the people of Tunisia, and supports the democratic aspirations of all people," Obama said. In fact, it was not until days later that the president made formal comments on the ongoing revolution in Egypt that was attempting to topple the government of President Hosni Mubarak.

America's continued roles in Iraq and Afghanistan led the president's foreign agenda in his State of the Union address. On Iraq, the president promised to maintain the full withdrawal of American troops by the end of 2011. "The Iraq war is coming to an end," the president said. And on Afghanistan, the president commended the work of American and Afghani troops in fighting al Qaeda and promoting global security. "Our purpose is clear," the president said. "By preventing the Taliban from reestablishing a stranglehold over the Afghan people, we will deny al Qaeda the safe haven that served as a launching pad for 9/11." He went on to say that the work to date will allow the United States to begin transferring more security responsibility to the Afghan people, which would lead to American troop withdrawal beginning in July 2011.

The president briefly discussed the work of the international community to end Iran and North Korea's continued march toward nuclear weapons stocks. Obama's comments on the subject were brief because his administration has not had many successes over the past year, and talks with Iran collapsed less than one week before he took to the podium for his State of the Union address.

REPUBLICAN RESPONSE

The Republican response to the president's State of the Union address was delivered by Rep. Paul Ryan, R-Wis., chairman of the House Budget Committee. In his response, Ryan blamed Obama for doing too little to fix the deficit problem, and called for a return to "limited government and free enterprise." But Ryan made the concession that no one person or political party could be held responsible for the current state of the economy. Instead, he called on leaders of Congress, the president, and the American people to come together to reduce spending and eliminate what he called the "crushing burden of debt."

Ryan described the investments of the Obama administration, including the various stimulus packages, as being sold to the American public with the promise of increasing growth. But, said Ryan, "after two years, the unemployment rate remains above 9% and government has added over $3 trillion to our debt." Ryan made it clear that the time to act is now. "Our debt is out of control. What was a fiscal challenge is now a fiscal crisis." He indicated that it would be up to his committee to draft and help pass a budget that would reflect the principles of limited, but effective, government. "We believe the days of business as usual must come to an end," Ryan said. "Endless borrowing is not a strategy; spending cuts have to come first."

Rep. Michele Bachmann, R-Minn., was chosen by the Tea Party arm of the Republican Party to deliver an additional response to Obama's State of the Union address. The response was carried only by CNN and streamed online. Bachmann directed her entire speech at Obama himself, criticizing him for creating "a bureaucracy that tells us which light bulbs to buy" rather than creating a "leaner, smarter government." Bachmann's response was criticized by Republican and Democratic leadership, who had previously asked her not to make comments on a night that was meant to be a show of unity following the tragedy in Tucson.

—Heather Kerrigan

Following is the full text of President Barack Obama's State of the Union address and the Republican response given by the chair of the House Budget Committee, Rep. Paul Ryan, R-Wis., both on January 25, 2011.

DOCUMENT   *The State of the Union Address*

January 25, 2011

Mr. Speaker, Mr. Vice President, members of Congress, distinguished guests, and fellow Americans:

Tonight I want to begin by congratulating the men and women of the 112th Congress, as well as your new Speaker, John Boehner. And as we mark this occasion, we're also mindful of the empty chair in this chamber, and we pray for the health of our colleague—and our friend—Gabby Giffords.

It's no secret that those of us here tonight have had our differences over the last two years. The debates have been contentious; we have fought fiercely for our beliefs. And that's a good thing. That's what a robust democracy demands. That's what helps set us apart as a nation.

But there's a reason the tragedy in Tucson gave us pause. Amid all the noise and passion and rancor of our public debate, Tucson reminded us that no matter who we are or where we come from, each of us is a part of something greater—something more consequential than party or political preference.

We are part of the American family. We believe that in a country where every race and faith and point of view can be found, we are still bound together as one people; that we share common hopes and a common creed; that the dreams of a little girl in Tucson are not so different than those of our own children, and that they all deserve the chance to be fulfilled.

That, too, is what sets us apart as a nation.

Now, by itself, this simple recognition won't usher in a new era of cooperation. What comes of this moment is up to us. What comes of this moment will be determined not by whether we can sit together tonight, but whether we can work together tomorrow.

I believe we can. And I believe we must. That's what the people who sent us here expect of us. With their votes, they've determined that governing will now be a shared responsibility between parties. New laws will only pass with support from Democrats and Republicans. We will move forward together, or not at all—for the challenges we face are bigger than party, and bigger than politics.

At stake right now is not who wins the next election—after all, we just had an election. At stake is whether new jobs and industries take root in this country, or somewhere else. It's whether the hard work and industry of our people is rewarded. It's whether we sustain the leadership that has made America not just a place on a map, but the light to the world.

We are poised for progress. Two years after the worst recession most of us have ever known, the stock market has come roaring back. Corporate profits are up. The economy is growing again.

But we have never measured progress by these yardsticks alone. We measure progress by the success of our people. By the jobs they can find and the quality of life those jobs offer. By the prospects of a small business owner who dreams of turning a good idea into a thriving enterprise. By the opportunities for a better life that we pass on to our children.

That's the project the American people want us to work on. Together.

We did that in December. Thanks to the tax cuts we passed, Americans' paychecks are a little bigger today. Every business can write off the full cost of new investments that they make this year. And these steps, taken by Democrats and Republicans, will grow the economy and add to the more than one million private sector jobs created last year.

But we have to do more. These steps we've taken over the last two years may have broken the back of this recession, but to win the future, we'll need to take on challenges that have been decades in the making.

Many people watching tonight can probably remember a time when finding a good job meant showing up at a nearby factory or a business downtown. You didn't always need a degree, and your competition was pretty much limited to your neighbors. If you worked hard, chances are you'd have a job for life, with a decent paycheck and good benefits and the occasional promotion. Maybe you'd even have the pride of seeing your kids work at the same company.

That world has changed. And for many, the change has been painful. I've seen it in the shuttered windows of once booming factories, and the vacant storefronts on once busy Main Streets. I've heard it in the frustrations of Americans who've seen their paychecks dwindle or their jobs disappear—proud men and women who feel like the rules have been changed in the middle of the game.

They're right. The rules have changed. In a single generation, revolutions in technology have transformed the way we live, work and do business. Steel mills that once needed 1,000 workers can now do the same work with 100. Today, just about any company can set up shop, hire workers, and sell their products wherever there's an Internet connection.

Meanwhile, nations like China and India realized that with some changes of their own, they could compete in this new world. And so they started educating their children earlier and longer, with greater emphasis on math and science. They're investing in research and new technologies. Just recently, China became the home to the world's largest private solar research facility, and the world's fastest computer.

So, yes, the world has changed. The competition for jobs is real. But this shouldn't discourage us. It should challenge us. Remember—for all the hits we've taken these last few years, for all the naysayers predicting our decline, America still has the largest, most prosperous economy in the world. No workers—no workers are more productive than ours. No country has more successful companies, or grants more patents to inventors and entrepreneurs. We're the home to the world's best colleges and universities, where more students come to study than any place on Earth.

What's more, we are the first nation to be founded for the sake of an idea—the idea that each of us deserves the chance to shape our own destiny. That's why centuries of pioneers and immigrants have risked everything to come here. It's why our students don't just memorize equations, but answer questions like "What do you think of that idea? What would you change about the world? What do you want to be when you grow up?"

The future is ours to win. But to get there, we can't just stand still. As Robert Kennedy told us, "The future is not a gift. It is an achievement." Sustaining the American Dream has never been about standing pat. It has required each generation to sacrifice, and struggle, and meet the demands of a new age.

And now it's our turn. We know what it takes to compete for the jobs and industries of our time. We need to out-innovate, out-educate, and out-build the rest of the world. We have to make America the best place on Earth to do business. We need to take responsibility for our deficit and reform our government. That's how our people will prosper. That's how we'll win the future. And tonight, I'd like to talk about how we get there.

The first step in winning the future is encouraging American innovation. None of us can predict with certainty what the next big industry will be or where the new jobs will come from. Thirty years ago, we couldn't know that something called the Internet would lead to an economic revolution. What we can do—what America does better than anyone else—is spark the creativity and imagination of our people. We're the nation that put cars in driveways and computers in offices; the nation of Edison and the Wright brothers; of Google and Facebook. In America, innovation doesn't just change our lives. It is how we make our living.

Our free enterprise system is what drives innovation. But because it's not always profitable for companies to invest in basic research, throughout our history, our government has provided cutting-edge scientists and inventors with the support that they need. That's what planted the seeds for the Internet. That's what helped make possible things like computer chips and GPS. Just think of all the good jobs—from manufacturing to retail—that have come from these breakthroughs.

Half a century ago, when the Soviets beat us into space with the launch of a satellite called Sputnik, we had no idea how we would beat them to the moon. The science wasn't even there yet. NASA didn't exist. But after investing in better research and education, we didn't just surpass the Soviets; we unleashed a wave of innovation that created new industries and millions of new jobs.

This is our generation's Sputnik moment. Two years ago, I said that we needed to reach a level of research and development we haven't seen since the height of the Space Race. And in a few weeks, I will be sending a budget to Congress that helps us meet that goal. We'll invest in biomedical research, information technology, and especially clean energy technology—an investment that will strengthen our security, protect our planet, and create countless new jobs for our people.

Already, we're seeing the promise of renewable energy. Robert and Gary Allen are brothers who run a small Michigan roofing company. After September 11th, they volunteered their best roofers to help repair the Pentagon. But half of their factory went unused, and the recession hit them hard. Today, with the help of a government loan, that empty space is being used to manufacture solar shingles that are being sold all across the country. In Robert's words, "We reinvented ourselves."

That's what Americans have done for over 200 years: reinvented ourselves. And to spur on more success stories like the Allen Brothers, we've begun to reinvent our energy policy. We're not just handing out money. We're issuing a challenge. We're telling America's scientists and engineers that if they assemble teams of the best minds in their fields, and focus on the hardest problems in clean energy, we'll fund the Apollo projects of our time.

At the California Institute of Technology, they're developing a way to turn sunlight and water into fuel for our cars. At Oak Ridge National Laboratory, they're using supercomputers to get a lot more power out of our nuclear facilities. With more research and incentives, we can break our dependence on oil with biofuels, and become the first country to have a million electric vehicles on the road by 2015.

We need to get behind this innovation. And to help pay for it, I'm asking Congress to eliminate the billions in taxpayer dollars we currently give to oil companies. I don't know if—I don't know if you've noticed, but they're doing just fine on their own. So instead of subsidizing yesterday's energy, let's invest in tomorrow's.

Now, clean energy breakthroughs will only translate into clean energy jobs if businesses know there will be a market for what they're selling. So tonight, I challenge you to join me in setting a new goal: By 2035, 80 percent of America's electricity will come from clean energy sources.

Some folks want wind and solar. Others want nuclear, clean coal and natural gas. To meet this goal, we will need them all—and I urge Democrats and Republicans to work together to make it happen.

Maintaining our leadership in research and technology is crucial to America's success. But if we want to win the future—if we want innovation to produce jobs in America and not overseas—then we also have to win the race to educate our kids.

Think about it. Over the next 10 years, nearly half of all new jobs will require education that goes beyond a high school education. And yet, as many as a quarter of our students aren't even finishing high school. The quality of our math and science education lags behind many other nations. America has fallen to ninth in the proportion of young people with a college degree. And so the question is whether all of us—as citizens, and as parents—are willing to do what's necessary to give every child a chance to succeed.

That responsibility begins not in our classrooms, but in our homes and communities. It's family that first instills the love of learning in a child. Only parents can make sure the TV is turned off and homework gets done. We need to teach our kids that it's not just the winner of the Super Bowl who deserves to be celebrated, but the winner of the science fair. We need to teach them that success is not a function of fame or PR, but of hard work and discipline.

Our schools share this responsibility. When a child walks into a classroom, it should be a place of high expectations and high performance. But too many schools don't meet this test. That's why instead of just pouring money into a system that's not working, we launched a competition called Race to the Top. To all 50 states, we said, "If you show us the most innovative plans to improve teacher quality and student achievement, we'll show you the money."

Race to the Top is the most meaningful reform of our public schools in a generation. For less than 1 percent of what we spend on education each year, it has led over 40 states to raise their standards for teaching and learning. And these standards were developed, by the way, not by Washington, but by Republican and Democratic governors throughout the country. And Race to the Top should be the approach we follow this year as we replace No Child Left Behind with a law that's more flexible and focused on what's best for our kids.

You see, we know what's possible from our children when reform isn't just a top-down mandate, but the work of local teachers and principals, school boards and communities. Take a school like Bruce Randolph in Denver. Three years ago, it was rated one of the worst schools in Colorado—located on turf between two rival gangs. But last May, 97 percent of the seniors received their diploma. Most will be the first in their families to go to college. And after the first year of the school's transformation, the principal who made it possible wiped away tears when a student said, "Thank you, Ms. Waters, for showing that we are smart and we can make it." That's what good schools can do, and we want good schools all across the country.

Let's also remember that after parents, the biggest impact on a child's success comes from the man or woman at the front of the classroom. In South Korea, teachers are known as "nation builders." Here in America, it's time we treated the people who educate our children with the same level of respect. We want to reward good teachers and stop making excuses for bad ones. And over the next 10 years, with so many baby boomers retiring from our classrooms, we want to prepare 100,000 new teachers in the fields of science and technology and engineering and math.

In fact, to every young person listening tonight who's contemplating their career choice: If you want to make a difference in the life of our nation; if you want to make a difference in the life of a child—become a teacher. Your country needs you.

Of course, the education race doesn't end with a high school diploma. To compete, higher education must be within the reach of every American. That's why we've ended the unwarranted taxpayer subsidies that went to banks, and used the savings to make college affordable for millions of students. And this year, I ask Congress to go further, and make permanent our tuition tax credit—worth $10,000 for four years of college. It's the right thing to do.

Because people need to be able to train for new jobs and careers in today's fast-changing economy, we're also revitalizing America's community colleges. Last month, I saw the promise of these schools at Forsyth Tech in North Carolina. Many of the students there used to work in the surrounding factories that have since left town. One mother of two, a woman named Kathy Proctor, had worked in the furniture industry since she was 18 years old. And she told me she's earning her degree in biotechnology now, at 55 years old, not just because the furniture jobs are gone, but because she wants to inspire her children to pursue their dreams, too. As Kathy said, "I hope it tells them to never give up."

If we take these steps—if we raise expectations for every child, and give them the best possible chance at an education, from the day they are born until the last job they take—we will reach the goal that I set two years ago: By the end of the decade, America will once again have the highest proportion of college graduates in the world.

One last point about education. Today, there are hundreds of thousands of students excelling in our schools who are not American citizens. Some are the children of undocumented workers, who had nothing to do with the actions of their parents. They grew up as Americans and pledge allegiance to our flag, and yet they live every day with the threat of deportation. Others come here from abroad to study in our colleges and universities. But as soon as they obtain advanced degrees, we send them back home to compete against us. It makes no sense.

Now, I strongly believe that we should take on, once and for all, the issue of illegal immigration. And I am prepared to work with Republicans and Democrats to protect our borders, enforce our laws and address the millions of undocumented workers who are now living in the shadows. I know that debate will be difficult. I know it will take time. But tonight, let's agree to make that effort. And let's stop expelling talented, responsible young people who could be staffing our research labs or starting a new business, who could be further enriching this nation.

The third step in winning the future is rebuilding America. To attract new businesses to our shores, we need the fastest, most reliable ways to move people, goods, and information—from high-speed rail to high-speed Internet.

Our infrastructure used to be the best, but our lead has slipped. South Korean homes now have greater Internet access than we do. Countries in Europe and Russia invest more in their roads and railways than we do. China is building faster trains and newer airports. Meanwhile, when our own engineers graded our nation's infrastructure, they gave us a "D."

We have to do better. America is the nation that built the transcontinental railroad, brought electricity to rural communities, constructed the Interstate Highway System. The jobs created by these projects didn't just come from laying down track or pavement. They came from businesses that opened near a town's new train station or the new off-ramp.

So over the last two years, we've begun rebuilding for the 21st century, a project that has meant thousands of good jobs for the hard-hit construction industry. And tonight, I'm proposing that we redouble those efforts.

We'll put more Americans to work repairing crumbling roads and bridges. We'll make sure this is fully paid for, attract private investment, and pick projects based [on] what's best for the economy, not politicians.

Within 25 years, our goal is to give 80 percent of Americans access to high-speed rail. This could allow you to go places in half the time it takes to travel by car. For some trips, it will be faster than flying—without the pat-down. As we speak, routes in California and the Midwest are already underway.

Within the next five years, we'll make it possible for businesses to deploy the next generation of high-speed wireless coverage to 98 percent of all Americans. This isn't just about—this isn't about faster Internet or fewer dropped calls. It's about connecting every part of America to the digital age. It's about a rural community in Iowa or Alabama where farmers and small business owners will be able to sell their products all over the world. It's about a firefighter who can download the design of a burning building onto a handheld device; a student who can take classes with a digital textbook; or a patient who can have face-to-face video chats with her doctor.

All these investments—in innovation, education, and infrastructure—will make America a better place to do business and create jobs. But to help our companies compete, we also have to knock down barriers that stand in the way of their success.

For example, over the years, a parade of lobbyists has rigged the tax code to benefit particular companies and industries. Those with accountants or lawyers to work the system can end up paying no taxes at all. But all the rest are hit with one of the highest corporate tax rates in the world. It makes no sense, and it has to change.

So tonight, I'm asking Democrats and Republicans to simplify the system. Get rid of the loopholes. Level the playing field. And use the savings to lower the corporate tax rate for the first time in 25 years—without adding to our deficit. It can be done.

To help businesses sell more products abroad, we set a goal of doubling our exports by 2014—because the more we export, the more jobs we create here at home. Already, our exports are up. Recently, we signed agreements with India and China that will support more than 250,000 jobs here in the United States. And last month, we finalized a trade agreement with South Korea that will support at least 70,000 American jobs. This agreement has unprecedented support from business and labor, Democrats and Republicans—and I ask this Congress to pass it as soon as possible.

Now, before I took office, I made it clear that we would enforce our trade agreements, and that I would only sign deals that keep faith with American workers and promote American jobs. That's what we did with Korea, and that's what I intend to do as we pursue agreements with Panama and Colombia and continue our Asia Pacific and global trade talks.

To reduce barriers to growth and investment, I've ordered a review of government regulations. When we find rules that put an unnecessary burden on businesses, we will fix them. But I will not hesitate to create or enforce common-sense safeguards to protect the American people. That's what we've done in this country for more than a century. It's why our food is safe to eat, our water is safe to drink, and our air is safe to breathe. It's why we have speed limits and child labor laws. It's why last year, we put in place consumer protections against hidden fees and penalties by credit card companies and new rules to prevent another financial crisis. And it's why we passed reform that finally prevents the health insurance industry from exploiting patients.

Now, I have heard rumors that a few of you still have concerns about our new health care law. So let me be the first to say that anything can be improved. If you have ideas about how to improve this law by making care better or more affordable, I am eager to work with you. We can start right now by correcting a flaw in the legislation that has placed an unnecessary bookkeeping burden on small businesses.

What I'm not willing to do—what I'm not willing to do is go back to the days when insurance companies could deny someone coverage because of a preexisting condition.

I'm not willing to tell James Howard, a brain cancer patient from Texas, that his treatment might not be covered. I'm not willing to tell Jim Houser, a small business man from Oregon, that he has to go back to paying $5,000 more to cover his employees. As we speak, this law is making prescription drugs cheaper for seniors and giving uninsured students a chance to stay on their patients'—parents' coverage.

So I say to this chamber tonight, instead of re-fighting the battles of the last two years, let's fix what needs fixing and let's move forward.

Now, the final critical step in winning the future is to make sure we aren't buried under a mountain of debt.

We are living with a legacy of deficit spending that began almost a decade ago. And in the wake of the financial crisis, some of that was necessary to keep credit flowing, save jobs, and put money in people's pockets.

But now that the worst of the recession is over, we have to confront the fact that our government spends more than it takes in. That is not sustainable. Every day, families sacrifice to live within their means. They deserve a government that does the same.

So tonight, I am proposing that starting this year, we freeze annual domestic spending for the next five years. Now, this would reduce the deficit by more than $400 billion over the next decade, and will bring discretionary spending to the lowest share of our economy since Dwight Eisenhower was President.

This freeze will require painful cuts. Already, we've frozen the salaries of hardworking federal employees for the next two years. I've proposed cuts to things I care deeply about, like community action programs. The Secretary of Defense has also agreed to cut tens of billions of dollars in spending that he and his generals believe our military can do without.

I recognize that some in this chamber have already proposed deeper cuts, and I'm willing to eliminate whatever we can honestly afford to do without. But let's make sure that we're not doing it on the backs of our most vulnerable citizens. And let's make sure that what we're cutting is really excess weight. Cutting the deficit by gutting our investments in innovation and education is like lightening an overloaded airplane by removing its engine. It may make you feel like you're flying high at first, but it won't take long before you feel the impact.

Now, most of the cuts and savings I've proposed only address annual domestic spending, which represents a little more than 12 percent of our budget. To make further progress, we have to stop pretending that cutting this kind of spending alone will be enough. It won't.

The bipartisan fiscal commission I created last year made this crystal clear. I don't agree with all their proposals, but they made important progress. And their conclusion is that the only way to tackle our deficit is to cut excessive spending wherever we find it—in domestic spending, defense spending, health care spending, and spending through tax breaks and loopholes.

This means further reducing health care costs, including programs like Medicare and Medicaid, which are the single biggest contributor to our long-term deficit. The health insurance law we passed last year will slow these rising costs, which is part of the reason that nonpartisan economists have said that repealing the health care law would add a quarter of a trillion dollars to our deficit. Still, I'm willing to look at other ideas to bring down costs, including one that Republicans suggested last year—medical malpractice reform to rein in frivolous lawsuits.

To put us on solid ground, we should also find a bipartisan solution to strengthen Social Security for future generations. We must do it without putting at risk current retirees, the most vulnerable, or people with disabilities; without slashing benefits for future generations; and without subjecting Americans' guaranteed retirement income to the whims of the stock market.

And if we truly care about our deficit, we simply can't afford a permanent extension of the tax cuts for the wealthiest 2 percent of Americans. Before we take money away from our schools or scholarships away from our students, we should ask millionaires to give up their tax break. It's not a matter of punishing their success. It's about promoting America's success.

In fact, the best thing we could do on taxes for all Americans is to simplify the individual tax code. This will be a tough job, but members of both parties have expressed an interest in doing this, and I am prepared to join them.

So now is the time to act. Now is the time for both sides and both houses of Congress—Democrats and Republicans—to forge a principled compromise that gets the job done. If we make the hard choices now to rein in our deficits, we can make the investments we need to win the future.

Let me take this one step further. We shouldn't just give our people a government that's more affordable. We should give them a government that's more competent and more efficient. We can't win the future with a government of the past.

We live and do business in the Information Age, but the last major reorganization of the government happened in the age of black-and-white TV. There are 12 different agencies that deal with exports. There are at least five different agencies that deal with housing policy. Then there's my favorite example: The Interior Department is in charge of salmon while they're in fresh water, but the Commerce Department handles them when they're in saltwater. I hear it gets even more complicated once they're smoked.

Now, we've made great strides over the last two years in using technology and getting rid of waste. Veterans can now download their electronic medical records with a click of the mouse. We're selling acres of federal office space that hasn't been used in years, and we'll cut through red tape to get rid of more. But we need to think bigger. In the coming months, my administration will develop a proposal to merge, consolidate, and reorganize the federal government in a way that best serves the goal of a more competitive America. I will submit that proposal to Congress for a vote—and we will push to get it passed.

In the coming year, we'll also work to rebuild people's faith in the institution of government. Because you deserve to know exactly how and where your tax dollars are being spent, you'll be able to go to a website and get that information for the very first time in history. Because you deserve to know when your elected officials are meeting with lobbyists, I ask Congress to do what the White House has already done—put that information online. And because the American people deserve to know that special interests aren't larding up legislation with pet projects, both parties in Congress should know this: If a bill comes to my desk with earmarks inside, I will veto it. I will veto it.

The 21st century government that's open and competent. A government that lives within its means. An economy that's driven by new skills and new ideas. Our success in this new and changing world will require reform, responsibility, and innovation. It will also require us to approach that world with a new level of engagement in our foreign affairs.

Just as jobs and businesses can now race across borders, so can new threats and new challenges. No single wall separates East and West. No one rival superpower is aligned against us.

And so we must defeat determined enemies, wherever they are, and build coalitions that cut across lines of region and race and religion. And America's moral example must always shine for all who yearn for freedom and justice and dignity. And because we've begun this work, tonight we can say that American leadership has been renewed and America's standing has been restored.

Look to Iraq, where nearly 100,000 of our brave men and women have left with their heads held high. American combat patrols have ended, violence is down, and a new government has been formed. This year, our civilians will forge a lasting partnership with the Iraqi people, while we finish the job of bringing our troops out of Iraq. America's commitment has been kept. The Iraq war is coming to an end.

Of course, as we speak, al Qaeda and their affiliates continue to plan attacks against us. Thanks to our intelligence and law enforcement professionals, we're disrupting plots and securing our cities and skies. And as extremists try to inspire acts of violence within our borders, we are responding with the strength of our communities, with respect for the rule of law, and with the conviction that American Muslims are a part of our American family.

We've also taken the fight to al Qaeda and their allies abroad. In Afghanistan, our troops have taken Taliban strongholds and trained Afghan security forces. Our purpose is clear: By preventing the Taliban from reestablishing a stranglehold over the Afghan people, we will deny al Qaeda the safe haven that served as a launching pad for 9/11.

Thanks to our heroic troops and civilians, fewer Afghans are under the control of the insurgency. There will be tough fighting ahead, and the Afghan government will need to deliver better governance. But we are strengthening the capacity of the Afghan people and building an enduring partnership with them. This year, we will work with nearly 50 countries to begin a transition to an Afghan lead. And this July, we will begin to bring our troops home.

In Pakistan, al Qaeda's leadership is under more pressure than at any point since 2001. Their leaders and operatives are being removed from the battlefield. Their safe havens are shrinking. And we've sent a message from the Afghan border to the Arabian Peninsula to all parts of the globe: We will not relent, we will not waver, and we will defeat you.

American leadership can also be seen in the effort to secure the worst weapons of war. Because Republicans and Democrats approved the New START treaty, far fewer nuclear weapons and launchers will be deployed. Because we rallied the world, nuclear materials are being locked down on every continent so they never fall into the hands of terrorists.

Because of a diplomatic effort to insist that Iran meet its obligations, the Iranian government now faces tougher sanctions, tighter sanctions than ever before. And on the Korean Peninsula, we stand with our ally South Korea, and insist that North Korea keeps its commitment to abandon nuclear weapons.

This is just a part of how we're shaping a world that favors peace and prosperity. With our European allies, we revitalized NATO and increased our cooperation on everything from counterterrorism to missile defense. We've reset our relationship with Russia, strengthened Asian alliances, built new partnerships with nations like India.

This March, I will travel to Brazil, Chile, and El Salvador to forge new alliances across the Americas. Around the globe, we're standing with those who take responsibility—helping farmers grow more food, supporting doctors who care for the sick, and combating the corruption that can rot a society and rob people of opportunity.

Recent events have shown us that what sets us apart must not just be our power—it must also be the purpose behind it. In south Sudan—with our assistance—the people were finally able to vote for independence after years of war. Thousands lined up before dawn. People danced in the streets. One man who lost four of his brothers at war summed up the scene around him: "This was a battlefield for most of my life," he said. "Now we want to be free."

And we saw that same desire to be free in Tunisia, where the will of the people proved more powerful than the writ of a dictator. And tonight, let us be clear: The United States of America stands with the people of Tunisia, and supports the democratic aspirations of all people.

We must never forget that the things we've struggled for, and fought for, live in the hearts of people everywhere. And we must always remember that the Americans who have borne the greatest burden in this struggle are the men and women who serve our country.

Tonight, let us speak with one voice in reaffirming that our nation is united in support of our troops and their families. Let us serve them as well as they've served us—by giving them the equipment they need, by providing them with the care and benefits that they have earned, and by enlisting our veterans in the great task of building our own nation.

Our troops come from every corner of this country—they're black, white, Latino, Asian, Native American. They are Christian and Hindu, Jewish and Muslim. And, yes, we know that some of them are gay. Starting this year, no American will be forbidden from serving the country they love because of who they love. And with that change, I call on all our college campuses to open their doors to our military recruiters and ROTC. It is time to leave behind the divisive battles of the past. It is time to move forward as one nation.

We should have no illusions about the work ahead of us. Reforming our schools, changing the way we use energy, reducing our deficit—none of this will be easy. All of it will take time. And it will be harder because we will argue about everything. The costs. The details. The letter of every law.

Of course, some countries don't have this problem. If the central government wants a railroad, they build a railroad, no matter how many homes get bulldozed. If they don't want a bad story in the newspaper, it doesn't get written.

And yet, as contentious and frustrating and messy as our democracy can sometimes be, I know there isn't a person here who would trade places with any other nation on Earth.

We may have differences in policy, but we all believe in the rights enshrined in our Constitution. We may have different opinions, but we believe in the same promise that says this is a place where you can make it if you try. We may have different backgrounds, but we believe in the same dream that says this is a country where anything is possible. No matter who you are. No matter where you come from.

That dream is why I can stand here before you tonight. That dream is why a working-class kid from Scranton can sit behind me. That dream is why someone who began by sweeping the floors of his father's Cincinnati bar can preside as Speaker of the House in the greatest nation on Earth.

That dream—that American Dream—is what drove the Allen Brothers to reinvent their roofing company for a new era. It's what drove those students at Forsyth Tech to learn a new skill and work towards the future. And that dream is the story of a small business owner named Brandon Fisher.

Brandon started a company in Berlin, Pennsylvania, that specializes in a new kind of drilling technology. And one day last summer, he saw the news that halfway across the world, 33 men were trapped in a Chilean mine, and no one knew how to save them.

But Brandon thought his company could help. And so he designed a rescue that would come to be known as Plan B. His employees worked around the clock to manufacture the necessary drilling equipment. And Brandon left for Chile.

Along with others, he began drilling a 2,000-foot hole into the ground, working three- or four-hour—three or four days at a time without any sleep. Thirty-seven days later, Plan B succeeded, and the miners were rescued. But because he didn't want all of the attention, Brandon wasn't there when the miners emerged. He'd already gone back home, back to work on his next project.

And later, one of his employees said of the rescue, "We proved that Center Rock is a little company, but we do big things."

We do big things.

From the earliest days of our founding, America has been the story of ordinary people who dare to dream. That's how we win the future.

We're a nation that says, "I might not have a lot of money, but I have this great idea for a new company." "I might not come from a family of college graduates, but I will be the first to get my degree." "I might not know those people in trouble, but I think I can help them, and I need to try." "I'm not sure how we'll reach that better place beyond the horizon, but I know we'll get there. I know we will."

We do big things.

The idea of America endures. Our destiny remains our choice. And tonight, more than two centuries later, it's because of our people that our future is hopeful, our journey goes forward, and the state of our union is strong.

Thank you. God bless you, and may God bless the United States of America.

SOURCE: The White House. Office of the Press Secretary. "Remarks by the President in State of the Union Address." January 25, 2011. http://www.whitehouse.gov/the-press-office/2011/01/25/remarks-president-state-union-address.

House Budget Committee Chairman Rep. Paul Ryan, R-Wis., Response to the President's Address

DOCUMENT

January 25, 2011

[Ellipses were used in the original document and do not represent text omissions.]

Good evening. I'm Congressman Paul Ryan from Janesville, Wisconsin—and Chairman here at the House Budget Committee.

President Obama just addressed a Congressional chamber filled with many new faces. One face we did not see tonight was that of our friend and colleague, Congresswoman Gabrielle Giffords of Arizona. We all miss Gabby and her cheerful spirit; and we are praying for her return to the House Chamber.

Earlier this month, President Obama spoke movingly at a memorial event for the six people who died on that violent morning in Tucson. Still, there are no words that can lift the sorrow that now engulfs the families and friends of the fallen.

What we can do is assure them that the nation is praying for them; that, in the words of the Psalmist, the Lord heals the broken hearted and binds up their wounds; and that over time grace will replace grief.

As Gabby continues to make encouraging progress, we must keep her and the others in our thoughts as we attend to the work now before us.

Tonight, the President focused a lot of attention on our economy in general—and on our deficit and debt in particular.

He was right to do so, and some of his words were reassuring. As Chairman of the House Budget Committee, I assure you that we want to work with the President to restrain federal spending.

In one of our first acts in the new majority, House Republicans voted to cut Congress's own budget. And just today, the House voted to restore the spending discipline that Washington sorely needs.

The reason is simple.

A few years ago, reducing spending was important. Today, it's imperative. Here's why.

We face a crushing burden of debt. The debt will soon eclipse our entire economy, and grow to catastrophic levels in the years ahead.

On this current path, when my three children—who are now 6, 7, and 8 years old—are raising their own children, the Federal government will double in size, and so will the taxes they pay.

No economy can sustain such high levels of debt and taxation. The next generation will inherit a stagnant economy and a diminished country.

Frankly, it's one of my greatest concerns as a parent—and I know many of you feel the same way.

Our debt is the product of acts by many presidents and many Congresses over many years. No one person or party is responsible for it.

There is no doubt the President came into office facing a severe fiscal and economic situation.

Unfortunately, instead of restoring the fundamentals of economic growth, he engaged in a stimulus spending spree that not only failed to deliver on its promise to create jobs, but also plunged us even deeper into debt.

The facts are clear: Since taking office, President Obama has signed into law spending increases of nearly 25 percent for domestic government agencies—an 84 percent increase when you include the failed stimulus.

All of this new government spending was sold as "investment." Yet after two years, the unemployment rate remains above 9% and government has added over $3 trillion to our debt.

Then the President and his party made matters even worse, by creating a new open-ended health care entitlement.

What we already know about the President's health care law is this: Costs are going up, premiums are rising, and millions of people will lose the coverage they currently have. Job creation is being stifled by all of its taxes, penalties, mandates and fees.

Businesses and unions from around the country are asking the Obama Administration for waivers from the mandates. Washington should not be in the business of picking winners and losers. The President mentioned the need for regulatory reform to ease the burden on American businesses. We agree—and we think his health care law would be a great place to start.

Last week, House Republicans voted for a full repeal of this law, as we pledged to do, and we will work to replace it with fiscally responsible, patient-centered reforms that actually reduce costs and expand coverage.

Health care spending is driving the explosive growth of our debt. And the President's law is accelerating our country toward bankruptcy.

Our debt is out of control. What was a fiscal challenge is now a fiscal crisis.

We cannot deny it; instead we must, as Americans, confront it responsibly.

And that is exactly what Republicans pledge to do.

Americans are skeptical of both political parties, and that skepticism is justified—especially when it comes to spending. So hold all of us accountable.

In this very room, the House will produce, debate, and advance a budget. Last year—in an unprecedented failure—Congress chose not to pass, or even propose a budget. The spending spree continued unchecked.

We owe you a better choice and a different vision.

Our forthcoming budget is our obligation to you—to show you how we intend to do things differently . . . how we will cut spending to get the debt down . . . help create jobs and prosperity . . . and reform government programs. If we act soon, and if we act responsibly, people in and near retirement will be protected.

These budget debates are not just about the programs of government; they're also about the purpose of government.

So I'd like to share with you the principles that guide us. They are anchored in the wisdom of the founders; in the spirit of the Declaration of Independence; and in the words of the American Constitution.

They have to do with the importance of limited government; and with the blessing of self-government.

We believe government's role is both vital and limited—to defend the nation from attack and provide for the common defense . . . to secure our borders . . . to protect innocent life . . . to uphold our laws and Constitutional rights . . . to ensure domestic tranquility and equal opportunity . . . and to help provide a safety not for those who cannot provide for themselves.

We believe that the government has an important role to create the conditions that promote entrepreneurship, upward mobility, and individual responsibility.

We believe, as our founders did, that "the pursuit of happiness" depends upon individual liberty; and individual liberty requires limited government.

Limited government also means effective government. When government takes on too many tasks, it usually doesn't do any of them very well. It's no coincidence that trust in government is at an all-time low now that the size of government is at an all-time high.

The President and the Democratic Leadership have shown, by their actions, that they believe government needs to increase its size and its reach, its price tag and its power.

Whether sold as "stimulus" or repackaged as "investment," their actions show they want a Federal government that controls too much; taxes too much; and spends too much in order to do too much.

And during the last two years, that is exactly what we have gotten—along with record deficits and debt—to the point where the President is now urging Congress to increase the debt limit.

We believe the days of business as usual must come to an end. We hold to a couple of simple convictions: Endless borrowing is not a strategy; spending cuts have to come first.

Our nation is approaching a tipping point.

We are at a moment, where if government's growth is left unchecked and unchallenged, America's best century will be considered our past century. This is a future in which we will transform our social safety net into a hammock, which lulls able-bodied people into lives of complacency and dependency.

Depending on bureaucracy to foster innovation, competitiveness, and wise consumer choices has never worked—and it won't work now.

We need to chart a new course.

Speaking candidly, as one citizen to another: We still have time … but not much time. If we continue down our current path, we know what our future will be.

Just take a look at what's happening to Greece, Ireland, the United Kingdom and other nations in Europe. They didn't act soon enough; and now their governments have been forced to impose painful austerity measures: large benefit cuts to seniors and huge tax increases on everybody.

Their day of reckoning has arrived. Ours is around the corner. That is why we must act now.

Some people will back away from this challenge. But I see this challenge as an opportunity to rebuild what Lincoln called the "central ideas" of the Republic.

We believe a renewed commitment to limited government will unshackle our economy and create millions of new jobs and opportunities for all people, of every background, to succeed and prosper. Under this approach, the spirit of initiative—not political clout—determines who succeeds.

Millions of families have fallen on hard times not because of our ideals of free enterprise—but because our leaders failed to live up to those ideals; because of poor decisions made in Washington and Wall Street that caused a financial crisis, squandered our savings, broke our trust, and crippled our economy.

Today, a similar kind of irresponsibility threatens not only our livelihoods but our way of life.

We need to reclaim our American system of limited government, low taxes, reasonable regulations, and sound money, which has blessed us with unprecedented prosperity. And it has done more to help the poor than any other economic system ever designed. That's the real secret to job creation—not borrowing and spending more money in Washington.

Limited government and free enterprise have helped make America the greatest nation on earth.

These are not easy times, but America is an exceptional nation. In all the chapters of human history, there has never been anything quite like America. The American story has been cherished, advanced, and defended over the centuries.

And it now falls to this generation to pass on to our children a nation that is stronger, more vibrant, more decent, and better than the one we inherited.

Thank you and good night.

SOURCE: Office of Congressman Paul Ryan. "Congressman Paul Ryan Delivers Republican Address to the Nation." January 26, 2011. http://paulryan.house.gov/News/DocumentSingle.aspx?DocumentID=221391.

OTHER HISTORIC DOCUMENTS OF INTEREST

FROM THIS VOLUME

- President Obama Remarks on the Debt Ceiling and Credit Downgrade, p. 423
- Evolving U.S. Involvement in Afghanistan, p. 435
- Remarks by President Obama and Defense Secretary Gates on Iraq Troop Withdrawal, p. 563
- Federal Deficit Reduction Committee Folds Without Conclusion, p. 618

FROM PREVIOUS *HISTORIC DOCUMENTS*

Two Financial Crisis
Reports Released

JANUARY 27 AND APRIL 13, 2011

January 2011 opened with bright economic news of decreasing unemployment and rising payrolls, but the year became a roller coaster ride as the stock market saw drastic fluctuations and consumer confidence wavered until late in the year. But the current state of the economy was not the only thing on the mind of government officials in early 2011. Instead, learning from the past mistakes of the economic crisis of 2007 to 2009 and implementing financial reforms came front and center in January and April when two reports were issued on the causes and impacts of the financial crisis. Fingers were pointed at both the Bush and Obama administrations as well as at the financial industry, and calls were made for the government to look into its financial regulatory policy and its own stake in the financial sector—specifically in the housing market.

CRISIS COMMISSION ISSUES REPORT

On January 27, 2011, the Financial Crisis Inquiry Commission (FCIC) released the first official government review of the financial crisis that began in 2007, the worst financial downturn in U.S. history since the Great Depression. In its nearly 550-page report, "The commission concluded that the crisis was avoidable and was caused by: Widespread failures in financial regulation, including the Federal Reserve's failure to stem the tide of toxic mortgages; Dramatic breakdowns in corporate governance including too many financial firms acting recklessly and taking on too much risk; AN explosive mix of excessive borrowing and risk by households and Wall Street that put the financial system on a collision course with crisis; Key policy makers ill prepared for the crisis, lacking a full understanding of the financial system they oversaw; And systemic breaches in accountability and ethics at all levels." Both the financial sector and the government ignored clear warning signs of impending financial crisis, placing too much faith in the idea that the financial markets would correct themselves before the unimaginable happened.

The report, which contained little new information, comprised interviews with multiple witnesses and comments gathered at twenty-one public hearings and meetings, forums, and roundtable discussions. Committee Chairman Phil Angelides said the crisis boiled down to both "human action and inaction," and warned that the crisis could be repeated if the government and the financial industry refuse to learn from their mistakes. "In many respects, our financial system is unchanged from the eve of this crisis," Angelides said. "We believe that much more needs to be done."

The committee report faulted a number of actors, finding that, "a crisis of this magnitude cannot be the work of a few bad actors. . . . The greatest tragedy would be to accept the refrain that no one could have seen this coming and thus nothing could have been done. If we accept this notion, it will happen again." The government players found to be at fault in the report included the administrations of presidents Barack Obama and George W. Bush; the Securities and Exchange Commission, the body tasked with protecting the financial industry; and the Federal Reserve. Of the latter, the report found that the Reserve had a "pivotal failure to stem the flow of toxic mortgages, which it could have done by setting prudent mortgage-lending standards."

The financial sector also bore responsibility in the report. The commission cited faulty corporate governance and risk management failure, excessive and risky borrowing, a breakdown in lending accountability, lobbyists who worked to weaken regulations, and credit rating agency approval for shaky mortgage-related securities. "Their ratings helped the market soar and their downgrades through 2007 and 2008 wreaked havoc across markets and firms," the report said of credit rating agencies.

Two dissents were filed by four Republican commission members—one was filed by three Republicans who said shock and panic brought down the financial institutions, while the second stated that the crisis had more to do with U.S. housing policy. In the former, committee members Bill Thomas, the vice chair of the committee and former California congressman, Keith Hennessey, the economic adviser to former president George W. Bush, and Douglas Holtz-Eakin, a former director of the Congressional Budget Office, called the majority report "too broad." In their dissent, the trio said the report "is more an account of bad events than a focused explanation of what happened and why. When everything is important, nothing is." Their dissent went on to find that the majority ignored parallel problems in foreign governments, more specifically in Asia and Europe, and also failed to distinguish between the causes of the financial crisis and its effects. The dissent also addressed the decision by the Bush administration to allow Lehman Brothers to fail, saying that the administration acted soundly because there was no legal or viable option at the time to keep the company afloat. The second dissent, filed by Peter J. Wallison, former White House counsel during the Iran-Contra Affair, ran for nearly 100 pages, associated the downfall with risky loans rather than deregulation or predatory lending, and criticized the long-running government policy of encouraging home ownership.

Additional criticism came from across the financial sector, faulting the report for not providing concrete steps to address the issues of the crisis, including what to do with mortgage giants Fannie Mae and Freddie Mac, which were taken under government control in 2008. The timing of the report garnered further criticism, because it was released six months after the Dodd-Frank regulatory overhaul bill went into effect, a bill which was meant to address the problems that sparked the financial crisis in 2007.

SENATE REPORT

On April 13, 2011, the Senate Permanent Subcommittee on Investigations, cochaired by Sens. Tom Coburn, R-Okla., and Carl Levin, D-Mich., released the findings of its own two-year investigation into the financial crisis. The committee drew its conclusions from testimony heard during four hearings held in the spring of 2010 and thousands of pages of financial documents. The 635-page report, "Wall Street and the Financial Crisis: Anatomy of a Financial Collapse," described the reckless business practices and other activities that led to the financial crisis that were ignored by banks and federal regulators. "The report pulls back the curtain on shoddy, risky, deceptive practices on the part of a lot of major financial institutions," Levin said. "The overwhelming evidence is that those institutions deceived their clients and deceived the public, and they were aided and abetted by deferential regulators and credit ratings agencies who had conflicts of interest."

A central role in the crisis, according to the report, was played by Washington Mutual, a mortgage lender that collapsed in 2008; the Office of Thrift Supervision, a government regulator; Standard & Poor's and Moody's Investors Service, two ratings agencies; and the two investment banks of Goldman Sachs and Deutsche Bank. The Office of Thrift Supervision took a significant amount of criticism in the report for its responsibility in overseeing Countrywide Financial, IndyMac, and Washington Mutual. According to the Senate report, the office did not interfere with lending practices at these institutions and instead expected executives to correct any problems they saw on their own. Between 2003 and 2008, approximately 500 instances of deficiencies at Washington Mutual were found, yet the office did nothing to impose or force change. The Office of Thrift Supervision was closed in 2010, and its functions are now a part of the Office of the Comptroller of the Currency.

The report also uncovered new information on Goldman Sachs's 2007 mortgage activity, claiming that it manipulated the mortgage market in order to protect itself from the housing collapse. Goldman Sachs stopped using some manipulation techniques in June 2007, when two hedge funds at Bear Sterns collapsed under bad mortgage debt. In response to the congressional report, Goldman Sachs said, "While we disagree with many of the conclusions of the report, we take seriously the issues explored by the subcommittee. We recently issued the results of a comprehensive examination of our business standards and practices and committed to making significant changes that will strengthen relationships with clients, improve transparency and disclose and enhance standards for the review, approval, and suitability of complex instruments." The Senate report also focused attention on Deutsche Bank, which was never before accused of any wrongdoing by the government, but which made bad mortgage bets. The report said the bank's activities amounted to little more than Ponzi scheme securities.

In addition to its findings of fault, the Senate report included nineteen recommendations for regulatory and industry changes. These recommendations included creating conflict-of-interest policies, requiring banks to hold higher reserves against risky mortgages, and asking federal regulators to examine the report findings for any violations of laws.

FANNIE MAE AND FREDDIE MAC

A question left open by both the FCIC and Senate reports was how to handle mortgage companies Fannie Mae and Freddie Mac. The two companies came under the government's control in 2008 in an effort to prevent a further collapse of the housing market, and have used $150 billion in Treasury funds to make up losses they experienced in the subprime mortgage crisis. When Congress passed the Dodd-Frank bill, a provision stated that the Treasury would be responsible for developing a plan to remove these two companies from government ownership. In February, Timothy Geithner, the U.S. Treasury Secretary, announced that he was drafting three options for congressional review pertaining to the desire for a reduced government role in Fannie Mae and Freddie Mac. One of the three possible options would see the government's withdrawal from the housing market other than in instances of low-income housing assistance, while the other two options would simply reduce the government's role in housing financing rather than eliminating it altogether.

By August, the Obama administration was still giving consideration to the three plans submitted by Geithner and drafting additional options for Congress that, the *Washington Post* reported, could include a continuing role in the financial side of the housing market.

The Treasury quickly rejected the idea that it was the president's desire for the government to maintain a financial role in the housing market, saying instead that the companies would be slowly "wound down" while the government reduced its role to a limited one. No matter which option the administration ultimately backs, it will be up to Congress to approve legislation to complete the full or partial withdrawal from Fannie Mae and Freddie Mac. It is expected that this process could take up to four years.

—Heather Kerrigan

Following is the edited text of the report issued by the Financial Crisis Inquiry Commission on January 27, 2011, containing its conclusions on the cause of the financial crisis; and a report by the Senate Permanent Subcommittee on Investigations, released on April 13, 2011, in regard to the causes of the financial crisis and recommendations to prevent future crises.

Financial Crisis Inquiry
Commission Conclusions

January 27, 2011

[A description of the purpose of the panel, its investigative work, and the state of the economy from the beginning of the crisis to the present has been omitted. All charts and graphs have been omitted.]

. . . Now to our major findings and conclusions, which are based on the facts contained in this report: they are offered with the hope that lessons may be learned to help avoid future catastrophe.

- **We conclude this financial crisis was avoidable.** The crisis was the result of human action and inaction, not of Mother Nature or computer models gone haywire. The captains of finance and the public stewards of our financial system ignored warnings and failed to question, understand, and manage evolving risks within a system essential to the well-being of the American public. Theirs was a big miss, not a stumble.

While the business cycle cannot be repealed, a crisis of this magnitude need not have occurred. To paraphrase Shakespeare, the fault lies not in the stars, but in us.

Despite the expressed view of many on Wall Street and in Washington that the crisis could not have been foreseen or avoided, there were warning signs. The tragedy was that they were ignored or discounted. There was an explosion in risky subprime lending and securitization, an unsustainable rise in housing prices, widespread reports of egregious and predatory lending practices, dramatic increases in household mortgage debt, and exponential growth in financial firms' trading activities, unregulated derivatives, and short-term "repo" lending markets, among many other red flags. Yet there was pervasive permissiveness; little meaningful action was taken to quell the threats in a timely manner.

The prime example is the Federal Reserve's pivotal failure to stem the flow of toxic mortgages, which it could have done by setting prudent mortgage-lending standards.

The Federal Reserve was the one entity empowered to do so and it did not. The record of our examination is replete with evidence of other failures: financial institutions made, bought, and sold mortgage securities they never examined, did not care to examine, or knew to be defective; firms depended on tens of billions of dollars of borrowing that had to be renewed each and every night, secured by subprime mortgage securities; and major firms and investors blindly relied on credit rating agencies as their arbiters of risk. What else could one expect on a highway where there were neither speed limits nor neatly painted lines?

- **We conclude widespread failures in financial regulation and supervision proved devastating to the stability of the nation's financial markets.** The sentries were not at their posts, in no small part due to the widely accepted faith in the self-correcting nature of the markets and the ability of financial institutions to effectively police themselves. More than 30 years of deregulation and reliance on self-regulation by financial institutions . . . had stripped away key safeguards, which could have helped avoid catastrophe. This approach had opened up gaps in oversight of critical areas with trillions of dollars at risk, such as the shadow banking system and over-the-counter derivatives markets. In addition, the government permitted financial firms to pick their preferred regulators in what became a race to the weakest supervisor.

Yet we do not accept the view that regulators lacked the power to protect the financial system. They had ample power in many arenas and they chose not to use it. To give just three examples: the Securities and Exchange Commission could have required more capital and halted risky practices at the big investment banks. It did not. The Federal Reserve Bank of New York and other regulators could have clamped down on Citigroup's excesses in the run-up to the crisis. They did not. Policy makers and regulators could have stopped the runaway mortgage securitization train. They did not. In case after case after case, regulators continued to rate the institutions they oversaw as safe and sound even in the face of mounting troubles, often downgrading them just before their collapse. And where regulators lacked authority, they could have sought it. Too often, they lacked the political will—in a political and ideological environment that constrained it—as well as the fortitude to critically challenge the institutions and the entire system they were entrusted to oversee. . . .

- **We conclude dramatic failures of corporate governance and risk management at many systemically important financial institutions were a key cause of this crisis.** There was a view that instincts for self-preservation inside major financial firms would shield them from fatal risk-taking without the need for a steady regulatory hand, which, the firms argued, would stifle innovation. Too many of these institutions acted recklessly, taking on too much risk, with too little capital, and with too much dependence on short-term funding. In many respects, this reflected a fundamental change in these institutions, particularly the large investment banks and bank holding companies, which focused their activities increasingly on risky trading activities that produced hefty profits. They took on enormous exposures in acquiring and supporting subprime lenders and creating, packaging, repackaging, and selling trillions of dollars in mortgage-related securities, including synthetic financial products. Like Icarus, they never feared flying ever closer to the sun.

Many of these institutions grew aggressively through poorly executed acquisition and integration strategies that made effective management more challenging. . . .

Financial institutions and credit rating agencies embraced mathematical models as reliable predictors of risks, replacing judgment in too many instances. Too often, risk management became risk justification.

Compensation systems—designed in an environment of cheap money, intense competition, and light regulation—too often rewarded the quick deal, the short-term gain—without proper consideration of long-term consequences. Often, those systems encouraged the big bet—where the payoff on the upside could be huge and the downside limited. This was the case up and down the line—from the corporate boardroom to the mortgage broker on the street.

Our examination revealed stunning instances of governance breakdowns and irresponsibility. . . .

- **We conclude a combination of excessive borrowing, risky investments, and lack of transparency put the financial system on a collision course with crisis.** Clearly, this vulnerability was related to failures of corporate governance and regulation, but it is significant enough by itself to warrant our attention here.

In the years leading up to the crisis, too many financial institutions, as well as too many households, borrowed to the hilt, leaving them vulnerable to financial distress or ruin if the value of their investments declined even modestly. For example, as of 2007, the five major investment banks—Bear Stearns, Goldman Sachs, Lehman Brothers, Merrill Lynch, and Morgan Stanley—were operating with extraordinarily thin capital. By one measure, their leverage ratios were as high as 40 to 1, meaning for every $40 in assets, there was only $1 in capital to cover losses. . . .

And the leverage was often hidden—in derivatives positions, in off-balance-sheet entities, and through "window dressing" of financial reports available to the investing public.

The kings of leverage were Fannie Mae and Freddie Mac, the two behemoth government-sponsored enterprises (GSEs). For example, by the end of 2007, Fannie's and Freddie's combined leverage ratio, including loans they owned and guaranteed, stood at 75 to 1.

But financial firms were not alone in the borrowing spree: from 2001 to 2007, national mortgage debt almost doubled, and the amount of mortgage debt per household rose more than 63 percent from $91,500 to $149,500, even while wages were essentially stagnant. When the housing downturn hit, heavily indebted financial firms and families alike were walloped.

The heavy debt taken on by some financial institutions was exacerbated by the risky assets they were acquiring with that debt. As the mortgage and real estate markets churned out riskier and riskier loans and securities, many financial institutions loaded up on them. . . .

- **We conclude the government was ill prepared for the crisis, and its inconsistent response added to the uncertainty and panic in the financial markets.** As part of our charge, it was appropriate to review government actions taken in response to the developing crisis, not just those policies or actions that preceded it, to determine if any of those responses contributed to or exacerbated the crisis.

As our report shows, key policy makers—the Treasury Department, the Federal Reserve Board, and the Federal Reserve Bank of New York—who were best positioned to watch over our markets were ill prepared for the events of 2007 and 2008. Other agencies were also behind the curve. They were hampered because they did not have a clear grasp of the financial system they were charged with overseeing, particularly as it had evolved in the years leading up to the crisis. . . . .

While there was some awareness of, or at least a debate about, the housing bubble, the record reflects that senior public officials did not recognize that a bursting of the bubble could threaten the entire financial system. . . .

In addition, the government's inconsistent handling of major financial institutions during the crisis—the decision to rescue Bear Stearns and then to place Fannie Mae and Freddie Mac into conservatorship, followed by its decision not to save Lehman Brothers and then to save AIG—increased uncertainty and panic in the market.

In making these observations, we deeply respect and appreciate the efforts made by Secretary Paulson, Chairman Bernanke, and Timothy Geithner, formerly president of the Federal Reserve Bank of New York and now treasury secretary, and so many others who labored to stabilize our financial system and our economy in the most chaotic and challenging of circumstances.

- **We conclude there was a systemic breakdown in accountability and ethics.** The integrity of our financial markets and the public's trust in those markets are essential to the economic well-being of our nation. The soundness and the sustained prosperity of the financial system and our economy rely on the notions of fair dealing, responsibility, and transparency. In our economy, we expect businesses and individuals to pursue profits, at the same time that they produce products and services of quality and conduct themselves well.

Unfortunately—as has been the case in past speculative booms and busts—we witnessed an erosion of standards of responsibility and ethics that exacerbated the financial crisis. This was not universal, but these breaches stretched from the ground level to the corporate suites. They resulted not only in significant financial consequences but also in damage to the trust of investors, businesses, and the public in the financial system. . . .

And the report documents that major financial institutions ineffectively sampled loans they were purchasing to package and sell to investors. They knew a significant percentage of the sampled loans did not meet their own underwriting standards or those of the originators. Nonetheless, they sold those securities to investors. The Commission's review of many prospectuses provided to investors found that this critical information was not disclosed.

THESE CONCLUSIONS must be viewed in the context of human nature and individual and societal responsibility. First, to pin this crisis on mortal flaws like greed and hubris would be simplistic. It was the failure to account for human weakness that is relevant to this crisis.

Second, we clearly believe the crisis was a result of human mistakes, misjudgments, and misdeeds that resulted in systemic failures for which our nation has paid dearly. As you read this report, you will see that specific firms and individuals acted irresponsibly. Yet a crisis of this magnitude cannot be the work of a few bad actors, and such was not the case here. At the same time, the breadth of this crisis does not mean that "everyone is at fault"; many firms and individuals did not participate in the excesses that spawned disaster.

We do place special responsibility with the public leaders charged with protecting our financial system, those entrusted to run our regulatory agencies, and the chief executives of companies whose failures drove us to crisis. These individuals sought and accepted positions of significant responsibility and obligation. Tone at the top does matter and, in this instance, we were let down. No one said "no."

But as a nation, we must also accept responsibility for what we permitted to occur. Collectively, but certainly not unanimously, we acquiesced to or embraced a system, a set of policies and actions, that gave rise to our present predicament. . . .

[Conclusions reached by the panel with regard to the specific components of the financial system, and competing conclusions as to the cause of the financial crisis, have been omitted.]

WHEN THIS COMMISSION began its work 18 months ago, some imagined that the events of 2008 and their consequences would be well behind us by the time we issued this report. Yet more than two years after the federal government intervened in an unprecedented manner in our financial markets, our country finds itself still grappling with the aftereffects of the calamity. Our financial system is, in many respects, still unchanged from what existed on the eve of the crisis. Indeed, in the wake of the crisis, the U.S. financial sector is now more concentrated than ever in the hands of a few large, systemically significant institutions.

While we have not been charged with making policy recommendations, the very purpose of our report has been to take stock of what happened so we can plot a new course. In our inquiry, we found dramatic breakdowns of corporate governance, profound lapses in regulatory oversight, and near fatal flaws in our financial system. We also found that a series of choices and actions led us toward a catastrophe for which we were ill prepared. These are serious matters that must be addressed and resolved to restore faith in our financial markets, to avoid the next crisis, and to rebuild a system of capital that provides the foundation for a new era of broadly shared prosperity.

The greatest tragedy would be to accept the refrain that no one could have seen this coming and thus nothing could have been done. If we accept this notion, it will happen again.

This report should not be viewed as the end of the nation's examination of this crisis. There is still much to learn, much to investigate, and much to fix.

This is our collective responsibility. It falls to us to make different choices if we want different results. . . .

[Chapters 1–22 have been omitted.]

Dissenting Statement of Commissioner Keith Hennessey, Commissioner Douglas Holtz-Eakin, and Vice Chairman Bill Thomas

Introduction

We have identified ten causes that are essential to explaining the crisis. . . .

We find areas of agreement with the majority's conclusions, but unfortunately the areas of disagreement are significant enough that we dissent and present our views in this report. . . .

How Our Approach Differs from Others'

During the course of the Commission's hearings and investigations, we heard frequent arguments that there was a single cause of the crisis. For some it was international capital flows or monetary policy; for others, housing policy; and for still others, it was insufficient regulation of an ambiguously defined shadow banking sector, or unregulated over-the-counter derivatives, or the greed of those in the financial sector and the political influence they had in Washington.

In each case, these arguments, when used as single-cause explanations, are too simplistic because they are incomplete. While some of these factors were essential contributors to the crisis, each is insufficient as a standalone explanation.

The majority's approach to explaining the crisis suffers from the opposite problem—it is too broad. Not everything that went wrong during the financial crisis caused the crisis, and while some causes were essential, others had only a minor impact. Not every regulatory change related to housing or the financial system prior to the crisis was a cause. The majority's almost 550-page report is more an account of bad events than a focused explanation of what happened and why. When everything is important, nothing is.

As an example, non-credit derivatives did not in any meaningful way cause or contribute to the financial crisis. Neither the Community Reinvestment Act nor removal of the Glass-Steagall firewall was a significant cause. The crisis can be explained without resorting to these factors.

We also reject as too simplistic the hypothesis that too little regulation caused the crisis, as well as its opposite, that too much regulation caused the crisis. We question this metric for determining the effectiveness of regulation. The *amount* of financial regulation should reflect the need to address particular failures in the financial system. For example, high-risk, nontraditional mortgage lending by nonbank lenders flourished in the 2000s and did tremendous damage in an ineffectively regulated environment, contributing to the financial crisis. Poorly designed government housing policies distorted market outcomes and contributed to the creation of unsound mortgages as well. Countrywide's irresponsible lending and AIG's failure were in part attributable to ineffective regulation and supervision, while Fannie Mae and Freddie Mac's failures were the result of policymakers using the power of government to blend public purpose with private gains and then socializing the losses. Both the "too little government" and "too much government" approaches are too broad-brush to explain the crisis.

The majority says the crisis was avoidable if only the United States had adopted across-the-board more restrictive regulations, in conjunction with more aggressive regulators and supervisors. This conclusion by the majority largely ignores the global nature of the crisis. . . .

These facts tell us that our explanation for the credit bubble should focus on factors common to both the United States and Europe, that the credit bubble is likely an essential cause of the U.S. housing bubble, and that U.S. housing policy is by itself an insufficient explanation of the crisis. Furthermore, any explanation that relies too heavily on a unique element of the U.S. regulatory or supervisory system is likely to be insufficient to explain why the same thing happened in parts of Europe. This moves inadequate international capital and liquidity standards up our list of causes, and it moves the differences between the regulation of U.S. commercial and investment banks down that list. . . .

[The remainder of the dissenting views, appendices, and notes have been omitted.]

SOURCE: Financial Crisis Inquiry Commission. "Final Report of the National Commission on the Causes of the Financial and Economic Crisis in the United States." January 27, 2011. http://www.gpo.gov/fdsys/pkg/GPO-FCIC/pdf/GPO-FCIC.pdf.

Senate Permanent Subcommittee on Investigations Report on the Financial Crisis

April 13, 2011

[A listing of the members of the subcommittee, the table of contents, and an overview of the subcommittee has been omitted.]

I. EXECUTIVE SUMMARY

A. Subcommittee Investigation

In November 2008, the Permanent Subcommittee on Investigations initiated its investigation into some of the key causes of the financial crisis. Since then, the Subcommittee has engaged in a wide-ranging inquiry, issuing subpoenas, conducting over 150 interviews and depositions, and consulting with dozens of government, academic, and private sector experts. The Subcommittee has accumulated and reviewed tens of millions of pages of documents, including court pleadings, filings with the Securities and Exchange Commission, trustee reports, prospectuses for public and private offerings, corporate board and committee minutes, mortgage transactions and analyses, memoranda, marketing materials, correspondence, and emails. The Subcommittee has also reviewed documents prepared by or sent to or from banking and securities regulators, including bank examination reports, reviews of securities firms, enforcement actions, analyses, memoranda, correspondence, and emails.

In April 2010, the Subcommittee held four hearings examining four root causes of the financial crisis. Using case studies detailed in thousands of pages of documents released at the hearings, the Subcommittee presented and examined evidence showing how high risk lending by U.S. financial institutions; regulatory failures; inflated credit ratings; and high risk, poor quality financial products designed and sold by some investment banks, contributed to the financial crisis. This Report expands on those hearings and the case studies they featured. The case studies are Washington Mutual Bank, the largest bank failure in U.S. history; the federal Office of Thrift Supervision which oversaw Washington Mutual's demise; Moody's and Standard & Poor's, the country's two largest credit rating agencies; and Goldman Sachs and Deutsche Bank, two leaders in the design, marketing, and sale of mortgage related securities. This Report devotes a chapter to how each of the four causative factors, as illustrated by the case studies, fueled the 2008 financial crisis, providing findings of fact, analysis of the issues, and recommendations for next steps. . . .

[An overview of the crisis and case studies on the Office of Thrift Supervision, Moody's and Standard & Poor's, and Goldman Sachs and Deutsche Bank have been omitted.]

C. Recommendations

The four causative factors examined in this Report are interconnected. Lenders introduced new levels of risk into the U.S. financial system by selling and securitizing complex home loans with high risk features and poor underwriting. The credit rating agencies labeled the resulting securities as safe investments, facilitating their purchase by institutional investors around the world. Federal banking regulators failed to ensure safe and sound lending practices and risk management, and stood on the sidelines as large financial institutions active in U.S. financial markets purchased billions of dollars in mortgage related securities containing high risk, poor quality mortgages. Investment banks magnified the risk to the system by engineering and promoting risky mortgage related structured finance products, and enabling investors to use naked credit default swaps and synthetic instruments to bet on the failure rather than the success of U.S. financial instruments. Some investment banks also ignored the conflicts of interest created by their products, placed their financial interests before those of their clients, and even bet against the very securities they were recommending and marketing to their clients. Together these factors produced a mortgage market saturated with high risk, poor quality mortgages and securities that, when they began incurring losses, caused financial institutions around the world to lose billions of dollars, produced rampant unemployment and foreclosures, and ruptured faith in U.S. capital markets.

Nearly three years later, the U.S. economy has yet to recover from the damage caused by the 2008 financial crisis. . . .

Recommendations on High Risk Lending

1. **Ensure "Qualified Mortgages" Are Low Risk.** Federal regulators should use their regulatory authority to ensure that all mortgages deemed to be "qualified residential mortgages" have a low risk of delinquency or default.

2. **Require Meaningful Risk Retention.** Federal regulators should issue a strong risk retention requirement under Section 941 by requiring the retention of not less than a 5% credit risk in each, or a representative sample of, an asset backed securitization's tranches, and by barring a hedging offset for a reasonable but limited period of time.

3. **Safeguard Against High Risk Products.** Federal banking regulators should safeguard taxpayer dollars by requiring banks with high risk structured finance products, including complex products with little or no reliable performance data, to meet conservative loss reserve, liquidity, and capital requirements.

4. **Require Greater Reserves for Negative Amortization Loans.** Federal banking regulators should use their regulatory authority to require banks issuing negatively amortizing loans that allow borrowers to defer payments of interest and principal, to maintain more conservative loss, liquidity, and capital reserves.

5. **Safeguard Bank Investment Portfolios.** Federal banking regulators should use the Section 620 banking activities study to identify high risk structured finance products and impose a reasonable limit on the amount of such high risk products that can be included in a bank's investment portfolio.

Recommendations on Regulatory Failures

1. **Complete OTS Dismantling.** The Office of the Comptroller of the Currency (OCC) should complete the dismantling of the Office of Thrift Supervision (OTS), despite attempts by some OTS officials to preserve the agency's identity and influence within the OCC.

2. **Strengthen Enforcement.** Federal banking regulators should conduct a review of their major financial institutions to identify those with ongoing, serious deficiencies, and review their enforcement approach to those institutions to eliminate any policy of deference to bank management, inflated CAMELS ratings, or use of short term profits to excuse high risk activities.

3. **Strengthen CAMELS Ratings.** Federal banking regulators should undertake a comprehensive review of the CAMELS ratings system to produce ratings that signal whether an institution is expected to operate in a safe and sound manner over a specified period of time, asset quality ratings that reflect embedded risks rather than short term profits, management ratings that reflect any ongoing failure to correct identified deficiencies, and composite ratings that discourage systemic risks.

4. **Evaluate Impacts of High Risk Lending.** The Financial Stability Oversight Council should undertake a study to identify high risk lending practices at financial institutions, and evaluate the nature and significance of the impacts that these practices may have on U.S. financial systems as a whole.

Recommendations on Inflated Credit Ratings

1. **Rank Credit Rating Agencies by Accuracy.** The SEC should use its regulatory authority to rank the Nationally Recognized Statistical Rating Organizations in terms of performance, in particular the accuracy of their ratings.

2. **Help Investors Hold CRAs Accountable.** The SEC should use its regulatory authority to facilitate the ability of investors to hold credit rating agencies accountable in civil lawsuits for inflated credit ratings, when a credit rating agency knowingly or recklessly fails to conduct a reasonable investigation of the rated security.

3. **Strengthen CRA Operations.** The SEC should use its inspection, examination, and regulatory authority to ensure credit rating agencies institute internal controls, credit rating methodologies, and employee conflict of interest safeguards that advance rating accuracy.

4. **Ensure CRAs Recognize Risk.** The SEC should use its inspection, examination, and regulatory authority to ensure credit rating agencies assign higher risk to financial instruments whose performance cannot be reliably predicted due to their novelty or complexity, or that rely on assets from parties with a record for issuing poor quality assets.

5. **Strengthen Disclosure.** The SEC should exercise its authority under the new Section 780-7(s) of Title 15 to ensure that the credit rating agencies complete the required new ratings forms by the end of the year and that the new forms provide comprehensible, consistent, and useful ratings information to investors, including by testing the proposed forms with actual investors.

6. **Reduce Ratings Reliance.** Federal regulators should reduce the federal government's reliance on privately issued credit ratings.

Recommendations on Investment Bank Abuses

1. **Review Structured Finance Transactions.** Federal regulators should review the RMBS, CDO, CDS, and ABX activities described in this Report to identify any violations of law and to examine ways to strengthen existing regulatory prohibitions against abusive practices involving structured finance products.

2. **Narrow Proprietary Trading Exceptions.** To ensure a meaningful ban on proprietary trading under Section 619, any exceptions to that ban, such as for marketmaking or risk-mitigating hedging activities, should be strictly limited in the implementing regulations to activities that serve clients or reduce risk.

3. **Design Strong Conflict of Interest Prohibitions.** Regulators implementing the conflict of interest prohibitions in Sections 619 and 621 should consider the types of conflicts of interest in the Goldman Sachs case study, as identified in Chapter VI(C)(6) of this Report.

4. **Study Bank Use of Structured Finance.** Regulators conducting the banking activities study under Section 620 should consider the role of federally insured banks in designing, marketing, and investing in structured finance products with risks that cannot be reliably measured and naked credit default swaps or synthetic financial instruments. . . .

[The remaining five sections of the report have been omitted.]

Source: Senate Permanent Subcommittee on Investigations. "Wall Street and the Financial Crisis: Anatomy of a Financial Collapse." April 13, 2011. http://hsgac.senate.gov/public/_files/Financial_Crisis/FinancialCrisisReport.pdf.

OTHER HISTORIC DOCUMENTS OF INTEREST

FROM PREVIOUS *HISTORIC DOCUMENTS*

February

DEPARTMENT OF JUSTICE DECLARES DEFENSE OF MARRIAGE ACT UNCONSTITUTIONAL

Arab Spring: King Abdullah II Reshuffles Cabinet (Jordan)

FEBRUARY 1 AND 27, AND OCTOBER 17, 2011

Following on the heels of other prodemocracy movements in the Middle East, Jordanians took to the streets in January to protest rising unemployment and high food and fuel prices. Unlike protesters in other nations, the demonstrators in Jordan did not want to see the end of King Abdullah II's monarchy, but rather government reforms that would take some power from the king and invest it instead in a body fairly elected by the people. The king responded to the demonstrations with some promises of democratic reform; however, he gave little indication of a timetable for these reforms to take place.

January Unrest

Swept up in the wave of prodemocracy movements in the Middle East, in January 2011, Jordanians took to the streets to protest rising unemployment and skyrocketing prices. The first protests were aimed at the power of King Abdullah II. However, directly criticizing the king is prohibited by law, so protesters instead focused on the king's government. The demonstrations were fueled by the nation's economic crisis, one element of which was a large underemployed youth population. More than two thirds of the unemployed in Jordan are under the age of thirty, and more than 50 percent of these youth have college degrees. Inflation has risen to more than 6 percent, wage growth has been slow, and the government is facing a deficit estimated at more than 5 percent of its gross domestic product (GDP). As one of the smallest Middle East economies, Jordan must rely heavily on foreign investment to bolster its economy.

Impending unrest was foreshadowed in 2010 when the rural, tribal areas of Jordan that have typically supported the government and military began to grow restless over the little economic investment in their area and a belief that the money that should have been slated for their development was instead lining the pockets of government officials. A group of retired soldiers issued a petition in May 2010 demanding that the king stop corruption, disenfranchise Jordanians of Palestinian descent, and stop liberal economic policies that benefited the wealthier urban areas. Additional unrest began brewing in other parts of the country following the November 2010 parliamentary elections, which had been boycotted by the Muslim Brotherhood's political action arm, the Islamic Action Front (IAF), because of accusations that the king had set up parliamentary districts to ensure his continued support rather than to allow for fair competition of seats.

Weekly protests began on January 14, 2011, but the protesters initially had little impact and no cohesive agenda to bring together other government opposition groups. On January 28, the IAF led its largest protest, which brought together members of trade unions and other leftist organizations. Similar protests broke out in the tribal area of Ma'an over the government's continuing neglect of rural Jordan. The protests in these areas, which continued into February, accused Queen Rania of keeping her friends and family rich while ignoring those of East Bank descent to instead promote Palestinian issues.

A significant difference between protests taking place in Jordan and those elsewhere in the Middle East is that no one in Jordan has called for the end of the king's regime. "There is no comparison between Egypt and Jordan. The people there demand a regime change, but here we ask for political reforms and an elected government," said IAF Secretary-General Hamzah Mansour. There is some belief among political analysts that the difference is caused by the tensions among the different societal groups, mainly made up of East Bankers, who are the original settlers of Jordan and make up a large part of the government and its security forces, and Palestinians, who make up much of the private sector and often benefit from the policies of the current government. Tensions between these groups are currently being kept in check by the king and could grow if he is removed from power.

King Abdullah Responds

King Abdullah II first responded to the unrest in the tribal areas by putting tribal loyalists in his government and increasing spending in tribal lands. To placate the IAF demonstrators, the king announced a $125 million subsidy for basic goods and fuel and an increase in the salaries of civil servants. He canceled sales taxes on fuel and lowered taxes on other basic necessities.

On February 1, the king took additional steps to work with the IAF on their grievances, and fired his cabinet and prime minister in an attempt to stave off violence. Prime Minister Samir Rifai was replaced by Marouf al-Bakhit, who had formerly served as prime minister, general, ambassador to Israel and Turkey, and also headed the committee that oversaw the Jordan-Israel peace treaty of 1994. Rifai had been accused by the IAF and trade unions of ignoring their demands, the people of Jordan, and the influence of the Muslim Brotherhood to instead focus on technocrats and business leaders who could increase his personal wealth. As the new prime minister, al-Bakhit was called on to "take tangible steps to social, political, and economic reform and give priority to dialogue with all segments of society," the palace said. These reforms would be necessary, according to the palace, to ensure a better life for the people of Jordan that cannot be reached without political reforms and an increase in political participation. The new cabinet was sworn in on February 9, with a number of members from the former cabinet retaining their posts, specifically the ministerial positions of interior, economy, and foreign affairs, allowing the former government to continue to hold a large amount of power in Jordan's affairs.

The Muslim Brotherhood, a group that has largely opposed the king's government, was invited to take part in the new government, but declined. The IAF was unhappy with the al-Bakhit choice and said that the protests would not end until he was replaced as well. The IAF took issue with elections al-Bakhit ran in 2007 that have been perceived as invalid. "He is not the right person to run things at this current state and get Jordan out of crisis," said Zaki Bani Rsheid, an IAF leader.

Protests Spread

True to their word, the IAF and its supporters continued their protests, which remained largely peaceful until a prodemocracy demonstrator was killed in the center of Amman on March 24 when supporters of the new government attacked a gathering of protesters. The violence that broke out after the incident was short lived, and peaceful protest resumed the following week.

The king responded to the growing discontent by attempting to promote national unity, but the IAF and Muslim Brotherhood refused to participate in any of the unity discussions. Their demands, which the government did not indicate that it would accept, included dissolution of the parliament and cabinet and new elections held under a revised election law. They further called for a new constitution that would allow for the prime minister to be directly elected rather than appointed by the king. To keep violence to a minimum, following the death of the protester the government set up specific areas in which protests could be held, giving government security forces a better ability to control any violence.

After the death of the prodemocracy demonstrator, the March 24 Youth opposition group took shape. The group held small protests and sit-ins around the capital government buildings. According to one young protester, the changes made by the king have to this point been only cosmetic and do not speak to the demands of the protesters. The changes "don't address the core issues that need to be implemented right away—and that includes a Parliament and a government that represents the people," the protester said. "We will continue our protests," and "we will not be intimidated and we will continue to demand that reforms be implemented on the ground," he continued.

JORDAN'S CHANGING GOVERNMENT

Since taking power twelve years earlier, King Abdullah II has changed his cabinet eight times. The short-lived cabinets are not uncommon in Jordan—over the past ninety years, the government has changed seventy-two times. The difference in the February 1 cabinet change was that it was the first overhaul done in response to public demands. Each cabinet change has maintained the political structure of Jordan's government—a weak political party system and an underrepresentative parliament that includes no opposition members.

As the protests continued, so did the changes taking place at the highest levels of Jordan's government. In May 2011, the justice and health ministers resigned after it became publicly known that a businessman who was convicted of corruption and bribery had been allowed by these two ministers to leave the country. The businessman subsequently went missing. The following month, King Abdullah II made his biggest concession to date to the prodemocracy protesters, announcing that he would no longer appoint the members of Jordan's government, but would instead allow the creation of a system based on parliamentary majority. No time frame for an election or for the changes to take place was announced, but the king hinted that it could take more than two years to put the changes in place. A National Dialogue Committee, first formed in March 2011, made recommendations on changes necessitated by the type of reform the king had promised. The committee recommended that the size of parliament be increased from 120 to 130, with seats split between a governorate level with 115 seats and a national level with 15 seats; that future elections be overseen by an independent panel rather than the Interior Ministry; and that requirements for political party formation be eased, reducing the number of members from 500 to 250, 25 of whom must be women. The strongest objection to these recommendations came from the IAF, who believed that the small number of nationally elected seats would benefit the monarchy, allowing it to continue holding the same power it does today.

By October, the government changed hands again. On October 17, the cabinet and prime minister were removed from office. "We have accepted the resignation of Prime Minister Marouf al-Bakhit, taking into consideration the views of the various sectors of society as well as a letter we have received from the parliamentary majority," the king said. Al-Bakhit's short time as prime minister had been wrought with problems. Shortly into his term, al-Bakhit was seen as doing nothing to reform the government, and further angered prodemocracy demonstrators by passing a new law that posed steep fines for falsely accusing anyone of corruption, a move seen by many as an attempt to subvert the power of the media. Under al-Bakhit's watch, attacks on opposition groups took place, and it is believed that al-Bakhit ordered or directly oversaw the attacks.

A new prime minister was quickly named. Awn Shawkat al-Khasawneh had previously served as a judge for the International Court of Justice since 2000. In Jordan, Khasawneh had held the positions of chief of the royal court and legal adviser. "Awn Khasawneh is known for his integrity and has no corruption issues in his past like the rest, and more importantly he has very high legal capabilities, which is essential now in this phase of constitutional amendments, laws, and legislation which will define the future of Jordan," said General Ali Habashneh, a spokesperson for retired military members who had recently opposed the king's government.

Although protesters were not asking for the fall of the king's Hashemite monarchy, questions remain as to his future and what power he will wield if a new government is formed. Because the constitution provides immunity to the king from being held responsible for any wrongdoing or problems within the country, it is difficult for opposition groups to hold him accountable for the state of the country. However, if the electoral reforms are adopted, the king's only current responsibility—appointing the cabinet, prime minister, and forty members of the upper house of parliament—will disappear, leaving him with little actual responsibility. The monarchy's future will largely rest on the outcome of government reforms and how those economically benefit the East Bankers, the group that often strongly supports the king. Until then, King Abdullah II will remain in a difficult position, balancing the competing interests of the East Bank and Palestinians, attempting to promote national unity, managing a still struggling economy that cannot provide a sufficient number of private sector jobs, reducing unsustainable budget deficits, and promoting Jordan's image abroad.

—Heather Kerrigan

Following is a press release issued by the King of Jordan on February 1, 2011, accepting the resignation of prime minister Samir Rifai; a press release issued by the King of Jordan on February 1, 2011, naming a new prime minister; a press release from Prime Minister Marouf al-Bakhit on February 27, 2011, outlining his government's platform; and a press release from the King of Jordan on October 17, 2011, calling for the formation of a new government.

DOCUMENT   *Prime Minister Samir Rifai Resigns*

February 1, 2011

A Royal decree has accepted the resignation of the government of Prime Minister Samir Rifai tendered to His Majesty today.

In a letter, the King thanked Rifai and his ministerial team for their efforts during their term in office.

"Since I entrusted you with forming your first government more than a year ago, you have worked sincerely and on transparent basis to implement our directives contained in the Letter of Designation and deal with challenges posed to the country to bring more achievements and a decent living to our people," The King said in his letter to Rifai.

His Majesty hailed achievements under Rifai's government, mainly reduction of the budget deficit, introduction of fiscal controls, launching projects with specific goals, organising parliamentary elections as well as its efforts to fight corruption.

In a reply letter to the King, Rifai said he was honored for the trust His Majesty had given him to shoulder the responsibility and pursue reform in various fields. . . .

Over the past year, Rifai said, his government had endeavoured to carry out the King's order of holding free, fair and transparent parliamentary elections and setting a "positive" relationship with the Lower House of Parliament in line with the constitution.

"The government had also formed a special committee tasked with political reform to expand popular participation in government and achieve development in all of the Kingdom's governorates," he wrote. . . .

SOURCE: Jordan News Agency (PETRA). "King Accepts Resignation of Rifai's Government." February 1, 2011. http://www.petra.gov.jo/Public_News/Nws_NewsDetails.aspx?site_id=1&lang=2&NewsID=20575&Type=A&CatID=-1&Search=&DateFrom=1/2/2011&DateTo=28/2/2011.

DOCUMENT   *King Names New Prime Minister*

February 1, 2011

His Majesty King Abdullah II on Tuesday asked Marouf Al Bakhit to form a new government after accepting the resignation of Prime Minister Samir Rifai's cabinet.

In the letter of desination [*sic*] to Bakhit, the King said the new government's major task should be "to take speedy practical and tangible steps to unleash a real political reform process that reflects our vision of comprehensive [*sic*] reform, modernisation and development." "Such a process should enable us to proceed with confidence along the path of bolstering democracy and building the nation that will open the door wide for achievement by all our dear people and secure them the safe and dignified life they are worthy of." Saying the current stage holds opportunity despite the challenges, His Majesty urged the incoming administration to build on and update national agenda programmes and proceed along the line set for the coming years in the letters of designation to the previous two governments.

He told Bakhit to take time and consult with all forces across the social and political spectra to put together his cabinet.

"We direct you to take the time to pick your ministerial team from the sons of Jordan who are capable, qualified and committed to the vision of comprehensive reform that upholds dialogue, openness, candor and transparency and reach out to our dear people," the King urged. Addressing the Prime Minister-Designate, the King hailed Bakhit as "a true and loyal soldier who could bear the responsibility with utmost fairness and dedication as you have always won my trust in all the posts you have held." The letter noted that since he came to power, the King had embraced comprehensive reform as the path to achievement while keeping abreast of the spirit of age which required launching the potentials of all Jordanians and empowering them through science, knowledge and training.

King Abdullah noted that he had made it clear that emphasis should be put on economic reform as a need to provide "best means of living to all people across the country", a goal that would not come about without political reform that brings citizens into the decision-making process.

He said political reform would build influential institutions encompassing effective and transparent programmes governed by up-to-date legislations befitting best democratic standards, but said the process was held back by imbalances and individuals who balked at change.

"The process has been marred by gaps and imbalances resulting from fear of change by some who resisted it to protect their own interests and the policies of appeasement which placed the private interest ahead of the public interest, hence costing the country dearly and denying it many opportunities for achievement," the letter went on.

King Abdullah asked Bakhit, a former Prime Minister, to conduct a comprehensive evaluation to come up with effective measures to address past mistakes and set a clear working strategy to press ahead with reform, through appraisal and updating of all laws governing political and civilian work and public freedoms.

The letter stressed that the elections law, "the pillar of real political development", is at the top of those legislations, which encompass laws related to political parties, assembly, municipalities, press and publication, access to information and others.

"Based on this, we look forward to your recommendations, in the earliest possible time, on a mechanism for a comprehensive, systematic national dialogue inclusive of all components and spectra of our society to reach consensus on a new elections law," read the letter.

It said the new law should emphasise an "inclusive national identy [sic]" and upgrade a collective partisan work where every one competes on serving the nation and citizens based on programmes and agree on all steps needed to accelerate democratisation "in a manner to guarantee maximum popular participation in decision-making."

"The government is duty-bound to take what is needed to promote civil society institutions, ensure free speech and create the atmosphere for a professional and independent media that take an unrestricted role, utilizing modern communications that should serve as a tool to disseminate and instill the culture of dialogue, not a means to spread misinformation and unjustly abuse individuals and institutions," the letter urged. . . .

Turning to the economy, the letter put the focus on creating better living conditions for citizens through increasing national productivity, raising growth and competitiveness while maximizing the potential to attract investment and create jobs. It also stressed an anti-corruption approach.

"You need to act within the parametres of the reformist economic approach through programmes and plans that guarantee best possible performance of the national economy, a real partnership between the public and private sectors, a fair distribution of development dividends, expansion of the middle class and protection of poor segments," it said.

"I should emphasise the need to build a strong institutional basis to combat all forms of corruption and take the utmost legal measures against anyone proven to have engaged in it," added the letter. . . .

SOURCE: Jordan News Agency (PETRA). "King Names Bakhit to Form New Govt, Urges Accelerated Reform." February 1, 2011. http://www.petra.gov.jo/Public_News/Nws_NewsDetails.aspx?site_id=1&lang=2&NewsID=20568&Type=A&CatID=-1&Search=&DateFrom=1/2/2011&DateTo=28/2/2011.

Prime Minister Bakhit Presents Governing Platform

February 27, 2011

Prime Minister Marouf Bakhit said on Sunday that overcoming challenges in the next stage required a strong will for reform and the courage for a rational review of social and economic policies.

Outlining his new government's manifesto to the Lower House of Parliament on the basis of which he will ask for confidence, Bakhit said the cabinet is implementing a real gradual reform approach to achieve national goals, stressing utmost clarity and transparency in an "equitable" relationship between legislative and executive authorities. "All what the government is doing will never come through an instantaneous policy of containment, but rather via a true, gradual method of reform to arrive at our national goals," he said. . . .

He said the government would review legislation pertaining to democratic and political life and grassroots participation, including the elections law, the public gatherings, political parties and municipalities laws and the decentralisation bill, in order to provide the conditions for political and popular participation and elevate the level of representation in national programmes and issues.

Bakhit pledged "a comprehensive" assessment of the national media leading to effective measures to address past mistakes and review legislation governing freedom of opinion, including the press and publications law, vowing that the government is "in one trench with a national media, both official and private, that is committed to the profession and objective of serving the country and the King." He also said the government would give the go-ahead for a teachers' association in response to demands by teachers and lawmakers.

Bakhit vowed to tackle financial and administrative corruption head-on, saying justice, equal opportunities and protection of public money are key to any reform process, and adding: there will be no justice, equal opportunities or development with corruption.

Turning to the economy, Bakhit said an open market economy would not last without controls, stressing a more effective economic approach that guarantees greater social justice.

He said the government would adopt a clear and transparent oil pricing mechanism taking into consideration the people's right to have oil derivatives at affordable prices, and telling lawmakers that the pricing approach would be on a quarterly basis instead of the current monthly criteria.

Bakhit also pledged support of the armed forces and security apparatuses and to offer their personnel and pensioners a decent life in order to help them to carry out their major role of presenting the country's bright image and its sublime values.

SOURCE: Jordan News Agency (PETRA). "PM Outlines Govt Platform to Parliament." February 27, 2011. http://www.petra.gov.jo/Public_News/Nws_NewsDetails.aspx?site_id=1&lang=2&NewsID=23218&Type=A&CatID=-1&Search=&DateFrom=1/2/2011&DateTo=28/2/2011.

King Calls for Formation of New Government

October 17, 2011

His Majesty King Abdullah II on Monday entrusted Dr. Own Khasawneh to for [*sic*] a new government to succeeded outgoing prime minister Marouf Bakhit whose resignation was accepted by the King today.

Following is the full text of the royal letter of designation to Khasawneh: In the Name of God, the Most Merciful, the Compassionate Peace, God's Mercy and Blessings be upon the Prophet Mohammad and his Family and Companions Your Excellency Awn Khasawneh, Peace and God's Mercy and Blessings be upon you, I extend my warmest and sincerest wishes for your good health, happiness and success.

For many years now I have known you as a loyal soldier of your country and I followed with interest your distinguished service as Chief of the Royal Hashemite Court under my father, His Majesty the late King Hussein bin Talal. Indeed, in all positions you served and all responsibilities you shouldered, you demonstrated great integrity, devotion and competence. . . .

Political reform characterises the current phase in the journey of our beloved Jordan. The latest constitutional amendments now require a comprehensive review and approval of much of the legislation governing political life in Jordan within the comprehensive reform vision. I have known you as a person of incorruptible integrity, with vast legal experience and international standing. I have also known you as a person who carries out his responsibilities with diligence, devotion and efficiency. Now, after accepting the resignation of Dr. Marouf Al-Bakhit's government, in light of many in-depth discussions with Jordanian civil society components and entities, and in light of the petition we received from a parliamentary majority, I hereby entrust you with the formation of a new government that will continue to move forward on all aspects of reform and modernisation, delivering on all the requirements of this phase, and building upon the accomplishments of previous governments.

Mr. Prime Minister, Completing the march towards political reform requires reviewing and introducing many laws and legislation in line with the new Constitution, which seeks to enhance public participation and the role of civil society in decision-making, within a framework of freedom, pluralism and the rule of law.

Accordingly, it is essential that: First, priority must be given to the completion of legislation and laws that regulate political life, at the forefront of which are the Election and Political Parties Laws. These should be agreed upon through an effective and constructive national dialogue with the entire political spectrum and civic institutions, before they are approved through the established constitutional channels. We remember God Almighty's injunction: And those who answer the call of their Lord and establish worship, and whose affairs are a matter of counsel and who spend of what We have bestowed on them, (Al-Shura, 42:38). Second, connected to these two laws, is the establishment of an independent commission to oversee the elections. This must include the ideal mechanism for achieving the highest degree of transparency, integrity and neutrality. All of this will set the groundwork for the next parliamentary elections. I emphasise that these elections must be free, fair and transparent. . . .

Third, there must be a comprehensive review of the issue of municipal elections. This is to ensure that these elections meet the highest standards of integrity and impartiality, so that municipalities may fulfil their main role of serving local communities. They must be established in a way that paves the way for future decentralisation and local governance plan.

Fourth, the government must spare no effort to enforce the principles of transparency, accountability and the rule of law. The government must also guarantee justice and equal opportunity, and fight favouritism and nepotism. Equally, the government must enhance the anti-corruption system so as to deter corruption before it occurs and hold the corrupt accountable without procrastination or delay, irrespective of their position, social status or any other considerations, so that citizens can see how serious and effective we are in countering this phenomenon, which undermines the credibility and authority of state institutions. All must be held accountable, and no one is above the law. . . .

Fifth, our national unity is a red line that we will not allow anyone to cross. It is not to be harmed in any way, shape or form, it must remain above any differences and disputes, always.

Sixth, media liberalisation must take place in tandem with the preservation of professionalism and credibility. The media must be open to all political opinions and orientations in a manner that ensures that all types of media print, audio-visual and online media serve as platforms for constructive national dialogue. . . . I emphasise here the need for all forms of expression—protests and peaceful marches—to be conducted in accordance with the law and to be based on respect for all opinions. . . .

Seventh, improving our citizens' living standards is our most critical priority and this demands that the government execute development, economic and social programmes. At the forefront of this is enhancing economic stability, boosting growth, tackling poverty and unemployment, improving the investment climate, attracting investments that create jobs especially for the youth and putting in place appropriate mechanisms to maximise benefits from the recently-established Fund for the Development of Governorates, in close coordination with local communities, each according to their needs and priorities. . . .

Eighth, we seek to implement the best possible approach to government administration, an approach based on consultation with local bodies, the private sector and civil society institutions, in order to identify priorities, suggest appropriate solutions, and then expedite implementation and completion, according to constitutional channels, without delays, postponements, favouritisms, and appeasement.

Ninth, as for our armed forces and our security services, they enjoy our utmost trust and make us all proud. They have my, and the Jordanian people's thanks and appreciation for their professionalism, proficiency, patience, self-control and true Jordanian conduct in dealing with what our country has witnessed in terms of demonstrations and/or public turmoil. They must receive all support they require in terms of training, preparation, equipment, and decent living so that they may continue to fulfil their duty to protect our beloved homeland and preserve its security, stability and accomplishments with efficiency and competence.

Tenth, our devotion to our Arab nation and our commitment to defend its just causes require the utmost consultation with our Arab brethren on all issues that concern our Arab and Islamic nations. Our cooperation with them, and joint Arab endeavour, must be encouraged and enhanced. In this framework, our brethren have welcomed Jordan to join the Gulf Cooperation Council. This is an invitation that we appreciate, as much as we appreciate their continuous support and solidarity, and in particular the supportive stands of my brother, the Custodian of the Two Holy Mosques. The government must work with our brothers in the GCC to achieve this goal and translate our joint vision into a tangible reality whose benefits all parties may reap. . . .

I also affirm to Your Excellency, and to the world at large, that any settlement regarding the Palestinian cause will never be at Jordan's expense or the expense of any of our national interests. Mr. Prime Minister, The primary mission of this government is to implement a political reform process with clear milestones, not just arbitrary timetables. The government must also draft legislation and laws and conduct municipal elections. This demands coordination between the legislative and executive branches, and neither must encroach upon the other. It also necessitates drawing a roadmap to achieve political reform based on clear foundations and criteria. Citizens must be kept abreast of achievements at each stage, as they materialise, for the challenges facing Jordan at this time are both great and complex. There are many political objectives that must be achieved as soon as possible together with the implementation of economic and social development programmes that will have a positive impact on the living standards of our citizens. I have great confidence in you, Mr. Prime Minister. I await your nominations, after the necessary consultations and within a reasonable timeframe that will allow you to choose ministers who are competent, experienced and committed to a vision of reform. Your ministers will share with you the burden of responsibility. You and your colleagues, the ministers, will have my full support, and I will be closely following up on your progress.

I beseech the Almighty to bless us all with success in serving Him and His servants in our beloved country and our Arab and Islamic nations.

SOURCE: Jordan News Agency (PETRA). "King Entrusts Awn Khasawneh to Form New Government." October 17, 2011. http://www.petra.gov.jo/Public_News/Nws_NewsDetails.aspx?site_id=1&lang=2&NewsID=46758&Type=A&CatID=-1&Search=&DateFrom=1/10/2011&DateTo=21/10/2011 and http://www.petra.gov.jo/Public_News/Nws_NewsDetails.aspx?site_id=1&lang=2&NewsID=46757&Type=A&CatID=-1&Search=&DateFrom=1/10/2011&DateTo=21/10/2011.

OTHER HISTORIC DOCUMENTS OF INTEREST

FROM THIS VOLUME

FROM PREVIOUS *HISTORIC DOCUMENTS*

Arab Spring: International Response to Mubarak's Resignation (Egypt)

FEBRUARY 11, 2011

Late January 2011 brought another prodemocracy movement to the Middle East, with Egyptians demonstrating in Cairo's Tahrir Square against the autocratic reign of President Hosni Mubarak. According to estimates, nearly one million people turned out to protest the regime, and after indicating that he would remain in power, on February 11, 2011, Mubarak resigned his position, handing power over to the nation's military. The jubilation in the streets quickly turned to disdain for the new leaders, who announced that they would not hand over power as planned following parliamentary elections, but would instead remain in control of the nation's government.

JANUARY PROTESTS

The revolution taking place in Tunisia that overthrew President Zine al-Abidine Ben Ali sparked Egyptians to rise up against the autocratic rule of their own president, Hosni Mubarak. Mubarak's reign began in 1981, and since that time he had managed to keep his dissenters quiet by governing under an emergency law originally meant to thwart terrorism. The law gave Mubarak's regime the power to arrest without reason, detain prisoners without charges or a trial, and stop any form of assembly. With the emergency laws and a strong security force behind him, Mubarak managed to stay in power even as he became increasingly unpopular. His hold on this power was partly due to general apathy among Egyptians and little cohesive opposition. The strongest opposition to Mubarak's rule was considered to be the Muslim Brotherhood, but after being banned from the country, it had little legitimacy among Egyptians.

Beginning on January 25, protesters took to the streets in what was called the April 6 Youth Movement, born out of a 2008 strike held on April 6, a "day of revolt against torture, poverty, corruption, and unemployment." The demonstrations, which brought together the Muslim Brotherhood and young Egyptians, took place in Cairo's Tahrir Square and in the outlying cities of Alexandria, Mansoura, and Suez. Demonstrators, frustrated by the failing economy, police brutality, and state corruption that they believed was led by Mubarak, called for greater democratic freedom and accountability for government leaders.

Many of those who came out to protest were initially driven by the Egyptian prodemocracy movement taking root on social media sites that were used to gain attention for the cause. More than one million Egyptians joined the demonstrations, using advice from Tunisian demonstrators on how to avoid the effects of tear gas by sniffing lemons, onions, and vinegar and how to use cardboard and plastic bottles to make a kind of armor for protection against rubber bullets. Mubarak's security forces had at first stood by, under orders to remain out of the fray, but it was not long before they began using force to break up the protests after they could no longer withstand homemade bombs and rocks being thrown at them. Members of the Egyptian military who had defected to join the protesters used their own guns to scatter Mubarak forces and leave protesters in control of Tahrir Square. The crackdown by security forces is thought to have caused at least 800 deaths. U.S. President Barack Obama spoke with Mubarak, encouraging him to respect the right of Egyptians to protest and not to harm those peacefully demonstrating. "Violence will not address the grievances of the Egyptian people. And suppressing ideas never succeeds in making them go away," Obama told Mubarak. "Surely, there will be difficult days to come, but the United States will continue to stand up for the rights of the Egyptian people and work with their government in pursuit of a future that is more just, more free, and more hopeful."

Mubarak's government was at first critical of the protesters, with Interior Minister Habib el-Adly criticizing the demonstrators and saying they would have no impact. The president's government further denied claims that events in Tunisia would have any effect on Egypt. It was not until late January when Mubarak took action to appease the protesters by firing his cabinet and choosing a new one. In his first statement following the protests, he said simply, "I have asked the government to present its resignation today." Protesters took little notice, and instead called on Mubarak to step down, but he gave no indication that he planned to leave his position.

Unrest in Egypt had been brewing for years before it came to the surface in January, and was mainly organized in secret meetings and through online venues. But Mubarak's forces often learned of the dissent and would jail leaders of the small opposition organizations. Discontent became stronger in 2010 over the continuing use of emergency rule; so, to avoid further dissent, Mubarak promised to grant the country more freedoms and only invoke the emergency law in cases of terrorism and drug trafficking. However, human rights activists said the new regulations for the application of the law were so loosely defined that the government could easily use it to detain innocent Egyptians.

Mubarak Resigns

On February 11, 2011, following eighteen days of protests, and a loss of support from his military, Mubarak made the decision to resign. A brief televised statement on state-run media was read by Mubarak's vice president, Omar Suleiman. "In these grave circumstances that the country is passing through, President Hosni Mubarak has decided to leave his position as president of the republic," Suleiman said. "He has mandated the Armed Forces Supreme Council [SCAF] to run the state."

In May, it was announced that Mubarak would stand trial for the killing of more than 800 demonstrators during his security force's crackdown on the protests and could face the death penalty if found guilty. Prosecutors listed his crimes as "intentional murder, attempted killing of some demonstrators . . . , misuse of influence and deliberately wasting public funds and unlawfully making private financial gains and profits." Following his resignation, Mubarak had been taken to a hospital in a Red Sea resort, where he was seeking medical treatment. Mubarak's trial began in August, and the former president was wheeled into the courtroom in a hospital bed. Witness testimony at the trial gave little evidence to whether Mubarak was guilty of any of the crimes of which he had been accused. Mubarak's opposition saw this as little more than his former military supporters trying to free him quickly without prosecution. In October, Mubarak's trial was postponed until December 28 while the validity of an appeal to replace the trial's judges was investigated. In early December, an Egyptian court rejected the appeal, and the final verdict is expected on June 2, 2012.

Following Mubarak's resignation, the military took control of the government and ruled through an eighteen-member body made up of top military leaders. After the elation of toppling Mubarak died down, fear spread as to whether the fall of Mubarak's regime would simply bring about military rule rather than freedom. The demonstrators had failed to come together politically during the eighteen days of protest to form a political party or coalition that could make a serious bid for control of the government.

After coming to power, the military quickly cracked down on any remaining demonstrations by keeping the emergency laws in place and announcing that it would not give up control until after parliamentary and presidential elections took place in late 2011 or in 2012. There was no guarantee that elections would take place that quickly, however, and communiqués from March indicated that the vote might come in 2013 or later. In October, the military revised its decision and announced that it would not hand over power after the elections, but would rather give parliament a subordinate role in the government. The military said it would retain the power of appointing a prime minister and cabinet.

POLITICAL TRANSITION

Following Mubarak's resignation, the SCAF said that elections would be scheduled for June 2011. Given the slow pace at which political parties were forming and registering, the SCAF decided to move the elections to September, and then finally scheduled them for November 28. The elections will be comprised of three separate votes running through January 10, each separated by fifteen days. A March 2011 referendum that was supported by 77.2 percent of voters, and hailed as the first real vote in Egypt's history, laid out the election laws for the November vote, and stated that after electing the upper and lower houses of parliament, members would need to choose the 100 members of the Constituent Assembly that would be tasked with drafting the new governing document. The Constituent Assembly would then be given six months to draft the document, and it would be voted on by the Egyptian people within fifteen days of completion. The elections would be overseen by the Supreme Electoral Commission, made up of Egyptian judges. A decision was made not to allow international election observers into the country as it was believed that would interfere with Egyptian sovereignty.

In July, a new election law was passed by the SCAF without voter approval. The new law would split the way in which parliamentary seats are allocated. Half would be selected in winner-take-all elections, while the other half would be chosen from party lists, with each party receiving a number of seats based on the percentage of the vote it received. Each party was required to submit a candidate list that included at least one female candidate, removing an earlier stipulation that the parliament must have sixty-four female members. The July law also changed some provisions as to who may run, lowering the age from thirty to twenty-five and maintaining that half of the seats must be for "workers and farmers." It would be up to the interim president to choose 10 of the 514 members of the lower house of parliament, while two thirds of the upper house seats would be elected and the other third would be left empty until a future presidential election. After this presidential election, it would be up to the winner to appoint members to fill those seats.

Without a constitution in place until after the election, the SCAF determined that to stave off some of the demonstrations that had been taking place, it would ask party leaders and other political experts to draft some constitutional principles that would guide the government until the Constituent Assembly drafted the official governing document. Proposals from party leaders included making all Egyptians, regardless of race, color, religion, or social status, equal and free under the law, a proposal that angered Islamists who thought this would make the state too secular. Other proposals included making Arabic the official language, creating a multiparty system and independent judiciary, limiting the role the military had in the government, and giving all Egyptians a right to expression, protest, and religion. In August, the groups tasked with drafting interim constitutional principles failed to agree on any of the proposals, and the government decided to instead await the Constituent Assembly's decisions.

Prior to the start of the election season, unrest broke out on November 18, with demonstrators protesting the military's retention of power. Tens of thousands turned out in Tahrir Square, and eventually more than 100,000 were thought to have joined the demonstration. In spite of the protests, the elections began as scheduled and featured 55 parties and approximately 6,600 candidates.

Regardless of how the military decides to retain power in Egypt, it is unclear how the parliamentary and presidential votes will turn out. There are fifty million eligible voters in Egypt, and up to 30 percent are thought to support Islamists and the Muslim Brotherhood. Fewer than 20 percent are Coptic Christian, a group heavily committed to democracy. That leaves 50 percent of the population undecided, and these voters are the ones the 6,600 parliamentary candidates will be vying for. Election results released in January 2012 showed the Muslim Brotherhood garnering a majority of votes.

Social Media's Role in the Uprising

While social media may not have caused the revolution in Egypt, it did accelerate its development. Prior to the start of demonstrations in January, and throughout, opposition groups including the April 6 Youth Movement, We Are All Khaled Said, the National Association for Change, and Kefaya used social media platforms to spread the demonstrators's messages around the world. Before the first January 25 protest, 85,000 pledged to attend what was dubbed Revolution Day on Facebook. Prodemocracy demonstrators continued to use Facebook, Twitter, and YouTube throughout their struggle to beam photos and videos of the protests and subsequent violence around the world.

On January 28, Mubarak shut down the Internet for five days to stop demonstrators from using social media outlets to gather and organize supporters. The move helped the prodemocracy movement gain additional support; Al Jazeera reported a tenfold increase in the number of protesters after the Internet blackout. The Internet outage also drew anger from outside the nation. "We support the universal rights of the Egyptian people including the rights to freedom of expression, association, and assembly. And we urge the Egyptian authorities not to prevent peaceful protests or block communications, including on social-media sites," said U.S. Secretary of State Hillary Rodham Clinton. On the eighth day of protests, when Internet access was restored, Egyptian preacher Amr Khaled, named by *Time* as one of the most influential people in the world, turned to his Facebook friends to describe the hope that the peaceful demonstrations brought him. "I have seen the wonderful view of civility among young people," Khaled wrote in Arabic.

—Heather Kerrigan

Following are statements by U.S. President Barack Obama, the United Nations, and the North Atlantic Treaty Organization (NATO) responding to the resignation of Egyptian President Hosni Mubarak on February 11, 2011.

President Obama on Mubarak's Resignation

February 11, 2011

Good afternoon, everybody. There are very few moments in our lives where we have the privilege to witness history taking place. This is one of those moments. This is one of those times. The people of Egypt have spoken, their voices have been heard, and Egypt will never be the same.

By stepping down, President Mubarak responded to the Egyptian people's hunger for change. But this is not the end of Egypt's transition. It's a beginning. I'm sure there will be difficult days ahead, and many questions remain unanswered. But I am confident that the people of Egypt can find the answers, and do so peacefully, constructively, and in the spirit of unity that has defined these last few weeks. For Egyptians have made it clear that nothing less than genuine democracy will carry the day.

The military has served patriotically and responsibly as a caretaker to the state, and will now have to ensure a transition that is credible in the eyes of the Egyptian people. That means protecting the rights of Egypt's citizens, lifting the emergency law, revising the constitution and other laws to make this change irreversible, and laying out a clear path to elections that are fair and free. Above all, this transition must bring all of Egypt's voices to the table. For the spirit of peaceful protest and perseverance that the Egyptian people have shown can serve as a powerful wind at the back of this change.

The United States will continue to be a friend and partner to Egypt. We stand ready to provide whatever assistance is necessary—and asked for—to pursue a credible transition to a democracy. I'm also confident that the same ingenuity and entrepreneurial spirit that the young people of Egypt have shown in recent days can be harnessed to create new opportunity—jobs and businesses that allow the extraordinary potential of this generation to take flight. And I know that a democratic Egypt can advance its role of responsible leadership not only in the region but around the world.

Egypt has played a pivotal role in human history for over 6,000 years. But over the last few weeks, the wheel of history turned at a blinding pace as the Egyptian people demanded their universal rights.

We saw mothers and fathers carrying their children on their shoulders to show them what true freedom might look like. We saw a young Egyptian say, "For the first time in my life, I really count. My voice is heard. Even though I'm only one person, this is the way real democracy works." We saw protesters chant "Selmiyya, selmiyya"—"We are peaceful"—again and again. We saw a military that would not fire bullets at the people they were sworn to protect. We saw doctors and nurses rushing into the streets to care for those who were wounded, volunteers checking protesters to ensure that they were unarmed.

We saw people of faith praying together and chanting—"Muslims, Christians, We are one." And though we know that the strains between faiths still divide too many in this world and no single event will close that chasm immediately, these scenes remind us that we need not be defined by our differences. We can be defined by the common humanity that we share.

And above all, we saw a new generation emerge—a generation that uses their own creativity and talent and technology to call for a government that represented their hopes and not their fears; a government that is responsive to their boundless aspirations. One Egyptian put it simply: "Most people have discovered in the last few days . . . that they are worth something, and this cannot be taken away from them anymore, ever."

This is the power of human dignity, and it can never be denied. Egyptians have inspired us, and they've done so by putting the lie to the idea that justice is best gained through violence. For in Egypt, it was the moral force of nonviolence—not terrorism, not mindless killing but nonviolence, moral force—that bent the arc of history toward justice once more.

And while the sights and sounds that we heard were entirely Egyptian, we can't help but hear the echoes of history, echoes from Germans tearing down a wall, Indonesian students taking to the streets, Gandhi leading his people down the path of justice.

As Martin Luther King said in celebrating the birth of a new nation in Ghana while trying to perfect his own, "There is something in the soul that cries out for freedom." Those were the cries that came from Tahrir Square, and the entire world has taken note.

Today belongs to the people of Egypt, and the American people are moved by these scenes in Cairo and across Egypt because of who we are as a people and the kind of world that we want our children to grow up in.

The word tahrir means "liberation." It is a word that speaks to that something in our souls that cries out for freedom. And forevermore it will remind us of the Egyptian people, of what they did, of the things that they stood for, and how they changed their country, and in doing so changed the world.

Thank you.

SOURCE: Executive Office of the President. "Remarks on the Situation in Egypt." February 11, 2011. *Compilation of Presidential Documents* 2011, no. 00081 (February 11, 2011). http://www.gpo.gov/fdsys/pkg/DCPD-201100081/pdf/DCPD-201100081.pdf.

UN Calls for Peaceful Transition in Egypt

February 11, 2011

Secretary-General Ban Ki-moon today called again for a transparent, orderly and peaceful transition in Egypt after hearing of President Hosni Mubarak's decision to step down after weeks of anti-government protests, and commended the Egyptian people for making their voices heard.

According to media reports, Vice-President Omar Suleiman announced on state television that Mr. Mubarak, who has been in power for 30 years, had resigned on Friday and had handed over power to the military.

"I respect what must have been a difficult decision, taken in the wider interests of the Egyptian people," Mr. Ban told reporters at United Nations Headquarters in New York.

"At this historic moment, I reiterate my call, made as recently as last night, for a transparent, orderly and peaceful transition that meets the legitimate aspirations of the

Egyptian people and includes free, fair and credible elections leading to the early establishment of civilian rule.

"I urge the interim authorities to chart a clear path forward with the participation of all stakeholders," he added.

In a statement issued by his spokesperson last night, Mr. Ban had emphasized that it is for the Egyptian people to determine their future.

"The voice of the Egyptian people, particularly the youth, has been heard, and it is for them to determine the future of their country," he stated today.

"I commend the people of Egypt for the peaceful and courageous and orderly manner in which they have exercised their legitimate rights. I call on all parties to continue in the same spirit."

He added that it is vital that human rights and civil liberties are fully respected, and that genuine and inclusive dialogue is assured, and reiterated the UN's readiness to assist the country.

In a related development, the UN High Commissioner for Refugees (UNHCR) reported today that amid the continuing political turmoil in Egypt, the agency has been working through key partners to provide financial support and medical help to refugees in Cairo while its staff have been manning telephone hotlines from their homes.

UNHCR's partner on the ground in Egypt, Caritas, is distributing financial help and offering medical support to refugees in Cairo who are particularly vulnerable at this time. There are 107,000 refugees and asylum-seekers in Egypt of which 39,680 are registered with UNHCR. Most refugees come from Sudan, Iraq, Somalia, Ethiopia and Eritrea.

SOURCE: United Nations. UN News Centre. "Egypt: UN Chief Urges Peaceful Transition After Mubarak Resignation." February 11, 2011. http://www.un.org/apps/news/story.asp?NewsID=37513.

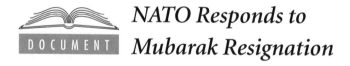

NATO Responds to Mubarak Resignation

February 11, 2011

I welcome President Mubarak's decision. I have consistently called for a speedy, orderly and peaceful transition to democracy, respecting the legitimate aspirations of the people of Egypt.

In the long run, no society can neglect the will of the people. Democracy means much more than majority rule—it also means respect for individual freedom, for minorities, human rights and the rule of law. These are the values on which our Alliance is based and the values we encourage our partners to respect. Egypt is a valued partner in our Mediterranean Dialogue and a pivotal country in the region. I am confident Egypt will continue to be a force for stability and security.

SOURCE: North Atlantic Treaty Organization. "Statement by the NATO Secretary General on Events in Egypt." February 11, 2011. http://www.nato.int/cps/en/natolive/news_70588.htm.

OTHER HISTORIC DOCUMENTS OF INTEREST

Wisconsin Passes Anti-Collective Bargaining Bill

FEBRUARY 11 AND MARCH 9 AND 10, 2011

The wave of 2010 midterm election Republican victories at the state and national level put into office a number of leaders interested in closing budget gaps by implementing strict spending limitations. Wisconsin was no exception. In February 2011, newly elected governor Scott Walker, a Republican, proposed a partial year budget bill that would close the state's budget gap for 2011 by requiring additional contributions from state employees to their pensions and health care plans. While these provisions were unpopular, what drew the most ire from the state's public employees, and brought tens of thousands of union members to protest in Madison, were provisions of the bill that would end most collective bargaining. Unions, backed by Democratic politicians from across the country, decried the move as an assault on public employee rights, but in the end, Walker emerged victorious and set off antiunion fights in other states.

BUDGET REPAIR BILL

In February, Wisconsin governor Scott Walker unveiled a budget repair bill intended to help balance the $137 million budget gap the state was facing for the fiscal year ending June 30, 2011, and the $3.6 billion shortfall expected during the 2011–2013 budget years. Walker's office reported that his budget repair would help save the state $30 million during fiscal year 2011 and $300 million over the next two years, leaving the state a $107 million reserve fund.

In order to close the budget gap, the 144-page budget repair plan called for higher pension and health insurance contributions from public employees and an end to collective bargaining for anything other than salaries. Public safety employees including local police, fire fighters, and state troopers were exempt from the collective bargaining restriction. Walker's office said the new bill would cost public employees 8 percent of their salary each year. Unions were quick to criticize Walker's plan because, in addition to restricting the right to collectively bargain, Walker was also removing the ability of unions to collect dues from state employees who are eligible but opt not to participate in a union. Union leaders argue that these employees should pay dues because they benefit from the negotiations at the bargaining table. This provision of Walker's bill, unions said, would only hurt union coffers, and have no impact on the state's budget. Unions called this a clear attempt by the governor to bust unions.

In unveiling his bill, Walker said he saw its provisions as the only way to avoid layoffs, up to 6,000 of which might otherwise be necessary. "I don't have anything to negotiate," Walker said. "We are broke in this state. We have been broke for years. People have ignored that for years and it's about time somebody stood up and told the truth. The truth is: We don't have any money to offer. We don't have finances to offer. This is what we have to offer," the governor said. Fearing backlash from public employees, Walker announced that the National Guard was prepared to respond if there was any unrest among state employees in response to the bill.

STRONG UNION HISTORY

Collective bargaining, the process through which an employer and a union, which represents the employees, negotiate over salary, benefits, and other employment conditions including hours and vacation time, has its roots in Wisconsin. The National Labor Relations Act of 1935 had previously granted collective bargaining rights to private sector employees, but not workers in the public sector. Wisconsin was the first state in the country to give public sector employees collective bargaining rights under the Public Employee Collective Bargaining Act of 1959. The rights first extended to local government employees and teachers, and in the 1970s were expanded to include state employees. Most states have now moved to afford public employees the right to collectively bargain. Since his election in 2010, Walker has opposed public employee unions, indicating his opinion that they serve little purpose today given the strong public service laws that exist. "I get why unions make sense in the private sector . . . but at the public level, it's the government, it's the people, who are the ones who are the employers," Walker said. "Whether someone is in the union or not . . . we protect sick leave, vacation time. We protect work rules."

DEMOCRATS FLEE, DEMONSTRATORS REMAIN

To avoid a vote on Walker's budget repair bill, fourteen Democratic state senators fled to Rockford, Illinois, where they remained for weeks, barring Republicans from having the quorum necessary to hold a vote on the bill. Republicans called on state troopers to bring the Democrats back; however, because they were not in Wisconsin, state troopers had no power to force their return. Walker issued strong words for the fourteen senators, calling them to return to the capitol and "do the job they're paid to do." According to Walker, "It's either a matter of making reductions and making modest requests of our government employees or making massive layoffs at a time when we don't need anyone else laid off."

As the standoff continued, Walker threatened the Democrats with $100 per day fines for each day of session they missed, withheld their paychecks, and said that he would issue layoff notices to 1,500 state employees. President Barack Obama stepped into the ring, backing the case of the fourteen senators and telling Walker, "I don't think it does anybody any good when public employees are denigrated or vilified or their rights are infringed upon."

While the Democrats remained in Illinois, tens of thousands of protesters gathered at the capitol to try to protect the collective bargaining rights of Wisconsin's 175,000 public employees, most of who would be affected by the budget repair bill. Public employees from around the country traveled to Wisconsin to show their support and held demonstrations in their own cities, as some political analysts predicted that Walker's bill, if passed, would lead to similar measures in other states. Large protests took place in California, Illinois, and New York. At a protest in Illinois, Sen. Dick Durbin, D-Ill., spoke to the crowd saying, "What's at stake in Wisconsin is the basic concept of liberty and freedom." He called Walker's bill a crusade against unions that would have a nationwide effect.

A number of protesters spent weeks sleeping on the floor inside the capitol building, peacefully protesting. Although there were few run-ins with the police, the capitol was closed to new protesters on February 28, and a circuit court judge in Madison issued a restraining order, calling for the building to be reopened. As the capitol closed, Democratic representative Nick Milroy attempted to enter the building to retrieve clothes from his office and was tackled by police. He admitted being somewhat aggressive in his attempt to get in, but noted, "I don't think I should be detained. I'm a state legislator. I have a state ID. I have access to the building."

SENATE AND ASSEMBLY VOTE

Without a quorum, Senate Republicans had few options to vote on the budget bill. The one option available to them, and the route they decided to take, involved removing the spending provisions from the budget repair bill, meaning that no Democrat was required to be present for the vote. Instead, the Senate voted strictly on the collective bargaining provisions of the bill. In a flurry of activity, the new, stripped-down bill went from Senate to conference committee, and back to the Senate. As word spread that Republicans were planning a vote, more demonstrators began gathering at the capitol. Legislators quickly voted to approve the bill on March 9, with one Republican voting in opposition.

Following passage in the Senate, the fourteen Democrats returned to Wisconsin to a hero's welcome from demonstrators and heavy criticism from Republicans. "Today, the most shameful 14 people in the state of Wisconsin are going to pat themselves on the back and smile for the cameras," said Senate majority leader Scott Fitzgerald. "They're going to pretend they're heroes for taking a three-week vacation. It is an absolute insult to the hundreds of thousands of Wisconsinites who are struggling to find a job, much less one they can run away from and go down to Illinois—with pay," he continued.

The state assembly voted one day later on the budget repair bill, having previously passed it in February with its spending provisions intact, 51 to 17 with 28 abstentions. The March vote on collective bargaining provisions went down party lines, 53 to 42. During the vote, Democratic members of the assembly shouted "Shame! Shame! Shame!" at the Republicans casting votes in favor of the bill. After passage, Walker commended the legislature. "I applaud all members of the Assembly for showing up, debating the legislation and participating in democracy," he said in a statement. Democrats continued to show their disdain for the bill. "Their disrespect for the people of Wisconsin and their rights is an outrage that will never be forgotten," said state Senator Mark Miller.

RECALLS, RESTRAINING ORDERS, AND THE RIPPLE EFFECT

Following the passage and signing of the collective bargaining bill, Dane County Circuit Judge Maryann Sumi issued a temporary restraining order to stop the bill from being published, arguing that the state constitution's open meetings provision may have been violated. "I do, therefore, restrain and enjoin the further implementation of 2011 Wisconsin Act 10," Sumi said. "The next step in implementation of that law would be the publication of that law by the secretary of state. He is restrained and enjoined from such publication until further order of this court." Despite Sumi's order, the legislation was published on the legislature's website, following state law that any new law must be published within ten working days of being signed to take effect.

Confusion over whether the law had indeed gone into effect landed the case at the state supreme court, which was tasked with deciding whether the Senate had violated the open meetings law by failing to give twenty-four hours's notice before a public meeting and limiting the number of members of the public in the chamber to twenty before closing the doors, a further violation of state law. The supreme court ruled to reinstate Walker's law, finding that the legislature, while subject to the constitution, is not subject to the open meetings law. The minority found the ruling flawed. Chief Justice Shirley Abrahamson wrote that the majority "make their own findings of fact, mischaracterize the parties' arguments, misinterpret statutes, minimize (if not eliminate) Wisconsin constitutional guarantees, and misstate case law, appearing to silently overrule case law dating back to at least 1891."

Although a number of lawsuits were filed against the law, the opposition took its case a step further and drafted recall petitions for eight Democratic and eight Republican lawmakers. Six of the petitions against Republicans and three of the petitions against Democrats were successful in securing enough signatures to trigger recall elections. Successful recall elections are rare, and most come on a local level involving mayoral or city council races. In California, the state which leads the nation in attempts to recall state legislators, only 2 of 107 recall attempts between 1911 and 1994 were successful. In the 2011 Wisconsin recall, Democrats gained only two seats, leaving both houses firmly in Republican hands.

In late 2011, a petition was circulated to recall Governor Walker. To be successful, 540,208 signatures were needed. The recall Walker petition garnered 900,900 valid signatures, and a recall election is set for June 5, 2012.

As feared by a number of Democrats and political analysts, the Walker bill had ramifications around the country. States including Alaska, Arizona, Colorado, Idaho, Indiana, Iowa, Kansas, Michigan, Nebraska, Nevada, New Hampshire, New Mexico, Oklahoma, Tennessee, and Washington all took up variations of Wisconsin's union law. In Ohio, Republican Governor John Kasich signed a law even stricter than Wisconsin's, which would remove collective bargaining and striking power from approximately 400,000 public employees in the state. In the Ohio bill, public safety employees were not exempt. The bill was signed in March, but enough signatures were collected to land the issue on the November 2011 ballot. A hard-fought battle on both sides, featuring strongly worded pro- and antiunion statements, ended with a resounding "no" vote from Ohio voters, allowing public employees to retain their collective bargaining rights.

As of March 2012, a federal district judge in Wisconsin ruled portions of Walker's collective bargaining law unconstitutional, stating that they violate equal protection rights afforded to state union members. Upon the ruling, public employee unions operating in the state regained their ability to collect membership dues.

—Heather Kerrigan

Following is a statement issued by Governor Scott Walker on February 11, 2011, upon the release of his budget repair bill; a March 9, 2011, press release from the American Federation of State, County and Municipal Employees (AFSCME) calling Governor Walker's budget bill "an affront to democracy"; and two statements by Governor Walker, on March 9 and 10, 2011, commending the Assembly and Senate on passage of his budget repair bill.

Governor Walker Introduces
Budget Repair Bill

February 11, 2011

Governor Walker today released details of his budget repair bill.

"We must take immediate action to ensure fiscal stability in our state," said Governor Walker. "This budget repair bill will meet the immediate needs of our state and give government the tools to deal with this and future budget crises."

The state of Wisconsin is facing an immediate deficit of $137 million for the current fiscal year which ends July 1. In addition, bill collectors are waiting to collect over $225 million for a prior raid of the Patients' Compensation Fund.

The budget repair bill will balance the budget and lay the foundation for a long-term sustainable budget through several measures without raising taxes, raiding segregated funds, or using accounting gimmicks.

First, it will require state employees to pay about 5.8% toward their pension (about the private sector national average) and about 12% of their healthcare benefits (about half the private sector national average). These changes will help the state save $30 million in the last three months of the current fiscal year.

"It's fair to ask public employees to make a pension payment of just over 5%, which is about the national average, and a premium payment of 12%, which is about half of the national average," said Governor Walker.

The budget repair will also restructure the state debt, lowering the state's interest rate, saving the state $165 million.

These changes will help the state fulfill its Medicaid spending on needy families of about $170 million; funding that the previous administration did not have in its budget. It will also allow the state to spend an additional $21 million in the Department of Corrections.

Additionally, the budget repair bill gives state and local governments the tools to manage spending reductions through changing some provisions of the state's collective bargaining laws.

The state's civil service system, among the strongest in the country, would remain in place. State and local employees could continue to bargain for base pay, they would not be able to bargain over other compensation measures. Local police, fire and state patrol would be exempted from the changes. Other reforms will include state and local governments not collecting union dues, annual certification will be required in a secret ballot, and any employee can opt out of paying union dues.

A full summary of the Governor's budget repair bill is below.

Fiscal Year 2010-11 Budget Adjustment Bill Items

Employee Compensation:

> **Pension contributions**: Currently, state, school district and municipal employees that are members of the Wisconsin Retirement System (WRS) generally pay little or nothing toward their pensions. The bill would require that employees of WRS employers,

and the City and County of Milwaukee contribute 50 percent of the annual pension payment. The payment amount for WRS employees is estimated to be 5.8 percent of salary in 2011.

Health insurance contributions: Currently, state employees on average pay approximately 6 percent of annual health insurance premiums. This bill will require that state employees pay at least 12.6 percent of the average cost of annual premiums. In addition, the bill would require changes to the plan design necessary to reduce current premiums by 5 percent. Local employers participating in the Public Employers Group Health insurance would be prohibited from paying more than 88 percent of the lowest cost plan. The bill would also authorize the Department of Employee Trust Funds to use $28 million of excess balances in reserve accounts for health insurance and pharmacy benefits to reduce health insurance premium costs.

Health insurance cost containment strategies: The bill directs the Department of Employee Trust Funds and the Group Insurance Board to implement health risk assessments and similar programs aimed at participant wellness, collect certain data related to assessing health care provider quality and effectiveness, and verify the status of dependents participating in the state health insurance program. In addition, it modifies the membership of the Group Insurance Board to require that the representative of the Attorney General be an attorney to ensure the board has access to legal advice among its membership.

Pension changes for elected officials and appointees: The bill modifies the pension calculation for elected officials and appointees to be the same as general occupation employees and teachers. Current law requires these positions to pay more and receive a different multiplier for pension calculation than general classification employees. Under the state constitution, this change will be effective for elected officials at the beginning of their next term of office.

Modifications to Wisconsin Retirement System and state health insurance plans: The bill directs the Department of Administration, Office of State Employment Relations and Department of Employee Trust Funds to study and report on possible changes to the Wisconsin Retirement System, including defined contribution plans and longer vesting periods. The three agencies must also study and report on changes to the current state health insurance plans, including health insurance purchasing exchanges, larger purchasing pools, and high-deductible insurance options.

General fund impact—Authorize the Department of Administration Secretary to lapse or transfer from GPR and PR appropriations (excluding PR appropriations to the University of Wisconsin) to the general fund estimated savings of approximately $30 million from implementing these provisions for state employees in the current fiscal year (2010–11). Segregated funds would retain any savings from these measures.

State and Local Government and School District Labor Relations:

Collective bargaining—The bill would make various changes to limit collective bargaining for most public employees to wages. Total wage increases could not exceed a cap based on the consumer price index (CPI) unless approved by referendum. Contracts would be limited to one year and wages would be frozen until the new contract is settled. Collective bargaining units are required to take annual votes to maintain certification as a union. Employers would be prohibited from collecting union dues and members of collective bargaining units would not be required to pay dues. These changes take effect upon the expiration of existing contracts. Local law enforcement and fire employees, and state troopers and inspectors would be exempt from these changes.

Career executive transfers—The bill would allow state employees in the career executive positions to be reassigned between agencies upon agreement of agency heads.

Limited term employees (LTE)—The bill would prohibit LTE's from being eligible for health insurance or participation in the Wisconsin Retirement System.

State employee absences and other work actions—If the Governor has declared a state of emergency, the bill authorizes appointing authorities to terminate any employees that are absent for three days without approval of the employer or any employees that participate in an organized action to stop or slow work.

Quality Health Care Authority—The bill repeals the authority of home health care workers under the Medicaid program to collectively bargain.

Child care labor relations—The bill repeals the authority of family child care workers to collectively bargain with the State.

University of Wisconsin Hospitals and Clinics (UWHC) Board and Authority— The bill repeals collective bargaining for UWHC employees. State positions currently employed by the UWHC Board are eliminated and the incumbents are transferred to the UWHC Authority.

University of Wisconsin faculty and academic staff—The bill repeals the authority of UW faculty and academic staff to collectively bargain.

Debt Restructuring—The bill authorizes the restructuring of principal payments in fiscal year 2010–11 on the state's general obligation bonds. These principal repayments will be paid in future years. Since the state is required to make debt service payments by March 15th, the bill must be enacted by February 25th to allow time to sell the refinancing bonds. This provision will reduce debt service costs by $165 million in fiscal year 2010–11. This savings will help address one-time costs to comply with the Injured Patients and Families Compensation Fund state Supreme Court decision and make payments under the Minnesota-Wisconsin tax reciprocity program.

Medicaid

Address FY11 Medicaid deficit—Medicaid costs are expected to exceed current GPR appropriations by $153 million. The bill would increase the Medicaid GPR appropriation to address this shortfall.

Authorize DHS to restructure program notwithstanding current law—Medicaid costs have increased dramatically due to the recession and expanded program eligibility. In order to reduce the growth in costs, the bill authorizes the Department of Health Services to make program changes notwithstanding limits in state law related to specific program provisions. The department is expected to develop new approaches on program benefits, eligibility determination and provider cost-effectiveness. The proposed changes will require passive approval of the Joint Committee on Finance before implementation.

Technical correction—Act 28 included language that required unused GPR expenditure authority in the Medicaid GPR appropriation at the end of the biennium to be carried over to the subsequent biennium. The bill repeals this provision in order to ensure unspent funds in Medicaid lapse to the general fund balance.

Aging and Disability Resource Centers (ADRC)—The bill transfers an estimated $3 million in savings in this appropriation to Medicaid. ADRC's are the intake and assessment element of the state's Family Care program.

Corrections—The bill provides $22 million GPR to address shortfalls in the Department of Corrections adult institutions appropriation. These shortfalls are due to health care costs, overtime, and reductions in salary and fringe benefit budgets under Act 28.

Temporary Assistance to Needy Families (TANF) Funding for Earned Income Tax Credit (EITC)—The bill allocates $37 million of excess TANF revenues to increase TANF funding for the EITC from $6.6 million to $43.6 million in fiscal year 2010–11. By increasing TANF funding, GPR funding for the EITC is reduced by a commensurate amount.

Income Augmentation Revenues—Allow the Department of Children and Families and Department of Health Services to utilize $6.5 million of already identified income augmentation revenues to meet fiscal year 2010–11 lapse requirements.

Act 28 Required Lapses by DOA Secretary—Under Act 28, the Department of Administration Secretary is required to lapse or transfer a total of $680 million in 2009–11 from appropriations made to executive branch agencies to the general fund. The bill would reduce this amount by $79 million to ensure the lapses can be met in the next five months as this was ineffectively addressed by the previous administration.

Lapse of Funding from Joint Committee on Finance (JCF) Appropriation—The JCF appropriation includes $4.5 million related to estimated fiscal year 2010–11 implementation costs of 2009 Wisconsin Act 100 (operating while intoxicated enforcement changes). This funding is not anticipated to be needed in fiscal year 2010–11 and the bill lapses these amounts to the general fund balance.

Sale of State Heating Plants—The bill authorizes the Department of Administration to sell state heating plants. The proceeds from any sale, net of remaining debt service, would be deposited in the budget stabilization fund.

Shift Key Cabinet Agency Positions to Unclassified Status—The bill creates unclassified positions for chief legal counsel, public information officer and legislative liaison activities in cabinet agencies. An equivalent number of classified positions are deleted to offset the new unclassified positions. These activities are critical to each cabinet agency's overall mission and should have direct accountability to the agency head.

SOURCE: Office of Governor Scott Walker. "Governor Walker Introduces Budget Repair." February 11, 2011. http://walker.wi.gov/Default.aspx?Page=bc59a45d-15ec-4677-8e73-9ddcdf8a1b36.

AFSCME Responds to Passage of Budget Repair Bill

March 9, 2011

On Wednesday, Wisconsin Governor Scott Walker and Republican state senators rammed through an anti-freedom bill that stripped nurses, teachers and EMTs of their rights to collectively bargain—the same rights enjoyed by just about every other Wisconsinite.

Wisconsin public employees represented by the American Federation of State, County and Municipal Employees (AFSCME) Councils 24, 40 and 48 said the following:

"Governor Walker's power grab is an affront to democracy. The voters will not stand for denying the rights of Wisconsin's public employees—and they will be held account-able for their actions at the ballot box," said Bob McLinn, President of AFSCME Council 24, and a correctional officer at Waupun Correctional Institution.

"Governor Walker and eighteen Republican senators handed us a setback, but we will win this war. This attack on the working and middle class will not stand—and we will take back our democracy in recall elections," said Brian Stafford, President of AFSCME District Council 48, and chief repair person for water distribution, City of Milwaukee.

"This is a sad day for democracy and for Wisconsin. But our state's nurses, teachers and EMTs will overcome. We will take back our government from the big moneyed inter-ests and reverse this attack on workers' rights," said Jim Garity, President of AFSCME Council 40, and a Jefferson County Highway Department equipment operator.

SOURCE: American Federation of State, County, and Municipal Employees. Press Room. "Wisconsin Public Employees: Ramming Through Anti-Freedom Bill 'An Affront to Democracy.'" March 9, 2011. http://www.afscme.org/news/press-room/press-releases/wisconsin-public-employees-ramming-through-anti-freedom-bill-an-affront-to-democracy.

Governor Walker on Senate Passage of Budget Repair

March 9, 2011

Today Governor Walker released the following statement regarding the action taken by the Legislature:

> The Senate Democrats have had three weeks to debate this bill and were offered repeated opportunities to come home, which they refused. In order to move the state forward, I applaud the Legislature's action today to stand up to the status quo and take a step in the right direction to balance the budget and reform government. The action today will help ensure Wisconsin has a business climate that allows the private sector to create 250,000 new jobs.

SOURCE: Office of Governor Scott Walker. "Governor Walker Statement on Legislative Action." March 9, 2011. http://walker.wi.gov/Default.aspx?Page=e8c615fb-6eb1-4757-aa2d-b7a60c17c5da.

Governor Walker on Assembly Passage of Budget Repair Bill

March 10, 2011

Today Governor Walker released the following statement regarding the action taken by the Legislature:

> *I applaud all members of the Assembly for showing up, debating the legislation and participating in democracy. Their action will save jobs, protect taxpayers, reform government, and help balance the budget. Moving forward we will continue to focus on ensuring Wisconsin has a business climate that allows the private sector to create 250,000 new jobs.*

SOURCE: Office of Governor Scott Walker. "Governor Walker Statement on Assembly Action." March 10, 2011. http://walker.wi.gov/Default.aspx?Page=bd36e523-8740-4e26-9ef9-b579e1ec3eca.

OTHER HISTORIC DOCUMENTS OF INTEREST

FROM PREVIOUS *HISTORIC DOCUMENTS*

- Schwarzenegger on His Inauguration as Governor of California, *2003*, p. 1005
- Impeachment and Conviction of Arizona Governor Mecham, *1988*, p. 249

Arab Spring: Violent Crackdown on Protesters in Bahrain

FEBRUARY 15 AND 28, MARCH 10, AND NOVEMBER 23, 2011

Unwilling to relinquish power as his counterparts in other Middle Eastern nations had in response to growing demonstrations, Bahraini King Hamad bin Isa al-Khalifa took a different tack, violently cracking down on protesters under the pretense of emergency law. Shiites were targeted in their homes and tortured or arrested without cause. Unable to break the will of the protesters, the king reversed course in November, establishing a commission to investigate the possible violations of human rights that took place in February and March 2011. The commission found significant evidence that the government and its security forces had been behind many deaths, illegal detentions, and incidents of unlawful torture. In response, King Hamad promised to declare torture illegal and work with his government to institute reforms to ensure the people of Bahrain were never again harmed by government security forces.

VIOLENT PROTESTS

After gaining independence from Great Britain in 1971, Bahrain became a traditional monarchy in 1975 and was ruled for twenty-five years by Emir Isa bin Salman al-Khalifa under a state of emergency. When his son, Hamad bin Isa al-Khalifa, came to power in 1999, ending the state of emergency and promising a constitutional monarchy, Bahrain was hailed internationally as a model for reform in the Middle East. In 2001, the new emir reneged on his promise and appointed a secondary parliament, meant to subvert the power of the elected parliament. A new constitution was written in 2002, but in the same year Emir Hamad proclaimed Bahrain a kingdom and named himself king. Elections for parliament were held in 2002, but Shiite Muslims, who make up approximately 70 percent of the population, were kept in the minority, leaving the Sunni minority in power.

Since 2009, unrest has been brewing in Shiite villages, where protests have called for the release of political prisoners thought to be held for disagreements with the Sunni leadership. In February and March 2011, sparked by demonstrations in Tunisia and Egypt, these protests came to the capital. Demonstrators, frustrated by housing, education, and employment discrimination against the Shiite majority, called for political reforms including a constitutional monarchy, an elected government, and the end of gerrymandering political districts that has left Shiites politically powerless. The protesters did not call for the overthrow of the king or his family.

Unarmed, and without a cohesive agenda or leadership structure, the demonstrators took to the streets on February 14 in what was called a Day of Rage demanding the release of prisoners. "We are only asking for political reforms, right of political participation, respect for human rights, stopping of systematic discrimination against Shias. All the demands are to do with human rights and nothing to do with the ruling family and their regime," said Nabeel Rajab of the Bahrain Center for Human Rights. Unexpectedly, young Sunnis quickly crossed the religious divide and joined Shia Muslims carrying banners and chanting, "We are neither Sunni nor Shia. We are Bahrainis." The social media site Twitter served as a virtual gathering place for protesters who used the hashtag #Feb14 to communicate with each other and gain support.

Clashes between government supporters and detractors turned bloody, and more than thirty were killed. Videos from the protests show government forces using tear gas, rubber bullets, batons, and shotguns on sleeping men, women, and children. The government in turn claimed that these protesters were armed and that the government had no other choice if it wanted to maintain the peace. The videos of the scene and eyewitness reports contradict this claim. The government began blocking individual users from uploading videos of the violence to social media sites before shutting down access to a number of websites for all users within Bahrain's borders. As the protests continued, King Hamad requested assistance from Saudi Arabia, which sent more than 1,000 troops, and the United Arab Emirates (UAE), which sent 500 troops. This marked the first time during the Arab Spring uprisings that a government requested foreign troop intervention.

Hundreds of thousands of Bahrain's citizens took part in the protests, helping the antigovernment demonstrators to take control of Pearl Square and its tower, where they stayed for weeks. In March, the government entered the square and, with the help of troops from Saudi Arabia and the UAE, forcibly removed the demonstrators and tore down the monument that had been their rallying point.

In the government's first public comment on the crackdown on demonstrations, foreign minister Khalid al-Khalifa called the government's action necessary because protesters were "polarizing the country" and bringing it to the "brink of the sectarian abyss." Following the dispersion of protesters from Pearl Square, the government declared a state of emergency, turning Bahrain into what some observers considered little more than a police state. Sunnis said they preferred the security to the intimidation spread by Shiite protesters. "If they manage to seize power, Sunnis in Bahrain will suffer and we'll see bloodshed and killings," said Sheikh Abdullatif al-Mahmoud, the Sunni spiritual leader in Bahrain. The Shiites strongly disagreed.

GOVERNMENT CRACKDOWN

The three-month-long state of emergency laws gave the government and its security forces the ability to take all measures necessary to "protect the safety of the country and its citizens." Security forces used these new rights to search homes without cause and take people into custody without charges. As many as 1,400 were thought to be arrested during the three-month crackdown, and many of the arrestees reported being tortured during their detention. Further steps taken against the Shiite demonstrators included firing as many as 3,600 government workers, and humiliating the population by allowing police forces to pull people from their homes at night and beat them in front of their families. Other forces painted pro-Hamad statements on the walls of community gathering places. To stop the flow of information, the government forced the editor of the country's only independent newspaper to resign and banned the opposition newspaper from the country for what it called "unethical" coverage and "fabricated" reports of demonstrations and crackdowns.

All of the government crackdowns followed initial promises from the king to compromise with the opposition and apologies for the killings during the demonstrations.

This goodwill was short lived. The state of emergency ended on June 1, 2011, but a heavy police presence remained.

In response to the number of Shiites who had been arrested during the government crackdown, the king formed a special security court to review all cases arising from demonstrations. This National Safety Court sentenced twenty medical workers to jail in late September, only to see their convictions overturned on appeal in October. The court sentenced an additional thirty-six people to fifteen- to twenty-five-year prison terms for taking part in the protests. Fourteen of these people were sentenced for beating a Pakistani to death and assembling for the demonstrations. Fifteen were sentenced for attempting to murder military personnel, and the remaining seven were sentenced for attempted murder.

KING HAMAD ESTABLISHES HUMAN RIGHTS INVESTIGATION COMMISSION

Responding to pressure by opposition groups, in June King Hamad established the Bahrain Independent Commission of Inquiry to investigate possible human rights abuses committed by the government during protest crackdowns. The king said that the commission was "completely independent and consists of international experts." There was little confidence in the panel on the part of outsiders, who knew the king had handpicked those involved.

In November, the panel released its report, confirming that human rights abuses, including torture, illegal detention, and use of excessive force, had been committed against Bahrainis involved in antigovernment protests. The report, comprising 9,000 interviews, statements, and complaints, was highly critical of officials in Bahrain. In announcing the release of the report, commission chair M. Cherif Bassiouni said, "The commission is of the view that the lack of accountability of officials within the security system in Bahrain has led to a culture of impunity, whereby security officials have few incentives to avoid mistreatment of prisoners or to take action to prevent mistreatment by other officials." Furthermore, Bassiouni said, "It was evident to the Commission that government security forces . . . violated the principles of necessity and proportionality while engaging with demonstrators."

In response, the king announced all torture to be illegal and said that those named in the report would be held responsible for their actions. "We are determined, God willing, to ensure that the painful events our beloved nation has just experienced are not repeated, but that we learn from them, and use our new insights as a catalyst for positive change," said Hamad. He went on to say that he hopes to never see Bahrain "paralyzed by intimidation and sabotage." The king promised to work with his government to reform the country's laws to ensure a similar situation never again arises. The commission recommended that the king work toward these reforms with opposition parties, but Hamad did not indicate in his speech whether he planned to follow through. In January 2012, Hamad announced changes to Bahrain's constitution, giving parliament the authority to approve, question, and remove members of the cabinet. Opposition groups dismissed the changes as insignificant and not in line with their demands to reform government.

PARLIAMENTARY ELECTIONS

Parliamentary elections were scheduled for September to replace the eighteen members of parliament from the Shiite group al-Wefaq who had resigned in February over the government's treatment of protesters. "We are no longer affiliated with this council, which

did not lift a finger in front of these massacres," the members said in their resignation letter. They further criticized the king's cabinet reshuffle for not going far enough. Mattar
Mattar, one of the members of parliament who resigned, said the reshuffle was a "negative
indicator for the willingness in the government to go for political reform." He continued,
"The changes in the government were very minor, and didn't reach the ministers who
were responsible for the blood."

Shiites boycotted the election, and protests continued in the streets over the lack of
political power for a majority of Bahrainis. Police used tear gas, stun grenades, and rubber
bullets to prevent the protests from affecting the elections. Only about 17 percent of eligible voters turned out. The government claims this is because voters were intimidated by
the protesters. "What is clear is that in areas where Bahrainis were allowed to freely exercise their democratic right, turnout was high. . . . what is also clear is that in areas where
they suffered sickening intimidation, turnout was low," said a press release from the Bahrain Information Affairs Authority. The government made an attempt to hide the low
turnout rates by banning television and news crews from entering polling stations.

—Heather Kerrigan

*Following is a press release issued on February 15, 2011, by Bahrain's Ministry of
Foreign Affairs, regarding the death of two prodemocracy demonstrators in Bahrain;
a statement by Bahrain's crown prince on February 28, 2011, calling for calm and
reform in the nation; a press release issued on March 10, 2011, discussing a call by
the UN Secretary General for government reform in Bahrain; and the edited text of
a speech given by the chair of the Bahrain Independent Commission of Inquiry on
November 23, 2011, announcing completion of a report related to the investigation
of possible human rights abuses during demonstrations.*

King Hamad on Death of Prodemocracy Demonstrators

February 15, 2011

Marking the birthday of prophet Mohammed (PBUH), His Majesty King Hamad bin Isa
Al Khalifa extended condolences, in an address to the nation today, to the families of the
two victims who lost their lives in the recent sad events in Bahrain.

A probe panel will be set up by Deputy Prime Minister Jawad bin Salim Al Arrayadh
to look into the causes of these events, HM the King revealed expressing deep regret over
the death of the two citizens.

The legislative power will be asked to investigate the phenomenon and propose the
needed legislation for it, he added pointing out that freedom of expression is a right guaranteed and organized by the constitution and that there is a law organizing peaceful
marches which was approved by an elected council. Therefore, everyone has to comply
with it.

He also pledged to continue the reform process unabatedly adding that 10 years ago,
on February 14, the doors were opened to freedoms and responsibility out of love for the

Bahraini people and for the sake of their dignity. "Bahrain has become a kingdom with full sovereignty, tolerant and advanced in all fields thanks to citizens' efforts," HM the King said vowing to work more in collaboration with the Bahraini people for a better Bahrain.

SOURCE: Kingdom of Bahrain. Ministry of Foreign Affairs. "HM King Hamad Addresses the Nation." February 15, 2011. http://www.mofa.gov.bh/Default.aspx?tabid=7824&language=en-US&ItemId=717.

Bahrain's Crown Prince Calls for Peaceful Reform

February 28, 2011

His Royal Highness the Crown Prince and Deputy Supreme Commander Prince Salman bin Hamad Al Khalifa has announced that the procedures and steps taken in the last few days in order to calm has achieved relatively quiet atmosphere that could return normal in preperation [*sic*] to start the National dialogue and crystalize visions.

This National Dialogue will reach the desire goal set by His Majesty to continue the reform process hand in hand with all parties hoping for reform and working seriously to have a brighter future and based on this messages will be sent for those involved to propose their ideas on the table of national dialogue to ensure the greatest measure of success.

In a statement by HRH Prince Salman said despite this positive sign, there are some who do not want to reform and work to obstacle it by unacceptable means, pointing that this obstruction damages the interests of citizens in the Kingdom of Bahrain through harming the economic and living conditions and disrupting life in several areas, causing harm to the private sector institutions and different sectors including banking, financial and economic fields.

HRH Prince Salman added that his national duty and mission he was charged by His Majesty drew all attention to the need for the immediate commencement of the comprehensive national dialogue and stop harming the everyone's interests.

SOURCE: Kingdom of Bahrain. Ministry of Foreign Affairs. "HRH the Crown Prince Statement." February 28, 2011. http://www.mofa.gov.bh/Default.aspx?tabid=7824&language=en-US&ItemId=827.

UN Calls for Reform in Bahrain

March 10, 2011

United Nations Secretary-General Ban Ki-moon on Thursday urged all parties in Bahrain to begin the national dialogue on reform and reconciliation, saying that it has created an opportunity for all sides to address political and constitutional reform and facilitate national reconciliation. Ban Ki-moon expressed concern at the apparent impasse in launching a national dialogue a few weeks after King Hamad bin Isa Al

Khalifa asked Crown Prince Salman bin Hamad Al Khalifa to initiate such a process, his spokesperson said in a statement.

"The Secretary-General calls on all parties in Bahrain to seize the moment and engage in a broad-based, peaceful and meaningful dialogue involving the political opposition and civil society in the interest of all Bahraini people," the spokesperson said.

Ban Ki-moon reiterated the readiness of the United Nations to provide support to nationally-led efforts, if requested to do so.

"The Secretary-General also calls on all of Bahrain's regional neighbours and the wider international community to support a dialogue process and an environment conducive for credible reforms in Bahrain," the spokesperson said.

SOURCE: Kingdom of Bahrain. Ministry of Foreign Affairs. "Statement Attributable to the Spokesperson for the Secretary-General on Bahrain." March 10, 2011. http://www.mofa.gov.bh/Default.aspx?tabid=7824&language=en-US&ItemId=894.

Commission Releases Findings of Human Rights Abuse Investigations

November 23, 2011

... Your Majesty,

Your Highnesses and Excellencies,

Ladies and Gentlemen,

The Bahrain Independent Commission of Inquiry (BICI) was mandated to prepare a report about the events that occurred in Bahrain during the months of February and March 2011 in addition to the subsequent related events. The Commission was also charged to make whatever recommendations it deemed appropriate for holding accountable those who had violated the rights and freedoms of individuals, and for preventing the recurrence of such incidents in the future. . . .

Your Majesty,

Your Highnesses and Excellencies,

Ladies and Gentlemen,

The Commission's work was not easy. We began our work in an atmosphere fraught with tension and were under immense pressure from the public, which was eager to have the testimonies of the many victims and witnesses heard. The Commission had to collect all the evidence, examine the documents and reports submitted to it, and conduct field visits, all of which were arduous tasks. The Commission also ensured the protection of witnesses that it heard and the confidentiality of information it received, which further complicated its work. In addition, the Commissioners and investigators worked to meet the expectations of Bahraini citizens to decisively intervene to prevent human rights violations regardless of the type of that violation or the perpetrator. Overall, the Commission received nearly 9,000 complaints, statements and testimonies and conducted dozens of on-site investigations throughout the country. The Commission also sought to resolve other problems including the dismissal and suspension of university students, employees, healthcare workers, and attempted to mitigate the negative effects of criminal prosecution.

The Commission created a database containing all the information that it gathered during its investigations. This information was divided into categories reflecting the different types of human rights violations committed during the period under investigation. This database contributed greatly to the Commission's work and in the preparation of its final report.

Following the categorization of the information in the database, the Commissioners analysed the available evidence in a manner that was objective and inclusive of all testimonies and statements. The Commission was assisted by its investigators as well as legal, medical, engineering and media experts. . . .

Your Majesty,

Your Highnesses and Excellencies,

Ladies and Gentlemen,

Allow me to summarise the general observations and recommendations of the report of the Bahrain Independent Commission of Inquiry:

1. The forceful confrontation of demonstrators involving the use of lethal force led to the death of civilians. This caused an increase in public anger, increased the number of persons participating in protests, and led to a palpable escalation in their demands. As protests continued into mid-March 2011, the general state of security in Bahrain deteriorated considerably. Sectarian clashes were reported in a number of areas, attacks on expatriates took place, violent clashes occurred between students at the University of Bahrain and other educational institutions, and major thoroughfares were blocked by protesters. This situation led the government to declare a State of National Safety on 15 March 2011.

2. HM King Hamad approved that HRH the Crown Prince engage in negotiations with various political parties with a view to reaching a peaceful resolution to the unfolding situation in Bahrain.

Notwithstanding the best efforts of HRH the Crown Prince, negotiations to reach a political solution were not successful. The Commission is of the view that if the initiative and proposals of HRH the Crown Prince had been accepted at the time it could have paved the way for significant constitutional, political and socio-economic reforms and precluded the ensuing negative consequences.

3. The Commission's investigations revealed that during a substantial number of the arrests carried out by law enforcement agencies arrest warrants were not presented to arrested individuals and arrested individuals were not informed of the reasons for their arrest. In many cases, government security forces resorted to the use of unnecessary and excessive force, and in a manner that sought to terrorise individuals, and to cause unnecessary damage to property.

4. The Commission's investigations revealed that many detainees were subjected to torture and other forms of physical and psychological abuse while in custody, which indicated patterns of behaviour by certain government agencies, especially with regard to certain categories of detainees. The extent of this physical and psychological mistreatment is evidence of a deliberate practice, which in some cases was aimed at extracting confessions and statements under duress, while in other cases was intended for the purpose of retribution and punishment. The most common techniques for mistreatment used on detainees included the following: blindfolding; handcuffing; enforced standing for prolonged periods; beating; punching; hitting the detainee with rubber hoses (including on the soles of feet), cables, whips, metal, wooden planks or other objects; electrocution; sleep-deprivation; exposure to extreme temperatures; verbal abuse; threats of rape; and insulting the detainee's religious sect (Shia). Generally, these measures fall within the meaning of torture as defined in the Convention Against Torture (CAT), to which Bahrain is a State Party. They also constitute violations of the Bahrain Criminal Code. These forced confessions have been used in criminal proceedings, either in the special courts established pursuant to the National Safety Decree or, in some cases, in the ordinary criminal courts.

5. The Commission is of the view that the lack of accountability of officials within the security system in Bahrain has led to a culture of impunity, whereby security officials have few incentives to avoid mistreatment of prisoners or to take action to prevent mistreatment by other officials.

6. It was evident to the Commission that government security forces, especially the Public Security Forces (PSF), violated the principles of necessity and proportionality while engaging with demonstrators, which are the generally applicable legal principles.

7. A large number of individuals were prosecuted before the National Safety Courts and imprisoned for violating articles 165, 168, 169, 179 and 180 of the Bahrain Penal Code. The text and application of these provisions raises questions about their conformity with international human rights law and the Constitution of Bahrain.

8. [sic] Numerous violations of due process rights were recorded by the Commission during proceedings before the National Safety Courts, which were composed of a presiding military judge and two civilian judges.

9. The manner in which the security and judicial agencies of the government of Bahrain interpreted the National Safety Decree opened the door for the perpetration of grave violations of human rights, including the arbitrary deprivation of life, torture and arbitrary detention. Detainees were kept for questioning for periods that, in some cases, extended to over two months during which they were neither brought before a judicial body or presented with any charges. The lack of judicial supervision, oversight or inspection of detention facilities operated by these security agencies allowed for the perpetration of human rights violations.

10. Thirty-five deaths occurred between 14 February and 15 April 2011, which are linked to the events of February/March 2011. Thirty of the thirty-five deaths were civilians, while five were security personnel. Investigations were opened by the different security and military agencies concerned, but the Commission has reservations with regard to the effectiveness of some investigations which only included statements by security personnel.

11. Between 21 March and 15 April 2011, security forces systematically raided homes in order to arrest individuals, and in so doing, terrorised the occupants of these homes. These arrests were carried out by masked individuals during night and pre-dawn raids. These individuals intentionally broke down doors and forcibly entered homes. These practices were often accompanied by sectarian insults and verbal abuse, and in some cases women were also exposed to such insults by security personnel.

Overall, the total number of persons arrested pursuant to Royal Decree No.18 of 2011 following the declaration of the State of National Safety was 2,929. Of those, 2,178 were released without any charges brought against them. The most prevalent charges made against persons brought before the National Safety Courts included: incitement of hate against the regime, illegal assembly, rioting, possession of anti-government leaflets, possession of material calling for the overthrow of the regime, inciting others to violence, threatening a civil servant, use of violence against a government official, premeditated murder, kidnapping, attempted murder, aggravated assault, membership in an illegally established society, and spreading rumours that undermine public interest. The majority of these charges involved the exercise of freedoms of opinion and expression that are guaranteed by the Bahrain Constitution and the International Covenant on Civil and Political Rights (ICCPR).

12. Many places of worship were demolished in the aftermath of the events of February/March 2011. . . .

13. In the aftermath of the February/March 2011 events, over two thousand public sector employees and over 2400 private sector employees were dismissed for their participation in, or support of, the protest movement, and on the grounds that these protests were unrelated to labour issues. The Commission, however, sees that the workers' protests that occurred were within the permissible bounds of the law.

14. A large number of university students were expelled or suspended in connection with their role in the events of February and March. The Commission finds that the universities applied arbitrary and unclear standards for issuing determinations and taking disciplinary action. The Commission welcomes, however, the move by the Ministry of Education, in conjunction with the University of Bahrain and Bahrain Polytechnic, to reverse the vast majority of disciplinary action taken against students.

15. The Commission received sufficient evidence to support the finding that Sunnis were targeted by some demonstrators, either because they professed loyalty to the regime or on the basis of their sectarian identity. Sunnis were subjected to verbal abuse, physical attacks and attacks on their private property as well as harassment.

16. The Commission finds sufficient evidence to establish that some expatriates, particularly South Asian workers, were exposed to attacks during the February/March events. Pakistanis, in particular, were targeted. Because of the atmosphere of fear which prevailed, some foreign nationals were afraid to return to their work and commercial activities. The Commission found that four expatriates were killed and many were injured by mobs as a result of these attacks.

17. The evidence presented to the Commission in relation to the involvement of the Islamic Republic of Iran in the internal affairs of Bahrain did not reveal a discernible link between specific incidents that occurred in Bahrain during February/March 2011 and Iran. In addition, the Commission has not found any evidence of human rights violations committed by the GCC-JSF units deployed in Bahrain, from 14 March 2011.

18. The Commission concluded that much of the material shown on national television contained derogatory language and inflammatory coverage of events, and some may have been defamatory. However, the Commission did not find evidence of media coverage that constituted hate speech. The Commission also identified numerous examples of defamation, harassment and, in some cases, incitement through social media websites. Both pro- and anti-government journalists were targeted through social media channels.

Your Majesty,

Your Highnesses and Excellencies,

Ladies and Gentlemen,

The Commission's report is not limited to outlining, compiling, and analysing the human rights violations that occurred in Bahrain during the period under investigation. Rather, the Commission also submitted the following recommendations to the Government of Bahrain:

1. To establish an independent and impartial national committee that consists of personalities of high standing representing the government, opposition political societies, and civil society to follow up monitor and implement the recommendations of the Commission. This committee should re-examine the laws and procedures that were applied in the aftermath of the events of February and March 2011 in order to make recommendations to the legislature for the appropriate amendments to existing laws and to develop new legislation, in line with the recommendations of this Commission.

2. To establish a national independent and impartial mechanism to hold accountable those in government who have committed unlawful or negligent acts resulting in the deaths, torture and mistreatment of civilians with a view to bringing legal and disciplinary action against such individuals, including those in positions of command, whether civilian or military, in accordance with the principle of superior responsibility.

3. To consider the Office of the Inspector General in the Ministry of Interior as a separate entity, independent of the Ministry's hierarchical control. The tasks of this office should include receiving complaints, and should protect the safety and privacy of complainants.

4. To amend the decree establishing the National Security Agency (NSA) in order to keep the organisation as an intelligence gathering agency without law enforcement or arrest authorities. Legislation should also be adopted to provide that the detention of individuals shall be governed by the Code of Criminal Procedure even during the application of a State of National Safety.

5. To adopt legislative measures requiring the Attorney General to investigate claims of torture and other forms of cruel, inhuman, or degrading treatment or punishment.

6. To allow for the review of all convictions rendered by the National Security Courts where fundamental principles of a fair trial were not respected.

7. To conduct effective investigations in all cases of deaths attributed to security forces and identify those responsible for these deaths. Likewise, all allegations of torture

and similar treatment should be investigated by an independent and impartial body. In addition, a standing independent body to investigate all complaints of torture or ill-treatment, excessive use of force or other abuses at the hands of the authorities should be established. The burden of proof to demonstrate that treatment complies with the prohibition of torture and other ill-treatment should be on the state.

8. To implement an extensive program of public order training for the public security forces, the National Security Agency and the Bahrain Defence Force, including their private security companies, in accordance with UN best practices in order to ensure future compliance with the Code of Conduct for Law Enforcement Officials.

9. To avoid detention without prompt access to lawyers and without access to the outside world, and, all cases of detention should be subject to effective monitoring by an independent body.

10. The Commission recommends that the government urgently establish, and implement vigorously, a programme for the integration into the security forces of personnel from all the communities in Bahrain.

11. To train the judiciary and prosecutorial personnel on the need to ensure that their activities contribute to the prevention and eradication of torture and ill-treatment.

12. To annul or mitigate convictions of persons charged with offences involving political expression that does not involve the incitement to violence, and to commute the death sentence for cases of murder arising out of the events of February/March 2011.

13. To compensate the families of the deceased victims in a manner that is commensurate with the gravity of their loss, and to compensate all victims of torture, ill-treatment, or prolonged incommunicado detention. In this respect, the Commission welcomes Royal Decree no. 30 of 2011 on the establishment of a compensation fund for victims, which was issued on 22 September 2011.

14. To ensure that the remaining dismissed employees have not been dismissed on the basis of their right to exercise freedom of expression, opinion, association or assembly.

15. To consider relaxing censorship on mass media and to allow the opposition greater access to television broadcasts, radio broadcasts and print media.

16. To undertake appropriate measures including legislative measures to prevent incitement to violence, hatred, sectarianism and other forms of incitement, which lead to the violation of internationally protected human rights.

17. To develop educational programmes at the primary, secondary, and high school levels and at the university level to promote religious, political and other forms of tolerance, as well as the promotion of human rights and the rule of law. In general, the Commission also recommends that the Government of Bahrain develop a national reconciliation program that addresses the grievances of groups which are, or perceive themselves, to be deprived of equal political, social and economic rights and benefits across all segments of Bahrain's population. . . .

SOURCE: Bahrain Independent Commission of Inquiry. "Prof M. Cherif Bassiouni's Speech on 23rd November." November 23, 2011. http://www.bici.org.bh/?page_id=235.

OTHER HISTORIC DOCUMENTS OF INTEREST

FROM THIS VOLUME

FROM PREVIOUS *HISTORIC DOCUMENTS*

Arab Spring: Crisis in Yemen Leads to Power Transfer

FEBRUARY 21, MARCH 26, SEPTEMBER 30, AND
NOVEMBER 14 AND 23, 2011

Yemen, a nation of great concern to the international community in helping to stop the spread of al Qaeda and its affiliates, became mired in a government transition battle in 2011, sparked by protests against the power of President Ali Abdullah Saleh. Saleh wavered between promising to accept international power transfer deals and using force to dispel the protesters. While other Middle East dictators were toppled, protesters feared that the attention of the international community would slowly drift away from the ongoing Yemeni struggle. To prevent this, youth activists who had initially used social media sites to garner support for their cause turned again to the power of the Internet to remind the nation and the world of the continuing struggle for democratic freedom. It was not until mid-November when Saleh finally agreed to cede power to his vice president, and did so only because he was able to avoid any future prosecution arising from his treatment of protesters. Saleh did not formally hand over power to his vice president, Abdu Rabbu Mansour Hadi, until February 25, 2012.

January Unrest

In January, mass demonstrations erupted in Yemen, one of the poorest countries in the Arab world, against President Ali Abdullah Saleh, who had been in power since 1978. The first demonstrations took place in southern Yemen in the capital of Sana'a. The protests began as constitutional reforms were debated in parliament that would eliminate presidential term limits. The protesters saw the reform as a tactic being used by Saleh to run for president again when his current term ended in 2013. As the protests gained steam, Saleh proposed a new set of reforms, including limiting presidential terms to two seven- or five-year terms and voter registration for all adults. But protesters said the term limits did not go far enough to ensure that Saleh would not run again or that he would not hand power directly over to his son. In proposing the reforms, Saleh rejected the claim, stating, "We are a republic. We reject bequeathing [the presidency]."

An opposition coalition formed in 2002, called the Joint Meetings Party (JMP), led the protests. The group included the Islah Party, the nation's main opposition party, which holds 20 percent of the seats in the legislature; the Yemeni Socialist Party; and other minor parties. The opposition movement struggled to articulate a political platform and had various divisions both among its members and within the individual parties. Mohammed al-Sabry, who headed the opposition coalition and the Islah party, called for constitutional amendments that would ensure that Saleh could not name himself or a member of his family as the next president. "We won't permit these corrupt leaders to stay in power and we are ready to sleep in the streets for our country's sake, in order to liberate it from the hands of the corrupt," al-Sabry said. Counterprotests began to take shape, and government supporters took to the streets, calling for a government that had the best interests of the Yemeni people in mind, regardless of whether that meant Saleh or his family could maintain a hold on the government.

January's mass demonstrations were not the first that the government of Yemen has faced. The nation has long had a separatist movement in the southern portion of the country and some rebellion in the northwest. Saleh has worked to keep the violence from reaching the capital by pitting tribes from the south and northwest against each other, alternately favoring whichever faction supported his government at a given time. North and South Yemen did not unite until 1990, with Saleh, who had led the North, assuming the role of president and Ali Salim al-Bidh, the South's leader, becoming vice president. The union of the two nations was fraught with tension, and al-Bidh often accused the North of attacks against his Yemeni Socialist Party. Al-Bidh stepped down from his seat in 1993 and demanded reforms that would appease those in the South. The ensuing political deadlock resulted in a three-month civil war in 1994. In June 1994, al-Bidh declared that he was forming a new Southern state, but the strength of the North's military ultimately toppled the South's fledgling government, reuniting the North and South under Saleh's rule. The South, home to most of the nation's oil, continues to claim that the government discriminates against it economically.

Saleh Responds

In response to the January protests, Saleh began both making concessions and using violence to crack down on demonstrations. Throughout the spring and summer of 2011, he successfully postponed either leaving office or changing his government, but said that he would not remain in the presidency beyond 2013. In February, Saleh proposed creating a national unity government if the protesters would end their demonstrations, but the opposition coalition refused, demanding the end of the regime. "The opposition decided to stand with the people's demand for the fall of the regime, and there is no going back from that," said al-Sabry. Saleh responded saying he would be happy to form a national unity government once the opposition was ready to name candidates, but said he would not stand by while they try "to reach power through chaos." said Saleh.

In early March, Saleh took a different route with the demonstrators, announcing that he would change the constitution to implement a parliamentary system in which the legislative and executive branches would be separated. The "government elected by the parliament would take control of the country's executive powers," said Saleh. The opposition coalition quickly rejected this proposal.

March 18 marked a turning point in the protests. Saleh ordered his forces to break up the demonstrations. Tens of thousands of demonstrators had gathered for noon prayers, and when they rose, government security forces and other supporters shot and killed more than 50 and injured more than 100 of the demonstrators. In response to the March 18 violence, Saleh fired his cabinet, but asked them to remain temporarily until a new government could be formed. Tribal leaders and army commanders responded to the violence by putting their support behind the demonstrators, leading to resignations of government officials in parliament including members of the ruling General People's Congress (JPC). Those who chose to leave the government said their decision was reached because they did not agree with the violence that was used against the protesters. Following the

March 18 incident, a state of emergency was declared, giving the government additional emergency powers of arrest, detention, and censorship.

As the United Nations called for an investigation into the shootings to be conducted by an independent and impartial body, Saleh proposed further constitutional reforms and promised to hold parliamentary elections by the end of 2011. A statement from his office said the president was "committed to undertaking all possible initiatives to reach a settlement" with the JMP to "prevent any future bloodshed of the Yemeni people." Saleh further accepted five requests submitted by the JMP, including the formation of a national unity government and a national committee to write a new constitution, the creation of a new electoral law, and the holding of a constitutional referendum, as well as parliamentary and presidential elections, by the end of 2011. "These accepted proposals have been submitted to the mediating party on the basis that this would end the current state of political turmoil facing the nation and paving [sic] the way for a smooth, peaceful and democratic transition," said a statement from Saleh's office. Although a number of their recommendations had been accepted, JMP spokesperson Mohammed Qahtan said, "Any offer that does not include the president's immediate resignation is rejected." By April, Saleh again made it clear that he had no intention of leaving office.

Unrest deepened in June when a bomb went off in a mosque in the presidential palace, wounding Saleh and sending him to Saudi Arabia to seek treatment. His disappearance from public life in Yemen while maintaining control of the government and its security forces made it clear to the protesters that Saleh would not leave his position easily. It was not until September when Saleh returned to the country. By mid-October, demonstrators entered progovernment areas and were met by sniper fire from Saleh's security forces. Saleh denied that his government was involved in the sniper attacks, stating in an interview, "It was done by the citizens first because the Yemenis are snipers."

SALEH VOWS TO LEAVE, REMAINS IN POWER

On April 7, as unrest grew, the Gulf Cooperation Council (GCC), a political alliance comprised of Bahrain, Kuwait, Oman, Qatar, Saudi Arabia, and the United Arab Emirates (UAE), worked on a proposal to help Saleh cede power to a temporary government led by his deputy within thirty days of signing the agreement. Although the JMP said it would accept the GCC proposal if protests were allowed to continue, leaders of the opposition demonstrations rejected it because it would have given Saleh and his family immunity from any future prosecution. The agreement was first set to be signed on May 1, then May 18, and then on May 22; when Saleh finally refused to sign it, he said that he would not take any action on the proposal until leaders of the opposition were present at the presidential palace for the signing ceremony. The deal went uncompleted, and Saleh blamed the opposition for creating a situation that could lead to civil war, saying, "If they remain stubborn, we will confront them everywhere with all possible means." He continued, "If they don't bow, and want to take the country into a civil war, let them be responsible for it and for the blood that was shed and that will be shed if they insist on their stupidity."

As the GCC worked on a proposal for the transfer of power, the JMP worked on another plan that would result in Saleh's exit at the end of 2011. Saleh initially agreed to sign that plan, but the proposal quickly broke down when the protesters decried it as not offering a fast enough exit for the president.

The GCC continued its work, and at times Saleh seemed prepared to accept a proposal for transition; but in the end he never agreed to anything. Part of the failure was caused by a lack of cohesion between the demands of the opposition in the government and those protesting in the streets. The opposition was willing to negotiate for the president to leave before 2012, but the protesters demanded his immediate departure. In October, Saleh indicated that he would step aside, only to retract his agreement the following day. His government had attempted to get the GCC to rewrite the proposal to allow Saleh to stay in office until elections scheduled for 2012 took place. Saleh's only other condition was that he and his family be able to escape prosecution.

On October 21, the United Nations Security Council became involved, passing a resolution calling on Saleh to immediately cede power "due to the lack of progress on a political settlement, and the potential for the further escalation of violence." A UN envoy to Yemen made similar comments on November 14, saying that the president must accept the GCC plan backed by the international community. Saleh appeared on state television in an interview stating that he would step down once a deal was in place and denying that he had refused earlier transition plans. "I already wanted to leave power in 2006," said Saleh. "As far as I'm concerned anyone that hangs onto power is a madman."

In mid-November, Saleh again agreed to immediately hand power to his deputy, vice president Abdu Rabbu Mansour Hadi, signing a deal in Saudi Arabia to end the political crisis. Saleh was expected to remain permanently in Saudi Arabia, but returned to Yemen in late November, sparking concern that he had no intention of straying from the public eye anytime soon. The agreement completed by the GCC gave Saleh immunity from prosecution if he transferred power. "Today marks a significant step forward for the Yemeni people in their quest for a unified, democratic, secure, and prosperous Yemen," said U.S. Secretary of State Hillary Rodham Clinton. The agreement was effective immediately; presidential elections were required to be held within ninety days, until which time Saleh would remain president in name only. The transitional government "will be responsible for rebuilding the economy and will undergo dialogue with the youth movements to ensure their support and participation in the political arena," said UN envoy to Yemen Jamal Benomar. Saleh formally ceded power on February 25, 2012, following the presidential election in which Hadi was the sole candidate and received 65 percent of the vote.

Even with Saleh out of power, political struggles will continue, caused by disagreements between tribes, government corruption, and declining oil revenues, which hold up most of the nation's economy. The new government will be further challenged by the high poverty rate, with half of the population living on $2 per day or less.

—Heather Kerrigan

Following is a statement from Yemeni President Ali Abdullah Saleh on February 21, 2011, calling on protesters to use the ballot box rather than violence to remove his regime from power; an edited transcript of an interview given by President Saleh on March 26, 2011, in regard to the crisis in Yemen; an interview given by President Saleh on September 30, 2011, addressing attempts at power transfer; an interview given by President Saleh on November 14, 2011, in which he denies refusing to transfer power; and a statement by U.S. Secretary of State Hillary Rodham Clinton on November 23, 2011, commending President Saleh and the Gulf Cooperation Council for working together on a peaceful power transfer.

President Saleh Calls on Protesters to Use Ballot Box

February 21, 2011

President Ali Abdullah Saleh said on Monday that whoever wants to reach power has to behave democratically through the ballot boxes either in the parliamentary or presidential elections away from chaos.

In a press conference in Sana'a today, he said that "the Yemeni people is a great nation and can differentiate between what is good and bad," adding "those people are copying others and the more concessions we provide, the more demands they ask for."

We ask those to come to dialogue table to make understanding clear, he said.

Saleh pointed out that the freedom of opinion is guaranteed by peaceful and democratic means and those who demand the regime to leave, they should go for voting boxes and respect the will of the Yemeni people as power is a responsibility and not a merit.

The president said that "we provided a package of reforms but the JMP, in particular, increased the ceiling of their demand to topple the regime which is unacceptable."

He thanked security systems for stopping clashes between the opponents and supports of the government, noting that they have strict directives not to use violence except in case of self protection.

The president expressed sorrow for what happened in Aden by some rioters who cased harm to state and private properties.

SOURCE: Yemen News Agency (SABA). "President: Power Can Be Reached Democratically Through Voting." February 21, 2011. http://www.presidentsaleh.gov.ye/shownews.php?lng=en&_nsid=9125&_newsctgry=4&_newsyr=2011.

President Saleh Addresses the Crisis in Yemen

March 26, 2011

An interview was aired on Sunday by Dubai-based pan-Arab news channel Al-Arabiya TV with President Ali Abdullah Saleh in Sana'a.

The interview was conducted by Muntaha al-Ramahi.

[Al-Ramahi]   Let me begin with the news that was disseminated and discussed today: namely, that a meeting was held over the past few hours at the residence of the vice president. It was attended by US and European envoys. An agreement was reached to the effect that you will hand over power to your vice president within 30 days and then other measures would follow. I am sorry; I should have said 60 days. This period has been specified for the transition of power. How true is this news?

[President Saleh]   I am happy to speak to Al-Arabiya, which is a balanced station in its reporting. What you mentioned is baseless. No meeting was held at the house of the vice president today. A meeting was held yesterday and the day before at the house of the vice president. It was attended by the leadership of the Joint JMP, Major General Ali Muhsin, and the US ambassador in order to look into ways and methods by which we can emerge from this crisis. It was agreed that the agenda of the meeting would be: 1. The president's speech in parliament. 2. The president's speech at the National Congress. 3. The plan that was presented by the clerics. 4. The five-point plan presented by the Joint Meeting Parties.

[Al-Ramahi]   No meeting was held at any time today, Saturday.

[President Saleh]   No meetings were held today. What was reported by news agencies and space channel television stations has no basis of the truth.

[Al-Ramahi]   The media cited statements by the foreign minister.

[President Saleh]   Our foreign minister denied this. He denied that this was attributed to him. This is not true. However, we are still adhering to dialogue on the points or topics that are being discussed; namely, how to extricate Yemen from this predicament.

[Al-Ramahi]   About these meetings which were attended by the US ambassador and the JMP and Major General Ali Muhsin. What did you agree on? What did you discuss? What did you approve?

[President Saleh]   The discussion was on how to emerge from this crisis. Naturally, they have conditions. Whenever the state presents an initiative, they raise the ceiling of their demands. They want the authorities to leave and they want power to be handed over immediately. We have no problem concerning the transfer power, but to whom and for whom? They propose the departure of the authorities, immediately—within hours, a day, two days, one month, or 60 days. These are their proposals, their demands, but we are adhering to our vision. We have specific points, mentioned in the president's speech in parliament, the points raised at the National Congress, and the points presented by the clerics. The points presented by the JMP are to a certain extent acceptable. These will be subjected to discussion in order to emerge from the crisis. We in power are not insisting on remaining in authority, but who should we hand over power to? It means to the unknown. They are looking continuously for the unknown. This means, throw it away, or let the people get rid of the authorities.

[Al-Ramahi]   This means that the discussion did not refer to who will take over once President Ali Abdullah Saleh decides to quit?

[President Saleh]   Not at all, this did not happen. . . .

[Al-Ramahi]   What is your vision about transferring power to the people?

[President Saleh]   My vision is this: You, the JMP, come. You are a minority. They stage protests in the streets and elsewhere. They hardly constitute 2.5 percent out of 25 million. They seek the support of 4,000 protesters. I have 1 million. If they stage a demonstration of 20,000, I can stage a 3 million-man demonstration. How can the minority twist the arm of the majority? This does not happen anywhere in the world. It is unacceptable that a minority of the society should twist the arm of the majority. You should have seen the million person rally in the Al-Sabain Square. That was a referendum on the legitimacy. Do they want to topple the political regime with 5 thousand? This is unacceptable, whether they are 5, 10, 20 thousands or even 1 million.

[Questions pertaining to demonstrations in other Middle Eastern nations have been omitted.]

[Al-Ramahi]   Do you not think there should be a clear vision of peaceful change and transfer of power?

[President Saleh]   Yes.

[Al-Ramahi]   For example, do you object to leaving power before the end of your term?

[President Saleh]   I do not have any objection or reservation. I do not cling to power.

[Al-Ramahi]   They may ask why this does not happen now in a certain way in order to spare blood.

[President Saleh]   No, this will lead to chaos and take the country to the unknown. I am responsible for the security and safety of this country. I must lead the country to the shore of safety. Let them come for talks about the way to transfer power peacefully and smoothly to the people but not to them. Transferring power to them is as far to them as the sun. Power will be transferred to the people, who will choose.

[Al-Ramahi]   What if the people choose them?

[President Saleh]   That will be welcome. If the people choose them, we will pay allegiance to them. We will welcome any political forces chosen by the people, but this should not be done through a coup or bloodshed. This will then be completely rejected.

[Al-Ramahi]   They say that they were staging protests in a peaceful manner for a long time. We know that these protests started several weeks ago, but what happened on bad Friday, 18 March, was the turning point that changed the equation.

[President Saleh]   This is true. We denounce and condemn what happened on Friday, and we are not pleased with it. Luckily, the police, the security forces, the army, and the cadres of the General People's Congress were not involved in it. That happened between them [protesters] and resident citizens. They protested in these areas for several weeks. No woman could go to the hospital or to a grocery for shopping. No child could go to school. No patient could go to the hospital. People in these neighborhoods lived in a state of terror. . . .

[Al-Ramahi]	They say that 52 people were killed by sniper fire mainly in the head and neck.
[President Saleh]	My information says about 41.
[Al-Ramahi]	Let us suppose they were 41, but the information available . . .
[President Saleh]	Seven to eight of them were not identified.
[Al-Ramahi]	They were reportedly hit in the head with sniper fire. Aiming directly at the head and chest cannot be done by ordinary citizens but trained snipers.
[President Saleh]	No, it was done by the citizens first because the Yemenis are snipers. . . .
[Al-Ramahi]	You said you are ready to step down if Maj Gen Ali Muhsin al-Ahmar also steps down with you at the same time. It was said then that he agreed and said: I have no ambition to assume power and I do not want to become president, and I agree to step down with you.
[President Saleh]	I am a constitutional president while he is an ordinary officer. I can issue a decree now dismissing him, but this is not the solution. Also he comes from the same family. I told him by telephone that in order to avoid bloodshed and avoid putting the blame on me and you, I can step down and depart, and let us depart together and save the people. That was said on telephone.
[Al-Ramahi]	This mean this conversation between you took place as part of a normal dialogue.
[President Saleh]	Normal dialogue.
[Al-Ramahi]	This is a very important point that we need to explain because it was reported in the media that agreement was reached between you and him to step down if he does not run for election.
[President Saleh]	No, that was a telephone conversation. I told him if we are going to be blamed for any bloodshed, let us get out of power because we do not want Ali Saleh and Ali Muhsin to be the reason for what happens, and we would then discuss a peaceful transfer of power. I am a constitutional president while he is an ordinary employee who can be sacked by a presidential decree. There is no room for comparison. . . .
[Al-Ramahi]	But there must be some way for a peaceful transition of power acceptable to the other side, perhaps within a short period of time, before the end of 2011, since you are saying that you do not want power anyway.
[President Saleh]	Yes, yes. For me, power . . .
[Al-Ramahi]	is no longer a dream or . . .
[President Saleh]	Power will not be in my culture. But I will stick to power until I transfer it peacefully. I will stick to power until a peaceful transition takes place, no matter what the price. But force and arm twisting are out of the question.

| [Al-Ramahi] | You know what happened in Egypt, for example. The Egyptian president was asked to leave immediately. He came under pressure from inside and outside the country. Finally the Army settled the matter and the president left immediately, as the people demanded. This must have influenced the positions of people in Yemen and Libya, who are talking about immediate departure. |

[President Saleh] The situation in Yemen is different from the situation in Egypt. Egypt and Yemen have different cultures. Yemen's culture is a tribal culture, while Egypt's culture is more civil. . . .

[Al-Ramahi] So we are not going to see a repetition of the Egyptian scenario: the president steps down and resigns from the party.

[President Saleh] No, no. I resign from power; I transfer it peacefully. A new power comes, but I am also a party leader. I established the party in 1982.

[Al-Ramahi] That is what frightens them. They say the president is maneuvering, saying he will hand over power but remain the leader of party that will emerge again.

[President Saleh] This is a party. Does anyone abandon his party? Should I abandon my supporters, friends, and leaders? This is not right. Millions of people took to the streets to declare support for me. Shall I abandon them tomorrow? I am not of the type that leaves the country and looks for residence in Jeddah, Paris, or Europe. I will have my residence in my hometown.

[Al-Ramahi] But you said on more than one occasion that you would not run again for president.

[President Saleh] This is true.

[Al-Ramahi] Even if you remain as the leader of the party, you will not run.

[President Saleh] Yes; this is true. I will not run.

[Al-Ramahi] And you said no to hereditary succession of power.

[President Saleh] No to hereditary succession of power. This is a pledge. This is a decision for the people: I will neither run nor pass the rule on to my children. But if I leave power by peaceful means I will leave with my head high, not humiliated. . . .

[Al-Ramahi] Do you seek to obtain any kind of immunity in case you step down? Do you want them to guarantee that you will have immunity so that no one can harm your excellency?

[President Saleh] I am not asking for this. I will immune myself by myself.

[Al-Ramahi] Yemeni President Ali Abdullah President Saleh, thank you very much for this interview.

SOURCE: Yemen News Agency (SABA). "President Saleh Talks on Yemen Current Crisis in Arabiya TV Interview." March 26, 2011. http://www.presidentsaleh.gov.ye/shownews.php?lng=en&_nsid=9228&_newsctgry=4&_newsyr=2011.

President Saleh Addresses Power Transfer

September 30, 2011

Yemeni President Ali Abdullah Saleh sat down Thursday for a brief interview with *The Washington Post* and *Time Magazine* in his presidential compound in the Yemeni capital, Sanaa. . . .

Q: You have authorized your deputy, Abed Rabbo Mansour Hadi, to sign the GCC initiative [a plan for a transfer of power crafted by the Gulf Cooperation Council, Yemen's Gulf neighbors]. Why don't you do it yourself, now that you are here? And if you could explain to me what is holding up the agreement, and how close is the government to signing it?

SALEH: First of all, the vice president was delegated according to a Republican declaration [a declaration by the president]. And there isn't any reason for it not to go through, whether I am in the country or out of it. There is nothing that would stop this declaration from going through.

Q: How close is the vice president to signing the agreement?

SALEH: The vice president is waiting for the other side. We are ready to sign the GCC initiative as it is. However, the JMP [the opposition coalition Joint Meetings Party] say that they want from this initiative one point: that the president or the vice president signs and that within 30 days [the president] leaves power. And then the 60 days that the GCC has mentioned—they [the JMP] say that is not enough for elections. What is important to [the JMP] is to remove the president from power, and the country would then go through chaos.

We are ready and willing to sign at any time. But we need to sign the GCC initiative as a whole, and we need timelines for the mechanism of executing it. . . . We are not holding onto power, we are willing to leave power as stated in the agreement, within the days and hours that will be agreed upon.

Q: Yet many say you are stalling. Three times you have offered to sign, only to back down at the last minute. Many in the international community think that you are buying time in order to consolidate power. What makes your commitment this time different?

SALEH: This is a misunderstanding. We are willing within the next hours and next days to sign it, if the JMP comes closer [to reaching an agreement]. We don't want to prolong it. And we don't want this crisis to continue. We want this country to get out of this crisis.

Q: And you are still committed to not running again when there are elections?

SALEH (laughing):   As for me, I will retire — since the opposition has helped bring the president closer to retirement through the criminal act that happened at the presidential mosque. . . .

SOURCE: Yemen News Agency (SABA). "Yemen's President Ali Abdullah Saleh Speaks." September 30, 2011. http://www.presidentsaleh.gov.ye/shownews.php?lng=en&_nsid=9539&_newsctgry=4&_newsyr=2011.

President Saleh Denies Refusal to Transfer Power

November 14, 2011

In an interview with FRANCE 24, President Ali Abdullah Saleh said he intended to step down within 90 days of reaching a deal on a power transfer plan that aims to end the political crisis in the country.

"When the Gulf initiative is agreed upon and signed and when a time frame is set for its implementation, and elections take place, the president will leave," President Saleh said in the interview.

The President said also he had given power to Vice-President Abdo Rabbo Mansour Hadi to negotiate a deal with the opposition on the formation of a transitional government and organising future presidential elections.

Saleh confirmed he has "never refused to sign the Gulf initiative" but wanted to "read it and work on a mechanism" to implement it.

"I already wanted to leave power in 2006," Saleh said, citing "exceptional circumstances" that forced him to remain as the head of state. "I have been in power for more than 33 years in Yemen. I've overcome lots of problems, there's been fascinating moments. But as far as I'm concerned anyone that hangs onto power is a madman."

The President also defended his record and continued to insist that he has clung to power in order to fight off the threat of regional and international Islamic terrorism. . . .

SOURCE: Yemen News Agency (SABA). "President Saleh Says He Never Refused to Sign Gulf Initiative." November 14, 2011. http://www.presidentsaleh.gov.ye/shownews.php?lng=en&_nsid=9624&_newsctgry=4&_newsyr=2011.

U.S. Secretary of State Applauds Yemen Power Transfer

November 23, 2011

The United States applauds the Yemeni government and the opposition for agreeing to a peaceful and orderly transition of power that is responsive to the aspirations of the Yemeni people. Today marks a significant step forward for the Yemeni people in their quest for a unified, democratic, secure, and prosperous Yemen. We commend the Gulf Cooperation Council for its invaluable role in leading efforts to broker this agreement and to support the Yemeni people. . . .

We urge all parties within Yemen to refrain from violence and to move swiftly to implement the terms of the agreement in good faith and with transparency—including credible presidential elections within 90 days. The United States, in coordination with our international partners, will continue to closely monitor and support Yemen's political transition. We look forward to strengthening our partnership with the Yemeni people and their new government as they address their political, economic, humanitarian, and security challenges.

SOURCE: U.S. State Department. Media Center. "Signing of GCC-Brokered Agreement in Yemen." November 23, 2011. http://www.state.gov/secretary/rm/2011/11/177749.htm.

OTHER HISTORIC DOCUMENTS OF INTEREST

FROM THIS VOLUME

- Arab Spring: Tunisian President Zine al-Abidine Ben Ali Resigns, p. 23
- Arab Spring: Violent Crackdown on Protesters in Bahrain, p. 113
- Arab Spring: International Response to Mubarak's Resignation (Egypt), p. 95
- Arab Spring: King Abdullah II Reshuffles Cabinet (Jordan), p. 85
- Arab Spring: Syrian Government's Violent Crackdown on Protests, p. 168
- Arab Spring: NATO and President Obama on the Death of Muammar Qaddafi, p. 555

FROM PREVIOUS *Historic Documents*

- U.S. Officials on Intercepted Package Bombs, *2010*, p. 533
- United Nations on Promoting Democracy in Arab Lands, *2005*, p. 269
- Clinton on the Bombing of the USS *Cole, 2000*, p. 861

Department of Justice Declares Defense of Marriage Act Unconstitutional

FEBRUARY 23 AND NOVEMBER 10, 2011

The Defense of Marriage Act (DOMA) is a U.S. federal law that defines marriage as the legal union between one man and one woman. It also codifies in law that states are not required to recognize same-sex marriages entered into in other states. Since its passage in 1996, DOMA has remained controversial, and the constitutionality of provisions within the Act has been challenged on numerous occasions in court. Until early 2011, the U.S. Department of Justice had defended the constitutionality of DOMA in many of these cases. However, on February 23, 2011, the Department of Justice, in consultation with President Barack Obama, announced its determination that Section 3 of DOMA was unconstitutional and that the department would no longer defend it in court. Although efforts have been made in Congress to repeal DOMA, a more likely outcome is that the legislation will be overturned by the courts.

ACT PASSES CONGRESS WITH WIDE SUPPORT

DOMA was introduced into the U.S. Congress in May 1996 and signed into law by President Bill Clinton on September 21, 1996. The legislation faced little opposition in the 104th Congress, where the Republican Party held the majority in both houses. The Act passed the House of Representatives by a margin of 342 to 67 and the Senate with 85 votes in favor and 14 opposed.

There are two key provisions in DOMA. First, no state shall be required to give effect to a law of any other state with respect to a same-sex marriage. Second, it defines the words *marriage* and *spouse* for purposes of federal law. The first substantive section allows each state or other political jurisdiction to decide whether or not it will grant legal status to same-sex marriages. At the time the bill was introduced, politicians in some states foresaw the legalization of same-sex marriage in a number of states. Owing to the Full Faith and Credit clause of the U.S. Constitution, which addresses the duties of all states in the union to respect "public acts, records, and judicial proceedings of every other state," the legalization of same-sex marriage in one state could potentially have had consequences for all other states. Indeed, if, as some states anticipated at the time, Hawaii allowed same-sex marriage under state law, other states could potentially have had to give "full faith and credit" to Hawaii's interpretation of marriage.

Under the Constitution, Congress maintains the authority to declare what effect one state's acts, records, and judicial proceedings will have in all other states. Invoking this authority is not without precedent. For example, the Parental Kidnapping Prevention Act of 1980 requires states to enforce child custody determinations made by another state. The public policy exception, a pillar of U.S. case law that falls under the choice of law doctrine, exempts any state from recognizing a law from another state if that law is deemed to be offensive to the receiving state's public policy. Choice of law principles in the United States may have prevented Hawaii's interpretation from being upheld in other states, but nonetheless around thirty states were concerned enough to initiate legislative efforts to prevent the recognition of same-sex marriage. DOMA gives states the right to refuse recognition of same-sex marriages approved by another state. Six states—Connecticut, Iowa, Massachusetts, New Hampshire, New York, and Vermont—plus the District of Columbia currently recognize same-sex marriages.

The second substantive provision in DOMA, Section 7, defines *marriage* and *spouse*: "In determining the meaning of any Act of Congress, or of any ruling, regulation, or interpretation of the various administrative bureaus and agencies of the United States, the word 'marriage' means only a legal union between one man and one woman as husband and wife, and the word 'spouse' refers only to a person of the opposite sex who is a husband or a wife."

DOMA's Impact

DOMA prevents federal agencies from recognizing same-sex marriages. This has a significant impact on the 1,138 benefits, rights, and privileges, as assessed by the U.S. Government Accountability Office (GAO), that are contingent, at least to an extent, on marital status. DOMA also has a significant impact on U.S. immigration law. Under DOMA, one spouse in a same-sex union may not sponsor the other for a "green card," which grants permanent residency to foreign-born individuals.

In its most recent report on the impact of DOMA, the GAO identified thirteen key areas that are affected by DOMA. These include social security and related programs, housing, and food stamps; veterans's benefits; taxation; federal civilian and military service benefits; employment benefits and related statutory provisions; immigration, naturalization, and aliens; Native Americans; trade, commerce, and intellectual property; financial disclosure and conflict of interest; crimes and family violence; loans, guarantees, and payments in agriculture; federal natural resources and related statutory provisions; and miscellaneous statutory provisions.

Waning DOMA Support

Subsequent to its passage by Congress, thirty-eight states enacted legislation to further bolster the principles enshrined in DOMA. Specifically, this state legislation defines marriage as a union between a man and a woman and asserts that this definition is public policy. The latter allows states to invoke the public policy exception standard as grounds to deny recognition of such marriages. The legislation also maintains that same-sex marriages from other states will not be legally recognized. Nevertheless, the public policy exception only applies to other states's laws, and not to judgments, which are judicial proceedings from another state. Thus, if a court rendered a judgment recognizing same-sex marriage, all other states would be required to recognize that judgment regardless of public policy against same-sex marriage. However, DOMA allows states to disregard such judgments. Some legal scholars have argued that this exception singles out same-sex couples, which could be a violation of the Equal Protection clause of the 14th Amendment.

DOMA has remained controversial. The administration of President George W. Bush supported DOMA and even sought to enshrine its principles in the Constitution. In February 2004, President Bush called for a constitutional amendment that would "fully protect marriage, while leaving the state legislatures free to make their own choices in defining legal arrangements other than marriage." The president stated that the Full Faith and Credit clause made DOMA vulnerable to opposition and that to ensure that DOMA would not be ruled unconstitutional by "activist courts," the Constitution would need to be amended. However, the Constitution was not subsequently amended during the Bush administration.

The stance on DOMA of the Obama administration is altogether different than that of its predecessor. President Barack Obama opposes DOMA, and has signalled that ideally he would like to see the legislation repealed by Congress. Despite the president's opposition, the Department of Justice has defended Section 3 of the Act in federal court in several cases since President Obama took office because it could advance reasonable arguments under the rational basis standard. According to the Department of Justice, each of the cases in which the department defended Section 3 of DOMA were considered in jurisdictions where binding court precedents state that laws that single out individuals based on sexual orientation are constitutional if there is a rational basis for their enactment.

However, Section 3 was subsequently challenged in the Second Circuit, which did not have such binding court precedents in this area. For the first time, the Department of Justice was forced to decide whether laws regarding sexual orientation should face a more rigorous or a more permissive standard of review. Under the former, laws that target minority groups with a history of discrimination are viewed with suspicion by the courts. The president, in consultation with the Department of Justice, concluded that a more rigorous standard should apply. Furthermore, President Obama concluded that Section 3 of DOMA, as applied to legally married same-sex couples, did not meet a higher standard of scrutiny and is therefore unconstitutional. As such, the president instructed the Department of Justice that it should not defend Section 3 of DOMA. Attorney General Eric Holder agreed with the president's decision. A statement to this effect was made public on February 23, 2011.

Holder cited two reasons for not defending the constitutionality of Section 3 of the Act. First, the Department of Justice found that not all arguments in favor of Section 3 are reasonable. Second, the president believes that Section 3 is unconstitutional. Although the administration indicated that it would no longer defend the constitutionality of Section 3 in court, it is required to uphold the law until it is repealed or it is struck down by a court. This means that the Department of Justice will not defend the Act in court if a lawsuit is filed charging that Section 3 is unconstitutional, but if, for example, an agency extends health benefits to same-sex couples, the Department of Justice would be required to step in and stop the action.

DOMA's Future

In November 2011 the Senate Judiciary Committee voted in favor of the Respect for Marriage Act by a margin of 10 to 8. The votes fell along party lines, with the Democratic senators voting in favor of the Act. The legislation would largely overturn DOMA. Nevertheless, the bill's sponsor, Sen. Dianne Feinstein, D-Calif., has acknowledged that the bill does not yet have the support of sixty senators needed in order to overcome a filibuster in the Senate. Moreover, in the event that the bill does pass the Senate, it would face intense opposition in the Republican-controlled House of Representatives. Timing is likely to be a crucial factor in the bill's passage. With a presidential election in November 2012, it is unlikely that either the Republicans or Democrats will be keen to see the repeal of DOMA as a major preelection issue. A more likely scenario is that DOMA will be overturned by the courts, which will find either Section 3 or Section 7, or perhaps both, unconstitutional.

—Hilary Ewing

The following is a press release issued by the U.S. Department of Justice on February 23, 2011, in which the department expresses its finding that the Defense of Marriage Act is unconstitutional; and a press release issued by Sen. Dianne Feinstein, D-Calif., on the Judiciary Committee passage of the DOMA repeal bill on November 10, 2011.

Department of Justice Statement on Defense of Marriage Act

February 23, 2011

The Attorney General made the following statement today about the Department's course of action in two lawsuits, *Pedersen v. OPM* and *Windsor v. United States*, challenging Section 3 of the Defense of Marriage Act (DOMA), which defines marriage for federal purposes as only between a man and a woman:

In the two years since this Administration took office, the Department of Justice has defended Section 3 of the Defense of Marriage Act on several occasions in federal court. Each of those cases evaluating Section 3 was considered in jurisdictions in which binding circuit court precedents hold that laws singling out people based on sexual orientation, as DOMA does, are constitutional if there is a rational basis for their enactment. While the President opposes DOMA and believes it should be repealed, the Department has defended it in court because we were able to advance reasonable arguments under that rational basis standard.

Section 3 of DOMA has now been challenged in the Second Circuit, however, which has no established or binding standard for how laws concerning sexual orientation should be treated. In these cases, the Administration faces for the first time the question of whether laws regarding sexual orientation are subject to the more permissive standard of review or whether a more rigorous standard, under which laws targeting minority groups with a history of discrimination are viewed with suspicion by the courts, should apply.

After careful consideration, including a review of my recommendation, the President has concluded that given a number of factors, including a documented history of discrimination, classifications based on sexual orientation should be subject to a more heightened standard of scrutiny. The President has also concluded that Section 3 of DOMA, as applied to legally married same-sex couples, fails to meet that standard and is therefore unconstitutional. Given that conclusion, the President has instructed the Department not to defend the statute in such cases. I fully concur with the President's determination.

Consequently, the Department will not defend the constitutionality of Section 3 of DOMA as applied to same-sex married couples in the two cases filed in the Second Circuit. We will, however, remain parties to the cases and continue to represent the interests of the United States throughout the litigation. I have informed Members of Congress of this decision, so Members who wish to defend the statute may pursue that option. The Department will also work closely with the courts to ensure that Congress has a full and fair opportunity to participate in pending litigation.

Furthermore, pursuant to the President's instructions, and upon further notification to Congress, I will instruct Department attorneys to advise courts in other pending DOMA litigation of the President's and my conclusions that a heightened standard should apply, that Section 3 is unconstitutional under that standard and that the Department will cease defense of Section 3.

The Department has a longstanding practice of defending the constitutionality of duly-enacted statutes if reasonable arguments can be made in their defense. At the same time, the Department in the past has declined to defend statutes despite the availability of professionally responsible arguments, in part because—as here—the Department does not consider every such argument to be a "reasonable" one. Moreover, the Department has declined to defend a statute in cases, like this one, where the President has concluded that the statute is unconstitutional.

Much of the legal landscape has changed in the 15 years since Congress passed DOMA. The Supreme Court has ruled that laws criminalizing homosexual conduct are unconstitutional. Congress has repealed the military's Don't Ask, Don't Tell policy. Several lower courts have ruled DOMA itself to be unconstitutional. Section 3 of DOMA will continue to remain in effect unless Congress repeals it or there is a final judicial finding that strikes it down, and the President has informed me that the Executive Branch will continue to enforce the law. But while both the wisdom and the legality of Section 3 of DOMA will continue to be the subject of both extensive litigation and public debate, this Administration will no longer assert its constitutionality in court.

SOURCE: U.S. Department of Justice. Office of Public Affairs. "Statement of the Attorney General on Litigation Involving the Defense of Marriage Act." February 23, 2011. http://www.justice.gov/opa/pr/2011/February/11-ag-222.html.

 # DOMA Repeal Bill Passes Senate Judiciary Committee

November 10, 2011

Legislation authored by Senator Dianne Feinstein (D-Calif.) to repeal the discriminatory *Defense of Marriage Act* (DOMA) passed the Senate Judiciary Committee today.

Senator Feinstein's *Respect for Marriage Act* (S. 598) would strike DOMA from federal law and provide legally married, same-sex couples the same federal benefits, rights and privileges as other married Americans.

"DOMA was wrong when it passed in 1996 and it is wrong now. There are 131,000 legally married, same-sex couples in this country who are denied more than 1,100 federal rights and protections because of this discriminatory law," Feinstein said. **"I don't know how long the battle for full equality will take, but we are on the cusp of change, and today's historic vote in the committee is an important step forward."**

Because of DOMA, there are more than 1,100 federal rights and protections that are denied to lawfully married same-sex couples. Specifically, these couples cannot:

- File joint federal income taxes and claim certain deductions;
- Receive spousal benefits under Social Security;
- Take unpaid leave under the *Family and Medical Leave Act*; or
- Obtain the protections of the estate tax when one spouse passes and wants to leave his or her possessions to another.

In addition to Senator Feinstein, *the Respect for Marriage Act* currently has 30 Senate cosponsors. Her legislation is supported by President Barack Obama.

Following are Senator Feinstein's remarks today:

"Mr. Chairman, I believe DOMA is discriminatory and should be stricken in its entirety from federal law. The Respect for Marriage Act will do that, and I urge my colleagues to report this bill to the floor cleanly, without any amendments.

When DOMA passed 15 years ago, no state permitted same-sex marriage. Today, 6 states and the District of Columbia do: Vermont, Connecticut, Iowa, New York, New Hampshire, and Massachusetts.

So, today there are 131,000-plus legally married same-sex couples in this country.

These changes reflect a firmly-established legal principle in this country: marriage is a legal preserve of the states.

DOMA infringes on this state authority by requiring the federal government to disregard state law, and deny more than 1,100 federal rights and benefits to which all other legally married couples are entitled.

Last week, Mr. Chairman, 70 businesses and other organizations joined in an amicus brief in the First Circuit in a case challenging the constitutionality of DOMA. They include Xerox, Exelon, CBS, Aetna, Time Warner, NIKE, Starbucks, Google, Microsoft, among many others.

They include legal and professional associations as well as three cities. The brief clearly indicates how DOMA is causing real problems in its discriminatory nature.

First, DOMA strips tax-free health coverage from spouses in same-sex marriages. This affects the employee's tax burden, increasing it on average by over $1,000 a year. It also increases the employer's payroll tax burden, which is based on the employee's wages.

DOMA strips spousal retirement protection under ERISA from same-sex married couples.

DOMA denies a same-sex spouse the right to continue health coverage under COBRA. It requires businesses to maintain two sets of books, which these petitioners say has produced additional cost—one for married employees with same-sex spouses, another for married employees with different-sex spouses.

It has compelled companies to hire costly compliance specialists. And, it imposes even greater costs on small businesses, which cannot afford outside experts.

So, I believe it's pretty clear that the time has come to repeal DOMA. When DOMA was passed, no one was affected, because no one was legally married, because no state had passed a law. That's changed now. We have 7 states, we have 131,000 married couples, and the discriminatory nature of DOMA is showing up throughout the business and professional communities of this country.

So I urge my colleagues to support this bill, end this discrimination, and vote no, please, on all amendments."

SOURCE: Sen. Dianne Feinstein. "Feinstein's DOMA Repeal Bill Passes Judiciary Committee." November 10, 2011. http://www.feinstein.senate.gov/public/index.cfm/2011/11/feinstein-s-doma-repeal-bill-passes-judiciary-committee.

OTHER HISTORIC DOCUMENTS OF INTEREST

FROM PREVIOUS *HISTORIC DOCUMENTS*

March

Supreme Court Rules on Picketers at Military Funerals

MARCH 2, 2011

The small Kansas-based Westboro Baptist Church has garnered national attention and public outrage for appearing at the funerals of soldiers who were killed in action with picket signs bearing hateful messages such as "Thank God for Dead Soldiers" and "God Hates Fags." A case brought by the father of one such fallen soldier was the focus of more attention than any other Supreme Court case during its 2010–2011 term. In *Snyder v. Phelps*, Chief Justice John Roberts, writing for the majority of the Court, acknowledged the great pain inflicted by the protesters, but nevertheless upheld Westboro's right to picket a military funeral. The First Amendment, on the facts of this case, he wrote, prohibits punishing the speaker for the pain caused by the speech. Strongly reaffirming fundamental First Amendment principles, he concluded that the United States has "chosen a different course—to protect even hurtful speech on public issues to ensure that we do not stifle public debate."

The history of cases involving the freedom of speech clause of the First Amendment—"Congress shall make no law . . . abridging the freedom of speech"—involves some highly controversial victors. The American Nazi Party won the right to march through a neighborhood in Skokie, Illinois, in which many Holocaust survivors resided, and *Hustler* magazine's sexual satire was held to be protected speech. As recently as last term, the Supreme Court, in another 8–1 decision, granted First Amendment protection for videos depicting cruelty toward animals. The *Snyder* case now brings Westboro Baptist Church into this rogue's gallery of First Amendment champions. Reasserting bedrock principles underlying the First Amendment, Roberts wrote that "the government may not prohibit the expression of an idea simply because society finds the idea itself offensive or disagreeable."

PARTIES TO THE LAWSUIT

Fred Phelps founded Westboro Baptist Church in Topeka, Kansas, in 1955. Its current membership is approximately forty and consists almost entirely of members of Phelps's family. Westboro Baptist Church members believe that sin has become "institutionalized" in America because of the lack of interest in and tolerance of sin, which for them includes homosexuality, divorce, remarriage, and the scandals of the Catholic Church. According to the Westboro Baptist Church, God hates and punishes the United States for this sin, particularly through the deaths of soldiers killed in Iraq and Afghanistan; the members of the church are called, like prophets and apostles, to warn of the wrath of God. For the past twenty years, the group has been drawing attention to its views by protesting at public events after issuing press releases to ensure that their protests will attract public attention. Church members travel the country picketing at funerals and memorial services for military dead. As grieving families mourn their children killed in action, church members carry picket signs such as "Thank God for Dead Soldiers," "Fags Doom Nations," "America is Doomed," "Priests Rape Boys," "You are Going to Hell," "God Hates Fags," and "Semper Fi Fags." They have not specifically targeted funerals of gay soldiers, but those of any fallen soldier. They have picketed approximately 600 funerals as of 2011. Their publicity strategy does not just target soldiers; they have also picketed at the funerals of police officers, firefighters, and the victims of natural disasters and shocking crimes. In 2011, after the deadly shooting spree in Tucson, Arizona, that targeted Rep. Gabrielle Giffords, D-Ariz., the group announced its intention to picket at the funeral of the nine-year-old girl killed in the attack. Their press release proclaimed that she was "better off dead" and drew national attention, although they later agreed not to picket in exchange for free radio air time.

Marine Lance Corporal Matthew Snyder died in the line of duty with his combat battalion in Anbar Province, Iraq. He was twenty years old and had been in Iraq for one month. His father, Albert Snyder, planned the funeral in a Catholic church in Westminster, Maryland, the town where Matthew had grown up. Local newspapers printed the time and location of the services.

Phelps, with two daughters and four grandchildren, flew to Maryland to protest and picket the funeral. Their press release announced that they were going "to picket the funeral of Lance Cpl. Matthew A. Snyder" because "God Almighty killed Lance Cpl. Snyder. He died in shame, not honor—for a fag nation cursed by God." They also informed the local authorities of their intent to picket and complied with police instructions in staging their demonstration. Signs carried by the picketers read: "God Hates the USA/Thank God for 9/11," "Thank God for IEDs," "Thank God for Dead Soldiers," "Priests Rape Boys," and "God Hates Fags," among other similar messages. The funeral procession passed within 200 to 300 feet of the picket signs, but Snyder stated that he did not see the content of the signs, just noticed their presence. He became aware of what they said watching a news broadcast of the event.

After the funeral, Matthew's father sued the church and its members for the intentional infliction of emotional distress, an action to recover for damages resulting from conduct that produces distress "so severe that no reasonable [person] could be expected to endure it" and which is itself "so outrageous in character and so extreme in degree as to go beyond all possible bounds of decency, and to be regarded as atrocious and utterly intolerable in a civilized community." Snyder testified he suffered from severe depression and was unable to separate thoughts of his dead son from thoughts of the picketing, that he often becomes tearful, angry, and physically ill when he thinks about it. Expert witnesses testified that the physical and mental trauma had exacerbated preexisting medical conditions. The jury awarded him $2.9 million in compensatory damages and $8 million in punitive damages. The judge reduced the punitive damages judgment, bringing the total award down to $5 million.

On appeal, the Fourth Circuit Court of Appeals in Richmond, Virginia, ruled for the Phelps family and their church, finding that Westboro's statements were entitled to First Amendment protection because, "notwithstanding the distasteful and repugnant nature of the words being challenged," the statements were hyperbolic rhetoric, not provably false on matters of public concern. The United States Supreme Court granted review of the case on March 8, 2010.

Court Reaffirms First Amendment Rights

In an 8–1 decision, the Supreme Court found that the First Amendment shields Westboro Baptist Church from tort liability for picketing Matthew's military funeral. Only Justice Samuel Alito dissented.

The majority opinion, written by Chief Justice John Roberts, turned primarily on whether Westboro's speech could be classified as concerning public or private issues. Unlike speech about purely private matters, "speech on public issues occupies the highest rung of hierarchy of First Amendment values, and is entitled to special protection." In deciding whether the speech deserves this "special protection," Roberts looked to the specific facts of the case including "what was said, where it was said, and how it was said."

First, the Court determined that the content of Westboro's message spoke to broad public issues. While the messages on the picket signs may, Roberts admitted, "fall short of refined social or political commentary," they nonetheless relate to broad issues of interest to society at large, specifically, "the political and moral conduct of the United States and its citizens, the fate of our Nation, homosexuality in the military, and scandals involving the Catholic clergy."

Then the Court looked at the other specific circumstances of the speech and rejected Snyder's contention that the context of the speech, a private funeral, should strip the public speech of constitutional protection. "The fact that Westboro spoke in connection with a funeral ... cannot by itself transform the nature of Westboro's speech." To reach this conclusion, the Court focused on the specific facts of this case, and described the holding as "narrow." The church members stayed on public land where picketing was lawful. They alerted local authorities before the protest and fully complied with all police directions about where to picket. The picketing was conducted under police supervision, a thousand feet from the church, and could not be heard or seen from the funeral service. Snyder himself testified that he had not been able to read the picket signs as he drove to the funeral. The protesters were quiet; there was no profanity or threats of violence. As there was no interference with the funeral itself, the Court concluded that Snyder was not distressed by the fact of the picketing, but rather by its content and viewpoint. Based on these facts, the Court found that the protesters speech could not "be restricted simply because it is upsetting or arouses contempt."

Justice Alito was the sole dissenter in this case, passionately arguing that the First Amendment should not license the "vicious verbal assault" inflicted on a parent who wanted only "what is surely the right of any parent who experiences such an incalculable loss: to bury his son in peace." Justice Alito outlined the almost limitless opportunities afforded the protesters to express their views, the countless other locations they could have protested. But, they intentionally employed a strategy of gaining media attention through the infliction of severe and lasting emotional injury on an ever growing list of innocent victims at a time of "acute emotional vulnerability." He rejected the majority contention that allowing family members a few hours to bury their loved ones in peace would in any way undermine public debate. "In order to have a society in which public issues can be openly and vigorously debated," he wrote, "it is not necessary to allow the brutalization of innocent victims like petitioner."

In a separate concurring opinion, Justice Stephen Breyer wrote to underscore that, in his view, this narrow ruling protected Westboro on the specific facts of this case and no more. He expressed his sympathy with Justice Alito's dissent and wrote separately to make clear that he did not read the holding to imply that the state is powerless to provide private individuals with protection in the most horrendous of circumstances.

IMPACT AND REACTION

The impact of this case will be a narrow one, carefully limited by the facts and addressing the kind of picketing that is conducted almost entirely by a single splinter church, made up of one single family. Forty-four states and the federal government have laws imposing restrictions on funeral picketing. These laws were not at issue in this case, but the Court acknowledged that even protected speech can be subject to reasonable restrictions on the time, place, or manner of the speech as long as such restrictions are content-neutral. Such restrictions have been upheld, for instance, to support laws requiring a buffer zone between protesters and an abortion clinic entrance. Maryland, where Snyder's son was buried, has a funeral picketing law, but it did not make a difference in this case, because the picketing here would have complied with the law prohibiting picketing within 100 feet of a funeral service or procession. Justice Roberts declined to evaluate the constitutionality of these laws, but suggested that laws such as these are the way to protect against disruptive and hurtful funeral protests.

Margie Phelps, Fred Phelps's daughter and the lawyer who argued his case before the Supreme Court, described the ruling as "ten times better than I had hoped for" and vowed to "quadruple" protests at funerals. Veterans groups pledged to continue to hold counter-protests. The Veterans of Foreign Wars national commander, Richard Eubank, expressing disappointment with the result, said that "Westboro Baptist Church may think they have won, but the VFW will continue to support community efforts to ensure no one hears their voice." The national commander of the American Legion, Jimmie L. Foster, pointed out the irony of protesting at "the funeral of an American hero who died defending the very freedoms this church abuses."

Snyder, who now cannot collect the $5 million judgment, described his first reaction to the ruling as "that eight justices don't have the common sense that God gave a goat," but said he is ready now to move on and try to find closure with his son's death.

—Melissa Feinberg

The following are excerpts from the U.S. Supreme Court ruling in Snyder v. Phelps, *in which the Court ruled 8–1 to uphold the First Amendment rights of those protesting at military funerals.*

`DOCUMENT`   ## *Snyder v. Phelps*

March 2, 2011

No. 09-751

Albert Snyder, Petitioner

v.

Fred W. Phelps, Sr., et al.

}

On writ of certiorari to the United States Court of Appeals for the Fourth Circuit

[March 2, 2011]

[Footnotes have been omitted.]

CHIEF JUSTICE ROBERTS delivered the opinion of the Court.

A jury held members of the Westboro Baptist Church liable for millions of dollars in damages for picketing near a soldier's funeral service. The picket signs reflected the church's view that the United States is overly tolerant of sin and that God kills American soldiers as punishment. The question presented is whether the First Amendment shields the church members from tort liability for their speech in this case. . . .

[Section I, containing a discussion of the facts in the case, has been omitted.]

II

To succeed on a claim for intentional infliction of emotional distress in Maryland, a plaintiff must demonstrate that the defendant intentionally or recklessly engaged in extreme and outrageous conduct that caused the plaintiff to suffer severe emotional distress. . . . The Free Speech Clause of the First Amendment—"Congress shall make no law . . . abridging the freedom of speech"—can serve as a defense in state tort suits, including suits for intentional infliction of emotional distress. . . .

Whether the First Amendment prohibits holding Westboro liable for its speech in this case turns largely on whether that speech is of public or private concern, as determined by all the circumstances of the case. "[S]peech on 'matters of public concern' . . . is 'at the heart of the First Amendment's protection.'" . . . The First Amendment reflects "a profound national commitment to the principle that debate on public issues should be uninhibited, robust, and wide-open." . . . That is because "speech concerning public affairs is more than self-expression; it is the essence of self-government." . . . Accordingly, "speech on public issues occupies the highest rung of the hierarchy of First Amendment values, and is entitled to special protection." . . .

"'[N]ot all speech is of equal First Amendment importance,'" however, and where matters of purely private significance are at issue, First Amendment protections are often less rigorous. . . . That is because restricting speech on purely private matters does not implicate the same constitutional concerns as limiting speech on matters of public interest: "[T]here is no threat to the free and robust debate of public issues; there is no potential interference with a meaningful dialogue of ideas"; and the "threat of liability" does not pose the risk of "a reaction of self-censorship" on matters of public import. . . .

We noted a short time ago, in considering whether public employee speech addressed a matter of public concern, that "the boundaries of the public concern test are not well defined." . . . Although that remains true today, we have articulated some guiding principles, principles that accord broad protection to speech to ensure that courts themselves do not become inadvertent censors.

Speech deals with matters of public concern when it can "be fairly considered as relating to any matter of political, social, or other concern to the community," *Connick, supra,* at 146, or when it "is a subject of legitimate news interest; that is, a subject of general interest and of value and concern to the public," *San Diego, supra,* at 83–84. . . . The arguably "inappropriate or controversial character of a statement is irrelevant to the question whether it deals with a matter of public concern." . . .

Deciding whether speech is of public or private concern requires us to examine the "'content, form, and context'" of that speech, "'as revealed by the whole record.'" . . . As in other First Amendment cases, the court is obligated "to 'make an independent examination of the whole record' in order to make sure that 'the judgment does not constitute a forbidden intrusion on the field of free expression.'" . . . In considering content, form, and context, no factor is dispositive, and it is necessary to evaluate all the circumstances of the speech, including what was said, where it was said, and how it was said.

The "content" of Westboro's signs plainly relates to broad issues of interest to society at large, rather than matters of "purely private concern." . . . The placards read "God Hates the USA/Thank God for 9/11," "America is Doomed," "Don't Pray for the USA," "Thank God for IEDs," "Fag Troops," "Semper Fi Fags," "God Hates Fags," "Maryland Taliban," "Fags Doom Nations," "Not Blessed Just Cursed," "Thank God for Dead Soldiers," "Pope in Hell," "Priests Rape Boys," "You're Going to Hell," and "God Hates You." . . . While these messages may fall short of refined social or political commentary, the issues they highlight—the political and moral conduct of the United States and its citizens, the fate of our Nation, homosexuality in the military, and scandals involving the Catholic clergy—are matters of public import. The signs certainly convey Westboro's position on those issues, in a manner designed, unlike the private speech in *Dun & Bradstreet*, to reach as broad a public audience as possible. And even if a few of the signs—such as "You're Going to Hell" and "God Hates You"—were viewed as containing messages related to Matthew Snyder or the Snyders specifically, that would not change the fact that the overall thrust and dominant theme of Westboro's demonstration spoke to broader public issues.

Apart from the content of Westboro's signs, Snyder contends that the "context" of the speech—its connection with his son's funeral—makes the speech a matter of private rather than public concern. The fact that Westboro spoke in connection with a funeral, however, cannot by itself transform the nature of Westboro's speech. Westboro's signs, displayed on public land next to a public street, reflect the fact that the church finds much to condemn in modern society. Its speech is "fairly characterized as constituting speech on a matter of public concern," *Connick*, 461 U. S., at 146, and the funeral setting does not alter that conclusion. . . .

Westboro's choice to convey its views in conjunction with Matthew Snyder's funeral made the expression of those views particularly hurtful to many, especially to Matthew's father. The record makes clear that the applicable legal term—"emotional distress"—fails to capture fully the anguish Westboro's choice added to Mr. Snyder's already incalculable grief. But Westboro conducted its picketing peacefully on matters of public concern at a public place adjacent to a public street. Such space occupies a "special position in terms of First Amendment protection." . . . "[W]e have repeatedly referred to public streets as the archetype of a traditional public forum," noting that "'[t]ime out of mind' public streets and sidewalks have been used for public assembly and debate." . . .

That said, "[e]ven protected speech is not equally permissible in all places and at all times." . . . Westboro's choice of where and when to conduct its picketing is not beyond the Government's regulatory reach—it is "subject to reasonable time, place, or manner restrictions" that are consistent with the standards announced in this Court's precedents. . . . Maryland now has a law imposing restrictions on funeral picketing, Md. Crim. Law Code Ann. §10–205 (Lexis Supp. 2010), as do 43 other States and the Federal Government. To the extent these laws are content neutral, they raise very different questions from the tort verdict at issue in this case. Maryland's law, however, was not in effect at the time of the events at issue here, so we have no occasion to consider how it might apply to facts such as those before us, or whether it or other similar regulations are constitutional.

We have identified a few limited situations where the location of targeted picketing can be regulated under provisions that the Court has determined to be content neutral. In *Frisby*, for example, we upheld a ban on such picketing "before or about" a particular residence, 487 U. S., at 477. In *Madsen* v. *Women's Health Center, Inc.*, we approved an injunction requiring a buffer zone between protesters and an abortion clinic entrance. The facts here are obviously quite different, both with respect to the activity being regulated and the means of restricting those activities.

Simply put, the church members had the right to be where they were. Westboro alerted local authorities to its funeral protest and fully complied with police guidance on where the picketing could be staged. The picketing was conducted under police supervision some 1,000 feet from the church, out of the sight of those at the church. The protest was not unruly; there was no shouting, profanity, or violence.

The record confirms that any distress occasioned by Westboro's picketing turned on the content and viewpoint of the message conveyed, rather than any interference with the funeral itself. A group of parishioners standing at the very spot where Westboro stood, holding signs that said "God Bless America" and "God Loves You," would not have been subjected to liability. It was what Westboro said that exposed it to tort damages.

Given that Westboro's speech was at a public place on a matter of public concern, that speech is entitled to "special protection" under the First Amendment. Such speech cannot be restricted simply because it is upsetting or arouses contempt. "If there is a bedrock principle underlying the First Amendment, it is that the government may not prohibit the expression of an idea simply because society finds the idea itself offensive or disagreeable." . . . Indeed, "the point of all speech protection . . . is to shield just those choices of content that in someone's eyes are misguided, or even hurtful." . . .

The jury here was instructed that it could hold Westboro liable for intentional infliction of emotional distress based on a finding that Westboro's picketing was "outrageous." "Outrageousness," however, is a highly malleable standard with "an inherent subjectiveness about it which would allow a jury to impose liability on the basis of the jurors' tastes or views, or perhaps on the basis of their dislike of a particular expression." . . . In a case such as this, a jury is "unlikely to be neutral with respect to the content of [the]speech," posing "a real danger of becoming an instrument for the suppression of . . . 'vehement, caustic, and sometimes unpleasan[t]'" expression. . . . Such a risk is unacceptable; "in public debate [we] must tolerate insulting, and even outrageous, speech in order to provide adequate 'breathing space' to the freedoms protected by the First Amendment." . . . What Westboro said, in the whole context of how and where it chose to say it, is entitled to "special protection" under the First Amendment, and that protection cannot be overcome by a jury finding that the picketing was outrageous.

For all these reasons, the jury verdict imposing tort liability on Westboro for intentional infliction of emotional distress must be set aside.

III

The jury also found Westboro liable for the state law torts of intrusion upon seclusion and civil conspiracy. The Court of Appeals did not examine these torts independently of the intentional infliction of emotional distress tort. Instead, the Court of Appeals reversed the District Court wholesale, holding that the judgment wrongly "attache[d] tort liability to constitutionally protected speech." . . .

Snyder argues that even assuming Westboro's speech is entitled to First Amendment protection generally, the church is not immunized from liability for intrusion upon seclusion because Snyder was a member of a captive audience at his son's funeral. . . . We do not agree. In most circumstances, "the Constitution does not permit the government to decide which types of otherwise protected speech are sufficiently offensive to require protection for the unwilling listener or viewer. Rather, . . . the burden normally falls upon the viewer to avoid further bombardment of [his] sensibilities simply by averting [his] eyes." . . . As a result, "[t]he ability of government, consonant with the Constitution, to shut off discourse solely to protect others from hearing it is . . . dependent upon a showing that substantial privacy interests are being invaded in an essentially intolerable manner." . . .

As a general matter, we have applied the captive audience doctrine only sparingly to protect unwilling listeners from protected speech. For example, we have upheld a statute allowing a homeowner to restrict the delivery of offensive mail to his home, see *Rowan v. Post Office Dept.*, 397 U. S. 728, 736–738 (1970), and an ordinance prohibiting picketing "before or about" any individual's residence, *Frisby*, 487 U. S., at 484–485.

Here, Westboro stayed well away from the memorial service. Snyder could see no more than the tops of the signs when driving to the funeral. And there is no indication that the picketing in any way interfered with the funeral service itself. We decline to expand the captive audience doctrine to the circumstances presented here.

Because we find that the First Amendment bars Snyder from recovery for intentional infliction of emotional distress or intrusion upon seclusion—the alleged unlawful activity Westboro conspired to accomplish—we must likewise hold that Snyder cannot recover for civil conspiracy based on those torts.

IV

Our holding today is narrow. We are required in First Amendment cases to carefully review the record, and the reach of our opinion here is limited by the particular facts before us. As we have noted, "the sensitivity and significance of the interests presented in clashes between First Amendment and [state law] rights counsel relying on limited principles that sweep no more broadly than the appropriate context of the instant case." . . .

Westboro believes that America is morally flawed; many Americans might feel the same about Westboro. Westboro's funeral picketing is certainly hurtful and its contribution to public discourse may be negligible. But Westboro addressed matters of public import on public property, in a peaceful manner, in full compliance with guidance of local officials. The speech was indeed planned to coincide with Matthew Snyder's funeral, but did not itself disrupt that funeral, and Westboro's choice to conduct its picketing at that time and place did not alter the nature of its speech.

Speech is powerful. It can stir people to action, move them to tears of both joy and sorrow, and—as it did here—inflict great pain. On the facts before us, we cannot react to that pain by punishing the speaker. As a Nation we have chosen a different course—to protect even hurtful speech on public issues to ensure that we do not stifle public debate. That choice requires that we shield Westboro from tort liability for its picketing in this case.

The judgment of the United States Court of Appeals for the Fourth Circuit is affirmed.

It is so ordered

[*The concurring statement of Justice Breyer has been omitted.*]

JUSTICE ALITO, dissenting.

Our profound national commitment to free and open debate is not a license for the vicious verbal assault that occurred in this case.

Petitioner Albert Snyder is not a public figure. He is simply a parent whose son, Marine Lance Corporal Matthew Snyder, was killed in Iraq. Mr. Snyder wanted what is surely the right of any parent who experiences such an incalculable loss: to bury his son in peace. But respondents, members of the Westboro Baptist Church, deprived him of that elementary right. They first issued a press release and thus turned Matthew's funeral into a tumultuous media event. They then appeared at the church, approached as closely as they could without trespassing, and launched a malevolent verbal attack on Matthew and his family at a time of acute emotional vulnerability. As a result, Albert Snyder suffered severe and lasting emotional injury. The Court now holds that the First Amendment protected respondents' right to brutalize Mr. Snyder. I cannot agree.

I

Respondents and other members of their church have strong opinions on certain moral, religious, and political issues, and the First Amendment ensures that they have almost limitless opportunities to express their views. They may write and distribute books, articles, and other texts; they may create and disseminate video and audio recordings; they may circulate petitions; they may speak to individuals and groups in public forums and in any private venue that wishes to accommodate them; they may picket peacefully in countless locations; they may appear on television and speak on the radio; they may post messages on the Internet and send out e-mails. And they may express their views in terms that are "uninhibited," "vehement," and "caustic." ...

It does not follow, however, that they may intentionally inflict severe emotional injury on private persons at a time of intense emotional sensitivity by launching vicious verbal attacks that make no contribution to public debate. To protect against such injury, "most if not all jurisdictions" permit recovery in tort for the intentional infliction of emotional distress (or IIED). . . .

[Sections II and III, containing information on the facts of the case and earlier court rulings, have been omitted.]

IV ...

[A discussion of state funeral picketing laws has been omitted.]

The real significance of these new laws is not that they obviate the need for IIED protection. Rather, their enactment dramatically illustrates the fundamental point that funerals are unique events at which special protection against emotional assaults is in order. At funerals, the emotional well-being of bereaved relatives is particularly vulnerable. Exploitation of a funeral for the purpose of attracting public attention "intrud[es] upon their ... grief," *ibid.*, and may permanently stain their memories of the final moments before a loved one is laid to rest. Allowing family members to have a few hours of peace without harassment does not undermine public debate. I would therefore hold that, in this setting, the First Amendment permits a private figure to recover for the intentional infliction of emotional distress caused by speech on a matter of private concern . . . .

[Section V, containing a discussion of lower court rulings on funeral picketing, has been omitted.]

VI

Respondents' outrageous conduct caused petitioner great injury, and the Court now compounds that injury by depriving petitioner of a judgment that acknowledges the wrong he suffered.

In order to have a society in which public issues can be openly and vigorously debated, it is not necessary to allow the brutalization of innocent victims like petitioner. I therefore respectfully dissent.

SOURCE: U.S. Supreme Court. *Snyder v. Phelps*, 562 U.S.__(2011). http://www.supremecourt.gov/opinions/10pdf/09-751.pdf.

OTHER HISTORIC DOCUMENTS OF INTEREST

FROM PREVIOUS *HISTORIC DOCUMENTS*

Japan Responds to Earthquake, Tsunami, and Nuclear Crisis

MARCH 11 AND 15, AND APRIL 1, 2011

On March 11, 2011, Japan was devastated by a massive earthquake and tsunami that struck the nation's northeastern coast with little warning. The natural disasters leveled towns, killed thousands, and caused a partial nuclear meltdown at one of the nation's nuclear power plants. The long-struggling economy took another hit when the earthquake and tsunami necessitated the closure of major ports, hindering production and exports. The crisis and the failure of government leaders to respond effectively afterwards caused Prime Minister Naoto Kan to lose his job in August 2011 and be replaced by the Democratic Party of Japan's Yoshihiko Noda. Noda became the sixth prime minister in five years.

EARTHQUAKE AND TSUNAMI

On March 11, 2011, at 2:46 p.m. local time, an earthquake struck off the coast of Japan, more than 150 miles northeast of Tokyo. Originally recorded at a magnitude of 8.8 on the Richter scale, the strength was later upgraded to a 9.0, making it the strongest recorded earthquake in Japanese history, and the fifth largest in the world since 1900. The quake caused a tsunami that washed away entire towns in the northern portion of Japan, pulling homes, cars, boats, trains, and the people in them out to sea. The tsunami was so strong that it triggered warnings on the west coasts of the United States and South America. "The earthquake, tsunami, and the nuclear incident have been the biggest crisis Japan has encountered in the 65 years since the end of the Second World War," Prime Minister Naoto Kan said. "We're under scrutiny on whether we, the Japanese people, can overcome this crisis."

Damage in the northern part of the nation was mainly localized, but completely devastated some towns, specifically those in Miyagi prefecture in the northeastern part of the country closest to the epicenter of the earthquake, where entire towns were completely wiped out. With more than 900,000 buildings destroyed or badly damaged and hundreds of thousands left homeless, Japanese citizens found themselves in community centers and makeshift shelters, where many stayed for months, living on straw mats on concrete floors, even in freezing cold temperatures. Here, they could find lists of those who had survived the disaster and those who had died. With limited Internet and telephone service, access to information on the fate of family members, friends, homes, and possessions was scarce. Added to this were rolling blackouts across the country, even in energy-hungry Tokyo, initiated in order to reduce the demand on the electric power system. Population centers like Tokyo came to a standstill as train service was suspended, stranding workers in their offices. Nearly 6 million households, or approximately 10 percent of the country, were left without power following the earthquake and tsunami and 1.5 million were left without water. Powerful aftershocks, which seismologists said could go on for a decade or more, put further stress on the already strained psyche of the Japanese people.

The strength and resilience of the Japanese people immediately shone through the damage, with citizens who had lost their entire families helping neighbors dig for loved ones and possessions. The prime minister did his part to try and rally his compatriots. "We Japanese had a lot of difficulties in the past, but we were able to overcome those difficulties to reach this peaceful and prosperous society we have been able to build," he said. "So with regard to the earthquake and tsunami, I am confident that the Japanese people can be united to work together."

INTERNATIONAL ASSISTANCE

As Japan sent 100,000 of its own troops for search, rescue, and recovery operations, and released $2.5 billion for relief efforts, assistance poured in from around the world, even from the smallest and most unlikely of sources, including Kandahar, Afghanistan. "I know $50,000 is not a lot of money for a country like Japan," said Kandahar's mayor Ghulam Haidar Hamidi, "but it is a show of appreciation from the Kandahar people." As of March 19, 2011, 128 countries and 33 international organizations offered assistance to Japan that included monetary resources, manpower, food, and rescue supplies. Even with the level of assistance, early in the recovery only 10 percent of supplies were being received by the people in the areas hardest hit by the earthquake and tsunami. "Rescue and relief operations are being hampered by continuous aftershocks, tsunami alerts and fires," the United Nations Office for the Coordination of Humanitarian Affairs said. "Many areas along the north-east coast remain isolated and unreachable."

Prior to March 11, the most devastating earthquake to strike Japan in recent history hit near the port city of Kobe in 1995. Until the March disaster, it was the most expensive natural disaster in history, causing $100 billion in damage. Using the Kobe disaster as a key indicator, the World Bank estimated that damage from the 2011 disasters could amount to between $122 billion and $235 billion, and that rebuilding could take up to five years. One bright spot in the World Bank report was in regards to trade. Immediately after the earthquake, all Japanese ports were closed costing the nation an estimated $3.4 billion each day. However, after the Kobe earthquake, which knocked out a major port, exports managed to recover to 85 percent of prequake levels within one year. "In the immediate future the biggest impact will be in terms of trade and finance," said World Bank economist Vikram Nehru in a news release. "We expect growth in Japan will pick up as reconstruction efforts accelerate."

NUCLEAR CRISIS

The twin disasters caused a major nuclear crisis at the Fukushima Daiichi Nuclear Power Station. Considered to be the worst nuclear crisis since the Chernobyl nuclear disaster in Ukraine in 1986, three reactors at the power station experienced explosions and leaked radioactive gas. The Japanese government was slow to release information on the effect of the disasters on the nuclear plant, and it was not until the International Atomic Energy Agency (IAEA) stepped in to assist that evacuations of those within a twelve-mile radius around the plant began.

The earthquake, tsunami, and subsequent loss of electricity caused the cooling system at the Fukushima Daiichi plant to fail, which permitted pressure to build up within the reactors. To help relieve the pressure, radioactive gas was intentionally released from the reactors, but Japanese health officials promised that the gas would cause no negative health effects. The release of pressure was not enough to prevent an explosion in one of the reactors, which led to a dangerous drop in water levels and exposed the fuel rods. The two other reactors that were fully online prior to the earthquake experienced similar explosions, and plant engineers rushed to use sea water to cool the reactors and cover exposed fuel rods. The United States offered coolant to the Japanese for the reactors, but it was refused. The exposed fuel rods raised fears of a full or partial meltdown of the power plant, although the IAEA cautioned that it was unlikely the disaster would turn into a crisis as severe as that at Chernobyl because of the containment structures in place.

The Japanese government faced domestic and international criticism for not informing the public quickly enough about the severity of the nuclear crisis. Withholding information in this manner is not uncommon in Japan. Former government officials came forward after the crisis to state that information had been withheld primarily to prevent additional evacuations in a country with little land to spare and to stop the questioning of government policy and the nuclear industry. Three top Japanese nuclear officials lost their jobs over the nuclear crisis, including the vice minister for economy, trade, and industry; the head of the Nuclear and Industrial Safety Agency; and the head of the Agency for Natural Resources and Energy.

Employees at the Fukushima Daiichi power plant, who were hailed in the local press as heroes, worked around the clock to prevent a meltdown. However, the impact of the release of radiation was quickly felt in Japan and in nearby countries. Radiation was found in crops and in the water supply. In Tokyo and five prefectures to the north and east, ninety-nine products including milk and vegetables were found to be contaminated. The government expected the number of contaminated products to rise as testing continued. More than 70 percent of food exports from Japan go to Hong Kong, the United States, China, Taiwan, and South Korea, and a number of those nations announced that they would begin testing all imports for radiation. Singapore, another key distribution point for Japanese goods, halted all fruit, vegetable, milk, seafood, and meat imports from certain parts of Japan. The government released an additional warning to farmers, asking them to delay planting rice and other ground crops for fear of soil contamination. Coastal areas of the United States and Canada increased radiation sampling because of the isotopes released into the Pacific Ocean, but only a minimal spike in radiation levels was found and it had no reported effects.

The nuclear crisis, sparked by the loss of electricity and subsequent cooling system failures, led to three of the nation's fifty-four nuclear reactors being permanently taken off-line. These three plants, which suffered extensive damage, had contributed 3 percent of Japan's power supply. Additional reactors were closed, and had their reopening postponed. By the end of 2011, only ten of the country's nuclear reactors were producing electricity. Prior to the disaster in March, nuclear power plants had been providing 30 percent of the nation's electricity. In an attempt to make up for some of the energy loss, power companies, including Tokyo Electric Power Company (TEPCO), ordered users to cut consumption by at least 15 percent, but recognized the move could only be a temporary measure. To close the energy gap, Japan's government will be forced to rethink its policy of decreasing importation and use of natural gas, coal, and oil, in favor of nuclear power. Outside of Japan, questions were raised around the world as to the safety of nuclear power. Taking perhaps the most drastic step to date, Germany made a decision to phase out all use of nuclear energy by 2022.

ECONOMIC RECOVERY

Japan's economic growth has largely been stagnant for the past two decades. Once an economic powerhouse, it had been predicted that Japan would surpass the United States as the world's largest economy by 2010. The country grew following World War II and then rode stock and real estate bubbles in the 1980s, challenging the dominant economies of the West. But in the late 1980s and early 1990s, the country fell into decline after the real estate and stock bubbles burst. Since that time, Japan's economy has been in a constant state of deflation. By the second quarter of 2010, China overtook Japan to become the world's second largest economy. In 2010, Japan's economy was the same size as it was in 1991, with a GDP of $5.7 trillion. Attempts made in early to mid-2010 to jump-start the economy with new spending measures and a $1 trillion budget have done little to raise the nation's economic prospects. In January 2011, Standard & Poor's, the credit rating agency, downgraded Japan's long-term sovereign debt rating to AA-, the first downgrade of Japanese government debt since 2002, stating that the country had no strategy to shore up its government debt.

Following the earthquake and tsunami, widespread fear of even greater economic crisis grew. Immediately after the dual disaster, the Bank of Japan injected $61.2 billion into the financial system, one day after pumping trillions into money markets and easing monetary policies. Despite the investments, stock markets fell around the world. A major fear of Japanese manufacturers—specifically those in the auto and technology industries—was that if forced to stop production at their plants for too long, the effects could be devastating. Downstream impact on companies that import materials and products from Japan were expected as well.

By November, a strong recovery was indicated, with an annualized rate of 6 percent growth in the third quarter of 2011. Exports and consumption began to rebound, with exports up 6.2 percent and private consumption up 1 percent. Factories and supply chains were quickly rebuilt and reestablished following the March disasters, and in the three months from July through September, Japan's GDP expanded 1.5 percent as compared to the previous quarter, making it the first expansion in four quarters.

—Heather Kerrigan

Following is a statement by Japanese Prime Minister Naoto Kan on March 11, 2011, in regard to the earthquake and tsunami; a statement by Prime Minister Kan on March 15, 2011, in regard to the nuclear crisis; and the edited text of a press conference held by Prime Minister Kan on April 1, 2011, responding to media inquiries on the earthquake recovery efforts and ongoing nuclear crisis.

Prime Minister Naoto Kan on the Earthquake and Tsunami

March 11, 2011

My fellow citizens, as you are already aware from reports on TV and on the radio, today at 2:46 PM an enormously powerful earthquake of Magnitude 8.4 struck, with its seismic center off the Sanriku coast. This has resulted in tremendous damage across a wide area, centered on the Tohoku district. I extend my heartfelt sympathy to those who have suffered.

As for our nuclear power facilities, a portion of them stopped their operations automatically. At present we have no reports of any radioactive materials or otherwise affecting the surrounding areas.

In light of these circumstances, I immediately established an emergency headquarters for response to disaster, with myself as the head. The government will make every possible effort to ensure the safety of the public and keep damage to the minimum possible extent.

I ask the public to continue to stay fully vigilant and to keep abreast of TV and radio reports, and I ask everyone to act calmly.

Source: Prime Minister of Japan and His Cabinet. Speeches and Statements. "Statement by Prime Minister Naoto Kan on Tohoku District—off the Pacific Ocean Earthquake." March 11, 2011. http://www.kantei.go.jp/foreign/kan/statement/201103/11kishahappyo_e.html.

Prime Minister Naoto Kan
on the Nuclear Crisis

March 15, 2011

I want to inform the people of Japan about the situation regarding the Fukushima Nuclear Power Stations. I urge you to please listen calmly to this information.

As I explained previously, the reactor at the Fukushima Daiichi Nuclear Power Station was shut off following the earthquake and tsunami, but none of the diesel engines that would normally power the emergency cooling system are in a functioning state. We have been using every means at our disposal to cool the nuclear reactors. However, the concentration of radioactivity being leaked into the vicinity of the station has risen considerably following hydrogen explosions caused by hydrogen produced at the Unit 1 and Unit 3 reactors, and a fire in the Unit 4 reactor. There is a heightened risk of even further leakage of radioactive material.

Most residents have already evacuated beyond the 20km radius of the Fukushima Daiichi Nuclear Power Station, but let me reiterate the need for everyone living within that radius to evacuate to a point outside of it.

Moreover, in view of the developing situation, those who are outside the 20km radius but still within a 30km radius should remain indoors in their house, office, or other structure, and not go outside. Further, with regard to the Fukushima Daini Nuclear Power Station, most people have already evacuated beyond a 10km radius but we are calling for everyone who remains within that radius to fully evacuate to a point beyond it.

At present we are doing everything possible to prevent further explosions or leakage of radioactive material. At this moment, Tokyo Electric Power Company (TEPCO) workers in particular are taking great personal risks in their tireless efforts to supply water to the reactor. I realize that people in Japan are greatly concerned about the situation but I sincerely urge everyone to act in a calm manner, bearing in mind the tremendous efforts underway to prevent further radiation leaks.

This concludes my request to the people of Japan at this moment.

Source: Prime Minister of Japan and His Cabinet. Speeches and Statements. "Message From the Prime Minister." March 15, 2011. http://www.kantei.go.jp/foreign/kan/statement/201103/15message_e.html.

Prime Minister Naoto Kan Holds Press Conference on Ongoing Recovery

DOCUMENT

April 1, 2011

CABINET PUBLIC RELATIONS SECRETARY: We will now begin the press conference with Prime Minister Naoto Kan. Prime Minister, your opening statement please.

Opening Statement by Prime Minister Naoto Kan

PRIME MINISTER KAN: Three weeks have now passed since the earthquake. A moment ago in a round robin Cabinet meeting we decided to officially name the disaster the Great East Japan Earthquake. I want to once again offer my heartfelt condolences to the families of those who perished in the earthquake, as well as my deepest sympathy for everyone affected by this disaster. To those in local governments, the Self-Defense Forces (SDF), fire departments, police bureaus, and to everyone else risking their lives to assist with the relief effort: you have my sincere respect. I am proud to command such incredible public servants.

I would also like to use this opportunity to once again express my gratitude for many offers of support Japan has received from all over the world.

Today is April 1. It is the start of a new fiscal year, and we have already successfully passed the budget as well as a portion of related legislation through the Diet. The Great East Japan Earthquake occurred after the budget had been submitted. We must now prioritize support for those affected by this disaster as well as policy toward reconstruction. To this end, although we already have a set budget, we will rescind a portion of it while beginning preparations of a supplementary budget. We will use some of the funds in the current budget to support those affected by the earthquake. We have been considering the necessity of implementing the budget for reconstruction in several stages in line with the requirements of this process. With the first round of funding, we will clear out rubble, build temporary housing, support reemployment and help businesses start to rebuild. We are currently preparing funding for this. I hope to finalize the first supplementary budget and submit it to the Diet within April.

We must then begin preparations toward reconstruction. In fact, we will go beyond mere reconstruction, creating an even better Tohoku and even better Japan. We are moving forward with the creation of a reconstruction plan that has this big dream at its core. I have received many opinions over the telephone from the mayors of each city, town and village in the disaster-stricken area. These opinions will be incorporated into the plan for instance, in some areas we will level parts of mountains in order to create plateaus for people to live on. Those residing in the area will then commute to the shoreline if they work in ports or the fisheries industry. We will create eco-towns, places which use biomass and plant-based fuel to provide natural heating. We will outfit cities with infrastructure to support the elderly. We aim to create new kinds of towns that will become models for the rest of the world.

In the course of reconstruction, reemployment will be a major issue. The disaster-stricken region is home to many parts manufacturers, farmers and fishermen. The area's fisheries industry in particular has always thrived. We must revitalize these primary industries without fail.

In drafting a plan for reconstruction we must call upon the opinions of experts and those with a stake in the future of the region. I hope to bring a group of such people together to form a Reconstruction Design Council by April 11, exactly one month after the disaster occurred. At the same time, we will create a system in the Government to actualize the proposals and plans created by this Council. I want to create this system within this month as well.

We have received many positive offers of cooperation for reconstruction activities from those in opposition parties. We will establish a system by which to promote cross-party cooperation. It is my absolute hope that we will be successful with this.

Next, I would like to discuss the Fukushima Nuclear Power Plants. We have carried out work thus far based on three principles, and we will continue to do so.

Our first principle is that we must prioritize the health and safety of the people of Japan.

Our second principle is that we must implement risk management initiatives to such an extent that some in the public feel we are being too cautious.

Our third principle is that we must conceive of every possible scenario and prepare response systems that can deal with each scenario should it occur.

We are currently proceeding with work under these three principles.

We are organizing our efforts around two cooperation initiatives in order to return the power plants to a stable condition.

The first hardly needs to be mentioned. The Government, Tokyo Electric Power Company (TEPCO) and related enterprises, the Japan Atomic Energy Commission (JAEC) and other expert groups are exerting every effort for cooperation to address this problem. We have been doing so for some time and will continue to do so.

The second is international cooperation. Experts from other countries, in particular the United States, are already fully involved in the response effort, participating in joint operations with us. I spoke with US President Obama a few days ago and he again promised the full cooperation of the United States. Yesterday, French President Sarkozy visited Japan and told me that as the leader of a country possessing advanced nuclear technology and as chair of the G8 and G20, he would offer France's full cooperation and would send experts to help us.

In addition, the International Atomic Energy Agency (IAEA) has dispatched experts, and is currently assisting us with a variety of operations. We are prepared for a long struggle at the power plants, and we will not give up until we have succeeded. We will continue to work with this resolve. Although we have caused much inconvenience to the people of Japan, I promise everyone that we will overcome this issue and restore the country to a state of complete safety.

The earthquake three weeks ago was truly horrific. However, in the time since then, I have seen some truly heart-warming scenes. People in and outside of Japan have come together to help our country overcome this disaster. Our efforts are now gathering momentum.

It has been sometimes said in Japan that the bonds between us Japanese are weakening. Since the earthquake, those in local governments, in industry, in NPOs, as well as many individuals across the country have voluntarily offered their support and cooperation to help us overcome this disaster. I believe that our renewed bonds will reach across the nation and lead us to a wonderful tomorrow. I am confident that we have a bright future ahead of us.

The late physicist Dr. Torahiko Terada wrote numerous essays about disaster. Among them, he noted that the practice of offering aid in times of trouble is deeply rooted in the nature of the Japanese as a custom passed down from generation to generation since ancient times.

I am certain that we will overcome the Great East Japan Earthquake, strengthen our mutual bonds and rebuild our great nation. With these opening remarks I pledge that I, my Cabinet, and everyone in the Government will make this happen. With this I conclude my opening remarks. Thank you for your attention.

Q&As

CABINET PUBLIC RELATIONS SECRETARY: We will now move on to the Q&A session. Although I will be calling on you to ask questions, we would appreciate it if you would still state your name and affiliation. Thank you. Aoyama-san, please.

REPORTER: I am Aoyama of Nippon TV. I would like to ask a question about Fukushima Daiichi Nuclear Power Plant. Three weeks have passed since the earthquake. It has been a time of great uncertainty not just for those living around the plant but for the entire nation, and this state continues. Up until now you have said that you cannot make any predictions, but what is your understanding of the current situation? Also, what steps or responses do you think should be undertaken to draw the situation at the plant to a close? Please tell us in detail what options there are to avoid the worst possible outcome. Additionally, please also tell us your frank thoughts about your objectives or goals for when you think this situation will calm down.

PRIME MINISTER KAN: I first wish to say that I am very sorry to those who have inconvenienced by calling for an evacuation around the power plants as well as those who have suffered losses regarding vegetables and other matters in various ways.

Regarding the current situation at the power plants, as I stated a moment ago we are gathering opinions from experts and working to stabilize the situation. At the current stage, we have not yet reached a point of sufficient stability. However, as I said earlier, we are preparing for every possibility, and I believe that we will definitely reach our goal.

As for a timeframe for this, at the current moment in time I cannot say anything for sure. We are working as hard as we can. This is all I can say. . . .

REPORTER: I am Yamaguchi of NHK. I would like to ask about reconstruction financing. You said that just reallocating a portion of the budget would not free up enough funds. Are you considering increasing the national debt? Or will you consider tax hikes? Are there other options? Please tell us your thoughts.

PRIME MINISTER KAN: As I said just now, although we have established a budget for the current fiscal year, we will be freezing a portion of this budget. It should be obvious that this alone will not be enough. How we can come up with the additional funding we need is going to be an important theme for the Reconstruction Design Council. At the same time, if we do not receive the cooperation or the agreement of opposition parties we will not be able to pass such a budget and related legislation, so I hope that we will be able to discuss this and reach a consensus. These are my thoughts on these issues. . . .

REPORTER: I am Sakajiri of the Asahi Shimbun. My question concerns the nuclear power plant. Previously, it seemed like Japan was trying to resolve this issue on its own, using the SDF and fire departments, but recently the emphasis has been placed on obtaining cooperation from the international community, as you mentioned in your opening statement. Put another way, does this mean that the situation is so serious that it requires the collective wisdom of the international community?

My other question concerns the specific options available for work at the power plants. The current situation at the Fukushima Daiichi Nuclear Power Plant is one in which reactors must be cooled by any means. While continuing the injection of pure water for this purpose, we must also work to treat contaminated water. Workers seem to be stuck running back and forth between two different jobs. Will this continue for some time, or are any other specific options feasible?

PRIME MINISTER KAN: Concerning the international community, the United States has been making various proposals from a very early stage. At least, as far as I know, we have gladly accepted almost all of their offers, and all that are necessary. Currently, discussion is being held every day, mainly at the Integrated Headquarters with the U.S. experts, and also with utility operators, the Nuclear and Industrial Safety Commissions (NISA), and the Nuclear Safety Commission (NSC). Various preparations are being made. In that sense, we have been cooperating with other countries, especially with the United States, on all matters, in order to respond to the nuclear incident, from the very beginning. In addition to the United States, France, the IAEA, and many other countries have proposed assistance regarding the nuclear incident, as I mentioned previously. We are going to receive a considerable amount of cooperation from them.

You also asked what options are available. This has been principally discussed by each group of experts, and based on their discussion we are proceeding with daily measures in a planned way. My understanding is that cooling is an extremely important operation and that this must be continued. At the same time, the resulting water contamination and other problems currently arising must be thoroughly addressed. We must see that the cooling operation leads to the full recovery of its functions. That I think is the first goal we must aim for. I hope this answers your question. . . .

REPORTER: I am Motobashira from Kahoku Online Network. My question concerns economic compensation for those affected by the disaster. Many people who are currently in evacuation shelters have lost everything due to the tsunami. I don't think the current Law to Provide Assistance for the Recovery of the Livelihoods of those Affected by Disasters would allow these people to rebuild houses and lead normal lives again in their home towns, due to the variability in the amount of allowance given. I believe the matter has also been discussed within the Government, I want to hear your current opinions about revising or expanding the scope of the said Law as well as generating employment in these regions, which will be a major issue going forward.

PRIME MINISTER KAN: I would like to again extend my words of apology and encouragement to all the people in Miyagi, Fukushima, Iwate, and other prefectures in the Tohoku Region, as well as a certain parts of the Kanto Region, who have suffered a tremendous loss and are having a difficult time.

Concerning the policy of assisting individual disaster victims, including whether or not the amount of allowance will be increased, as you suggested, to the extent possible I would like to do my best to provide them with sufficient assistance.

Concerning employment, I think some of these people can be hired for various kinds of work handled by local governments, such as the clearing of rubble. And then we must revive the industrial infrastructure to generate new jobs and recover lost jobs. I think that process is extremely important. . . .

REPORTER: I am Nanao from Nico Nico Douga. The evacuation zones around the Fukushima Daiichi and Daini Nuclear Power Plants are still being disputed, and the people, especially those living around the zone, are not sure what to trust.

When you met with President Sarkozy yesterday, a proposal was made to discuss the safety standards of nuclear power plants at the G8 and in other international fora. In addition to this, do you have any intention to set an international standard about evacuation zones in the event of a nuclear accident? Don't you think that this would give assurance to the people and prevent harmful rumors from arising?

PRIME MINISTER KAN: I exchanged opinions on various topics yesterday with President Sarkozy. Among these topics, we talked about discussing and establishing international safety standards about the safety of nuclear reactors and power plants during an international meeting. We didn't discuss if the topics should include a standard rule about evacuation zones. I said that such a rule is needed for nuclear reactors, as a start.

Currently, as you are aware, the NSC gives advice to the Government from the perspective of experts. These experts make proposals based on various kinds of monitoring operations and in consideration of the various efforts being made at the nuclear power plants. The scope of the safety measures has been decided based on such proposals, and we have been assuring the people that there will be no threat to human health as long as they observe these standards. . . .

REPORTER: I am Indo from the Nihon Keizai Shimbun. I would like to ask about your overall vision for the nuclear energy policy. Yesterday, I believe President Sarkozy sent out the message that in terms of safety, discussions will be conducted out of a need to establish rigorous standards, and that France will be going ahead with its nuclear energy policy.

You indicated you will consider Japan's nuclear energy policy bearing in mind the verifications made about the accident. However, news reports about your meeting with Japanese Communist Party (JCP) Leader Kazuo Shii prior to your meeting with Mr. Sarkozy only headlined the energy plan being reviewed. Are your intentions to move forward with nuclear energy? Or are you considering alternative energies and scrapping nuclear power programs altogether? Which is your overall vision?

PRIME MINISTER KAN: First of all, the accident is of course the biggest in Japan's history of nuclear power accidents. Internationally, while there has been an even bigger accident, the ongoing incident is one of the biggest accidents to unfold. Therefore, first and foremost, the starting point for beginning anew must be to conduct a thorough verification once this problem has stabilized to some extent. I believe everybody will agree with me on this.

And so, in that context, we will begin with a thorough verification from the stage that this problem is a little more stabilized. I believe through the verifications, it will gradually become clear what level of safety will need to be ensured to reassure the people of Japan and so on. Rather than having some vision in advance, we will start with verifications. Although reference has been made to reviewing the energy policy, what I was saying is that the existing plans for nuclear power plants obviously need to be reviewed under the forthcoming verifications to see whether sufficient safety is ensured or not. I was not making a conclusive statement about abandoning all plans or going forward with all plans. . . .

REPORTER: I am Hatakeyama, a freelance reporter. I have a question about the shelter in place advisory for the 20 to 30km zone. The emergency response manuals for nuclear power accidents of the IAEA, the U.S. Environmental Protection Agency, France, and the European Commission state that wooden buildings are hardly expected to reduce external radiation exposure. Furthermore, with regards to shelter in place to reduce internal radiation exposure due to inhalation, the manuals recommend a period not exceeding around 48 hours as permissible. Beyond that, they say the sheltering measure should be removed or an evacuation should be decided to cope with the situation. Already three weeks have passed. Twenty thousand people still remain in the shelter in place zone, and this being a sheltering zone, supplies are not reaching smoothly and peoples' lives are extremely inconvenienced. Nevertheless, the shelter in place measure, which cannot be expected to reduce internal radiation exposure, has not been removed. Could you tell us why?

PRIME MINISTER KAN: First, as I have noted earlier, these decisions about evacuation or sheltering are made in respect to the advice sought and received from the NSC in principle, while of course we also seek the various opinions of many others. Such was the process behind arriving at the current decision that, while in principle areas beyond the 20 km zone are safe, people living in the 20 to 30km zone will be alright if they stay indoors.

However, as you mentioned, we are also aware of the fact that problems slightly different from the safety issues are arising in peoples' day-to-day lives, such as for instance supplies are extremely difficult to reach the 20 to 30km zone. The respective municipalities and response headquarters are responding. At the same time, we are also exchanging views with the NSC and the local municipalities on how these problems should be coped with, including what is socially appropriate. That is where we are right now. . . .

Source: Prime Minister of Japan and His Cabinet. Speeches and Statements. "Press Conference by Prime Minister Naoto Kan." April 1, 2011. http://www.kantei.go.jp/foreign/kan/statement/201104/01kaiken_e .html.

Other Historic Documents of Interest

From previous *Historic Documents*

- China Surpasses Japan to Become the World's Second Largest Economy, *2010*, p. 360
- Democratic Party Wins Landmark Election in Japan, *2009*, p. 449
- Japanese Prime Minister on Economic Crisis, *1998*, p. 532
- Chernobyl Nuclear Accident, *1986*, p. 383

Arab Spring: Syrian Government's Violent Crackdown on Protests

MARCH 18 AND 26, AND NOVEMBER 23, 2011

Inspired by the events taking place across the Middle East in early 2011, protesters in Syria began coming together to decry the actions of the government of President Bashar al-Assad and his security forces, specifically those involving unlawful torture and detention. The protesters first called on the government to end corruption and institute political reform that would end one-party rule, but after Assad's government violently cracked down on the protests, killing at least 3,500 and arresting countless others, the object of their demands became Assad's removal from office. Assad made a number of promises of reform to the protesters, only to continue using force to dispel their demonstrations. Syria has long been secretive about its internal affairs, keeping its borders closed to most foreigners, making it difficult for the United Nations and other international groups to work with the government to end the violence and foster more transparent governance. In early 2012, former UN Secretary General Kofi Annan negotiated a ceasefire with Assad, set to take effect on April 10. Although Assad agreed to the terms of the ceasefire, there is no indication that he will follow through.

INSPIRED BY ARAB SPRING

Demonstrations against the government of President Bashar al-Assad began in March 2011 in the small southern city of Dara'a, where protesters spoke out against the treatment of students who were arrested and tortured by government security forces for writing antigovernment graffiti. In response to the demonstrations, Assad called the protesters "terrorists" and sent tanks into the region.

Following the events in Dara'a, peaceful protests spread to Al Ladhiqiyah, Baniyas, Damascus, Dayr Az Zawr, Homs, Hama, and Idlib. Inspired by the ongoing protests around the Middle East, on March 15 Syrians came together in Damascus for what they called a Day of Dignity. When the protesters gathered in Damascus, their first calls were for an end to government corruption and new political reforms. When the government failed to cooperate and instead used violence to dispel the protesters, their objective became the downfall of Assad's regime. Large military operations took place in Dara'a on April 25 in the government's strongest show of force to date. During the demonstrations, thousands were arrested or injured, and another 10,000 fled to safety in Turkey. After his cabinet resigned on March 29, Assad sought to quell the demonstrations by appointing a new prime minister and calling for an end to emergency laws that had been in place for decades. However, the lifting of the state of emergency was immediately followed by another round of violent crackdowns on protesters. Additional tanks moved into cities where uprisings were starting, and security forces were given the authority to fire on demonstrators. Assad appeared on national television in March, stating that the government had been targeted by violent demonstrators, and claiming that a number of the protests were fueled by foreign governments. Assad said his government was "facing a great conspiracy," and that those involved were spreading misinformation concerning the government response to the demonstrations in an effort to gain support for their cause.

Prior to the March uprising, Syrians enjoyed few Internet freedoms, and Assad kept tight control over the flow of information. Following periodic Internet outages, Assad's government shut down most Internet and mobile data access in June. Activists were undeterred and began smuggling phones and computers across the Syrian border, using them to upload videos and photos of the violence to those outside of the country, who would disseminate the information. According to an NBC News report from inside Syria, some activists had acquired encryption software from the U.S. State Department that allowed them to work around government firewalls. Unlike people of other nations swept up in prodemocracy movements during the spring of 2011 who took to social media outlets to organize protests, activists in Syria used websites like Facebook, Twitter, and YouTube mainly to keep international media outlets apprised of the situation in the country.

Long fraught with ethnic divisions, Syria experienced earlier discontent in 1982 when the Muslim Brotherhood led demonstrations against the government, which responded by sending in troops and killing at least 10,000 people. Many leaders in the opposition movement were jailed and never seen again. Assad, who belongs to the minority Alawite sect in a nation where Sunnis make up a majority of the population, has retained power by instilling fear in the population, commanding the loyalty of his sect, and maintaining a strong hold over the government's security forces.

Assad Responds

Assad made a number of indications that he would be willing to work with the opposition. The protesters demanded the end of Assad's regime, an end to the forty-eight-year state of emergency, an end to torture and killings, a release of political prisoners, a transition to democracy, freedom of the media, an independent judiciary, and compensation for political exiles.

In April, Assad responded to the demands of the protesters by promising some political reform, but reiterated that he had no intention of stepping down from his post. Assad offered to officially end the state of emergency on April 21, form a new government, and give citizens new rights to participate in peaceful demonstrations. Assad also offered amnesty for political prisoners beginning on May 31, a review of possible constitutional reforms, and a review of a new election law that would allow for political parties other than the Baath Party to form in the nation. To make good on his promises of government reform, on June 1 Assad formed the National Dialogue Committee, a group which he said would be tasked with making recommendations to his government on how to move Syria from one-party to multiparty rule. Less than a week later, however, Assad inflamed demonstrators by again calling their acts criminal and condemning the deaths of government military and security forces.

In an effort to force Assad to act, in October members of the opposition formed the Syrian National Council to bring together groups with the goal of overthrowing Assad's government. The new coalition featured members of the Damascus Declaration group, the Syrian Muslim Brotherhood, Kurdish factions, Local Coordination Committees, and other tribal and independent opposition groups. The Syrian National Council refused to work with Assad's government toward reform; opposed foreign military intervention in the nation; and promoted human rights, an independent judiciary, press freedom, and democracy. Two other coalition groups formed in August and September of 2011. The first, the Free Syrian Army (FSA), was created by army deserters who wanted to "work hand in hand with the people to achieve freedom and dignity, topple the regime, protect the revolution and the country's resources and stand up to the irresponsible military machine which is protecting the regime." The group claimed to have a membership of 15,000 by October 2011. The National Coordination Committee, formed in September 2011, was comprised of opposition blocs in Syria and called for peaceful change, no military intervention, and for Assad's government to play a role in a transition to democracy, fearing chaos if the current government were to simply be toppled.

During the summer and fall of 2011, Assad made a number of indications that he was working to follow through on government reform. On August 4, he announced new rules governing political parties and a new election law. On August 28, Assad announced the writing of a new law governing media coverage that would increase journalists's access to information and prevent them from being jailed. In September, the president proposed holding elections on December 14 that would be held under the new election laws and include members of various political parties. By October, Assad said that he had established another committee that was being placed in charge of preparing a new constitution for the country that would be voted on by the public within four months.

In November, Assad promised, in line with an agreement with the Arab League, to withdraw his troops from cities where demonstrations were taking place and to direct these troops to stop killing protesters. This peace deal would help Syria move toward additional political reforms, working in cooperation with opposition groups. Assad also followed through on his political prisoner amnesty promise, releasing 553 detainees on November 5 and another 1,180 on November 15.

Despite the progress, crackdowns intensified and the country grew closer to civil war. Syrian military forces carried out operations against protesters in Homs, Dara'a, Hama, Dayr Az Zawr, and Rif Damascus. The forces made funerals and any other public gatherings a target of their violence. Assad said on November 20 that if any innocent civilians had been killed during these crackdowns, it was a mistake, and would be investigated at a later date. He called the military actions necessary to protect the citizens of Syria and stop those who intended to throw the nation into chaos.

INTERNATIONAL REACTION

Since the beginning of Assad's crackdown on demonstrations, nations around the world called on the Syrian leader to stop hindering peaceful protests and killing those involved. The United Nations expressed concern when the first hints of violence broke out in March in Dara'a. "It is the responsibility of the Government in Syria to listen to the legitimate aspirations of the people and address them through inclusive political dialogue and genuine reforms, not repression," said UN Secretary General Ban Ki-moon.

Once the agreements Assad had worked out with the Arab League fell through and the violence continued, world leaders called on Assad to step down from his position. On November 22, Turkey's government called on Assad to resign. "For the welfare of your own people and the region, just leave that seat," said Turkey's Prime Minister Recep Tayyip Erdogan. "If you want to see someone who has fought until death against his own people, just look at Nazi Germany, just look at Hitler, at Mussolini, at Nicolae Ceausescu in

Romania." He continued, "If you cannot draw any lessons from these, then look at the Libyan leader who was killed just 32 days ago."

In November, the United Nations General Assembly Human Rights Committee issued a condemnation of Assad's crackdown on the protests. Syria's ambassador to the United Nations said the condemnation had no meaning for his country. "Despite the fact that the draft resolution was basically presented by three European states, however it is no secret that the United States of America is ... the main mind behind the political campaign against my country," said Bashar Jaafari. "This draft resolution has no relevance to human rights, other than it is part of an adversarial American policy against my country." Jaafari further accused the United States of attempting to topple Assad's regime.

Human Rights Abuses

On November 23, 2011, the United Nations General Assembly Human Rights Council issued a report on human rights violations in Syria. According to the report, "The substantial body of evidence gathered by the commission indicates that these gross violations of human rights have been committed by Syrian military and security forces since the beginning of the protests in March 2011." The report found that those killed by government forces from March 2011 through November 2011 numbered at least 3,500. The General Assembly's report called on Assad's government "to put an immediate end to the ongoing gross human rights violations, to initiate independent and impartial investigations of these violations and to bring perpetrators to justice."

—Heather Kerrigan

Following are two press releases issued by the United Nations on March 18 and March 26, 2011, expressing concern at the Syrian government's violent crackdown on antigovernment demonstrations; and a report issued on November 23, 2011, by the United Nations General Assembly Human Rights Council on human rights violations committed by the Syrian government against antigovernment demonstrators.

United Nations Secretary General Expresses Concern Over Use of Force in Syria

March 18, 2011

Secretary-General Ban Ki-moon has voiced concern about today's reported killing of unarmed demonstrators in a Syrian town, describing the use of lethal force against peaceful protesters as unacceptable.

Media reports state that at least two people died after security forces opened fire at the protest in the southern town of Der'a earlier today.

Syria is one of many countries in the Middle East and North Africa to face public protests this year amid widespread calls for reform in the region.

In a statement issued by his spokesperson Mr. Ban urged Syrian authorities "to refrain from violence and to abide by their international commitments regarding human rights, which guarantee the freedom of opinion and expression, including the freedom of the press and the right to peaceful assembly."

The Secretary-General stressed that, "as elsewhere, it is the responsibility of the Government in Syria to listen to the legitimate aspirations of the people and address them through inclusive political dialogue and genuine reforms, not repression."

The deaths of the Syrian demonstrators have occurred on the same day that security forces opened fire on peaceful protesters in Yemen, killing more than 30 people. Protests and violent clashes have also taken place in recent weeks in Bahrain.

SOURCE: United Nations. UN News Centre. "Killing of Syrian Protesters Sparks Concern From UN Chief." March 18, 2011. http://www.un.org/apps/news/story.asp?NewsID=37819&Cr=syria&Cr1=.

DOCUMENT

UN Human Rights Chief Expresses Concern Over Violence in Syria

March 26, 2011

The United Nations human rights chief on Saturday urged Syria to listen to the voices of its people who are rising up and demanding change in the country, warning that continued killing of protesters will only lead to more anger and violence.

The demonstrations in Syria are part of a broader protest movement that has swept the Middle East and North Africa since the start of the year, toppling long-standing regimes in Tunisia and Egypt and leading to fierce fighting in Libya.

Media reports say around 55 people have been killed in unrest in Syria over the past week, including two children.

High Commissioner for Human Rights Navi Pillay called on Syria "to draw lessons from recent events across the Middle East and North Africa which clearly demonstrate that violent repression of peaceful protest not only does not resolve the grievances of people taking to the streets, it risks creating a downward spiral of anger, violence, killings and chaos."

She pointed out that the use of force by authorities in other countries has not succeeded in quelling discontent, but only led to fuelling frustration and anger.

Indeed, she added, the use of force to suppress initial peaceful protests in Tunisia, Egypt, Libya, Yemen and Bahrain only contributed to a rapid deterioration in the situation, as well as many deaths and injuries.

"If those governments had responded more thoughtfully, without violence, to the demands of the people, so much death, so much destruction, so much of the fear and uncertainty faced by ordinary people could have been averted," said Ms. Pillay.

"The Syrian people are no different to the other populations in the region. They want to enjoy the fundamental human rights which they have been denied for so long."

She stressed the need for the Government to guarantee protesters' legitimate rights to peaceful expression and assembly, listen and work to resolve the real issues they are raising and take rapid action to tackle the underlying human rights deficits that have led to their discontent.

On Thursday, the Syrian Government announced a set of political and economic reforms, including holding consultations on ending the state of emergency that has been in place since 1963.

Yet, the very next day the violent repression of protests by security forces continued—something Ms. Pillay found "particularly disturbing."

"Actions speak much louder than words," she said. "To announce a package of long-overdue and very welcome reforms, and then to open fire at protestors in the streets the very next day sends diametrically opposite signals and seriously undermines trust."

The High Commissioner stressed the need for an independent, impartial and transparent investigation into the killings that have occurred recently, and called for the immediate release of all detained protesters and human rights defenders.

SOURCE: United Nations. UN News Centre. "Syria's Violent Repression of Protests Risks Fuelling Further Anger—UN Official." March 26, 2011. http://www.un.org/apps/news/story.asp?NewsID=37905&Cr=Syria&Cr1=.

UN Issues Report on Human Rights Abuses in Syria

DOCUMENT

November 23, 2011

SUMMARY

The deteriorating situation in the Syrian Arab Republic prompted the Human Rights Council to establish an independent international commission of inquiry to investigate alleged violations of human rights since March 2011. From the end of September until mid-November 2011, the commission held meetings with Member States from all regional groups, regional organizations, including the League of Arab States and the Organization of Islamic Cooperation, non-governmental organizations, human rights defenders, journalists and experts. It interviewed 223 victims and witnesses of alleged human rights violations, including civilians and defectors from the military and the security forces. In the present report, the commission documents patterns of summary execution, arbitrary arrest, enforced disappearance, torture, including sexual violence, as well as violations of children's rights.

The substantial body of evidence gathered by the commission indicates that these gross violations of human rights have been committed by Syrian military and security forces since the beginning of the protests in March 2011. The commission is gravely concerned that crimes against humanity have been committed in different locations in the Syrian Arab Republic during the period under review. It calls upon the Government of the Syrian Arab Republic to put an immediate end to the ongoing gross human rights violations, to initiate independent and impartial investigations of these violations and to bring perpetrators to justice. The commission also addresses specific recommendations to opposition groups, the Human Rights Council, regional organizations and States Members of the United Nations.

The commission deeply regrets that, despite many requests, the Government failed to engage in dialogue and to grant the commission access to the country. The Government informed the commission that it would examine the possibility of cooperating with the commission once the work of its own independent special legal commission was completed. The commission reiterates its call for immediate and unhindered access to the Syrian Arab Republic. . . .

[The footnotes, table of contents, and background on the human rights abuse, have been omitted.]

III. EVENTS AND HUMAN RIGHTS VIOLATIONS SINCE MARCH 2011

A. Sequence of events

27. In February 2011, limited protests broke out around issues such as rural poverty, corruption, freedom of expression, democratic rights and the release of political prisoners. Subsequent protests called for respect for human rights, and demanded far-reaching economic, legal and political reforms. By mid-March, peaceful protests erupted in Dar'a in response to the detention and torture of a group of children accused of painting anti-Government graffiti on public buildings. Following the suppression by State forces of peaceful protests, including firing at a funeral procession, civilian marches in support of Dar'a spread to a number of cities, including some suburbs of Al Ladhiqiyah, Baniyas, Damascus, Dayr Az Zawr, Homs, Hama and Idlib.

28. On 25 April, Syrian armed forces undertook the first wide-scale military operation in Dar'a. Since then, protests have continued across the country, with an increasingly violent response by State forces. Other major military operations were carried out in different locations. On 8 November, OHCHR estimated that at least 3,500 civilians had been killed by State forces since March 2011. Thousands are also reported to have been detained, tortured and ill-treated. Homs, Hama and Dar'a reportedly suffered the highest number of casualties.

29. Numerous defections from military and security forces have occurred since the onset of the protests, and have, by many accounts, increased in recent months. An unknown number of defectors have organized themselves into the "Free Syrian Army", which has claimed responsibility for armed attacks against both military and security forces (although there is no reliable information on the size, structure, capability and operations of this body). Colonel Riad Al Asaad, who declared his defection in July, is said to be in charge of the Free Syrian Army.

30. From the start of the protests, the Government has claimed to be the target of attacks by armed gangs and terrorists, some of whom it accused of being funded by foreign sources. On 30 March 2011, in his national address, President Al Assad asserted that the Syrian Arab Republic was "facing a great conspiracy" at the hands of "imperialist forces". He stated that conspirators had spread false information, incited sectarian tension and used violence. He contended that they were supported inside the country by media groups and others.

31. In April, the President announced several steps towards political and legal reform. These steps included the formation of a new Government, the lifting of the state of emergency, the abolition of the Supreme State Security Court, the granting of general amnesties and new regulations on the right of citizens to participate in peaceful demonstrations.

32. On 2 June, the President announced the establishment of the National Dialogue Commission, responsible for preparing consultations as part of a transitional process towards a multiparty democracy. Several leading opposition figures boycotted the meeting because of the continued violence used against protesters.

33. On 6 June, the President stated that members of the military and security forces, as well as innocent people, had been killed in acts of sabotage and terror. While admitting that the State should work tirelessly to meet the demands of its people, he affirmed that among those demanding change was a small group of criminals and religious extremists attempting to spread chaos. The Government news agency increasingly reported armed attacks against State forces in cities, including Homs, Hama, Idlib and Talkalakh.

34. The Government has since announced a number of policy initiatives as part of the reform process, including Decree No. 100 of 3 August, promulgating a new law on political parties, and Decree No. 101 of 3 August, promulgating a general law on elections. Local elections were announced for 12 December, and a new law on the media was introduced on 2 September. On 16 October, the President established a national committee tasked with preparing a draft constitution, which would be subject to a referendum within four months.

35. On 3 August, the Security Council issued a presidential statement condemning the ongoing violence against protesters by Syrian forces and calling on restraint from all sides. It also called on the Syrian Arab Republic to implement political reforms and to cooperate with OHCHR. On 4 October, China and the Russian Federation vetoed a draft resolution of the Security Council, in which the Council recommended possible measures against the Syrian Arab Republic under Article 41 of the Charter of the United Nations.

36. A number of States and regional organizations have imposed sanctions on the Syrian Arab Republic.

37. On 7 October, the Government of the Syrian Arab Republic reiterated that the country was being subjected to a series of criminal attacks by armed terrorist groups and an unprecedented media campaign of lies and allegations, supported by certain western States. According to the Government, the groups involved had committed offences against the Syrian people, including acts of theft, murder and vandalism, and they were exploiting peaceful demonstrations to create anarchy. The Government also claimed that 1,100 members of State forces had been killed by terrorists and armed gangs. It pointed out that, while many protests had been conducted in full legality, others had been held without notification and disrupted public order.

38. On 2 November, the Council of the League of Arab States announced that the Syrian Arab Republic had agreed on a workplan to end violence and protect citizens. The Government also pledged to release all those detained in relation to the recent events, to remove armed elements from cities and inhabited areas, and to give the specialized organizations of the League and Arab and international media access to the country. The Council mandated a ministerial committee of the League to oversee and report on the implementation of the workplan. According to the Government, 553 detainees were

released pursuant to the agreement. Continued violence and the non-implementation of the agreement prompted the League, on 12 November, to adopt a resolution suspending Syrian activities within the organization. The resolution also imposed economic and political sanctions on the country, and reiterated the previous demand that the Syrian Arab Republic withdraw its armed forces from cities and residential areas. The League urged its Member States to recall their ambassadors from Damascus. The measures came into force on 16 November. On 15 November, 1,180 prisoners were also released.

39.   In November, military and security forces carried out operations in Homs, Dar'a, Hama, Dayr Az Zawr and Rif Damascus, targeting public assemblies and funeral processions. In Homs, the operations were conducted in the residential areas of Alqaseer, Bab Amr, Bab Al Sibaa, Bab Hood and Karm Al Zaitoon. According to eyewitnesses, tanks deployed in and around the city frequently fired at residential buildings. It is estimated that, in a three-week period until 13 November, 260 civilians were killed. According to information received, a small number of defectors claiming to be part of the Free Syrian Army engaged in operations against State forces, killing and injuring members of military and security forces.

40.   On 20 November, in an interview published by *The Sunday Times*, President Al Assad explained that his Government did not have a policy to treat the public harshly; its aim was to fight militants to restore stability and protect civilians. He added that any "mistakes" committed by officials would be addressed by the independent special legal commission.

B. Excessive use of force and extrajudicial executions

41.   According to individual testimonies, including those of defectors who have acknowledged their role in policing and quelling the protests, State forces shot indiscriminately at unarmed protestors. Most were shot in the upper body, including in the head. Defectors from military and security forces told the commission that they had received orders to shoot at unarmed protesters without warning. In some instances, however, commanders of operations ordered protesters to disperse and issued warnings prior to opening fire. In some cases, non-lethal means were used prior to or at the same time as live ammunition.

42.   The commission received several testimonies indicating that military and security forces and *Shabbiha* militias had planned and conducted joint operations with "shoot to kill" orders to crush demonstrations. Such operations were conducted in the centre of Al Ladhiqiyah around Sheikh Daher Square in early April, and also in the Ramel suburb of Al Ladhiqiyah on 13 and 14 August. During the latter incident, at least 20 people, including children, were reportedly killed. In other incidents, officers ordered their personnel to attack protesters without warning, hitting them with batons.

43.   A defector described to the commission the rationale for deployment and the orders that were given to his army battalion on 1 May:

> *Our commanding officer told us that there were armed conspirators and terrorists attacking civilians and burning Government buildings. We went into Telbisa on that day. We did not see any armed group. The protestors called for freedom. They carried olive branches and marched with their children. We were ordered to either disperse*

the crowd or eliminate everybody, including children. The orders were to fire in the air and immediately after to shoot at people. No time was allowed between one action and the other. We opened fire; I was there. We used machine guns and other weapons. There were many people on the ground, injured or killed.

44. The rationale for the use of force and orders to open fire on demonstrators were echoed in numerous testimonies of other former soldiers who had been dispatched to different locations and at different times. For example, on 29 April, thousands of people walked from nearby villages to the town of Dar'a to bring food, water and medicine to the local population. When they reached the Sayda residence complex, they were ambushed by security forces. More than 40 people were reportedly killed, including women and children.

45. The commission is aware of acts of violence committed by some demonstrators. However, it notes that the majority of civilians were killed in the context of peaceful demonstrations. Accounts collected by the commission, including those of defectors, indicated that protesters were largely unarmed and determined to claim their rights and express their discontent peacefully.

46. Snipers were responsible for many casualties. On some occasions, snipers appeared to be targeting leaders of the march and those using loudspeakers or carrying cameras and mobile phones. The commission heard several accounts of how those who were trying to rescue the wounded and collect the bodies of demonstrators also came under sniper fire. The commission documented several cases in Dar'a, Hama and Al Ladhiqiyah.

47. Checkpoints and roadblocks were set up to prevent people from moving freely and joining demonstrations, especially on Fridays. Defectors who were deployed at checkpoints told the commission about "black lists" with names of people wanted by the authorities. They were given instructions to search for weapons and, in some cases, given orders to shoot. A soldier who manned two checkpoints in the Dar'a governorate, from April to August, was given orders "to search everybody and if any demonstrators try to pass through, to fire at them".

48. Several defectors witnessed the killing of their comrades who refused to execute orders to fire at civilians. A number of conscripts were allegedly killed by security forces on 25 April in Dar'a during a large-scale military operation. The soldiers in the first row were given orders to aim directly at residential areas, but chose to fire in the air to avoid civilian casualties. Security forces posted behind shot them for refusing orders, thus killing dozens of conscripts.

49. Civilians bore the brunt of the violence as cities were blockaded and curfews imposed. The commission heard many testimonies describing how those who ventured outside their homes were shot by snipers. Many of the reported cases occurred in Dar'a, Jisr Al Shughour and Homs. A lawyer told how security forces took positions in old Dar'a during the operation in April. Snipers were deployed on the hospital rooftop and other buildings. "They targeted anyone who moved", he said. Two of his cousins were killed on the street by snipers.

50. A number of cases was documented of injured people who were taken to military hospitals, where they were beaten and tortured during interrogation. Torture and killings reportedly took place in the Homs Military Hospital by security forces dressed as doctors and allegedly acting with the complicity of medical personnel. As people became afraid

of going to public hospitals, makeshift clinics were set up in mosques and private houses, which also became targets. This was the case of the Omari Mosque in Dar'a, which was raided on 23 March. Several of the injured and some medical personnel were killed there.

51. According to the Government, global media inaccurately reported the use of weapons against civilians to discredit the Syrian Arab Republic. Security forces were deployed to the demonstrations to keep the peace, but many of them were killed, including unarmed police officers. For instance, in the city of Homs, 12 police officers were reportedly murdered. The Government claimed that security forces were not usually armed when policing demonstrations. It also claimed that the information on the use of tanks was false, and that they were used solely for rescuing overwhelmed police officers who had no means of defending themselves. . . .

[The remainder of the report, containing information on arbitrary detentions and torture, sexual violence, violations of children's rights, displacement, criminal violations under international law, government responsibility, and annexes, has been omitted.]

SOURCE: United Nations. Office of the High Commissioner for Human Rights. "Report of the Independent International Commission of Inquiry on the Syrian Arab Republic." November 23, 2011. http://www2 .ohchr.org/english/bodies/hrcouncil/specialsession/17/docs/A-HRC-S-17-2-Add1.pdf.

OTHER HISTORIC DOCUMENTS OF INTEREST

FROM THIS VOLUME

- Arab Spring: Tunisian President Zine al-Abidine Ben Ali Resigns, p. 23
- Arab Spring: Violent Crackdown on Protesters in Bahrain, p. 113
- Arab Spring: International Response to Mubarak's Resignation (Egypt), p. 95
- Arab Spring: King Abdullah II Reshuffles Cabinet (Jordan), p. 85
- Arab Spring: Crisis in Yemen Leads to Power Transfer, p. 125
- Arab Spring: NATO and President Obama on the Death of Muammar Qaddafi, p. 555

FROM PREVIOUS *HISTORIC DOCUMENTS*

- US and Israeli Officials on Violence in Lebanon, Peace Talks With Syria, *2008*, p. 182
- United Nations on Promoting Democracy in Arab Lands, *2005*, p. 269

April

Department of Justice on Military Trials for Guantánamo Detainees

APRIL 4, 2011

From the beginning of his administration in 2009, President Barack Obama made closing the detention center at the U.S. Naval Station at Guantánamo Bay, Cuba, and reevaluating the country's military commission system top priorities. Yet on March 7, 2011, Obama issued Executive Order 13567, which caused many to question whether these goals would be achieved. The order lifted the president's previously imposed suspension of all military commission proceedings and established a formal system for the long-term detention of those held at Guantánamo. While a disappointment to many human rights organizations, the president's order earned praise from Republican lawmakers and spurred the ultimate codification of long-term detention procedures through the National Defense Authorization Act of 2012.

Less than a month after the president's executive order, the Department of Justice announced that the alleged September 11 conspirators would be tried before a military tribunal instead of in federal court. Charges against the five men were filed on May 31, 2011. At the same time, the military commission system resumed the trial of another alleged terrorist, Abd al-Rahim al-Nashiri, suspected in the 2000 bombing of the USS *Cole*.

REFORMING A SYSTEM OF WARTIME JUSTICE

Former President George W. Bush established the military commission system by executive order in November 2001, shortly after the attacks of September 11, with the intention of using the system to try those detained during the war on terror. The system was highly controversial from its inception, as military commissions typically require defendants to forgo certain rights they would enjoy in civilian courts and allow some forms of evidence that elsewhere might be considered questionable.

Throughout the 2008 presidential campaign, then-Sen. Barack Obama had promised to close the Guantánamo Bay detention center. Days after taking office in January 2009, he issued Executive Order 13492, calling for the center to be closed within one year and suspending all current and pending proceedings before military commissions until that system could be fully reviewed. The order established a special task force to review the case of each detainee to determine who could be brought to trial and declared that any detainees remaining at Guantánamo at the time of the facility's closure would be returned to their home country, released, transferred to a third country, or transferred to another detention facility within the United States.

Lawmakers and law enforcement officials challenged Obama's order from the beginning. Congress created the first obstacle to the order's implementation when it denied Obama's request for $80 million to support the facility's closure. The administration also faced challenges to transferring detainees to domestic prisons. Municipal officials in

Standish, Michigan, and Thomson, Illinois, initially offered to hold detainees at their maximum-security prisons, but congressional opposition prevented any transfer agreements. Then, in June 2009, Congress banned the transfer of Guantánamo detainees into the United States, except for prosecution, as part of a supplemental war-funding bill. This meant the administration would need to find third-party countries willing to accept any detainees deemed suitable for release and transfer. This process became further complicated following an attempted bombing of an airplane over Detroit on Christmas Day 2009, a plot allegedly devised by a Yemeni al Qaeda affiliate. This prompted Obama to halt all transfers of detainees to Yemen.

Support for trying detainees in civilian courts instead of before military commissions also crumbled. In April 2009, the Department of Justice lawyer leading the Guantánamo review task force informed Obama that only about 20 of the remaining 172 detainees could be prosecuted—in many cases because the intelligence gathered on the detainees would not stand up in civilian court. Plans to bring Khalid Sheikh Mohammed, the alleged mastermind of the September 11 attacks, and his co-conspirators to trial in Manhattan also faltered in January 2010, after New York City Mayor Michael Bloomberg withdrew his initial support and the New York City Police Department estimated it would cost $200 million annually to provide security around the courthouse for the duration of the case. Attorney General Eric Holder and his staff considered moving the trial to Otisville, New York, a village approximately seventy miles from New York City, but local officials noted they did not have the infrastructure to manage the anticipated influx of people. Support for civilian trials further diminished after the sentencing of Ahmed Ghailani, the first Guantánamo detainee brought to the United States for prosecution in federal court. He had been accused of participating in the 1998 bombings of U.S. embassies in Tanzania and Kenya. Of the 285 charges filed against him, Ghailani was found guilty only of one—conspiracy. Although he received a life sentence, critics claimed the outcome was too close a call and cited it as proof that civilian trials would result in terrorists being freed. Congress delivered what was perhaps the final blow to civilian trials in December 2010, when lawmakers barred the administration from bringing any detainees into the United States, even for prosecution, under the National Defense Authorization Act of 2011.

Obama was successful in securing several reforms to the military commission system. Signed in October, the 2009 Military Commissions Act excluded evidence obtained from detainees through torture or cruel, inhuman, or degrading treatment; gave defendants the right to attend their entire trial, examine all evidence presented against them, cross-examine witnesses, and call their own witnesses; and permitted appeals to the U.S. Court of Military Commission Review. However, as 2010 drew to a close, it seemed likely that the commission system would remain largely unchanged and that holding civilian trials for detainees would be impossible.

New Guantánamo Detainee Policy

On March 7, 2011, Obama issued Executive Order 13567, effectively reversing his suspension of military commission proceedings and allowing trials to resume. The order also established new rules for the prolonged detention of prisoners who the Guantánamo Bay review task force had determined could not be tried. The new rules called for the secretary of defense to coordinate an initial review of each remaining detainee's case within a year of the order's announcement. The review would consist of a hearing before a

Periodic Review Board, made up of representatives from the Departments of State, Justice, Homeland Security, and Defense, and would determine whether the continued detention of a particular detainee was "necessary to protect against a significant threat to the security of the United States," or if he or she could be released. Thereafter, detainees would receive full reviews every three years, with file reviews, in which a detainee's file is updated with any new information, every six months.

Obama claimed the new rules would "broaden our ability to bring terrorists to justice, provide oversight for our actions, and ensure the humane treatment of detainees." Republican lawmakers mostly praised the move, with Rep. Peter King, R-N.Y., chair of the House Committee on Homeland Security, describing the order as "clearly another step in the right direction." Reaction from Democrats was mixed, and human rights groups came out strongly against the order. "The best way to get America out of the Guantánamo morass is to use the most effective and reliable tool we have: our criminal justice system. Instead, the Obama administration has done just the opposite and chosen to institutionalize unlawful indefinite detention . . . and to revive the illegitimate Guantánamo military commissions," said the American Civil Liberties Union (ACLU) in a statement.

ALLEGED SEPTEMBER 11 CONSPIRATORS TO FACE COMMISSION

The Department of Justice soon followed Obama's reversal with one of its own. On April 4, Attorney General Holder announced that Khalid Sheikh Mohammed and his alleged co-conspirators would be tried before a military tribunal instead of in federal court. Holder explained that charges previously filed against the men, who also included Walid bin Attash, Ramzi bin al-Shibh, Ali Abdul Aziz Ali, and Mustafa al-Hawsawi, in the U.S. District Court for the Southern District of New York had been dismissed, and their cases referred to the Department of Defense. In announcing the decision, Holder accused Congress of tying the administration's hands and taking "one of the nation's most tested counterterrorism tools off the table" by preventing the transfer of any detainees to the United States for civilian trials. "We cannot allow a trial to be further delayed for the victims of the 9/11 attacks or their families," Holder said. "I have full faith and confidence in the reformed military commission system to appropriately handle this case as it proceeds."

On May 31, military prosecutors refiled charges against the men, including murder in violation of the law of war, attacking civilians and civilian objects, hijacking aircraft, and terrorism. All five men were to be tried jointly, but no trial date had been set. Prosecutors were expected to seek the death penalty.

COMMISSIONS RESUME

While the Department of Defense began preparing its case against the alleged 9/11 conspirators, the military commission system officially resumed proceedings in the trial of Abd al-Rahim al-Nashiri, the primary suspect in the 2000 bombing of the USS *Cole*. Al-Nashiri's case was the first new commission case to move forward under the Obama administration, and was viewed by many as a test run for the prosecution of Khalid Sheikh Mohammed. Al-Nashiri was also the first "high-value" detainee to receive a trial. It was well known that he was held at a secret Central Intelligence Agency (CIA) prison before being transferred to Guantánamo Bay and was subjected to "enhanced interrogation techniques," including waterboarding and mock executions. Given these circumstances, his legal team was expected to question the validity of evidence submitted against him.

The Department of Defense announced the charges filed against al-Nashiri on September 28. They included murder and terrorism and carried the death penalty with a conviction. A trial date was tentatively set for November 2012.

CODIFYING PROLONGED DETENTIONS

Congress meanwhile had been working on a number of provisions in the National Defense Authorization Act of 2012 that would effectively codify the system of long-term detentions established by Obama's executive order. Yet the bill included several other detention-related items that stirred debate. For one, it mandated military detention for any individual suspected of being a member of al Qaeda or its associates and being involved in a terrorist plot against the United States, even if that individual was captured in the United States. It also required the secretary of defense to certify that any detainees transferred out of Guantánamo would not commit future hostile acts, which many expected to be a significant barrier to future transfers. The Obama administration noted it had "serious reservations" about several provisions, including one that would have eliminated executive branch authority to use civilian courts for terrorism cases against foreign nationals, and another that could have denied U.S. citizens suspected of terrorism the right to trial. Congress made several changes to the bill to address these concerns, including the addition of an amendment to preserve current law concerning the detention of U.S. citizens and lawful resident aliens. Obama signed it on December 31. Human rights organizations and other critics of the legislation continue to question whether the bill may be interpreted differently by future presidents, opening the door to possible infringements on U.S. citizens' rights.

—Linda Fecteau

Following are three documents from the U.S. Department of Justice, all released on April 4, 2011. The first is a press release detailing the department's decision to try the five alleged 9/11 conspirators in a military commission; the second is a statement from Attorney General Eric Holder announcing the decision to move the conspirators from federal court to a military commission; and the third details the indictment filed against the conspirators in federal court, which was dismissed.

Justice Department Announces Military Commissions for Guantánamo Detainees

April 4, 2011

The Justice Department today announced that the cases involving Khalid Sheikh Mohammed and four other Guantanamo Bay detainees accused of conspiring to commit the Sept. 11, 2001 terror attacks have been referred to the Defense Department to proceed in military commissions and that the federal indictment against these defendants that was returned under seal by a grand jury in the Southern District of New York on Dec. 14, 2009 has been unsealed and dismissed.

"As the indictment unsealed today reveals, we were prepared to bring a powerful case against the 9/11 defendants in federal court, and had this case proceeded as planned, I'm confident our justice system would have performed with the same distinction that has been its hallmark for more than two hundred years," said Attorney General Eric Holder. "Unfortunately, Members of Congress have intervened and imposed restrictions blocking the administration from bringing any Guantanamo detainees to trial in the United States. While we will continue to seek to repeal those restrictions, we cannot allow a trial to be further delayed for the victims of the 9/11 attacks or their families. I have full faith and confidence in the reformed military commission system to appropriately handle this case as it proceeds."

The Attorney General, in consultation with the Secretary of Defense, determined that Khalid Sheikh Mohammed, Walid Bin Attash, Ramzi Bin Al-Shibh, Ali Abdul Aziz Ali and Mustafa Al-Hawsawi are eligible for military commission charges and referred their cases to the Defense Department.

Earlier today, federal prosecutors from the Southern District of New York and the Eastern District of Virginia unsealed and moved to dismiss the indictment returned in federal court in Manhattan that charged these defendants for their roles in the Sept. 11, 2001 attacks that damaged or destroyed four commercial aircraft in New York, Virginia and Pennsylvania; the Twin Towers of the World Trade Center and surrounding property in New York; and the Pentagon in Virginia, resulting in the deaths of 2,976 persons. A federal judge today granted the motion to dismiss the indictment.

The 10-count, 80-page indictment charged each of the defendants with conspiracy to commit acts of terrorism transcending national boundaries; acts of terrorism transcending national boundaries; conspiracy to commit violent acts and destroy aircraft; violence on and destruction of aircraft; conspiracy to commit aircraft piracy; aircraft piracy; murder of U.S. officers and employees; destruction of property by means of fire and explosives; and conspiracy to kill Americans.

The federal indictment specifically alleged that Khalid Sheikh Mohammed, who was closely associated with Usama Bin Laden and, who in 1999 proposed to Bin Laden a terror plot that would use airplanes as missiles to crash into buildings, served as the operational leader of the Sept. 11, 2001 plot. Walid Bin Attash participated in the plot, by among other things collecting information on matters related to airport and airplane security measures, according to the indictment.

Ramzi Bin Al-Shibh, according to the indictment, tried to become one of the pilot hijackers, but repeatedly failed to obtain a visa for entry into the United States and instead managed the plot by among other things sending money to hijackers in the United States from abroad. Ali Abdul Aziz Ali allegedly facilitated the plot by among other things sending money to hijackers in the United States from abroad. Mustafa Al-Hawsawi allegedly facilitated the plot by among other things helping hijackers travel to the United States and facilitating their efforts upon arrival.

Attorney General Holder thanked federal prosecutors from the U.S. Attorney's Offices for the Southern District of New York and the Eastern District of Virginia, as well as the hundreds of federal agents and analysts from across the government who spent years investigating and working to bring federal charges against these defendants.

The military commission system was substantially reformed by the Military Commissions Act of 2009, which the administration worked with Congress to enact, as well as the 2010 revised Manual for Military Commissions.

Source: U.S. Department of Justice. "Justice Department Refers Five Accused 9/11 Plotters to Military Commissions." April 4, 2011. http://www.justice.gov/opa/pr/2011/April/11-ag-421.html.

Attorney General Holder on Prosecution of the 9/11 Conspirators

April 4, 2011

In November 2009, I announced that Khalid Sheikh Mohammed and four other individuals would stand trial in federal court for their roles in the terrorist attacks on our country on September 11, 2001.

As I said then, the decision between federal courts and military commissions was not an easy one to make. I began my review of this case with an open mind and with just one goal: to look at the facts, look at the law, and choose the venue where we could achieve swift and sure justice most effectively for the victims of those horrendous attacks and their family members. After consulting with prosecutors from both the Department of Justice and Department of Defense and after thoroughly studying the case, it became clear to me that the best venue for prosecution was in federal court. I stand by that decision today.

As the indictment unsealed today reveals, we were prepared to bring a powerful case against Khalid Sheikh Mohammed and his four co-conspirators—one of the most well-researched and documented cases I have ever seen in my decades of experience as a prosecutor. We had carefully evaluated the evidence and concluded that we could prove the defendants' guilt while adhering to the bedrock traditions and values of our laws. We had consulted extensively with the intelligence community and developed detailed plans for handling classified evidence. Had this case proceeded in Manhattan or in an alternative venue in the United States, as I seriously explored in the past year, I am confident that our justice system would have performed with the same distinction that has been its hallmark for over two hundred years.

Unfortunately, since I made that decision, Members of Congress have intervened and imposed restrictions blocking the administration from bringing any Guantanamo detainees to trial in the United States, regardless of the venue. As the President has said, those unwise and unwarranted restrictions undermine our counterterrorism efforts and could harm our national security. Decisions about who, where and how to prosecute have always been—and must remain—the responsibility of the executive branch. Members of Congress simply do not have access to the evidence and other information necessary to make prosecution judgments. Yet they have taken one of the nation's most tested counterterrorism tools off the table and tied our hands in a way that could have serious ramifications. We will continue to seek to repeal those restrictions.

But we must face a simple truth: those restrictions are unlikely to be repealed in the immediate future. And we simply cannot allow a trial to be delayed any longer for the victims of the 9/11 attacks or for their family members who have waited for nearly a decade for justice. I have talked to these family members on many occasions over the last two years. Like many Americans, they differ on where the 9/11 conspirators should be prosecuted, but there is one thing on which they all agree: We must bring the conspirators to justice.

So today I am referring the cases of Khalid Sheikh Mohammed, Walid Muhammad Bin Attash, Ramzi Bin Al Shibh, Ali Abdul-Aziz Ali, and Mustafa Ahmed Al Hawsawi to the Department of Defense to proceed in military commissions. Furthermore, I have directed prosecutors to move to dismiss the indictment that was handed down under seal in the Southern District of New York in December, 2009, and a judge has granted that motion.

Prosecutors from both the Departments of Defense and Justice have been working together since the beginning of this matter, and I have full faith and confidence in the military commission system to appropriately handle this case as it proceeds. The Department of Justice will continue to offer all the support necessary as this critically important matter moves forward. The administration worked with Congress to substantially reform military commissions in 2009, and I believe they can deliver fair trials and just verdicts. For the victims of these heinous attacks and their families, that justice is long overdue, and it must not be delayed any longer.

Since I made the decision to prosecute the alleged 9/11 conspirators, the effectiveness of our federal courts and the thousands of prosecutors, judges, law enforcement officers, and defense attorneys who work in them have been subjected to a number of unfair, and often unfounded, criticisms. Too many people—many of whom certainly know better—have expressed doubts about our time-honored and time-tested system of justice. That's not only misguided, it's wrong. The fact is, federal courts have proven to be an unparalleled instrument for bringing terrorists to justice. Our courts have convicted hundreds of terrorists since September 11, and our prisons safely and securely hold hundreds today, many of them serving long sentences. There is no other tool that has demonstrated the ability to both incapacitate terrorists and collect intelligence from them over such a diverse range of circumstances as our traditional justice system. Our national security demands that we continue to prosecute terrorists in federal court, and we will do so. Our heritage, our values, and our legacy to future generations also demand that we have full faith and confidence in a court system that has distinguished this nation throughout its history.

Finally, I want to thank the prosecutors from the Southern District of New York and the Eastern District of Virginia who have spent countless hours working to bring this case to trial. They are some of the most dedicated and patriotic Americans I have ever encountered, and our nation is safer because of the work they do every day. They have honored their country through their efforts on this case, and I thank them for it. I am proud of each and every one of them.

Sadly, this case has been marked by needless controversy since the beginning. But despite all the argument and debate it has engendered, the prosecution of Khalid Sheikh Mohammed and his co-conspirators should never have been about settling ideological arguments or scoring political points. At the end of our indictment appear the names of 2,976 people who were killed in the attacks on that deadly September day nearly ten years ago. Innocent Americans and citizens of foreign countries alike who were murdered by ruthless terrorists intent on crippling our nation and attacking the values that we hold dear. This case has always been about delivering justice for those victims, and for their surviving loved ones. Nothing else. It is my sincere hope that, through the actions we take today, we will finally be able to deliver the justice they have so long deserved.

SOURCE: U.S. Department of Justice. "Statement of the Attorney General on the Prosecution of the 9/11 Conspirators." April 4, 2011. http://www.justice.gov/iso/opa/ag/speeches/2011/ag-speech-110404.html.

Federal Indictments Against 9/11 Conspirators

DOCUMENT

April 4, 2011

UNITED STATES DISTRICT COURT

SOUTHERN DISTRICT OF NEW YORK

NOLLE PROSEQUI

AND UNSEALING ORDER

(S14) 93 Cr. 180 (KTD)

UNITED STATES OF AMERICA

- v. -

KHALID SHEIKH MOHAMMED,

a/k/a "Mukhtar,"

a/k/a "Mukhtar al-Baluchi,"

a/k/a "Al-Mukh,"

a/k/a "Abdulrahman Abdullah al-Ghamdi,"

a/k/a "Salem All,"

WALID BIN ATTASH,

a/k/a "Khallad Bin Attash,"

a/k/a "Saleh Saeed Mohammed Bin Yousaf,"

a/k/a "Tawfiq Muhammad Salih Bin Rashid,"

a/k/a "Silver,"

RAMZI BIN AL-SHIBH,

a/k/a "Abu Ubaydah,"

a/k/a "Ahad Abdollahi Sabet,"

ALI ABDUL AZIZ ALI,

a/k/a "Aliosh,"

a/k/a "Ali A,"

a/k/a "Isam Mansur,"

a/k/a "Ammar al-Baluchi," a

/k/a "Hani," and

MUSTAFA AL-HAWSAWI,

a/k/a "Hashem Abdulrahman,"

a/k/a "Hashem Abdollahi,"

a/k/a "Mustafa Ahmed,"

a/k/a "Zaher,"

a/k/a "Khal,"

Defendants.

1. The filing of this nolle prosequi will dismiss this federal criminal indictment against the defendants KHALID SHEIKH MOHAMMED, a/k/a "Mukhtar," a/k/a "Mukhtar al-Baluchi," a/k/a "Al-Mukh," a/k/a "Abdulrahman Abdullah al-Ghamdi," a/k/a "Salem Ali," WALID BIN ATTASH, a/k/a "Khallad Bin Attash," a/k/a "Saleh Saeed Mohammed Bin Yousaf," a/k/a "Tawfiq Muhammad Salih Bin Rashid," a/k/a "Silver," RAMZI BIN AL-SHIBH, a/k/a "Abu Ubaydah," a/k/a "Ahad Abdollahi Sabet," ALI ABDUL AZIZ ALI, a/k/a "Aliosh," a/k/a "Ali A," a/k/a "Isam Mansur," a/k/a "Ammar al-Baluchi," a/k/a "Hani," and MUSTAFA AL-HAWSAWI, a/k/a "Hashem Abdulrahman," a/k/a "Hashem Abdollahi," a/k/a "Mustafa Ahmed," a/k/a "Zaher," a/k/a "Khal."

2. On December 14, 2009, Indictment (S14) 93 Cr. 180 (KTD) was returned and, upon Sealed Affirmation and Application of the Government, ordered to be filed under seal. The Indictment charges the defendants with various offenses relating to the terrorist attacks on September 11, 2001. In particular, the Indictment charges the defendants in ten counts as follows:

   a. Count One: Conspiracy to Commit Acts of Terrorism Transcending National Boundaries, in violation of Title 18, United States Code, Section 2332b(a)(2) & (c)(1)(a);
   b. Count Two: Acts of Terrorism Transcending National Boundaries, in violation of Title 18, United States Code, Sections 2332b(a)(l) & (c)(1)(A), and 2;
   c. Count Three: Conspiracy to Commit Violent Acts and Destroy Aircraft, in violation of Title 18, United States Code, Sections 32(a)(7) and 34;
   d. Count Four: Violence on and Destruction of Aircraft, in violation of Title 18, United States Code, Sections 32(a)(1) & (5), 34, and 2;
   e. Count Five: Conspiracy to Commit Aircraft Piracy, in violation of Title 49, United States Code, Section 46502(a)(1)(A) & (a)(2)(B);
   f. Count Six: Aircraft Piracy, in violation of Title 49, United States Code, Section 46502(a)(1)(A) & (a)(2)(B), and Title 18, United States Code, Section 2;
   g. Count Seven: Murder of a United States Officer and Employee, in violation of Title 18, United States Code, Sections 1111, 1114, and 2;
   h. Count Eight: Murder of a United States Officer and Employee, in violation of Title 18, United States Code, Sections 1111, 1114, and 2;

    i. Count Nine: Destruction of Commercial Property, in violation of Title 18, United States Code, Sections 844(i) and 2; and

    j. Count Ten: Conspiracy to Kill Americans, in violation of Title 18, United States Code, Section 2332(b). The indictment also contains a notice of special findings to support death sentences, pursuant to Title 18, United States Code, Sections 3591 and 3592.

3. In December 2010, the United States Congress enacted the Ike Skelton National Defense Authorization Act for Fiscal Year 2011, Section 1032 of which bars the use of funds authorized to be appropriated by the Act to transfer the defendants from the United States Naval Station, Guantanamo Bay, Cuba, to the United States, even for prosecution. In light of this opposition by Congress to a federal criminal prosecution, the Government does not believe there is any reasonable likelihood that the defendants will be tried in this forum in the near future.

4. Both the public generally, and the victims of the terrorist attacks of September 11, 2001, and their families specifically, have a strong interest in seeing the defendants prosecuted in some forum. Because a timely prosecution in federal court does not appear feasible, the Attorney General intends to refer this matter to the Department of Defense to proceed in military commissions.

5. In light of the foregoing, the Attorney General has directed that the undersigned seek dismissal of Indictment (S14) 93 Cr. 180 (KTD). Accordingly, we hereby direct, with leave of the Court, that an order of nolle prosequi be filed as to defendants KHALID SHEIKH MOHAMMED, a/k/a "Mukhtar," a/k/a "Mukhtar al-Baluchi," a/k/a "Al-Mukh," a/k/a "Abdulrahman Abdullah al-Ghamdi," a/k/a "Salem Ali," WALID BIN ATTASH, a/k/a "Khallad Bin Attash," a/k/a "Saleh Saeed Mohammed Bin Yousaf," a/k/a "Tawfiq Muhammad Salih Bin Rashid," a/k/a "Silver," RAMZI BIN AL-SHIBH, a/k/a "Abu Ubaydah," a/k/a "Ahad Abdollahi Sabet," ALI ABDUL AZIZ ALI, a/k/a "Aliosh," a/k/a "Ali A," a/k/a "Isam Mansur," a/k/a "Ammar al-Baluchi," a/k/a "Hani," and MUSTAFA AL-HAWSAWI, a/k/a "Hashem Abdulrahman," a/k/a "Hashem Abdollahi," a/k/a "Mustafa Ahmed," a/k/a "Zaher," a/k/a "Khal," with respect to Indictment (S14) 93 Cr. 180 (KTD).

6. Upon dismissal of the Indictment, there is no longer any basis for maintaining Indictment (S14) 93 Cr. 180 (KTD); the Government's Affirmation and Application of December 14, 2009; or the Order of the same date, signed by the Honorable James C. Francis IV, United States Magistrate Judge, under seal. Accordingly, the undersigned further ask that Indictment (S14) 93 Cr. 180 (KTD); the Government's Affirmation and Application of December 14, 2009; and the Order of the same date, signed by Magistrate Judge Francis, all under docket (S14) 93 Cr. 18 0 (KTD), be unsealed and entered on the docket.

PREET BHARARA

United States Attorney

Southern District of New York

NEIL H. MacBRIDE

United States Attorney

Eastern District of Virginia

SO ORDERED:

THE HONORABLE KEVIN THOMAS DUFFY

United States District Judge Southern District of New York

SOURCE: U.S. Department of Justice. "Nolle Prosequi and Unsealing Order." April 4, 2011. http://www .justice.gov/opa/documents/nolle-unsealing-order.pdf.

OTHER HISTORIC DOCUMENTS OF INTEREST

FROM PREVIOUS *Historic Documents*

- Justice Department Announces Khalid Sheikh Mohammed Will Be Tried in New York City, *2009*, p. 552
- President Obama Calls for the Closure of Detention Facilities at Guantánamo Bay, *2009*, p. 31
- U.S. Supreme Court on Guantánamo Bay Detainees, *2008*, p. 226
- Khalid Sheikh Mohammed Charged for His Role in the 9/11 Attacks, *2008*, p. 49
- Appeals Court on Prisoners Held at Guantanamo Bay, Cuba, *2005*, p. 446
- Supreme Court on Detentions in Terrorism Cases, *2004*, p. 375

Bipartisan FY2011 Budget Agreement Averts Government Shutdown

APRIL 8 AND APRIL 12, 2011

The U.S. political scene in early 2011 was dominated by the federal budget deadlock. Despite already being more than a third of the way into the 2011 fiscal year, Congress had yet to approve a budget, relying instead on temporary spending authorizations to keep the federal government funded. By mid-February the Republican-dominated House of Representatives had passed a budget with $61 billion in spending cuts. However, the Senate, with a Democratic majority, along with President Barack Obama, opposed the budget and indicated it would not be passed. In the weeks leading up to April 8, 2011 (the deadline for passage of the FY2011 budget or another continuing resolution), extended negotiations took place between the leaders of both parties and President Obama. With no agreement imminent, federal agencies prepared to shut down. One of the last sticking points was $80 million in federal funding for Planned Parenthood, an organization that provides health care services to low-income women. In the end, a deal was struck between the two parties just hours ahead of the midnight deadline. The budget deal included $38.5 billion in spending cuts, the largest nondefense spending cut in U.S. history and the most significant overall decline in spending since the end of World War II.

2011 Budget Faces Severe Delays

The first real test for the Republicans in the wake of the November 2010 midterm elections, when the party won a majority in the House, was to rein in the federal budget deficit. In line with the budget procedures spelled out in the Budget and Accounting Act of 1921, President Obama submitted a budget request to Congress in February 2010 that included requests for appropriations for all federal executive departments and independent agencies for fiscal year 2011. Efforts to pass the budget before the start of the 2011 fiscal year in October 2010 failed, so seven consecutive continuing resolutions, or temporary spending authorizations, were passed to provide funding at or near fiscal year 2010 levels.

Negotiations culminated on February 19, 2011, when the House approved a budget package with spending cuts worth $61 billion, which were designed to cover the remaining seven months of the fiscal year. The proposed package had no chance of passage, however, because of strong opposition from President Obama and the Democratic Party, which held a majority in the Senate. By late February, a group of moderate senators from both parties were working on a compromise based on the recommendations of the National Commission on Fiscal Responsibility and Reform, a bipartisan presidential commission led by former Republican Senator Alan Simpson, and the chief-of-staff under former President Bill Clinton, Erskine Bowles. The commission, which issued a report in December 2010, was mandated to improve the country's fiscal situation in the short term and improve fiscal sustainability over the long term. The commission's recommendations were widely rejected by both Republicans and Democrats, but nonetheless proved to be a solid starting point for negotiations.

A continuing resolution passed by the House on March 16 added an additional $6 billion in spending cuts to the $61 billion already proposed by the Republicans. The measure, which met with significant resistance from Senate Democrats, who were unwilling to cut spending to the extent proposed, passed the Senate on March 17. The stalemate over a full-year spending agreement looked set to continue, until mid-March, when pressure mounted to solve the budget crisis. A growing number of House Republicans, many of whom were associated with the Tea Party, proclaimed there would be no more continuing resolutions. Without either a temporary spending authorization or a budget deal, the federal government would effectively be shut down. Republicans further demanded that all of their proposed cuts be implemented or they would not support a separate measure to raise the federal government debt ceiling. Failure to raise the debt ceiling would likely have serious financial and economic consequences for the United States. Finally, with frustration over the stalemate mounting, sixty-four senators—with an equal number from each party—urged President Obama to step in to the negotiations to help reach a compromise.

FEDERAL GOVERNMENT PREPARES FOR SHUTDOWN AS NEGOTIATIONS INTENSIFY

By March, many government agencies were preparing for a potential shutdown, which would affect approximately 800,000 federal employees. These workers would be furloughed, meaning that they would not receive pay or benefits for as long as the shutdown continued. The agencies and functions affected would have been widespread, although no crucial functions, such as air traffic controllers, would be affected. But many other government entities, including the U.S. Park Service (which is responsible for the operation of the nation's national parks and monuments), the Securities and Exchange Commission, the Social Security Administration, and even the Central Intelligence Agency, would be affected to some degree. Staff at federal agencies were divided into two groups—essential and nonessential workers—with the latter facing furlough.

Weeks of negotiations and partisan political bickering ensued in the wake of the March continuing resolution. The deadline for reaching a new agreement was April 8—if a compromise could not be found by midnight, another stopgap measure to keep federal agencies funded would be necessary to avoid a shutdown. President Obama and key party leaders, including Speaker of the House John Boehner, R-Ohio, and Senate Majority Leader Harry Reid, D-Nev., all sought to reach a resolution. Negotiations continued through the night of April 7 and into the morning of April 8, but failed. Sen. Reid announced that Republicans and Democrats had agreed to approximately $38 billion in spending cuts, but the Republicans were holding up the final deal because of funding to Planned Parenthood.

The disagreement over the funding of Planned Parenthood became the centerpiece of the stalemate. Planned Parenthood receives around $80 million a year from the U.S. government through Title X, which provides grants to women's health centers with the proviso that funds cannot be used to pay for abortions. Republicans argued that Title X funding to Planned Parenthood freed up financial resources that were then spent on providing abortion services. The party proposed cutting federal funds to the organization and instead giving states Title X money to distribute to health groups of their choosing. Democrats rejected the plan, arguing that giving states the authority to decide which health groups to fund would allow Republican governors to deny funds to Planned Parenthood and other women's health providers.

Reid described the holdup over Planned Parenthood funding as "indefensible," but Boehner shot back that negotiations were stalled over spending and asked, "When will the White House and when will Senate Democrats get serious about cutting spending?" As the day progressed, political aides noted that progress was being made on the issue. Even Republicans with steadfast anti-abortion views, including Sen. Tom Coburn, R-Okla., indicated that a compromise could be made and that it was necessary to end the stalemate.

Yet by mid-afternoon on April 8, a deal remained elusive. Boehner called on the Senate to pass a resolution that would see the military fully funded for the remainder of the fiscal year, cut $12 billion in spending from the 2011 budget, and provide funding for the federal government to operate for one week. Democratic senators rejected the plan, and President Obama indicated he would veto such a measure.

A Deal Beats the Deadline

At nearly 11 p.m. on April 8, Boehner called a closed-door meeting where he described to his party's rank and file the deal that had been negotiated with the Democrats. Both the Republican and Democratic parties soon announced that a deal had been struck. The budget did not include provisions to restrict funding to Planned Parenthood. After the announcement, President Obama said that some of the spending cuts agreed to by Democrats "will be painful." In a joint statement, Boehner and Reid announced that the agreement would cut $78.5 billion from the president's FY2011 budget proposal, and that a temporary spending bridge before final passage of this agreement would stop a federal government shutdown. "We have agreed to an historic amount of cuts for the remainder of this fiscal year, as well as a short-term bridge that will give us time to avoid a shutdown while we get that agreement through both houses and to the President," said Boehner and Reid in a joint statement.

Both Republicans and Democrats claimed a political victory in the wake of the budget deal. But not all Republicans were happy with the outcome. Indeed, fifty-nine Republicans broke rank and voted against the deal on the grounds that there was too much compromise with the Democrats. Nevertheless, the $38.5 billion in spending cuts was well above what President Obama and the Democrats had initially proposed, and the compromise included several policy riders that Democrats had initially been unwilling to even consider.

Total spending in the final 2011 budget topped $1 trillion, a decrease of $38.5 billion from 2010 spending levels. Cuts touched nearly every area of government, from agriculture to education and even homeland security. One key area that was left untouched, however, was defense, which saw a funding increase of around $5 billion to $513 billion. Meanwhile, the Departments of Labor, Health and Human Services, Education, and related agencies saw cuts equivalent to nearly 3.4 percent, bringing funding down to around $158 billion. According to a report issued by the House Appropriations Committee Chair Hal Rogers, R-Ky., funding for more than fifty-five programs in the Departments of Labor, Health and Human Services, Education, and related agencies was eliminated. In addition to specific program cuts, all nondefense programs, projects, and accounts saw an across-the-board funding cut of 0.2 percent.

—Hilary Ewing

Following is a joint statement from Senate Majority Leader Harry Reid and House Speaker John Boehner on April 8, 2011, on the bipartisan spending agreement; a statement by President Barack Obama on April 8, 2011, announcing the budget agreement that prevented a government shutdown; and a summary of the final fiscal year 2011 continuing resolution, released on April 12, 2011.

House and Senate Leaders Announce Spending Agreement

April 8, 2011

House Speaker John Boehner (R-OH) and Senate Majority Leader Harry Reid (D-NV) tonight released the following statement:

"We have agreed to an historic amount of cuts for the remainder of this fiscal year, as well as a short-term bridge that will give us time to avoid a shutdown while we get that agreement through both houses and to the President. We will cut $78.5 billion below the President's 2011 budget proposal, and we have reached an agreement on the policy riders. In the meantime, we will pass a short-term resolution to keep the government running through Thursday. That short-term bridge will cut the first $2 billion of the total savings."

SOURCE: Representative John Boehner. "Joint Statement From Speaker Boehner & Senate Majority Leader Reid on Bipartisan Agreement to Cut Spending, Keep Government Open." April 8, 2011. http://boehner .house.gov/News/DocumentSingle.aspx?DocumentID=235059.

President Obama on FY2011 Budget Agreement

April 8, 2011

Good evening. Behind me, through the window, you can see the Washington Monument, visited each year by hundreds of thousands from around the world. The people who travel here come to learn about our history and to be inspired by the example of our democracy, a place where citizens of different backgrounds and beliefs can still come together as one nation. Tomorrow, I'm pleased to announce that the Washington Monument, as well as the entire Federal Government, will be open for business. And that's because today Americans of different beliefs came together again.

In the final hours before our Government would have been forced to shut down, leaders in both parties reached an agreement that will allow our small businesses to get the loans they need, our families to get the mortgages they applied for, and hundreds of thousands of Americans to show up at work and take home their paychecks on time, including our brave men and women in uniform.

This agreement between Democrats and Republicans, on behalf of all Americans, is on a budget that invests in our future while making the largest annual spending cut in our history. Like any worthwhile compromise, both sides had to make tough decisions and give ground on issues that were important to them. And I certainly did that.

Some of the cuts we agreed to will be painful. Programs people rely on will be cut back. Needed infrastructure projects will be delayed. And I would not have made these cuts in better circumstances.

But beginning to live within our means is the only way to protect those investments that will help America compete for new jobs: investments in our kids' education and student loans, in clean energy and life-saving medical research. We protected the investments we need to win the future.

At the same time, we also made sure that at the end of the day, this was a debate about spending cuts, not social issues like women's health and the protection of our air and water. These are important issues that deserve discussion, just not during a debate about our budget.

I want to think Speaker Boehner and Senator Reid for their leadership and their dedication during this process. A few months ago, I was able to sign a tax cut for American families because both parties worked through their differences and found common ground. Now the same cooperation will make possible the biggest annual spending cut in history, and it's my sincere hope that we can continue to come together as we face the many difficult challenges that lie ahead, from creating jobs and growing our economy to educating our children and reducing our deficit. That's what the American people expect us to do. That's why they sent us here.

A few days ago, I received a letter from a mother in Longmont, Colorado. Over the year, her son's eighth grade class saved up money and worked on projects so that next week they could take a class trip to Washington, D.C. They even have an appointment to lay a wreath on the Tomb of the Unknown Soldier.

The mother wrote that for the last few days the kids in her son's class had been worried and upset that they might have to cancel their trip because of a shutdown. She asked those of us in Washington to get past our petty grievances and make things right. And she said, "Remember, the future of this country is not for us. It's for our children."

Today we acted on behalf of our children's future. And next week, when 50 eighth graders from Colorado arrive in our nation's capital, I hope they get a chance to look up at the Washington Monument and feel the sense of pride and possibility that defines America, a land of many that has always found a way to move forward as one.

Thank you.

SOURCE: Executive Office of the President. "Remarks on the Federal Budget." April 8, 2011. *Compilation of Presidential Documents* 2011, no. 00245 (April 8, 2011). http://www.gpo.gov/fdsys/pkg/DCPD-201100245/pdf/DCPD-201100245.pdf.

Summary of the Final FY2011 Continuing Resolution

April 12, 2011

[All footnotes have been omitted.]

The negotiated agreement between the House, Senate, and White House on a final Fiscal Year 2011 Continuing Resolution will prevent a government shutdown, fund the entire federal government until September 30, 2011, and provide essential funding for national defense. In addition, the legislation will cut an unparalleled nearly $40 billion in federal spending.

When this agreement is signed into law, Congress will have taken the unprecedented step of passing the largest non-defense spending cut in the history of our nation—tens of billions larger than any other non-defense reduction, and the biggest overall reduction since World War II. This remarkable accomplishment is the result of hard-fought negotiations that required all sides to come together to find common ground.

It has been the goal of this new Republican majority to keep precious tax dollars where they are needed most—in the hands of businesses and individuals across the nation so that they can create jobs and grow our economy. The final Continuing Resolution will allow Congress to further this goal, continuing the trend of budget reductions to dig our nation out of our dangerous deficits and debt for years to come.

A summary of the final Continuing Resolution (CR) follows:

Overall Spending Limit: The final CR will include a total of $1.049 trillion in funding, a nearly $40 billion reduction from last year's (fiscal year 2010) levels. This includes the $12 billion in reductions previously approved by Congress and signed into law under the previous three continuing resolutions, as well as nearly $28 billion in additional new spending cuts.

Agriculture: The CR funds Agriculture programs at $20 billion, which is $3 billion below the fiscal year 2010 enacted level and $3.2 billion below the President's 2011 budget request.

The bill provides $1 billion for Food Safety and Inspection, which is $10 million below the fiscal year 2010 level, while allowing for uninterrupted meat, poultry, and egg products inspection activities of the agency. The bill also reduces Agricultural Credit Programs by $433 million, Agricultural Research Service by $64 million, and the National Institute for Food and Agriculture by $125.9 million below the fiscal year 2010 levels.

The CR also includes $6.75 billion for the Special Supplemental Feeding Program for Women, Infants and Children (WIC), which allows the program to support more than 9 million income-eligible mothers, infants, and children up to 5 years of age.

Commerce, Justice, Science: The Commerce, Justice, Science section of the CR contains a total of $53.4 billion, a $10.9 billion, or 17%, reduction from fiscal year 2010 levels, and a reduction of $7.1 billion, or 12%, from the President's fiscal year 2011 request.

The CR provides funding above fiscal year 2010 levels for National Institute of Standards and Technology research and manufacturing programs, as well as critical FBI national security and prisons/detention requirements. Justice Department appropriations are reduced by $946 million below fiscal year 2010 . . . and Commerce Department appropriations are cut by $6.5 billion below fiscal year 2010. The bill also includes $18.5 billion for NASA and fully funds the newly authorized exploration program.

This section of the CR also prohibits funding for: the establishment of a Climate Service at the National Oceanic and Atmospheric Administration; the approval of new fisheries catch-share programs in certain fisheries; and for NASA and the Office of Science and Technology Policy to engage in bilateral activities with China.

Defense Funding: The Department of Defense is funded at $513 billion in the CR—approximately $5 billion above last year—providing the necessary resources for the safety of our troops and the success of our nation's military actions. The bill also includes an additional $157.8 billion for overseas contingency operations (emergency funding) to advance our missions abroad.

The Defense section of this legislation includes $126.7 billion for military personnel, providing for 1,432,400 active duty and 846,200 reserve troops. In addition, the bill contains a total of $165.6 billion for operations and maintenance, $102.1 billion for procurement, $75 billion for research and development, and $31.4 billion for Defense health programs. This legislation eliminates all Defense earmark account funding, a cut of $4.2 billion from last year's level.

The CR also includes language preventing Guantanamo Bay detainees from being transferred into the United States for any purpose, prevents the construction or modification of detention facilities within the U.S. for the housing of detainees, and requires the Secretary of Defense to provide a certification to Congress that a transfer of any detainee to any foreign country or entity will not jeopardize the safety of the U.S. or its citizens. This language is virtually identical to existing law that was included in the National Defense Authorization Act.

Energy and Water: The Energy and Water section is funded at $31.8 billion in the CR. This is a 10% reduction—or $3.6 billion—from the President's fiscal year 2011 request, and a 5% reduction—or $1.7 billion—from fiscal year 2010 levels. These significant cuts further the House Republican commitment to deficit reduction and reining in the size of government, while at the same time protecting American security, providing support for private sector growth, and promoting a balanced national energy supply.

The bill funds the Army Corps of Engineers at the President's request level of $4.9 billion, supports existing applications for renewable energy loan guarantees at the Department of Energy, and provides a $697 million (7%) increase for the National Nuclear Security Administration to ensure adequate funding for critical components of our national defense.

Financial Services: The Financial Services and General Government section of the CR contains a total of $22 billion, a $2.4 billion, or 10%, reduction from fiscal year 2010 levels, and a reduction of $3.4 billion, or 14%, from the President's fiscal year 2011 request.

The CR reduces most Treasury and Executive Office of the President accounts and reduces funding for construction of new federal buildings by more than $800 million. The bill provides a $13 million increase over last year for the Inspector General of Troubled Asset Relief Program (TARP) to provide strong oversight of the billions of dollars remaining in TARP assets and continues current funding for drug task forces and programs to assist small businesses.

The CR restores a long-standing provision against the use of federal and local funds for abortions in the District of Columbia. The bill also includes the reauthorization of the DC Opportunity Scholarships, along with a $2.3 million funding increase, to stop the termination of the program and allow new students to participate. The legislation also eliminates four Administration "Czars," including the "Health Care Czar," the "Climate Change Czar," the "Car Czar," and the "Urban Affairs Czar."

Homeland Security: A total of $41.8 billion in discretionary funding is provided for the Department of Homeland Security (DHS) for fiscal year 2011. This is $784 million, or 2%, below FY 2010, and $1.9 billion, or 4%, below the President's fiscal year 2011 request.

All critical frontline operations for DHS—including Customs and Border Protection, Immigration and Customs Enforcement, the Transportation Security Agency, the Coast Guard, and the Secret Service are sufficiently funded to meet mission requirements and sustain staffing levels. This includes funding for 21,370 Border Patrol agents, 33,400 ICE detention beds, and military pay and allowances for the U.S. Coast Guard. The bill reduces

CBP's Border Security Fencing, Infrastructure, and Technology (BSFIT) account to the President's request, reduces FEMA first responder grants by $786 million, eliminates $264 million in funding that was previously targeted to earmarks, and rescinds $557 million in unobligated and lapsed balances from prior year funds. The bill also caps the amount of TSA screener personnel at 46,000.

Interior: The CR includes $29.6 billion in discretionary funding in the Interior and Environment section of the bill, which is 8.1%, or $2.62 billion, below the fiscal year 2010 enacted level and 8.5%, or $2.8 billion, below the President's request.

The Environmental Protection Agency (EPA) is reduced by $1.6 billion, a 16% decrease from last year's level. The cuts to the EPA alone represent 61% of the bill's reduction compared to last year's level. . . .

Funding levels for operational accounts bill-wide are largely sustained to prevent layoffs and the closure of national parks and forests, wildlife refuges, Smithsonian museums and other sites. In addition, the legislation contains language reinstating the Fish and Wildlife Service's original determination to delist wolves in states with approved management plans in place. It returns management of wolf populations in Idaho, Montana, Oregon, Washington, and Utah to the states. The bill also includes a limitation on the use of funds to implement the Bureau of Land Management's "Wild Lands" policy.

Labor, HHS, Education and Related Agencies

The Labor, HHS, Education and Related Agencies section of the CR contains a total of $157.7 billion, roughly a $5.5 billion, or 3.36%, reduction from fiscal year 2010 levels. The bill is also nearly $13 billion, or 7.6 percent, below the President's fiscal year 2011 request.

The CR preserves funding for large education programs that fund elementary and secondary schools as well as special education and provides a modest increase for Head Start to ensure that all children currently enrolled will continue to receive services, while making prudent reductions in lower priority areas. In addition, the bill continues the Pell Grant Program at the current maximum award level of $4,860.

The CR terminates funding for more than 55 programs, for a total savings of well over $1 billion. In addition, the bill cuts two programs funded in ObamaCare. . . . The bill makes reforms to the Pell Grant Program that are estimated to save more than $35 billion over the next 10 years by eliminating the ability of students to draw down two Pell Grant awards at the same time. Finally, the CR will return Title X funding to fiscal year 2008 levels.

Legislative Branch: Legislative Branch is reduced by $103 million from last year's levels. Of this amount, funding for the U.S. House is reduced by $55 million from last year—or 53% of the total cut—and reflects a 5% cut in Member, Committee, and Leadership office expenses except for the Appropriations Committee, which offered a larger cut of 9%.

Military Construction/Veterans Affairs: Military Construction/Veterans Affairs programs will receive $73.3 billion in discretionary funding—a decrease of $2.7 billion below the President's fiscal year 2011 request and a decrease of $3.3 billion below last year's level. Within this funding, the bill provides critical and necessary resources for veterans' health and benefits, including an increase of $13.8 billion for the Department of Veterans affairs over last year's level.

State and Foreign Operations: The funding level for the State Department and Foreign Operations in the CR is a total of $48.3 billion—a $504 million reduction from last year's level and an $8.4 billion reduction from the President's fiscal year 2011 request.

This section of the legislation includes a prohibition on pay raises for foreign services officers, a $377 million cut to U.S. contributions to the United Nations and international organizations, and a $130 million cut to international banks and financial institutions. In addition, the bill reduces family planning activities by $73 million—and includes a reduction in the UN Population Fund to fiscal year 2008 levels. The bill also maintains pro-life policy provisions carried in fiscal year 2010.

Transportation, Housing and Urban Development: The Transportation, Housing, Urban Development and Related Agencies section of the CR contains a total of $55.5 billion, a $12.3 billion, or 18%, reduction from fiscal year 2010 levels, and a reduction of $13.2 billion, or 20%, from the President's fiscal year 2011 request.

For the Department of Transportation, the bill eliminates new funding for High Speed Rail and rescinds $400 million in previous year funds, for a total reduction of $2.9 billion from fiscal year 2010 levels. The bill reduces funding for transit by a total of $991 million and includes a total of $528 million in new funding for the "TIGER" grant program. While the majority of programs funded by the Highway Trust Fund remain at fiscal year 2010 levels, the bill contains total contract authority rescissions of $3.2 billion, of which $630 million is comprised of old earmarks.

For the Department of Housing and Urban Development, the Community Development Fund program was reduced $942 million, for a fiscal year 2011 funding level of $3.5 billion. The Section 8 program is funded at a level of $18.4 billion with $16.7 billion for voucher renewals, $1.45 billion for administrative fees, $35 million for Section 811 mainstream voucher renewals, and $50 million for HUD-Veterans Affairs Supportive Housing (VASH) vouchers.

SOURCE: House Appropriations Committee. "Summary—Final Fiscal Year 2011 Continuing Resolution." April 12, 2011. http://appropriations.house.gov/_files/41211SummaryFinalFY2011CR.pdf.

OTHER HISTORIC DOCUMENTS OF INTEREST

FROM THIS VOLUME

FROM PREVIOUS *HISTORIC DOCUMENTS*

Goodluck Jonathan on His Inauguration as President of Nigeria

APRIL 18 AND MAY 29, 2011

Nigeria is home to an estimated 250 ethnic groups, with distinct cultural, linguistic, and religious traditions. Given the abundance of subcultures that formed independent Nigeria after the exit of the British colonial representatives in 1960, it is not surprising that Nigerians often view their religion, not their nationality, as their primary identity. Since the transition from military rule to a fledgling democracy in 1999, Nigeria's religious and regional fault lines have been deepened by competition for resources, resentment toward endemic corruption, and a series of irregular elections. Communal tensions have traditionally been eased by a "gentleman's agreement" in which the presidency rotates every term between a northern Muslim and a southern Christian. Christian nominees traditionally have Muslim running mates and Muslim nominees traditionally have Christian running mates. In practice, this has been facilitated by alternative nominations of Christian and Muslim presidential candidates by the People's Democratic Party (PDP), which has held the office since the switch to representative government in 1999. In 2011, however, Nigerian President Goodluck Jonathan, a Christian, announced that he would seek a second term, violating the long-standing tradition of Muslim-Christian rotation.

BUILDUP TO VIOLENCE

The election in 2007 was widely viewed as compromised, fostering a sense of public disenfranchisement. Many poll stations had delayed openings during the balloting, and some were not opened at all. The ruling PDP's Muslim candidate, Umaru Yar'Adua, was sworn in amid reports of electoral violence. Following the death in 2010 of President Yar'Adua, who had struggled with a long illness during his term, his Christian vice president, Goodluck Jonathan, took office. When President Jonathan announced that he would stand for a subsequent term in 2011, Muslims protested that he was dishonoring precedent, which held that a Muslim should hold the office for the next term. Although the elections were considered a transparent and credible improvement upon the 2007 poll, President Jonathan's compelling mandate—winning a sizeable percentage more of the vote than his nearest rival—prompted accusations of fraud. These assertions were accompanied by widespread rioting following his acceptance of the office.

2011 ELECTIONS

Civic organizations appealed for peace in the run-up to the April 2011 balloting. The reinstatement of the Independent National Electoral Commission (INEC) by the Electoral Reform Act of 2010 bolstered public confidence that the new government would be more representative. Improved transparency deterred some violence and supported turnout, even after the postponement of the election because paper ballots did not arrive in time. Millions cast their votes and expressed confidence that the 2011 election would be fairer than the last, although some Nigerian poll watchers secured the integrity of the results under duress. The poll was generally acknowledged to be credible, despite isolated reports of voter intimidation and late poll office openings. Nevertheless, Muslim groups watched the victory of Jonathan with dismay. Rioting spread in Nigeria's northern and central regions, with violence escalating during the subsequent gubernatorial and local campaigns.

Although religion is the most obvious motivator in recent outbreaks of political violence, the roles of religion, socioeconomics, and the perception of official impunity are intertwined in explanations of enduring conflict in Nigeria. The president appealed to alienated constituencies in his April 2011 acceptance speech. President Jonathan struck a conciliatory note, describing erstwhile rivals "not as opponents, but as partners," positing that "even in our diversity, the progress of Nigeria remains paramount to all." He also emphasized the country's common monotheism, taking office "with a heart full of gratitude to Almighty God" and with thanks to his Muslim vice president. This note of unity permeated the address, which presented a vision of a harmonious citizenry and inclusive government working together to realize both Nigeria's economic potential and its full transition to democracy. Jonathan ended the speech with a rejection of electoral violence and an expression of gratitude for national and international election monitors and reporters whose "fair observations" benefited the electoral outcome.

The inaugural address echoed these themes of ecumenical cooperation toward national progress; transparent, representative government; and disavowal of violence by Nigeria's distinct communities and their leaders. The president praised the faith of voters who participated in the election and promised to begin a "decade of development" in which detractors would not be allowed to undermine progress in favor of their individual religious or economic interests. Instead, the president pledged "to forge a united Nigeria: a land of justice, opportunity and plenty." Specific policy proposals included power sector reform, heretofore a bastion of corruption and inefficiency, despite its potential to contribute to national wealth. The president acknowledged that peace in the violent and resource-rich Niger Delta Region would need to precede reform, however. He closed with a request that Nigerians who fought for decolonization commit themselves equally to securing full democratization.

CONSEQUENCES AND ONGOING CHALLENGES

Public grievances, however, did not dissipate in 2011 following the inauguration. Although the government launched plans to improve access to education, health care, and electricity, living standards stagnated, and Muslim groups remained resentful of the president's mandate. Community tensions were exacerbated by the government's apparent inability to respond effectively to attacks by Boko Haram, an Islamist group that promotes the nationwide adoption of Islamic sharia law. These attacks included a car bombing of the United Nations headquarters in the capital Abuja, in central Nigeria, on August 26, 2011. Boko Haram is considered by some to be an insurgency, and this—its first attack on foreign interests in the country—was viewed as an escalation of its conflict with the central government. Boko Haram's activities have raised the risk of reprisals between religious groups, with Muslim worshippers at Ramadan services suffering an attack a few days later, on August 29, in the troubled central city of Jos. Some saw the coordinated assaults on Christmas Day services that year as revenge for the Ramadan violence, although Boko Haram claimed responsibility. Multiple outbreaks of mayhem transpired in the aftermath, with the Christian Association of Nigeria (CAN) warning that it would "respond appropriately" to any future attacks on Christians. Perhaps taking a cue from the president's pleas, the Sultan of Sokoto, the symbolic head of Islam in Nigeria, condemned Boko Haram as evil. Nevertheless, its influence appeared to grow apace: Boko Haram called for all Christians to leave northern Nigeria in January 2012, prompting complaints that the government was not protecting the public. Likewise, Boko Haram urged Muslims to leave southern Nigeria for the North, citing unsubstantiated claims that they faced the risk of renewed violence. Despite assurances by the president that the law would be "enforced without fear or favor," critics accused officials of both faiths of offering rhetoric and prayers for national welfare instead of effective action.

For its part, the government was outwardly consumed with security and development concerns following the election. To the extent religion played a role in government, officials sought to pacify the public by emphasizing inclusiveness in their rhetoric and power sharing in their practices to preempt communal violence where possible. It was less effective, however, in neutralizing active provokers of the violence.

Notwithstanding religious tensions, the policy agenda was dominated by economic initiatives in early 2012. The removal of costly fuel subsidies proved nearly as explosive as sectarian provocations, with riots and protests hampering logistics and daily life throughout the country in January. Major roads were blocked and officials' houses set on fire, prompting the imposition of curfews in multiple Nigerian states as residents increasingly retaliated against security forces with impunity. While the government claimed that the $8 billion saved in the subsidy cut would be reinvested to provide better services and public transportation, the population remained unconvinced. The price of gas doubled to $3.50 per gallon causing crippling nationwide strikes and threatening the livelihoods of Nigerians, who typically subsist on a daily income of $2. Small businesses were faced with prohibitive operating costs due to their dependence on oil-fueled generators during Nigeria's frequent power outages.

By tradition, Nigerians see fuel subsidies as a right. Low fuel prices are viewed as the only benefit the people derive from Nigeria's status as a major oil exporter, as corruption in the industry otherwise prevents energy profits from benefiting the wider society. The Nigeria Labour Conference, the country's largest trade union, urged the public to demand reinstatement of the subsidy, which had artificially depressed gas prices for more than two decades. Although the cut was expected to bolster public coffers, activists still viewed it as unjust, given the past largesse the energy sector had provided to scores of government officials heedless of the public interest.

Mismanagement over the past few decades has severely reduced Nigeria's refining capacity and—despite its status as one of Africa's chief oil exporters—rendered it dependent upon imported gas. The public backlash over the end of the fuel subsidy reflected widespread frustration with the corruption that has traditionally characterized oversight of Nigeria's national and natural resources. The demonstrations attracted widespread support, despite reports that criminal elements were attempting to infiltrate them and leverage the disorder for their own purposes. Ironically, the protests achieved what the government could not—joining Muslims and Christians in a common cause. That solidarity, however, may prove short-lived if the government fails to secure the vision for development outlined in President Jonathan's acceptance speech and inaugural address.

—Anastazia Clouting

Following is the edited transcript of a speech given on April 18, 2011, by Nigerian President Goodluck Jonathan upon his reelection; and the edited transcript of President Jonathan's inaugural address on May 29, 2011.

President Goodluck Jonathan Accepts Presidency

DOCUMENT

April 18, 2011

My dear country men and women.

This is a new dawn! Our nation has spoken. At the end of intense and hard fought campaigns by all the political parties, our people spoke through the ballot. In every city, town, village, ward and voting unit, Nigerians stood in the sun, some in the rain, some walked long distances and all waited patiently, to vote.

With a heart full of gratitude to Almighty God, I want to thank Nigerians for the great sacrifice and overwhelming national mandate you have just given to me, to preside over the affairs of this nation for the next four years.

We have, by this election, reaffirmed our unity as one nation under God; reiterated our faith in democracy; and underscored our determination to fully join the free world where only the will of the people is the foundation of governance. We will not let you down. We will not let Nigeria down.

My brothers and sisters, fellow citizens, we are all winners. In this context, there is no victor and no vanquished. Nigerians have proved to the world that we are capable of holding free, fair and credible elections. With the evident national spread of our victory, we have demonstrated that even in our diversity, the progress of Nigeria remains paramount to all.

This is a victory for the sustenance of our democracy; a victory which all Nigerians irrespective of creed, ethnicity, or state of origin should celebrate. It is a triumph for our common destiny as a people with shared ideals, shared dreams and shared hopes.

I congratulate the candidates of the other political parties. I regard them not as opponents, but as partners. Indeed, some of them have held high public office in the past. . . .

When I declared my intention to run for the office of President under the ticket of the Peoples Democratic Party, I reflected on my humble background and the long journey that brought me to that moment.

Eight months later, I stand before you as the winner of the 2011 Presidential election. I am humbled by your overwhelming mandate.

During that declaration, I said that I had no enemies. Let me say it again, I have no enemies to fight.

Indeed, I reassure all Nigerians that we would continue to run a government that is committed to fairness, equity and justice for all.

The progress we seek for our country is in our collective hands. I am confident that with this new spirit of national reawakening and our sense of collective ownership of the

Nigerian project, a firm foundation has been laid for participatory governance and progress.

Together we will build a new economy that is strong and dynamic and underpinned by a patriotic work ethic. Together we will remake our society to emphasize the most noble of our national values, and together we shall recreate a great nation welded in unity and harmony; a nation marching towards collective progress in which no one is left behind.

This election is the renewal of hope. As we march towards our centenary as a nation in the year 2014, this election will be remembered as that which reaffirmed our faith and strengthened the bond of our union. We found within ourselves the basis for our national confidence. We demonstrated that we are making great strides in consolidating democratic governance. This election is further evidence that Nigeria is secure, that we are stable; and most of all, that the future of Nigeria is bright.

Now, we must all unite. We must quickly move away from partisan battlegrounds and find the national common ground. We must show the world that this nation of many people will always find the love, the courage and the path to move forward as one. Let us join hands to build a prosperous nation. This is the challenge of our generation. This is our unfinished task. On my part, I promise to run an all-inclusive government.

It is on this note that I am greatly pained at reports of incidences of unnecessary violence and loss of lives and property in some parts of the country over the past twenty four hours.

I enjoin our political and religious leaders, in their usual sense of patriotism to call on their followers to eschew all acts of bitterness and violence. As I have always stated, nobody's political ambition is worth the blood of any Nigerian.

I thank all the nations of the world, their leaders and our friends for their goodwill. I thank our friends from the national and international media, religious leaders, civil society, voluntary organizations, development partners and our talented diaspora Nigerians that are reporting, monitoring or participating in our elections. We have benefitted from their fair observations.

My special thanks go to all our public services, security agencies, academia, members of the National Youth Service Corps and emergency services. These men, women and youth are making huge sacrifices towards the success of the 2011 elections.

I wish to express my profound thanks to Vice President Mohammed Namadi Sambo. He brought strength and commitment to our ticket. I am equally grateful to the leadership and members of the PDP; the governors of the 36 states of the Federation; members of the Presidential Campaign Council and all our supporters across the nation for their great sense of dedication, faith and exemplary conduct.

Now is the time for all Nigerians to reach out to their neighbours. I want all of us to join hands in brotherhood, party affiliation or preferred candidate notwithstanding. We are all Nigerians and I will President to all. This is the new dawn we crave. What is now required is a new commitment, national solidarity and re-dedication to service.

Come, join me. Let's continue on the road of national transformation.

Let us all thank our merciful God for this day. Let us all continue to pray for God's guidance in the years ahead.

I thank you and May God bless Nigeria.

SOURCE: The State House, Abuja. "Acceptance Speech by President Goodluck Ebele Jonathan, following his declaration as the winner of the 2011 presidential election on Monday, April 18, 2011." April 18, 2011. http://www.nigeriafirst.org/article_11013.shtml.

President Goodluck Jonathan
Delivers Inaugural Address

DOCUMENT

May 29, 2011

My Dear Compatriots, I stand in humble gratitude to you, this day, having just sworn to the oath of office as President, Commander-in-Chief of the Armed Forces of our great nation.

I thank you all, fellow citizens, for the trust and confidence, which you have demonstrated through the power of your vote. I want to assure you, that I will do my utmost at all times, to continue to deserve your trust. . . .

Your Excellencies, distinguished ladies and gentlemen, earlier this year, over seventy-three million eligible Nigerians endured all manner of inconvenience just to secure their voters cards, in order to exercise the right to choose those that will govern them.

At the polls, we saw the most dramatic expressions of the hunger for democracy. Stories of courage and patriotism were repeated in many ways, including how fellow citizens helped physically challenged voters into polling stations to enable them exercise their franchise. The inspiring story of the one hundred and three year-old man, and many like him across the country, who struggled against the physical limitations of age to cast their vote, is noteworthy.

Such determination derives from the typical Nigerian spirit of resilience in the face of the greatest of odds. That spirit has, over the years, stirred our hopes, doused our fears, and encouraged us to gather ourselves to build a strong nation even when others doubted our capacity.

Today, our unity is firm, and our purpose is strong. Our determination unshakable. Together, we will unite our nation and improve the living standards of all our peoples whether in the North or in the South; in the East or in the West. Our decade of development has begun. The march is on. The day of transformation begins today. We will not allow anyone exploit differences in creed or tongue, to set us one against another. Let me at this point congratulate the elected governors, senators, members of the House of Representatives and those of the State Houses of Assembly for their victories at the polls.

I am mindful that I represent the shared aspiration of all our people to forge a united Nigeria: a land of justice, opportunity and plenty. Confident that a people that are truly committed to a noble ideal, cannot be denied the realisation of their vision, I assure you that this dream of Nigeria, that is so deeply felt by millions, will indeed come to reality.

A decade ago, it would have been a mere daydream to think that a citizen from a minority ethnic group could galvanise national support, on an unprecedented scale, to discard ancient prejudices, and win the people's mandate as President of our beloved country. That result emanated from the toil and sacrifice of innumerable individuals and institutions, many of whom may never get to receive public appreciation for their effort. . . .

The success of the 2011 elections and the widespread acclaim which the exercise received was due to the uncommon patriotism and diligence exhibited by many Nigerians, including members of the Armed Forces, National Youth Service Corps (NYSC) and others. Unfortunately, despite the free, fair and transparent manner the elections were conducted, a senseless wave of violence in some parts of the country led to the death of ten members of the NYSC and others. These brave men and women paid the supreme sacrifice in the service of our fatherland. They are heroes of our democracy. We offer our heartfelt prayers and condolences in respect of all those who lost their lives.

In the days ahead, those of us that you have elected to serve must show that we are men and women with the patriotism and passion, to match the hopes and aspirations of you, the great people of this country. We must demonstrate the leadership, statesmanship, vision, capacity, and sacrifice, to transform our nation. We must strengthen common grounds, develop new areas of understanding and collaboration, and seek fresh ideas, that will enrich our national consensus. It is the supreme task of this generation to give hope to the hopeless, strength to the weak and protection to the defenceless.

Fellow citizens, the leadership we have pledged is decidedly transformative. The transformation will be achieved in all the critical sectors, by harnessing the creative energies of our people.

We must grow the economy, create jobs, and generate enduring happiness for our people. I have great confidence in the ability of Nigerians to transform this country. The urgent task of my administration is to provide a suitable environment, for productive activities to flourish. I therefore call on the good people of Nigeria, to enlist as agents of this great transformation. My dear countrymen and women, being a Nigerian is a blessing. It is also a great responsibility. We must make a vow that, together, we will make the Nigerian Enterprise thrive.

The leadership and the followership must strive to convert our vast human and natural resources into the force that leads to a greater Nigeria. The Nigeria of our dreams must be built on hard work and not on short cuts. Let me salute the Nigerian workers who build our communities, cities and country. They deserve fair rewards, and so do the women that raise our children, and the rural dwellers that grow our food.

The moment is right. The signs are heart-warming. We are ready to take off on the path of sustained growth and economic development. In our economic strategy, there will be appropriate policy support to the real sector of the economy, so that Small and Medium Enterprises may thrive. Nigeria is blessed with enormous natural wealth, and my Administration will continue to encourage locally owned enterprises to take advantage of our resources in growing the domestic economy. A robust private sector is vital to providing jobs for our rapidly expanding population. But this must be a collaborative effort.

We must form technical and financial partnerships with global businesses and organizations. We live in an age where no country can survive on its own; countries depend on each other for economic well-being. Nigeria is no different. Returns on investment in Nigeria remain among the highest in the world. We will continue to welcome sustainable investment in our economy.

We will push programs and policies that will benefit both local and foreign businesses, but we must emphasize mutual benefits and win-win relationships. The overall ongoing reforms in the banking and financial sectors are therefore designed to support the real sector of the economy.

To drive our overall economic vision, the power sector reform is at the heart of our industrialization strategy. I call on all stakeholders, to cooperate with my administration, to ensure the success of the reforms.

Over the next four years, attention will be focused on rebuilding our infrastructure. We will create greater access to quality education and improved health care delivery. We will pay special attention to the agricultural sector, to enable it play its role of ensuring food security and massive job creation for our people.

The creation of the Nigerian Sovereign Investment Authority will immensely contribute to strengthening our fiscal framework, by institutionalizing savings of our commodity-related revenues. With this mechanism in place, we will avoid the boom and bust cycles, and mitigate our exposure to oil price volatility.

The lesson we have learnt is that the resolution of the Niger Delta issue is crucial for the health of the nation's economy. In the interest of justice, equity and national unity, we shall actively promote the development of the region. I believe that peace is a necessary condition for development.

Fellow citizens, in every decision, I shall always place the common good before all else. The bane of corruption shall be met by the overwhelming force of our collective determination, to rid our nation of this scourge. The fight against corruption is a war in which we must all enlist, so that the limited resources of this nation will be used for the growth of our common wealth.

I am confident that we have every reason to look to the future with hope. We owe ourselves and posterity the duty of making this country respectable in the comity of nations. Nigeria, as a responsible member of the international community, will remain committed to the maintenance of global peace and security. We will continue to play an active role in the United Nations. Our role in the African Union, ECOWAS, and the Gulf of Guinea will be enhanced to ensure greater human and energy security.

Your Excellencies, Distinguished Ladies and Gentlemen, this is a new dawn for Africa. We fought for decolonization. We will now fight for democratization. Nigeria, in partnership with the African Union, will lead the process for democracy and development in Africa. In particular, we will support the consolidation of democracy, good governance and human rights in the continent. Africa must develop its vast resources to tackle poverty and under-development.

Conscious of the negative effect of insecurity on growth and development, my Administration will seek collaboration at bilateral and multilateral levels, to improve our capability in combating trans-border crimes. In this regard, we will intensify our advocacy against the illicit trades in small arms and light weapons, which have become the catalyst for conflicts on the African continent. All Nigerian diplomatic missions abroad are to accord this vision of defending the dignity of humanity the highest priority.

My fellow countrymen and women, Nigeria is not just a land of promise; it shall be a nation where positive change will continue to take place, for the good of our people. The time for lamentation is over. This is the era of transformation. This is the time for action. But Nigeria can only be transformed if we all play our parts with commitment and sincerity. Cynicism and skepticism will not help our journey to greatness. Let us all believe in a new Nigeria. Let us work together to build a great country that we will all be proud of. This, is our hour.

Fellow Compatriots, lift your gaze towards the horizon. Look ahead, and you will see a great future, that we can secure with unity, hard work and collective sacrifice.

Join me now as we begin the journey of transforming Nigeria.

- I will continue to fight, for your future, because I am one of you.
- I will continue to fight, for improved medical care for all our citizens.
- I will continue to fight for all citizens to have access to first class education.

- I will continue to fight for electricity to be available to all our citizens.
- I will continue to fight for an efficient and affordable public transport system for all our people.
- I will continue to fight for jobs to be created through productive partnerships.

You have trusted me with your mandate, and I will never, never let you down.

I know your pain, because I have been there. Look beyond the hardship you have endured. See a new beginning; a new direction; a new spirit.

Nigerians, I want you to start to dream again. What you see in your dreams, we can achieve together. I call upon all the Presidential candidates who contested with me to join hands with us as we begin the transformation of our country.

Let us work together; let us build together; let us bequeath a greater Nigeria to the generations to come.

I thank you! God bless you all! And God bless the Federal Republic of Nigeria.

SOURCE: The State House, Abuja. "President Goodluck Jonathan's Inauguration Speech May 29, 2011." May 29, 2011. http://www.nigeriafirst.org/article_11151.shtml.

OTHER HISTORIC DOCUMENTS OF INTEREST

FROM PREVIOUS *HISTORIC DOCUMENTS*

House and EPA Release Reports on Natural Gas Drilling

APRIL 16 AND DECEMBER 8, 2011

For hundreds of years, the United States has taken minerals from the ground. From the 1800s on, coal has been mined and turned into energy, and in the 1900s, glass, coke, and steel were the products of industrial mining. Today, the United States is hoping natural gas can cure its dependence on foreign oil. But the rush to drill deep into the Earth has not been without concern. Forecasting what is available in natural gas reserves is difficult. The Environmental Protection Agency (EPA) estimates that natural gas wells will produce fuel for approximately 110 years, but that range is based on limited data and guesswork. There is additional concern surrounding the extraction process, known as hydraulic fracturing, or fracking, and the chemicals used to remove natural gas from deep underground. Environmental groups and residents near drilling sites question whether chemicals are leaking into the groundwater and aquifers, or being released into the air, causing harm to human health. There is a lack of information about the costs of drilling versus its benefits. The first reports were that natural gas drilling was relatively cheap, but drillers now know that active wells are surrounded by large, often less-productive wells that can be more costly to drill than their benefits warrant.

Natural Gas Drilling in the United States

One of the world's largest known natural gas fields has drawn particular attention from people on both sides of the debate. The Marcellus Shale Deposit runs under New York, Ohio, Pennsylvania, and West Virginia, and was expected to account for 6 percent of the U.S. gas supply in 2011. That number could more than double by 2020. In 2011, all four states debated how drilling should take place, where it would be allowed, and the value for the state. In Ohio, where drilling is currently taking place, the state's Republican governor, John Kasich, has supported opening more public lands to drilling and entered into an agreement with Pennsylvania to dispose of some of that state's wastewater drilling by-product. In New York, Democratic Governor Andrew Cuomo worked to lift a state moratorium on fracking, and a decision is expected in 2012. In West Virginia, Democratic Governor Earl Ray Tomblin strongly supports the natural gas drilling taking place in his state and penned a column entitled "Our Future: Marcellus Shale," writing, "West Virginia can help bring an end to our nation's reliance on foreign sources of energy, while being environmentally responsible within our borders. . . . I am mindful that the steps we take today will allow our economy to blossom, giving rise to greater educational and employment opportunities for our citizens." In 2011, the state's legislature passed a bill to weaken regulations on natural gas drilling.

Some of the fiercest debate has come out of Pennsylvania, where drilling is fast and furious. The state currently has 4,000 natural gas wells and is projected to add 2,500 more wells each year during the coming decades. The economic benefits for the state are well documented. A Pennsylvania State University study reported that drilling helped bring the state 23,000 new jobs. The drilling boom brought in revenue through busy hotels, stores, and restaurants, and has benefited residents with the installation of new roads. Drilling in Pennsylvania has not been without incident, however. Sixty-five wells drilled in 2011 were cited for bad cementing and casing, which can lead to dangerous chemical leaks. And the *New York Times* ran a series of reports on natural gas drilling, some featuring Pennsylvania homeowners who had leased their land for drilling, only to later develop medical problems after being exposed to arsenic and benzene, two chemicals used in the extraction of natural gas. In an effort to protect residents, the state senate and assembly have passed separate bills to regulate drilling, but the two houses have not yet agreed on one bill. Pennsylvania Governor Tom Corbett was a vocal opponent to a Delaware River Basin Commission decision to postpone a vote on new drilling rules for the watershed, which supplies drinking water to fifteen million people, many of them in New York and Pennsylvania.

FRACKING CONCERNS

Natural gas drilling raises a number of concerns, the most significant of which is the method for extracting natural gas deposits known as hydraulic fracturing, or fracking. The process involves pumping large amounts of water, sand, and chemicals into the ground to crack shale deposits and free bubbles of gas, releasing them to the surface where the gas can be collected and transported for use.

The primary concerns are the chemicals used by the drilling companies to extract the natural gas deposits, their by-products, and disposal. In 2005, Vice President Dick Cheney helped to push through an amendment to the Safe Drinking Water Act that exempts fracking from regulation, meaning that companies do not need to disclose what chemicals they are using in the process. The drillers maintain that revealing such information would force them to divulge proprietary secrets. The drilling industry announced plans to start a public database to disclose their fracking chemicals. However, reporting to the database will be voluntary, and the release of information on proprietary chemicals will not be mandatory, nor is any data required to be factually accurate.

States involved in natural gas drilling have expressed concern about how to handle the wastewater by-product of fracking, which can contain salts, radionuclides, and volatile organic compounds hazardous to human health. Typically, drilling companies can pump the by-product into wells deep below the Earth's surface. But in places like Pennsylvania, the state's geological structure makes this impossible. So, drilling companies in Pennsylvania have paid wastewater treatment plants for processing or have trucked the chemicals to other states where they are pumped into the ground. Many of the processing facilities that received the wastewater by-product were not equipped to remove the harmful chemicals it contained and ended up pumping contaminated water back into waterways. Because of this, the Pennsylvania Department of Environmental Protection asked drilling companies to stop sending their by-products to water treatment plants, although at this time they are under no compulsion to do so.

Questions about the economic impact of drilling are abundant. Studies have been released extolling the benefits of drilling, particularly the jobs it creates in the drilling area. But an Ohio State University study called "Economic Value of Shale Natural Gas in Ohio" claims that these studies have overstated the economic benefits. "Even if the natural gas industry experiences significant job growth, its employment share is too small to have any significant effect on unemployment rates and on the economy (with the exception of remote rural areas such as in rural Western North Dakota)." The report continues, "From a national perspective greater natural gas production will displace other fossil fuels and their workers as they are no longer needed, in particular coal."

There is also the economic impact on individuals to consider. A number of leases allow oil and gas companies to drill for natural gas on private land, and many landowners, drawn in by the prospect of annual payments and royalties, enter into these leases without fully understanding their terms. A number of banks have become reluctant to back mortgages for homes within three miles of a well for fear that home values would plummet if the area becomes a brownfield. Some leases do not require landowner compensation for water contamination or damage to livestock, crops, or property. Others allow the companies to store chemicals, cut down trees, or build roads through the landowner's property. And many of the leases allow for extension without the landowner's approval.

At least eight states have taken action to protect landowners by requiring drilling companies to compensate for any property damage caused by natural gas extraction. And a growing number of attorneys general—specifically those in New York, Ohio, and Pennsylvania—have issued warnings to landowners to proceed with caution before signing drilling leases. In other states, landowners have taken matters into their own hands. Landowners in Pennsylvania, Texas, and Virginia have filed class action lawsuits. The suits claim that drilling companies deducted the costs of drilling activities from the payments landowners received for allowing drilling on their land.

House Report on Fracking Chemicals

On April 16, 2011, Democrats on the U. S. House of Representatives Committee on Energy and Commerce released the findings of its study into the types of chemicals and the amounts used by fourteen leading oil and gas companies from 2005 to 2009. This was the first national inventory of fracking chemicals on a comprehensive scale.

The House report found that the fourteen companies used more than 780 million gallons of fracking products between 2005 and 2009, not including water. The 2,500 products used in the fracking process contained 750 different chemicals and other components, some of which were harmless, but others, like lead and benzene, are considered extremely hazardous. During the time frame of the study, the companies used twenty-nine chemicals that are known or possible human carcinogens, regulated under the Safe Drinking Water Act because of risk to human health, or listed as hazardous air pollutants under the Clean Air Act. Menthol, a hazardous air pollutant, was the most widely used chemical. Ninety-seven million gallons of 279 different products were used in fracking by the fourteen companies that contained at least one chemical or component listed as proprietary or a trade secret.

Rep. Diana DeGette, D-Colo., said she found it "deeply disturbing to discover the content and quantity of toxic chemicals, like benzene and lead, being injected into the ground without the knowledge of the communities whose health could be affected." Drilling companies found the House study methods flawed: "This report uses the same sleight of hand deployed in the last report on diesel use—it compiles overall product volumes, not the volumes of the hazardous chemicals contained within those products," said Matt Armstrong, an energy attorney at Bracewell & Giuliani, which represents some of the drilling companies. "This generates big numbers but provides no context for the use of these chemicals over the many thousands of frac jobs that were conducted within the time frame of this report," he said.

EPA and National Academy of Sciences Reports

Ongoing fracking in Pennsylvania led the EPA to conduct one of its first investigations into the effects the process has on water and overall human health in the United States. The draft report, released in December 2011, linked groundwater contamination in Pavillion, Wyoming, to fracking. Democrats used the report as a call to overturn the 2005 amendment to the Safe Drinking Water Act. "These draft findings reinforce the need for state and federal regulators to ensure that hydraulic fracturing of natural-gas wells proceeds with the strongest possible safeguards in place to protect public health and the environment," said Rep. Henry Waxman, D-Calif. Opposition to the report came from Wyoming's governor, Matt Mead, who called the findings "scientifically questionable." The EPA did issue caveats along with the report, one noting that many fracking wells differ from the ones it explored in its report.

In May 2011, the National Academy of Sciences released a report on the impact of fracking with data collected by Duke University scientists from sixty-eight drinking water samples. The scientists found potentially harmful levels of methane near drilling sites in New York and Pennsylvania, specifically in those aquifers that overlay the Marcellus and Utica shale deposits. Methane was detected in fifty-one of the sixty drinking water wells in the area, regardless of whether drilling had taken place nearby, but methane levels increased as scientists sampled nearer to natural gas wells. "Greater stewardship, data, and possibly regulation are needed to ensure the sustainable future of shale-gas extraction and to improve public confidence in its use," the report concluded.

Stronger Drilling Regulations

In August 2011, a Department of Energy panel, known as the Natural Gas Subcommittee, made recommendations on improving the safety and overall impact of natural gas drilling, noting—significantly—that drinking water contamination caused by fracking is improbable. The subcommittee, created by President Obama and Energy Secretary Steven Chu, had been heavily criticized by state legislators, scientists, and environmental groups for its makeup, mainly because six of the seven members on the panel had ties to the drilling industry. Additional criticism came from Congressional Republicans and others who said the work by the committee undermined the work of the EPA. The committee's report noted that shale gas could provide great economic and environmental benefits for the United States, but that protecting public health would require additional regulations. To ensure higher drilling standards, the committee called for better tracking and disposal of waste; stricter air pollution standards; the creation of a database to monitor drilling operations; the elimination of diesel fuel from fracking; and disclosure of the full list of chemicals used in the process. The committee also noted in its report that further study would be needed to determine whether fracking is more harmful to the environment than the extraction of coal or other fuels. To determine this, the committee called on federal officials to finance research on safer and more efficient drilling techniques, paying for any necessary studies or regulatory changes by levying additional fees and taxes on drilling companies.

—Heather Kerrigan

Following is the edited text of the House Energy and Commerce Committee report on chemicals used during the hydraulic fracturing process, issued on April 16, 2011; and the edited text of a draft report issued by the Environmental Protection Agency on the effects of hydraulic fracturing in Wyoming.

House Releases Report on Fracking Chemicals

April 16, 2011

[The list of committee members, table of contents, footnotes, and tables have been omitted.]

I. EXECUTIVE SUMMARY

Hydraulic fracturing has helped to expand natural gas production in the United States, unlocking large natural gas supplies in shale and other unconventional formations across the country. As a result of hydraulic fracturing and advances in horizontal drilling technology, natural gas production in 2010 reached the highest level in decades. According to new estimates by the Energy Information Administration (EIA), the United States possesses natural gas resources sufficient to supply the United States for approximately 110 years.

As the use of hydraulic fracturing has grown, so have concerns about its environmental and public health impacts. One concern is that hydraulic fracturing fluids used to fracture rock formations contain numerous chemicals that could harm human health and the environment, especially if they enter drinking water supplies. The opposition of many oil and gas companies to public disclosure of the chemicals they use has compounded this concern.

Last Congress, the Committee on Energy and Commerce launched an investigation to examine the practice of hydraulic fracturing in the United States. As part of that inquiry, the Committee asked the 14 leading oil and gas service companies to disclose the types and volumes of the hydraulic fracturing products they used in their fluids between 2005 and 2009 and the chemical contents of those products. This report summarizes the information provided to the Committee.

Between 2005 and 2009, the 14 oil and gas service companies used more than 2,500 hydraulic fracturing products containing 750 chemicals and other components. Overall, these companies used 780 million gallons of hydraulic fracturing products—not including water added at the well site—between 2005 and 2009.

Some of the components used in the hydraulic fracturing products were common and generally harmless, such as salt and citric acid. Some were unexpected, such as instant coffee and walnut hulls. And some were extremely toxic, such as benzene and lead. . . .

The most widely used chemical in hydraulic fracturing during this time period, as measured by the number of compounds containing the chemical, was methanol.

Methanol, which was used in 342 hydraulic fracturing products, is a hazardous air pollutant and is on the candidate list for potential regulation under the Safe Drinking Water Act. Some of the other most widely used chemicals were isopropyl alcohol (used in 274 products), 2-butoxyethanol (used in 126 products), and ethylene glycol (used in 119 products).

Between 2005 and 2009, the oil and gas service companies used hydraulic fracturing products containing 29 chemicals that are (1) known or possible human carcinogens, (2) regulated under the Safe Drinking Water Act for their risks to human health, or (3) listed as hazardous air pollutants under the Clean Air Act. These 29 chemicals were components of more than 650 different products used in hydraulic fracturing.

The BTEX compounds—benzene, toluene, xylene, and ethylbenzene—appeared in 60 of the hydraulic fracturing products used between 2005 and 2009. Each BTEX compound is a regulated contaminant under the Safe Drinking Water Act and a hazardous air pollutant under the Clean Air Act. Benzene also is a known human carcinogen. The hydraulic fracturing companies injected 11.4 million gallons of products containing at least one BTEX chemical over the five year period.

In many instances, the oil and gas service companies were unable to provide the Committee with a complete chemical makeup of the hydraulic fracturing fluids they used. Between 2005 and 2009, the companies used 94 million gallons of 279 products that contained at least one chemical or component that the manufacturers deemed proprietary or a trade secret. Committee staff requested that these companies disclose this proprietary information. Although some companies did provide information about these proprietary fluids, in most cases the companies stated that they did not have access to proprietary information about products they purchased "off the shelf" from chemical suppliers. In these cases, the companies are injecting fluids containing chemicals that they themselves cannot identify.

[Sections II–V, containing information on the background of the study, methodology, hydraulic fracturing components, and proprietary chemicals, have been omitted.]

VI. CONCLUSION

Hydraulic fracturing has opened access to vast domestic reserves of natural gas that could provide an important stepping stone to a clean energy future. Yet questions about the safety of hydraulic fracturing persist, which are compounded by the secrecy surrounding the chemicals used in hydraulic fracturing fluids. This analysis is the most comprehensive national assessment to date of the types and volumes of chemical used in the hydraulic fracturing process. It shows that between 2005 and 2009, the 14 leading hydraulic fracturing companies in the United States used over 2,500 hydraulic fracturing products containing 750 compounds. More than 650 of these products contained chemicals that are known or possible human carcinogens, regulated under the Safe Drinking Water Act, or listed as hazardous air pollutants.

[Appendix A has been omitted.]

Source: House Committee on Energy and Commerce. Democratic Site. "Chemicals in Hydraulic Fracturing." April 16, 2011. http://democrats.energycommerce.house.gov/sites/default/files/documents/Hydraulic%20Fracturing%20Report%204.18.11.pdf.

EPA Report on the Effects of Fracking in Wyoming

December 8, 2011

[The notice, foreword, acknowledgments, table of contents, figures, and tables have all been omitted.]

EXTENDED ABSTRACT

In response to complaints by domestic well owners regarding objectionable taste and odor problems in well water, the U.S. Environmental Protection Agency initiated a ground water investigation near the town of Pavillion, Wyoming under authority of the Comprehensive Environmental Response, Compensation, and Liability Act. The Wind River Formation is the principal source of domestic, municipal, and stock (ranch, agricultural) water in the area of Pavillion and meets the Agency's definition of an Underground Source of Drinking Water. Domestic wells in the area of investigation overlie the Pavillion gas field which consists of 169 production wells which extract gas from the lower Wind River Formation and underlying Fort Union Formation. Hydraulic fracturing in gas production wells occurred as shallow as 372 meters below ground surface with associated surface casing as shallow as 110 meters below ground surface. Domestic and stock wells in the area are screened as deep as 244 meters below ground surface. With the exception of two production wells, surface casing of gas production wells do not extend below the maximum depth of domestic wells in the area of investigation. At least 33 surface pits previously used for the storage/disposal of drilling wastes and produced and flowback waters are present in the area. The objective of the Agency's investigation was to determine the presence, not extent, of ground water contamination in the formation and if possible to differentiate shallow source terms (pits, septic systems, agricultural and domestic practices) from deeper source terms (gas production wells).

The Agency conducted four sampling events (Phase I–IV) beginning in March 2009 and ending in April, 2011. Ground water samples were collected from domestic wells and two municipal wells in the town of Pavillion in Phase I. Detection of methane and dissolved hydrocarbons in several domestic wells prompted collection of a second round of samples in January, 2010 (Phase II). During this phase, EPA collected additional ground water samples from domestic and stock wells and ground water samples from 3 shallow monitoring wells and soil samples near the perimeter of three known pit locations. Detection of elevated levels of methane and diesel range organics (DRO) in deep domestic wells prompted the Agency to install 2 deep monitoring wells screened at 233–239 meters (MW01) and 293–299 meters (MW02) below ground surface, respectively, in June 2010 to better evaluate to deeper sources of contamination. The expense of drilling deep wells while utilizing blowout prevention was the primary limiting factor in the number of monitoring wells installed. In September 2010 (Phase III), EPA collected gas samples from well casing from MW01 and MW02. In October 2010, EPA collected ground water samples from MW01 and MW02 in addition to a number of domestic wells. In April 2011 (Phase IV), EPA resampled the 2 deep monitoring wells to compare previous findings and to expand the analyte list to include glycols, alcohols, and low molecular weight acids.

Detection of high concentrations of benzene, xylenes, gasoline range organics, diesel range organics, and total purgeable hydrocarbons in ground water samples from shallow monitoring wells near pits indicates that pits are a source of shallow ground water contamination in the area of investigation. When considered separately, pits represent potential source terms for localized ground water plumes of unknown extent. When considered as whole they represent potential broader contamination of shallow ground water. A number of stock and domestic wells in the area of investigation are fairly shallow (e.g., < 30 meters below ground surface) representing potential receptor pathways.

Determination of the sources of inorganic and organic geochemical anomalies in deeper ground water was considerably more complex than determination of sources in shallow media necessitating the use of mulitiple [*sic*] lines of reasoning approach common to complex scientific investigations. pH values in MW01 and MW01 are highly alkaline (11.2–12.0) with up to 94% of the total alkalinity contributed by hydroxide suggesting addition of a strong base as the causative factor. Reaction path modeling indicates that sodium-sulfate composition of ground water typical of deeper portions of the Wind River Formation provides little resistance to elevation of pH with small addition of potassium hydroxide. Potassium hydroxide was used in a crosslinker and in a solvent at this site.

The inorganic geochemistry of ground water from the deep monitoring wells is distinctive from that in the domestic wells and expected composition in the Wind River formation. Potassium concentration in MW02 (43.6 milligrams per liter) and MW01 (54.9 milligrams per liter) is between 14.5 and 18.3 times values in domestic wells and expected values in the formation. Chloride concentration in monitoring well MW02 (466 milligrams per liter) is 18 times the mean chloride concentration (25.6 milligrams per liter) observed in ground water from domestic wells and expected in the formation. Chloride enrichment in this well is significant because regional anion trends show decreasing chloride concentration with depth. In addition, the monitoring wells show low calcium, sodium, and sulfate concentrations compared to the general trend observed in domestic well waters. The formulation of fracture fluid provided for carbon dioxide foam hydraulic fracturing jobs typically consisted of 6% potassium chloride. Potassium metaborate was used in crosslinkers. Potassium hydroxide was used in a crosslinker and in a solvent. Ammonium chloride was used in crosslinker.

A number of synthetic organic compounds were detected in MW01 and MW02. Isopropanol was detected in MW01 and MW02 at 212 and 581 micrograms per liter, respectively. Diethylene glycol was detected in MW01 and MW02 at 226 and 1570 micrograms per liter, respectively. Triethylene glycol was detected in MW01 and MW02 at 46 and 310 micrograms per liter, respectively. Another synthetic compound, *tert*-butyl alcohol, was detected in MW02 at a concentration of 4470 micrograms per liter. Isopropanol was used in a biocide, in a surfactant, in breakers, and in foaming agents. Diethylene glycol was used in a foaming agent and in a solvent. Triethylene glycol was used in a solvent. *Tert*-butyl alcohol is a known breakdown product of methyl *tert*-butyl ether (a fuel additive) and *tert*-butyl hydroperoxide (a gel breaker used in hydraulic fracturing). Material Safety Data Sheets do not indicate that fuel or tert-butyl hydroperoxide were used in the Pavillion gas field. However, Material Safety Data Sheets do not contain proprietary information and the chemical ingredients of many additives. The source of *tert*-butyl alcohol remains unresolved. However, *tert*-butyl alcohol is not expected to occur naturally in ground water.

Benzene, toluene, ethylbenzene, and xylenes (BTEX) were detected in MW02 at concentrations of 246, 617, 67, and 750 micrograms per liter, respectively. Trimethylbenzenes were detected in MW02 at 105 micrograms per liter. Gasoline range organics were detected in MW01 and MW02 at 592 and 3710 micrograms per liter. Diesel range organics were detected in MW01 and MW02 at 924 and 4050 micrograms per liter, respectively. Aromatic solvent (typically BTEX mixture) was used in a breaker. Diesel oil (mixture of saturated and aromatic hydrocarbons including naphthalenes and alkylbenzenes) was used in a guar polymer slurry/liquid gel concentrate and in a solvent. Petroleum raffinates (mixture of paraffinic, cycloparaffinic, olefinic, and aromatic hydrocarbons) were used in a breaker. Heavy aromatic petroleum naphtha (mixture of paraffinic, cycloparaffinic and aromatic hydrocarbons) was used in surfactants and in a solvent. Toluene and xylene were used in flow enhancers and a breaker.

Detections of organic chemicals were more numerous and exhibited higher concentrations in the deeper of the two monitoring wells. Natural breakdown products of organic contaminants like BTEX and glycols include acetate and benzoic acid. These breakdown products are more enriched in the shallower of the two monitoring wells, suggesting upward/lateral migration with natural degradation and accumulation of daughter products. Hydraulic gradients are currently undefined in the area of investigation. However, there are flowing conditions in a number of deep stock wells suggesting that upward gradients exist in the area of investigation.

Alternative explanations were carefully considered to explain individual sets of data. However, when considered together with other lines of evidence, the data indicates likely impact to ground water that can be explained by hydraulic fracturing. A review of well completion reports and cement bond/variable density logs in the area around MW01 and MW02 indicates instances of sporadic bonding outside production casing directly above intervals of hydraulic fracturing. Also, there is little lateral and vertical continuity of hydraulically fractured tight sandstones and no lithologic barrier (laterally continuous shale units) to stop upward vertical migration of aqueous constituents of hydraulic fracturing in the event of excursion from fractures. In the event of excursion from sandstone units, vertical migration of fluids could also occur via nearby wellbores. For instance, at one production well, the cement bond/variable density log indicates no cement until 671 m below ground surface. Hydraulic fracturing occurred above this depth at nearby production wells.

A similar lines of reasoning approach was utilized to evaluate the presence of gas in monitoring and domestic wells. A comparison of gas composition and stable carbon isotope values indicate that gas in production and monitoring wells is of similar thermogenic origin and has undergone little or no degradation. A similar evaluation in domestic wells suggests the presence of gas of thermogenic origin undergoing biodegradation. This observation is consistent with a pattern of dispersion and degradation with upward migration observed for organic compounds.

Elevated levels of dissolved methane in domestic wells generally increase in those wells in proximity to gas production wells. Near surface concentrations of methane appear highest in the area encompassing MW01. Ground water is saturated with methane at MW01 which is screened at a depth (239 meters below ground surface) typical of deeper domestic wells in the area. A blowout occurred during drilling of a domestic well at a depth of only 159 meters below ground surface close to MW01. A mud-gas log conducted in 1980 (prior to intensive gas production well installation) located only 300 m from the location of the blowout does not indicate a gas show (distinctive peaks on a gas chromatograph) within 300 meters of the surface. Again, with the exception of two production wells, surface casing of gas production wells do not extend below the maximum depth of domestic wells in the area of investigation. A number of production wells in the vicinity of MW01 have sporadic bonding or no cement over large vertical instances. Again, alternate explanations of data have been considered. Although some natural migration of gas would be expected above a gas field such as Pavillion, data suggest that enhanced migration of gas has occurred within ground water at depths used for domestic water supply and to domestic wells. Further investigation would be needed to determine the extent of gas migration and the fate and transport processes influencing migration to domestic wells.

[Sections 1.0–3.0, containing information on the site background, research methods, results, and discussion, have been omitted.]

4.0

CONCLUSIONS

A lines of reasoning approach utilized at this site best supports an explanation that inorganic and organic constituents associated with hydraulic fracturing have contaminated ground water at and below the depth used for domestic water supply. However, further investigation would be needed to determine if organic compounds associated with hydraulic fracturing have migrated to domestic wells in the area of investigation. A lines of evidence approach also indicates that gas production activities have likely enhanced gas migration at and below depths used for domestic water supply and to domestic wells in the area of investigation.

Hydraulic fracturing in the Pavillion gas field occurred into zones of producible gas located within an Underground Source of Drinking Water (USDW).

Hydraulic fracturing for coal-bed methane recovery is often shallow and occurs directly into USDWs (EPA 2004). TDS less than 10,000 mg/L in produced water is common throughout the Rocky Mountain portion of the United States (USGS 2011; Dahm et al. 2011). Ground water contamination with constituents such as those found at Pavillion is typically infeasible or too expensive to remediate or restore (GAO 1989). Collection of baseline data prior to hydraulic fracturing is necessary to reduce investigative costs and to verify or refute impacts to ground water.

Finally, this investigation supports recommendations made by the U.S. Department of Energy Panel (DOE 2011a, b) on the need for collection of baseline data, greater transparency on chemical composition of hydraulic fracturing fluids, and greater emphasis on well construction and integrity requirements and testing. As stated by the panel, implementation of these recommendations would decrease the likelihood of impact to ground water and increase public confidence in the technology.

[References and appendixes have been omitted.]

SOURCE: Environmental Protection Agency. "Investigation of Ground Water Contamination Near Pavillion, Wyoming." December 8, 2011. http://www.epa.gov/region8/superfund/wy/pavillion/EPA_ReportOnPavillion_Dec-8-2011.pdf.

OTHER HISTORIC DOCUMENTS OF INTEREST

FROM THIS VOLUME

Prime Minister Cameron on the Royal Wedding and Succession Law Changes

APRIL 29 AND OCTOBER 28, 2011

The British Royal Family is closely watched around the world through times of triumph and scandal. In the United Kingdom, the monarchy receives mixed reviews—there are those who prefer to maintain it as is through taxpayer funding, and those who prefer to see what they consider an obsolete system abolished. In 2011, these competing opinions received global attention when the royal wedding of Prince William and Catherine Middleton took place in April. The notion of an antiquated system that no longer fits in today's society received an upgrade in October when members of the Commonwealth voted to end male primogeniture and abolish some of the limits on whom a monarch can marry.

ROYAL WEDDING

On April 29, 2011, the second in line to the British throne, Prince William, married his longtime girlfriend, Catherine Middleton, in a ceremony at Westminster Abbey that captured worldwide attention. "This is, as every wedding day should be, a day of hope," said the Bishop of London during his wedding address. The British royal family hoped the pageantry of the long-anticipated nuptials would boost its image, while the British government hoped the event would improve public sentiment mired in fears of recession, unemployment, and a new austerity program. "It's a great moment for Britain, a moment when everyone is celebrating and it's being watched round the world where people will see lots of things they love about Britain," said Prime Minister David Cameron. As opposed to the last great wedding in 1981 between Prince William's parents, Charles and Diana, during which 750 million tuned in around the world to watch the ceremony, an estimated two billion joined the global audience in 2011 to watch the prince marry a commoner. Despite global enthusiasm, the British press featured stories indicating that less half of British citizens were interested in the wedding.

The wedding brought to the surface the class issues that still exist in the United Kingdom. The British press criticized Middleton for being a social climber. Her family has its roots in manual labor and mining, but her parents worked their way up to build a multimillion-dollar party wares company. "In the UK, we are all deeply obsessed with the issue of class. When the royal wedding was announced, newspaper inches were devoted to Kate's background," said Lee Elliot Major, a research director at Sutton Trust, a British organization aimed at improving the educational outcomes of the less fortunate. "In England, particularly, you walk into a room and a lot of people will be assessing, whether it's consciously or subconsciously, where you are in the social-class rankings," said Major. Still, the global press painted a portrait of a modern-day fairy tale—one that many hoped would be different from the ill-fated marriage of William's parents.

SUPPORT FOR THE MONARCHY AND REPUBLICANISM

The wedding was viewed as an important step in improving the image of the monarchy and solidifying its position in Britain. William and Catherine, who following their marriage became the Duke and Duchess of Cambridge, were readily aware of this fact, as well as the state of the British economy, and took both into consideration when planning the wedding. The event required a delicate balance between being too plain and risking disappointment, or being too opulent and risking public backlash in a time of recession. In an effort to combat the latter, the bride's parents made clear their intention to pay for a portion of the festivities, which were estimated to cost tens of millions of dollars.

Under Britain's unwritten constitution, the monarch is the head of state, head of the armed forces, and defender of the faith. In reality, the role is more ceremonial with political decisions left to Parliament. This apolitical position has aided the monarchy in maintaining its image and respect in the current antipolitical environment. Tristram Hunt, a member of Parliament representing the Labour Party, believes that people view the monarchy positively because it represents "continuity, tradition, and dignity." Opinion polls generally favor the monarchy, and approval remains above 60 percent. According to private polling conducted by Buckingham Palace, the wedding did little to change public opinion. Following the death of Princess Diana in August 1997, 48 percent of Britons polled believed the country would be worse off without the monarchy. Today, that number has grown to 63 percent. Two-thirds of British citizens believe the monarchy is still relevant to life in the United Kingdom, and 60 percent believe the monarchy is good for the nation's image around the world.

Public opinion of the monarchy rests on its ability to appear accessible to the public, a tradition started by King George V. Queen Elizabeth II, the reigning monarch, capitalizes on this, attending hundreds of public events each year, and reaching out to the public in annual televised addresses. Her profile will be elevated even further in 2012 when she celebrates sixty years of rule. But the support the queen enjoys is not as readily apparent for her son, Charles, who will ascend the throne following Elizabeth's death. Some polling has shown public favor for skipping Charles in favor of William.

But both supporters and opponents of the monarchy admit that the level of approval it enjoys comes largely from disinterest. "Ninety days out of 100, the British attitude to the monarchy is like our attitude to the sky: we know it exists, and we don't really think about it that much," said Peter Morgan, who wrote the 2006 movie *The Queen*. "We can't make up our minds what we want of the royals," Morgan said. "Whether we want to pay them, whether they should pay for themselves. Whether we want to reform them, empower them, fade them out. We never resolve our conflicting attitudes or come to any conclusion, least of all the one that's staring us all in the face—namely, that we're really quite happy with the way that it is," said Morgan.

It is this attitude that monarchy opponents, known as Republicans, are using to support their goal of abolishing the monarchy by 2025. According to Graham Smith, who leads Republicans in the United Kingdom, the monarchy can only survive on the same indifference Morgan notes. "It is indifference which sustains the monarchy rather than love and support, and when you have these bit set piece events, all it does is start to make people think about it again," said Smith. Republicanism is not a new phenomenon in Britain. Its roots reach back to Oliver Cromwell's civil war in the 1640s, to more current events like Edward VIII's abdication in 1936 to marry American divorcée Wallis Simpson. More recently, Queen Elizabeth's children have put a negative spotlight on the monarchy with three divorces, financial indiscretions, and love affairs splashed across British tabloids. Smith said the 2011 wedding was the best opportunity to remind British citizens and the world that the monarchy is archaic and has no place in current society, especially given its cost to taxpayers, which is reported to be just under $65 million per year or $1.03 annually per British citizen. Republicans say the cost continues to entrench Britain in a state of class warfare. "The monarchy is not a luxury," says Graham. "It's an imposition and an obstacle to serious political reform."

Such reforms, Graham notes, have become increasingly necessary as the British population continues to change. Of the more than sixty million people in the United Kingdom, three million are immigrants from the past two decades from Eastern Europe, the Middle East, and Africa. These immigrants have settled mainly in London where nearly one-third of the population is foreign born. Religion plays a key factor in the changing face of Britain. Seventy percent of the population belongs to the protestant Church of England, of which the Queen is head, but only 5 percent consider themselves regular churchgoers, thus negating one of the monarchy's key duties as defender of the faith. The nation also has approximately 2.5 million Muslims, some of whom have supported abolishment of the state-sanctioned Church of England. But Morgan finds that, contrary to Republican belief, whether Queen Elizabeth, Charles, or William is on the throne, adapting to changing demographics will not be an obstacle. "Never underestimate the British monarchy's ability to adapt, reorganize its molecular configuration and survive. They'll be here long, long, long after we've all gone," said Morgan.

SUCCESSION RULE CHANGE

In October 2011, the sixteen nations that recognize the Queen as head of state took an important step toward modernization by voting to change the succession policy known as primogeniture that dates back at least 1,000 years. The policy, enshrined in English common law, gives male precedence in succession to the throne. Eleven previous attempts have been made in the British Parliament to overturn primogeniture, the most recent coming in January 2011, but none have been successful. In October, both the Queen and Prime Minister Cameron came to the annual meeting of the Commonwealth countries, held in Perth, Australia, supportive of a change. "The idea that a younger son should become monarch instead of an elder daughter simply because he's a man . . . This way of thinking is at odds with the modern countries that we've all become," said Cameron.

With their vote, the Commonwealth nations agreed to work together to amend succession law to allow a female heir, if older than a male heir, to automatically become Queen rather than her brother becoming King. The new rules will come into play for any children of the Duke and Duchess of Cambridge. "Put simply, if the Duke and Duchess of Cambridge were to have a little girl, that girl would one day be our Queen," said Cameron.

A second change, this one dealing with religion, was made to the monarchy's rules during the Commonwealth meeting. During certain points in British history, Catholics have been persecuted by a number of laws that have included prohibiting them from serving in the army, voting, inheriting land, joining a "learned profession," or holding public office. This anti-Catholic sentiment began after Henry VIII broke with the Vatican in the 1500s. Since then, all of these provisions have been phased out but one—the one that disallowed members of the monarchy from ascending to the throne if married to a Roman Catholic. The change made at the Commonwealth meeting will allow members of the monarchy to marry Roman Catholics and ascend to the throne; however, the restriction on Catholics ascending to the throne was maintained, primarily because of the link between the monarch and the Church of England. "Let me be clear," Cameron said, "the monarch must be in communion with the Church of England because he or she is head of that church." But, Cameron said, "It is simply wrong that they should be denied the chance to marry a Catholic if they wish to do so." The British Parliament is required to vote for the primogeniture and religion changes to take effect. Hearings were held in late 2011 on the topic in the House of Commons, and the body is expected to vote on the issue in its next session.

—Heather Kerrigan

Following is an announcement from the press secretary to Queen Elizabeth II on the titles given to Prince William and his wife Catherine upon their marriage on April 29, 2011; a press release from Prime Minister David Cameron congratulating the new Duke and Duchess of Cambridge on their marriage on April 29, 2011; and the edited transcript of a joint press conference held on October 28, 2011, by Prime Minister Cameron of the United Kingdom and Prime Minister Julia Gillard of Australia on changes to the monarchy's rules of succession.

Queen Announces Titles for Prince William and Catherine Middleton

April 29, 2011

The Queen has today been pleased to confer a Dukedom on Prince William of Wales. His titles will be Duke of Cambridge, Earl of Strathearn and Baron Carrickfergus.

Prince William thus becomes His Royal Highness The Duke of Cambridge and Miss Catherine Middleton on marriage will become Her Royal Highness The Duchess of Cambridge.

BACKGROUND:

DUKEDOM: Cambridge:

In 1706 George Augustus (subsequently George II) the only son of George Ludwig, Elector of Hanover (subsequently George I of Great Britain) was created with other titles Duke of Cambridge. On the accession of his father to the throne in 1714 he also became Duke of Cornwall and was created Prince of Wales. On his own accession to the throne in 1727 the Dukedom of Cambridge merged with The Crown and ceased.

Cambridge was previously a Royal Dukedom and four sons of James, Duke of York (afterwards James II) who died in infancy were all created Duke of Cambridge. As an Earldom Cambridge was a medieval Royal title. Edward IV was Duke of York and Earl of Cambridge till proclaimed King of England in 1461 when his titles merged with The Crown.

His father and grandfather both Richard Plantagenet were both Earls of Cambridge and the latter was also Duke of York. Edmund of Langley, 5th son of Edward III and great-grandfather of Edward IV, was created Earl of Cambridge in 1362 and Duke of York in 1385.

The Dukedom of Cambridge created in 1801 became extinct on the death of the 2nd Duke of Cambridge in 1904. Cambridge existed as a Marquessate from 1917 when it was conferred on Queen Mary's brother till 1981 when the 2nd Marquess died and the title became extinct.

EARLDOM: Strathearn

Strathearn has had Royal connections since Robert Stewart, High Steward of Scotland, was created Earl of Strathearn in 1357. In 1371 he succeeded his Uncle as King of Scotland becoming Robert II and the Earldom merged with The Crown Robert II created his 5th son David, Earl of Strathearn in 1371. Subsequently in 1427 the 6th son of Robert II was created Earl of Strathearn.

In 1766 George III's younger brother Prince Henry Frederick was created Duke of Cumberland and Strathearn. He died without issue in 1790 and in 1799 Queen Victoria's father was created Duke of Kent and Strathearn. These Dukedoms became extinct on his death in 1820. Finally, Prince Arthur William Patrick Albert, 3rd son of Queen Victoria was created Duke of Connaught and Strathearn in 1874. He died in 1942 and was succeeded by his grandson who died the following year 1943 since when Strathearn as a title has been extinct.

BARONY: Carrickfergus:

An Irish Viscountcy of Chichester of Carrickfergus now held by the Marquess of Donegall was created in 1625 but Carrickfergus alone only existed as a title between 1841 and 1883. The 3rd Marquess of Donegall was created Baron Ennishowen and Carrickfergus, of Ennishowen, co: Donegal and Carrickfergus, co: Antrim. He died in 1883 being succeeded by his brother and the Barony became extinct.

Carrickfergus is County Antrim's oldest town. The word means Rock of Fergus and as an urban settlement it predates Belfast. It is on the north shore of Belfast Lough and is the site of Carrickfergus Castle which dates from circa 1180 and is one of the best preserved Castles in Ireland.

SOURCE: The British Monarchy. "Announcement of Titles, 29 April 2011." April 29, 2011. http://www .royal.gov.uk/LatestNewsandDiary/Pressreleases/2011/Announcementoftitles29April2011.aspx.

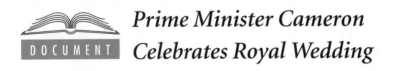

Prime Minister Cameron Celebrates Royal Wedding

April 29, 2011

Prime Minister David Cameron and his wife Samantha have hosted a street party in Downing Street to celebrate the marriage of Prince William and Catherine Middleton.

Guests included children from local schools and representatives of Age UK, Contact the Elderly and Save the Children, as well as young charity fundraisers.

Red, white and blue bunting was hung on the street and live coverage of celebrations elsewhere and replays of key moments from the service were broadcast on a big screen.

David and Samantha Cameron, who attended the wedding in Westminster Abbey and reception at Buckingham Palace, mingled with guests at the street party.

Speaking this afternoon, Mr Cameron said the ceremony had been "incredibly romantic and moving".

He added:

"It was beautiful to see two people who really love each other and who are incredibly happy at an amazing ceremony.

"It's a day when we see "the new team". It was incredibly romantic and moving.

"It's a great moment for Britain, a moment when everyone is celebrating and it's being watched round the world where people will see lots of things they love about Britain.

"The ceremonial, the pageantry, the Royal Family, the institution—but also this beautiful young couple who love each other very much."

Earlier this week, children helped Mrs Cameron bake cakes in the No 10 kitchen for the Downing Street party, and they returned today to sample their handiwork.

Food and drink was donated or made by Downing Street staff and an ice cream tricycle with umbrella served children treats.

SOURCE: Office of the British Prime Minister. "Downing Street Celebrates the Royal Wedding." April 29, 2011. http://www.number10.gov.uk/news/downing-street-celebrates-the-royal-wedding/.

Commonwealth Revises Monarchy's Rules of Succession

October 28, 2011

PM [Julia Gillard]: Thank you very much, I'm delighted to be able to introduce Prime Minister Cameron, who has an important announcement to make.

PRIME MINISTER.

CAMERON: Well, thank you very much and I'm grateful to Prime Minister Gillard for hosting the meeting that we've just had today. This has been, I believe, something of an historic moment. This has been the first time that the Queen's 16 realms have acted together as one single group. From the Pacific to the North Atlantic we are diverse countries, united not just by our association through the Commonwealth, but by sharing one head of state.

For us in Britain, some of the issues we've been looking at date back to the very beginnings of the English Crown. Others to the *Bill of Rights* in 1688 and the *Act of Settlement* in 1701. All 16 realms here today share this rich constitutional inheritance, but at the same time, the great strength of our constitutional approach is its ability to evolve.

Attitudes have changed fundamentally over the centuries and some outdated rules, like some of the rules on succession, just don't make sense to us anymore: the idea that a younger son should become monarch instead of an elder daughter simply because he's a man, or that a future monarch can marry someone of any faith, except a Catholic. This way of thinking is at odds with the modern countries that we've all become.

People have been talking about changing the rules for some time, but when there are 16 countries sharing the same head of state and each have their own constitutional, legal and political concerns, it's absolutely right that we should all discuss this together. That's why I asked Prime Minister Gillard for the opportunity to chair this meeting today with the heads of government from all 16 nations. I'm very pleased to say that we've reached a unanimous agreement on two changes to the rules of succession.

First, we will end the male primogenitor rule so that in future the order of succession should be determined simply by the order of birth. We've agreed to introduce this for all decedents from the Prince of Wales. Put simply, if the Duke and Duchess of Cambridge were to have a little girl, that girl would one day be our Queen.

Second, we've agreed to scrap the rule which says that no one who marries a Roman Catholic can become monarch. Let me be clear, the monarch must be in communion with the Church of England, because he or she is the head of that church. But it is simply wrong that they should be denied the chance to marry a Catholic if they wish to do so. After all, they're already quite free to marry someone of any other faith. We agreed today that this has to change.

Across the 16 realms we'll now work together through an international group and within each country to bring forward the necessary measures to implement these changes at the same time. For historic reasons, the UK needs to publish its legislation first and we'll make sure that what we bring forward is acceptable to all countries. Of course, Her Majesty will play her normal role in any legislation, her Private Secretary, Sir Christopher Geidt, was present at this meeting and we will now advise Her Majesty of this unanimous agreement.

Finally, let me say a word about Her Majesty the Queen. I know we're all delighted to see Her Majesty with us here in Perth and we're looking forward to the many celebrations that will mark Her Majesty's Diamond Jubilee, 60 years on the throne, next summer. Today, Buckingham Palace has announced the creation of the Queen Elizabeth Diamond Jubilee Trust, which will be chaired by Sir John Major. This will honour 60 years of extraordinary public service by Her Majesty The Queen, and it will seek to further Her Majesty's work across the Commonwealth, reflecting her commitment to helping those in need, including by tackling curable disease and promoting education and culture.

I'm delighted that Prime Minister Gillard and I can confirm that both the British and Australian Governments will play their part in supporting this Trust, and for our part, we'll be making a multi-million pound donation. We're encouraging other countries that are here today to make a contribution too. At the same time, we hope individuals and businesses across the Commonwealth may also choose to mark the Jubilee by supporting the Trust in their own way. Together, we will help make this a fitting tribute to a very, very special anniversary.

Thank you.

Prime Minister.

PM: Thank you, Prime Minister Cameron. Prime Minister Cameron, can I congratulate you on leading this initiative. Can I offer you that congratulations both as a prime minister and as a woman, and can I say I am absolutely delighted that this moment in history is happening here in Perth. To our modern minds these seem like simple and very rational changes, that there would no longer be a discrimination against women in the way in which the line of succession works, and that we would not continue the religious prohibition against marriage to a Catholic.

These things seem straightforward, but just because they seem straightforward to our modern minds doesn't mean that we should underestimate their historical significance, changing as they will for all time the way in which the Monarchy works and changing its history. So I'm very glad this moment in history has been made in Perth.

Prime Minister, I am in a position where I can inform you that I have consulted with each of our State Premiers and each Australian state gives its in principle agreement to these changes and the Australian nation gives its in principle agreement to these changes, and we look forward to working with you and with your officials on now doing the technical work that needs to be done to ensure that we, along with other realm countries, enact the necessary legislation. In Australia that does need to be legislation at both the Federal and at the level of each state.

Prime Minister, can I also congratulate you on the initiative to set up the Diamond Jubilee Trust, the Queen Elizabeth Diamond Jubilee Trust. The Queen has been received here in Australia on this visit with a great deal of affection and I know that Australians will be very excited to celebrate her Diamond Jubilee next year.

It seems very appropriate and fitting to mark a lifetime of dedication and service through a Trust which will honour the things that the Queen has been so passionate about. So as an Australian Government, we will make a contribution and we will be doing everything we can to encourage businesses in Australia to also make donations to this Trust.

Prime Minister Cameron, with the Queen here this week in Perth, I want to just reflect very briefly when she first came to Australia as Monarch. She came in 1954, it was a very extensive tour. She went to every Australian capital city, apart from Darwin, she crisscrossed the country, she went to some 70 country towns on that visit. When she came here to Perth, Perth was in the grips of a polio epidemic.

Now, I mention this historical footnote because you and I tomorrow will be saying some things about our dedication to see the global eradication of polio in the four countries where it still continues to exist, three of them Commonwealth countries.

But once again, thank you very much for your leadership on this change. I'm very enthusiastic about it, you would expect the first Australian woman prime minister to be very enthusiastic about a change which equals equality for women in a new area. . . .

[Questions from the media have been omitted.]

SOURCE: Office of the Prime Minister of Australia. Press Office. "Transcript of Joint Press Conference With Prime Minister Cameron." October 28, 2011. http://www.pm.gov.au/press-office/transcript-joint-press-conference-prime-minister-cameron.

OTHER HISTORIC DOCUMENTS OF INTEREST

FROM PREVIOUS *HISTORIC DOCUMENTS*

May

U.S. and Pakistan Officials on Death of Osama bin Laden

MAY 1 AND 2, 2011

Following the attacks of September 11, 2001, Presidents George W. Bush and Barack Obama, and the U.S. intelligence community, focused on finding the perpetrators and bringing them to justice. As the leader of al Qaeda, the terrorist organization responsible for the attacks, Osama bin Laden became their primary target. Officials unsuccessfully sought to locate bin Laden for nearly ten years, but in 2011, the intelligence community tracked him to a compound in Pakistan and Navy SEALs conducted a raid that resulted in his death.

A Wanted Man

It is believed that Osama bin Muhammad bin Awad bin Laden was born in 1957, one of fifty children of a billionaire contractor who owned his own construction company in Saudi Arabia. As a student, bin Laden was educated in Wahhabism, a puritanical, anti-Western strain of Islam. He earned his degree at King Abdulaziz University in Jidda, Saudi Arabia, where he began forming his militant tendencies. He became involved with the Muslim Brotherhood, an Islamic group that believes much of the Muslim world lives in violation of the true meaning of the Koran. He was also influenced by two Islamic scholars, one of whom taught his students that jihad, or holy war, was the responsibility of all Muslims until the lands once held by Islam were reclaimed.

In 1988, bin Laden cofounded al Qaeda as a way to coordinate the efforts of various groups that were fighting the Soviet Union in Afghanistan. When the Soviets withdrew in 1989, bin Laden viewed it as an opportunity to expand the organization in an effort to re-create Islam's historical political power and topple "infidel" governments through jihad. He created businesses to obtain and transport weapons, chemicals, and money; created training camps for soldiers; set up a media office; and established councils to approve his plans. Throughout the 1990s, al Qaeda also developed a network of relationships with other extremist organizations, including the Taliban, which largely owes its rise to political power in Afghanistan to bin Laden's aid.

With the Soviets out of Afghanistan, bin Laden turned his attention to the United States. Officials suspect bin Laden orchestrated the 1993 bombing of the World Trade Center in New York City, in which six people were killed. In 1996, al Qaeda officially announced jihad against the United States, and in 1998, bin Laden declared it the duty of every Muslim to "kill Americans wherever they are found." He also led al Qaeda to bomb the U.S. embassies in Tanzania and Kenya in 1998, and attack the USS *Cole* in 2000. However, bin Laden is best known for the attacks of September 11, 2011, in which nearly 3,000 people lost their lives as hijacked airplanes crashed into the twin towers of the World Trade Center, the Pentagon, and a field in Pennsylvania.

As the United States prepared for war in Afghanistan following those attacks, bin Laden received safe haven and support from that country's Taliban-controlled government. When U.S. and allied forces successfully drove the Taliban from power in November 2001, bin Laden fled to Tora Bora in the Afghan mountains, and ultimately escaped across the border into Pakistan. U.S. officials offered $25 million for information leading to bin Laden's capture or death.

Finding bin Laden

In August 2010, President Obama received a briefing on a possible lead to the whereabouts of bin Laden. Officials had gathered information on individuals within bin Laden's inner circle, including his personal couriers. Detainees said one courier in particular possibly lived with bin Laden. Officials traced the man and his brother to the compound where they lived in Abbottabad, Pakistan. The location surprised many, as Abbottabad is an affluent suburb located approximately thirty-five miles north of Islamabad, and bin Laden was originally suspected to be hiding in the remote mountainous tribal regions near the Pakistan-Afghanistan border. Abbottabad is also home to a Pakistani military base and a military academy for the Pakistani army. The compound itself was unique; it was roughly eight times larger than other homes in the area and was surrounded by twelve- to eighteen-foot walls topped with barbed wire. Given the high value of the property and knowing the courier lacked any substantial wealth, intelligence analysts concluded the compound had been built for the purpose of hiding someone important.

After months of attempting to confirm whether bin Laden was indeed in the compound, Obama administration officials determined in February 2011 that they had sufficient evidence to develop a plan for his capture or killing at the suspected location. In March, Obama held a series of meetings with the National Security Council to form those plans, and on April 29 he gave the order for a raid on the compound.

The raid occurred in the early morning hours of May 1, when helicopters carrying a seventy-nine-man Navy SEAL team flew to bin Laden's compound from Afghanistan. The team reportedly came from a Virginia-based unit that previously raided targets near war zones in Yemen and Somalia, with its more recent missions occurring in Afghanistan. Known as SEAL Team 6, the team was known for working closely and frequently with the Central Intelligence Agency (CIA), and the men who ultimately entered bin Laden's compound were considered top members of their unit.

The original plan called for one helicopter to hover over the main building of the compound as the SEALs climbed a rope down to the roof, while another would drop a team of men within the compound grounds. However, one of the helicopters experienced a mechanical failure and was intentionally crashed by the crew inside the compound. Twenty-four of the men entered the compound and fought their way through the first floor, killing the courier and his brother as they proceeded to bin Laden's rooms. The team reportedly asked bin Laden to surrender but shot him in the head and chest when he refused, killing him. The team took his body with them for identification, and left the compound roughly forty minutes after they had arrived. They also took with them what was described as "a robust collection of materials" that intelligence officials hoped would reveal valuable information about other al Qaeda operatives. In keeping with Islamic custom, the SEAL team later buried bin Laden at sea. No one on the SEAL team was injured during the raid.

U.S. officials did not share their intelligence on the compound with Pakistani leaders, nor did they provide any advance notice that they were conducting the raid. Once the helicopters entered Pakistan's air space, the U.S. informed officials that an operation was under way against a "high value target" and, following the raid's completion, updated them on the intent and results of the operation.

That evening, at 11:35 p.m. Eastern time, Obama addressed the nation live, to announce bin Laden's death. While declaring that justice had been done for the families who lost loved ones on September 11, Obama also cautioned that the U.S. fight against terrorism was not over. "The death of bin Laden marks the most significant achievement to date in our Nation's effort to defeat Al Qaida," he said. "Yet his death does not mark the end of our effort. There's no doubt that Al Qaida will continue to pursue attacks against us. We must—and we will—remain vigilant at home and abroad." Obama also reaffirmed that the United States was not at war with Islam, and acknowledged Pakistan's collaboration on counterterrorism efforts, noting that, "going forward, it is essential that Pakistan continue to join us in the fight against Al Qaida and its affiliates."

A NATION CELEBRATES

The news of bin Laden's death was greeted with celebration in the United States. Crowds took to the streets outside the White House in Washington, D.C., and at Times Square and Ground Zero in New York City, with many people chanting, "U.S.A.! U.S.A.!" Former President George W. Bush, who had initiated the most recent search for bin Laden, released a statement saying, "This momentous achievement marks a victory for America, for people who seek peace around the world, and for all those who lost loved ones on September 11, 2011. The fight against terror goes on, but tonight America has sent an unmistakable message: No matter how long it takes, justice will be done." The Council on American-Islamic Relations also welcomed bin Laden's death, noting that, "in addition to the killing of thousands of Americans, he and al Qaeda caused the deaths of countless Muslims worldwide."

Officials did caution that the United States would need to remain vigilant, particularly because al Qaeda or its sympathizers may try to retaliate for bin Laden's death. Secretary of State Hillary Rodham Clinton acknowledged, "even as we mark this milestone, we should not forget that the battle to stop al Qaeda and its syndicate of terror will not end with the death of bin Laden. Indeed, we must take this opportunity to renew our resolve and redouble our efforts." The State Department issued a worldwide travel warning for citizens as well as guidance on enhanced security measures for U.S. embassies, while military bases were ordered to a higher state of readiness.

QUESTIONS FOR PAKISTAN

While the Pakistan Ministry of Foreign Affairs issued a statement applauding bin Laden's death, U.S. officials questioned whether someone or some organization within Pakistan had been supporting bin Laden while he was in hiding. Although the United States had been providing billions of dollars in military and civilian assistance to Pakistan since 2001, strategic differences between the two countries with regard to forming a new government in Afghanistan had led to tensions. For one, the United States favored a strong, centralized Afghan government with a large army, while Pakistan preferred a looser system of government with smaller-scale defense systems that it could potentially influence. U.S. drone strikes against suspected terrorist sites in Pakistan further increased tensions, fomenting negative public opinion and ultimately leading Pakistani officials to demand an end to all drone strikes. In addition, U.S. officials had acknowledged that in some instances they had not shared intelligence information with the Pakistanis, because they did not believe they could always be trusted.

In the days after bin Laden's death, John Brennan, Obama's chief counterterrorism adviser, said it was "inconceivable that bin Laden did not have a support system" in Pakistan that enabled him to live comfortably in such a noticeable building, and in such proximity to the military in Abbottabad. Obama admitted the same suspicion in an interview with CBS's *60 Minutes* news program. "We think that there had to be some sort of support network for bin Laden inside of Pakistan," he said. "But we don't know who or what that support network was."

Pakistan's Ministry of Foreign Affairs affirmed the country's commitment to continue working with the United States to eliminate terrorism but took several steps that appeared to undercut that commitment, including releasing the name of the CIA's station chief in Islamabad and asking the Pentagon to withdraw military advisers. However, Pakistani officials did allow CIA officers to interview bin Laden's wives and examine his former compound for additional evidence.

FUTURE IMPACT

U.S. officials are unsure what impact bin Laden's death will have on al Qaeda. The organization announced on June 16 that Ayman al-Zawahiri would succeed bin Laden as its leader. Officials noted that he is less charismatic and not as well respected as his predecessor, raising the question of whether he can maintain the loyalty of al Qaeda's followers. Some believe bin Laden's death sends a message to the Taliban, as it fights to regain power in Afghanistan, to give up its efforts, renounce al Qaeda, and join the democratic political process. It remains to be seen whether bin Laden's former followers will make him into a martyr, or if his death will be a turning point in the war in Afghanistan and the broader war on terror.

—Linda Fecteau

Following is a statement by President Barack Obama delivered on May 1, 2011, following the successful United States operation to kill Osama bin Laden; a statement by the Foreign Ministry of Pakistan on May 2, 2011, applauding the death of Osama bin Laden; and a statement by Secretary of State Hillary Rodham Clinton on May 2, 2011, honoring the work of the United States and its allies in the death of Osama bin Laden.

Obama Remarks on the Death of Osama bin Laden

May 1, 2011

Good evening. Tonight I can report to the American people and to the world that the United States has conducted an operation that killed Usama bin Laden, the leader of Al Qaida and a terrorist who's responsible for the murder of thousands of innocent men, women, and children.

It was nearly 10 years ago that a bright September day was darkened by the worst attack on the American people in our history. The images of 9/11 are seared into our national memory: hijacked planes cutting through a cloudless September sky; the Twin Towers collapsing to the ground; black smoke billowing up from the Pentagon; the wreckage of Flight 93 in Shanksville, Pennsylvania, where the actions of heroic citizens saved even more heartbreak and destruction.

And yet we know that the worst images are those that were unseen to the world: the empty seat at the dinner table; children who were forced to grow up without their mother or their father; parents who would never know the feeling of their child's embrace; nearly 3,000 citizens taken from us, leaving a gaping hole in our hearts.

On September 11, 2001, in our time of grief, the American people came together. We offered our neighbors a hand, and we offered the wounded our blood. We reaffirmed our ties to each other and our love of community and country. On that day, no matter where we came from, what God we prayed to, or what race or ethnicity we were, we were united as one American family.

We were also united in our resolve to protect our Nation and to bring those who committed this vicious attack to justice. We quickly learned that the 9/11 attacks were carried out by Al Qaida, an organization headed by Usama bin Laden, which had openly declared war on the United States and was committed to killing innocents in our country and around the globe. And so we went to war against Al Qaida to protect our citizens, our friends, and our allies.

Over the last 10 years, thanks to the tireless and heroic work of our military and our counterterrorism professionals, we've made great strides in that effort. We've disrupted terrorist attacks and strengthened our homeland defense. In Afghanistan, we removed the Taliban Government, which had given bin Laden and Al Qaida safe haven and support. And around the globe, we worked with our friends and allies to capture or kill scores of Al Qaida terrorists, including several who were a part of the 9/11 plot.

Yet Usama bin Laden avoided capture and escaped across the Afghan border into Pakistan. Meanwhile, Al Qaida continued to operate from along that border and operate through its affiliates across the world.

And so shortly after taking office, I directed Leon Panetta, the Director of the CIA, to make the killing or capture of bin Laden the top priority of our war against Al Qaida, even as we continued our broader efforts to disrupt, dismantle, and defeat his network.

Then, last August, after years of painstaking work by our intelligence community, I was briefed on a possible lead to bin Laden. It was far from certain, and it took many months to run this thread to ground. I met repeatedly with my national security team as we developed more information about the possibility that we had located bin Laden hiding within a compound deep inside Pakistan. And finally, last week, I determined that we had enough intelligence to take action and authorized an operation to get Usama bin Laden and bring him to justice.

Today, at my direction, the United States launched a targeted operation against that compound in Abbottabad, Pakistan. A small team of Americans carried out the operation with extraordinary courage and capability. No Americans were harmed. They took care to avoid civilian casualties. After a firefight, they killed Usama bin Laden and took custody of his body.

For over two decades, bin Laden has been Al Qaida's leader and symbol and has continued to plot attacks against our country and our friends and allies. The death of bin Laden marks the most significant achievement to date in our Nation's effort to defeat Al Qaida.

Yet his death does not mark the end of our effort. There's no doubt that Al Qaida will continue to pursue attacks against us. We must—and we will—remain vigilant at home and abroad.

As we do, we must also reaffirm that the United States is not—and never will be—at war with Islam. I've made clear, just as President Bush did shortly after 9/11, that our war is not against Islam. Bin Laden was not a Muslim leader; he was a mass murderer of Muslims. Indeed, Al Qaida has slaughtered scores of Muslims in many countries, including our own. So his demise should be welcomed by all who believe in peace and human dignity.

Over the years, I've repeatedly made clear that we would take action within Pakistan if we knew where bin Laden was. That is what we've done. But it's important to note that our counterterrorism cooperation with Pakistan helped lead us to bin Laden and the compound where he was hiding. Indeed, bin Laden had declared war against Pakistan as well and ordered attacks against the Pakistani people.

Tonight I called President Zardari, and my team has also spoken with their Pakistani counterparts. They agree that this is a good and historic day for both of our nations. And going forward, it is essential that Pakistan continue to join us in the fight against Al Qaida and its affiliates.

The American people did not choose this fight. It came to our shores and started with the senseless slaughter of our citizens. After nearly 10 years of service, struggle, and sacrifice, we know well the costs of war. These efforts weigh on me every time I, as Commander in Chief, have to sign a letter to a family that has lost a loved one or look into the eyes of a servicemember who's been gravely wounded.

So Americans understand the costs of war. Yet as a country, we will never tolerate our security being threatened nor stand idly by when our people have been killed. We will be relentless in defense of our citizens and our friends and allies. We will be true to the values that make us who we are. And on nights like this one, we can say to those families who have lost loved ones to Al Qaida's terror: Justice has been done.

Tonight we give thanks to the countless intelligence and counterterrorism professionals who've worked tirelessly to achieve this outcome. The American people do not see their work nor know their names, but tonight they feel the satisfaction of their work and the result of their pursuit of justice.

We give thanks for the men who carried out this operation, for they exemplify the professionalism, patriotism, and unparalleled courage of those who serve our country. And they are part of a generation that has borne the heaviest share of the burden since that September day.

Finally, let me say to the families who lost loved ones on 9/11 that we have never forgotten your loss nor wavered in our commitment to see that we do whatever it takes to prevent another attack on our shores.

And tonight let us think back to the sense of unity that prevailed on 9/11. I know that it has, at times, frayed. Yet today's achievement is a testament to the greatness of our country and the determination of the American people.

The cause of securing our country is not complete. But tonight we are once again reminded that America can do whatever we set our mind to. That is the story of our history, whether it's the pursuit of prosperity for our people or the struggle for equality for all our citizens, our commitment to stand up for our values abroad and our sacrifices to make the world a safer place.

Let us remember that we can do these things not just because of wealth or power, but because of who we are: one nation under God, indivisible, with liberty and justice for all.

Thank you. May God bless you, and may God bless the United States of America.

SOURCE: U.S. Executive Office of the President. "Remarks on the Death of Al Qaida Terrorist Organization Leader Usama bin Laden." May 1, 2011. *Daily Compilation of Presidential Documents* 2010, no. 00314 (May 1, 2011). http://www.gpo.gov/fdsys/pkg/DCPD-201100314/pdf/DCPD-201100314.pdf.

Pakistan Ministry of Foreign Affairs on the Death of Osama bin Laden

May 2, 2011

In an intelligence driven operation, Osama Bin Ladin was killed in the surroundings of Abbottabad in the early hours of this morning. This operation was conducted by the US forces in accordance with declared US policy that Osama bin Ladin will be eliminated in a direct action by the US forces, wherever found in the world.

Earlier today, President Obama telephoned President Zardari on the successful US operation which resulted in killing of Osama bin Ladin.

Osama bin Ladin's death illustrates the resolve of the international community including Pakistan to fight and eliminate terrorism. It constitutes a major setback to terrorist organizations around the world.

Al-Qaeda had declared war on Pakistan. Scores of Al-Qaeda sponsored terrorist attacks resulted in deaths of thousands of innocent Pakistani men, women and children. Almost, 30,000 Pakistani civilians lost their lives in terrorist attacks in the last few years. More than 5,000 Pakistani security and armed forces officials have been martyred in Pakistan's campaign against Al-Qaeda, other terrorist organizations and affiliates.

Pakistan has played a significant role in efforts to eliminate terrorism. We have had extremely effective intelligence sharing arrangements with several intelligence agencies including that of the US. We will continue to support international efforts against terrorism.

It is Pakistan's stated policy that it will not allow its soil to be used in terrorist attacks against any country. Pakistan's political leadership, parliament, state institutions and the whole nation are fully united in their resolve to eliminate terrorism.

SOURCE: Pakistan Ministry of Foreign Affairs. "Death of Osama bin Ladin." May 2, 2011. http://www.mofa.gov.pk/mfa/pages/article.aspx?id=234&type=1.

Secretary of State Clinton on the Killing of Osama bin Laden

May 2, 2011

Well, good morning. As President Obama said last night, Usama bin Ladin is dead, and justice has been done. And today, I want to say a few words about what this means for our efforts going forward.

First, I want to offer my thoughts and prayers to the thousands of families whose loved ones were killed in Usama bin Ladin's campaign of terror and violence, from the embassy bombings in Africa, to the strike on the U.S.S. Cole, to the attacks of September 11, 2001, and so many more. These were not just attacks against Americans, although we suffered grievous losses; these were attacks against the whole world. In London and Madrid, Bali, Istanbul, and many other places, innocent people—most of them Muslims—were targeted in markets and mosques, in subway stations, and on airplanes, each attack motivated by a violent ideology that holds no value for human life or regard for human dignity. I know that nothing can make up for the loss of the victims or fill the voids they left, but I hope their families can now find some comfort in the fact that justice has been served.

Second, I want to join the President in honoring the courage and commitment of the brave men and women who serve our country and have worked tirelessly and relentlessly for more than a decade to track down and bring Usama bin Ladin, this terrorist, to justice. From our troops and our intelligence experts, to our diplomats and our law enforcement officials, this has been a broad, deep, very impressive effort.

Here at the State Department, we have worked to forge a worldwide anti-terror network. We have drawn together the effort and energy of friends, partners, and allies on every continent. Our partnerships, including our close cooperation with Pakistan, have helped put unprecedented pressure on al-Qaida and its leadership. Continued cooperation will be just as important in the days ahead, because even as we mark this milestone, we should not forget that the battle to stop al-Qaida and its syndicate of terror will not end with the death of bin Ladin. Indeed, we must take this opportunity to renew our resolve and redouble our efforts.

In Afghanistan, we will continue taking the fight to al-Qaida and their Taliban allies, while working to support the Afghan people as they build a stronger government and begin to take responsibility for their own security. We are implementing the strategy for transition approved by NATO at the summit in Lisbon, and we are supporting an Afghan-led political process that seeks to isolate al-Qaida and end the insurgency. Our message to the Taliban remains the same, but today it may have even greater resonance: You cannot wait us out. You cannot defeat us. But you can make the choice to abandon al-Qaida and participate in a peaceful political process.

In Pakistan we are committed to supporting the people and government as they defend their own democracy from violent extremism. Indeed, as the President said, bin Ladin had also declared war on Pakistan. He had ordered the killings of many innocent Pakistani men, women, and children. In recent years, the cooperation between our governments, militaries, and law enforcement agencies increased pressure on al-Qaida and the Taliban, and this progress must continue and we are committed to our partnership.

History will record that bin Ladin's death came at a time of great movements toward freedom and democracy, at a time when the people across the Middle East and North Africa are rejecting the extremist narratives and charting a path of peaceful progress based on universal rights and aspirations. There is no better rebuke to al-Qaida and its heinous ideology.

All over the world we will press forward, bolstering our partnerships, strengthening our networks, investing in a positive vision of peace and progress, and relentlessly pursuing the murderers who target innocent people. The fight continues, and we will never waver. Now I know there are some who doubted this day would ever come, who questioned our resolve and our reach. But let us remind ourselves, this is America. We rise to the challenge, we persevere, and we get the job done.

I am reminded especially today of the heroism and humanity that marked the difficult days after 9/11. In New York, where I was a senator, our community was devastated; but we pulled through. Ten years later, that American spirit remains as powerful as ever, and it will continue to prevail. So this is a day, not only for Americans, but also for people all over the world who look to a more peaceful and secure future—yes, with continued vigilance, but more so with growing hope and renewed faith in what is possible.

Thank you all very much.

SOURCE: U.S. Department of State. "Remarks on the Killing of Usama bin Ladin." May 2, 2011. http://www.state.gov/secretary/rm/2011/05/162339.htm.

OTHER HISTORIC DOCUMENTS OF INTEREST

FROM THIS VOLUME

- Department of Justice on Military Trials for Guantánamo Detainees, p. 181

FROM PREVIOUS *HISTORIC DOCUMENTS*

- United Nations on the al Qaeda Terrorist Network and the Taliban, *2004*, p. 534
- Joint Congressional Panel on September 11 Attacks, *2003*, p. 544
- British Government on Osama Bin Laden, *2001*, p. 802
- Bush and Blair on the Start of the War in Afghanistan, *2001*, p. 686
- Bush on Terrorist Attacks Against the United States, *2001*, p. 614
- Defense Department on USS *Cole* Attack, *2001*, p. 3

Hamas and Fatah Agree to Historic Reconciliation Pact; Palestine Requests UN Membership

MAY 3 AND 4, AND SEPTEMBER 23, 2011

The relationship between Palestinian factions Hamas and Fatah has long been fraught with tension, and the 2006 parliamentary elections brought divisions between the two groups to the surface. Hamas won a surprise victory and, after a brief civil war, seized power of the Gaza Strip from Fatah in June 2007. By taking control of Gaza, Hamas was able to limit the influence of the Palestinian Authority (PA) and Palestine's president, Mahmoud Abbas, a member of Fatah. One of the key disagreements between the two factions is Palestine's relationship with Israel. Fatah prefers a peace agreement with the nation, while Hamas has bombed Israel and does not recognize its existence. With peace talks with Israel at a standstill in 2011, Hamas and Fatah, swept up in the impact of Arab Spring, worked with the Egyptian government, which served as a mediator, to reach their own reconciliation agreement. Palestine used this request as the starting point for their September bid for full UN membership.

Previous Reconciliation Work

Seeking to maintain its legitimacy in the region after losing the 2006 parliamentary elections, Fatah turned to Israel to establish a peace agreement that would remove Israeli troops from Palestine. Hamas opposed any peace agreement with Israel, stating its belief that Israel had no rights in Palestine and should be destroyed. Hamas and Israel had a ceasefire agreement, but it ended in 2008 and sparked the Israel-Gaza conflict of 2008 to 2009. Palestinian President Mahmoud Abbas came close to an agreement with then-Israeli Prime Minister Ehud Olmert in 2008, but when his successor, Benjamin Netanyahu, took office in 2009, Abbas met resistance to any peace agreement. Talks almost immediately broke down. "He wanted Israeli troops in the valley and on the heights for 40 years," Abbas remarked of Netanyahu's plans for Palestine. "That means a continuation of the occupation."

Despite the differences between Fatah and Hamas on peace with Israel, Egypt worked to broker a reconciliation pact between the two factions. In late 2009, a reconciliation pact was drafted in Cairo and signed by Fatah and Abbas. Hamas refused to sign the agreement, and two further attempts at gaining a Hamas signature were delayed because of a number of disagreements still unresolved between the two factions.

In February 2010, talks were renewed between Hamas and Fatah and held in the Gaza Strip, where the parties worked to reconcile their differences. No agreement was reached at the meetings, and renewed talks in Damascus in November 2010 failed to culminate in any agreement because Fatah and Hamas could not agree on who should control security on the West Bank and in the Gaza Strip.

Few were aware of the renewed peace talks taking place in secret meetings with Egypt in 2011, but at the time when the reconciliation pact was announced in April, there was little speculation as to the driving forces behind it. Abbas's plans for retirement and Fatah's failure to reach a peace agreement with Israel contributed to the April agreement, but the larger impact of the Arab Spring seemed to heighten awareness among the two groups of an immediate need for a reconciliation pact. Egypt's new government, if only interim, was hopeful to mark its growing influence in the region by acting as negotiator in the talks, and with increasing uncertainty surrounding Syria's government, Hamas, which is based in Syria, began seeking closer ties to Egypt's new government.

RECONCILIATION REACHED IN 2011

After the fall of Hosni Mubarak's government in Egypt in February 2011, Nabil el-Araby, the new Egyptian foreign minister, invited Hamas to Cairo to discuss renewing the reconciliation discussions. "The foreign minister told them, 'We do not want to talk about a "peace process",'" said Egyptian foreign ministry spokesperson Menha Bakhoum. "We want a peace, and the only way to talk about peace is to end the divisions," Bakhoum said. Hamas agreed to rejoin the discussions only after Egypt agreed to open the Egypt-Gaza border that had remained virtually closed for most of Mubarak's reign.

It was not until March when the reconciliation process began to gather momentum. On March 15, 10,000 demonstrators took to the streets in Palestine in the largest unauthorized demonstration since Hamas gained control of the government in 2007. The protesters called for Hamas-Fatah unity and quickly gained the attention of the warring factions and their leadership, sparking recognition that discontent in other Middle Eastern nations had reached Palestine's borders.

The secret reconciliation negotiations resulted in a pact that was agreed to in principle in April, and both Abbas and Khaled Meshaal, the leader of Hamas, signed the formal version on May 4 in Cairo. As a show of goodwill, prior to the official signing ceremony, Fatah-controlled Palestine TV was allowed to broadcast from Gaza for the first time since 2007. Hamas official Ismail Radwan was invited by Fatah to comment on the reconciliation pact during the broadcast. "Today we end a dark chapter in our recent history," Radwan said. "It's time now to work together . . . With the support of our people and the Arab brothers, we will make this agreement work." The government also allowed the display of Fatah banners that had previously been banned in the streets.

The ceremony held on May 4 to mark the signing of the agreement nearly became its downfall, when Abbas demanded that he be the only speaker at the signing ceremony and sit alone at the podium to emphasize his position in Palestine. Meshaal was already scheduled to speak on the program, but the two sides quickly reached an agreement in which Meshaal sat in the ceremony hall rather than joining Abbas on stage and gave only brief remarks. It was exactly this type of embarrassment that the Egyptian government wanted to avoid and as such there was no live feed of the ceremony and the signing was held privately. However, the international community did not overlook the importance of the event. The United Nations, the European Union, and the Arab League all sent representatives to witness the signing.

In his brief remarks during the ceremony, Meshaal told the audience multiple times his belief that Palestinians, be they supporters of Hamas or Fatah, only have a disagreement with Israel, not with each other. "Our aim is to establish a free and completely sovereign Palestinian state on the West Bank and Gaza Strip, whose capital is Jerusalem, without any settlers and without giving up a single inch of land and without giving up on the right of return [of Palestinian refugees]." Abbas hinted of the change to come for Palestine during his remarks. "Four black years have affected the interests of Palestinians. Now we meet to assert a unified will," Abbas said. "Our people have always rejected this rift. All factions will now have to show that they have learned from this difficult experience, and that they will accept a democratic government through the coming elections," he continued.

The signed reconciliation pact contained five major components. Hamas and Fatah agreed to work together to form an interim unity government, which would replace the two governments currently in Palestine, and a twelve-judge election tribunal. The interim government would be made up of independent technocrats and current Hamas and Fatah leaders would not be included. The new government would be in charge of preparing the country for elections to choose a parliament and president, which the pact stated would be held within one year. Hamas and Fatah further agreed to unify their security forces, and the two groups planned to create an oversight committee that would regulate security and assist in the unification. A committee will be set up to review changes to the Palestine Liberation Organization (PLO), an organization established in 1964 to support Palestinian issues, which could mean inclusion in the group for Hamas. Fatah makes up the largest portion of PLO membership, and Abbas is the group's current chair. By including Hamas in the PLO, the group could further complicate its two-decade long attempt at peace negotiations with Israel. Finally, the Palestinian Legislative Council (PLC) will be reactivated after being barred from legislative activity in 2007. Hamas and Fatah also agreed to continue talks on the release of all political prisoners held by either side after the signing of the agreement. Language specific to this was not included in the final text of the agreement.

REMAINING DISAGREEMENTS AND OBSTACLES TO FULL RECONCILIATION

Israel was one of the biggest dissenters to any agreement between Fatah and Hamas. Following the signing of the reconciliation pact, Netanyahu stopped tax revenue payments from being sent to the Palestinian Authority (PA). He also began encouraging the United States and the European Union to cut funding for the organization. "When . . . the head of the Palestinian Authority embraces Hamas, an organization that two days ago condemned the American action against Bin Laden, praises Bin Laden to the gills as some great martyr for emulation, when he embraces this organization that is committed to Israel's destruction, fires rockets on our cities . . . this is a tremendous setback for peace, and a great advance for terror," Netanyahu said of the agreement.

Internal disagreements between Hamas and Fatah will also act as obstacles to full reconciliation. Fatah still desires a peace agreement with Israel, which Hamas has continued to oppose. And Palestine now faces the alienation of the West. The PA had enjoyed the West's support in the past, and received millions of dollars each year from the U.S. Congress. Now, that funding remains in jeopardy. At the time of the agreement, the House of Representatives and Senate made no announcement about whether the reconciliation pact would affect funding. The State Department, which continues to label Hamas as a terrorist organization, did not take an immediate stance on reconciliation but stated instead that it would review the pact and watch its implementation before taking an official position.

Security is also a concern for maintaining the pact. Fatah and Hamas are continuing negotiations on how security should be controlled in the West Bank and the Gaza Strip, and until an agreement is reached, each area will be policed separately, with Fatah running security in the West Bank and Hamas handling the Gaza Strip.

To ensure that the reconciliation pact is actualized despite these challenges, the Arab League will supervise its implementation and Egypt has set up a committee to assist with oversight as well. "The Arab League will have a role in the follow-up with the Palestinians on the reconciliation process to ensure the process unfolds in due course," said League spokesperson Hisham Youssef.

PALESTINE REQUESTS UN MEMBERSHIP

During his term as president of the PA, Abbas made clear his desire for United Nations membership. But he recognized that membership was unlikely to be granted until Hamas and Fatah reached a reconciliation agreement. With the agreement signed, in September Palestine submitted a formal request for admission into the United Nations as a full member. "I do not believe that anyone with a shred of conscience can reject our application for a full membership in the United Nations and our admission as an independent state," Abbas said in a speech before the General Assembly. Palestine currently has observer status with the international organization.

In order to receive full membership, Palestine required the support of nine of the fifteen members on the Security Council; however, any vote against the measure by one of the five permanent members—China, France, Russia, the United Kingdom, or the United States—would disqualify Palestine. If Palestine received Security Council approval, a vote of the General Assembly would be held with two-thirds necessary for approval.

The United States came out strongly against Palestine's bid, and both the House and Senate threatened to cut the $100 million in annual funding the PA receives from the United States if the bid continued. In remarks before the UN General Assembly, President Barack Obama called on Palestine to first work out its differences with Israel before asking for UN recognition. The UK and France indicated that they would abstain from a vote on Palestine's membership, citing concerns that any hope of an Israel-Palestine peace deal would be squandered by granting Palestine membership in the United Nations.

In November, the Security Council failed to approve Palestine's request for membership. Abbas vowed to continue working toward membership, and will most likely take the route of asking the General Assembly to upgrade its current membership to nonmember observer status. Palestine enjoys broad support in the General Assembly, and there are indications that an application could be approved.

—Heather Kerrigan

Following is the text of the agreement between Hamas and Fatah, released on May 3, 2011; a statement by Israeli Prime Minister Benjamin Netanyahu on May 4, 2011, in opposition to the agreement; and the text of Palestine's September 23, 2011, request for UN membership.

Hamas-Fatah Reconciliation Agreement

May 3, 2011

Under the auspices of Egypt, delegations from the Fatah and Hamas movements met in Cairo on April 27, 2011 to discuss the issues concerning ending the political division and the achievement of national unity. On top of the issues were some reservations related to the Palestinian National Unity Accord made in 2009.

Both political parties mutually agreed that the basis of understanding made during the meeting are committing to both parties in the implementation of the Palestinian National Reconciliation Agreement. The basis of understanding agreed upon by Fatah and Hamas are as follows:

1. ELECTIONS

A. Election Committee:

Both Fatah and Hamas agree to identify the names of the members of the Central Election Commission in agreement with the Palestinian factions. This list will then be submitted to the Palestinian President who will issue a decree of the reformation of the committee.

B. Electoral Court:

Both Fatah and Hamas agree on the nomination of no more than twelve judges to be members of the Electoral Court. This list will then be submitted to the Palestinian President in order to take the necessary legal actions to form the Electoral Court in agreement with the Palestinian factions.

C. Timing of Elections:

The Legislative, Presidential, and the Palestinian National Council elections will be conducted at the same time exactly one year after the signing of the Palestinian National Reconciliation Agreement.

2. PALESTINE LIBERATION ORGANIZATION

The political parties of both Fatah and Hamas agree that the tasks and decisions of the provisional interim leadership cannot be hindered or obstructed, but in a manner that is not conflicting with the authorities of the Executive Committee of the Palestine Liberation Organization.

3. SECURITY

It was emphasized that the formation of the Higher Security Committee which will be formed by a decree of the Palestinian President and will consist of professional officers in consensus.

4. Government

A. Formation of the Government:

Both Fatah and Hamas agree to form a Palestinian government and to appoint the Prime Minister and Ministers in consensus between them.

B. Functions of the Government:

1. Preparation of necessary condition for the conduction of Presidential, Legislative and the Palestinian National Council elections.

2. Supervising and addressing the prevalent issues regarding the internal Palestinian reconciliation resulting from the state of division.

3. Follow-up of the reconstruction operations in the Gaza Strip and the efforts to end the siege and blockade that is imposed on it.

4. Continuation of the implementation of the provisions of the Palestinian National Accord.

5. To resolve the civil and administrative problems that resulted from the division.

6. Unification of the Palestinian National Authority institutions in the West Bank, Gaza Strip and Jerusalem.

7. To fix the status of the associations, Non-Governmental Organizations and charities.

5. Legislative Council:

Both Fatah and Hamas agree to reactivate the Palestinian Legislative Council in accordance to the Basic Law.

Source: Al Mubadara: Palestinian National Initiative. "Text of the Agreement Between Fatah and Hamas." May 3, 2011. http://www.almubadara.org/details.php?id=fj0p26a1333y0gf14q6wm.

Prime Minister Netanyahu Reacts to Hamas-Fatah Agreement

May 4, 2011

"What happened today in Cairo is a tremendous blow to peace and a great victory for terrorism. Three days ago, terrorism was dealt a resounding defeat with the elimination of Osama bin Laden. Today, in Cairo, it had a victory."

In signing this deal, Palestinian Authority President Mahmoud Abbas had "embraced" an organization that had condemned the American operation against the al-Qaida leader and called him a "great martyr," Netanyahu said. "When he embraces this organization, which is committed to Israel's destruction and fires rockets on our cities, this is a tremendous setback for peace and a great advancement for terror. What we hope will happen is that we find peace, and the only way we can make peace is with our neighbors who want peace. Those who want to eliminate us, those who practice terror, are not partners for peace."

SOURCE: Office of the Prime Minister of Israel. Briefing Room. "PM Netanyahu Comments on Palestinian Authority-Hamas Reconciliation Agreement." May 4, 2011. http://www.pmo.gov.il/PMOEng/Archive/Press+Releases/2011/05/spokehamas040511.htm.

Palestine Submits Request for UN Membership

September 23, 2011

NOTE BY THE SECRETARY-GENERAL

In accordance with rule 135 of the rules of procedure of the General Assembly and rule 59 of the provisional rules of procedure of the Security Council, the Secretary-General has the honour to circulate herewith the attached application of Palestine for admission to membership in the United Nations, contained in a letter received on 23 September 2011 from its President (see annex I). He also has the honour to circulate a further letter, dated 23 September 2011, received from him at the same time (see annex II).

ANNEX I

Letter received on 23 September 2011 from the President of Palestine to the Secretary-General Application of the State of Palestine for admission to membership in the United Nations

I have the profound honour, on behalf of the Palestinian people, to submit this application of the State of Palestine for admission to membership in the United Nations.

This application for membership is being submitted based on the Palestinian people's natural, legal and historic rights and based on United Nations General Assembly resolution 181 (II) of 29 November 1947 as well as the Declaration of Independence of the State of Palestine of 15 November 1988 and the acknowledgement by the General Assembly of this Declaration in resolution 43/177 of 15 December 1988.

In this connection, the State of Palestine affirms its commitment to the achievement of a just, lasting and comprehensive resolution of the Israeli-Palestinian conflict based on the vision of two-States living side by side in peace and security, as endorsed by the United Nations Security Council and General Assembly and the international community as a whole and based on international law and all relevant United Nations resolutions.

For the purpose of this application for admission, a declaration made pursuant to rule 58 of the provisional rules of procedure of the Security Council and rule 134 of the rules of procedure of the General Assembly is appended to this letter (see enclosure).

I should be grateful if you would transmit this letter of application and the declaration to the Presidents of the Security Council and the General Assembly as soon as possible.

(*Signed*) Mahmoud **Abbas**

President of the State of Palestine

Chairman of the Executive Committee of
the Palestine Liberation Organization

Enclosure

Declaration

In connection with the application of the State of Palestine for admission to membership in the United Nations, I have the honour, in my capacity as the President of the State of Palestine and as the Chairman of the Executive Committee of the Palestine Liberation Organization, the sole legitimate representative of the
Palestinian people, to solemnly declare that the State of Palestine is a peace-loving nation and that it accepts the obligations contained in the Charter of the United Nations and solemnly undertakes to fulfill them.

(*Signed*) Mahmoud **Abbas**

President of the State of Palestine

Chairman of the Executive Committee of
the Palestine Liberation Organization

Annex II

Letter dated 23 September 2011 from the President of Palestine to the Secretary-General
After decades of displacement, dispossession and the foreign military occupation of my people and with the successful culmination of our State-building program, which has been endorsed by the international community, including the Quartet of the Middle East Peace Process, it is with great pride and honour that I have submitted to you an application for the admission of the State of Palestine to full membership in the United Nations.

On 15 November 1988, the Palestine National Council (PNC) declared the Statehood of Palestine in exercise of the Palestinian people's inalienable right to self-determination. The Declaration of Independence of the State of Palestine was acknowledged by the United Nations General Assembly in resolution 43/177 of 15 December 1988. The right of the Palestinian people to self-determination and independence and the vision of a two-State solution to the Israeli-Palestinian conflict have been firmly established by General Assembly in numerous resolutions, including, inter alia, resolutions 181 (II) (1947), 3236 (XXIX) (1974), 2649 (XXV) (1970), 2672 (XXV) (1970), 65/16 (2010) and 65/202 (2010) as well as by United Nations Security Council resolutions 242 (1967), 338 (1973) and 1397 (2002) and by the International Court of Justice Advisory Opinion of 9 July 2004 (on the Legal Consequences of the Construction of a Wall in the Occupied Palestinian Territory).

Furthermore, the vast majority of the international community has stood in support of our inalienable rights as a people, including to statehood, by according bilateral recognition to the State of Palestine on the basis of the 4 June 1967 borders, with East Jerusalem as its capital, and the number of such recognitions continues to rise with each passing day.

Palestine's application for membership is made consistent with the rights of the Palestine refugees in accordance with international law and the relevant United Nations resolutions, including General Assembly resolution 194 (III) (1948), and with the status of the Palestine Liberation Organization (PLO) as the sole legitimate representative of the Palestinian people.

The Palestinian leadership reaffirms the historic commitment of the Palestine Liberation Organization of 9 September 1993. Further, the Palestinian leadership stands committed to resume negotiations on all final status issues—Jerusalem, the Palestine refugees, settlements, borders, security and water—on the basis of the internationally endorsed terms of reference, including the relevant United Nations resolutions, the Madrid principles, including the principle of land for peace, the Arab Peace Initiative and the Quartet Roadmap, which specifically requires a freeze of all Israeli settlement activities.

At this juncture, we appeal to the United Nations to recall the instructions contained in General Assembly resolution 181 (II) (1947) and that "sympathetic consideration" be given to application of the State of Palestine for admission to the United Nations.

Accordingly, I have had the honour to present to Your Excellency the application of the State of Palestine to be a full member of the United Nations as well as a declaration made pursuant to rule 58 of the provisional rules of procedure of the Security Council and rule 134 of the rules of procedure of the General Assembly. I respectfully request that this letter be conveyed to the Security Council and the General Assembly without delay.

(*Signed*) Mahmoud **Abbas**

President of the State of Palestine

Chairman of the Executive Committee of
the Palestine Liberation Organization

SOURCE: United Nations. "Application of Palestine for Admission to Membership in the United Nations." September 23, 2011. http://unispal.un.org/UNISPAL.nsf/47D4E277B48D9D3685256DDC00612265/ F6CF1ED25A5D8FE9852579170050C37F.

OTHER HISTORIC DOCUMENTS OF INTEREST

FROM THIS VOLUME

■ Israel and Palestine Remark on Prisoner Swap, p. 549

FROM PREVIOUS *HISTORIC DOCUMENTS*

Supreme Court Rules on Legal Arizona Workers Act

MAY 26, 2011

Congressional inaction on passing stronger immigration laws has prompted a number of states to take action themselves as the influx of illegal Hispanic immigrants continues to have a significant impact. In 2010 and 2011, states including Alabama, Arizona, Georgia, and South Carolina have all passed varying regulations on illegal immigrants. In 2011, the immigration fight centered on Arizona, where a state law allowing for the revocation of business licenses from those companies found to knowingly hire illegal immigrants came up against the federal government assertion that its own laws preempt state regulation. The case came before the Supreme Court, where the divided justices ruled 5–3 that Arizona's law was not in conflict with federal law, giving states a possible loophole to supersede federal immigration authority.

Legal Arizona Workers Act

Arizona was one of the early adopters of state-based immigration policy, in 2007 passing into law the Legal Arizona Workers Act (LAWA). The law was signed by then-governor Janet Napolitano, a Democrat. LAWA bars employers from knowingly hiring illegal immigrants. The state defines illegal immigrants as "an alien who does not have the legal right or authorization under federal law to work in the United States." Those businesses that do so repeatedly are in jeopardy of having their business licenses revoked. In addition, LAWA requires employers in the state to use the federal E-Verify system to match Social Security and drivers's license numbers to government documents for verification of an individual's legal status to work in the United States. The law went into effect on January 1, 2008, and affects hiring practices after December 31, 2007.

To date, LAWA has been used infrequently to revoke the business licenses of anyone found in noncompliance. But that did not stop businesses and civil rights groups from filing suit, arguing that the law violated federal immigration policy. Both a federal judge and a federal appeals court upheld the law, stating that LAWA did not preempt federal law. The U.S. Chamber of Commerce took up the case, appealing to the Supreme Court for a review of Arizona's law. The Chamber argued that there are two key issues in LAWA that are unconstitutional—state preemption of federal law and mandated use of the E-Verify system.

Arguments in the Case

The Chamber of Commerce rested their preemption argument on the federal Immigration Reform and Control Act of 1986 (IRCA), which allows the federal government to impose sanctions on employers who knowingly hire illegal immigrants. This law prohibits states from using civil or criminal punishment without first receiving federal approval against those who hire illegal immigrants. The Chamber, in cooperation with the U.S. Department of Justice, argued that IRCA preempts LAWA. According to the Chamber's argument, IRCA prohibits states from the enactment of "any State or local law imposing civil or criminal sanctions (other than through licensing and similar laws) upon those who employ, or recruit or refer for a fee for employment, unauthorized aliens." Although the IRCA includes the licensing provision, the Chamber argued that federal law limits the scope of the licensing restriction, barring it from being used to exempt those who are revoking business licenses. The Chamber additionally argued that LAWA is not a genuine licensing law because it deals with the revoking of, rather than the distribution of, licenses.

The Chamber also looked to earlier Supreme Court cases to support its argument. In 1976, ten years before Congress took action through IRCA, the Court ruled on the case of *DeCanas v. Bica,* which focused on the federal-state partnership on restricting the right of illegal immigrants to work in the United States. The Court ruled that "[p]ower to regulate immigration is unquestionably exclusively a federal power."

The second claim brought by the Chamber dealt with the E-Verify system. E-Verify is a federal, web-based program used to determine a person's legal status in the country, and therefore that person's eligibility to work. The Department of Homeland Security and the Social Security Administration run the program, which reviews credentials presented by job candidates to determine if they are credible. Use of the federal system is voluntary, except under LAWA. The Chamber argued that LAWA's E-Verify stipulation creates tension between state and federal law. When tensions between the two sectors of government arise, it is federal law or mandate that preempts state decisions.

The State of Arizona, represented in the case by Apache County Attorney Michael Whiting, argued that federal inaction provoked the state to enact its own laws to protect businesses and citizens from unlawful immigrant workers. Arizona claimed that it was protected under IRCA's licensing provision, and that no conflict existed that would not allow enforcement of both federal and state immigration policy in Arizona.

Justice Antonin Scalia was sympathetic to Arizona's LAWA regulations, quoting the state's argument that "That is the only option the government left us." Justice Stephen Breyer, on the other hand, backed the Congressional approach through IRCA as balanced to ensure that illegal aliens do not get jobs but that those of Hispanic descent are not discriminated against. "How do you reconcile that with Arizona's law?" he asked.

VICTORY FOR STATE RIGHTS

In a landmark decision on state rights to sanction employers and place requirements on them when it comes to illegal immigration, on May 26, 2011, the Supreme Court ruled 5–3 that federal law does not prohibit Arizona from taking away the business licenses of those Arizona companies that knowingly hire illegal immigrants. Additionally, federal law does not stop Arizona from requiring employers to use the federal E-Verify system to ensure that employees have the legal right to work in the United States. Chief Justice John Roberts wrote the majority opinion, joined in full by Justices Scalia, Samuel Alito, and Anthony Kennedy, and joined in part by Justice Clarence Thomas, a strong supporter of state's rights. Justice Breyer wrote for the dissent, joined by Justice Ruth Bader Ginsburg; Justice Sonia Sotomayor wrote her own dissent. Justice Elena Kagan recused herself from the case because of her earlier involvement with the government's case against LAWA during her time as U.S. Solicitor General.

In the opinion of the majority, the case hinged on the word "licensing" and what it means in the context of IRCA. Federal law, Roberts wrote, "expressly preempts some state powers dealing with the employment of unauthorized aliens and it expressly preserves others." He continued, "We hold that Arizona's licensing law falls well within the confines of the authority Congress chose to leave to the states and therefore is not expressly preempted." If Congress had intended a more specific prohibition on state sanctions for employers, the majority wrote, it would have said so, rather than offering a broad exemption of "licensing and similar laws." Roberts took note of the Chamber's argument that revocation of licenses and granting of licenses are two separate ideas under IRCA. "There is no basis in law, fact, or logic for deeming a law that grants licenses a licensing law, but a law that suspends or revokes those very licenses something else altogether," he wrote. The majority noted that while LAWA's punishment of license revocation is more significant than punishment under federal law, this punishment still fell within the licensing exemption of IRCA. In sum, Roberts wrote, "Arizona has taken the route least likely to cause tension with federal law."

The dissent argued that LAWA goes well beyond Congress's intention in IRCA. "Congress did not intend its 'licensing' language to create so broad an exemption," wrote Breyer, cautioning that a literal interpretation of IRCA could give states the right to revoke drivers's licenses, marriage licenses, or dog licenses based on the legal employment status of a state resident. Giving broad interpretation to IRCA's licensing exemption, as Roberts did, "facilitates the creation of 'obstacles to the accomplishment and execution of the full purposes and objectives of Congress,'" wrote Breyer. Breyer also expressed concern that the Arizona law could lead to discrimination of those from Hispanic backgrounds or to state witch hunts for businesses suspected of hiring illegal immigrants. Employers, Breyer said, "will hesitate to hire those they fear will turn out to lack the right to work in the United States." Breyer argued that this would threaten the antidiscriminatory policies of IRCA. In his opinion, Roberts refuted this notion, writing that it is logical to believe that employers will follow the law, "both the law barring the employment of unauthorized aliens and the law prohibiting discrimination."

In her own dissent, Sotomayor wrote that the majority decision gives states the right to "determine for themselves whether someone has employed an unauthorized alien so long as they do so in conjunction with licensing sanctions." Sotomayor wrote that she would prefer that Arizona be able to sanction businesses only after the federal government determined that a business had knowingly hired illegal immigrants. She also noted that Congress did not intend the licensing exemption to be treated the way the majority read it. "I cannot believe that Congress intended for the 50 states and countless localities to implement their own distinct enforcement and adjudication procedures for deciding whether employers have employed unauthorized aliens."

On the issue of LAWA's mandated use of E-Verify, the majority found that because no federal law regulates the use of E-Verify, there is no conflict between the federal and state law. The Court also noted that President Barack Obama had ordered all federal contractors to use E-Verify in order to be eligible to receive a federal contract. When this issue was challenged, the Obama administration wrote that its own mandate was legal, while Arizona's was not because "the State of Arizona is not the Secretary of Homeland Security." In his dissent, Breyer wrote that it was incorrect of Arizona to require businesses to use a federal pilot program that he called "prone to error."

FUTURE IMPACT OF *CHAMBER OF COMMERCE V. WHITING*

Typically, federal law has been considered to supersede state law in immigration policy, but the decision in *Chamber of Commerce v. Whiting* shows that there may be a loophole, which could allow for the creation and enforcement of fifty state immigration policies rather than one unified federal policy. States wanting to use this loophole, however, would have to narrowly focus their immigration policies to fit within the licensing provision of IRCA to only revoke business licenses but not use fines or other forms of punishment for businesses hiring illegal immigrants.

It remains to be seen whether the *Chamber of Commerce v. Whiting* ruling will impact how the Court might rule on Arizona's other immigration law, Senate Bill 1070, when it takes up the issue in 2012. The Support Our Law Enforcement and Safe Neighborhoods Act, passed in the Arizona legislature in 2010, is considered the toughest regulation of immigration to date in the United States. Two of the law's main provisions have sparked significant controversy, including a requirement for police to verify the legal status of those suspected of being illegal immigrants and a requirement that legal immigrants carry proper documentation of their legal status at all times. SB 1070 is not a licensing law, and the Court did not mention it in its *Chamber v. Whiting* decision. In the summer of 2010, a federal judge issued an injunction against SB 1070 for the reason of preemption. The Ninth Circuit Court of Appeals agreed, and in December 2011, the Supreme Court decided to hear the case. In the case of *United States v. Arizona*, the federal government argues that the Arizona law violates the federal government's right to set immigration policy.

—Heather Kerrigan

The following are excerpts from the U.S. Supreme Court ruling in Chamber of Commerce v. Whiting, *in which the Court ruled 5–3 that Arizona is within its rights to revoke the business license of any state company that it finds has knowingly hired undocumented workers and to require employers to use the federal E-Verify system to check whether employees are authorized to work in the United States.*

DOCUMENT   *Chamber of Commerce v. Whiting*

May 26, 2011

[Footnotes have been omitted.]

No. 09-115

Chamber of Commerce of the United States of America, et al., Petitioners

v.

Michael B. Whiting et al.

On writ of certiorari to the United States Court of Appeals for the Ninth Circuit

[May 26, 2011]

CHIEF JUSTICE ROBERTS delivered the opinion of the Court, except as to Parts II–B and III–B.

Federal immigration law expressly preempts "any State or local law imposing civil or criminal sanctions (other than through licensing and similar laws) upon those who employ . . . unauthorized aliens." A recently enacted Arizona statute—the Legal Arizona Workers Act—provides that the licenses of state employers that knowingly or intentionally employ unauthorized aliens may be, and in certain circumstances must be, suspended or revoked. The law also requires that all Arizona employers use a federal electronic verification system to confirm that the workers they employ are legally authorized workers. The question presented is whether federal immigration law preempts those provisions of Arizona law. Because we conclude that the State's licensing provisions fall squarely within the federal statute's savings clause and that the Arizona regulation does not otherwise conflict with federal law, we hold that the Arizona law is not preempted. . . .

[Section I, part A, containing background on immigration legislation and its impacts, including the Immigration Reform and Control Act of 1986 (IRCA), has been omitted.]

[Section I, part B, containing information on the Legal Arizona Workers Act, has been omitted.]

[Section I, part C, containing additional background information on the case, has been omitted.]

II

The Chamber of Commerce argues that Arizona's law is expressly preempted by IRCA's text and impliedly preempted because it conflicts with federal law. We address each of the Chamber's arguments in turn.

A

When a federal law contains an express preemption clause, we "focus on the plain wording of the clause, which necessarily contains the best evidence of Congress' preemptive intent."

IRCA expressly preempts States from imposing "civil or criminal sanctions" on those who employ unauthorized aliens, "other than through licensing and similar laws." The Arizona law, on its face, purports to impose sanctions through licensing laws. The state law authorizes state courts to suspend or revoke an employer's business licenses if that certificate, approval, registration, charter or similar form of authorization that is required by law and that is issued by any agency for the purposes of operating a business in" the State. That definition largely parrots the definition of "license" that Congress codified in the Administrative Procedure Act.

Apart from that general definition, the Arizona law specifically includes within its definition of "license" documents such as articles of incorporation, certificates of partnership, and grants of authority to foreign companies to transact business in the State. These examples have clear counterparts in the APA definition just quoted. . . . .

The Chamber and the United States as *amicus* argue that the Arizona law is not a "licensing" law because it operates only to suspend and revoke licenses rather than to grant them. Again, this construction of the term runs contrary to the definition that Congress itself has codified. . . . It is also contrary to common sense. There is no basis in law, fact, or logic for deeming a law that grants licenses a licensing law, but a law that suspends or revokes those very licenses something else altogether.

In much the same vein, the Chamber argues that Congress's repeal of "AWPA's separate prohibition concerning unauthorized workers belies any suggestion that IRCA meant to authorize each of the 50 States . . . to impose its own separate prohibition," and that Congress instead wanted uniformity in immigration law enforcement. JUSTICE BREYER also objects to the departure from "one centralized enforcement scheme" under federal law. But Congress expressly preserved the ability of the States to impose their own sanctions through licensing; that—like our federal system in general—necessarily entails the prospect of some departure from homogeneity. And as for "separate prohibition[s]," it is worth recalling that the Arizona licensing law is based exclusively on the federal prohibition—a court reviewing a complaint under the Arizona law may "consider only the federal government's determination" with respect to "whether an employee is an unauthorized alien." . . .

IRCA expressly preempts some state powers dealing with the employment of unauthorized aliens and it expressly preserves others. We hold that Arizona's licensing law falls well within the confines of the authority Congress chose to leave to the States and therefore is not expressly preempted.

B

As an alternative to its express preemption argument, the Chamber contends that Arizona's law is impliedly preempted because it conflicts with federal law. At its broadest level, the Chamber's argument is that Congress "intended the federal system to be exclusive," and that any state system therefore necessarily conflicts with federal law. But Arizona's procedures simply implement the sanctions that Congress expressly allowed Arizona to pursue through licensing laws. Given that Congress specifically preserved such authority for the States, it stands to reason that Congress did not intend to prevent the States from using appropriate tools to exercise that authority.

And here Arizona went the extra mile in ensuring that its law closely tracks IRCA's provisions in all material respects. . . .

The federal determination on which the State must rely is provided under 8 U. S. C. §1373(c). That provision requires the Federal Government to "verify or ascertain" an individual's "citizenship or immigration status" in response to a state request. . . . In any event, if the information provided under §1373(c) does not confirm that an employee is an unauthorized alien, then the State cannot prove its case. . . .

Apart from the mechanics of the Arizona law, the Chamber argues more generally that the law is preempted because it upsets the balance that Congress sought to strike when enacting IRCA. In the Chamber's view, IRCA reflects Congress's careful balancing of several policy considerations—deterring unauthorized alien employment, avoiding burdens on employers, protecting employee privacy, and guarding against employment discrimination. . . .

As an initial matter, the cases on which the Chamber relies in advancing this argument all involve uniquely federal areas of regulation. Regulating in-state businesses through licensing laws has never been considered such an area of dominant federal concern.

Furthermore, those cases all concern state actions that directly interfered with the operation of the federal program. . . .

The Chamber and JUSTICE BREYER assert that employers will err on the side of discrimination rather than risk the "'business death penalty'" by "hiring unauthorized workers." That is not the choice. License termination is not an available sanction simply for "hiring unauthorized workers." Only far more egregious violations of the law trigger that consequence. The Arizona law covers only knowing or intentional violations. The law's permanent licensing sanctions do not come into play until a second knowing or intentional violation at the same business location, and only if the second violation occurs while the employer is still on probation for the first. These limits ensure that licensing sanctions are imposed only when an employer's conduct fully justifies them. An employer acting in good faith need have no fear of the sanctions. . . .

All that is required to avoid sanctions under the Legal Arizona Workers Act is to refrain from knowingly or intentionally violating the employment law. Employers enjoy safe harbors from liability when they use the I–9 system and E-Verify—as Arizona law requires them to do. The most rational path for employers is to obey the law—both the law barring the employment of unauthorized aliens and the law prohibiting discrimination—and there is no reason to suppose that Arizona employers will choose not to do so.

As with any piece of legislation, Congress did indeed seek to strike a balance among a variety of interests when it enacted IRCA. Part of that balance, however, involved allocating authority between the Federal Government and the States. The principle that Congress adopted in doing so was not that the Federal Government can impose large sanctions, and the States only small ones. IRCA instead preserved state authority over a particular category of sanctions—those imposed "through licensing and similar laws."

Of course Arizona hopes that its law will result in more effective enforcement of the prohibition on employing unauthorized aliens. But in preserving to the States the authority to impose sanctions through licensing laws, Congress did not intend to preserve only those state laws that would have no effect. The balancing process that culminated in IRCA resulted in a ban on hiring unauthorized aliens, and the state law here simply seeks to enforce that ban.

Implied preemption analysis does not justify a "freewheeling judicial inquiry into whether a state statute is in tension with federal objectives"; such an endeavor "would undercut the principle that it is Congress rather than the courts that preempts state law." Our precedents "establish that a high threshold must be met if a state law is to be pre-empted for conflicting with the purposes of a federal Act." That threshold is not met here.

III. . .

[A discussion of the Arizona law's requirement of the use of the E-Verify system has been omitted.]

***

IRCA expressly reserves to the States the authority to impose sanctions on employers hiring unauthorized workers, through licensing and similar laws. In exercising that authority, Arizona has taken the route least likely to cause tension with federal law. It uses the Federal Government's own definition of "unauthorized alien," it relies solely on the Federal

Government's own determination of who is an unauthorized alien, and it requires Arizona employers to use the Federal Government's own system for checking employee status. If even this gives rise to impermissible conflicts with federal law, then there really is no way for the State to implement licensing sanctions, contrary to the express terms of the savings clause.

Because Arizona's unauthorized alien employment law fits within the confines of IRCA's savings clause and does not conflict with federal immigration law, the judgment of the United States Court of Appeals for the Ninth Circuit is affirmed.

It is so ordered.

JUSTICE KAGAN took no part in the consideration or decision of this case.

JUSTICE BREYER, with whom JUSTICE GINSBURG joins, dissenting.

The federal Immigration Reform and Control Act of 1986 (Act or IRCA) pre-empts "any State or local law imposing civil or criminal sanctions (other than through licensing and similar laws) upon those who employ, or recruit, or refer for a fee for employment, unauthorized aliens." The state law before us, the Legal Arizona Workers Act, imposes civil sanctions upon those who employ unauthorized aliens. The state law before us, the Legal Arizona Workers Act, imposes civil sanctions upon those who employ unauthorized aliens.

Thus the state law falls within the federal Act's general preemption rule and is pre-empted—unless it also falls within that rule's exception for "licensing and similar laws." Unlike the Court, I do not believe the state law falls within this exception, and I consequently would hold it pre-empted.

Arizona calls its state statute a "licensing law," and the statute uses the word "licensing." But the statute strays beyond the bounds of the federal licensing exception, for it defines "license" to include articles of incorporation and partnership certificates, indeed *virtually every* state-law authorization for *any* firm, corporation, or partnership to do business in the State. Congress did not intend its "licensing" language to create so broad an exemption, for doing so would permit States to eviscerate the federal Act's preemption provision, indeed to subvert the Act itself, by undermining Congress' efforts (1) to protect lawful workers from national-origin-based discrimination and (2) to protect lawful employers against erroneous prosecution or punishment. . . .

I. . .

[Section A, which discusses the IRCA's verification requirements, has been omitted.]

B

The Act reconciles these competing objectives in several ways: First, the Act prohibits employers from hiring an alien knowing that the alien is unauthorized to work in the United States. Second, the Act provides an easy-to-use mechanism that will allow employers to determine legality: the I–9 form. In completing an I–9 form, the employer certifies that he or she has examined one or two documents (*e.g.*, a passport, or a driver's license along with a Social Security card) that tend to confirm the worker's identity and employability. Completion of the form in good faith immunizes the employer from liability, even if the worker turns out to be unauthorized. . . . Third, the Act creates a central enforcement mechanism. . . .

Fourth, the Act makes it "an unfair immigration-related employment practice . . . to discriminate against any individual" in respect to employment "because of such individual's national origin." Fifth, the Act sets forth a carefully calibrated sanction system. The penalties for hiring unauthorized aliens are graduated to prevent the Act from unduly burdening employers who are not serious offenders. . . .

C. . .

Second, Arizona's law subjects lawful employers to increased burdens and risks of erroneous prosecution. In addition to the Arizona law's severely burdensome sanctions, the law's procedures create enforcement risks not present in the federal system. . . . A related provision of the state law aggravates the risk of erroneous prosecutions. . . .

So what is the employer to do? What statute gives an employer whom the State proceeds against in state court the right to conduct discovery against the Federal Government? The Arizona statute, like the federal statute, says that the employer's use of an I–9 form provides a defense. But there is a hitch. The federal Act says that neither the I–9 form, nor "any information contained in or appended to" the form, "may . . . be used for purposes other than for enforcement of this" federal Act. So how can the employer present a defense, say, that the Government's information base is flawed? The majority takes the view that the forms are not *necessary* to receive the benefit of the affirmative defense. . . .

And that is my basic point. Either directly or through the uncertainty that it creates, the Arizona statute will impose additional burdens upon lawful employers and consequently lead those employers to erect ever stronger safeguards against the hiring of unauthorized aliens—without counterbalancing protection against unlawful discrimination. . . .

III

I would therefore read the words "licensing and similar laws" as covering state licensing systems applicable primarily to the licensing of firms in the business of recruiting or referring workers for employment, such as the state agricultural labor contractor licensing schemes in existence when the federal Act was created. This reading is consistent with the provision's history and language, and it minimizes the risk of harm of the kind just described. . . .

[Additional discussion of the IRCA has been omitted.]

Thus, reading the phrase as limited in scope to laws licensing businesses that recruit or refer workers for employment is consistent with the statute's language, with the relevant history, and with other statutory provisions in the Act. That reading prevents state law from undermining the Act and from turning the pre-emption clause on its head. That is why I consider it the better reading of the statute.

IV

Another section of the Arizona statute requires "every employer, after hiring an employee," to "verify the employment eligibility of the employee" through the Federal Government's E-Verify program. This state provision makes participation in the federal E-Verify system *mandatory* for virtually all Arizona employers. The federal law governing the E-Verify program, however, creates a program that is *voluntary.* By making mandatory that which federal law seeks to make voluntary, the state provision stands as a significant "'obstacle to the accomplishment and execution of the full purposes and objectives of Congress,'" and it is consequently pre-empted.

The federal statute itself makes clear that participation in the E-Verify program is voluntary. . . .

[Additional discussion of the E-Verify system has been omitted.]

For these reasons I would hold that the federal Act, including its E-Verify provisions, pre-empts Arizona's state law. With respect, I dissent from the majority's contrary holdings.

JUSTICE SOTOMAYOR, dissenting.

. . . The Court reads IRCA's saving clause—which preserves from pre-emption state "licensing and similar laws," 8 U. S. C. §1324a(h)(2)—to permit States to determine for themselves whether someone has employed an unauthorized alien so long as they do so in conjunction with licensing sanctions. . . .Congress could not plausibly have intended for the saving clause to operate in the way the majority reads it to do. . . .Because the Legal Arizona Workers Act instead creates a separate state mechanism for Arizona state courts to determine whether a person has employed an unauthorized alien, I would hold that it falls outside the saving clause and is pre-empted.

I would also hold that federal law pre-empts the provision of the Arizona Act making mandatory the use of E-Verify, the federal electronic verification system. . . .

I

A

I begin with the plain text of IRCA's pre-emption clause. IRCA expressly pre-empts States from "imposing civil or criminal sanctions (other than through licensing and similar laws) upon those who employ, or recruit or refer for a fee for employment, unauthorized aliens." The Arizona Act, all agree, imposes civil sanctions upon those who employ unauthorized aliens. The Act thus escapes express pre-emption only if it falls within IRCA's parenthetical saving clause for "licensing and similar laws.". . .

[Section B, containing a review of the IRCA, has been omitted.]

C

IRCA's saving clause must be construed against this backdrop. Focusing primarily on the text of the saving clause, Arizona and the majority read the clause to permit States to determine themselves whether a person has employed an unauthorized alien, so long as they do so in connection with licensing sanctions. This interpretation overlooks the broader statutory context and renders the statutory scheme "[in]coherent and [in]consistent.". . .

Equally problematic is the fact that employers charged under a state enforcement scheme with hiring unauthorized aliens are foreclosed from using I–9 forms in their defense in the state proceedings. Like IRCA, the Arizona Act confers an affirmative defense on employers who comply in good faith with IRCA's verification requirement. As discussed above, however, IRCA prohibits an employer from using the I–9 form to establish that affirmative defense under Arizona law. Not to worry, the majority says: The employer can establish the affirmative defense through office policies and testimony of employees. But Congress made the I–9 verification system and accompanying good-faith defense central to IRCA. . . .

Furthermore, given Congress' express goal of "unifor[m]" enforcement of "the immigration laws of the United States," IRCA §115, 100 Stat. 3384, I cannot believe that Congress intended for the 50 States and countless localities to implement their own distinct enforcement and adjudication procedures for deciding whether employers have employed unauthorized aliens. Reading the saving clause as the majority does subjects employers to a patchwork of enforcement schemes similar to the one that Congress sought to displace when it enacted IRCA. Having carefully constructed a uniform federal scheme for determining whether a person has employed an unauthorized alien, Congress could not plausibly have meant to create such a gaping hole in that scheme through the undefined, parenthetical phrase "licensing and similar laws."

In sum, the statutory scheme as a whole defeats Arizona's and the majority's reading of the saving clause. . . .

To render IRCA's saving clause consistent with the statutory scheme, I read the saving clause to permit States to impose licensing sanctions following a final federal determination that a person has violated §1324a(a)(1)(A) by knowingly hiring, recruiting, or refer ring for a fee an unauthorized alien. This interpretation both is faithful to the saving clause's text, see *supra*, at 2– 3, and best reconciles the saving clause with IRCA's "careful regulatory scheme," *Locke*, 529 U. S., at 106. . . .

I do not mean to suggest that the mere existence of a comprehensive federal scheme necessarily reveals a congressional intent to oust state remedies. . . .

Under my construction of the saving clause, the Arizona Act cannot escape preemption. . . .

II

I agree with the conclusion reached by JUSTICE BREYER in Part IV of his dissenting opinion that federal law impliedly pre-empts the provision in the Arizona Act requiring all Arizona employers to use the federal E-Verify program. . . .

[Additional remarks on the E-Verify program have been omitted.]

***

For these reasons, I cannot agree with either of the Court's holdings in this case. I respectfully dissent.

SOURCE: U.S. Supreme Court. *Chamber of Commerce v. Whiting*, 563 U.S. (2011). http://www.supremecourt .gov/opinions/10pdf/09-115.pdf.

OTHER HISTORIC DOCUMENTS OF INTEREST

FROM PREVIOUS *HISTORIC DOCUMENTS*

June

National Cancer Institute on Possible New Breast Cancer and Melanoma Treatments

JUNE 14 AND JULY 19, 2011

Breast cancer is the second-leading cause of cancer death for women in the United States following lung cancer. The disease affects 1.3 million women worldwide each year, with 500,000 succumbing to the disease. The number of melanoma cases has also been growing in part because of unprotected exposure to the sun, greater use of tanning salons, and better disease detection. In 2010, there were 68,000 new cases and 8,700 deaths linked to melanoma in the United States, according to the American Cancer Society. Just ten years earlier, there were 48,000 new cases and 7,700 deaths. Melanoma affects more young people than other types of cancer, and the five-year survival rate for metastatic melanoma patients is 15 percent. With diagnoses on the rise, studies on various drugs to treat and prevent melanoma and breast cancer have been increasing. In 2011, the results of significant clinical trials were released, with positive results.

AROMATASE INHIBITOR BREAST CANCER STUDY

Exemestane, known best by its brand name Aromasin, a drug developed by Pfizer Inc., is currently approved in the United States to treat breast cancer and help prevent recurrence. But a study released in 2011 suggests that Aromasin may also prevent breast cancer from developing in women who are at high risk for the disease, including women over age sixty, postmenopausal women, and those who have abnormal biopsies. Aromasin is one of a group of drugs known as an aromatase inhibitor that works to block estrogen in postmenopausal women, a key factor in fueling tumor growth in two-thirds of all breast cancer cases, according to the National Institutes of Health.

The Aromasin study, funded by Pfizer and sponsored by the National Cancer Institute, followed a group of 4,560 women who were at least sixty years old or who had been diagnosed with precancerous lesions. Beginning in 2004, the women in the study were split into two groups. Half of the group received a placebo, and the other half took Aromasin. The study ran for three years, and the women were provided with annual mammograms and checkups.

At the conclusion of the third year, eleven women in the Aromasin group were diagnosed with invasive breast cancer compared to thirty-two in the placebo group. Women who took Aromasin were therefore 65 percent less likely to develop invasive breast cancer than those who took a placebo instead. The women in the Aromasin group who had previously received hormone-replacement therapy had an even greater success rate, reducing their cancer risk by 70 percent. On a broader scale, if Aromasin were approved for breast cancer prevention, ninety-four women would need to take the drug for three years to prevent one incident of breast cancer. This number drops to twenty-six after five years of taking an aromatase inhibitor.

The Aromasin study was the first to look at aromatase inhibitors as possible cancer prevention drugs. Previous studies on cancer prevention treatments looked at the drugs tamoxifen and raloxifene, which reduced the risk of breast cancer by 50 percent and 38 percent, respectively, in older women who took the drug for five years. The difference shown in the Aromasin study, in addition to its higher success rate, is that it does not carry a higher risk of endocrine cancer or blood clots like tamoxifen and raloxifene. In fact, women participating in the Aromasin study had no increased risk of serious side effects. Eighty-eight percent of women in the Aromasin group reported some form of side effect, with the most common being arthritis and hot flashes, while 85 percent of those in the placebo group reported side effects. Tamoxifen and raloxifene have been approved for cancer prevention, but their side effects, that additionally include strokes, leg cramps, and joint pain, mean that many women do not use the drugs. Research on tamoxifen shows that only about 4 percent of the two million women who could benefit from the drug actually choose to take it.

Dr. Paul Goss, the lead investigator on the study, presented the results at the annual American Society of Clinical Oncology (ASCO) meeting saying, "There's a very safe therapy that looks highly effective in preventing breast cancer." Goss did admit that more follow-up was still necessary to confirm the effects of Aromasin, but that he was optimistic that the results would be maintained in later studies. Reaction from the health community was generally positive. "This is the first study to show that a new class of drugs, aromatase inhibitors, have the ability to prevent breast cancer in high-risk women," said Dr. Jennifer Litton, a breast cancer specialist at MD Anderson Cancer Center in Houston. But there were still some concerns with a few aspects of the study, including its short span of only three years, the lack of evidence that cancer survival was improved, and no information on whether women would need to take the drug for life.

In May, Pfizer's patent for Aromasin expired, and drug manufacturers have produced generic versions of the aromatase inhibitor, which have been approved to treat early stage breast cancer. For Aromasin to be approved by the Food and Drug Administration (FDA) to prevent breast cancer, Pfizer would need to go through a costly approval process, and because it has lost patent protection, the company is unlikely to do so. The generic drug manufacturers can apply for FDA prevention approval, but it is unknown whether insurance companies would be more or less likely to pay for generic versions of the drug used for this purpose. Regardless of FDA approval, a more significant hurdle to overcome would be promotion of widespread use of aromatase inhibitors for breast cancer prevention. Currently, these drugs are prescribed by oncologists, but for prevention, both family doctors and gynecologists would need to become comfortable prescribing the drug, an education campaign that could prove challenging, especially because there are still no 100 percent accurate methods to predict who is at risk of developing breast cancer, and would therefore benefit from the drug.

Two Possible Alternative Breast Cancer Drug Treatments

In December, the results of two clinical trials on the drugs pertuzumab, produced by Genentech, and everolimus, made by Novartis, were released and show that the drugs may be able to delay the worsening of advanced breast cancer by several months.

The Genentech study on pertuzumab was completed to determine if the drug, when taken in conjunction with Genentech's Herceptin, used for patients who have tumors with an elevated level of protein Her2, can prolong the lives of late-stage cancer patients. The study involved 808 participants who were split into two groups, one of which received a placebo with Herceptin and a chemotherapy drug called docetaxel, while the other group received a combination of pertuzumab, Herceptin, and docetaxel. Those in the pertuzumab group went an average of 18.5 months before the tumors worsened or the participant died, a measure known as progression-free survival. Those in the placebo group had a progression-free survival average of 12.4 months. Researchers did note that in addition to the positive results, the use of pertuzumab showed no increase in cardiac dysfunction, a side effect of Herceptin. Currently, Genentech cannot market pertuzumab in the United States and Europe, but the company is expected to apply for the right to do so.

Novartis's drug everolimus inhibits the protein mTOR and is used for tumors that have become resistant to hormone therapy. Currently, the drug is sold in the United States to treat kidney cancer and some rare tumors. The everolimus study looked at 724 postmenopausal women with hormone receptor–positive metastatic breast cancer. One group received a placebo, while the other received everolimus in conjunction with exemestane. The group taking everolimus and exemestane had a progression-free survival of 7.4 months while the placebo group had a 3.2-month progression-free survival average. Novaris is expected to apply for approval to market everolimus in the United States for the treatment of breast cancer.

Although both the pertuzumab and everolimus trials show the drugs may be able to prolong lives, the researchers cannot yet say that with absolutely certainty and agreed that additional research is necessary.

DRUG TREATMENTS FOR ADVANCED MELANOMA

The results of two studies released in 2011 looked at the drugs vemurafenib and ipilimumab and their effectiveness in prolonging the lives of those with advanced melanoma. Vemurafenib, used to attack a gene mutation that accelerates tumor growth, and ipilimumab, which uses the body's immune system to fight the disease, both proved successful in the studies.

In 2002, scientists discovered a mutation in the gene BRAF. It is this mutation that encourages cell growth, and half of all melanoma patients have the BRAF mutation. Vemurafenib, researchers believe, can inhibit the mutation in BRAF, and thus shrink the tumors of about a quarter of those with melanoma. The vemurafenib study, sponsored by Roche and led by Dr. Paul Chapman of the Memorial Sloan-Kettering Cancer Center in New York, took place in three phases and consisted of 675 participants. Half of the group was given vemurafenib, while the other half took an older chemotherapy drug. Early study results showed that 48 percent of those taking vemurafenib had tumor shrinkage that lasted more than one month, while the chemotherapy drug group had only 5.5 percent tumor shrinkage. After six months of study, 84 percent of the vemurafenib group was still alive, compared to only 64 percent of those in the chemotherapy drug group. Because of the significant reduction in mortality, researchers stopped the trial early to give patients in the chemotherapy group the ability to switch to vemurafenib. Because the trial was ended early, no median survival rate is known. However, comparing vemurafenib to the only FDA-approved chemotherapy drug for melanoma, dacarbazine, approximately 90 percent of patients benefit from vemurafenib, while only 10 percent of patients have benefited from dacarbazine, which has been in use since 1975. "These are truly striking results," said ASCO president Dr. George Sledge.

Without a median survival rate, additional research is necessary, but scientists are optimistic. The side effects reported during the study were relatively minor—38 percent of patients in the study had to stop taking vemurafenib early or lower their dose because of side effects including joint pain and rash. Some participants also reported minor skin cancers, but they were easily treated and removed. Because the drug does not yet have FDA approval, the cost of treatment is unknown, but is expected to reach tens of thousands of dollars per year. The drug has been criticized because it stops working after approximately nine to ten months, but researchers pointed to the fact that the drug begins working within seventy-two hours, thus giving those with a serious form of cancer additional months to live.

The ipilimumab trial was paid for by Bristol-Meyers and included 502 patients with late-stage melanoma. Half of the participants were given ipilimumab combined with decarbazine, while the other half took a placebo and decarbazine. Those taking the placebo extended their median survival to 9.1 months, while those taking ipilimumab extended their median survival to 11.2 months. After three years of taking each drug, 20.8 percent of those taking the ipilimumab combination were still alive, while only 12.2 percent of those taking the placebo and decarbazine were still alive. The FDA gave approval to the drug in March under the brand name Yervoy, and treatment costs approximately $120,000 for one course. One course of the drug, when combined with decarbazine, works for approximately nineteen months. Decarbazine by itself works for only approximately eight months. Two concerns to arise out of the study were the length of time the drug takes to work and the seriousness of side effects because ipilimumab unleashes the immune system. In the study, the most significant side effect was liver damage.

The vemurafenib and ipilimumab studies show that the drugs cannot cure melanoma, but can add months to the lifespan of someone with an advanced stage of the disease. However, based on the study results, more than half of the patients suffering from metastatic melanoma would not benefit from the use of either drug.

—Heather Kerrigan

Following is a bulletin from the National Cancer Institute, issued on June 14, 2011, regarding clinical trials showing evidence that the aromatase inhibitor drug, exemestane, reduces the risk of breast cancer; and a July 19, 2011, news release from the National Cancer Institute on the results of clinical trials of new therapies for melanoma patients.

National Cancer Institute
on Breast Cancer Drugs

June 14, 2011

The list of drugs that have been shown to reduce a woman's chance of developing breast cancer can now be expanded from two to three. Clinical trial results presented at the American Society of Clinical Oncology's (ASCO) annual meeting last week showed that the aromatase inhibitor exemestane (Aromasin)—commonly used to treat early and advanced-stage breast cancer—substantially reduced the risk of invasive breast cancer in postmenopausal women at high risk of developing the disease.

The findings were also published online June 4 in the *New England Journal of Medicine* (*NEJM*).

At 3 years of follow-up, women who took exemestane were 65 percent less likely than women who took a placebo to develop breast cancer. This is the largest reduction in risk seen in any of the four large breast cancer prevention trials that have been conducted to date. In previous trials, daily use of tamoxifen or raloxifene reduced breast cancer risk by approximately 50 percent and 38 percent, respectively, after 5 years of follow-up; both drugs were eventually approved by the Food and Drug Administration (FDA) to reduce breast cancer risk.

Some researchers cautioned that 3 years of follow-up might not be long enough to determine the extent of any serious side effects, including osteoporosis, from long-term use of aromatase inhibitors in this patient population.

Despite the limited follow-up, the trial's principal investigator, Dr. Paul Goss of Harvard Medical School, said the findings were enough to establish exemestane "as a new option for breast cancer prevention in postmenopausal women." All women older than 60, who by virtue of their age alone have an increased breast cancer risk, "should be made aware of these results," he continued.

Sponsored by the National Cancer Institute of Canada, the trial, dubbed MAP.3, enrolled 4,560 women at increased risk of developing breast cancer. A high-risk determination was made based on at least one of several risk factors: age of 60 years or older; a history of abnormal breast cell growth or having had a noninvasive lesion known as ductal carcinoma *in situ* (DCIS); or an elevated 5-year score on the Gail model, a commonly used breast cancer risk model.

Participants were randomly assigned to take exemestane or a placebo daily for 5 years. Overall, 11 women assigned to exemestane developed an invasive breast cancer compared with 32 women who took the placebo. Exemestane use also led to statistically significant reductions in the development of DCIS, Dr. Goss said, and the invasive tumors that did develop in women taking exemestane were less aggressive than those in the placebo group.

UNDERSTANDING THE SIDE EFFECTS

Importantly, Dr. Goss stressed, women taking exemestane had no increased risk of serious side effects. "We looked for serious toxicities, but we did not find them," he said. The incidence of osteoporosis, cardiac events, and bone fractures were identical for women taking exemestane and for those taking the placebo. However, women who took exemestane had a small, but not statistically significant increase in menopausal symptoms, such as hot flashes and joint pain.

Overall, approximately 30 percent of participants stopped taking exemestane because of side effects, about 10 percent each year. This is similar to what is seen in clinical practice in women taking an aromatase inhibitor as an adjuvant treatment for early-stage breast cancer.

The data from the MAP.3 trial indicate that exemestane provides another option for risk reduction in the appropriate women, said Dr. Worta McCaskill-Stevens of NCI's Division of Cancer Prevention (DCP). "But when thinking about prevention women ask [about] the duration of use of the drug and [want] a clear understanding of its potential side effects," she cautioned.

Of particular concern is severe joint pain, or arthralgia, whose incidence has been relatively high in women being treated for cancer with aromatase inhibitors.

Several studies, however, have shown that women continued to experience the benefits of treatment after stopping aromatase inhibitors—a phenomenon known as a carry-over effect—and that they have fewer adverse events. The women who participated in MAP.3 will have to be followed to better assess the extent and significance of long-term side effects, especially osteoporosis, she stressed.

Overall, because of the short follow-up in the trial, it's too early to definitively understand the drug's risks, Dr. McCaskill-Stevens added. "We can't say that the adverse events in this group of women will be the same as those seen in women receiving an aromatase inhibitor for treatment," she continued. "That's a different patient population as it relates to assessing benefit and risk."

Dr. Victor Vogel, director of the cancer institute at Geisinger Health System in Danville, PA, who was involved in the tamoxifen and raloxifene prevention trials, called the risk reduction findings with exemestane "very impressive." Many of exemestane's side effects can be prevented and treated with monitoring, he explained.

Even if a woman stops taking exemestane for risk reduction because of side effects, Dr. Goss believes, the effort will have been worthwhile. "We feel comfortable that if a woman takes [exemestane] for 6 months or a year, she's gained benefit," he said.

Several clinical trials currently under way should provide more information about the safety and possible side effects of aromatase inhibitors when used for breast cancer risk reduction, explained Dr. Leslie Ford of DCP.

The British IBIS-2 trial is comparing the aromatase inhibitor anastrazole with a placebo in women at high risk of breast cancer. And a U.S. trial being led by the National Surgical Adjuvant Breast and Bowel Project is comparing the aromatase inhibitor letrozole with tamoxifen in postmenopausal women with DCIS.

More Choices in the Clinic

The failure of tamoxifen and raloxifene to break through into the clinic has been well documented, with women and their doctors citing toxicity as one of their chief concerns. "The good news is that exemestane has a completely different toxicity profile," said Dr. Susan Domchek, director of the Cancer Risk Evaluation Program at the University of Pennsylvania Abramson Cancer Center, who was a site investigator on the trial. "For some women, exemestane will be viewed as a nice choice because of that difference."

As Dr. Vogel stressed, it's not medical oncologists but primary care physicians who would talk with women about their breast cancer risk and whether they should consider taking a drug for prevention. This group of clinicians, along with women themselves, needs to be educated about breast cancer prevention, he explained.

"We need to train primary care physicians about how to do risk assessment; how to counsel these patients," said Dr. Vogel. "And we need to ensure that reimbursement is available so that doctors get paid for taking the time to counsel their patients about preventive interventions."

Several research groups are developing tools to help clinicians with some of the risk assessment and counseling issues, Dr. Domchek noted. In an accompanying editorial in *NEJM*, Drs. Nancy Davidson and Thomas Kensler of the University of Pittsburgh Cancer Institute noted the need to better identify "high-risk cohorts and biomarkers that can predict response to a particular intervention."

Indeed, as Dr. Andrew Seidman of Memorial Sloan-Kettering Cancer Center noted, unlike with blood pressure or cholesterol medicines, one cannot measure whether tamoxifen, raloxifene, or exemestane is having its intended preventive effect. "There's no feedback loop," he said, to let doctors and women know whether the drug is having the intended effect.

The patent for exemestane expired in 2010, and Pfizer, which manufactures the drug, has not said whether it will apply to the FDA to market exemestane for breast cancer risk reduction.

—Carmen Phillips

SOURCE: National Cancer Institute. *NCI Cancer Bulletin,* Volume 8, Number 12. "Exemestane Substantially Reduces Breast Cancer Risk." June 14, 2011. http://www.cancer.gov/ncicancerbulletin/061411/page4.

DOCUMENT

National Cancer Institute on Melanoma Treatment

July 19, 2011

The highly anticipated findings from two phase III clinical trials of new therapies for patients with metastatic melanoma did not disappoint those in attendance at the 2011 American Society of Clinical Oncology (ASCO) annual meeting in Chicago.

The trials confirmed that the molecularly targeted agent vemurafenib and the immunotherapy agent ipilimumab (Yervoy™) offer valuable new options for a disease in which effective treatments have been lacking.

After decades of almost no progress, this new research represents a welcome and long-awaited change, remarked Lynn Schuchter, M.D., leader of the melanoma program at the University of Pennsylvania Abramson Cancer Center.

"I think it's a time for celebration for our patients," she said, "for hope."

VEMURAFENIB: EARLY PHASE III RESULTS AGAIN SHOW STRONG, RAPID RESPONSES

The vemurafenib trial, called BRIM3, enrolled 675 patients with newly diagnosed, inoperable metastatic melanoma, all of whom had tumors with the *BRAF* mutation that is targeted by the agent. The patients were randomly assigned to receive either vemurafenib or the chemotherapy drug dacarbazine, the standard treatment for most patients with advanced disease. At the first planned interim analysis of trial data at 3 months, there were already statistically significant reductions in the risk of death (63 percent) and disease progression (74 percent) in patients being treated with vemurafenib compared with patients receiving dacarbazine. (The results were published in the Jun. 30, 2011, issue of the *New England Journal of Medicine* (*NEJM*); see the journal abstract.)

Almost half of the patients taking vemurafenib had substantial tumor regressions, compared with fewer than 6 percent of the patients being treated with dacarbazine. Because of the dramatic effect on tumors, patients receiving dacarbazine were switched to vemurafenib, which may complicate the trial's overall survival analysis, several researchers noted.

At the time of the first interim analysis, "we had just finished accrual to the trial," explained the trial's lead investigator, Paul Chapman, M.D., of Memorial Sloan-Kettering Cancer Center. "So this is unprecedented to report a trial this early. . . and yet [the survival] curves separated very early."

However, the trial hasn't gone on long enough to calculate a median overall survival, he noted.

The tumor response rate, although strong, was substantially less than what had been seen in the phase I and II trials of vemurafenib. Even though patients who respond to the treatment typically do so within 2 months of beginning treatment, that is not always the case, Dr. Chapman noted. And given the short follow up, he believes the response rate "will creep up."

The results also confirm that most tumor responses peak after approximately 6 months and that the disease will return. So a priority will be identifying therapies that can help overcome tumor resistance, he said.

Serious toxic effects occurred in fewer than 10 percent of patients on vemurafenib, and common side effects of the drug included joint pain; sun sensitivity; and forms of nonmelanoma skin cancer, primarily squamous cell carcinoma (SCC), which occurred in 18 percent of patients. SCC lesions can easily be excised by dermatologists, Dr. Chapman explained, and there have been no cases of metastatic SCC in any of the vemurafenib trials.

Nevertheless, nearly 40 percent of patients taking vemurafenib in the phase III trial had to stop treatment temporarily or have their dose reduced because of side effects.

IPILIMUMAB: A SUBSET OF PATIENTS HAVE PROLONGED RESPONSES

Results from the ipilimumab trial were far more mature than those from the vemurafenib trial. Five hundred and two patients with metastatic melanoma were randomly assigned to receive the immunotherapy in combination with dacarbazine or dacarbazine alone. Median overall survival improved by just 2 months: 11.2 months for those receiving combination therapy versus 9.1 months for those receiving dacarbazine alone. (The results were published Jun. 30, 2011, in *NEJM*; see the journal abstract.)

But those figures don't tell the whole story, said the trial's lead investigator, Jedd Wolchok, M.D., Ph.D., also of Memorial Sloan-Kettering Cancer Center. He pointed to the 1-, 2-, and 3-year survival rates, which were all superior in patients who received ipilimumab. At 3 years, approximately 21 percent of patients in the ipilimumab arm were still alive compared with 12 percent in the chemotherapy-only arm.

There was also a 24 percent improvement in progression-free survival in the ipilimumab group, but no statistically significant difference in tumor shrinkage was found between the groups. The duration of the tumor response was 19.3 months in the ipilimumab arm and 8.1 months in the dacarbazine arm. The greater response duration and survival at 3 years is "consistent with an immunotherapy," Dr. Wolchok said, because immunotherapies are more likely to keep tumors in check than to produce significant tumor shrinkage.

High-grade adverse events occurred in nearly twice as many patients in the ipilimumab arm (56 percent) as the dacarbazine alone arm (27 percent). Although fewer patients receiving ipilimumab had high-grade diarrhea and colitis (swelling of the large intestine) than in previous trials, Dr. Wolchok explained, liver toxicity was substantially more frequent than previously seen, which he said was likely due to the combination with dacarbazine.

WHICH TREATMENT WHEN?

Until the Food and Drug Administration (FDA) approved ipilimumab in March 2011, there were essentially two options for treating advanced melanoma: dacarbazine, which in most patients produces at most modest improvements in survival or symptomatic benefit, and interleukin-2, a highly toxic therapy that induces long-term remissions in only a small percentage of patients.

Roche and Plexxikon, the companies that co-developed vemurafenib, submitted an application for approval to the FDA in May 2011, with the expectation of a decision by the end of the year. So, although both ipilimumab and vemurafenib will be options for patients with metastatic disease, a key clinical question remains: Which therapy should be used first in patients whose tumors have the *BRAF* mutation that is targeted by vemurafenib?

Because vemurafenib can lead to such rapid tumor regression, many researchers at the meeting suggested that vemurafenib would typically be the preferred first-line option for these patients.

During the meeting's plenary session, Kim A. Margolin, M.D., of the University of Washington laid out a potential pattern of use for these patients. "Vemurafenib is appropriate for patients who have symptoms and need to respond fast," she said. "For those with limited tumor burden and limited symptoms, whose long-term goal is durable benefit and who are not in urgent need of the physical and emotional relief associated with quick tumor regression, ipilimumab may well be the preferred choice."

Because of the serious liver side effects attributed to dacarbazine in the trial, however, she advised that ipilimumab be used alone.

Dr. Schuchter was quick to respond with how she will handle such patients. "I'll put them on a trial," she said. With studies rapidly identifying mechanisms of tumor resistance and potentially effective combinations of therapies, she continued, "we can further characterize patient tumors" by their different genetic abnormalities "and direct them to [trials testing] the right targeted therapies."

A clinical trial "is clearly the top priority," agreed Sekwon Jang, M.D., a medical oncologist at Washington Hospital Center who primarily treats melanoma patients. "We're going to have many more clinical trial options for patients," he said.

On the day before the ASCO meeting began, in fact, Roche and Bristol-Myers Squibb, the manufacturers of ipilimumab, announced that they had entered into a collaborative agreement to conduct clinical trials testing the agents in combination.

If a patient cannot be enrolled in a clinical trial for some reason, Dr. Schuchter said, vemurafenib would likely be her first-line therapy of choice for most patients with *BRAF* mutations.

During an education session on melanoma therapy, Antoni Ribas, M.D., of UCLA's Jonsson Comprehensive Cancer Center, who has been involved in studies of both agents, said he hoped that ipilimumab's less robust response rate compared with that of vemurafenib will not deter oncologists from using it. "It's unquestionable that ipilimumab has a positive impact on overall survival," he said.

Based on the clinical trial data, he continued, it's clear that a modest proportion of patients will have long, objective responses "and are probably cured."

SOURCE: National Cancer Institute. Clinical Trial Results. "New Therapies Offer Valuable Options for Patients With Melanoma." July 19, 2011. http://www.cancer.gov/clinicaltrials/results/summary/2011/melanoma-ASCO0611.

OTHER HISTORIC DOCUMENTS OF INTEREST

FROM PREVIOUS *HISTORIC DOCUMENTS*

NOAA on 2011 Extreme Weather

JUNE 14, AUGUST 19, SEPTEMBER 8, AND DECEMBER 7, 2011

According to federal analysis, 2011 was one of the most extreme weather years on record in the United States. By December, the National Oceanic and Atmospheric Administration (NOAA) reported twelve weather events that each caused at least $1 billion in damage, the most reported since 2008. More than 1,000 people were killed by extreme weather events in 2011, nearly double the annual average. The year started off with extreme weather in January in central and eastern states that were affected by a blizzard, causing an estimated $4 billion in damage and leaving Chicago with a record 24-hour snow total of twenty inches. The year also had the deadliest tornadoes in recent history, many of which hit heavily populated areas. Rainfall in the spring in the Midwest and South led to record crests along the Mississippi River and flooding in the Lower Mississippi River Valley with damage totaling $2 billion to $4 billion. And while some states had more rain than they had experienced in years, other parts of the country, particularly the South and West, were dealing with the driest spring on record that sparked massive wildfires causing livestock and land losses. In a December speech, NOAA Administrator Jane Lubchenco warned that the New Year would not mark the end of extreme weather events in the United States. "What's likely down the road on the weather-climate front? [I]ncreased overall warming; amplified water cycle; and more extreme events and more variability . . . more wild weather and wild swings in weather," she said.

AN ACTIVE TORNADO SEASON

The spring and summer of 2011 brought one of the most active and destructive tornado seasons in recent history. Through the first half of the year, seven severe storms and tornadoes caused more than $1 billion in damage, the most property damage caused by severe storms and tornadoes since record keeping began in 1980. In total, the United States experienced more than 1,600 tornadoes in 2011, all of which have an anticipated total cost of $28 billion. Six of these tornadoes were given the highest NOAA rating of EF-5 on the Enhanced Fujita scale. By the end of the year, the number of those killed in the record outbreak of tornadoes stood at 553, the most since 1936.

In just the months of March, April, and May, 1,150 tornadoes were confirmed, with the largest number experienced in April. April 27 had the highest number of tornadoes on a single day in modern record at 199. The deadliest and most destructive tornado of 2011 hit Joplin, Missouri, near the Kansas border, on May 22. Residents received a twenty-four-minute warning before the tornado touched down around dinnertime, cutting a six-mile swath and reaching wind speeds of 200 miles per hour. One-quarter of the city was destroyed, including 2,000 buildings and 7,000 homes, while vital resources such as power lines and water treatment and sewage plants suffered extensive damage. Thousands were injured during the storm and 158 were killed. The tornado caused an estimated $3 billion in damage. "This is a horrific and traumatic storm that has been total devastation for a significant portion of this town," said Missouri Governor Jay Nixon.

RECORD PRECIPITATION BRINGS RECORD FLOODS

Higher-than-normal rainfall in the spring and summer of 2011 in the South and Midwest led to flooding in Arkansas, Illinois, Kentucky, Louisiana, Mississippi, Missouri, and Tennessee, with Kentucky, Mississippi, and Tennessee being declared federal disaster areas. The flooding heavily affected the Mississippi River and its tributaries, leading to thousands of evacuation orders along the river's path. Some areas of the Mississippi reached record crests comparable to those last seen in 1927 and 1933.

The swelling river and its tributaries flooded farmland and placed excessive strain on the levees and reservoirs that were built after severe flooding in the 1920s and 1930s. The billions of dollars spent on these floodways were questioned as the river continued to swell and the Army Corps of Engineers was forced to make difficult decisions, in one instance blowing up a two-mile levee section in Missouri, flooding 130,000 acres of farmland, in an effort to save 100 homes across the border in Cairo, Illinois. "These are very tough decisions to make. No matter which way you go, somebody is not being saved," said Charles Dowding, an infrastructure expert at Northwestern University. The flooding placed additional focus on methods being undertaken by some cities and states before the 2011 weather events to purchase homes and farmland along flood plains and relocate levees from the river's edge. These practices follow a centuries-old Dutch tradition aimed at keeping lowlands dry. "For decades, we've treated levees as the only line of defense," said Andrew Fahlund, senior vice president of American Rivers, a waterway advocacy group. "They ought to be the last line of defense," he said.

The impact of heavy rain and flooding did not stop at devastated farmlands and rising river levels. Because of stream-flow rates during the spring and summer, the level of nitrogen flowing from the Mississippi River into the Gulf of Mexico increased significantly. An increase in nitrogen removes the oxygen from the water that marine life requires to survive. This creates what is known as a hypoxic zone, or dead zone, where little marine life exists. NOAA scientists estimated that the additional nitrogen caused by 2011 flooding would increase the Gulf's hypoxic zone to approximately the size of New Hampshire.

EXTREME DROUGHT AND SUBSEQUENT WILDFIRES

While the Northern plains, Ohio Valley, and Northeast experienced record-breaking rainfall in the spring, in the South and West, drier-than-normal conditions caused debilitating drought brought on by higher-than-average spring and summer temperatures. By August, Louisiana, New Mexico, Oklahoma, and Texas all reported 100 percent of their states experiencing drought. Texas was the hardest hit, with more than 90 percent of the state categorized as experiencing "extreme" or "exceptional" drought. The effects of the drought in Texas devastated farmland and livestock. Many farmers had to sell off cattle because they could no longer afford to feed them. But while the drought was regionalized, the effects will be felt across the United States, according to David Anderson, an economist with the Texas AgriLife Extension Service at Texas A&M University. "The long-term effect is higher prices for consumers over the next couple of years," he said. "Every cow that's gone now is a cow that won't have a calf next year. Two, three years down the road, we'll have much higher beef prices because of the drought we have now." NOAA's National Climatic Data Center predicts that the lack of rainfall across portions of the United States and ensuing drought had an economic impact upwards of $10 billion.

One year earlier, during the summer of 2010, the South and West experienced adequate rainfall that gave ground vegetation the opportunity to grow in abundance. The subsequent dry winter and spring months killed this new vegetation. Coupled with the extreme heat, the nation's lower half had the perfect recipe for wildfires. Arizona, New Mexico, and Texas all experienced record-breaking wildfires in 2011. More than 73,000 wildfires in 2011 burned 8.7 million acres. Texas made up nearly half of that total, with more than 3.7 million acres burned. In some instances during the spring and summer, the state was spending $1 million per day to control the fires. The biggest wildfire in Texas took place in Bastrop County, east of the state capital in Austin. Thousands of people were evacuated and hundreds of homes were destroyed. The cost of the damage caused by wildfires across the United States in 2011 is expected to top $1 billion.

WHY IS EXTREME WEATHER INCREASING?

Since the 1980s, extreme weather has become more common, partly due to climate change. "Extremes of precipitation are generally increasing because the planet is actually warming and more water is evaporating from the oceans," said Tom Karl, the director of NOAA's National Climatic Data Center. "This extra water vapor in the atmosphere then enables rain and snow events to become more extensive and intense than they might otherwise be," said Karl. On the other side of this, it is likely that droughts will become stronger as well, but weather patterns years in advance are difficult to predict.

The 2011 weather can also be blamed on La Niña and cold Arctic air in the southern United States late in 2010. The droughts experienced through the South in 2011 that led to wildfires are characteristic of La Niña. "[I]t's a La Niña year, which means the Pacific is cold in terms of the ocean, and that changes the air path around the Continental United States," said M. Sanjayan, a lead scientist at the Nature Conservancy. The last significant La Niña occurred approximately five years ago, and some NOAA climate scientists are predicting 2012 to be a La Niña year as well.

Weather events caused by precipitation, or a lack thereof, are becoming more common worldwide, partly because climate change leads to warmer temperatures giving more energy and water to the atmosphere to fuel storms. The Intergovernmental Panel on Climate Change (IPCC) issued a report in 2011 projecting worse heat waves, droughts, and greater economic impact from extreme weather events during the next decade. These "unprecedented extreme weather and climate events" are being caused partly by growing populations and increasing development around the world.

—Heather Kerrigan

Following are four documents from the National Oceanic and Atmospheric Administration. The first, released on June 14, 2011, details the effects of record flooding along the Mississippi River in 2011; the second, released on August 19, 2011, outlines damage caused by 2011 tornadoes; the third, released on September 8, 2011, gives information on the high 2011 summer temperatures; and the fourth, released on December 7, 2011, is a speech given by NOAA Administrator Jane Lubchenco, Ph.D., on 2011 extreme weather events and how NOAA works to predict and manage such events.

NOAA on Effect of Flooding Along the Mississippi River

June 14, 2011

The Gulf of Mexico's hypoxic zone is predicted to be the largest ever recorded due to extreme flooding of the Mississippi River this spring, according to an annual forecast by a team of NOAA-supported scientists from the Louisiana Universities Marine Consortium, Louisiana State University and the University of Michigan. The forecast is based on Mississippi River nutrient inputs compiled annually by the U.S. Geological Survey (USGS).

Scientists are predicting the area could measure between 8,500 and 9,421 square miles, or an area roughly the size of New Hampshire. If it does reach those levels it will be the largest since mapping of the Gulf "dead zone" began in 1985. The largest hypoxic zone measured to date occurred in 2002 and encompassed more than 8,400 square miles.

The average over the past five years is approximately 6,000 square miles of impacted waters, much larger than the 1,900 square miles which is the target goal set by the Gulf of Mexico/Mississippi River Watershed Nutrient Task Force. This collaboration between NOAA, USGS and university scientists facilitates understanding links between activities in the Mississippi River watershed and downstream impacts to the northern Gulf of Mexico. Long-term data sets on nutrient loads and the extent of the hypoxic zone have improved forecast models used by management agencies to understand the nutrient reductions required to reduce the size of the hypoxic zone.

Hypoxia is caused by excessive nutrient pollution, often from human activities such as agriculture that results in too little oxygen to support most marine life in bottom and near-bottom water. The hypoxic zone off the coast of Louisiana and Texas forms each summer and threatens valuable commercial and recreational Gulf fisheries. In 2009, the dockside value of commercial fisheries in the Gulf was $629 million. Nearly three million recreational fishers further contributed more than $1 billion to the Gulf economy taking 22 million fishing trips.

"This ecological forecast is a good example of NOAA applied science," said Jane Lubchenco, Ph.D., under secretary of commerce for oceans and atmosphere and NOAA administrator. "While there is some uncertainty regarding the size, position and timing of this year's hypoxic zone in the Gulf, the forecast models are in overall agreement that hypoxia will be larger than we have typically seen in recent years."

During May 2011 stream-flow rates in the Mississippi and Atchafalaya Rivers were nearly twice that of normal conditions. This significantly increased the amount of nitrogen transported by the rivers into the Gulf. According to USGS estimates, 164,000 metric tons of nitrogen (in the form of nitrite plus nitrate) were transported by the Mississippi and Atchafalaya Rivers to the northern Gulf. The amount of nitrogen transported to the Gulf in May 2011 was 35 percent higher than average May nitrogen loads estimated in the last 32 years.

"The USGS monitoring network and modeling activities for water quantity and quality helps us 'connect the dots' to see how increased nutrient run-off in the Mississippi watershed during a historic spring flood event impacts the health of the ocean many hundreds of miles away," said Marcia McNutt, Ph.D., USGS director. "This work on Gulf hypoxia is a great example of interagency teamwork between NOAA and USGS to work across the land-sea boundary."

Coastal and water resource managers nationwide require new and better integrated information and services to adapt to the uncertainty of future climate and land-use changes, an aging water delivery infrastructure, and an increasing demand on limited resources. NOAA and USGS, as well as the U.S. Army Corps of Engineers, have signed an agreement that will further facilitate collaboration in the future. These agencies, with complementary missions in water science, observation, prediction and management, have formed this partnership to unify their commitment to address the nation's water resources information and management needs.

This year's forecast is just one example of NOAA's growing ecological forecasting capabilities, supported by both NOAA and USGS science, which allow for the protection of valuable resources using scientific, ecosystem-based approaches.

The actual size of the 2011 hypoxic zone will be released following a NOAA-supported monitoring survey led by the Louisiana Universities Marine Consortium between July 25 and August 6. Collecting these data is an annual requirement of the Mississippi River/Gulf of Mexico Watershed Nutrient Task Force Action Plan.

NOAA has been funding investigations and forecast development for the dead zone in the Gulf of Mexico since 1990 and currently oversees the two national hypoxia programs authorized by the Harmful Algal Bloom and Hypoxia Research and Control Act.

NOAA's mission is to understand and predict changes in the Earth's environment, from the depths of the ocean to the surface of the sun, and to conserve and manage our coastal and marine resources. Find us on Facebook.

SOURCE: National Oceanic and Atmospheric Administration. "Major Flooding on the Mississippi River Predicted to Cause Largest Gulf of Mexico Dead Zone Ever Recorded." June 14, 2011. http://www .noaanews.noaa.gov/stories2011/20110614_deadzone.html.

DOCUMENT *NOAA Information on 2011 Tornadoes*

August 19, 2011

Preliminary tornado statistics including records set in 2011

May 2011

On May 24, 2011, deadly tornadoes claimed 18 additional lives in Oklahoma (10), Kansas (2), and Arkansas (6). . . .

- On Sunday, May 22, 2011, an EF-5 tornado hit the city of Joplin, Mo., leaving an estimated 157 people dead.
  - The Joplin tornado is the deadliest single tornado since modern recordkeeping began in 1950 and is ranked as the 7th deadliest in U.S. history.
  - The deadliest tornado on record in the U.S. was on March 18, 1925. The "Tri-State Tornado" (MO, IL, IN) had a 291-mile path, was rated F5 based on a historical assessment, and caused 695 fatalities.

- o The EF-5 Joplin tornado had winds in excess of 200 mph, was ¾ of a mile wide, and had a track lasting six miles. . . .
- o The NWS Springfield forecast office issued a tornado warning with a lead time of 24 minutes for Joplin at 5:17 p.m. (local time). At 5:41 p.m., the local storm report stated: "NUMEROUS REPORTS OF TORNADO ON THE GROUND WEST OF JOPLIN AND POWER FLASHES." The damage path began at South Black Cat Road and Newton Road.
- o The NWS Storm Prediction Center highlighted southwest Missouri for the potential for severe weather several days prior to Sunday's storm. SPC also issued a tornado watch more than four hours in advance of the tornado touching down.

- The Marion County long-track EF5 of 27 April 2011 claimed 78 lives.
- NWS's preliminary estimate about 320 tornadoes occurred during the month of May 2011. There were 177 fatalities in May (157 of those in the Joplin EF5 tornado alone).

- o The record number of tornadoes during the *month of May* was 542 tornadoes set in May 2003.
- o The average number of tornadoes for the month of May during the past decade is 298.
- o May is historically the most active month for tornadoes.
- o This was the deadliest May since 1933.
- o The deadliest May for tornadoes in the U.S. occurred in 1896, with 502 deaths.

2011 Year-to-Date (and record annual) Statistics

- NWS's preliminary estimate is that there have been approximately 1,665 tornadoes so far this year.

- o The previous yearly record number of tornadoes was set in 2004 with 1,817.
- o The overall yearly average number of tornadoes for the past decade is 1,274.

- The preliminary estimated number of tornado fatalities so far this year is 549. NWS records indicate that there were 370 tornado fatalities before the Joplin event. There were 157 fatalities from the Joplin tornado. An additional 18 fatalities were reported in KS, OK, and AR from a tornado outbreak on May 24, 2011, along with 3 deaths in MA on June 1, 2011, and 1 death in OK on August 10, 2011.

- o 2011 is preliminarily the 4th deadliest tornado year in U.S. history.

April 2011

- April 2011 is ranked as the most active tornado month on record with 753 tornadoes. . . .There were an estimated 364 fatalities.

- o The previous record was set in April 1974 with 267 tornadoes.
- o The average number of tornadoes for the month of April during the past decade is 161.
- o The previous record number of tornadoes during *any month* was 542 tornadoes set in May 2003.

- NWS records indicate 321 people were killed during the April 25–28 tornado outbreak.
- NWS records indicate 364 people were killed during the entire month of April 2011....

[Tables have been omitted.]

SOURCE: National Oceanic and Atmospheric Administration. "2011 Tornado Information." August 19, 2011. http://www.noaanews.noaa.gov/2011_tornado_information.html.

NOAA Reports Second-Warmest Summer on Record

DOCUMENT

September 8, 2011

The blistering heat experienced by the nation during August, as well as the June through August months, marks the second warmest summer on record according to scientists at NOAA's National Climatic Data Center (NCDC) in Asheville, N.C. The persistent heat, combined with below-average precipitation across the southern U.S. during August and the three summer months, continued a record-breaking drought across the region.

The average U.S. temperature in August was 75.7 degrees F, which is 3.0 degrees above the long-term (1901-2000) average, while the summertime temperature was 74.5 degrees F, which is 2.4 degrees above average. The warmest August on record for the contiguous United States was 75.8 degrees F in 1983, while its warmest summer on record at 74.6 degrees F occurred in 1936. Precipitation across the nation during August averaged 2.31 inches, 0.29 inches below the long-term average. The nationwide summer precipitation was 1.0 inch below average.

This monthly analysis, based on records dating back to 1895, is part of the suite of climate services NOAA provides.

U.S. CLIMATE HIGHLIGHTS—AUGUST

- Excessive heat in six states—Arizona, Colorado, New Mexico, Texas, Oklahoma, and Louisiana—resulted in their warmest August on record. This year ranked in the top ten warmest August for five other states: Florida (3rd), Georgia (4th), Utah (5th), Wyoming (8th), and South Carolina (9th).The Southwest and South also had their warmest August on record.
- Only nine of the lower 48 states experienced August temperatures near average, and no state had August average temperatures below average.
- Wetter-than-normal conditions were widespread across the Northeastern United States, which had its second wettest August, as well as parts of the Northern Plains and California. Drier-than-normal conditions reigned across the interior West, the Midwest, and the South....
- Despite record rainfall in parts of the country, drought covered about one-third of the contiguous United States, according to the U.S. Drought Monitor. The Palmer Hydrologic Drought Index indicated that parts of Louisiana, New Mexico, Oklahoma

and Texas are experiencing drought of greater intensity, but not yet duration, than those of the 1930s and 1950s. Drought intensity refers to the rate at which surface and ground water is lost, due to a combination of several factors, including evaporation and lack of precipitation.

- An analysis of Texas statewide tree-ring records dating back to 1550 indicates that the summer 2011 drought in Texas is matched by only one summer (1789), indicating that the summer 2011 drought appears to be unusual even in the context of the multi-century tree-ring record.

U.S. climate highlights—Summer

- Texas, Oklahoma, New Mexico, and Louisiana had their warmest (June–August) summers on record. Average summer temperatures in Texas and Oklahoma, at 86.8 degrees F and 86.5 degrees F, respectively, exceeded the previous seasonal statewide average temperature record for any state during any season. The previous warmest summer statewide average temperature was in Oklahoma, during 1934 at 85.2 degrees F.
- Fifteen states had a summer average temperature ranking among their top ten warmest. West of the Rockies, a persistent trough brought below-average temperatures to the Pacific Northwest, where Washington and Oregon were the only states across the lower 48 to have below-average summer temperatures.
- Texas had its driest summer on record, with a statewide average of 2.44 inches of rain. This is 5.29 inches below the long-term average, and 1.04 inches less than the previous driest summer in 1956. New Mexico had its second driest summer and Oklahoma its third driest summer. New Jersey and California had their wettest summers on record with 22.50 inches and 1.93 inches, respectively.
- The U.S. Climate Extremes Index, a measure of the percent area of the country experiencing extreme climate conditions, was nearly four times the average value was during summer 2011. This is the third largest summer value of the record, which dates to 1910. The major drivers were extremes in warm minimum and maximum temperatures and in the wet and dry tails of the Palmer Drought Severity Index.
- Based on NOAA's Residential Energy Demand Temperature Index, the contiguous U.S. temperature-related energy demand was 22.3 percent above average during summer. This is the largest such value during the index's period of record, which dates to 1895.

Other U.S. climate highlights

- During the six-month period (March–August), much-above-average temperatures dominated the southern and eastern United States. New Mexico, Oklahoma, Texas, Louisiana, South Carolina, and Florida, all experienced their warmest March–August on record. Cooler-than-average temperatures dominated the West and Northwest.
- For the year-to-date period, the average statewide temperature for Texas was 69.9 degrees F, the warmest such period on record for the state. This bests the previous record for the year-to-date period of 69.8 degrees F in 2000.

- For precipitation year-to-date, New Mexico, Texas, and Louisiana have all had their driest January–August periods on record, while Ohio, Pennsylvania, New York, New Jersey, and Connecticut were record wet during the same period. . . .

Source: National Oceanic and Atmospheric Administration. "U.S. Experiences Second Warmest Summer on Record." September 8, 2011. http://www.noaanews.noaa.gov/stories2011/20110908_auguststats.html.

NOAA Administrator on
Extreme Weather Events

December 8, 2011

. . . THE EXTERNAL LANDCAPE

This is a challenging time for the nation and for science.

- The economy is in bad shape, but beginning to show some positive signs.
- Extraordinary numbers of Americans are without jobs.
- The public holds a record low opinion of government.
- Our science is being questioned; and
- Pressure to reduce federal spending is fierce.

The irony is that the demand for services provided by agencies like NOAA is at an all-time high and growing.

One reason for this demand is the increase in number and intensity of extreme events—

- . . . from heat records set in every single state this year—at one time this summer about ½ of the people in the US were under a heat advisory or heat warning.
- . . . to last week's hurricane force winds that hit parts of CA, UT, NV, AZ, NM and WY with winds reaching 97mph in Pasadena.

NOAA has been busy predicting the weather-related extreme events we've seen this year.

However, our capacity to continuing to do so is seriously threatened by downward pressure on our budgets. Budgets and politics threaten observations, research, modeling and delivery of information and other services.

Our ability to do and fund research to better understand the causes of weather extreme events and our ability to improve the effectiveness of response to our warnings are all at great risk.

Today, I will focus on the unusual weather patterns we're seeing and what I believe we need to do to better predict and manage them. I hope many of you will work with us to innovate new approaches to succeed together in this tough environment.

A YEAR OF EXTREMES: 12 BILLION-DOLLAR DISASTERS

2011 is already in the record books as a year of historic extreme events.

One of those new records is the number of events totaling at least $1Billion in damages.

Today, NOAA announces in 2011, there have now been 12 extreme weather events each totaling at least $1B. The previous record was 9, set in 2008. . . .

Earlier this year, we announced there were 10 to date; today we announce numbers 11th and 12th:

- The June 18–21 tornadoes;
- And the split of the spring/summer drought/heat waves in Texas as a separate event from the record Texas wildfires during the summer and fall.

The aggregate damage from these 12 events is approximately $52 billion.

We have not finished tallying damages caused by additional extreme events, such as the pre-Halloween winter storm that impacted the Northeast and the wind/flood damage from Tropical Storm Lee, so stay tuned for the final total # of $1B events and the aggregate damage total.

Please note that damages totaling less than a billion dollars individually are not included in this tally, even though many of them represent additional significant financial losses.

And the economic losses are far from the full picture. More than 1,000 people died from these disasters. Deaths this year are almost double the yearly average (~600).

Each of these events is a huge disaster for victims who experience them; collectively, they are an unprecedented challenge for the Nation—for the safety of citizens, the bottom line for businesses, and the societal stresses they engender.

Timely, accurate, and reliable weather warnings and forecasts are essential to our collective well-being, but also to the Nation's ability to recover and prosper.

Now, I've emphasized how unusual this year has been, but a single year can just be an anomaly. Is that the case here? What are we documenting across years? And what might we expect in the future?

Globally, according to Munich Re, the frequency of extreme events has risen steadily over the past 20 years. The number of meteorological and hydrological events each tripled in that time. . . .

[Information on the IPCC study and NOAA's weather monitoring and prediction capabilities has been omitted.]

DECONSTRUCTING CLIMATE TRENDS: What's driving the increase since the 1970s?

Deconstructing the index reveals what is driving the trend: in this case it is extremes in maximum and minimum temperature, too little and too much water, and 1-day heavy precipitation.

These graphs are individual elements of NOAA's U.S. Climate Extremes Index. The vertical axes continue to be the percent of the country affected by the given extreme. All graphs are for the January to October period, each year from 1910 to 2011.

These are the primary components that are driving the changes in the Climate Extremes Index: extremes in maximum and minimum temperature, too much and too little soil moisture, and 1-day heavy precipitation events.

Extremes in maximum temperature mean unusually warm or cold daily high temperatures—either in the top 10% or bottom 10% of maximum temperatures. You can visually see that since 1970, more of the country is experiencing unusually warm highs (the red bars) and less of the country is experiencing unusually cool highs (the blue bars).

But, more striking is the change in the extremes in minimum temperature related to unusually warm or cold nighttime lows. More of the country is experiencing unusually warm nights, and less of the country is experiencing unusually cool nights. Warm overnight lows are related to heat stress in both people and plants and animals—they never get a chance to cool off—so this data set is of particular importance to those managing the response to the extremes.

What does the Index tell us about too much or too little soil water? The green bars show the percent of the country in extremely wet conditions, and the brown bars show extremely dry conditions.

While the country has had periods of more severe drought—for example, during the "Dust Bowl" years of the 30's—we've never seen the country get both drier and wetter at the same time as this graph shows in the past decade.

And finally, the 1-day heavy precipitation graph shows more single days with precipitation much above normal (top 10%). This is important for hydrological engineers, water resource managers, and emergency managers in flood-prone areas, among others.

A variety of observations, taken over time, and used in well-crafted ensembles, can improve understanding and management of extremes.

These observational data—our historical record—are the vital input to models critical to predicting and projecting the future state of the Earth system. . . .

[Information on NOAA resources has been omitted.]

THE PATH FORWARD

What's likely down the road on the weather-climate front? increased overall warming; amplified water cycle; and more extreme events and more variability, i.e. more wild weather and wild swings in weather. . . .

Source: National Oceanic and Atmospheric Administration. "Predicting and Managing Extreme Events." December 7, 2011. http://www.noaanews.noaa.gov/stories2011/20111207_speech_agu.html.

Other Historic Documents of Interest

From this volume

- 2011 Durban Climate Change Conference; Canada Leaves Kyoto, p. 670

From previous *Historic Documents*

- Intergovernmental Panel of Scientists on Climate Change, *2007*, p. 657
- EPA Report on Global Warming, *2002*, p. 298
- Committee of Scientists on the Impact of Global Warming, *2000*, p. 337

New York Legalizes Same-Sex Marriage

JUNE 14, JUNE 22, AND JUNE 24, 2011

As in the national debate, same-sex marriage has been a contentious issue in New York State, where voters and their representatives are less liberal overall than those in the state's namesake city, where the gay rights movement had its roots. In 1969, at the Stonewall Inn bar in Greenwich Village, gay rights advocates rioted against the police, and it was this event that is said to have been a key turning point in the gay rights movement. But in recent years, the attitudes of those across the state have been shifting on gay marriage. A 2011 Quinnipiac poll found that 58 percent of New York voters supported allowing same-sex couples in the state to marry. A similar poll conducted in 2004 found support at only 37 percent. Democrats in the state legislature, led by the governor, used this momentum to pass a bill on June 24, 2011, allowing same-sex couples to marry.

HISTORY OF SAME-SEX MARRIAGE IN NEW YORK

Prior to 2011, New York's Domestic Relations Law did not extend marriage rights to same-sex couples, leaving the fight over same-sex marriage to the courts, legislature, and executive branch. In 2004, Mayor Jason West of New Paltz, New York, began marrying same-sex couples in his city. As a result, the Ulster County district attorney charged him with misdemeanors. The charges were ultimately dropped in July 2005. In response to Mayor West's actions, then-Attorney General Eliot Spitzer, a supporter of gay marriage, asked municipal clerks not to issue marriage licenses to same-sex couples until the state legislature had an opportunity for review. Following Spitzer's announcement, five lawsuits were filed regarding the state's definition of marriage. Four of these lawsuits failed and one succeeded, but that successful case was later overturned. With their mixed results, the five cases were joined in *Hernandez v. Robles* and presented before the state Court of Appeals on May 31, 2006. The court ruled in July that same-sex couples had no constitutional right to marry in New York and stated that the issue of whether to allow same-sex marriage was up to the legislature.

When Spitzer campaigned for governor in 2006, he promised to use the court's decision and push for same-sex marriage rights in the legislature. "We will not ask whether this proposition of legalizing same-sex marriage is popular or unpopular; we will not ask if it's hard or easy; we will simply ask if it's right or wrong," Spitzer told supporters. "I think we know in this room what the answer to that question is," he said. Spitzer's successful election bid was quickly followed by a push in the state legislature to legalize same-sex marriage and the state Assembly passed a bill in 2007, but it failed in the Senate, where Republicans held a majority of the seats.

Little momentum was gained in the same-sex marriage legislative fight after the 2007 attempt, with Democrats waiting until the next election cycle in 2008 to attempt to gain additional seats in the Senate that could mean additional votes for their cause. During that waiting period, Spitzer resigned his post as governor on May 12, 2008, and David Paterson,

Spitzer's lieutenant governor, assumed the governorship. Paterson strongly supported same-sex marriage and on April 9 issued a promise to continue working for same-sex marriage rights during his term. "We will push on and bring full marriage equality in New York State," Paterson said.

On November 4, 2008, Democrats gained a majority of seats in the New York Senate, and the party continued its push for same-sex marriage rights. The Assembly again passed a bill, only to watch it be rejected in the Senate by a vote of 38 to 24 with no Republican support and eight Democrats in opposition to the measure. Before the end of his gubernatorial term in 2010, Paterson made an attempt to work with the legislature on lame-duck passage of same-sex marriage rights, but he received little support and legislation was never introduced. Supporters and opponents of same-sex marriage considered the issue dead until at least 2011 when a new legislature would be elected. When asked by reporters what he thought it would take to pass same-sex marriage legislation in New York, Paterson responded, "Get rid of the lobbyists."

CUOMO SUPPORT, CONSERVATIVE OPPOSITION

During his election campaign in 2010, then-Attorney General Andrew Cuomo, a Democrat, promised supporters that he would make same-sex marriage legislation a top priority in his administration. Cuomo faced criticism on the issue from those who pointed to his work on his father's 1977 run for mayor of New York City, which featured homophobic posters, and his own reluctance to endorse the idea of same-sex marriage, waiting until 2006 to make public his stance on the issue.

Once in office, Cuomo placed the blame for same-sex marriage legislation failure squarely on disorganized gay-rights organizations operating in the state. To ensure that one of his top campaign priorities would succeed, Cuomo sent an aide from his administration to work with gay-rights organizations to formulate a clear message to deliver to voters. This coordination resulted in the formation of New Yorkers United for Marriage, a group that included the Empire State Pride Agenda, the Human Rights Campaign, Freedom to Marry, Marriage Equality New York, and the Log Cabin Republicans.

The group's bid for same-sex marriage rights met opposition from conservative religious organizations, namely the Roman Catholic Church, and the New York Conservative Party, a political party formed in 1962 as a more conservative alternative to the Republican Party. Resistance from the Catholic Church was not as strong as Cuomo's office had expected, and Archbishop Timothy Dolan did not actively campaign against the bill, choosing instead to issue only brief remarks on radio programs in opposition to the movement. Cuomo extended an olive branch to the Church, inviting its lawyers and Dolan to meet with him to share their concerns about the measure. The New York Conservative Party chose to focus its opposition on individual lawmakers, promising that any Republican lawmaker who voted for same-sex marriage would not be supported, and would in fact be actively opposed by the Conservative Party during the 2012 campaign and election cycle.

TEN TENSE DAYS IN THE LEGISLATURE

The odds of passing same-sex marriage legislation in 2011, even with the strong support of the governor, seemed unlikely because the state Senate was back in the hands of Republicans, who held a one-seat majority. Nationwide, a Republican-controlled legislature had never before passed a bill allowing same-sex marriage. Added to this was increasing pressure from voters to focus the legislative agenda on economic issues facing the state rather than social concerns.

Regardless of the political climate in New York, the state Assembly again passed a same-sex marriage bill by a vote of 80 to 63 on June 15. The measure went to the Senate, where a number of tense negotiations and closed-door meetings took place in the ten days leading up to the vote while Democrats scrambled to secure support. Republican senators met in closed-door meetings with Governor Cuomo, who pushed them to support the bill regardless of the election threat from the Conservative Party. It was rumored each day that a vote on the bill would come to the floor within hours, but the vote never materialized until June 24, when one was finally called following a nine-hour closed-door debate. Senate majority leader Dean Skelos announced that he would not push members of his party to vote one way or the other on the bill, and also stated that he would not delay the vote any longer. "The days of just bottling up things, and using these as excuses not to have votes—as far as I'm concerned as leader, it's over with," said Skelos, who ultimately cast a "no" vote on the bill.

When the votes were tallied, the measure had passed the Senate 33 to 29, with the support of twenty-nine Democrats and four Republicans. Only one Democratic Senator, Rubén Díaz, cast a no vote on the bill, stating, "God, not Albany, has settled the definition of marriage, a long time ago." Republican support was key for passage of the legislation. Some of the Republican support came from members who had voted against earlier legislation for same-sex marriage, calling their 2011 vote one in support of civil rights. "I cannot deny a person, a human being, a taxpayer, a worker, the people of my district and across this state, the State of New York, and those people who make this the great state that it is the same rights that I have with my wife," said Republican Senator Mike Grisanti. Some Democrats changed their 2009 votes as well. Senate Democrat Joseph Addabo Jr. noted that when he cast a "no" vote in 2009, 79 percent of his constituents who wrote to him opposed the measure, but in 2011, 80 percent wrote to him in support of same-sex marriage.

Governor Cuomo signed the legislation just before midnight on June 24. "New York has finally torn down the barrier that has prevented same-sex couples from exercising the freedom to marry and from receiving the fundamental protections that so many couples and families take for granted," the governor said in a statement. "With the world watching, the Legislature, by a bipartisan vote, has said that all New Yorkers are equal under the law."

The legislation signed by the governor included strong protections for religious organizations that do not support same-sex marriage. The language protecting these groups, which gives them the opportunity to decline performing wedding services for same-sex couples, was added to ensure final passage in the Senate and will insulate the groups from discrimination lawsuits. The new law allowing same-sex couples to marry in New York did not include a residency requirement, meaning that same-sex couples from around the country would be able to marry in New York. The law went into effect one month after receiving the governor's signature.

REACTION, FALLOUT, AND A NATIONWIDE MOVEMENT

New York became the sixth, and largest, state to legalize same-sex marriage, joining Connecticut, Iowa, Massachusetts, New Hampshire, Vermont, and Washington, D.C. New York joined New Hampshire and Vermont to become only the third state to use a legislative measure, rather than a court order, to legalize same-sex marriage.

Following passage in New York, gay rights advocates nationwide hoped that other states would take notice and pass similar legislation. "This victory sends a message that marriage equality across the country will be a reality very soon," said Joe Solmonese, president of the Human Rights Campaign. As of 2011, however, thirty-seven states had "defense of marriage" laws that defined marriage as between a man and a woman, and the year brought mixed success for same-sex marriage supporters. Maryland and Rhode Island were unable to pass same-sex marriage legislation. Delaware, Hawaii, and Illinois passed legislation in 2011 to allow same-sex couples to enter into civil unions, which gives them some but not all of the benefits enjoyed by married couples. Pennsylvania is currently considering a constitutional amendment that would make same-sex marriage legal within its borders, and in Minnesota, the 2012 ballot will ask voters whether the state should define marriage as between a man and a woman. Thirty-one states have put similar questions on their ballots in the past, and in all cases voters have approved this definition of marriage.

In New York, opposition to the new law was swift. On July 12, the Barker, New York, town clerk resigned her position because of her objection to same-sex marriage and her unwillingness to sign marriage certificates for same-sex couples. Two weeks earlier, the town clerk from Volney gave power to her deputy to sign marriage certificates for same-sex couples because she too opposed the new legislation. On July 25, New Yorkers for Constitutional Freedoms filed a lawsuit with the state Supreme Court seeking an injunction against the law. The group argued that the legislature had violated the state's open meetings law. The suit was given permission to proceed in November, but no date was set for a trial.

—Heather Kerrigan

Following is the text of New York's same-sex marriage legislation, released on June 14, 2011; a statement written by New York state senator Rubén Díaz and chair of the state Conservative Party, Michael Long, released on June 22, 2011, in opposition to same-sex marriage legislation; and a statement by New York Governor Andrew Cuomo upon passage of the same-sex marriage legislation on June 24, 2011.

DOCUMENT   *New York Marriage Equality Act*

June 14, 2011

STATE OF NEW YORK

8354

2011-2012 Regular Sessions

IN ASSEMBLY

June 14, 2011

Introduced by M. of A. O'donnell, Gottfried, Glick, Titone, Kellner, Bronson, J. Rivera, Silver, Farrell, Sayward, Lentol, Nolan, Weisen Berg, Arroyo, Brennan, Dinowitz, Hoyt, Lifton, Millman, Cahill, Paulin, Reilly, Bing, Jeffries, Jaffee, Rosenthal, Kavanagh, Dendekk Er, Schimel, Hevesi, Benedetto, Schroeder, J. Miller, Lavine, Lancman, Linares, Moya,

Roberts, Simotas, Abinanti, Braunstein—Multi-Sponsored By—M. of A. Aubry, Boyland, Brook-Krasny, Canestrari, Cook, Duprey, Englebright, Latimer, V. Lopez, Lupardo, Magnarelli, Mceneny, Morelle, Ortiz, Pretlow, Ramos, N. Rivera, P. Rivera, Rodriguez, Russell, Sweeney, Thiele, Titus, Weprin, Wright, Zebrowski—(at request of the governor)—read once and referred to the committee on judiciary an act to amend the domestic relations law, in relation to the ability to marry the people of the state of New York, represented in senate and assembly, do enact as follows:

Section 1. This act shall be known and may be cited as the "Marriage Equality Act".

S 2. Legislative intent. Marriage is a fundamental human right. Same sex couples should have the same access as others to the protections, responsibilities, rights, obligations, and benefits of civil marriage. Stable family relationships help build a stronger society. For the welfare of the community and in fairness to all New Yorkers, this act formally recognizes otherwise-valid marriages without regard to whether the parties are of the same or different sex. It is the intent of the legislature that the marriages of same-sex and different-sex couples be treated equally in all respects under the law. The omission from this act of changes to other provisions of law shall not be construed as a legislative intent to preserve any legal distinction between same-sex couples and different-sex couples with respect to marriage. The legislature intends that all provisions of law EXPLANATION—Matter in ITALICS (underscored) is new; matter in brackets [ ] is old law to be omitted.

LBD12066-04-1

A. 8354   2

which utilize gender-specific terms in reference to the parties to a marriage, or which in any other way may be inconsistent with this act be construed in a gender-neutral manner or in any way necessary to effectuate the intent of this act.

S 3. The domestic relations law is amended by adding two new sections 10-a and 10-b to read as follows:

S 10-A. Parties to a marriage.

1. A marriage that is otherwise valid shall be valid regardless of whether the parties to the marriage are of the same or different sex.

2. No government treatment or legal status, effect, right, benefit, privilege, protection or responsibility relating to marriage, whether deriving from statute, administrative or court rule, public policy, common law or any other source of law, shall differ based on the parties to the marriage being or having been of the same sex rather than a different sex. When necessary to implement the rights and responsibilities of spouses under the law, all gender-specific language or terms shall be construed in a gender-neutral manner in all such sources of law.

S 10-B. Application.

1. Notwithstanding any other provision of law, pursuant to subdivision nine of section two hundred ninety-two of the executive law, a corporation incorporated under the benevolent orders law or described in the benevolent orders law but formed under any other law of this state or a religious corporation incorporated under the education law or the religious corporations laws shall be deemed to be in its nature distinctly private and therefore, shall not be required to provide accommodations, advantages, facilities or privileges related to the solemnization or celebration of a marriage.

2. A refusal by a benevolent organization or a religious corporation, incorporated under the education law or the religious corporations law, to provide accommodations, advantages, facilities or privileges in connection with section ten-a of this article shall not create a civil claim or cause of action.

3. pursuant to subdivision eleven of section two hundred ninety-six of the executive law, nothing in this article shall be deemed or construed to prohibit any religious or denominational institution or organization, or any organization operated for charitable or educational purposes, which is operated, supervised or controlled by or in connection with a religious organization from limiting employment or sales or rental of housing accommodations or admission to or giving preference to persons of the same religion or denomination or from taking such action as is calculated by such organization to promote the religious principles for which it is established or maintained.

S 4. Section 13 of the domestic relations law, as amended by chapter 720 of the laws of 1957, is amended to read as follows:

S 13. Marriage licenses. It shall be necessary for all persons intended to be married in New York state to obtain a marriage license from a town or city clerk in New York state and to deliver said license, within sixty days, to the clergyman or magistrate who is to officiate before the marriage ceremony may be performed. In case of a marriage contracted pursuant to subdivision four of section eleven of this chapter, such license shall be delivered to the judge of the court of record before whom the acknowledgment is to be taken. If either party to the marriage resides upon an island located not less than twenty-five miles from the office or residence of the town clerk of the town of which such island is a part, and if such office or residence is not on such island such license may be obtained from any justice of the peace residing on

A. 8354   3

such island, and such justice, in respect to powers and duties relating to marriage licenses, shall be subject to the provisions of this article governing town clerks and shall file all statements or affidavits received by him while acting under the provisions of this section with the town clerk of such town. No application for a marriage license shall be denied on the ground that the parties are of the same, or a different, sex.

S 5. Subdivision 1 of section 11 of the domestic relations law, as amended by chapter 319 of the laws of 1959, is amended and a new subdivision 1-a is added to read as follows:

1. A clergyman or minister of any religion, or by the senior leader, or any of the other leaders, of The Society for Ethical Culture in the city of New York, having its principal office in the borough of Manhattan, or by the leader of The Brooklyn Society for Ethical Culture, having its principal office in the borough of Brooklyn of the city of New York, or of the Westchester Ethical Society, having its principal office in Westchester county, or of the Ethical Culture Society of Long Island, having its principal office in Nassau county, or of the Riverdale-Yonkers Ethical Society having its principal office in Bronx county, or by the leader of any other Ethical Culture Society affiliated with the American Ethical Union; provided that no clergyman or minister as defined in section two of the religious corporations law, or society for ethical culture leader shall be required to solemnize any marriage when acting in his or her capacity under this subdivision.

1-A. A refusal by a clergyman or minister as defined in section two of the religious corporations law, or society for ethical culture leader to solemnize any marriage under this subdivision shall not create a civil claim or cause of action.

S 6. This act shall take effect on the thirtieth day after it shall have become a law.

Source: New York State Senate. "A8354-2011: Enacts the Marriage Equality Act Relating to Ability of Individuals to Marry." June 14, 2011. http://open.nysenate.gov/legislation/bill/A8354-2011.

Statement in Opposition to the Marriage Equality Act

June 22, 2011

We are two lifelong New Yorkers who do not agree about many things. We are of different races, religions, and political parties. One of us is a Bronx liberal Democrat, the other of us heads the Conservative party.

But we agree on at least three great truths:

First, marriage is and should remain the union of husband and wife. Same-sex marriage is a government takeover of an institution the government did not create and should not redefine.

Second, gay marriage is not inevitable. The mainstream media widely retailed a misconstrued version of Sen. Rev. Diaz's remarks in Albany this week. We both agree, as Senator Diaz said, that if a gay-marriage bill passes it will be because the GOP caved for no discernible good reason at all.

Third, as practical pols we agree: If gay marriage passes, it is Republicans across the state who will pay the biggest price.

Politics is a team sport. The decision of senate Republicans to take up this bill, and thus help enable Governor Cuomo's goal to pass gay marriage, will affect the way voters across the state view the Republican party—especially if Republican state senators told voters one thing during the campaign, and now propose to change their votes at Governor Cuomo's behest.

The National Organization for Marriage released a poll of registered New Yorkers, conducted this past weekend. Fifty-seven percent of New York voters agree that "marriage should only be between a man and a woman" versus 32 percent who disagree. Meanwhile, the new NOM poll shows that only about one in four New York voters (26 percent) prefer legislators in Albany to decide this issue, while 59 percent say the issue of marriage should be decided by the voters in New York.

Other polls with different wordings have produced widely different results—but there is no poll that puts gay marriage high on the priority list of any significant number of voters. And even those polls most favorable to gay marriage continue to show that solid majorities of Republican voters have not shifted at all in their opposition to gay marriage.

If gay marriage advocates honestly believe they have a super-majority of New Yorkers in their corner, they should join with us to agree to permit a referendum to decide this issue. If they do not, their claims to represent the majority will ring rather hollow.

This gay-marriage bill is not in the best interests of New York, it is not the choice of New Yorkers, and it is decidedly against the interests of the Republican party.

Republicans have conferenced for four days without reaching agreement on what to do about gay marriage in New York. The enormous public outpouring against the bill—Sen. Greg Ball said 60 percent of calls have opposed it in his district—and the hundreds of people who showed up to rally against gay marriage yesterday must have made state senate Republicans aware that they have a real problem on their hands.

The last time the Republican party caved on a deeply important social issue—abortion—it destroyed the party's prospects for years. And for what? To help Andrew Cuomo run for president? As Brian Brown, president of NOM, quipped:

> Selling your principles in order to get elected is wrong, selling your principles to help get the other guy get elected is just plain dumb.

Memo to GOP leadership: Kill this bill, and let the people of New York decide the future of marriage.

—Sen. Rev. Ruben Diaz is a Democratic state senator from the Bronx. Michael Long is the chairman of the Conservative Party of New York State.

Source: New York State Senator Ruben Diaz. "If the NY Senate Passes Gay Marriage, It's Republicans Who Will Take the Heat." June 22, 2011. http://www.nysenate.gov/press-release/if-ny-senate-passes-gay-marriage-it-s-republicans-who-will-take-heat.

DOCUMENT

Governor Cuomo Announces Passage of the Marriage Equality Act

June 24, 2011

Governor Andrew M. Cuomo today announced passage of the Marriage Equality Act, granting same-sex couples the freedom to marry under the law, as well as hundreds of rights, benefits, and protections that have been limited to married couples of the opposite sex.

"New York has finally torn down the barrier that has prevented same-sex couples from exercising the freedom to marry and from receiving the fundamental protections that so many couples and families take for granted," Governor Cuomo said. "With the world watching, the Legislature, by a bipartisan vote, has said that all New Yorkers are equal under the law. With this vote, marriage equality will become a reality in our state, delivering long overdue fairness and legal security to thousands of New Yorkers."

"I commend Majority Leader Dean Skelos and Minority Leader John Sampson for their leadership and Senator Tom Duane for his lifetime commitment to fighting for equality for all New Yorkers," Governor Cuomo continued. "I also thank Assembly Speaker Sheldon Silver and Assemblyman Danny O'Donnell for ushering this measure through their chamber."

The Marriage Equality Act amends New York's Domestic Relations Law to state:

- A marriage that is otherwise valid shall be valid regardless of whether the parties to the marriage are of the same or different sex
- No government treatment or legal status, effect, right, benefit, privilege, protection or responsibility relating to marriage shall differ based on the parties to the marriage being the same sex or a different sex
- No application for a marriage license shall be denied on the ground that the parties are of the same or a different sex

The Marriage Equality Act was amended to include protections for religious organizations. The Act states that no religious entity, benevolent organization or not-for-profit corporation that is operated, supervised or controlled by a religious entity, or their employees can be required to perform marriage ceremonies or provide their facilities for marriage ceremonies, consistent with their religious principles. In addition, religious entities will not be subject to any legal action for refusing marriage ceremonies. The Act will grant equal access to the government-created legal institution of civil marriage while leaving the religious institution of marriage to its own separate and fully autonomous sphere. Additionally, the Act was amended to include a clause that states that if any part is deemed invalid through the judicial process and after all appeals in the courts, the entire Act would be considered invalid.

The Act was made a reality thanks largely to New Yorkers United for Marriage, a coalition of leading New York LGBT rights organizations who have fought so that all couples in New York have the freedom to marry. The partners include Empire State Pride Agenda, Freedom to Marry, Human Rights Campaign, Marriage Equality New York, and Log Cabin Republicans.

SOURCE: Office of the Governor of New York. Press Office. "Governor Cuomo Announces Passage of Marriage Equality Act." June 24, 2011. http://www.governor.ny.gov/press/062411passageofmarriageequality.

OTHER HISTORIC DOCUMENTS OF INTEREST

FROM PREVIOUS *HISTORIC DOCUMENTS*

Supreme Court Rules on EPA's Authority to Regulate Carbon Dioxide Emissions

JUNE 20, 2011

On June 20, 2011, the U.S. Supreme Court unanimously blocked a lawsuit brought by six states, New York City, and three private land trusts against four private power companies and the federal Tennessee Valley Authority. The states had claimed that the combined 650 million tons of carbon dioxide released into the atmosphere by these power companies each year contributed to global warming and constituted a dangerous "public nuisance." Plaintiffs in this case sought an order from the courts capping the carbon dioxide emissions and reducing them by a specified percentage each year. The Supreme Court, although split on whether the plaintiffs had standing to even bring the lawsuit, were unanimous that the Clean Air Act gave the exclusive authority to regulate greenhouse gases such as carbon dioxide to the federal government and thereby extinguished the rights of states to sue directly in federal court. Justice Ruth Bader Ginsburg, writing on this point for the unanimous Court, noted that the Environmental Protection Agency (EPA) has undertaken regulation of greenhouse gases and has committed to issuing a final rule for greenhouse gas standards for fossil-fuel-fired power plants by May 2012. Only if the EPA fails to issue rules or if the states are still unsatisfied with the EPA's regulations do they have the right under the Clean Air Act to take the EPA to federal court to compel enforcement. Beyond ensuring that the EPA fulfills the mandate of the Clean Air Act, there is, the Court ruled, no independent role for the courts to regulate greenhouse gases.

BACKGROUND OF THE CASE

The lawsuit, *American Electric Power Co. v. Connecticut*, was originally filed in 2004 by eight states, New York City, and three private land trusts. The states were California, Connecticut, Iowa, New Jersey, New York, Rhode Island, Vermont, and Wisconsin, but New Jersey and Wisconsin, under new governors, backed out of the lawsuit. According to the plaintiffs, the power companies they sued were the "five largest emitters of carbon dioxide in the United States." Together, their annual emissions constitute 25 percent of the greenhouse gases released by power companies in the United States, 10 percent of the emissions from all domestic human activities, and 2.5 percent of all human-generated carbon dioxide emissions worldwide. By contributing to global climate change, the plaintiffs alleged, the emissions threaten habitats, infrastructure, and health, in violation of the federal common law of interstate nuisance, a cause of action usually used for localized pollution. They sought an injunction limiting and reducing the defendants's release of greenhouse gases.

The federal trial court dismissed the lawsuit against the power companies, saying that the issues presented required the "balancing of economic, environmental, foreign policy and national security interests involved." Issues like these are generally "consigned to the political branches, not the judiciary." Without ever addressing the merits of the case, the district court rejected the lawsuit for presenting "non-justiciable political questions." On appeal, the United States Court of Appeals for the Second Circuit reversed, finding that the plaintiffs had stated a claim under the "federal common law of nuisance." The Supreme Court agreed to hear the case. Because Supreme Court Justice Sonia Sotamayor had been sitting on the Second Circuit bench when the case was argued, she recused herself from the case when it reached the Supreme Court, leaving the case to be heard by the remaining eight justices.

In the seven years between the initial filing of *American Electric Power Co. v. Connecticut* and when it reached the Supreme Court, the legal and political landscape had changed dramatically. In 2004, the states had felt the need to sue to reduce the emissions contributing to global warming because the President George W. Bush administration would not regulate carbon dioxide as an air pollutant, arguing that such regulation was outside the scope of the Clean Air Act and that, in any event, it would be unwise to do so. In 2007, the Supreme Court, in the landmark case of *Massachusetts v. EPA*, undercut the administration's legal position. The Court held that greenhouse gases are within the meaning of "air pollutants" under the governing Clean Air Act provisions and, therefore, the EPA was required to issue regulations unless it had a scientific basis for refusal. "Because EPA had authority to set greenhouse gas emission standards and had offered no 'reasoned explanation' for failing to do so," the Court concluded, "the agency had not acted in 'accordance with law.'"

After the new directive from the Supreme Court and a change in administrations, the EPA started regulating greenhouse gases. The Barack Obama administration settled other parallel lawsuits, filed in large part by the same states that were plaintiffs in *American Electric Power Co. v. Connecticut,* by agreeing to issue such greenhouse gas regulations for fossil-fuel-fired power plants according to a schedule that calls for a final rule by May 26, 2012.

The Clean Air Act is triggered when the EPA concludes that pollutants "cause, or contribute to, air pollution which may reasonably be anticipated to endanger public health or welfare." In December 2009, the agency concluded, after an exhaustive review of the scientific evidence, that greenhouse gases satisfy this requirement. First, finding that mean global temperatures demonstrate an "'unambiguous warming trend over the last 100 years,' and particularly 'over the past 30 years,'" the agency concluded that, although scientists don't all agree on the causes or consequences of this rise in temperatures, "'compelling' evidence" supported attributing the climate change to the release of greenhouse gases from human activities. Dangers resulting from these emissions, the EPA determined, include heat-related deaths; coastal inundation and erosion caused by melting icecaps and rising sea levels; more frequent and intense hurricanes, floods and other "extreme weather events" that cause death and destroy infrastructure; drought due to reductions in mountain snowpack and shifting precipitation patterns; destruction of ecosystems supporting animals and plants; and potentially significant disruptions of food production. The EPA concluded these findings were sufficient to support the regulation of greenhouse gases under the Clean Air Act.

Together with the Department of Transportation, the EPA subsequently issued final joint regulations to curb greenhouse gases from light-duty trucks and initiated joint rule making covering medium and heavy-duty vehicles. In November 2011, the EPA released proposed standards requiring cars and trucks to achieve significantly higher fuel economy by 2025, with final regulations due in the summer of 2012. The EPA also began phasing in requirements that new or modified industrial polluters use the "best available" technology to limit greenhouse gases.

While *American Electric Power Co. v. Connecticut* was working its way through the lower courts, the EPA commenced rule making to set limits on the greenhouse gas emissions from new, modified, and existing fossil-fuel fired power plants that were at issue in the case. The agency conducted listening sessions, took public comment, and, as required by the settlement of other lawsuits, proposed a schedule for establishing greenhouse gas standards for fossil-fuel-fired power plants that called for the release of a final rule by May 2012.

THE SUPREME COURT RULES: STATES HAVE TO WAIT FOR THE EPA

Eight justices ruled on the case of *American Electric Power Co. v. Connecticut*, with Justice Sotomayor sitting out. On the threshold issue, whether the case presented only the kind of political issues that the federal courts lack the authority to adjudicate, the Court was split 4-4. Because the Court was equally divided on this point, they left in place the Second Circuit opinion that allowed jurisdiction in the case, and then proceeded to the merits of the case, on which they were unanimous.

Writing for the Court, Justice Ruth Bader Ginsburg ruled that the Clean Air Act and the EPA actions that it authorizes "displace any federal common law right to seek abatement of carbon-dioxide emissions from fossil-fuel fired power plants." Congress, she wrote, delegated the power to decide these issues to the EPA exclusively and the EPA is required to establish standards for the emission of greenhouse gases. If the EPA does not set such standards, states and private parties may petition for a rule making and the agency's response is then reviewable in federal court, or if the plaintiffs are dissatisfied with the outcome of the EPA's rule making, the Clean Air Act gives them recourse under federal law that could ultimately lead to review by the Supreme Court. This is "the same relief the plaintiffs seek by invoking federal common law. We see no room for a parallel track," the Court concluded.

Given the complexity of the scientific issues and the need to balance competing interests, Justice Ginsburg wrote that "It is altogether fitting that Congress designated an expert agency, here, EPA, as best suited to serve as primary regulator of greenhouse gas emissions." The agency's expertise makes it better equipped to take on the complex balancing required to determine what amount of carbon-dioxide emissions is "unreasonable" than would be "individual district judges issuing ad hoc, case-by-case injunctions."

The Court cautioned that it "endorses no particular view of the complicated issues related to carbon-dioxide emissions and climate change." Further, the Court left open the issue of whether the plaintiffs would have been able to sue under state nuisance law in the states where the offending power plants are located.

IMPACT OF THE RULING

This opinion limited the ability of states and environmental advocates to press directly for faster action on climate change issues than the government is currently providing, but it did strongly reassert the ability of the EPA to place limits on the release of carbon dioxide. It may result in more pressure on the EPA to promulgate regulations governing the emission of greenhouse gases. David Doniger, an attorney for the Natural Resources Defense Council who was involved in the case, emphasized that "now the EPA must act without delay." But, the EPA has missed several of its deadlines heading toward its commitment to release a final rule by May. After an announced delay in September 2011, EPA Administrator Lisa Jackson stated that "greenhouse gases for power plants is first on the docket," and that the EPA would soon be announcing a new schedule. The EPA did publish, on December 21, 2011, the Mercury Air and Toxics Standard, the first national standards for mercury and acid gases released from power plants. This rule impacts the same power plants that release greenhouse gases, and Jeff Holmstead, a former EPA official, stated that the EPA could win significant greenhouse gas reductions indirectly through regulations such as this one focusing on mercury pollution.

The anticipated EPA greenhouse gas regulation impacts the politically controversial issue of climate change and is coming during a politically fraught presidential election season. Business and Republican interests are putting intense pressure on President Obama to cut environmental regulations that they claim have hurt the economy. In April 2011, arguing that proposed regulations would kill jobs, the Republican-controlled House attempted to modify the Clean Air Act to strip the EPA of jurisdiction to regulate carbon dioxide emissions. The legislation passed the House but died in the Senate.

—Melissa Feinberg

The following are excerpts from the U.S. Supreme Court ruling in American Electric Power Co. v. Connecticut, *in which the Court ruled 8–0 to uphold the Environmental Protection Agency's right to regulate carbon dioxide emissions.*

American Electric Power Co. v. Connecticut

June 20, 2011

[Footnotes have been omitted.]

No. 10-174

American Electric Power Company, Inc., et al., Petitioners

v.

Connecticut et al.

On writ of certiorari to the United States Court of Appeals for the Second Circuit

[June 20, 2011]

JUSTICE GINSBURG delivered the opinion of the Court.

We address in this opinion the question whether the plaintiffs (several States, the city of New York, and three private land trusts) can maintain federal common law public nuisance claims against carbon-dioxide emitters (four private power companies and the federal Tennessee Valley Authority). As relief, the plaintiffs ask for a decree setting carbon-dioxide emissions for each defendant at an initial cap, to be further reduced annually. The Clean Air Act and the Environmental Protection Agency action the Act authorizes, we hold, displace the claims the plaintiffs seek to pursue. . . .

[Sections I–III, containing background information, the facts of the case, and previous precedents, have been omitted.]

IV. . .

[Section A, containing earlier decisions of the Court, has been omitted.]

"[W]hen Congress addresses a question previously governed by a decision rested on federal common law," the Court has explained, "the need for such an unusual exercise of law-making by federal courts disappears." Legislative displacement of federal common law does not require the "same sort of evidence of a clear and manifest [congressional] purpose" demanded for preemption of state law. "'[D]ue regard for the presuppositions of our embracing federal system . . . as a promoter of democracy,'" *id.*, at 316 (quoting *San Diego Building Trades Council* v. *Garmon*, 359 U. S. 236, 243 (1959)), does not enter the calculus, for it is primarily the office of Congress, not the federal courts, to prescribe national policy in areas of special federal interest. The test for whether congressional legislation excludes the declaration of federal common law is simply whether the statute "speak[s] directly to [the] question" at issue.

We hold that the Clean Air Act and the EPA actions it authorizes displace any federal common law right to seek abatement of carbon-dioxide emissions from fossil-fuel fired power plants. *Massachusetts* made plain that emissions of carbon dioxide qualify as air pollution subject to regulation under the Act. And we think it equally plain that the Act "speaks directly" to emissions of carbon dioxide from the defendants' plants.

Section 111 of the Act directs the EPA Administrator to list "categories of stationary sources" that "in [her] judgment . . . caus[e], or contribut[e] significantly to, air pollution which may reasonably be anticipated to endanger public health or welfare." Once EPA lists a category, the agency must establish standards of performance for emission of pollutants from new or modified sources within that category. And, most relevant here, §7411(d) then requires regulation of existing sources within the same category. For existing sources, EPA issues emissions guidelines, see 40 C. F. R. §60.22, .23 (2009); in compliance with those guidelines and subject to federal oversight, the States then issue performance standards for stationary sources within their jurisdiction, §7411(d)(1).

The Act provides multiple avenues for enforcement. EPA may delegate implementation and enforcement authority to the States, §7411(c)(1), (d)(1), but the agency retains the power to inspect and monitor regulated sources, to impose administrative penalties for noncompliance, and to commence civil actions against polluters in federal court. In specified circumstances, the Act imposes criminal penalties on any person who knowingly violates emissions standards issued under §7411. And the Act provides for private enforcement. If States (or EPA) fail to enforce emissions limits against regulated sources, the Act permits "any person" to bring a civil enforcement action in federal court.

If EPA does not *set* emissions limits for a particular pollutant or source of pollution, States and private parties may petition for a rulemaking on the matter, and EPA's response will be reviewable in federal court. As earlier noted, see *supra*, at 3, EPA is currently engaged in a §7411 rulemaking to set standards for greenhouse gas emissions from fossil-fuel fired power plants. To settle litigation brought under §7607(b) by a group that included the majority of the plaintiffs in this very case, the agency agreed to complete that rulemaking by May 2012. The Act itself thus provides a means to seek limits on emissions of carbon dioxide from domestic power plants—the same relief the plaintiffs seek by invoking federal common law. We see no room for a parallel track.

C

The plaintiffs argue, as the Second Circuit held, that federal common law is not displaced until EPA actually exercises its regulatory authority, *i.e.*, until it sets standards governing emissions from the defendants' plants. We disagree.

The sewage discharges at issue in *Milwaukee II*, we do not overlook, were subject to effluent limits set by EPA; under the displacing statute, "[e]very point source discharge" of water pollution was "prohibited unless covered by a permit." As *Milwaukee II* made clear, however, the relevant question for purposes of displacement is "whether the field has been occupied, not whether it has been occupied in a particular manner." Of necessity, Congress selects different regulatory regimes to address different problems. Congress could hardly preemptively prohibit every discharge of carbon dioxide unless covered by a permit. After all, we each emit carbon dioxide merely by breathing.

The Clean Air Act is no less an exercise of the legislature's "considered judgment" concerning the regulation of air pollution because it permits emissions *until* EPA acts. The critical point is that Congress delegated to EPA the decision whether and how to regulate carbon-dioxide emissions from power plants; the delegation is what displaces federal common law. Indeed, were EPA to decline to regulate carbon-dioxide emissions altogether at the conclusion of its ongoing §7411 rulemaking, the federal courts would have no warrant to employ the federal common law of nuisance to upset the agency's expert determination.

EPA's judgment, we hasten to add, would not escape judicial review. Federal courts, we earlier observed, see *supra*, at 11, can review agency action (or a final rule declining to take action) to ensure compliance with the statute Congress enacted. As we have noted, see *supra*, at 10, the Clean Air Act directs EPA to establish emissions standards for categories of stationary sources that, "in [the Administrator's] judgment," "caus[e], or contribut[e] significantly to, air pollution which may reasonably be anticipated to endanger public health or welfare." "[T]he use of the word 'judgment,'" we explained in *Massachusetts*, "is not a roving license to ignore the statutory text." "It is but a direction to exercise discretion within defined statutory limits." *Ibid.* EPA may not decline to regulate carbon dioxide emissions from power plants if refusal to act would be "arbitrary, capricious, an abuse of discretion, or otherwise not in accordance with law." If the plaintiffs in this case are dissatisfied with the outcome of EPA's forthcoming rulemaking, their recourse under federal law is to seek Court of Appeals review, and, ultimately, to petition for certiorari in this Court.

Indeed, this prescribed order of decisionmaking—the first decider under the Act is the expert administrative agency, the second, federal judges—is yet another reason to resist setting emissions standards by judicial decree under federal tort law. The appropriate amount of regulation in any particular greenhouse gas-producing sector cannot be prescribed in a vacuum: as with other questions of national or international policy, informed assessment of competing interests is required. Along with the environmental benefit potentially achievable, our Nation's energy needs and the possibility of economic disruption must weigh in the balance.

The Clean Air Act entrusts such complex balancing to EPA in the first instance, in combination with state regulators. Each "standard of performance" EPA sets must "tak[e] into account the cost of achieving [emissions] reduction and any non air quality health and environmental impact and energy requirements." EPA may "distinguish among classes, types, and sizes" of stationary sources in apportioning responsibility for emissions reductions. And the agency may waive compliance with emission limits to permit a facility to test drive an "innovative technological system" that has "not [yet] been adequately demonstrated." The Act envisions extensive cooperation between federal and state authorities, see §7401(a), (b), generally permitting each State to take the first cut at determining how best to achieve EPA emissions standards within its domain, see §7411 (c)(1), (d)(1)–(2).

It is altogether fitting that Congress designated an expert agency, here, EPA, as best suited to serve as primary regulator of greenhouse gas emissions. The expert agency is surely better equipped to do the job than individual district judges issuing ad hoc, case-by-case injunctions. Federal judges lack the scientific, economic, and technological resources an agency can utilize in coping with issues of this order. Judges may not commission scientific studies or convene groups of experts for advice, or issue rules under notice-and-comment procedures inviting input by any interested person, or seek the counsel of regulators in the States where the defendants are located. Rather, judges are confined by a record comprising the evidence the parties present. Moreover, federal district judges, sitting as sole adjudicators, lack authority to render precedential decisions binding other judges, even members of the same court.

Notwithstanding these disabilities, the plaintiffs propose that individual federal judges determine, in the first instance, what amount of carbon-dioxide emissions is "unreasonable," App. 103, 145, and then decide what level of reduction is "practical, feasible and economically viable," App. 58, 119. These determinations would be made for the defendants named in the two lawsuits launched by the plaintiffs. Similar suits could be mounted, counsel for the States and New York City estimated, against "thousands or hundreds or tens" of other defendants fitting the description "large contributors" to carbon-dioxide emissions.

The judgments the plaintiffs would commit to federal judges, in suits that could be filed in any federal district, cannot be reconciled with the decisionmaking scheme Congress enacted. The Second Circuit erred, we hold, in ruling that federal judges may set limits on greenhouse gas emissions in face of a law empowering EPA to set the same limits, subject to judicial review only to ensure against action "arbitrary, capricious, . . . or otherwise not in accordance with law."

V

The plaintiffs also sought relief under state law, in particular, the law of each State where the defendants operate power plants. The Second Circuit did not reach the state law claims because it held that federal common law governed. In light of our holding that the Clean Air Act displaces federal common law, the availability *vel non* of a state lawsuit depends, *inter alia*, on the preemptive effect of the federal Act. None of the parties have briefed preemption or otherwise addressed the availability of a claim under state nuisance law. We therefore leave the matter open for consideration on remand.

* * *

For the reasons stated, we reverse the judgment of the Second Circuit and remand the case for further proceedings consistent with this opinion.

It is so ordered.

JUSTICE SOTOMAYOR took no part in the consideration or decision of this case.

SOURCE: U.S. Supreme Court. *American Electric Power Co. v. Connecticut*, 564 U.S.__(2011). http://www .supremecourt.gov/opinions/10pdf/10-174.pdf.

OTHER HISTORIC DOCUMENTS OF INTEREST

FROM PREVIOUS *HISTORIC DOCUMENTS*

Supreme Court Rules on Wal-Mart Class Action Suit

JUNE 20, 2011

On June 20, 2011, the U.S. Supreme Court ruled 5–4 in *Wal-Mart Stores v. Dukes,* rejecting what it characterized as "one of the most expansive class actions ever." The nationwide class action lawsuit, brought against Wal-Mart on behalf of nearly 1.5 million current and former female employees, had alleged that the nation's largest private employer had unlawfully discriminated in both pay and promotions against its female employees. The Supreme Court didn't decide if there had in fact been discrimination—just that the case could not proceed as a class action. Justice Antonin Scalia, writing for the majority, concluded that the Wal-Mart employees did not have enough in common to justify joining together as a single, huge class action. The case was one of the most closely watched business-related cases to come to the Supreme Court in years and is likely to have a sweeping impact, making it much harder for workers to join together to sue large companies and causing lower courts to reexamine other pending employee class actions to determine if they meet the new vigorous common interest requirement.

The Case Against Wal-Mart

Wal-Mart is the nation's largest private employer, operating 3,400 individual stores employing more than one million people. While it has a stated corporate policy against discrimination in employment decisions, it leaves pay and promotion decisions to the broad discretion of local managers. Vacancies are not regularly posted and most promotion decisions are filled in a manner characterized as a "tap on the shoulder" process, giving managers broad discretion over which shoulders to tap.

In 1998, lawyers filed a class action lawsuit in a California district court on behalf of "all women employed at any Wal-Mart domestic retail store at any time since December 26, 1998." Such class actions are a type of lawsuit that allows a large group of individuals to join together to pursue claims that they all share in common. Class actions are useful in cases where the size of the injury may not justify each individual to sue on their own, but, if they join together in a "class," they can pool resources and share in the result. To be certified, representatives of the class must as a threshold prove that the class is so numerous that joinder of all members is impracticable; there are questions of law or fact common to the class; the claims or defenses of the representative parties are typical of the claims or defenses of the class; and the representative parties will fairly and adequately protect the interests of the class.

Betty Dukes worked at the Wal-Mart in Pittsburg, California, and claims that she was repeatedly passed over for promotion while males were promoted. As one of three named plaintiffs who sought to represent the female members of the class, she and the other plaintiffs alleged that the company discriminates based on gender in pay and promotions, relying on gender stereotypes and prejudices. Wal-Mart, they allege, permits those prejudices to infect all personnel decisions by leaving pay and promotions in the hands of "a nearly all male managerial workforce" using "arbitrary and subjective criteria." The plaintiffs presented statistical evidence that, while women fill 70 percent of the hourly jobs, they hold only 33 percent of management positions. Women are also paid less than men in every region and "'that the salary gap widens over time even for men and women hired into the same jobs at the same time.'" An expert testified that, after correcting for job performance, store location, and length of time with the company, these statistics "'can be explained only by gender discrimination.'" Plaintiffs also testified to their own experiences to suggest that gender bias "suffused Wal-Mart's company culture." In one example, company managers routinely referred to female associates as "little Janie Q's." The district court ruled that the requirements for a class action were met, and certified the class of past and present female employees of Wal-Mart.

When Wal-Mart appealed the class certification, the Ninth Circuit Court of Appeals, in a special *en banc* hearing, affirmed the district court's order certifying the class of female employees. Wal-Mart then appealed to the Supreme Court.

THE COURT'S DECISION

On the main issue in this case, whether female employees could be certified as a single class and sue Wal-Mart in a single trial, the Supreme Court split 5–4 along its ideological divide. Justice Antonin Scalia, the justice who has been the most skeptical of class actions, wrote the majority opinion, joined by Chief Justice John Roberts and Justices Samuel Alito, Anthony Kennedy, and Clarence Thomas.

Justice Scalia defined the crux of the case as whether the plaintiffs could satisfy the requirement that members of a class share common questions of law or fact. "Here," he wrote, "respondents wish to sue about literally millions of employment decisions at once. Without some glue holding the alleged *reasons* for all those decisions together, it will be impossible to say that examination of all the class members' claims for relief will produce a common answer to the crucial question *why was I disfavored.*" Scalia found this necessary "glue" to be lacking. He cited Wal-Mart's explicit policy forbidding discrimination and found that the plaintiff's statistical evidence was "worlds away" from showing the significant proof of the general companywide policy of discrimination in pay or promotions that would be required to satisfy the class action rules. The company's policy against sex bias together with its delegation of discretion in workplace decisions to the regions "is just the opposite of a uniform employment practice that would provide the commonality needed for a class action; it is a policy *against having* uniform employment practices. It is also a very common and presumptively reasonable way of doing business." Merely showing that some lower-level supervisors used their discretion in a way that has a disparate impact on women does not, he wrote, "lead to the conclusion that every employee in a company using a system of discretion has such a claim in common."

Justice Ruth Bader Ginsburg, who had spent much of her career before joining the high court specializing in gender equality issues, wrote for the dissent, joined by Justices Stephen Breyer and the two other female justices, Elena Kagan and Sonia Sotomayor. The dissenters agreed with the majority that the case had been filed as the wrong kind of class action, but, rather than ruling that they could not meet the standard of commonality under any kind of class action, and thus disqualifying the class "at the starting gate," the dissent would have given the class action plaintiffs the chance on remand to prove that there were adequate issues in common under the appropriate version of class action. Justice Ginsburg wrote, "The practice of delegating to supervisors large discretion to make personnel decisions, uncontrolled by formal standards, has long been known to have the potential to produce disparate effects." When the managers with the discretion are predominantly male and steeped in a corporate culture that perpetuates gender stereotypes, Ginsberg wrote that the risk they will fall prey to biases knowingly or unknowingly is heightened. Antidiscrimination claims exist not only when practices are motivated by a discriminatory intent, but also when they produce discriminatory results. On these points the dissent was more persuaded than was the majority that the plaintiff's evidence, both statistical and the class members's own tales of their experiences, suggested that gender bias suffused the company culture at Wal-Mart. Whether the pay and promotions policy of delegated discretion in fact violated the law is an issue, the dissent argued, that all plaintiffs would have in common.

Sharply Divided Reaction

While the reaction to the Supreme Court's ruling was sharply divided, most agreed that it was an expansive rejection of large employment discrimination class action suits that would make it much harder for victims of discrimination to join together to seek justice in the courts. It will be harder both to sue as a group, but also to find lawyers who will fight small individual cases against large companies. In a statement released just after the decision, the plaintiffs's attorneys declared, "The court's ruling erects substantially higher barriers for working women and men to vindicate rights to be free from employment discrimination." Nan Aron of the Alliance for Justice, a nonprofit judicial advocacy group, placed this case in context, finding it to be "another in a long series of cases where the conservative majority has used a radical reformulation of the law to erect a wall of privilege and protection around big business."

Other critics worried that the case will create what Marcia Greenberger, president of the National Women's Law Center, called a "perverse incentive." The larger a company is, the more decentralized and the more discretion left to local managers, the less likely that company is to face class action lawsuits. The large companies may be able to protect themselves as long as they have a well-publicized policy against discrimination, even if they turn a blind eye to the discretion exercised by managers. After the ruling in this case, Greenberger concluded, in the absence of a plainly discriminatory corporate policy, employees will have trouble bringing a class action suit for the actions of individual managers who break the rules based on general statistics of bias.

Business groups, by contrast, were thrilled with the result in *Wal-Mart Stores v. Dukes,* seeing it as a victory to businesses that are trying to fend off mega-class actions designed to intimidate them into settling. In a statement about the decision, Robin Conrad of the U.S. Chamber of Commerce applauded the ruling for protecting businesses from what she described as an abusive legal tactic to force businesses "to choose between settling meritless lawsuits or potentially facing financial ruin." Our economy, she said, "would be better served if businesses could spend more resources creating jobs and fewer resources fighting frivolous litigation."

The Wal-Mart case has already started to have a profound impact on pending class action cases against large companies. As reported in the *Wall Street Journal,* in anticipation of a favorable ruling, Best Buy Company was able to settle a multimillion-dollar suit by workers alleging systematic discrimination against women and minorities for a monetary award of only $290,000 to be divided among the nine named plaintiffs. There are currently other large discrimination class actions pending against companies such as Costco Wholesale Corp., units of Cigna Corp., Bayer, Toshiba Corp., and Deere & Co. It is likely that the certification of all these class actions will be reexamined. The impact of the Court's ruling in *Wal-Mart Stores v. Dukes* is likely to extend beyond employment actions to affect all sorts of other class actions, including actions by investors and consumers.

While expressing disappointment with the Court's ruling, Joseph Sellers, the lawyer who represented the class of female Wal-Mart employees, stated his belief that he can continue the case against Wal-Mart by breaking the class action into pieces in order to bring the case as a series of smaller cases and he is currently lining up lawyers around the country to bring these cases. "What we will look for," Sellers stated, "on a region- or store-wide basis is some evidence to which we can attribute to top-level people in the region or in the store, some more general bias toward women. I don't read the majority as saying you can never have a class where there is evidence attributable to higher-level people." Wal-Mart lawyer Ted Boutrous, however, feels confident that the *Dukes* case will close the door on any type of lawsuit against them, other than those brought by single employees with individual claims.

—Melissa Feinberg

The following are excerpts from the U.S. Supreme Court ruling in Wal-Mart Stores v. Dukes, *in which the Court ruled 5–4 that the female plaintiffs in the case did not have enough in common to be able to bring a class action lawsuit against the mega retailer.*

DOCUMENT   *Wal-Mart Stores v. Dukes*

June 20, 2011

[Footnotes have been omitted.]

No. 10-277

Wal-Mart Stores, Inc., Petitioner

v.

Betty Dukes et al.

On writ of certiorari to the United States Court of Appeals for the Ninth Circuit

[June 20, 2011]

JUSTICE SCALIA delivered the opinion of the Court.

We are presented with one of the most expansive class actions ever. The District Court and the Court of Appeals approved the certification of a class comprising about one and a half million plaintiffs, current and former female employees of petitioner Wal-Mart who allege that the discretion exercised by their local supervisors over pay and promotion matters violates Title VII by discriminating against women. In addition to injunctive and declaratory relief, the plaintiffs seek an award of backpay. We consider whether the certification of the plaintiff class was consistent with Federal Rules of Civil Procedure 23(a) and (b)(2). . . .

[Section I, containing the facts and background in the case, has been omitted.]

II

The class action is "an exception to the usual rule that litigation is conducted by and on behalf of the individual named parties only." In order to justify a departure from that rule, "a class representative must be part of the class and 'possess the same interest and suffer the same injury' as the class members." Rule 23(a) ensures that the named plaintiffs are appropriate representatives of the class whose claims they wish to litigate. The Rule's four requirements— numerosity, commonality, typicality, and adequate representation—"effectively 'limit the class claims to those fairly encompassed by the named plaintiff's claims.'"

A

The crux of this case is commonality—the rule requiring a plaintiff to show that "there are questions of law or fact common to the class." That language is easy to misread, since "[a]ny competently crafted class complaint literally raises common 'questions.'" For example: Do all of us plaintiffs indeed work for Wal-Mart? Do our managers have discretion over pay? Is that an unlawful employment practice? What remedies should we get? Reciting these questions is not sufficient to obtain class certification. Commonality requires the plaintiff to demonstrate that the class members "have suffered the same injury," *Falcon, supra,* at 157. This does not mean merely that they have all suffered a violation of the same provision of law. Title VII, for example, can be violated in many ways—by intentional discrimination, or by hiring and promotion criteria that result in disparate impact, and by the use of these practices on the part of many different superiors in a single company. Quite obviously, the mere claim by employees of the same company that they have suffered a Title VII injury, or even a disparate impact Title VII injury, gives no cause to believe that all their claims can productively be litigated at once. Their claims must depend upon a common contention—for example, the assertion of discriminatory bias on the part of the same supervisor. That common contention, moreover, must be of such a nature that it is capable of classwide resolution—which means that determination of its truth or falsity will resolve an issue that is central to the validity of each one of the claims in one stroke.

"What matters to class certification . . . is not the raising of common 'questions'— even in droves—but, rather the capacity of a classwide proceeding to generate common *answers* apt to drive the resolution of the litigation. Dissimilarities within the proposed class are what have the potential to impede the generation of common answers."

Rule 23 does not set forth a mere pleading standard. A party seeking class certification must affirmatively demonstrate his compliance with the Rule—that is, he must be prepared to prove that there are *in fact* sufficiently numerous parties, common questions of law or fact, etc. We recognized in *Falcon* that "sometimes it may be necessary for the court to probe behind the pleadings before coming to rest on the certification question," 457 U. S., at 160, and that certification is proper only if "the trial court is satisfied, after a rigorous analysis, that the prerequisites of Rule 23(a) have been satisfied," *id.*, at 161; see *id.*, at 160 ("[A]ctual, not presumed, conformance with Rule 23(a) remains . . . indispensable"). Frequently that "rigorous analysis" will entail some overlap with the merits of the plaintiff's underlying claim. That cannot be helped. "'[T]he class determination generally involves considerations that are enmeshed in the factual and legal issues comprising the plaintiff's cause of action.'". . .

In this case, proof of commonality necessarily overlaps with respondents' merits contention that Wal-Mart engages in a *pattern or practice* of discrimination. That is so because, in resolving an individual's Title VII claim, the crux of the inquiry is "the reason for a particular employment decision," *Cooper* v. *Federal Reserve Bank of Richmond*, 467 U. S. 867, 876 (1984). Here respondents wish to sue about literally millions of employment decisions at once. Without some glue holding the alleged *reasons* for all those decisions together, it will be impossible to say that examination of all the class members' claims for relief will produce a common answer to the crucial question *why was I disfavored.*

B

This Court's opinion in *Falcon* describes how the commonality issue must be approached. There an employee who claimed that he was deliberately denied a promotion on account of race obtained certification of a class comprising all employees wrongfully denied promotions and all applicants wrongfully denied jobs. We rejected that composite class for lack of commonality and typicality, explaining:

> "Conceptually, there is a wide gap between (a) an individual's claim that he has been denied a promotion [or higher pay] on discriminatory grounds, and his otherwise unsupported allegation that the company has a policy of discrimination, and (b) the existence of a class of persons who have suffered the same injury as that individual, such that the individual's claim and the class claim will share common questions of law or fact and that the individual's claim will be typical of the class claims."

Falcon suggested two ways in which that conceptual gap might be bridged. First, if the employer "used a biased testing procedure to evaluate both applicants for employment and incumbent employees, a class action on behalf of every applicant or employee who might have been prejudiced by the test clearly would satisfy the commonality and typicality requirements of Rule 23(a)." Second, "[s]ignificant proof that an employer operated under a general policy of discrimination conceivably could justify a class of both applicants and employees if the discrimination manifested itself in hiring and promotion practices in the same general fashion, such as through entirely subjective decisionmaking processes." We think that statement precisely describes respondents' burden in this case. . . .

The second manner of bridging the gap requires "significant proof" that Wal-Mart "operated under a general policy of discrimination." That is entirely absent here. Wal-Mart's announced policy forbids sex discrimination, see App. 1567a–1596a, and as the District Court recognized the company imposes penalties for denials of equal employment opportunity, 222 F. R. D., at 154. The only evidence of a "general policy of discrimination" respondents produced was the testimony of Dr. William Bielby, their sociological expert. Relying on "social framework" analysis, Bielby testified that Wal-Mart has a "strong corporate culture," that makes it "'vulnerable'" to "gender bias." He could not, however, "determine with any specificity how regularly stereotypes play a meaningful role in employment decisions at Wal-Mart. At his deposition . . . Dr. Bielby conceded that he could not calculate whether 0.5 percent or 95 percent of the employment decisions at Wal-Mart might be determined by stereotyped thinking." The parties dispute whether Bielby's testimony even met the standards for the admission of expert testimony under Federal Rule of Evidence 702 and our *Daubert* case, see *Daubert* v. *Merrell Dow Pharmaceuticals, Inc.*, 509 U. S. 579 (1993). The District Court concluded that *Daubert* did not apply to expert testimony at the certification stage of class-action proceedings. We doubt that is so, but even if properly considered, Bielby's testimony does nothing to advance respondents' case. "[W]hether 0.5 percent or 95 percent of the employment decisions at Wal-Mart might be determined by stereotyped thinking" is the essential question on which respondents' theory of commonality depends. If Bielby admittedly has no answer to that question, we can safely disregard what he has to say. It is worlds away from "significant proof" that Wal-Mart "operated under a general policy of discrimination."

C

The only corporate policy that the plaintiffs' evidence convincingly establishes is Wal-Mart's "policy" of *allowing discretion* by local supervisors over employment matters. On its face, of course, that is just the opposite of a uniform employment practice that would provide the commonality needed for a class action; it is a policy *against having* uniform employment practices. It is also a very common and presumptively reasonable way of doing business—one that we have said "should itself raise no inference of discriminatory conduct," *Watson* v. *Fort Worth Bank & Trust*, 487 U. S. 977, 990 (1988).

To be sure, we have recognized that, "in appropriate cases," giving discretion to lower-level supervisors can be the basis of Title VII liability under a disparate-impact theory—since "an employer's undisciplined system of subjective decisionmaking [can have] precisely the same effects as a system pervaded by impermissible intentional discrimination." But the recognition that this type of Title VII claim "can" exist does not lead to the conclusion that every employee in a company using a system of discretion has such a claim in common. To the contrary, left to their own devices most managers in any corporation—and surely most managers in a corporation that forbids sex discrimination—would select sex-neutral, performance-based criteria for hiring and promotion that produce no actionable disparity at all. Others may choose to reward various attributes that produce disparate impact—such as scores on general aptitude tests or educational achievements, see *Griggs* v. *Duke Power Co.*, 401 U. S. 424, 431–432 (1971). And still other managers may be guilty of intentional discrimination that produces a sex based disparity. In such a company, demonstrating the invalidity of one manager's use of discretion will do nothing to demonstrate the invalidity of another's. A party seeking to certify a nationwide class will be unable to show that all the employees' Title VII claims will in fact depend on the answers to common questions.

Respondents have not identified a common mode of exercising discretion that pervades the entire company—aside from their reliance on Dr. Bielby's social frameworks analysis that we have rejected. In a company of Wal-Mart's size and geographical scope, it is quite unbelievable that all managers would exercise their discretion in a common way without some common direction. Respondents attempt to make that showing by means of statistical and anecdotal evidence, but their evidence falls well short.

The statistical evidence consists primarily of regression analyses performed by Dr. Richard Drogin, a statistician, and Dr. Marc Bendick, a labor economist. Drogin conducted his analysis region-by-region, comparing the number of women promoted into management positions with the percentage of women in the available pool of hourly workers. After considering regional and national data, Drogin concluded that "there are statistically significant disparities between men and women at Wal-Mart . . . [and] these disparities . . . can be explained only by gender discrimination." Bendick compared work-force data from Wal-Mart and competitive retailers and concluded that Wal-Mart "promotes a lower percentage of women than its competitors."

Even if they are taken at face value, these studies are insufficient to establish that respondents' theory can be proved on a classwide basis. In *Falcon*, we held that one named plaintiff's experience of discrimination was insufficient to infer that "discriminatory treatment is typical of [the employer's employment] practices." A similar failure of inference arises here. As Judge Ikuta observed in her dissent, "[i]nformation about disparities at the regional and national level does not establish the existence of disparities at individual stores, let alone raise the inference that a company-wide policy of discrimination is implemented by discretionary decisions at the store and district level." A regional pay disparity, for example, may be attributable to only a small set of Wal-Mart stores, and cannot by itself establish the uniform, store-by-store disparity upon which the plaintiffs' theory of commonality depends.

There is another, more fundamental, respect in which respondents' statistical proof fails. Even if it established (as it does not) a pay or promotion pattern that differs from the nationwide figures or the regional figures in *all* of Wal-Mart's 3,400 stores, that would still not demonstrate that commonality of issue exists. Some managers will claim that the availability of women, or qualified women, or interested women, in their stores' area does not mirror the national or regional statistics. And almost all of them will claim to have been applying some sex-neutral, performance-based criteria—whose nature and effects will differ from store to store. In the landmark case of ours which held that giving discretion to lower-level supervisors can be the basis of Title VII liability under a disparate-impact theory, the plurality opinion *conditioned* that holding on the corollary that merely proving that the discretionary system has produced a racial or sexual disparity *is not enough*. "[T]he plaintiff must begin by identifying the specific employment practice that is challenged." That is all the more necessary when a class of plaintiffs is sought to be certified. Other than the bare existence of delegated discretion, respondents have identified no "specific employment practice"—much less one that ties all their 1.5 million claims together. Merely showing that Wal-Mart's policy of discretion has produced an overall sex-based disparity does not suffice.

Respondents' anecdotal evidence suffers from the same defects, and in addition is too weak to raise any inference that all the individual, discretionary personnel decisions are discriminatory. In *Teamsters* v. *United States*, 431 U. S. 324 (1977), in addition to substantial statistical evidence of company-wide discrimination, the Government (as plaintiff) produced about 40 specific accounts of racial discrimination from particular individuals. That number was significant because the company involved had only 6,472 employees, of whom 571 were minorities, *id.*, at 337, and the class itself consisted of around 334 persons, *United States* v. *T.I.M.E.-D. C., Inc.*, 517 F. 2d 299, 308 (CA5 1975), overruled on other grounds, *Teamsters, supra*. The 40 anecdotes thus represented roughly one account for every eight members of the class. Moreover, the Court of Appeals noted that the anecdotes came from individuals "spread throughout" the company who "for the most part" worked at the company's operational centers that employed the largest numbers of the class members. Here, by contrast, respondents filed some 120 affidavits reporting experiences of discrimination—about 1 for every 12,500 class members—relating to only some 235 out of Wal-Mart's 3,400 stores. More than half of these reports are concentrated in only six States (Alabama, California, Florida, Missouri, Texas, and Wisconsin); half of all States have only one or two anecdotes; and 14 States have no anecdotes about Wal-Mart's operations at all. Even if every single one of these accounts is true, that would not demonstrate that the entire company "operate[s] under a general policy of discrimination," *Falcon, supra,* at 159, n. 15, which is what respondents must show to certify a companywide class. . . .

[Section III, which contains information on the respondents's claims for back pay, has been omitted.]

***

The judgment of the Court of Appeals is *Reversed.*
JUSTICE GINSBURG, with whom JUSTICE BREYER, JUSTICE SOTOMAYOR, and JUSTICE KAGAN join, concurring in part and dissenting in part. . . .

[The dissent's introduction and Section I, which contain information on the decision of the majority, facts in the case, and earlier precedents, have been omitted.]

II

A

The Court gives no credence to the key dispute common to the class: whether Wal-Mart's discretionary pay and promotion policies are discriminatory. "What matters," the Court asserts, "is not the raising of common 'questions,'" but whether there are "[d]issimilarities within the proposed class" that "have the potential to impede the generation of common answers.". . .

B

The "dissimilarities" approach leads the Court to train its attention on what distinguishes individual class members, rather than on what unites them. Given the lack of standards for pay and promotions, the majority says, "demonstrating the invalidity of one manager's use of discretion will do nothing to demonstrate the invalidity of another's." Wal-Mart's delegation of discretion over pay and promotions is a policy uniform throughout all stores. The very nature of discretion is that people will exercise it in various ways. A system of delegated discretion, *Watson* held, is a practice actionable under Title VII when it produces discriminatory outcomes. A finding that Wal-Mart's pay and promotions practices in fact violate the law would be the first step in the usual order of proof for plaintiffs seeking individual remedies for company-wide discrimination. That each individual employee's unique circumstances will ultimately determine whether she is entitled to backpay or damages, §2000e–5(g)(2)(A) (barring backpay if a plaintiff "was refused . . . advancement

... for any reason other than discrimination"), should not factor into the Rule 23(a)(2) determination.

***

The Court errs in importing a "dissimilarities" notion suited to Rule 23(b)(3) into the Rule 23(a) commonality inquiry. I therefore cannot join Part II of the Court's opinion.

Source: U.S. Supreme Court. *Wal-Mart Stores, Inc. v. Dukes,* 564 U.S.__(2011). http://www.supremecourt .gov/opinions/10pdf/10-277.pdf.

OTHER HISTORIC DOCUMENTS OF INTEREST

FROM PREVIOUS *HISTORIC DOCUMENTS*

Supreme Court Rules on Generic Drug Labeling

JUNE 23, 2011

In 2011, the Supreme Court ruled for the third time in as many years on federal preemption in state medical labeling lawsuits. In the case of *Pliva v. Mensing*, the Court heard arguments from two women harmed by the generic drug metoclopramide, and two generic manufacturers of the drug, Pliva and Actavis. In what was considered a follow-up to the 2009 case of *Wyeth v. Levine*, in which the Court ruled on brand name drugs, the *Pliva* case asked the Court to decide whether generic drug manufacturers can be sued under state law for failing to warn consumers of the side effects of the drug or if federal Food and Drug Administration (FDA) regulations preempt these state failure-to-warn claims by denying generics the same ability to change their warning labels as their brand name counterparts enjoy. On June 23, 2011, the Court issued a victory for generic drug manufacturers, finding that FDA regulations do in fact preempt state failure-to-warn claims, leaving those harmed by generic drugs with no judicial recourse at the state level.

METOCLOPRAMIDE AND TARDIVE DYSKINESIA

Pliva v. Mensing stems from lower court rulings in cases filed by Gladys Mensing and Julie Demahy, both of whom used the generic drug equivalent of Reglan, metoclopramide. Mensing began taking the drug in 2001 for diabetic gastroparisis. She took the drug for four years and subsequently developed tardive dyskinesia, a severe neurological disorder. Demahy began taking metoclopramide in 2002 for gastroesophageal reflux disorder, and also took the drug for four years before developing tardive dyskinesia. Mensing and Demahy sued in separate cases, each claiming that the generic manufacturer had failed to include information on the warning label regarding growing evidence of the risk of tardive dyskinesia associated with long-term use of metoclopramide. The pair further claimed that the generic drug companies, Pliva in the case of Mensing and Actavis in the case of Demahy, had promoted the drug for long-term use.

At the time Demahy and Mensing took metoclopramide, the warning label read "therapy longer than 12 weeks has not been evaluated and cannot be recommended." In 2004, the label was amended to state that the drug should not be used for more than twelve weeks; however, in the cases of Mensing and Demahy, use of the drug continued despite the change. By the time Mensing and Demahy developed tardive dyskinesia, no warnings appeared on metoclopramide warning of a connection to the disease. It was not until 2009 that the FDA stepped in and required both Reglan and generic manufacturers of metoclopramide to add a boxed warning on their drug labels indicating that there is an increased risk of tardive dyskinesia associated with long-term use of the drug.

In an attempt to dismiss the cases, Pliva and Actavis argued in district court that the Hatch-Waxman amendments of the Food, Drug, and Cosmetic Act (FDCA), which require generic drugs to display the same warning labels as their brand name drug counterpart, preempt state failure-to-warn suits. The district courts granted dismissal in part in both cases. When Demahy appealed to the Fifth Circuit Court, this ruling was reversed and the court found that federal law does not preempt state failure-to-warn claims. The Eighth Circuit Court also did not find federal preemption in Mensing's case.

Both generic manufacturers appealed the rulings to the U.S. Supreme Court. Before deciding to hear the case, the Court asked for the opinion of the federal government. The government stated that the circuit courts had ruled correctly and that no preemption was at issue in the case. The Court, however, decided to hear the case, which consolidated three separate cases against Pliva and Actavis.

Pliva, Mensing, and Demahy Arguments

In their arguments before the Court, Mensing and Demahy relied on the Constitution's Supremacy Clause. This provision states that federal law can preempt state law in one of three ways: through language in a federal act; passage of federal laws that occupy the field, thus leaving no room for state interpretation; or if the state law conflicts with the federal law, and compliance with both is impossible, or the state law becomes an obstacle to complying with the federal law as intended by Congress.

On the third method of preemption, the plaintiffs argued that the generic drug manufacturers in question could not prove that they could not comply with both the FDA regulations and state failure-to-warn laws. The plaintiffs stated that the manufacturers could have asked the FDA for a label change or issued letters to health-care providers to warn them of the link between metoclopramide and tardive dyskinesia. In fact, the plaintiffs noted, in addition to the health-care provider letters, the generic manufacturers could have undertaken the prior approval supplement, changes being effected, or citizen petition processes to ensure that drug users were well aware of the link. Because the burden lies with the defendant in preemption cases, the plaintiffs stated that Pliva and Actavis could make no argument that the FDA would not have allowed for a stronger warning on metoclopramide labels.

The plaintiffs also argued that state failure-to-warn does not obstruct the intent of federal law. The plaintiffs rested this idea on the 2009 case of *Wyeth v. Levine,* in which the Court ruled that FDA labeling regulations could not stop brand name pharmaceutical companies from being sued in state court. According to the Court, there was no express preemption intended by Congress in the FDCA for brand name drugs. Demahy and Mensing said that *Levine* finds that state liability in fact complements federal law by allowing those harmed by a drug to seek judicial recourse. On the other hand, preemption would actually damage federal attempts to reduce health care costs, increase drug safety, and encourage the use of generics. Because the Hatch-Waxman amendments include no federal preemption, a ruling in favor of the generic drug manufacturers would violate federal law. Finding preemption in the case would leave generic manufacturers without responsibility for the costs related to injury from use of their drugs and would encourage consumers to seek more costly brand name drugs.

In rebuttal, Pliva argued that they could not be sued in state court for failure-to-warn because the FDA requires generic drug manufacturers to have the same labels as their name brand drug counterparts and gives generic drug manufacturers no method for issuing stronger warnings. Because generic and brand name drugs are inherently different in this respect, generic drug manufacturers cannot be held to a higher state standard, as federal law makes label changes impossible. Pliva did concede that generic drug manufacturers have the responsibility to report problems to the FDA, but that these responsibilities do not extend to the involvement of third parties, meaning the manufacturers cannot be sued over this responsibility.

In addition to arguing that they could not add safety warnings to their labels until Reglan did so, the defendants additionally argued against the plaintiffs's claims of issuing warnings through other means, stating that issuing letters to health-care professionals would be a violation of FDCA and other FDA regulations. Issuing these letters, Pliva said, would be akin to changing a warning label. Morton Grove Pharmaceuticals, Inc. and Impax Laboratories, who filed briefs for the court but were not party to the case, took this argument even further, stating that taking steps to let the FDA know about potential side effects of the drug would violate the Court's decision in *Buckman Co. v. Plaintiffs' Legal Committee*, in which the Court ruled that the review process for medical devices preempted state claims because of the manufacturers's fraudulent misrepresentation to the FDA. The briefs filed by Morton Grove and Impax Laboratories went on to indicate that state failure-to-warn claims would place substantial cost on the FDA and an additional burden on generic drug manufacturers that Congress never intended to be in place.

VICTORY FOR GENERIC DRUG MANUFACTURERS

The case of *Pliva v. Mensing* marked the third time since 2008 that the Court ruled on labeling preemption, each time issuing contradictory rulings to those delivered previously. In its final opinion on June 23, the Court ruled 5–4 to reverse the circuit court decisions, finding that generic drug companies cannot be sued in state courts for failing to provide labeling that adequately describes side effects. Justice Clarence Thomas wrote the majority opinion, with Justice Antonin Scalia and Chief Justice John Roberts joining in full and Justice Anthony Kennedy joining in part. In its decision, the Court reviewed FDA regulations and how they apply to generic drug manufacturers. In this review, the majority relied on the Constitution's Supremacy Clause and found impossibility for any generic drug manufacturer to comply with both state failure-to-warn claims and FDA regulations. "It was not lawful under federal law for the Manufacturers to do what state law required of them," wrote Thomas. "And even if they had fulfilled their federal duty to ask for FDA assistance, they would not have satisfied the requirements of state law. If the Manufacturers had independently changed their labels to satisfy their state-law duty, they would have violated federal law," Thomas wrote. Ultimately, the majority ruled, federal regulations conflict with and preempt state lawsuits on generic drug failure-to-warn claims. In his opinion, Thomas did "acknowledge the unfortunate hand" that was dealt to Mensing and Demahy, but ultimately ruled that they had no judicial recourse in state court.

Justice Sonia Sotomayor wrote the dissenting opinion, and was joined by Justices Ruth Bader Ginsburg, Stephen Breyer, and Elena Kagan. The majority's ruling, Sotomayor wrote, "invents new principles of pre-emption law out of thin air to justify its dilution of the impossibility standard." While the majority chose to recognize inherent differences between generic and brand name drug manufacturers in FDA regulations, the dissent did not, accusing the majority of contradicting the decision in *Wyeth v. Levine* and the principles of the Hatch-Waxman amendments, which consider generic and brand name drugs to be the same under federal law. By removing the protection of Hatch-Waxman, the dissent wrote, "whether a consumer harmed by inadequate warnings can obtain relief turns solely on the happenstance of whether her pharmacist filled her prescription with a brand-name or generic drug." Sotomayor concluded that the majority's opinion would reduce consumer demand for generic drugs. "Today's decision leads to so many absurd consequences that I cannot fathom that Congress would have intended to pre-empt state law in these cases," she wrote.

REACTION AND IMPACT

Reaction from the victors in the case was swift. "The Supreme Court hit the nail on the head today by making clear that federal law does not permit states to hold generic drug manufacturers liable for using the very warnings federal law required them to use," said Jay Lefkowitz, a lawyer for the drug companies. Bob Billings, the executive director of the Generic Pharmaceutical Association, said that had the Court ruled differently, it would have put "the generic drug manufacturer in the impossible position of defending the content of a label that they are required by law to use and prevented by law from changing."

Those who opposed the Court's decision did so mainly because it left those harmed by generic drugs with little recourse. "Three out of four patients just lost the right to sue" for generic drug use complications, said Louis Bograd, counsel at the Center for Constitutional Litigation, hinting to the fact that generic drugs account for 70 percent of all drugs sold in the United States today. The Court's ruling left generic drug users "without any legal remedy," he said.

By removing judicial recourse through state court for those injured by generic drugs, drug manufacturers can now avoid some liability for injury caused by their products. This, said opponents to the ruling, undermines the FDA's ability to follow-through on the principles of the Hatch-Waxman amendments.

—Heather Kerrigan

The following are excerpts from the U.S. Supreme Court ruling in Pliva v. Mensing, *in which the Court ruled 5–4 that generic drug manufacturers cannot be sued under state law for providing inadequate warning labels.*

DOCUMENT *Pliva v. Mensing*

June 23, 2011

[Footnotes have been omitted.]

Nos. 09-993, 09-1039 and 09-1501

Pliva, Inc., et al., Petitioners

v.

Gladys Mensing

Actavis Elizabeth, LLC, Petitioner

v.

Gladys Mensing

Actavis, Inc., Petitioner

v.

Julie Demahy

On writs of certiorari to the United States Courts of Appeals for the Eighth and Fifth Circuits

[June 23, 2011]

JUSTICE THOMAS delivered the opinion of the Court, except as to Part III–B–2.

These consolidated lawsuits involve state tort-law claims based on certain drug manufacturers' alleged failure to provide adequate warning labels for generic metoclopramide. The question presented is whether federal drug regulations applicable to generic drug manufacturers directly conflict with, and thus pre-empt, these state-law claims. We hold that they do. . . .

[Section I, containing the background of the case before the Court, has been omitted.]

II

Pre-emption analysis requires us to compare federal and state law. We therefore begin by identifying the state tort duties and federal labeling requirements applicable to the Manufacturers.

A

It is undisputed that Minnesota and Louisiana tort law require a drug manufacturer that is or should be aware of its product's danger to label that product in a way that renders it reasonably safe. . . . In both States, a duty to warn falls specifically on the manufacturer. . . .

Mensing and Demahy have pleaded that the Manufacturers knew or should have known of the high risk of tardive dyskinesia inherent in the long-term use of their product. They have also pleaded that the Manufacturers knew or should have known that their labels did not adequately warn of that risk. The parties do not dispute that, if these allegations are true, state law required the Manufacturers to use a different, safer label.

B

Federal law imposes far more complex drug labeling requirements. We begin with what is not in dispute. Under the 1962 Drug Amendments to the Federal Food, Drug, and Cosmetic Act, 76 Stat. 780, 21 U. S. C. §301 *et seq.*, a manufacturer seeking federal approval to market a new drug must prove that it is safe and effective and that the proposed label is accurate and adequate.. . .

Originally, the same rules applied to all drugs. In 1984, however, Congress passed the Drug Price Competition and Patent Term Restoration Act, 98 Stat. 1585, commonly called the Hatch-Waxman Amendments. Under this law, "generic drugs" can gain FDA approval simply by showing equivalence to a reference listed drug that has already been approved by the FDA. . . .

As a result, brand-name and generic drug manufacturers have different federal drug labeling duties. A brand name manufacturer seeking new drug approval is responsible for the accuracy and adequacy of its label. A manufacturer seeking generic drug approval, on the other hand, is responsible for ensuring that its warning label is the same as the brand name's.

The parties do not disagree. What is in dispute is whether, and to what extent, generic manufacturers may change their labels *after* initial FDA approval. Mensing and Demahy contend that federal law provided several avenues through which the Manufacturers could have altered their metoclopramide labels in time to prevent the injuries here. The FDA, however, tells us that it interprets its regulations to require that the warning labels of a brand-name drug and its generic copy must always be the same—thus, generic drug manufacturers have an ongoing federal duty of "sameness." . . .

1

First, Mensing and Demahy urge that the FDA's "changes-being-effected" (CBE) process allowed the Manufacturers to change their labels when necessary. . . .

The FDA denies that the Manufacturers could have used the CBE process to unilaterally strengthen their warning labels. The agency interprets the CBE regulation to allow changes to generic drug labels only when a generic drug manufacturer changes its label to match an updated brand-name label or to follow the FDA's instructions. . . .

2

Next, Mensing and Demahy contend that the Manufacturers could have used "Dear Doctor" letters to send additional warnings to prescribing physicians and other healthcare professionals. Again, the FDA disagrees, and we defer to the agency's views.

The FDA argues that Dear Doctor letters qualify as "labeling." . . . Thus, any such letters must be "consistent with and not contrary to [the drug's] approved . . .labeling." Moreover, if generic drug manufacturers, but not the brand-name manufacturer, sent such letters, that would inaccurately imply a therapeutic difference between the brand and generic drugs and thus could be impermissibly "misleading." . . .

3

Though the FDA denies that the Manufacturers could have used the CBE process or Dear Doctor letters to strengthen their warning labels, the agency asserts that a different avenue existed for changing generic drug labels. According to the FDA, the Manufacturers could have proposed—indeed, were required to propose—stronger warning labels to the agency if they believed such warnings were needed. . . .

The Manufacturers and the FDA disagree over whether this alleged duty to request a strengthened label actually existed. . . .Because we ultimately find pre-emption even assuming such a duty existed, we do not resolve the matter.

C

To summarize, the relevant state and federal requirements are these: State tort law places a duty directly on all drug manufacturers to adequately and safely label their products.

Taking Mensing and Demahy's allegations as true, this duty required the Manufacturers to use a different, stronger label than the label they actually used. Federal drug regulations, as interpreted by the FDA, prevented the Manufacturers from independently changing their generic drugs' safety labels. But, we assume, federal law also required the Manufacturers to ask for FDA assistance in convincing the brand-name manufacturer to adopt a stronger label, so that all corresponding generic drug manufacturers could do so as well. We turn now to the question of pre-emption.

III

The Supremacy Clause establishes that federal law "shall be the supreme Law of the Land . . . any Thing in the Constitution or Laws of any State to the Contrary notwithstanding." Where state and federal law "directly conflict," state law must give way. We have held that state and federal law conflict where it is "impossible for a private party to comply with both state and federal requirements."

A

We find impossibility here. It was not lawful under federal law for the Manufacturers to do what state law required of them. And even if they had fulfilled their federal duty to ask for FDA assistance, they would not have satisfied the requirements of state law.

If the Manufacturers had independently changed their labels to satisfy their state-law duty, they would have violated federal law. . . .

The federal duty to ask the FDA for help in strengthening the corresponding brand-name label, assuming such a duty exists, does not change this analysis. Although requesting FDA assistance would have satisfied the Manufacturers' federal duty, it would not have satisfied their state tort-law duty to provide adequate labeling. State law demanded a safer label; it did not instruct the Manufacturers to communicate with the FDA about the possibility of a safer label. . . .

B

1

Mensing and Demahy contend that, while their state law claims do not turn on whether the Manufacturers asked the FDA for assistance in changing their labels, the Manufacturers' federal affirmative defense of pre-emption does. . . .

This raises the novel question whether conflict preemption should take into account these possible actions by the FDA and the brand-name manufacturer. Here, what federal law permitted the Manufacturers to do could have changed, even absent a change in the law itself, depending on the actions of the FDA and the brand-name manufacturer. . . .

Mensing and Demahy assert that when a private party's ability to comply with state law depends on approval and assistance from the FDA, proving pre-emption requires that party to demonstrate that the FDA would not have allowed compliance with state law. Here, they argue, the Manufacturers cannot bear their burden of proving impossibility because they did not even *try* to start the process that might ultimately have allowed them to use a safer label. This is a fair argument, but we reject it.

The question for "impossibility" is whether the private party could independently do under federal law what state law requires of it. Accepting Mensing and Demahy's argument would render conflict pre-emption largely meaningless because it would make most conflicts between state and federal law illusory. . . .

If these conjectures suffice to prevent federal and state law from conflicting for Supremacy Clause purposes, it is unclear when, outside of express pre-emption, the Supremacy Clause would have any force. . . .

2

Moreover, the text of the Clause—that federal law shall be supreme, "any Thing in the Constitution or Laws of any State to the Contrary notwithstanding"—plainly contemplates conflict pre-emption by describing federal law as effectively repealing contrary state law. . . . The *non obstante* provision in the Supremacy Clause therefore suggests that federal law should be understood to impliedly repeal conflicting state law. Further, the provision suggests that courts should not strain to find ways to reconcile federal law with seemingly conflicting state law. . . .

To consider in our pre-emption analysis the contingencies inherent in these cases. . . would be inconsistent with the *non obstante* provision of the Supremacy Clause. The Manufacturers would be required continually to prove the counterfactual conduct of the FDA and brand name manufacturer in order to establish the supremacy of federal law. We do not think the Supremacy Clause contemplates that sort of contingent supremacy. . . . When the "ordinary meaning" of federal law blocks a private party from independently accomplishing what state law requires, that party has established pre-emption.

3

To be sure, whether a private party can act sufficiently independently under federal law to do what state law requires may sometimes be difficult to determine. But this is not such a case. Before the Manufacturers could satisfy state law, the FDA—a federal agency—had to undertake special effort permitting them to do so. . . .

Here, state law imposed a duty on the Manufacturers to take a certain action, and federal law barred them from taking that action. The only action the Manufacturers could independently take—asking for the FDA's help—is not a matter of state-law concern. Mensing and Demahy's tort claims are pre-empted.

C. . .

We recognize that from the perspective of Mensing and Demahy, finding pre-emption here but not in *Wyeth* makes little sense. . . . But because pharmacists, acting in full accord with state law, substituted generic metoclopramide instead, federal law pre-empts these lawsuits. We acknowledge the unfortunate hand that federal drug regulation has dealt Mensing, Demahy, and others similarly situated.

But "it is not this Court's task to decide whether the statutory scheme established by Congress is unusual or even bizarre." It is beyond dispute that the federal statutes and regulations that apply to brand name drug manufacturers are meaningfully different than those that apply to generic drug manufacturers. Indeed, it is the special, and different, regulation of generic drugs that allowed the generic drug market to expand, bringing more drugs more quickly and cheaply to the public. But different federal statutes and regulations may, as here, lead to different pre-emption results. We will not distort the Supremacy Clause in order to create similar preemption across a dissimilar statutory scheme. As always, Congress and the FDA retain the authority to change the law and regulations if they so desire.

* * *

The judgments of the Fifth and Eighth Circuits are reversed, and the cases are remanded for further proceedings consistent with this opinion.

It is so ordered.

JUSTICE SOTOMAYOR, with whom JUSTICE GINSBURG, JUSTICE BREYER, and JUSTICE KAGAN join, dissenting.

The Court today invokes the doctrine of impossibility pre-emption to hold that federal law immunizes generic drug manufacturers from all state-law failure-to-warn claims because they cannot unilaterally change their labels. I cannot agree. We have traditionally held defendants claiming impossibility to a demanding standard: Until today, the mere possibility of impossibility had not been enough to establish pre-emption.

The Food and Drug Administration (FDA) permits—and, the Court assumes, requires—generic-drug manufacturers to propose a label change to the FDA when they believe that their labels are inadequate. . . .Although generic manufacturers may be able to show impossibility in some cases, petitioners, generic manufacturers of metoclopramide (Manufacturers), have shown only that they *might* have been unable to comply with both federal law and their state-law duties to warn respondents Gladys Mensing and Julie Demahy. This, I would hold, is insufficient to sustain their burden.

The Court strains to reach the opposite conclusion. It invents new principles of pre-emption law out of thin air to justify its dilution of the impossibility standard. It effectively rewrites our decision in *Wyeth* v. *Levine*, 555 U. S. 555 (2009), which holds that federal law does not pre-empt failure-to-warn claims against brand-name drug manufacturers. And a plurality of the Court tosses aside our repeated admonition that courts should hesitate to conclude that Congress intended to pre-empt state laws governing health and safety. As a result of today's decision, whether a consumer harmed by inadequate warnings can obtain relief turns solely on the happenstance of whether her pharmacist filled her prescription with a brand-name or generic drug. The Court gets one thing right: This outcome "makes little sense."

I

A

Today's decision affects 75 percent of all prescription drugs dispensed in this country. The dominant position of generic drugs in the prescription drug market is the result of a series of legislative measures, both federal and state. . . .

[A discussion of legislative efforts regarding generic drugs has been omitted.]

B

As noted, to obtain FDA approval a generic manufacturer must generally show that its drug is the same as an approved brand-name drug. It need not conduct clinical trials to prove the safety and efficacy of the drug. This does not mean, however, that a generic manufacturer has no duty under federal law to ensure the safety of its products. . . .

Generic manufacturers, the majority assumes, also bear responsibility under federal law for monitoring the adequacy of their warnings. I agree with the majority's conclusion that generic manufacturers are not permitted unilaterally to change their labels through the "changes-being-effected" (CBE) process or to issue additional warnings through "Dear Doctor" letters. . . .

II

This brings me to the Manufacturers' pre-emption defense. State law obliged the Manufacturers to warn of dangers to users. The Manufacturers contend, and the majority agrees, that federal law pre-empts respondents' failure-to-warn claims because, under federal law, the Manufacturers could not have provided additional warnings to respondents without the exercise of judgment by the FDA. I cannot endorse this novel conception of impossibility pre-emption. . . .

[Section A on the analysis of preemption has been omitted.]

B

Federal law impliedly pre-empts state law when state and federal law "conflict"—*i.e.*, when "it is impossible for a private party to comply with both state and federal law" or when state law "stands as an obstacle to the accomplishment and execution of the full purposes and objectives of Congress." The Manufacturers rely solely on the former ground of pre-emption.
    Impossibility pre-emption, we have emphasized, "is a demanding defense." . . .

[Additional discussion of the Manufacturers's argument has been omitted.]

This is not to say that generic manufacturers could never show impossibility. If a generic-manufacturer defendant proposed a label change to the FDA but the FDA rejected the proposal, it would be impossible for that defendant to comply with a state-law duty to warn. Likewise, impossibility would be established if the FDA had not yet responded to a generic manufacturer's request for a label change at the time a plaintiff's injuries arose. . . .
    This conclusion flows naturally from the overarching principles governing our pre-emption doctrine. . . .This presumption against preemption has particular force when the Federal Government has afforded defendants a mechanism for complying with state law, even when that mechanism requires federal agency action. . . .Any other approach threatens to infringe the States' authority over traditional matters of state interest—such as the failure-to-warn claims here—when Congress expressed no intent to pre-empt state law.

C

The majority concedes that the Manufacturers might have been able to accomplish under federal law what state law requires. To reach the conclusion that the Manufacturers have nonetheless satisfied their burden to show impossibility, the majority invents a new preemption rule: "The question for 'impossibility' is whether the private party could *independently* do under federal law what state law requires of it." Because the Manufacturers could not have changed their labels without the exercise of judgment by the FDA, the majority holds, compliance with both state and federal law was impossible in these cases.

The majority's new test has no basis in our precedents. . . .

With so little support in our case law, the majority understandably turns to other rationales. . . .

[Notes on earlier Court cases have been omitted.]

The plurality's new theory of the Supremacy Clause is a direct assault on these precedents. Whereas we have long presumed that federal law does not pre-empt, or repeal, state law, the plurality today reads the Supremacy Clause to operate as a provision instructing courts "*not* to apply the general presumption against implied repeals.". . .

That the plurality finds it necessary to resort to this novel theory of the Supremacy Clause—a theory advocated by no party or *amici* in these cases—is telling. Proper application of the longstanding presumption *against* pre-emption compels the conclusion that federal law does not render compliance with state law impossible merely because it requires an actor to seek federal agency approval. . . .

III

Today's decision leads to so many absurd consequences that I cannot fathom that Congress would have intended to pre-empt state law in these cases.

First, the majority's pre-emption analysis strips generic drug consumers of compensation when they are injured by inadequate warnings. . . .

Second, the majority's decision creates a gap in the parallel federal-state regulatory scheme in a way that could have troubling consequences for drug safety. . . .

Finally, today's decision undoes the core principle of the Hatch-Waxman Amendments that generic and brand name drugs are the "same" in nearly all respects. . . .

Today's decision introduces a critical distinction between brand-name and generic drugs. Consumers of brand-name drugs can sue manufacturers for inadequate warnings; consumers of generic drugs cannot. These divergent liability rules threaten to reduce consumer demand for generics, at least among consumers who can afford brand-name drugs. They may pose "an ethical dilemma" for prescribing physicians. And they may well cause the States to rethink their longstanding efforts to promote generic use through generic substitution laws. . . .

Nothing in the Court's opinion convinces me that, in enacting the requirement that generic labels match their corresponding brand-name labels, Congress intended these absurd results. . . . With respect, I dissent.

SOURCE: U.S. Supreme Court. *Pliva, Inc. v. Mensing,* 564 U.S.__(2011). http://www.supremecourt.gov/opinions/10pdf/09-993.pdf.

OTHER HISTORIC DOCUMENTS OF INTEREST

FROM PREVIOUS *HISTORIC DOCUMENTS*

- FDA Officials on Protecting Patients From Unsafe Drugs, *2004,* p. 850

Supreme Court Rules on California's Violent Video Game Ban

JUNE 27, 2011

In a ruling variously described as an epic win for the First Amendment or a cynical preference for corporations over children, the U.S. Supreme Court, on June 27, 2011, struck down a California law that barred the sale or rental of violent video games to children in a 7–2 decision. *Brown v. Entertainment Merchants Association* was the latest in a series of recent controversial First Amendment rulings in which the Court has protected the free speech rights of funeral protesters, videos depicting cruelty to animals, and the political speech of corporations. The Supreme Court did not come easily to the result in this case. It grappled with how old constitutional principles dating back hundreds of years can be applied to the new technology of video gaming and whether the different constitutional treatment of sexuality and violence could still be justified. There were four very different opinions in this case that at times read like a testy conversation between the justices.

CALIFORNIA'S VIDEO GAME BAN

California State Senator Leland Yee, a child psychologist, wrote the law at issue in this case. It imposed a $1,000 fine on anyone who sells or rents violent video games to minors. It targets games "in which the range of options available to a player includes killing, maiming, dismembering, or sexually assaulting an image of a human being, if those acts are depicted" in a manner that "[a] reasonable person, considering the game as a whole, would find appeals to a deviant or morbid interest of minors," and that "is patently offensive to prevailing standards in the community as to what is suitable for minors." The law, mirroring similar laws about obscene material, applies only to games that, as a whole, "lack serious literary, artistic, political, or scientific value for minors." This law was passed in 2005 and signed into law by then-Governor Arnold Schwarzenegger, but never took effect as it was immediately challenged by the video game and software industries. The lower courts found that the law violated the First Amendment and California appealed to the Supreme Court.

FOUR OPINIONS

The majority opinion upheld the lower court's decision that banning the sale of violent video games to minors violates the freedom of speech protections of the First Amendment. Written by Justice Antonin Scalia, the opinion was joined by Justices Anthony Kennedy, Ruth Bader Ginsburg, Sonia Sotomayor, and Elena Kagan.

Justice Scalia rejected the idea that video games, although a new and different medium for communication, were in any relevant way different from existing media, such as books, plays, and movies, which are clearly protected by the First Amendment. Like older media, video games communicate ideas "through many familiar literary devices (such as characters, dialogue, plot, and music) and through features distinctive to the medium (such as the player's interaction with the virtual world)." For this reason, Scalia argued, the First Amendment protects them and government has no power to restrict their expression because of their ideas, subject matter, or content, unless it can demonstrate that regulation is justified by a compelling government interest and is narrowly drawn to serve that interest. Scalia found that California could not meet that standard.

Justice Samuel Alito, joined by Chief Justice John Roberts, concurred with Scalia that the California law was unconstitutional, but only on the limited grounds that it was unconstitutionally vague. On the First Amendment issues, Alito wrote that the Court had acted prematurely in jumping to the conclusion that the new technology of video gaming is the same as older media such as books and movies. Scalia's majority opinion was "too quick to dismiss the possibility that the experience of playing video games," Alito wrote, "may be very different from anything that we have seen before." He then recounted in detail the astounding violence of some games that are already on the market where victims cry out in agony and beg for mercy, as they are "dismembered, decapitated, disemboweled, set on fire, and chopped into little pieces." Current video gamers can reenact the killings at Columbine and Virginia Tech, or play games the goal of which is to rape a mother and her daughters, or to engage in "'ethnic cleansing'" where they can choose to gun down African Americans, Latinos, or Jews. He noted that the industry forecasts that video games will soon be seen in three dimensions and provide sensory feedback such that children will be able to "'actually feel the splatting blood from the blown-off head' of a victim." The Court should not, he concluded, have dismissed the possibility out of hand that the experience of playing such video games is fundamentally different from the experience of reading a book and may, for at least some minors, have quite different results.

Justice Scalia was unmoved by the horrors feared by this concurring opinion. "Justice Alito," he responded, "recounts all these disgusting video games in order to disgust us— but disgust is not a valid basis for restricting expression." Scalia minimizes the dangers of video gaming, making the case that similar arguments about the dangers to children have historically been made against new forms of entertainment. In the 1800s, dime novels were blamed for juvenile delinquency, and then, when motion pictures were introduced, there were laws censoring movies because of their capacity to be "'used for evil'" that were later held unconstitutional. In the late 1940s and early 1950s, comic books were blamed for fostering a "'preoccupation with violence and horror'" among the youth. And more recently, television and music lyrics have prompted similar reactions. Justice Scalia also rejected the argument that because video games are interactive, they are essentially different from other protected speech. He saw the interactivity of video games as different only in degree, rather than in kind, as all literature is also interactive, drawing in the reader and making him or her identify with the characters.

Also disagreeing with the majority opinion, Justice Clarence Thomas wrote a dissent from an "originalist" perspective, asking how the Constitution's founders would have originally understood "the freedom of speech" at the time the First Amendment was adopted. Justice Thomas engaged in a lengthy historical analysis of the existing views about minors, starting from the puritan tradition through the founding generation, before determining that the drafters of the First Amendment "would not have understood 'the freedom of speech' to include a right to speak to children without going through their parents." Because minors lacked free speech rights at that time, the California law banning the sale of certain material directly to children without parental consent should not, Thomas concludes, "'abridg[e] the freedom of speech' within the original meaning of the First Amendment."

Justice Scalia, as another "originalist" on the Court, generally joined with Justice Thomas, but this time he dismissed the dissent, responding that Thomas "cites no case, state or federal, supporting this view, and to our knowledge there is none." Minors are, Scalia cites from an earlier case, "entitled to a significant measure of First Amendment protection, and only in relatively narrow and well-defined circumstances may government bar public dissemination of protected materials to them." To hold otherwise, Scalia elaborates, would allow, for example, the government to make it a crime to let people under 18 enter a political rally or go to a church without parents' prior consent. In the absence of any precedent for this kind of state control or of any compelling justification for such restrictions, these laws must be unconstitutional.

Finally, Justice Stephen Breyer also took on the majority opinion in his own dissent. He agreed that video games have expressive and artistic elements and are therefore constitutionally protected, and cannot be regulated without satisfying the strictest standard of review, but he believed California had satisfied that standard. Providing a long list of scientific studies analyzing exposure to violent video games, Breyer concluded that "unlike the majority, I would find sufficient grounds in these studies and expert opinions for the court to defer to an elected legislature's conclusion that the video games in question are particularly likely to harm children." The majority opinion, Breyer wrote, creates the anomaly that laws can constitutionally prohibit the sale of material that falls well short of obscenity to minors, but not material that is extremely violent. "What sense does it make to forbid selling to a 13-year-old boy a magazine with an image of a nude woman, while protecting a sale to that 13-year-old of an interactive video game in which he actively, but virtually, binds and gags the woman, then tortures and kills her," Breyer wrote.

REACTION AND IMPACT

Reaction to the Court's decision from the video game industry was one of relief. Michael Gallager, president and CEO of the Entertainment Software Association, the game industry's trade group, applauded the decision for letting "parents not government bureaucrats, have the right to decide what is appropriate for their children." He added that the video gaming industry would continue improving its parental controls and voluntary rating system. The current rating system, implemented by the Entertainment Software Rating Board, is designed to inform consumers about the content of the games and encourages stores to refrain from renting or selling games rated AO (Adults Only) to minors, and to rent or sell games rated for age seventeen or older (M) to minors only with parental consent. Recently, a Federal Trade Commission undercover shopper survey found that video game retailers continue to vigorously enforce these ratings governing age and content. In fact, it found the enforcement of these voluntary standards to be substantially better by game retailers than by CD retailers and movie theaters. John Morris, general counsel for the Center for Democracy and Technology, a technology lobbying group that supported the video game industry, expressed pleasure that the "Supreme Court has embraced the idea that voluntary ratings systems are one of the best ways to assist parents in determining what kinds of content their children can view." He predicted that the video game industry would "develop user empowerment tools that will help parents achieve this goal in a much more effective—and constitutional—way than the California law."

The California state senator who wrote the law rejected by the Supreme Court released a statement accusing the Court of having "once again put the interests of corporate America before the interests of children." State Senator Yee wrote, "It is simply wrong that the video game industry can be allowed to put their profit margins over the rights of parents and the well-being of children." James Steyer, the CEO of the parents's advocacy group Common Sense Media, also expressed disappointment in the Court's ruling, respectfully disagreeing with the First Amendment analysis. "[T]his is a sanity issue," he wrote, "not a censorship issue." And it is an issue that will only get bigger, he added, "now that children can download even to their cell phones."

—Melissa Feinberg

The following are excerpts from the U.S. Supreme Court ruling in Brown v. Entertainment Merchants Association, *in which the Court ruled 7–2 to overturn California's ban on the sale of violent video games to minors.*

Brown v. Entertainment Merchants Association

June 27, 2011

[Footnotes have been omitted.]

No. 08-1448

Edmund G. Brown, Jr., Governor of California, et al., Petitioners

v.

Entertainment Merchants Association et al.

On writ of certiorari to the United States Court of Appeals for the Ninth Circuit

[June 27, 2011]

JUSTICE SCALIA delivered the opinion of the Court.
    We consider whether a California law imposing restrictions on violent video games comports with the First Amendment. . . .

[Section I, containing background information on the case, has been omitted.]

II

California correctly acknowledges that video games qualify for First Amendment protection. The Free Speech Clause exists principally to protect discourse on public matters, but we have long recognized that it is difficult to distinguish politics from entertainment, and dangerous to try. "Everyone is familiar with instances of propaganda through fiction. What is one man's amusement, teaches another's doctrine." Like the protected books, plays, and movies that preceded them, video games communicate ideas—and even social messages—through many familiar literary devices (such as characters, dialogue, plot, and music) and through features distinctive to the medium (such as the player's interaction with the virtual world). That suffices to confer First Amendment protection. Under our Constitution, "esthetic and moral judgments about art and literature . . . are for the individual to make, not for the Government to decree, even with the mandate or approval of a majority." And whatever the challenges of applying the Constitution to ever-advancing technology, "the basic principles of freedom of speech and the press, like the First Amendment's command, do not vary" when a new and different medium for communication appears. The most basic of those principles is this: "[A]s a general matter, . . . government has no power to restrict expression because of its message, its ideas, its subject matter, or its content." There are of course exceptions. "'From 1791 to the present,' . . . the First Amendment has 'permitted restrictions upon the content of speech in a few limited areas,' and has never 'include[d] a freedom to disregard these traditional limitations.'" These limited areas—such as obscenity, *Roth* v. *United States*, 354 U. S. 476, 483 (1957), incitement, *Brandenburg* v. *Ohio*, 395 U. S. 444, 447–449 (1969) *(per curiam)*, and fighting words, *Chaplinsky* v. *New Hampshire*, 315 U. S. 568, 572 (1942)—represent "well-defined and narrowly limited classes of speech, the prevention and punishment of which have never been thought to raise any Constitutional problem," *id.*, at 571–572.

Last Term, in *Stevens*, we held that new categories of unprotected speech may not be added to the list by a legislature that concludes certain speech is too harmful to be tolerated. *Stevens* concerned a federal statute purporting to criminalize the creation, sale, or possession of certain depictions of animal cruelty. The statute covered depictions "in which a living animal is intentionally maimed, mutilated, tortured, wounded, or killed" if that harm to the animal was illegal where the "the creation, sale, or possession t[ook] place," §48(c)(1). A saving clause largely borrowed from our obscenity jurisprudence, see *Miller* v. *California*, 413 U. S. 15, 24 (1973), exempted depictions with "serious religious, political, scientific, educational, journalistic, historical, or artistic value," §48(b). We held that statute to be an impermissible content-based restriction on speech. There was no American tradition of forbidding the *depiction of* animal cruelty—though States have long had laws against *committing* it.

The Government argued in *Stevens* that lack of a historical warrant did not matter; that it could create new categories of unprotected speech by applying a "simple balancing test" that weighs the value of a particular category of speech against its social costs and then punishes that category of speech if it fails the test. We emphatically rejected that "startling and dangerous" proposition. "Maybe there are some categories of speech that have been historically unprotected, but have not yet been specifically identified or discussed as such in our case law." But without persuasive evidence that a novel restriction on content is part of a long (if heretofore unrecognized) tradition of proscription, a legislature may not revise the "judgment [of] the American people," embodied in the First Amendment, "that the benefits of its restrictions on the Government outweigh the costs."

That holding controls this case. As in *Stevens*, California has tried to make violent-speech regulation look like obscenity regulation by appending a saving clause required for the latter. That does not suffice. Our cases have been clear that the obscenity exception to the First Amendment does not cover whatever a legislature finds shocking, but only depictions of "sexual conduct," Miller, supra, at 24. . . .

Because speech about violence is not obscene, it is of no consequence that California's statute mimics the New York statute regulating obscenity-for-minors that we upheld in *Ginsberg* v. *New York*, 390 U. S. 629 (1968). That case approved a prohibition on the sale to minors of *sexual* material that would be obscene from the perspective of a child. We held that the legislature could "adjus[t] the definition of obscenity 'to social realities by permitting the appeal of this type of material to be assessed in terms of the sexual interests . . .' of . . . minors. " And because "obscenity is not protected expression," the New York statute could be sustained so long as the legislature's judgment that the proscribed materials were harmful to children "was not irrational." The California Act is something else entirely. It does not adjust the boundaries of an existing category of unprotected speech to ensure that a definition designed for adults is not uncritically applied to children. California does not argue that it is empowered to prohibit selling offensively violent works *to adults*—and it is wise not to, since that is but a hair's breadth from the argument rejected in *Stevens*. Instead, it wishes to create a wholly new category of content-based regulation that is permissible only for speech directed at children.

That is unprecedented and mistaken. "[M]inors are entitled to a significant measure of First Amendment protection, and only in relatively narrow and well-defined circumstances may government bar public dissemination of protected materials to them." No doubt a State possesses legitimate power to protect children from harm, *Ginsberg*, *supra*, at 640–641; *Prince* v. *Massachusetts*, 321 U. S. 158, 165 (1944), but that does not include a free-floating power to restrict the ideas to which children may be exposed. "Speech that is neither obscene as to youths nor subject to some other legitimate proscription cannot be suppressed solely to protect the young from ideas or images that a legislative body thinks unsuitable for them."

California's argument would fare better if there were a longstanding tradition in this country of specially restricting children's access to depictions of violence, but there is none. Certainly the *books* we give children to read—or read to them when they are younger—contain no shortage of gore. Grimm's Fairy Tales, for example, are grim indeed. As her just deserts for trying to poison Snow White, the wicked queen is made to dance in red hot slippers "till she fell dead on the floor, a sad example of envy and jealousy." Cinderella's evil stepsisters have their eyes pecked out by doves And Hansel and Gretel (children!) kill their captor by baking her in an oven. . . .

JUSTICE ALITO has done considerable independent research to identify, see *post*, at 14–15, nn. "Victims are dismembered, decapitated, disemboweled, set on fire, and chopped into little pieces. . . . Blood gushes, splatters, and pools." JUSTICE ALITO recounts all these disgusting video games in order to disgust us—but disgust is not a valid basis for restricting expression. And the same is true of JUSTICE ALITO's description, *post*, at 14–15, of those video games he has discovered that have a racial or ethnic motive for their violence—"'ethnic cleansing' [of] . . . African Americans, Latinos, or Jews." To what end does he relate this? Does it somehow increase the "aggressiveness" that California wishes to suppress? Who knows? But it does arouse the reader's ire, and the reader's desire to put an end to this horrible message. Thus, ironically, JUSTICE ALITO's argument highlights the precise danger posed by the California Act: that the *ideas* expressed by speech—whether it be violence, or gore, or racism—and not its objective effects, may be the real reason for governmental proscription.

III

Because the Act imposes a restriction on the content of protected speech, it is invalid unless California can demonstrate that it passes strict scrutiny—that is, unless it is justified by a compelling government interest and is narrowly drawn to serve that interest. The State must specifically identify an "actual problem" in need of solving, *Playboy*, 529 U. S., at 822–823, and the curtailment of free speech must be actually necessary to the solution, see *R. A. V., supra*, at 395. That is a demanding standard. "It is rare that a regulation restricting speech because of its content will ever be permissible."

California cannot meet that standard. At the outset, it acknowledges that it cannot show a direct causal link between violent video games and harm to minors. Rather, relying upon our decision in *Turner Broadcasting System, Inc.* v. *FCC*, 512 U. S. 622 (1994), the State claims that it need not produce such proof because the legislature can make a predictive judgment that such a link exists, based on competing psychological studies. But reliance on *Turner Broadcasting* is misplaced. That decision applied *intermediate scrutiny* to a content-neutral regulation. California's burden is much higher, and because it bears the risk of uncertainty, see *Playboy, supra*, at 816–817, ambiguous proof will not suffice.

The State's evidence is not compelling. California relies primarily on the research of Dr. Craig Anderson and a few other research psychologists whose studies purport to show a connection between exposure to violent video games and harmful effects on children. These studies have been rejected by every court to consider them, and with good reason: They do not prove that violent video games *cause* minors to *act* aggressively (which would at least be a beginning). Instead, "[n]early all of the research is based on correlation, not evidence of causation, and most of the studies suffer from significant, admitted flaws in methodology." They show at best some correlation between exposure to violent entertainment and minuscule real-world effects, such as children's feeling more aggressive or making louder noises in the few minutes after playing a violent game than after playing a nonviolent game. . . .

[Additional information on evidence in the case presented by the State of California has been omitted.]

* * *

California's effort to regulate violent video games is the latest episode in a long series of failed attempts to censor violent entertainment for minors. While we have pointed out above that some of the evidence brought forward to support the harmfulness of video games is unpersuasive, we do not mean to demean or disparage the concerns that underlie the attempt to regulate them—concerns that may and doubtless do prompt a good deal of parental oversight. We have no business passing judgment on the view of the California Legislature that violent video games (or, for that matter, any other forms of speech) corrupt the young or harm their moral development. Our task is only to say whether or not such works constitute a "well-defined and narrowly limited clas[s] of speech, the prevention and punishment of which have never been thought to raise any Constitutional problem," *Chaplinsky*, 315 U. S., at 571–572 (the answer plainly is no); and if not, whether the regulation of such works is justified by that high degree of necessity we have described as a compelling state interest (it is not). Even where the protection of children is the object, the constitutional limits on governmental action apply. . . .

We affirm the judgment below.

It is so ordered.

JUSTICE ALITO, with whom THE CHIEF JUSTICE joins, concurring in the judgment.

The California statute that is before us in this case represents a pioneering effort to address what the state legislature and others regard as a potentially serious social problem: the effect of exceptionally violent video games on impressionable minors, who often spend countless hours immersed in the alternative worlds that these games create. Although the California statute is well intentioned, its terms are not framed with the precision that the Constitution demands, and I therefore agree with the Court that this particular law cannot be sustained.

I disagree, however, with the approach taken in the Court's opinion. In considering the application of unchanging constitutional principles to new and rapidly evolving technology, this Court should proceed with caution. We should make every effort to understand the new technology. We should take into account the possibility that developing technology may have important societal implications that will become apparent only with time. We should not jump to the conclusion that new technology is fundamentally the same as some older thing with which we are familiar. And we should not hastily dismiss the judgment of legislators, who may be in a better position than we are to assess the implications of new technology. The opinion of the Court exhibits none of this caution.

In the view of the Court, all those concerned about the effects of violent video games—federal and state legislators, educators, social scientists, and parents—are unduly fearful, for violent video games really present no serious problem. Spending hour upon hour controlling the actions of a character who guns down scores of innocent victims is not different in "kind" from reading a description of violence in a work of literature.

The Court is sure of this; I am not. There are reasons to suspect that the experience of playing violent video games just might be very different from reading a book, listening to the radio, or watching a movie or a television show. . . .

[Sections I and II, containing a review of the case, its evidence, and the majority opinion, have been omitted.]

[The dissent written by Justice Clarence Thomas has been omitted.]

JUSTICE BREYER, dissenting. . . .

[Sections I–III, reviewing the facts in the case and earlier precedents, have been omitted.]

IV

The upshot is that California's statute, as applied to its heartland of applications (*i.e.,* buyers under 17; extremely violent, realistic video games), imposes a restriction on speech that is modest at most. That restriction is justified by a compelling interest (supplementing parents' efforts to prevent their children from purchasing potentially harmful violent, interactive material). And there is no equally effective, less restrictive alternative. California's statute is consequently constitutional on its face—though litigants remain free to challenge the statute as applied in particular instances, including any effort by the State to apply it to minors aged 17.

I add that the majority's different conclusion creates a serious anomaly in First Amendment law. *Ginsberg* makes clear that a State can prohibit the sale to minors of depictions of nudity; today the Court makes clear that a State cannot prohibit the sale to minors of the most violent interactive video games. But what sense does it make to forbid selling to a 13-year-old boy a magazine with an image of a nude woman, while protecting a sale to that 13-year-old of an interactive video game in which he actively, but virtually, binds and gags the woman, then tortures and kills her? What kind of First Amendment would permit the government to protect children by restricting sales of that extremely violent video game *only* when the woman—bound, gagged, tortured, and killed—is also topless?

This anomaly is not compelled by the First Amendment. It disappears once one recognizes that extreme violence, where interactive, and *without literary, artistic, or similar justification,* can prove at least as, if not more, harmful to children as photographs of nudity. And the record here is more than adequate to support such a view. That is why I believe that *Ginsberg* controls the outcome here *a fortiori.* And it is why I believe California's law is constitutional on its face.

This case is ultimately less about censorship than it is about education. Our Constitution cannot succeed in securing the liberties it seeks to protect unless we can raise future generations committed cooperatively to making our system of government work. Education, however, is about choices. Sometimes, children need to learn by making choices for themselves. Other times, choices are made for children—by their parents, by their teachers, and by the people acting democratically through their governments. In my view, the First Amendment does not disable government from helping parents make such a choice here—a choice not to have their children buy extremely violent, interactive video games, which they more than reasonably fear pose only the risk of harm to those children.

For these reasons, I respectfully dissent. . . .

[The appendices of Justice Breyer's dissent have been omitted.]

Source: U.S. Supreme Court. *Brown v. Entertainment Merchants Association,* 564 U.S.__(2011). http://www.supremecourt.gov/opinions/10pdf/08-1448.pdf.

OTHER HISTORIC DOCUMENTS OF INTEREST

FROM PREVIOUS *HISTORIC DOCUMENTS*

JULY

Economic Impact of the Recession on States

JULY 1, 14, AND 24, 2011

The November 2010 elections that resulted in Republicans winning a majority of state legislatures and governorships meant that in 2011, states would be run by more fiscally conservative leaders. "Under our administration," said newly installed Wisconsin Governor Scott Walker, "state government will do only what is necessary—no more, no less." Few ambitious agendas were announced as the governors gave their State of the State addresses in early 2011, with a focus placed instead on continuing to cut. Regardless of party affiliation, however, state leaders across the country faced difficult fiscal realities and hard budgetary choices. Maryland's Democratic Governor Martin O'Malley announced that the state's 2011 budget would "feel a lot more painful than the last few."

Constitutional requirements for states to balance their budgets meant tough decisions for lawmakers. Many states chose to make significant spending cuts, which mainly impacted education, health care, employee compensation, and services for the elderly and disabled. Other states employed tax hikes to balance their budgets. In 2011, these cuts and tax hikes affected states in different ways. In Missouri, cuts to public defender services meant that offices had to stop accepting new cases. In California, state workers continued "Furlough Fridays," which forced employees to take one unpaid day off each week. Corrections took a hit in a number of states. Once a large portion of state budgets, many states now have to reconsider how they deal with first-time or nonviolent offenders, choosing to place them in rehabilitation programs rather than in overcrowded prisons. Spending was also down for K–12 education. In Hawaii, this meant four-day school weeks to avoid teacher layoffs. A national survey indicated that forty-four states had to lay off school personnel for the 2010–2011 school year, and two-thirds expected to do the same for the 2011–2012 school year. In Minnesota, a $5 billion budget gap coupled with tax increase disagreements between the governor and legislature resulted in a two-week shutdown of state government in July.

The slow economic recovery following the 2007 to 2009 recession, with state revenue still well below its peak in 2008, left little room for optimism. "You might have some ridiculously high-sounding revenue growth . . . but that's because the base is so low," said Scott Pattison, executive director of the National Association of State Budget Officers (NASBO), adding, "Don't assume happy days are here again." This pessimistic outlook was maintained through most of 2011, as tax revenue struggled to keep up with state expenditures.

RECESSION LEADS TO SLOW RECOVERY

During the recession that officially ended in 2009, states took a significant hit, mainly because of lost tax revenue. In the second quarter of 2009, income tax collections were down by 27 percent from the same time the previous year. Since peaking in 2008, by 2011 state tax collections were down 6 percent, or 11 percent when adjusted for inflation. Although overall tax revenues were slowly improving, property taxes continued to decline as home values fell. The biggest problem faced by states as revenue struggled to keep up was increased demand for government services. As more people lost their jobs or saw their income reduced, the demand for food stamps and other financial services, most specifically Medicaid, increased. States struggled to meet demand, especially in the wake of the end of funds from the American Recovery and Reinvestment Act of 2009 (ARRA) handed down by the federal government. In total, the federal government had given $145 billion to state and local governments, of which $90 billion was allocated specifically to cover Medicaid. Total assistance only covered approximately 40 percent of state budget gaps. The recovery that began in fiscal year 2011 and would continue into FY2012 would not be enough to make up for the lost ARRA funds. The federal government had anticipated that ARRA money would last long enough to get states back into a financially stable position before running out. This hope didn't materialize, and at the start of 2011, states were well aware that they were mostly on their own. "We have a $13 trillion national debt," said Oregon Governor John Kitzhaber, a Democrat. "I don't think we're looking at a whole lot of new money going down to the states from the federal government."

There was a bright spot for state governments in 2011, however—revenues had been increasing during the past six quarters. Approximately two-thirds of state revenue comes from taxes, service charges, and other miscellaneous sources such as royalties and special assessments. The remainder comes from grants. For FY2012, which runs from July 2011 to June 2012 in most states, higher general fund revenue was included in the budget, but it is still more than 3 percent lower than spending in FY2008. In FY2012, revenue collections were expected to come from an increase of 5.2 percent in personal income tax, a 0.1 percent decrease in corporate income tax, and a 0.3 percent decrease in sales tax. The decline in sales tax was related to temporary tax increases implemented by states in 2009 and 2010 to shore up budgets that were not renewed. In fact, states predicted a $584 million decline in new taxes and fees, the first net reduction since FY2007. Additionally, fewer mid-year budget cuts were expected. "I wouldn't say states have recovered, but I would say that states are on the road to recovery," said Lucy Dadayan, a senior policy analyst at the Nelson A. Rockefeller Institute of Government.

Individual states reported slow but positive growth at the end of FY2011. In Tennessee, state sales tax collections were up for the fifteen months before the close of the fiscal year, and revenues were 4 percent higher than in FY2010. However, revenues in Tennessee were not expected to return to pre-recession levels until FY2014. In New York, Comptroller Thomas DiNapoli admitted that the state's fiscal situation "is tenuous" but noted that tax collections were hundreds of millions of dollars higher than anticipated. In nearby Massachusetts, revenue was up more than 10 percent over FY2010, higher than the state had predicted. And in Virginia, the state closed out its fiscal year with a $311 million surplus, caused in part by tax collection that unexpectedly jumped 5.8 percent.

Minnesota Government Shuts Down

The continuing financial impact of the recession may have been most strongly felt in Minnesota. On July 1, 2011, the State of Minnesota experienced its second shutdown in state history. The first took place in 2005 and was relatively short with few government services closing. The 2011 shutdown came because the Democratic governor, Mark Dayton, and the Republican majority in the legislature could not agree on a two-year budget plan. The core argument was how to close a $5 billion budget gap. "I don't want to see this shutdown occur ... But I think there are basic principles and the well-being of millions of people in Minnesota that would be damaged not just for the next week or whatever long it takes, but the next two years and beyond with these kind of permanent cuts in personal care attendants and home health services and college tuition increases," Dayton said. In an effort to keep the state running, the legislature had passed a $34 billion two-year budget that included no tax increases, but Dayton vetoed the measure calling on the legislature to raise taxes on the wealthy to help close the budget gap.

When the government closed for business on July 1, approximately 22,000 state employees were laid off. Only essential services remained open, including public safety; public health maintenance of immediate concern; benefit and medical payments to individuals; and custodial care for correctional facilities, nursing homes, and veterans homes. Schools also remained open, and local governments continued to receive state aid payments. However, road construction was suspended, and all rest stops and state parks were closed. Republicans in the legislature urged the governor to call a special session to solve the budget crisis as estimates showed that the shutdown was costing millions of dollars in lost productivity.

The longest shutdown in state history came to an end on July 14, when the governor and Republicans announced a compromise. The compromise featured no tax increases and a number of spending cuts that Republicans had demanded during earlier negotiations were not included either. To close the budget gap, the state will delay payments to schools and borrow against payments expected to come in from the tobacco industry. Neither side got all of what it wanted, but Dayton said, "Public sentiment was shifting to 'Let's get this over with, regardless of what it takes.'" The agreement left open a number of questions for the next biennial budget, but a new legislature will be installed by then, and Dayton said it would be up to voters to decide "if they want this divided government to continue."

FUTURE ECONOMIC CHALLENGES FACING STATES

Slow growth in 2011 won't be enough to help states avoid future challenges. One challenge plaguing states is the job market. While the private sector enjoyed job growth in 2011, the public sector, and more specifically state and local governments, continued to shed jobs. According to the Bureau of Labor Statistics, since August 2008, states have cut 120,000 jobs and local governments have cut 527,000 jobs. Growth in the private sector still has a ways to go before it produces positive results for states as well. "Jobs have been extraordinarily slow to recover," said Donald Boyd, a senior fellow at the Rockefeller Institute. "You can't get much income tax growth without job and wage growth. People can't open up their pocket books if they don't have money to spend."

In the coming years, Medicaid is expected to make up a larger portion of state spending because of higher enrollment, an end of ARRA funds, and health care costs that are increasing faster than the economy has grown. In 2011, states were spending more on Medicaid than on any other part of their budgets. "It's hard for me to believe that Medicaid won't be the largest part of total state spending for quite awhile," said Pattison, adding, "that's pretty unbelievable." To make up for increased health care costs and the number of residents on Medicaid, a number of states lowered reimbursement rates for doctors and reduced the number of services covered. In Arizona, Medicaid coverage for organ transplants ended, leaving more than 100 Medicaid recipients on donor rolls without the likelihood of being able to pay for the cost of a transplant if a match came up. In Illinois, the state chose to stop paying its medical bills, causing some doctors and pharmacists to turn away Medicaid patients or risk bankruptcy.

Internally, the unfunded pensions and retiree health care problems that have plagued states for years show no signs of letting up. The defined benefit pension plans given to state workers are no longer a guarantee. In total, states face a $1 trillion shortfall between what they are required to pay retirees and what they have on hand. These retirement costs are being pushed onto current and former employees, who already bear a significant economic burden. In Colorado, Minnesota, and South Dakota, lawsuits were filed when the states asked retirees to pay more for their benefits. The retirees in these cases argued that the states cannot take back promises made many years ago.

But even these problems, coupled with a continuing decline in federal aid to states, are unlikely to result in states declaring bankruptcy as some local governments have done, or defaulting on their obligations. "I don't expect any states to default on any loan," said Pattison. "I cannot imagine an elected official who wants their legacy to be default, especially at the state level. What governor is going to want to be remembered for that," Pattison asked. No state government has defaulted since the 1800s.

—Heather Kerrigan

Following is a statement by Minnesota Senate Majority Leader Amy Koch on the shutdown of state government services on July 1, 2011; a press release on July 14, 2011, from Minnesota State Representative Kurt Zellers on a budget agreement; and a statement by Minnesota Governor Mark Dayton, released on July 24, 2011, describing the compromise that ended the state government shutdown.

Minnesota Majority Leader on State Government Shutdown

July 1, 2011

Senate Majority Leader Amy Koch (R-Buffalo) issued the following statement regarding Governor Dayton's decision to shut down state government:

"I am deeply disappointed in Gov. Dayton's decision to allow the State of Minnesota's government to shut down. We have been working tirelessly to meet Gov. Dayton's funding requests that in many cases, we matched 100 percent of the way. We met several times in order to bridge the gap between our differences over more complicated areas of the budget and left thinking that a budget agreement was imminent. Unfortunately, Gov. Dayton has chosen to prioritize his rigid, tax-and-spend ideology, rather than prioritize the best interests of Minnesotans as we move into the holiday weekend.

I am also troubled by Gov. Dayton's rejection of a temporary "lights on" funding bill that would have allowed government services and amenities to continue uninterrupted.

The Governor's decision is a major disappointment to me, members of the Legislature and to the citizens that we all represent. We will continue working on a solution to the state budget deficit when the time is appropriate."

Source: Office of State Senator Amy T. Koch. "Statement From Senate Majority Leader Amy Koch on Governor Dayton's Decision to Shut Down State Government." July 1, 2011. http://www.senate.leg.state .mn.us/members/member_pr_display.php?ls=&id=4066.

Minnesota Republican Leadership Announce Budget Deal

July 14, 2011

Republican Legislative Leadership met with Governor Dayton today for over three hours and agreed to a conditional budget offer to end the longest state government shutdown in recent history. The budget deal reached spends $34 billion from the General Fund, without raising taxes.

"The budget agreement in place does not raise taxes, makes targeted reductions in eight budget areas and slows the exponential growth of state spending," said Senate Majority Leader Amy Koch (R-Buffalo).

"Republicans have said all along that we do not need a tax increase to balance the budget and today Governor Mark Dayton agreed," said Speaker of the House Kurt Zellers (R-Maple Grove). "The best thing we can do to improve Minnesota's economy and create jobs is keep the tax burden down. We appreciate Governor Dayton's willingness to compromise in the best interests of the state of Minnesota. Our agreement today will result in a budget that is balanced without tax increases and a state that is back to work."

"I am pleased that we were finally able to come together with Gov. Dayton and agree to a plan that gets Minnesota moving again," said Senator Koch. "This government shutdown had a rippling effect of individuals, families and businesses all over Minnesota. Having an agreement in place is a certain sign of relief for those most adversely affected by the shutdown."

Speaker Zellers and Senate Majority Leader Koch expect to finalize details of the agreement over the next few days and have bills ready for a Special Legislative Session as early as next week.

SOURCE: Office of State Representative Kurt Zellers. "Republican Legislative Leaders Reach Budget Agreement to End State Government Shutdown Without Raising Taxes." July 14, 2011. http://www .house.leg.state.mn.us/members/pressrelease.asp?pressid=4877&party=2&memid=10811.

Gov. Dayton on Budget Compromise

July 24, 2011

The budget agreement I reached with Republican legislative leaders last week was a true compromise: no one was happy with it. However, after two weeks of the state government shutdown, I decided that someone had to take the initiative to resolve the stalemate.

So, I did.

After four days and nights of intense negotiations, the final agreement was not entirely what I believed was best for Minnesota. However, I knew that it was the best option available to Minnesota.

It achieved four top priorities.

First, it put Minnesota back to work. It became very clear to me that Republican legislators would never vote for a tax increase, not even on millionaires and multi-millionaires. Thus, the shutdown threatened to go on, and on, and on. That would have been far too damaging to the lives of far too many Minnesotans.

Second, the agreement set the State's biennial budget at $35.7 billion, $1.5 billion higher than the Republicans' "All Cuts" proposal. What that additional spending does for the people of Minnesota and their essential services was worth fighting for. From preventing cuts in special education, to increasing the state's per-pupil funding by $50/student for each year of the biennium, the first real increase school districts have received for many years.

From reducing by $50 million the savage cuts to the University of Minnesota, which the Regents said would raise tuitions by as much as 12% this fall, to preventing reductions in the hours of personal care attendants, whose assistance makes it possible for Minnesotans with disabilities to live more independent and productive lives.

From protecting home care health services to senior citizens, which enable them to live in their own homes rather than being forced into nursing homes, to preventing many thousands of Minnesotans from being forced out of affordable health care.

I could not have expected a better spending level, no matter how long the negotiations dragged on.

Third, the agreement included a $500 million bonding bill, which the Republican leaders had opposed all session. Those important projects, from needed improvements at the University of Minnesota and MnSCU campuses, to repairs at Early Childhood Learning Centers, to rebuilding the Coon Rapids Dam to stop the invasion of Asian carp, will create several thousand new jobs throughout Minnesota.

Fourth, just as important as what was in the final bills, is what was not in them. The Republicans' promise to withdraw all of their social policy legislation was crucial to the agreement. Their earlier proposals, from banning stem cell research, to prohibiting women's rights to choice, to an arbitrary 15% cut in state government employees, to eliminating teacher tenure, to slashing collective bargaining rights, ALL were eliminated.

I regret not being able to persuade Republican legislators that making Minnesota's taxes fairer by increasing state income taxes on the richest 2% of Minnesotans was in almost everyone's best interests. However, it became painfully clear that nothing would budge them from their anti-tax convictions.

Instead, they insisted upon the unwise path of additional borrowing: $700 million more in the "school shift," which will have to be repaid to the school districts, and another $640 million by issuing "tobacco bonds," which are state debt secured by proceeds from the tobacco settlement. They will need to explain to Minnesotans why an additional $1.34 billion in debt is better than raising taxes on our wealthiest citizens.

And I will continue to do my utmost to persuade Minnesotans that asking our richest citizens to pay their fair share of taxes is good public policy, and to send legislators to St. Paul who agree with me.

Some people accuse me of "caving". I don't agree. While the framework of the final agreement was originally proposed by the Republican leaders, what I agreed to was very different. All of the reactionary social policy items were removed, to the consternation of many legislators and their allies. $500 million in bonding was added. And many thousands of Minnesotans were spared a budget that would have been very hard on them.

Some of my friends are upset that I didn't get everything they or I wanted from the negotiations. Well, I wasn't negotiating with myself! The legislative leaders across the table were also passionate about their beliefs, budgets, and policies, however different they were from mine. Neither of us was going to agree to anything other than a true compromise, where both sides kept but also lost some of what they wanted.

I believe that, as people learn the details of our agreement and compare those results with the initial Republican bills, most will better understand and appreciate how much we gained and how much we saved. I hope that most Minnesotans will come to understand and appreciate that, painful and costly as the shutdown was, it was much less painful and far less costly than not only the loss of $1.5 billion in essential services for this biennium, but also the loss of an additional $1.5 billion for those services in the next biennium, and in the next, and in the next.

Now that the legislature has finally adjourned for this year, I look forward to making state government better serve the people of Minnesota at lower costs, and to bringing more jobs to our state.

SOURCE: Office of Governor Mark Dayton. Newsroom. "Ending the Shutdown Through Compromise." July 24, 2011. http://mn.gov/governor/newsroom/pressreleasedetail.jsp?id=102-14649.

OTHER HISTORIC DOCUMENTS OF INTEREST

FROM PREVIOUS *HISTORIC DOCUMENTS*

Republican Presidential Candidates on Jobs and Economic Growth

JULY 5, SEPTEMBER 6, SEPTEMBER 29, AND OCTOBER 17, 2011

In early 2011, the race for the Republican presidential nomination began in earnest. A large pool of contenders jockeyed for front-runner status while hammering away at the policies of President Barack Obama. Despite the news coverage, by April polls indicated that few Americans could name the candidates running for the nomination or were enthusiastic about their options. Throughout the summer, candidates entered and left the Republican field, and speculation about who might still enter the race increased. It was not until December when the field seemed narrowed to the four most likely contenders—former Pennsylvania Senator Rick Santorum, former Massachusetts Governor Mitt Romney, former Speaker of the House Newt Gingrich, and Texas Representative Ron Paul. Each worked diligently to vie for support with polls showing a new front-runner every few weeks.

EARLY PRIMARY ISSUES

In the early part of the primary season, Sharia law and the impact of Islam on America took center stage. Some candidates crisscrossed the country citing Sharia law, the moral and religious code of Islam, as a threat to America. "Creeping Sharia is a huge issue here in the United States," said former Pennsylvania Senator Rick Santorum. "The enemy is motivated by an interpretation of Islam, Sharia, that is antithetical to American civilization," he said. Other candidates made clear that their position was not about religion, but rather about protecting U.S. law. "We should have a federal law that says Sharia law cannot be recognized by any court in the United States," said former Speaker of the House Newt Gingrich. And others, like Texas Representative Ron Paul, disagreed that Sharia had a significant impact on the United States. "You have radicals in all religions, if there is some way to incite them, their numbers will grow," said Paul.

The start of the campaign was also marked by a number of conservative groups asking candidates to sign pledges on issues ranging from marriage rights to balanced budget amendments to abortion. The purpose of the pledges, according to these groups, was to hold candidates accountable if they were elected. Santorum, one of the most enthusiastic pledge signers, said, "At a time when voters have grown skeptical about politicians and candidates who run on a certain platform only to backtrack once elected, signing a pledge is a good way to strengthen our political promises." Many candidates signed the Cap, Cut, and Balance pledge, written by Tea Party organizations, that would hold Congress to its current spending levels and require a Constitutional balanced budget amendment. Santorum and Minnesota Representative Michelle Bachmann ended up in a pledge controversy when they signed a marriage vow written by an evangelical Christian group. The pledge called on them to block same sex marriage, oppose women in military combat roles, support childbearing and reproduction, and be faithful to their spouses. The pledge also included a statement indicating that black children were more likely to be raised by both parents under slavery than after the election of President Barack Obama. Bachmann claimed that the statement was not in any pledge that she signed, and the phrase was later removed after public backlash. Former Massachusetts Governor Mitt Romney called the pledge "undignified and inappropriate for a presidential campaign."

Speculative Candidates and Drop Outs

May ended speculation on a number of possible candidates including Indiana Governor Mitch Daniels, New Jersey Governor Chris Christie, former Mississippi Governor Haley Barbour, Donald Trump, and former Arkansas Governor Mike Huckabee. Speculation on Trump's candidacy began in early 2011, when he spoke at the Conservative Political Action Conference (CPAC). He topped polls early in the year, but a May 4 poll by Quinnipiac found that 58 percent of Americans said they would not vote for him. Political analysts argued that if he had officially joined the race, his numbers would have improved. In announcing that he would not run, Trump told supporters, "Ultimately, business is my greatest passion and I am not ready to leave the private sector."

Christie, a state budget hawk who supporters expected could draw moderate voters and would push a conservative fiscal agenda if elected, had to again announce that he would not run for the nomination on October 4, after being pressured by donors and top Republicans to reconsider entering the race. "Now is not my time," Christie said, adding that he would also not run for vice president. "I don't think there's anybody . . . in America who would . . . necessarily think my personality is best suited to being number two," Christie told supporters.

Sarah Palin, the 2008 vice presidential nominee, increased speculation about a possible run for the top spot when she launched a bus tour across the country in 2010. In May 2011, she bought a house in Arizona, further adding to speculation that she would set up a campaign headquarters there. But on October 5, pressured by a number of Republicans, Palin withdrew her name from consideration. "I believe that at this time, I can be more effective in a decisive role to help elect other true public servants to office—from the nation's governors to congressional seats and the presidency," Palin said.

Bachmann a favorite of the Tea Party, began her campaign in June and was instantly a top contender heading into the August 13 Ames, Iowa, straw poll, which she won, beating out second-place Paul. The Bachmann campaign lost momentum after the straw poll, however, because of her poor performance at the Republican debates, and she was heavily criticized for a comment during a debate about a voter who approached her to say that her daughter had become mentally handicapped after being vaccinated for human papillomavirus (HPV). In response to the comment, two bioethics professors offered up more than $10,000 for the woman to come forward and present verifiable evidence to support her claim. The American Academy of Pediatrics released a statement that there was "absolutely no scientific validity" to the comment. Bachmann dropped her bid in January 2012.

Rick Perry, the governor of Texas, was recruited to run for the nomination as part of a draft campaign, and entered the race on August 13. Perry instantly shot to the front of the pack, but weak debate performances and support for college tuition breaks for illegal immigrants hurt his credibility among conservatives. Although Perry had a solid economic record in Texas, he had little national experience to draw on and consistently turned everything back to his record as governor. On January 19, Perry withdrew his name from consideration.

Herman Cain, a radio talk show host and the former executive of Godfather's Pizza, entered the race in May, and at the time only 29 percent of Republicans knew who he was, according to a Gallup poll. Cain had no elected political experience and first caught national attention in 1994 when he challenged former President Bill Clinton at a town hall on health care. To win the September Florida straw poll and challenge Romney and Perry for the top spot in the polls, Cain drew heavily on his background of growing up poor in Georgia, working his way through school, becoming a business leader, and battling cancer. Cain's candidacy appealed to conservatives tired of being labeled racist for opposing President Obama. "Tea Party people love him," said Jenny Beth Martin, cofounder of the Tea Party Patriots. "He's not a senator or a governor. He's just a mister." Cain ran on what he considered "common-sense business solutions" and proposed replacing the federal income tax with a consumption tax. He drew criticism for offering few details on foreign policy, and garnered negative attention when he stumbled during an editorial board meeting when asked about the president's policy in Libya. Ultimately, Cain's campaign was brought down by sexual harassment claims made by women who worked with him at the National Restaurant Association while he led the organization from 1996 to 1999. Cain maintained that he was "falsely accused" but ultimately dropped his bid for the nomination on December 3.

Debates

The first debate was held by Fox News on May 5, and only included former Minnesota Governor Tim Pawlenty, Paul, Santorum, Cain, and former New Mexico Governor Gary Johnson. Cain was considered the winner of the debate, but little weight was given to the outcome because none of the candidates considered front-runners at the time were in attendance. In September, debates started in earnest and by the end of the year, more than ten major Republican debates had been held.

Romney was the strongest performer during the early debates, staking a position of not being over-the-top to appeal to Tea Party voters, and using muted language, calling Obama a "big-spending liberal" rather than a socialist, as some other candidates had. During the December debates, Gingrich, who had overtaken Romney in national polls, sparred with the former governor on policy recommendations and character. Romney attacked Gingrich's proposal to mine the moon for minerals while Gingrich attacked Romney's claims that Gingrich is a career politician stating, "The only reason you didn't become a career politician is you lost to Teddy Kennedy in 1994." Gingrich was popular for being combative with debate moderators, and became a front-runner in Florida, Iowa, and South Carolina, three of the first four primary states, following his December debate performances.

Four Top Candidates

By the end of the year, Gingrich, Romney, Santorum, and Paul emerged as top contenders for the Republican nomination. The Gingrich campaign got off to a bad start in May when he called the House Republican plan on Medicare "right-wing social engineering," defended part of Obama's health care law, and refused to comment on up to $500,000 in debt he had previously owed at Tiffany, the jewelry store. By June, Gingrich's senior staff resigned en masse, citing disagreement over the path of the campaign. Gingrich hoped to capitalize on his time as Speaker of the House in the 1990s, releasing an updated Contract with America to lay out his economic policy. It was not until September that Gingrich's polling numbers surged, which pollsters attributed to voter unease with Perry and Romney.

Romney, who also ran for the nomination in 2008, was a front-runner throughout 2011, but he alienated some conservatives because of his Massachusetts universal health care plan that was used as a blueprint for Obama's health care law, and also for shifting positions on social issues, including gun ownership. Republicans expressed concern that he may not be a strong enough candidate to compete against Obama, especially in the age of Tea Party dominance and pitchfork populism, which prefers new candidates to those with years of political experience. Given this, Romney decided to rely heavily on his business experience gained at Bain Capital, a financial services and asset management company he cofounded, to promote his economic policies and experience.

Paul, who ran for the nomination in both 1998 and 2008, used the Tea Party as a key to his success in the election cycle, sharing its values like decreased spending, fixing the national debt, not compromising, and not trusting the Republican establishment. The Texas Libertarian told voters that the "time has come around to the point where the people are agreeing with much of what I've been saying for thirty years." Paul was the most fiscally conservative of the candidates, proposing to eliminate five federal agencies. However, he also supported legalizing heroin and immediately ending almost all overseas involvement.

Santorum, who lost his Senate seat during the 2006 midterm elections, was not seen as a top contender in the race until early 2012. Like the other Republican candidates, Santorum stumped on reducing the size and scope of the federal government and opening up innovation and opportunity in the private sector. Santorum also tried to carve himself a spot as the most socially conservative contender vying for the Republican nomination, telling voters he prayed to decide whether to run for president and advocating for a family values–oriented society.

—Heather Kerrigan

Following are the jobs and economic growth platforms released by the Republican presidential front-runners. Rick Santorum's jobs plan was released on July 5, 2011; Mitt Romney's plan for economic turnaround was released on September 6, 2011; Newt Gingrich released his 21st Century Contract With America on September 29, 2011; and Ron Paul announced his economic blueprint on October 17, 2011.

DOCUMENT   *Rick Santorum Releases Jobs Plan*

July 5, 2011

. . . The Santorum vision to unlock American economic greatness and open up the job market again focuses on five simple points to create growth, spur innovation, and ensure prosperity—all centered on freeing the American people and free-enterprise:

WE MUST REDUCE THE SIZE AND SCOPE OF A GOVERNMENT THAT IS STIFLING JOB CREATION

Historically, the federal government has been 18% of America's gross domestic product. If we hope to not be served the fate of the western European countries now embattled with debt crisis after debt crisis, we must return to our historical norms. This starts by first cutting government spending, capping future government spending, and finally enacting a Balanced Budget Amendment to our constitution.

Creating a tax structure that does not punish, but encourages innovation and entrepreneurship

First and foremost, America must no longer have a tax regime that punishes the individual, the small business, or the corporation but encourages growth in America. Rick Santorum believes we need to reduce taxes on individuals across the board, making the system simpler, flatter, and fairer. Likewise, we must cut the corporate tax rate in half, so that we can once again be competitive with the rest of the industrialized world. However, we must go further and cut the tax rate to zero for all manufacturers irrespective of the tax paying entity so we can keep jobs in America. Manufacturing has epitomized the loss of American jobs and innovation over the past several decades, and by reinvigorating this crucial sector of our economy the multiplier effect on our entire economy will spur on economic and job growth not seen in three decades. We must also permanently extend the current Capital Gains and Dividend Tax rates, repeal the Death Tax, and repatriate taxable income outside the United States at a rate of 5% to induce job creation here in America rather than abroad. And, we must not only encourage innovation, but celebrate it by no longer holding entrepreneurs hostage year-in and year-out through the tax code's treatment of the research and development of new and promising discoveries—regardless of whether it is the next ground-breaking cancer treatment or a component for a fuel-efficient engine.

Removing the regulatory burdens that hold our economic engine back

The first thing nearly every executive will tell you, from sole proprietors to CEOs of international conglomerates: the existing federal regulatory structure in untenable. From the enactment of the boondoggle of ObamaCare to the CO_2 regulations of the EPA, President Obama has single-handedly placed weight after weight on our job market and economy as a whole—and Rick Santorum would immediately repeal the regulatory alphabet soup implemented by the Obama Administration. This also means ensuring that government agencies stay within their intended framework, most notably the National Labor Relations Board (NLRB) that has diverted from its purpose of protecting the rights of workers to doing the political work of President Obama's staunches union allies. Furthermore, while legislation pending before Congress is a start, Rick Santorum believes we need to streamline the patent process to unclog the patent backlog and encourage innovation in America. And likewise, to ensure America remains the global beacon of biotechnology, we must reform the transparency of the Food and Drug Administration's approval process so entrepreneurs and investors alike can have surety in the process. Finally, Rick Santorum believes that each new federal law and reauthorization of existing laws should be simpler and limit the ability of federal agencies to expand upon the law through regulation.

Ensuring global capital and credit markets believe in America again

We must repeal the burdensome Sarbanes-Oxley law that not only did not prevent the financial crisis, but chased capital overseas. At the same time, we must repeal Dodd-Frank before it can be fully-implemented and start from scratch to enact real reform that ensures the 2008 financial crisis does not happen again but at the same time does not place impediments in the way of capital formation and credit availability for average Americans. Rick Santorum believes we should not enshrine "too big to fail," and both of these laws do just that.

TAP AMERICA'S VAST DOMESTIC RESOURCES TO POWER OUR 21ST CENTURY ECONOMY

Rick Santorum believes we need to stop being naïve, put aside our dreams of "green jobs," and focus on the great domestic resources at our disposal. This means we need an all-of-the-above energy policy that utilizes oil, natural gas, coal, and nuclear energy to power our economy and empower the American worker. To do this, we must start by eliminating the Obama Administration's roadblocks to oil exploration in the Gulf of Mexico, along the Outer Continental Shelf, and onshore—including in ANWR. Furthermore, no new natural gas regulations, such as those being debated by Congress, should be enacted. The states are regulating the natural gas industry and there is no reason for the federal government to get involved. Federal regulation for federal regulation's sake serves no purpose—and in this instance it not only impedes job growth, but weakens our national security.

SOURCE: Rick Santorum for President. "The Courage to Fight for American Jobs." July 5, 2011. http://www.ricksantorum.com/news/2011/07/courage-fight-american-jobs.

Mitt Romney Releases Economic Turnaround Plan

September 6, 2011

[The introductory press release and a list of bills and executive orders Romney would submit on day one of his presidency have been omitted.]

MITT ROMNEY'S PLAN FOR JOBS AND ECONOMIC GROWTH

... Tax Policy

Mitt Romney will push for a fundamental redesign of our tax system. He recognizes the need to simplify the system. He also recognizes the need both to lower rates and to broaden the tax base so that taxation becomes an instrument for promoting economic growth. As president, Romney will hold the line on individual income tax rates and eliminate taxes on interest, dividends, and capital gains for low- and middle-income taxpayers. He will eliminate the estate tax. And he will pursue a conservative overhaul that applies lower and flatter rates to a broader tax base.

Romney will also reform the corporate tax system. He will immediately lower the corporate income tax rate, and then explore opportunities to further lower the marginal rate while broadening the tax base. He will also begin the process of transitioning to a territorial corporate tax system. A territorial system must be designed to encourage multinational companies to bring their profits back into the U.S. and it must avoid the creation of incentives for outsourcing.

Regulatory Policy

Mitt Romney will act swiftly to tear down the vast edifice of regulations the Obama Administration has imposed on the economy. He will also seek to make structural changes to the federal bureaucracy that ensure economic growth remains front and center when regulatory decisions are made. As president, Romney will work to repeal laws like Obamacare and Dodd-Frank that have given bureaucrats unprecedented discretion to craft unpredictable, job-killing regulations by the thousands of pages.

Romney will also initiate the immediate review of all Obama-era regulations with the goal of eliminating any that unduly burden the economy and job creation. And he will impose a regulatory cap on all agencies at zero dollars, meaning that an agency issuing a new regulation must go through a budget-like process and identify offsetting cost reductions from the existing regulatory burden. Other initiatives in a Romney Administration will include a new, cost-conscious approach to environmental regulation; an increased role for Congress in the approval of new regulations; and reforms to the legal liability system.

Trade Policy

Mitt Romney sees free trade as essential to restoring robust economic growth that creates jobs. The productivity and ingenuity of the American workforce are unparalleled—when American business and workers are able to compete on a level playing field, they have proved they can win. Romney will work to open foreign markets for American goods and services on terms that work for America. Specifically, Romney will submit pending Free Trade Agreements to Congress, conclude the Trans-Pacific Partnership negotiations, and seek Trade Promotion Authority to pursue new trading relationships. Romney will also create the "Reagan Economic Zone," a multilateral trading bloc open to any country committed to the principles of open markets and free enterprise.

While continuing to open new frontiers, Romney will also ensure that existing trade agreements are enforced. Romney will seek to build a constructive relationship with China on the basis of mutual respect, while also making clear that the United States will no longer tolerate Chinese practices that unfairly benefit their economy at the expense of ours. As president, Romney will take unilateral action and also partner with other nations affected by China's refusal to participate responsibly in the global economy.

Energy Policy

Mitt Romney will pursue an energy policy that puts conservative principles into action: significant regulatory reform, support for increased production, and a government that focuses on funding basic research instead of chasing fads and picking winners. Romney will streamline federal regulation of energy exploration and development so that the government acts as a facilitator of those activities instead of as an obstacle to them. He will create one-stop shops and impose fixed timelines for standard permits and approvals, and he will accelerate the process for companies with established safety records seeking to employ approved practices in approved areas.

Under this robust and efficient regulatory framework, Romney will significantly expand the areas available for energy development—including in the Gulf of Mexico, the Outer Continental Shelf, Western lands, and Alaska. He will also strengthen partnerships with Canada and Mexico to expand opportunities for American companies in the development of those nations' resources. And he will encourage continued development of unconventional reserves like shale gas and oil that hold enormous promise for expanding the base of U.S. reserves.

Labor Policy

Mitt Romney will protect the worker rights and employer flexibility crucial to innovation, economic growth, and job creation. As president, Romney's first step in improving labor policy will be to ensure that our labor laws create a stable and level playing field on which businesses can operate. This means he will appoint to the National Labor Relations Board (NLRB) experienced individuals with a respect for the law and an even-handed approach to labor relations. Rather than seek to impose his own vision for the future of labor law via executive fiat and bureaucratic subterfuge, Romney will take the conservative approach and work with Congress to amend the outdated portions of the existing statutory framework, setting it on a stronger footing appropriate to contemporary conditions.

Specifically, Romney will seek amendments to the National Labor Relations Act that protect free enterprise, free choice, and free speech. . . .

Human Capital Policy

Mitt Romney sees two important objectives that America can pursue immediately to build on the extraordinary traditional strengths of its workforce. The first is to retrain American workers to ensure that they have the education and skills to match the jobs of today's economy. The second is to attract the best and brightest from around the world. As president, Romney will focus retraining efforts on a partnership that brings together the states and the private sector. He will consolidate federal programs and then block grant major funding streams to states. Federal policy will be structured to encourage the use of Personal Reemployment Accounts that empower workers to put retraining funds to efficient use and that encourage employers to provide on-the-job training.

Romney will also press for an immigration policy that maximizes America's economic potential. The United States needs to attract and retain job creators from wherever they come. Romney will raise the ceiling on the number of visas issued to holders of advanced degrees in math, science, and engineering who have job offers in those fields from U.S. companies. Romney will also work to establish a policy that staples a green card to the diploma of every eligible student visa holder who graduates from an American university with an advanced degree in math, science, or engineering.

Fiscal Policy

The only recipe for fiscal health and a thriving private economy is a government that spends within its means. Mitt Romney will immediately move to cut spending and cap it at 20 percent of GDP. As spending comes under control, he will pursue further cuts that would allow caps to be set even lower so as to guarantee future fiscal stability. As a first step in this direction, Romney will move immediately to cut non-security discretionary spending by 5 percent.

But more will be required to bring the budget under control. Romney will also work to reform Medicaid, converting it to a federal block grant administered by the states, and he will provide the leadership necessary to make progress in reforming other entitlement programs. He will undertake a fundamental restructuring of the federal government that places the burden on the federal agency to establish why a program or service must be provided at the federal level and gives to the private sector and the states whatever functions they can perform more effectively. Finally, he will pursue a Balanced Budget Amendment to ensure that the out-of-control borrowing and spending of the Obama Administration is never repeated. . . .

Source: Romney for President, Inc. "Fact Sheet: Mitt Romney's Plan to Turn Around the Economy." September 6, 2011. http://www.mittromney.com/news/press/2011/09/fact-sheet-mitt-romneys-plan-turn-around-economy.

Newt Gingrich's 21st Century Contract With America

September 29, 2011

[A letter from Gingrich preceding the legislative proposals has been omitted.]

Legislative Proposals

1. **Repeal Obamacare** and pass a replacement that saves lives and money by empowering patients and doctors, not bureaucrats and politicians.

2. **Return to robust job creation** with a bold set of tax cuts and regulatory reforms that will free American entrepreneurs to invest and hire, as well as by reforming the Federal Reserve and creating a training requirement for extended federal unemployment benefits to encourage work and improve the quality of our workforce.

3. **Unleash America's full energy production potential** in oil, natural gas, coal, biofuels, wind, nuclear oil shale and more, creating jobs, stimulating a sustainable manufacturing boom, lowering gasoline and other energy prices, increasing government revenues, and bolstering national security.

4. **Save Medicare and Social Security** by giving Americans more choices and tools to live longer, healthier lives with greater financial independence.

5. **Balance the federal budget** by freeing job-creators to grow the economy, reforming entitlements, and implementing waste cutting and productivity improvement systems such as Lean Six Sigma to eliminate waste and fraud. Pass a balanced budget amendment to keep it balanced.

6. **Control the border by January 1, 2014** and establish English as the official language of government; reform the legal visa system, and make it much easier to deport criminals and gang members while making it easier for law abiding visitors to come to the US.

7. **Revitalize our national security system** to meet 21st century threats by restructuring and adequately funding our security agencies to function within a grand strategy for victory over those who seek to kill us or limit American power.

8. **Maximize the speed and impact of medical breakthroughs** by removing unnecessary obstacles that block new treatments from reaching patients and emphasizing research spending towards urgent national priorities, like brain science with its impact on Alzheimer's, autism, Parkinson's, mental health and other conditions knowledge of the brain will help solve.

9. **Restore the proper role of the judicial branch** by using the clearly delineated powers available to the president and Congress to correct, limit, or replace judges who violate the Constitution.

10. **Enforce the Tenth Amendment** by starting an orderly transfer of power and responsibility from the federal government back "to the states, respectively, or to the people," as the Constitution requires. Over the next year, state and local officials and citizens will be asked to identify the areas which can be transferred back home.

SOURCE: Newt 2012. "21st Century Contract With America." September 29, 2011. http://www.newt.org/sites/newt.org/files/volunteer/docs/21stcenturyB%20copy.pdf.

Ron Paul Announces Plan to Restore Economy

October 17, 2011

EXECUTIVE SUMMARY

Synopsis:

. . . Ron Paul's "Plan to Restore America" slams on the brakes and puts America on a return to constitutional government. It is bold but achievable. Through the bully pulpit of the presidency, the power of the Veto, and, most importantly, the united voice of freedom-loving Americans, we can implement fundamental reforms.

Delivers a True Balanced Budget in year three of Dr. Paul's Presidency:

Ron Paul is the ONLY candidate who doesn't just talk about balancing the budget, but who has a full plan to get it done.

Spending:

Cuts $1 trillion in spending during the first year of Ron Paul's presidency, eliminating five cabinet departments (Energy, HUD, Commerce, Interior, and Education), abolishing the Transportation Security Administration and returning responsibility for security to private property owners, abolishing corporate subsidies, stopping foreign aid, ending foreign wars, and returning most other spending to 2006 levels.

Entitlements:

Honors our promise to our seniors and veterans, while allowing young workers to opt out. Block-grants Medicaid and other welfare programs to allow States the flexibility and ingenuity they need to solve their own unique problems without harming those currently relying on the programs.

Cutting Government Waste:

Makes a 10% reduction in the federal workforce, slashes Congressional pay and perks, and curbs excessive federal travel. To stand with the American People, President Paul will take a salary of $39,336, approximately equal to the median personal income of the American worker.

Taxes:

Lowers the corporate tax rate to 15%, making America competitive in the global market. Allows American companies to repatriate capital without additional taxation, spurring trillions in new investment. Extends all Bush tax cuts. Abolishes the Death Tax. Ends taxes on personal savings, allowing families to build a nest egg.

Regulation:

Repeals ObamaCare, Dodd-Frank, and Sarbanes-Oxley. Mandates REINS-style requirements for thorough Congressional review and authorization before implementing any new regulations issued by bureaucrats. President Paul will also cancel all onerous regulations previously issued by Executive Order.

Monetary Policy:

Conducts a full audit of the Federal Reserve and implements competing currency legislation to strengthen the dollar and stabilize inflation.

Conclusion:

Dr. Paul is the only candidate with a plan to cut spending and truly balance the budget. This is the only plan that will deliver what America needs in these difficult times: Major regulatory relief, large spending cuts, sound monetary policy, and a balanced budget. . . .

[The charts and graphs have been omitted.]

SOURCE: Ron Paul 2012 Presidential Campaign Committee Inc. "Ron Paul's 'Plan to Restore America.'" October 17, 2011. http://c3244172.r72.cf0.rackcdn.com/wp-content/uploads/2011/10/RestoreAmericaPlan .pdf.

OTHER HISTORIC DOCUMENTS OF INTEREST

NASA on End of Space Shuttle Program, Future of U.S. Space Exploration

---

JULY 8, JULY 12, AND JULY 21, 2011

In the summer of 2011, the National Aeronautics and Space Administration (NASA) and the American public prepared to say good-bye to the space shuttle program. After thirty years of scientific discovery and advancement mixed with cost overruns, program delays, and technological and safety failures, NASA retired its remaining shuttle fleet and began focusing on new goals for space exploration set forth by the administration of President Barack Obama.

End of an Era

The shuttle program began as an effort to establish a system for inexpensive, reliable transportation into low-Earth orbit. NASA designed the shuttle for repeated use, initially envisioning fifty launches per year, with the capability to carry satellites and other large payloads into space. Once construction began on the International Space Station, the shuttle also became the primary vehicle for transporting staff and supplies to the space-based laboratory.

The shuttle fleet originally consisted of five vehicles—*Discovery, Atlantis, Endeavour, Columbia,* and *Challenger. Columbia* made the first flight of the program on April 12, 1981. However, only three of the shuttles remained in service until the end of the program. In the shuttle program's first tragedy, *Challenger* exploded during takeoff on January 28, 1986, killing all seven people on board. The explosion was later traced to a failed O-ring, a seal connecting sections of the shuttle's rocket boosters, which likely froze in the unusually cold temperatures and caused a fuel leak. Then in 2003, *Columbia* broke apart as it attempted to re-enter Earth's atmosphere. An investigation into the incident determined that a piece of insulating foam on the shuttle's external fuel tank broke off during launch, hitting and damaging the heat shield tiles on the shuttle's left wing. The damage compromised the shuttle's ability to protect against the extreme heat of re-entry, causing it to slowly break apart and leading to the deaths of the seven-member crew.

Both tragedies served to highlight the risks of the shuttle program, but also called attention to the technological and safety issues that often caused NASA to delay or cancel flights. Program scrutiny intensified after the *Columbia* Accident Investigation Board released a report in August 2003 pointing to the "broken safety culture" at NASA and claiming that various missteps and organizational problems at the agency were as much to blame for the *Columbia* tragedy as the technical problems plaguing the shuttle. The report also noted that schedule pressures and an insufficient budget led NASA to de-emphasize the shuttle program's risk while placing success over safety. Among its recommendations for resolving these issues was a call for a significant increase in funding for NASA. Yet lawmakers questioned whether maintaining manned spaceflight was worth the investment, particularly given the country's mounting deficit, and considering the costs of the shuttle program to date. When the program launched, NASA had estimated each flight would cost approximately $7 million, but the true cost was closer to $1 billion. Various estimates of the program's total cost fall between $193 billion and $211 billion.

These considerations, and the knowledge that the shuttle fleet had nearly reached the end of its useful life, led then- President George W. Bush to call for an end to the shuttle program in January 2004. In unveiling his proposed NASA budget on January 14, Bush set a new goal for the agency—to return to the Moon no later than 2020 and eventually build and use a lunar base as a launching pad for missions to Mars. Bush said NASA would retire its remaining space shuttles by 2010 and replace them with a new crew exploration vehicle capable of traveling to the Moon. The president said he would seek an additional $11 billion over the next five years to begin research for the new program, and directed NASA to divert an additional $11 billion from existing programs to develop the technology necessary to go back to the Moon. Space policy experts questioned Bush's funding requests early on, expressing concerns that his proposed budget was not fiscally realistic, and that it did not take into account organizational realities within the agency.

In an effort to meet these new goals, NASA began work to develop a new spacecraft and launch system to replace the shuttle. Yet the project, named Constellation, was short-lived. On February 1, 2010, President Barack Obama announced an end to the program in making his annual budget request for NASA. His administration concluded that Constellation, which had already cost $9 billion, was "over budget, behind schedule, and lacking in innovation," and that increased collaboration between NASA and the private sector would result in a program that was more cost-efficient. Administration officials had authorized an independent review of NASA's programs in 2009, which concluded that Constellation would not be workable unless it received an additional $3 billion per year in restored funding. The review panel outlined several alternatives to the Constellation program, and advocated for a "flexible path" approach to spaceflight that would rely on private industry to conduct manned flights to and from low-Earth orbit while NASA focused on developing a new heavy-lift rocket and vehicle that could support deep space flight. In line with these recommendations, Obama set a goal of conducting a manned flight to an asteroid by 2025 and a mission to Mars in the 2030s. His budget request included $6 billion to stimulate commercial development of low-Earth orbit manned spaceflight capabilities and $3.1 billion for NASA to develop technologies for the heavy-lift rockets necessary for deep space flight.

THE SHUTTLE'S FINAL FLIGHT

As lawmakers and NASA administrators continued mapping the agency's future, the country prepared for the shuttle's final flight. Scheduled for takeoff on July 8, 2011, the shuttle *Atlantis* would carry a four-person crew and more than 9,000 pounds of supplies to the International Space Station. The mission also involved an experiment called the Robotic Refueling Mission, which was designed to test the tools and technologies needed for robotic refueling of satellites in space.

When *Atlantis* landed back at NASA's Kennedy Space Center in Cape Canaveral, Florida, on July 21, 2011, it marked the end of a storied program that, while flawed, boasted a number of achievements. The program's five shuttles had launched and repaired the Hubble Space Telescope, built the space station, and carried the country's first female and minority astronauts into space. A total of 355 individuals from sixteen countries flew 135 missions aboard the shuttle, which travelled more than 542 million miles and hosted more than 2,000 varied scientific experiments.

Emotions ran high among *Atlantis*'s crew and the 2,000 spectators who gathered at the runway to watch the shuttle return home. "I saw grown men and grown women crying today–tears of joy to be sure," said shuttle launch director Mike Leinbach, and crew member Rex Walheim later told reporters that he and the rest of the crew all became choked up. NASA Administrator Charles Bolden took the opportunity to assure Americans that the agency remained committed to continuing human spaceflight and ensuring the United States remained a leader in space for years to come. "The future is bright for human spaceflight and for NASA," Bolden said. "That future begins today."

Beyond the Shuttle

The future of which Bolden spoke relied in part on collaboration with international partners and commercial entities. NASA signed a deal with Russia to provide U.S. astronauts with twelve round-trip flights to the International Space Station at a cost of $753 million, or $62.7 million per seat, until an American company is able to provide the same service. The agency will also contract with private company SpaceX to fly supply missions to the space station through 2016.

NASA also began working with private companies to develop and test a new rocket powerful enough to launch future deep space missions. Several companies already have rockets in development that could be modified to meet NASA's needs. This includes SpaceX's Falcon 9. NASA awarded the company a $75 million contract to work on upgrading the medium-lift rocket, which SpaceX said could be ready for manned spaceflight by 2014. The Spaceship Company, owned by Virgin Group Chairman Sir Richard Branson and Burt Rutan, is also working on two vehicles that will offer suborbital spaceflights to the public, and eventually plans to offer orbital flights and satellite launches. Other companies such as Blue Origin, Space Adventures, and XCOR Aerospace are also working to develop launch vehicles for both manned and unmanned flights, and it is possible their technologies and designs could provide an inexpensive starting point for NASA's heavy-lift rocket. In testimony before the House Committee on Science, Space, and Technology, Bolden told lawmakers that NASA was evaluating all options for the new launch system and had conducted an analysis of alternatives to compare the advantages and disadvantages of various technical designs, which included collecting industry suggestions and comments. Bolden said NASA's goal was to have a launch system in place for an unmanned developmental flight or mission in late 2017. He also noted such extensive research efforts were intended to ensure the agency's future programs would be more efficient, affordable, and sustainable.

At the same time, NASA restarted its work on the *Orion* Crew Exploration Vehicle, originally begun under the cancelled Constellation program. Bolden told lawmakers he had determined that *Orion* could still meet the needs of NASA's new deep space–focused program, and that continuing its development would prevent a waste of already spent resources. The *Orion* vehicle is intended to support a crew of four people for up to twenty-one-day missions, but can be modified to support longer missions.

LOCAL IMPACT

While NASA planned for the next chapter of human spaceflight, communities in Florida and Texas worried about the impact the shuttle program's end would have on their local economies, particularly as agency employees and contractors faced layoffs. At the peak of the shuttle program, about 32,000 people worked at the Kennedy Space Center alone. A 2008 study conducted by NASA found that the agency accounted for approximately $4.1 billion in economic output for Florida and 40,802 jobs, both at its own facilities, and at high-tech businesses serving the space program. The facility's visitor center also helped drive the tourism industry, attracting 1.6 million out-of-state visitors each year.

Yet with the shuttle program's end, NASA completed several rounds of layoffs, leaving approximately 8,000 employees in place at the Florida center. Similar layoffs occurred at the Johnson Space Center in Houston. While many former NASA employees, particularly those with science and engineering skills, have been able to find new jobs in other sectors, business development officials expect a negative ripple effect in both regions stemming from the agency's downsizing.

FUTURE CHALLENGES

The loss of personnel may also create future challenges for NASA. While staffing cuts were necessary in light of the shuttle program's end, some question whether those layoffs, and the choice by some personnel to leave before layoffs began, will result in a brain drain at the agency that could hinder the success of future projects. The agency's astronaut corps has also dwindled to 60 from a high of 149 in 2000. According to chief astronaut Peggy Whitson, NASA needs to maintain that number in order to be able to complete future missions. Officials acknowledge it may be difficult to sustain morale and attract and retain astronauts and other employees without a project similar in clarity, scope, and ambition to the shuttle program in place.

NASA is likely to continue facing budget challenges that could delay its new commercial and deep space projects. In November 2011, Congress approved a $17.8 billion budget for the agency, less than what President Obama had requested. That total includes $406 million to support NASA's collaboration with commercial companies to develop a new low-Earth orbit spaceflight program, less than half the amount the agency originally requested. Due to the lack of funding, NASA administrators have suggested the commercial program may have to be pushed back from a 2015 launch to 2017.

—Linda Fecteau

Following is a press release from the National Aeronautics and Space Administration (NASA), released on July 8, 2011, marking the launch of the final mission of NASA's space shuttle program; the edited transcript of testimony given by NASA Administrator Charles Bolden on July 12, 2011, before a Congressional panel on the future of the space program in the United States; and two press releases from NASA, both on July 21, 2011, marking the final space shuttle landing.

NASA Marks Start of Final Space Shuttle Mission

July 8, 2011

Space shuttle Commander Chris Ferguson and his three crewmates are on their way to the International Space Station after launching from NASA's Kennedy Space Center at 11:29 a.m. EDT Friday. STS-135 is the final mission of NASA's Space Shuttle Program.

"With today's final launch of the space shuttle we turn the page on a remarkable period in America's history in space, while beginning the next chapter in our nation's extraordinary story of exploration," Administrator Charles Bolden said. "Tomorrow's destinations will inspire new generations of explorers, and the shuttle pioneers have made the next chapter of human spaceflight possible."

The STS-135 crew consists of Ferguson, Pilot Doug Hurley, Mission Specialists Sandy Magnus and Rex Walheim. They will deliver the Raffaello multi-purpose logistics module filled with more than 8,000 pounds of supplies and spare parts to sustain space station operations after the shuttles are retired.

"The shuttle's always going to be a reflection to what a great nation can do when it dares to be bold and commits to follow through," Ferguson said shortly before liftoff. "We're not ending the journey today . . . we're completing a chapter of a journey that will never end."

The mission includes flying the Robotic Refueling Mission, an experiment designed to demonstrate and test the tools, technologies and techniques needed for robotic refueling of satellites in space, even satellites not designed for servicing. The crew also will return with an ammonia pump that recently failed on the station. Engineers want to understand why the pump failed and improve designs for future spacecraft.

Atlantis is on a 12-day mission and scheduled to dock to the station at 11:06 a.m. on Sunday.

STS-135 is the 135th shuttle flight, the 33rd flight for Atlantis and the 37th shuttle mission dedicated to station assembly and maintenance. NASA's Web coverage of STS-135 includes mission information, a press kit, interactive features, news conference images, graphics and videos. . . .

SOURCE: National Aeronautics and Space Administration. Press Release Archives. "NASA's Final Space Shuttle Mission Begins With Atlantis' Launch." July 8, 2011. http://www.nasa.gov/home/hqnews/2011/jul/HQ_11-216_STS-135_Launch.html.

NASA Administrator Bolden on Future of Space Program

July 12, 2011

Chairman Hall and Members of the Committee, thank you for the opportunity to appear before you today to discuss the future of NASA's human spaceflight program, and in particular the progress NASA is making on developing the next-generation human spaceflight transportation systems known as the Space Launch System (SLS) and the Multi-Purpose Crew Vehicle (MPCV), as well as their associated mission and ground support elements and other programs.

With passage of the NASA Authorization Act of 2010 (P.L. 111-267) on October 11, 2010, NASA has a clear direction for our human spaceflight programs. NASA appreciates the significant effort made in advancing this important bipartisan legislation, and we look forward to working with you to shape a promising future for our Nation's human space-flight programs. With the enactment of the FY 2011 Full-Year Continuing Appropriations Act (P.L. 112-10), NASA is aggressively moving forward with our next-generation human spaceflight system development efforts as authorized.

The President's FY 2012 budget request continues to focus Agency efforts on a vigor-ous path of innovation and technological development leading to an array of challenging and inspiring missions to destinations with an incredible potential for discovery, increasing our knowledge of our solar system, developing technologies to improve life, expanding our presence in space, increasing space commerce, and engaging the public. The request sup-ports an aggressive launch rate of about 40 missions from FY 2011 through FY 2012, including U.S. and international flights to the International Space Station (ISS) as well as science missions flown to Earth orbit and beyond. Within the human spaceflight arena, our foremost priority is safely and productively conducting our current human spaceflight endeavor. The FY 2012 budget request also maintains a strong commitment to human spaceflight beyond low-Earth orbit (LEO) via a capability-driven architecture that will focus on increasingly complex missions as we develop the technical expertise to reach des-tinations ever deeper into our solar system. At present, as designated by the President, our initial destination for a human mission is a crewed flight to an asteroid by 2025, followed by a human mission to Mars in the mid-2030's. Our post-Shuttle human spaceflight plan also focuses on utilization and operation of the ISS and on establishing a U.S. commercial cargo and crew capability to reach this National Laboratory. It establishes critical priorities and invests in the technologies and excellent science, aeronautics research, and education programs that will help us win the future.

In terms of our next-generation human spaceflight system, the SLS and MPCV will be capable of transporting astronauts to multiple destinations beyond LEO. The capabilities provided by these two vehicle systems are necessary for all activities beyond LEO. While our plan calls for the initial destination for human flight beyond LEO to target an asteroid by 2025, other destinations could include cis-lunar space such as the Earth-Moon Lagrange points, the lunar surface, and eventually Mars and its moons. All of these places hold incredible information for us—information that we probably do not even know exists at this point. Compelling missions to advance exploration will be enabled by coupling these spacecraft systems with others needed for particular missions. This journey begins with the SLS and MPCV as the first important core elements of the evolutionary exploration approach to accomplishing a broad spectrum of missions.

To date, as NASA has reported to the Committee, the Agency has determined that the beyond-LEO version of the Orion Crew Exploration Vehicle is NASA's new MPCV, and as such, the current Orion contract with Lockheed Martin Corporation is being used through at least the development phase of the vehicle.

NASA has been working expeditiously to complete assessments of SLS design options and develop a final integrated proposal for MPCV/Orion and SLS. NASA has been conduct-ing detailed technical analysis since the enactment of the NASA Authorization Act of 2010, and is working towards selecting a technical approach that will meet the intent of the SLS configuration described in the NASA Authorization of 2010 and enable the Nation to conduct a sustainable program of exploration. NASA's intent is that the design would evolve over time to meet the end goals of the SLS configuration in the Authorization Act. NASA is exploring strategic approaches that would be adaptable to modifications in annual funding and still make significant progress toward the end design. The SLS and MPCV teams are continuing to develop an integrated development plan that will be affordable in the near term and over the long run. In doing so, we are striving to design an evolvable and interoperable human spaceflight transportation system that will serve us for decades to come as we explore multiple compelling mission destinations. Due diligence will ensure the best value for the taxpayer with respect to cost, risk, schedule, performance, and impacts to critical NASA and industrial skills and capabilities in this multi-billion dollar endeavor.

While NASA has made significant progress to date on both the SLS and the MPCV, much work remains ahead for the Agency, as we finalize development plans and acquisition decisions per normal Agency processes for the SLS—decisions that must remain consistent with NASA's Strategic Plan and Agency commitments, as well as the NASA Authorization Act of 2010.

In a constrained budget environment, NASA knows how important it is to identify ways to make our programs and projects more efficient, so finding and incorporating these efficiencies remains a primary goal. We have embraced the challenge to deliver human spaceflight systems for lower cost, and the opportunity to become more efficient, innovative and agile in our programs. For example, we are revising the management of our requirements, contracts, and projects and incorporating approaches to ensure affordability in the near term and over the long run. This includes the use of focused insight/oversight, specifying to industry—where appropriate—what we need instead of how to build it, designing for cost-effective operations, increasing the use of common components and parts, and wisely consolidating infrastructure.

The remainder of my testimony will address progress made to date on the SLS and MPCV Programs, as well as outlining the work ahead of us in order to ensure that we develop systems that reflect the NASA Authorization Act of 2010 using an affordable, sustainable and realistic approach.

However, before I explore those topics, I would like to take a moment to personally recognize the thousands of NASA civil servants and industry team members who have worked selflessly for countless hours, often under difficult circumstances and in a turbulent environment, to make our human spaceflight programs and projects productive and successful. In the days ahead, these incredible and talented employees will continue to do whatever it takes to make sure that the United States remains the world's leader in human spaceflight. After all, they do not know how to commit to anything less. I would also like to thank the Committee for its continued strong support for NASA's human spaceflight programs and their value to the Nation, especially as we work hard to finalize details of a well-thought-out strategy for our next-generation human spaceflight programs.

[The following six and a half pages have been omitted and include further details on NASA's research and development of a space launch system and multi-purpose crew vehicle.]

In conclusion, Americans and people worldwide have turned to NASA for inspiration throughout our history—our work gives people an opportunity to imagine what is barely possible, and we at NASA get to turn those dreams into real achievements for all humankind.

With the passage of the NASA Authorization Act of 2010, NASA has a clear direction and is making plans for moving the Agency forward. Today, we have a roadmap to even more historic achievements that will spur innovation, employ Americans in fulfilling jobs, and engage people around the world as we enter an exciting new era in space. NASA appreciates the significant effort that has gone into advancing this bipartisan legislation.

Let me assure you that NASA is committed to meeting the spaceflight goals of the Nation and fulfilling the requirements of the NASA Authorization Act of 2010. As such, we are committed to developing an affordable, sustainable, and realistic next-generation human spaceflight system that will enable human exploration, scientific discovery, broad commercial benefits, and inspirational missions that are in the best interests of the Nation. We look forward to working with you and other Members of Congress as we finalize our strategy for achieving human spaceflight to many destinations in our solar system.

Chairman Hall and Members of the Committee, I would like to conclude my remarks by thanking you again for your continued support for NASA and its human spaceflight programs. I would be pleased to respond to any questions you or the other Members of the Committee may have.

Source: National Aeronautics and Space Administration. "Statement of The Honorable Charles F. Bolden, Jr., Administrator, National Aeronautics and Space Administration, Before the Committee on Science, Space and Technology." July 12, 2011. http://www.nasa.gov/pdf/569239main_Bolden_2011_0712_HSST-finalx.pdf.

NASA Administrator on Final Space Shuttle Landing

July 21, 2011

NASA Administrator Charles Bolden today issued this statement about the final landing of the Space Shuttle Program:

"At today's final landing of the space shuttle, we had the rare opportunity to witness history. We turned the page on a remarkable era and began the next chapter in our nation's extraordinary story of exploration.

The brave astronauts of STS-135 are emblematic of the shuttle program. Skilled professionals from diverse backgrounds who propelled America to continued leadership in space with the shuttle's many successes. It is my great honor today to welcome them home.

I salute them and all of the men and women who have flown shuttle missions since the very first launch on April 12, 1981.

The shuttle program brought our nation many firsts. Many proud moments, some of which I was privileged to experience myself as a shuttle commander. I was proud to be part of the shuttle program and will carry those experiences with me for the rest of my life.

As we move forward, we stand on the shoulders of these astronauts and the thousands of people who supported them on the ground—as well as those who cheered their triumphs and mourned their tragedies.

This final shuttle flight marks the end of an era, but today, we recommit ourselves to continuing human spaceflight and taking the necessary—and difficult—steps to ensure America's leadership in human spaceflight for years to come.

I want to send American astronauts where we've never been before by focusing our resources on exploration and innovation, while leveraging private sector support to take Americans to the International Space Station in low Earth orbit.

With the bold path President Obama and Congress have set us on, we will continue the grand tradition of exploration.

Children who dream of being astronauts today may not fly on the space shuttle . . . but, one day, they may walk on Mars. The future belongs to us. And just like those who came before us, we have an obligation to set an ambitious course and take an inspired nation along for the journey.

I'm ready to get on with the next big challenge.

The future is bright for human spaceflight and for NASA. American ingenuity is alive and well. And it will fire up our economy and help us win the future, but only if we dream big and imagine endless possibilities. That future begins today."

SOURCE: National Aeronautics and Space Administration. Press Release Archives. "NASA Administrator Commemorates Final Space Shuttle Landing." July 21, 2011. http://www.nasa.gov/home/hqnews/2011/jul/HQ_11-241_Bolden_Statement.html.

NASA Marks End of Space Shuttle Program

July 21, 2011

Wrapping up 30 years of unmatched achievements and blazing a trail for the next era of U.S. human spaceflight, NASA's storied Space Shuttle Program came to a "wheels stop" on Thursday at the conclusion of its 135th mission.

Shuttle Atlantis and its four-astronaut crew glided home for the final time, ending a 13-day journey of more than five million miles with a landing at 5:57 a.m. EDT at NASA's Kennedy Space Center in Florida. It was the 26th night landing (20th night and 78th total landings at Kennedy) and the 133rd landing in shuttle history.

"The brave astronauts of STS-135 are emblematic of the shuttle program—skilled professionals from diverse backgrounds who propelled America to continued leadership in space with the shuttle's many successes," NASA Administrator Charles Bolden said. "This final shuttle flight marks the end of an era, but today, we recommit ourselves to continuing human spaceflight and taking the necessary—and difficult—steps to ensure America's leadership in human spaceflight for years to come."

Since STS-1 launched on April 12, 1981, 355 individuals from 16 countries flew 852 times aboard the shuttle. The five shuttles traveled more than 542 million miles and hosted more than 2,000 experiments in the fields of Earth, astronomy, biological and materials sciences.

The shuttles docked with two space stations, the Russian Mir and the International Space Station. Shuttles deployed 180 payloads, including satellites, returned 52 from space and retrieved, repaired and redeployed seven spacecraft.

The STS-135 crew consisted of Commander Chris Ferguson, Pilot Doug Hurley, Mission Specialists Sandra Magnus and Rex Walheim. They delivered more than 9,400 pounds of spare parts, spare equipment and other supplies in the Raffaello multi-purpose logistics module—including 2,677 pounds of food—that will sustain space station operations for the next year. The 21-foot long, 15-foot diameter Raffaello brought back nearly 5,700 pounds of unneeded materials from the station . . . .

SOURCE: National Aeronautics and Space Administration. Press Release Archives. "NASA's Proud Space Shuttle Program Ends With Atlantis Landing." July 21, 2011. http://www.nasa.gov/home/hqnews/2011/jul/HQ_11-240_Atlantis_Lands.html.

OTHER HISTORIC DOCUMENTS OF INTEREST

FROM PREVIOUS *HISTORIC DOCUMENTS*

- NASA on the Return of the Shuttle Discovery to Space, *2005*, p. 498
- Investigating Board on the Columbia Space Shuttle Disaster, *2003*, p. 631
- John Glenn's Return to Space on Shuttle Mission, *1998*, p. 776
- Challenger Accident Commission Report, *1986*, p. 515
- Space Shuttle Mission Report, *1981*, p. 417

Consumer Financial Protection Bureau Director Nomination and Hearing

JULY 18, JULY 21, AND SEPTEMBER 6, 2011

The Consumer Financial Protection Bureau (CFPB) was created by the Dodd-Frank financial reform legislation signed by President Barack Obama in July 2010. Dodd-Frank has been under attack since its inception, and by the time the agency officially opened on July 21, 2011, there were already twenty bills pending in Congress to undo some of the legislation's provisions.

The Bureau is considered to be the federal response to consumer complaints about deceptive lending practices that led to the 2007–2008 credit crisis and subsequent economic meltdown. By creating the CFPB, Dodd-Frank merged consumer protection responsibility from being spread across seven agencies into one single agency charged with protecting consumers from deceptive financial practices. Until a director was appointed to lead the CFPB, however, it would not be able to fully assume its consumer financial protection responsibilities, a point of significant partisan bickering on Capitol Hill in 2011.

CFPB GOALS

The official language establishing the CFPB said the Bureau will "implement and, where applicable, enforce Federal consumer financial law consistently for the purpose of ensuring that all consumers have access to markets for consumer financial products and services and that markets for consumer financial products and services are fair, transparent and competitive." With this authority, the CFPB would investigate and enforce consumer protection law, issue subpoenas and require testimony in federal court, and write and enforce new standards for financial products. The Bureau was expected to look at mortgage lending, credit cards, payday loans, banking fees, and a host of other consumer financial products. The Bureau's reach does have limits, however. Those not under the purview of the new department include larger banks, automobile dealers, and real estate brokers.

A larger goal of the Bureau would be consumer education and watching for major violations of mortgage disclosure laws or other problems that cause consumers to undertake risky borrowing decisions. "This means ensuring that consumers get the information they need to make the financial decisions they believe are best for themselves and their families—that prices are clear up front, that risks are visible, and that nothing is buried in fine print. In a market that works, consumers should be able to make direct comparisons among products and no provider should be able to build, or feel pressure to build, a business model around unfair, deceptive, or abusive practices," the Bureau's website states.

The idea of a consumer protection bureau in the federal government was the idea of Elizabeth Warren, a Harvard law professor, who first proposed the body in 2007. "Personal responsibility will always play a critical role in dealing with credit cards, just as personal responsibility remains a central feature in the safe use of any other product. But a Financial Product Safety Commission could eliminate some of the most egregious tricks and traps in the credit industry," she said at the time. President Barack Obama brought Warren on board in September 2010, not as director of the CFPB but as special assistant to the president who would have oversight of the day-to-day Bureau activities. By not giving her the director position, Obama ensured that she would not need to be confirmed by the Senate.

SUPPORT AND OPPOSITION

Many Republicans and lobbyists from the banking industry oppose the Bureau, arguing that Wall Street did not cause the financial crisis, but it can help solve it. By adding additional regulation of financial markets through the Bureau, they argue, the government is hindering recovery. "The fact is that any attempt to manage the market is unlikely to work, and the cost of that management ends up being borne by the consumer," said David John, the lead financial markets analyst with the Heritage Foundation, a conservative think tank. Opponents also expressed concerns about the funding method for the Bureau—it does not go through the Congressional appropriations and budget process— and whether consumers would have to absorb the costs of any new regulations. They also expressed concern that the additional regulations and costs would lead to a decrease in the availability of products and would put some small financial institutions out of business.

One of the biggest points of contention in Congress was the power structure within the Bureau. "This agency . . . will have unprecedented reach and control over individual consumer decisions—but an unprecedented lack of oversight and accountability," said Sen. Mitch McConnell, R-Ky. As established by Dodd-Frank, the Bureau has one director who is advised by a six-member panel made up of finance and consumer protection experts appointed through recommendation from regional Federal Reserve Bank presidents. A group of regulators, known as the Financial Stability Oversight Council, made up of nine federal regulatory agency heads and chaired by Treasury Secretary Timothy Geithner, can block Bureau regulations. Opponents preferred that the director have less power and be replaced by a board in an effort to add additional checks and balances.

While banking and finance lobbyists spent $50 million trying to change how the Bureau was set up under Dodd-Frank, supporters promoted the Bureau as a necessary part of continuing economic recovery and establishing stability for consumers. "Unfortunately for consumers, financial abuses continue today, making the CFPB's success as important as ever," said Mike Calhoun, president of the Center for Responsible Lending. "The CFPB, with its consumer protection mission, is the best place to establish basic rules of the road to enhance both consumer protection and a robust competitive market," Calhoun told the Senate Banking and Finance committee.

According to a poll conducted by the Center for Responsible Lending, three-quarters of likely voters supported the idea of the CFPB. "There's still a populist view out there among the population that the banks are responsible for the economic downturn and it's about time we start regulating for consumer protection," said Robert Clarke, former Comptroller of the Currency under former presidents Ronald Reagan and George H. W. Bush.

OPEN FOR BUSINESS

Despite having existed since 2010, on July 21, 2011, the CFPB officially opened for business. "The Consumer Financial Protection Bureau (CFPB) hit the ground running this week, launching functions and issuing a variety of required rules and reports that represent important steps in making the CFPB operational and effective from the start," the Bureau said in a press release. Before its official opening, the Bureau completed some basic tasks allowed under Dodd-Frank, including working with credit card companies, mortgage companies, and consumers to simplify disclosure forms and helping service members more easily access financial assistance. The Bureau also strived to make the public aware of its mission and tried to get its message out through Twitter, Facebook, Flickr, an interactive website, blog, and YouTube videos. Because the Bureau plans to rely heavily on feedback, consumer knowledge of its existence was paramount.

DIRECTOR DEBATE

Under Dodd-Frank, the CFPB cannot fully function until a director is installed. Without a director, the agency can only oversee that banks are complying with current laws, but cannot write certain new rules or supervise some financial companies. It could, however, enforce twenty consumer financial laws and file lawsuits immediately if it saw wrongdoing at the 110 banks it had the power to investigate upon its creation. It could also write rules and issue orders about the laws over which it gained oversight from the seven agencies whose consumer protection responsibilities were consolidated under its auspices.

It was clear, given the amount of contention surrounding the CFPB, that confirming a director would not be easy. In May 2011, forty-four Republican senators sent a letter to President Obama, stating that they would not vote for any of Obama's nominees to lead the CFPB, instead calling on the president to replace the director position with a board of directors. "Until President Obama addresses our concerns by supporting a few reasonable structural changes, we will not confirm anyone to lead it," said Sen. Richard Shelby, R-Ala., in a written statement.

In July 2011, Obama ignored this threat and nominated Richard Cordray, former Ohio attorney general, to be director of the Bureau. "Richard Cordray has spent his career advocating for middle-class families, from his tenure as Ohio's attorney general to his most recent role as heading up the enforcement division at the C.F.P.B. and looking out for ordinary people in our financial system," Obama said.

Cordray grew up in Ohio and attended Michigan State University, Oxford, and the University of Chicago Law School. After graduation, he served as a Supreme Court clerk, state representative, Ohio State University law professor, worked in a private law practice, and was state treasurer and treasurer of Franklin County, Ohio, before winning a special election in 2008 to become Ohio's attorney general. In this position, he aggressively investigated foreclosure practices and the settlements he won totaled $2 billion. After losing reelection to former Senator Mike DeWine in 2010, Cordray came to the CFPB as director of the enforcement division.

Obama passed over Warren for the position of director because, although some Democrats liked her, she never received full support from Obama or Geithner, who did not like her independence or outspokenness. After Cordray's nomination, Warren stepped down but gave the nominee high praise. "Rich has always had my strong support because he is tough and he is smart—and that's exactly the combination this new agency needs," Warren said.

During his confirmation hearings before the Senate Banking and Finance committee, Cordray promised to focus the Bureau's enforcement powers on nonbank companies like private mortgage lenders and money transfer agencies that have often been outside the realm of federal regulation. He also announced that he planned to reduce the number of consumer finance regulations and impose few new regulations. "My main objectives in consumer protection . . . were to help empower people to make better-informed financial decisions for themselves and their families and to stop the scams and frauds that not only cheat consumers but also undercut law-abiding businesses," said Cordray.

Although Democrats and Republicans on the committee did not disagree on Cordray's qualifications, Republicans still strongly fought the nomination, preferring to change the Bureau to be governed by a board. "The director will single-handedly determine the financial products consumers can buy, as well as which consumers have access to credit and which do not," said Sen. Shelby. He continued, "It is staggering the amount of control the director will exert over the daily financial choices available to Americans." Democrats in turn argued that blocking the nomination—and therefore stopping the Bureau from assuming its full powers—would be detrimental. "[I]t will not only be bad for consumers if his nomination is hijacked, it will be bad for the country if he continues to be treated as a pawn in a cynical Washington game," said Sen. Charles Schumer, D-N.Y.

In December, a Republican filibuster blocked the Cordray nomination from being approved. However, on January 4, 2012, President Obama used his recess appointment power to install Cordray into the position. "I am not going to stand by while a minority in the Senate puts party ideology ahead of the people we were elected to serve," Obama said. The appointment set off a firestorm in Congress over questions of whether it was legal. In an effort to block a recess appointment, House and Senate Republicans had been holding "pro forma" sessions during the winter holidays during which members would gavel in and gavel out after a few minutes without conducting any business. Republicans argued that the appointment was illegal. "By opening this door, the White House is saying it can appoint any person at any time to any position it chooses without the advice and consent of the Senate," said Sen. Orrin Hatch, R-Utah. The Obama legal team disagreed, arguing that because Congress conducted no formal business during its pro forma sessions, it was technically in recess. "Can the Senate, through form, render a constitutional power of the executive obsolete? Our view is that the answer to that question is clearly no," said White House Counsel Kathryn Ruemmler. Cordray's appointment will stand unless it is challenged in court, and there is some speculation that the Supreme Court may end up reviewing the nomination if a lawsuit is filed in relation to CFPB regulations.

—Heather Kerrigan

Following is a statement by President Barack Obama on July 18, 2011, nominating Richard Cordray to the position of director of the Consumer Financial Protection Bureau (CFPB); a press release issued by the CFPB on July 21, 2011, marking its official first day of business; comments made by Senators Tim Johnson and Richard Shelby on September 6, 2011, during Cordray's nomination hearing; and the opening statement given by Cordray on September 6, 2011, during his nomination hearing before the Senate Banking, Housing, and Urban Affairs Committee.

President Obama Nominates CFPB Director

July 18, 2011

Good afternoon, everybody. It has been almost 3 years since the financial crisis pulled the economy into a deep recession. And millions of families are still hurting because of it. They're trying to get by on one income instead of two, on fewer shifts at the plant or at the hospital. They're cutting expenses, giving up on a family night out so there's money for groceries. And for a lot of families, things were tough even before the recession.

So we've got to get the economy growing faster and make sure that small businesses can hire again, so that an entrepreneur out there can sell a new product, so that the middle class is getting stronger again, and so folks feel confident in their futures and their children's futures.

That's why we can't let politics stand in the way of doing the right thing in Washington. . . .

One of the biggest problems was that the tables were tilted against ordinary people in the financial system. . . .

That's why we passed financial reform a year ago. It was a commonsense law that did three things. First, it made taxpayer-funded bailouts illegal, so taxpayers don't have to foot the bill if a big bank goes under. Second, it said to Wall Street firms, you can't take the same kind of reckless risks that led to the crisis. And third, it put in place the stronger—the strongest consumer protections in history.

Now, to make sure that these protections worked—so ordinary people were dealt with fairly, so they could make informed decisions about their finances—we didn't just change the law. We changed the way the Government did business. For years, the job of protecting consumers was divided up in a lot of different agencies. So if you had a problem with a mortgage lender, you called one place. If you had a problem with a credit card company, you called somebody else. It meant there were a lot of people who were responsible, but that meant nobody was responsible.

And we changed that. We cut the bureaucracy and put one consumer watchdog in charge, with just one job: looking out for regular people in the financial system . . . .

. . . Already, the agency is starting to do a whole bunch of things that are going to be important for consumers: making sure loan contracts and credit card terms are simpler and written in plain English. Already, thanks to the leadership of the bureau, we're seeing men and women in uniform who are getting more protections against fraud and deception when it comes to financial practices. And as part of her charge, I asked Elizabeth [Warren] to find the best possible choice for Director of the bureau.

And that's who we found in Richard Cordray. Richard was one of the first people that Elizabeth [Warren] recruited, and he's helped stand up the bureau's enforcement division over the past 6 months. . . . So I am proud to nominate Richard Cordray to this post. . . .

The fact is the financial crisis and the recession were not the result of normal economic cycles or just a run of bad luck. They were abuses and there was a lack of smart regulations. So we're not just going to shrug our shoulders and hope it doesn't happen again. We're not going to go back to the status quo where consumers couldn't count on getting protections that they deserved. We're not going to go back to a time when our whole economy was vulnerable to a massive financial crisis. That's why reform matters. That's why this bureau matters. I will fight any efforts to repeal or undermine the important changes that we passed. And we are going to stand up this bureau and make sure it is doing the right thing for middle class families all across the country. . . .

I look forward to working with Richard Cordray as this bureau stands up on behalf of consumers all across the country. I want to thank both Elizabeth and Tim Geithner for the extraordinary work that they've done over at Treasury to make sure that, a year after we passed this law, it is already having an impact and it's going to have impact for years to come.

SOURCE: U.S. Executive Office of the President. "Remarks on the Nomination of Richard A. Cordray To Be Director of the Consumer Financial Protection Bureau and an Exchange With Reporters." July 18, 2011. *Daily Compilation of Presidential Documents* 2011, no. 00511 (July 18, 2011). http://www.gpo.gov/fdsys/pkg/DCPD-201100511/pdf/DCPD-201100511.pdf.

| DOCUMENT | *CFPB Officially Opens* |

July 21, 2011

The Consumer Financial Protection Bureau (CFPB) hit the ground running this week, launching functions and issuing a variety of required rules and reports that represent important steps in making the CFPB operational and effective from the start.

"Two years ago, the consumer agency was just barely an idea. A year ago it became law. And this week, the CFPB will open its doors and begin to make a difference in the marketplace," said Elizabeth Warren, Special Advisor to the Secretary of the Treasury on the CFPB. "This agency is ready to be a cop on the beat for American families—and I couldn't be prouder."

Today, the CFPB is sending introductory letters to the CEOs of the depository institutions—generally large banks and their bank affiliates—that are subject to CFPB supervision. These letters, which outline the agency's approach to supervision and examination, mark the beginning of the CFPB's regular communications with the institutions it supervises. In addition, the CFPB's Enforcement team is ready to begin enforcing federal consumer financial laws, when necessary.

The CFPB's Consumer Response Center began accepting credit card complaints today on its newly redesigned website, ConsumerFinance.gov, and through a toll-free number. It will also refer distressed homeowners to housing counselors via the Homeowner's HOPE Hotline. Over the coming months, the agency will expand its Consumer Response Center to handle complaints about other consumer financial products and services under its jurisdiction.

To enable the CFPB to perform its functions under the Dodd-Frank Wall Street Reform and Consumer Protection Act (Dodd-Frank Act), the agency will publish the following:

- A final list of the regulations of the transferor agencies that will be enforceable by the CFPB, as required by Section 1063(i) of the Dodd-Frank Act.

- A series of interim rules to create records and information procedures. These include rules to implement the Privacy Act and the Freedom of Information Act, and to establish a process by which parties may seek testimony or records from the CFPB for use in litigation. Also included are confidentiality rules, required by the Dodd-Frank Act, describing how the CFPB will treat information it obtains.
- An interim rule, implementing Section 1052 of the Dodd-Frank Act, concerning the CFPB's conduct of investigations of potential violations of any provision of federal consumer financial law. . . .
- An interim rule providing for a fair and expeditious process for the resolution of administrative enforcement actions, as required by Section 1053(e) of the Dodd-Frank Act. . . .
- An interim rule specifying procedures for state officials—such as attorneys general—to notify the CFPB of actions or proceedings they undertake to enforce Title X of the Dodd-Frank Act, as required by Section 1042(c) of the Act. This rule will help to ensure that the CFPB is aware of actions being initiated under Title X and that the law is being enforced in a consistent and efficient manner.

In addition, the following reports were required by Congress and issued by the CFPB this week:

- A report examining the differences between credit scores sold to consumers and scores used by lenders to make credit decisions. The report covers the process of developing credit scoring models, why different scoring models may produce different scores for the same consumer, how different scoring models are used by creditors in the marketplace, what credit scores are available to consumers for purchase, and ways that differences between the scores provided to creditors and those provided to consumers may disadvantage consumers. The report is required by Section 1078(b) of the Dodd-Frank Act.
- A report that recommends principles for maximizing transparency and disclosure of exchange rate information for consumers making remittance transfers, and examines the incentives and challenges related to using remittance data in credit scores. The report is required by Section 1073(e) of the Dodd-Frank Act.
- A report on three plans pertaining to the CFPB staff: (1) a training and workforce development plan, including an identification of skill and technical expertise needs, a description of the steps taken to foster innovation and creativity, and a leadership development and succession plan; (2) a workplace flexibilities plan covering items such as telework, flexible work schedules, and parental leave benefits; and (3) a recruitment and retention plan that includes provisions on targeting highly qualified applicant pools with diverse backgrounds, streamlined employment application processes, and the collection of information to measure indicators of hiring effectiveness. The report is required by Section 1067(b) of the Dodd-Frank Act.

SOURCE: Consumer Financial Protection Bureau. Press Releases. "Consumer Financial Protection Bureau Ready to Help Consumers on Day One." July 21, 2011. http://www.consumerfinance.gov/pressrelease/consumer-financial-protection-bureau-ready-to-help-consumers-on-day-one/.

Sen. Johnson on the Consumer Financial Protection Bureau

September 6, 2011

On our next panel, we will consider the nomination of Richard Cordray to be the first Director of the Consumer Financial Protection Bureau.

Mr. Cordray, welcome to the Senate Banking Committee and a warm welcome to your family and friends who are here this afternoon.

The CFPB was born out of the failure by prudential regulators to hold financial companies accountable for complying with consumer protection laws. Congress created the CFPB to be a robust and independent agency focused on protecting consumers, like military families and older Americans, from abusive financial products. The CFPB was also created to streamline disclosures so consumers can make the best financial choices for themselves and their families. In fact, one of the CFPB's first projects is to simplify the long, confusing mortgage disclosure forms.

The CFPB is an agency that the American people want. A recent bipartisan survey shows that Americans strongly support the creation of the CFPB.

The Director of the CFPB will play an important role in maintaining the agency's independence, promoting an equitable and transparent consumer financial market place and exercising enforcement of consumer protection laws.

On July 18th, President Obama nominated Mr. Cordray to be the first ever Director of the CFPB.

The purpose of today's hearing *should* be to consider whether Mr. Cordray is qualified for that job. Instead, a vocal minority is playing games with the process and holding Mr. Cordray's nomination hostage. This political gamesmanship is preventing Americans from receiving the consumer protections they deserve and putting community banks and credit unions at a competitive disadvantage to nonbank financial companies.

This vocal minority insists on rehashing the same debate Congress had last year when it created the CFPB as an accountable yet independent regulator. . . .

So the misleading claim of no CFPB accountability—drummed up by special interests and put forth by a vocal minority—should be exposed for what it is: an attempt to destroy the Bureau's ability to do its job of protecting American consumers. . . .

. . . Richard Cordray has spent his career in public service caring about people. He has taken the time to understand and come up with the best, most practical solutions for their problems.

Mr. Cordray supports small business and honest companies. He has been a member of his local chamber of commerce for 22 years. He believes in leveling the playing field so that small companies can compete fairly and that playing by the rules is good for business. . . .

Mr. Cordray also believes that people and corporations must be responsible for their own behavior and if they act responsibly they should get a fair shake.

It is my hope that, if confirmed, Mr. Cordray will use his knowledge and experience as a law enforcement official and public servant to better protect American consumers and to enhance the quality of our consumer financial markets.

We have seen many important nominations blocked in the Senate and denied an up-and-down vote on confirmation. The stability of our financial system, and of our economy, is simply too important to be put at risk by political games. It's time to allow the CFPB to do its job to the fullest extent of its authority with a Senate-confirmed Director in place. . . .

SOURCE: U.S. Senate Committee on Banking, Housing, and Urban Affairs. "Opening Statement of Chairman Tim Johnson." September 6, 2011. http://banking.senate.gov/public/index.cfm?FuseAction=Files.View&FileStore_id=9a808a8c-0d68-40e3-b779-96c2ccf795a0.

Sen. Shelby on the Consumer Financial Protection Bureau

DOCUMENT

September 6, 2011

Thank you, Mr. Chairman.

I don't think it will be a surprise to anyone to hear that we believe that today's hearing is premature. We do not believe that the Committee should consider any nominee to be the Director of the Bureau of Consumer Financial Protection until reforms are adopted to make the Bureau accountable to the American people.

Earlier this year, 43 of my Senate colleagues and I sent a letter to President Obama expressing our serious concerns about the Bureau's lack of accountability. We also proposed three reasonable reforms to the structure of the bureau.

We had hoped to work with the majority to address this issue before the President nominated a Director. Unfortunately, neither the President nor the majority has made any effort to work with us to improve the accountability of the Bureau. Instead, the President has nominated Mr. Cordray to be the first Director.

It is regrettable that the President and the majority have chosen to ignore our request rather than work with us to improve the Bureau's accountability. It may be good politics for them, but it is certainly bad police for American people.

One of our nation's founding principles is that the government should be accountable to the people. Yet, the majority structured the Bureau to grant its Director unprecedented authority over the lives of the American people without any effective checks.

All of the Bureau's power is concentrated in the hands of its Director . . . It is staggering the amount of control the Director will exert over the daily financial choices available to Americans.

Despite having such broad powers, however, there is no meaningful check on the Director's authority. The Director cannot be removed except on extremely limited grounds of inefficiency, malfeasance, or neglect of duty. . . . In addition, bank regulators do not have a meaningful ability to ensure that the Director's actions do not needlessly undermine the safety-and-soundness of our banks. While some claim that the Financial Stability Oversight Council could overrule the Director, this so-called check is simply illusory. . . .

No one person should have so much unfettered power over the American people. It blatantly violates the spirit of our democratic system of government. Our pursuit of better consumer protections should not require us to compromise our basic Constitutional values. This should be something on which we can all agree.

Moreover, the principle involved will have real consequences. Unless the Bureau is reformed, it is only a matter of time before this concentration of power is abused or misused to the detriment of American consumers and the economy. . . .

In closing, the Chairman today has attempted to turn the phrase "vocal minority" into a pejorative. Over the years, however, Senators from both parties have agreed upon rules governing this chamber that are designed to protect the rights of the minority. The requests made by this particular vocal minority seek only to preserve the system of checks and balances embodied in the Constitution—that is not what I would call a radical undertaking.

Thank you, Mr. Chairman.

SOURCE: U.S. Senate Committee on Banking, Housing, and Urban Affairs. "Statement of Senator Richard C. Shelby." September 6, 2011. http://banking.senate.gov/public/index.cfm?FuseAction=Files .View&FileStore_id=e905128a-65a3-4c10-9eb0-3c30b54d1fb1.

Richard Cordray Nomination
Hearing Opening Statement

September 6, 2011

Thank you, Chairman Johnson, Ranking Member Shelby, and members of the Committee. I am honored to be here today as the nominee for the position of Director of the Consumer Financial Protection Bureau.

I am glad to have my wife Peggy and my twins Danny and Holly here with me today. I deeply appreciate the confidence that President Obama has shown by nominating me to serve as the first Director of the Bureau. I thank Professor Elizabeth Warren for all her painstaking and thoughtful work to turn the Bureau from an abstract idea into a tangible, vibrant new agency. And I am grateful to the Committee members for all your personal courtesy and advice over the past month.

From childhood, my parents taught me the value of work that seeks to improve the lives of others. My Dad, Frank, now 93, spent his entire career in programs that served children and adults who have developmental disabilities. My Mom, Ruth, who died of cancer when I was in college, founded the first foster grandparent program for the developmentally disabled in Ohio, in addition to doing all the things that a mother does to raise three rambunctious boys.

After completing degrees in political theory, economics, and law, I worked for years as an attorney in the private sector with individual and business clients, and was in and out of public service, including a brief stint in the Ohio legislature. In 2002, however, my life took a different direction when I became the Franklin County Treasurer.

The job required me to develop managerial skills and the knowledge needed to run a financial office and safeguard public funds. But there was also another, very significant dimension of the county treasurer work. From the beginning, I set out to collect millions of dollars of unpaid property taxes. The people who evade their taxes take advantage of all the law-abiding taxpayers and businesses who meet their obligations. I thought that was wrong, and I tried to fix it by leveling the playing field.

As I went about that task, I was deeply impressed by the importance of consumer finance issues and the growing difficulties they pose for families and households. Although I found that many delinquent taxpayers were not willing to pay their share until we moved aggressively to enforce the law against them, I also found something different and note-worthy: many individuals did not want to be in trouble, and wanted to pay their share, but were in tough circumstances through no fault of their own. Sometimes it was because of the loss of a job. Other times I would find that it was because of a death or serious illness in their family or because of a divorce that heaped on the added expense of running two households instead of just one.

Out of these experiences, I developed a strong resolve to address these kinds of finan-cial difficulties that confront communities. . . .

Later I became the State Treasurer. In that position, it was my primary duty to protect the public's money during the financial crisis, a job I fulfilled by steering clear of risky investments. In addition, I continued to work on consumer issues. . . .

Before coming to the Bureau as the chief of Enforcement, I also served as the Ohio Attorney General. There too, with a different set of tools, my main objectives in consumer protection were to help empower people to make sound financial decisions in managing their affairs. . . .

These are the experiences that brought me to the Consumer Financial Protection Bureau, where I have found that Congress provided us with both a range of tools and the resources to analyze and address the problems that we face. . . .

At the Bureau, our bigger and more flexible toolbox includes research reports, rule-making, market guidance, consumer education and empowerment, and the ability to supervise and examine both large banks and many nonbank institutions. I know from my own experience that lawsuits can be a very slow, wasteful, and needlessly acrimonious way to solve a problem. The supervisory tool, in particular, offers the prospect of resolving compliance issues more quickly and effectively without resorting to litigation. We are con-tinuing to build our capacity to make effective use of this entire range of tools.

Enforcement, of course, will still have an important role at the Consumer Bureau. If people are ignoring or evading consumer protections laws—and seeking to gain an unfair advantage over their law-abiding competitors—then litigation is an essential tool, and we will use it judiciously.

I also am convinced that the Bureau will find many opportunities to streamline regu-lations and disclosures. . . .

In closing, Chairman Johnson, Ranking Member Shelby, and members of this Commit-tee, I very much appreciate your consideration. If I were to have the privilege of being con-firmed as the first Director of the new Consumer Financial Protection Bureau, I promise that you will have one person who will always be accountable to you for how we are carrying out the laws laid down by Congress and I will be eager to hear your thoughts about how we should do our work. Thank you again, and I will be pleased to answer your questions.

SOURCE: U.S. Senate Committee on Banking, Housing, and Urban Affairs. "Opening Statement of Richard Cordray, Nominee for Director of the Consumer Financial Protection Bureau, Before the Committee on Banking, Housing, and Urban Affairs, United States Senate." September 6, 2011. http://banking.senate .gov/public/index.cfm?FuseAction=Files.View&FileStore_id=34fb5952-05b5-409f-801a-d9471615ff3c.

OTHER HISTORIC DOCUMENTS OF INTEREST

FROM PREVIOUS *HISTORIC DOCUMENTS*

- Senate Debates Dodd–Frank Wall Street Reform Legislation, *2010,* p. 165
- Federal Reserve Board Chair Announces End of Recession, *2009,* p. 430
- Federal Reserve and Economists on the U.S. Financial Crisis at Year-End, *2008,* p. 557
- Federal Reserve Board on the State of the U.S. Economy, *2007,* p. 449

Testimony in British Phone-Hacking Scandal

JULY 19, 2011

Journalism in the United Kingdom is a highly competitive industry, and British newspapers, which would be considered tabloids in some parts of the world, are known for undertaking frowned upon tactics to get the best stories. The British public expects the media to go for blood and produce flashy headlines that are occasionally truth bending. Despite the unscrupulous reporting tactics, the United Kingdom has some of the tightest restrictions on media in the Western world, including a tough libel law and privacy code.

In mid-2011, British tabloid journalism reached its breaking point, when a massive phone hacking scandal led by the *News of the World* was exposed, with those affected ranging from celebrities and the royal family to murder victims and war veterans. The scandal forced the closure of the newspaper and left open questions of how far into the culture of British journalism the scandal reached.

RUPERT MURDOCH'S *NEWS OF THE WORLD*

One component of News Corp., the media empire owned by media mogul Rupert Murdoch, is News International, the British newspaper arm of the company. News International comprises a group of newspapers that sees themselves as having significant influence in British life and politics. In 1992, for example, *The Sun*, one of Murdoch's British papers, featured a headline "It's The Sun Wot Won It" after the Conservative Party, which had been heavily backed by the paper, won a parliamentary election. This trend continued over time. In 1997, Murdoch's papers supported the Labour Party and Tony Blair won the prime minister's seat. The papers later supported the Tories, who triumphed in the 2010 election.

Murdoch's British newspapers cover sports stars, celebrities, the monarchy, politicians, and any other topic that will help sell papers, although they have been criticized around the world for a lack of serious reporting. *News of the World (NoW)*, a Sunday tabloid publication, was one of Murdoch's papers published by News Group Newspapers, an arm of News International. The paper was the nation's best-selling weekly, and had been in print for 168 years. Each week, the paper sold more than 2.8 million copies.

After allegations that the staff of the paper had been involved in illegal phone hacking that dated back to 2002, the paper was forced to announce its closure on July 7, 2011. On July 10, 2011, *NoW* published its final edition with the headline "Thank You and Goodbye." The last edition highlighted the work of the paper over nearly two centuries, stating, "We have saved children from paedos and nailed 250 evil crooks." The final edition also featured a full-page editorial apology. "Quite simply, we lost our way. Phones were hacked and for that this newspaper is truly sorry. There is no justification for this appalling wrongdoing. No justification for the pain caused to victims, nor for the deep stain it has left on a great history," the editorial read.

At the closure of the paper, staff expressed both sadness for the end of an era and anger at those who had been involved in phone hacking. Most of the anger was directed at News International chief Rebekah Brooks, who staff said had attempted to play the victim. Brooks was the *NoW* editor from 2000 to 2003, after which she took higher positions as editor of *The Sun* and chief executive at News International. Rather than devoting the newspaper's final pages to speculation on who at News International had knowledge of or was involved in phone hacking, Colin Myler, the newspaper's editor at the time of its closure, told staff, "We wanted to go out with dignity." The proceeds from the paper's last edition were donated to three charities.

PHONE HACKING ALLEGATIONS

For years, allegations had been made that *NoW* was involved in hacking cell phone voice mail. According to these allegations, many of which were made by competitors and potential hacking victims, *NoW* hired private investigators to hack into the cell phone mailboxes of celebrities, politicians, and journalists. As more details came to light, however, the public learned that hacking extended to murder victims, victims of the July 2005 London terrorist attacks, and soldiers killed in Iraq and Afghanistan. Initially, *NoW* responded to the allegations by stating that the hacking was the work of one rogue reporter and a private investigator. Those running the company, however, claimed to have no knowledge about the phone hacking.

The earliest concerns about *NoW* phone hacking stemmed from a 2005 story about a knee injury suffered by Prince William. After a 2006 police investigation, in 2007 *NoW* Royal Editor Clive Goodman was jailed for four months, and the private investigator he worked with, Glenn Mulcaire, was jailed for six months. The pair admitted to hacking the voice mail of royal family aides. Police confiscated files from Mulcaire's home that contained names and information on numerous celebrities and other public figures, leading police to believe that the scandal might be deeper than one story about a knee injury; however, they took no additional steps to investigate.

In 2009, the British newspaper *The Guardian* made claims that *NoW* had hacked as many as 3,000 phones and had paid off people, including police, to keep the hacking under wraps. *NoW* immediately dismissed the allegations and the Press Complaints Commission, an independent regulatory body for British media, criticized the story for lacking any hard evidence to support the hacking claims. In response to the allegations, the House of Commons Culture, Media and Sport Select Committee interviewed News International leadership, including Andy Coulson, a former *NoW* editor and communications director for Prime Minister David Cameron. A report released by the committee in February 2010 found that *NoW* executives had "collective amnesia" regarding phone hacking. The report also criticized News International for "deliberate attempts to thwart investigations" and was highly critical of the 2006 police investigation. However, it produced no evidence that leadership at News International or *NoW* had knowledge of phone hacking.

The scandal reached a breaking point in April 2011, when *NoW* acknowledged its role in hacking voice mails. Murdoch ran newspaper articles admitting "serious wrongdoing" and apologizing to the British public. Brooks, along with a number of other senior executives, resigned her position at News International, and was later arrested and released by police. In July, public outcry over the scandal reached a fever point when *The Guardian* released information claiming that the phone of a missing and later murdered schoolgirl,

Milly Dowler, had also been hacked. Brooks had been editor of *NoW* at the time Dowler's phone was hacked, and when the girl's voice mailbox was accessed, it led her parents to believe that, before her body was discovered, she may still have been alive.

INQUIRIES

The Metropolitan Police and the British government conducted a number of inquiries in response to hacking allegations. The first investigation took place in 2006 after the Prince William knee injury story, but it produced no evidence of phone hacking beyond royal aides and was heavily criticized by the British public and politicians for being incomplete. In 2009, despite the charges made by *The Guardian*, the Metropolitan Police announced that it would not renew the 2006 hacking investigation.

Under political pressure, police reopened the case in January 2011. On the same day the police investigation reopened, *NoW* fired assistant editor Ian Edmondson for e-mails he saved on the company computer system indicating knowledge of voice mail hacking. Edmondson was later arrested and questioned as part of the hacking investigation. As the hacking scandal continued to unfold, John Yates, then Scotland Yard assistant commissioner, expressed "extreme regret" for not reopening the case in 2009 and resigned his position. Police Commissioner Sir Paul Stephenson also resigned. When called before Parliament's Home Affairs Select Committee, officers blamed the decision not to reopen the case in 2009 on a News International attempt to stop the investigation.

News International produced e-mails proving that during his time with *NoW*, Coulson had authorized payments to police officers who in turn provided *NoW* with information. The Metropolitan Police extended its investigation into bribes allegedly taken by officers from 2003 to 2007, which were supposedly for contact information for members of the royal family. The police accused News International of leaking information on their payouts to the press to undermine the police investigation. During the investigation, questions were raised as to whether officers's phones were hacked during the initial 2006 investigation, and whether this indicated that police had purposefully botched the investigation to prevent any information gathered from their hacked phones from being released.

In 2011, Prime Minister Cameron announced a two-part inquiry into British media to be led by Lord Justice Brian Leveson. The first part of the inquiry would look at "the culture, practices and ethics" of media outlets in the United Kingdom and the relationship between journalists, police, and politicians. The second inquiry would review illegal actions undertaken by newspapers and police during the initial phone hacking investigation in 2006. The hearings in the first inquiry opened on November 14, and the investigating body was charged with gathering evidence from phone hacking victims. A report from Lord Justice Leveson was expected in 2012.

In Parliament, the Culture, Media and Sport Select Committee began its own hearings into the hacking scandal, calling current and former *NoW* and News International executives and staff to testify. On July 19, 2011, Murdoch and his son James were called to testify alongside Brooks. All three denied knowing the extent of phone hacking until late 2010, and Brooks noted that once they had information on hacking, News International acted "quickly and decisively" to deal with the situation. Rupert Murdoch claimed his staff misled him as to the extent of the hacking, while his son claimed he was unaware that the hacking was anything more than the work of one rogue reporter. On August 16, 2011, the committee released a letter received from Goodman that stated that discussion of phone hacking was typical and widespread at *NoW*. Goodman further alleged that he was told he could have his job back if he did not name any executives with knowledge of hacking if called to testify.

In September, Myler and Tom Crone, the former editor and legal manager of *NoW*, respectively, appeared before the committee, claiming that they had informed James Murdoch of the extent of phone hacking prior to late 2010. On November 10, James Murdoch refuted this claim when he was again called to testify before Parliament, stating that these former company executives provided "misleading" information.

ADDITIONAL QUESTIONS

The phone hacking scandal, investigations, and *NoW* closure left open a number of questions on media regulation and ethics, and the relationship between politicians, police, and journalists. Cameron called on former Parliamentary Commission for Standards Commissioner Elizabeth Filkin to "examine the ethical considerations that should, in future, underpin the relationship between the Metropolitan Police and the media." Filkin concluded that the relationship between journalists and police had caused "serious harm" and eroded public trust in the media and police. A similar report, by Her Majesty's Inspectorate of Constabulary, was set up to "consider instances of undue influence, inappropriate contractual arrangements and other abuses of power in police relationships with the media and other parties."

The value of the Press Complaints Commission is also being reviewed. In its last issue, *NoW* defended the Commission and supported its continued existence. "It needs more power and more resources. We do not need government legislation. That would be a disaster for democracy and for a free press," the paper stated in an editorial. Cameron, on the other hand, claimed the Commission had failed public confidence and should be disbanded.

The impact of phone hacking did not stop at British borders. On July 14, 2011, the Federal Bureau of Investigation (FBI) opened an investigation to find out whether phones of 9/11 victims were hacked by News Corp., which has significant media holdings in the United States. One day later, Attorney General Eric Holder announced that the Department of Justice would investigate whether News Corp. had violated the Foreign Corrupt Practices Act, which could lead to possible charges under U.S. anti-corruption laws.

—Heather Kerrigan

Following is an edited transcript of the testimony given by Rupert Murdoch, James Murdoch, and Rebekah Brooks with regard to the News of the World *phone hacking scandal, on July 19, 2011.*

DOCUMENT *Testimony on Phone Hacking Scandal*

July 19, 2011

[Neither witnesses nor Members have corrected the record.]

[The list of present members of Parliament has been omitted.]

Witnesses: **Rupert Murdoch**, Chairman and Chief Executive Officer, News Corporation, and **James Murdoch**, Chairman, News International, gave evidence. . . .

Q153 Chair: Perhaps I might start with Mr James Murdoch. You made a statement on 7 July in which you stated that the paper had made statements to Parliament without being in full possession of the facts, and that was wrong. You essentially admitted that Parliament had been misled in what we had been told. Can you tell us to what extent we were misled, and when you became aware of that?. . .

James Murdoch: Subsequent to our discovery of that information in one of the civil trials at the end of 2010, which I believe was the Sienna Miller case—a civil trial around illegal voicemail interceptions—the company immediately went to look at additional records around the individual involved. We alerted—the company alerted the police, who restarted on that basis the investigation that is now under way, and since then the company has admitted liability to victims of illegal voicemail interceptions, has apologised unreservedly, which I repeat today, to those victims, and the company also set up a compensation scheme independently managed by a former High Court judge to be able to deal with legitimate claims from victims of those terrible incidents of voicemail interceptions. . . .

Q158 Chair: Have you carried out your own investigation since the discovery of this information to find out the extent of involvement in phone hacking in the *News of the World*?

James Murdoch: We have established a group in the company, co-operating very closely with the police on their investigation. . . .

Q161 Mr Watson: In October 2010, did you still believe it to be true when you made your Thatcher speech and you said, "Let me be clear: we will vigorously pursue the truth—and we will not tolerate wrongdoing."?

Rupert Murdoch: Yes.

Q162 Mr Watson: So if you were not lying then, somebody lied to you. Who was it?

Rupert Murdoch: I don't know. That is what the police are investigating, and we are helping them with.

Q163 Mr Watson: But you acknowledge that you were misled.

Rupert Murdoch: Clearly.

Q164 Mr Watson: Can I take you back to 2003? Are you aware that in March of that year, Rebekah Brooks gave evidence to this Committee admitting paying police?

Rupert Murdoch: I am now aware of that. I was not aware at the time. I am also aware that she amended that considerably, very quickly afterwards.

Q165 Mr Watson: I think that she amended it seven or eight years afterwards.

Rupert Murdoch: Oh, I'm sorry.

Q166 Mr Watson: Did you or anyone else at your organisation investigate this at the time?

Rupert Murdoch: No.

Q167 Mr Watson: Can you explain why?

Rupert Murdoch: I didn't know of it, I'm sorry. Allow me to say something? This is not an excuse. Maybe it is an explanation of my laxity. The *News of the World* is less than 1% of our company. I employ 53,000 people around the world who are proud and great and ethical and distinguished people—professionals in their line. Perhaps I am spread watching and appointing people whom I trust to run those divisions.

Q168 Mr Watson: Mr Murdoch, I do accept that you have many distinguished people who work for your company. You are ultimately responsible for the corporate governance of News Corp. . .If I can take you forward to 2006: when Clive Goodman was arrested and subsequently convicted of intercepting voicemails, were you made aware of that?

Rupert Murdoch: I think so. I was certainly made aware of when they were convicted.

Q169 Mr Watson: What did News International do subsequent to the arrest of Clive Goodman and Glenn Mulcaire to get to the facts?

Rupert Murdoch: We worked with the police on further investigation and eventually we appointed—very quickly appointed—a very leading firm of lawyers in the City to investigate it further.

[A line of questioning regarding e-mail hacking, blackmail, and staff compensation has been omitted.]

Q196 Mr Watson: . . . Mr Murdoch, at what point did you find out that criminality was endemic at *News of the World?*

Rupert Murdoch: Endemic is a very hard, wide-ranging word. I also have to be extremely careful not to prejudice the course of justice, which is taking place now. It has been disclosed. I became aware as it became apparent. I was absolutely shocked and appalled and ashamed when I heard about the Milly Dowler case, only two weeks ago, eight days before I was graciously received by the Dowlers.

Q197 Mr Watson: Did you read our last report into the matter, where we referred to the collective amnesia of your executives who gave evidence to our Committee?

Rupert Murdoch: I haven't heard that. I don't know who made that particular charge.

Q198 Mr Watson: A parliamentary inquiry found your senior executives in the UK guilty of collective amnesia and nobody brought it to your attention. I do not see why you do not think that that is very serious.

Rupert Murdoch: But you're not really saying amnesia, you're really saying lying.

Q199 Mr Watson: We found your executives guilty of collective amnesia. I would have thought that someone would like to bring that to your attention—that it would concern you. Did they forget?

Rupert Murdoch: No. . . .

Q202 Mr Watson: . . .Mr Murdoch, why was no one fired in April, when News International finally admitted that *News of the World* had been engaged in criminal interception of voicemails?

Rupert Murdoch: It was not our job to get in the course of justice. It was up to the police to bring the charges and to carry out their investigation, which we were 100% co-operating with.

Q203 Mr Watson: But in April the company admitted liability for phone hacking, and nobody took responsibility for it then. No one was fired. The company admitted that they had been involved in criminal wrongdoing and no one was fired. Why was that?

Rupert Murdoch: There were people in the company who apparently were guilty. We have to find them and we have to deal with them appropriately.

James Murdoch: Mr Watson, if I can clarify: most of the individuals involved or implicated in the allegations that were there had long since left the company. Some that were still there—you mentioned one—exited the business as soon as evidence of wrongdoing was found. . . .

Q205 Mr Watson: Did you close the paper down because of the criminality?

Rupert Murdoch: Yes, we felt ashamed at what had happened and thought we ought to bring it to a close.

Q206 Mr Watson: People lied to you and lied to their readers.

Rupert Murdoch: We had broken our trust with our readers; the important point was that we had broken our trust with our readers.

Q207 Mr Watson: Are you aware that there are other forms of illicit surveillance being used by private investigators, which were used by News International?

Rupert Murdoch: Other forms of?

Q208 Mr Watson: Illicit surveillance. Computer hacking, tracking on cars.

Rupert Murdoch: No. I think all news organisations have used private detectives, and do so in their investigations from time to time, but not illegally.

[A line of questioning on visiting the prime minister has been omitted.]

Q230 Jim Sheridan: . . .Mr Murdoch, do you accept that ultimately you are responsible for this whole fiasco?

Rupert Murdoch: No.

[Questions about tax payments have been omitted.]

Q240 Dr Coffey: Mr Murdoch, who made the recommendation to close down the *News of the World* to the board of News Corp?

Rupert Murdoch: It was the result of a discussion between my son and I, and senior executives. . . .

[Questions about the financial state of News International and payments to potential hacking victims have been omitted.]

Q251 Dr Coffey: I appreciate Mr Murdoch's statement at the beginning. Given that you have been in the media spotlight and perhaps, I expect, not appreciated the attention you have had, without wishing to suppress investigative journalism, will this make you think again about how you approach your headlines and targets in future? That could be people from Hillsborough 96 to celebrities to others. Will you think again about what your headlines will say in future?

Rupert Murdoch: I think all our editors certainly will. I am not aware of any transgressions. It is a matter of taste. It is a very difficult issue. We have in this country a wonderful variety of voices and they are naturally very competitive. I am sure there are headlines that occasionally give offence, but it is not intentional.

James Murdoch: It is important to say that one of the lessons, if you will, from all of this for us is, we do need to think as a business as well as an industry in this country more forcefully and thoughtfully about our journalistic ethics, about what exactly the codes of conduct should be around the whole area.

[Questions about out-of-court settlements and former staff members have been omitted.]

Q313 Philip Davies: It seems on the face of it that the *News of the World* was sacrificed to try and protect Rebekah Brooks' position at News International. In effect, instead of her departure being announced, the *News of the World* was offered up as an alternative to try to deal with the whole thing. Do you now regret making that decision? Do you regret closing the *News of the World* to try to save Rebekah Brooks? In hindsight, do you wish that you had accepted her resignation to start with, so that that paper with a fine tradition could continue and all the people who are now out of work or are struggling to find a job could still be in work?

Rupert Murdoch: I regret very much the fate of people who will not be able to find work. The two decisions were absolutely and totally unrelated.

[Questions about legal fees, a letter from Harbottle & Lewis, and day-to-day newspaper operations have been omitted.]

Q370 Alan Keen: I will leave some of the more mundane issues. It became clear from the first couple of questions to you, Rupert Murdoch, that you have been kept in the dark quite a bit on some of these real serious issues. Is there no—

Rupert Murdoch: Nobody has kept me in the dark. I may have been lax in not asking more, but it was such a tiny part of our business.

Q371 Alan Keen: I understand that, but obviously you have come to this point—you would not be here if it was not extremely serious.

Rupert Murdoch: It has become extremely serious.

Q372 Alan Keen: Are there no written rules that certain things have to be reported straight to the very top. It sounds as if there are no such rules; it is left to the trust—

Rupert Murdoch: Anything that is seen as a crisis comes to me.

James Murdoch: Mr Keen, may I? It is important to know that there is a difference between being kept in the dark, and a company that is a large company, the management of which is delegated to managers of different companies within the group, and so on and so forth. To suggest that my father or myself were kept in the dark is a different thing from saying that the management and the running of these businesses is often delegated either to the chief executive of a different company, an editor, a managing editor or an editorial floor, and decision making has to be there. . . .

Q373 Alan Keen: . . . Who really is responsible? . . . What has gone wrong?

James Murdoch: Mr Keen, that is a good question. But that is not to say that we are saying—and I am not saying—that somebody should have told me. To my knowledge, certain things were not known. When new information came to light with respect to my knowledge of these events—to my understanding, when new information came to light—the company acted on it. . . .

[Questions about relationships within News of the World *have been omitted.]*

Q377 Damian Collins: . . . Mr Rupert Murdoch, you said earlier that we live in a transparent society. Do you think it is right that people in public life can expect total privacy in a society like that?

Rupert Murdoch: No.

Q378 Damian Collins: Where do you think the limits of that lie? . . .

Rupert Murdoch: I think phone hacking is something quite different. But I do believe that investigative journalism, particularly competitive, does lead to a more transparent and open society, inconvenient though that may be to many people. And I think we are a better society because of it. I think we are probably a more open society than even the United States. . . .

Q381 Damian Collins: So, James Murdoch, you would be very clear that within your company and within your organisation, senior people should have been very aware that phone hacking was not only illegal, but totally unacceptable.

James Murdoch: I think, particularly in light of the successful prosecutions and convictions of the individuals involved in 2007, it could not be taken more seriously. If new evidence emerges, as it has in cases, the company acts on it very, very quickly. . . .

Q385 Damian Collins: Do you think there was a pressure on editors of your newspapers that leads them to take risks and break boundaries? In the *News of the World*, there was illegal action and wrongdoing, and people broke the law in order to get scoops.

Rupert Murdoch: No, I think that's totally wrong. There is no excuse for breaking the law at any time. . . .

Q388 Damian Collins: One final question, you said in your interview that you gave to *The Wall Street Journal* that you thought that your fellow executives at News Corporation had handled this crisis very well with just a few minor mistakes. Do you stand by that statement or do you believe the level of mistakes was far greater than that?

Rupert Murdoch: They seem very big now. What we did was terrible, but you're talking about handling the crisis. . . . Were mistakes made within the organisation? Absolutely. Were people that I trusted or that they trusted badly betrayed? Yes.

[Questions about financial settlements reached by News of the World *have been omitted.]*

Q394 Louise Mensch: . . . Can I ask you very specifically—Mr James Murdoch first—when did you become aware that the phones not merely of celebrities and members of the royal family but of victims of crime had been hacked? When did you become aware that the phone of the murder victim, Milly Dowler, had been hacked?

James Murdoch: The terrible instance of voicemail interception around the Milly Dowler case only came to my attention when it was reported in the press a few weeks ago and it was—

Q395 Louise Mensch: So only when *The Guardian* reported it.

James Murdoch: I can tell you, it was a total shock. That was the first I had heard of it and became aware of it.

Q396 Louise Mensch: Is that the same for hacking of other victims of crime? In other words, have you been made aware prior to the Milly Dowler story breaking that your reporters hacked into the phones of any other crime victims?

James Murdoch: No, I had not been made aware of that. . . .

Q399 Louise Mensch: . . . have you received any information that gives you cause for concern that employees of News Corp or contractors of News Corp may have indulged in that kind of hacking?

James Murdoch: No. Not at this moment. We have only seen the allegations that have been made in the press—I think it was in *The Mirror* or something like that.

[Questions about possible phone hacking in other territories, British journalistic behavior, and the Harbottle & Lewis file of evidence have been omitted.]

Q411 Louise Mensch: . . . This terrible thing happened on your watch. Mr Murdoch, have you considered resigning?

Rupert Murdoch: No.

Q412 Louise Mensch: Why not?

Rupert Murdoch: Because I feel that people I trusted—I am not saying who, and I don't know what level—have let me down. I think that they behaved disgracefully and betrayed the company and me, and it is for them to pay. Frankly, I think that I am the best person to clean this up.

[Questions about staff payments and Murdoch's closing statement have been omitted.]

Witness: **Rebekah Brooks**, former Chief Executive, News International, gave evidence. . . .

Q420 Chair: . . . Perhaps I can invite you to comment on whether you now accept that the statement issued saying that *News of the World* journalists had not accessed voicemails, or indeed instructed investigators to do so, is actually untrue.

Rebekah Brooks: Again, as you have heard in the last few hours, the fact is that since the Sienna Miller civil documents came into our possession at the end of December 2010, that was the first time that we, the senior management of the company at the time, had actually seen some documentary evidence actually relating to a current employee. I think that we acted quickly and decisively then, when we had that information. . . .

Q421 Chair: So until you saw the evidence that was produced in the Sienna Miller case, you continued to believe that the only person in the *News of the World* who had been implicated in phone hacking was Clive Goodman.

Rebekah Brooks: . . . . It was only when we saw the Sienna Miller documentation that we realised the severity of the situation.

[Questions about lawyers representing News of the World *have been omitted.]*

Q427 Mr Watson: To answer my question, you extensively worked with private investigators. Is that the answer?

Rebekah Brooks: No. What I said was that the use of private detectives in the late '90s and 2000 was a practice of Fleet Street, and after Operation Motorman and "What price privacy now?" Fleet Street reviewed this practice and in the main the use of private detectives was stopped. Don't forget that at the time, as you are aware, it was all about the Data Protection Acts and changes that were made. That's why we had the committee in 2003.

Q428 Mr Watson: For the third time, how extensively did you work with private detectives?

Rebekah Brooks: The *News of the World* employed private detectives, like most newspapers in Fleet Street.

Q429 Mr Watson: So it's fair to say that you were aware of, and approved payments to, private detectives.

Rebekah Brooks: I was aware that *News of the World* used private detectives under my editorship, yes.

Q430 Mr Watson: So you would have approved payments to them.

Rebekah Brooks: That's not how it works, but I was aware that we used them.

[Questions about payments and private investigators have been omitted.]

Q477 Mr Watson: One last question: do you have any regrets?

Rebekah Brooks: Of course I have regrets . . . .

Q478 Louise Mensch: . . . On the wider culture of hacking, blagging and private detectives in Fleet street, to what extent did the *News of the World* feel justified, in its internal culture, in using those practices because everybody was doing it? . . .

Rebekah Brooks: . . . As far as I was concerned, the failings of all newspapers in not understanding the extent of the use of private investigators across Fleet street was held to account then. . . .

Q479 Louise Mensch: The Committee in 2003 concluded that there was widespread evidence of despicable practices across the media, including blagging and payments to the police. I appreciate the legal sensitivities involved in this question, but I will put it to you anyway. In your evidence to the Committee in 2003, you were asked if you had paid the police, and you clearly said, "We have paid the police in the past." May I suggest to you that the manner in which you said that implied that so do all tabloid newspapers? I am not asking you to make specific allegations, but in your general knowledge, were payments to the police widespread across Fleet street, or were they confined to News International titles?

Rebekah Brooks: . . . I can say that I have never paid a policeman myself; I have never knowingly sanctioned a payment to a police officer. . . .

[Questions about the culture of Fleet Street, lost e-mails, and legal fees have been omitted.]

Q510 Damian Collins: This is potentially something that happened under your watch, as ever, so if it is proven that it was the case, would you take personal responsibility for what happened under your editorship of the newspaper?

Rebekah Brooks: I would take responsibility, absolutely. . . .

[Questions about Milly Dowler have been omitted.]

Q548 Dr Coffey: Final question from me: do you have any regrets about any of the headlines that you have done, now that you have been in the spotlight yourself? You have been subject to quite a lot of media spotlight. Does this make you regret any one at all?

Rebekah Brooks: I don't think that you would find any editor in Fleet Street who did not feel that with some headlines that they had published, they had made some mistakes, and I am no different to that—there have been mistakes. On the other hand, despite, as you say, being in the spotlight recently and having read lots of criticism that is justified and lots of criticism that was totally spurious, I would defend the right of a free press from my entire career. . . .

[Questions about other NoW employees and internal communications have been omitted.]

Q558 Philip Davies: When our report was published in early 2010, when you were chief executive of News International, there were certain things that we obviously reported. We found that the evidence from the people from News International was wholly unsatisfactory. We referred to the collective amnesia in our report, and we felt it was inconceivable that Clive Goodman was a rogue reporter, as had been passed on to us. We referred to the "for Neville" e-mail in there—all that kind of stuff. When you were chief executive of News International, at the time the report was published, did you read the report that we published?

Rebekah Brooks: Yes, I did. I'm not saying that I read every single word, but I read a large majority of it. I particularly read the criticisms that were addressed to the company, and I can only hope that, from the evidence you have heard from us today, you know that we have really stepped up our investigation. . . . I think that everyone involved in 2007 would say now that mistakes were made. But I hope that you feel that we have responded appropriately and responsibly since we saw the information in 2010.

Q559 Philip Davies: So when you read the report did that make you think, "Well blow me, there are some things that don't stack up. We might not have any evidence, I might not know anything about these people, but there is clearly something that is not quite right here"? Did that prompt any activity on your part as chief executive of News International to say, "Well, you know, let's go back over this because there is something not right here"?

Rebekah Brooks: . . . It was only when we had the information in December 2010 that we did something about it. . . .

[Questions about journalists's relationships with politicians have been omitted.]

Q576 Paul Farrelly: . . . Would you agree, Ms Brooks, that part of the public concern here is about the closeness of the police and now politicians to *News of the World* and News International?

Rebekah Brooks: I think the public's concern overwhelmingly, on the interception of voicemails, is the idea that anybody could intercept the voicemails of victims of crime. I think that is their overwhelming concern.

Q577 Paul Farrelly: But there has been a lot of concern voiced over the closeness of police and politicians and *News of the World* and News International; would you agree, as a matter of fact?

Rebekah Brooks: I have seen that the *News of the World* has been singled out for that closeness. I think if you were going to address it—you know this more than anyone on the Committee because of your career as a journalist—it is wholly unfair in discussing the closeness of police and politicians to the media to single out the *News of the World*. . . .

Source: Parliament of the United Kingdom. Committee on Culture, Media, and Sport. "Oral Evidence Taken Before the Culture, Media and Sport, Phone Hacking." July 19, 2011. http://www.publications .parliament.uk/pa/cm201012/cmselect/cmcumeds/uc903-ii/uc90301.htm.

United Nations Responds
to Famine in Somalia

JULY 20, AUGUST 3, AUGUST 17, AND SEPTEMBER 8, 2011

The ongoing troubles in Somalia deepened in 2011 after a drought sank parts of the nation into a severe food crisis and subsequent famine. Twenty years ago Somalia's government collapsed and a series of Transitional Federal Governments have ruled since. These temporary governments have largely been unsuccessful in stopping militants from seizing portions of the country and adequately providing for its citizens. The warring factions have been unable to set up necessary government agencies that can coordinate aid and assist with disease prevention, hampering the 2011 global aid effort. Al Shabab forces that control many portions of the country, including the capital and southern regions, caused additional difficulties. The Islamist militant group with ties to al Qaeda forced Western aid organizations from the country in 2010, and by 2011, these groups were reluctant to return to provide vitally important aid.

2011 Crisis

The United Nations does not often qualify food shortages as famine. In the past two decades, only a few have been categorized as such. Famine is only declared when "acute malnutrition rates among children exceed 30 percent, more than 2 people per 10,000 die per day and people are not able to access food and other basic necessities." Famine hit Somalia in 1991–1992 and killed hundreds of thousands, mainly in the southern portion of the country. But in that year, the global community was far more willing to intervene, despite lawless thugs who ruled portions of the country. The United Nations and United States worked closely together, with the United States sending 25,000 troops to Somalia to allow aid shipments to get to those affected by the famine. The nation was flooded with food aid, but lawless militias gained power by stealing food and profiting by selling it at high prices. The peacekeeping groups left Somalia in 1993 after two American Black Hawk helicopters were shot down. Although the U.S.-led operation was said to have saved 110,000 from dying of famine-related malnutrition or disease, according to the Refugee Policy Group, 240,000 were killed by the famine in 1994.

In 2011, Somalia was hit by the worst drought in sixty years, leading to the worst food crisis in two decades, with food prices rising 270 percent from 2010 to 2011. The drought didn't catch anyone off guard—it was predicted by the U.S. government's Famine Early Warning Systems Network in 2010. The system is intended to help aid groups know when to prepare for famine and position aid. "There has been a catastrophic breakdown of the world's collective responsibility," said Fran Equiza, a regional director at Oxfam, an international organization dedicated to lifting people out of poverty. "The warning signs have been seen for months, and the world has been slow to act," she said. But the continuing tenuous political situation limited aid organizations in how they could respond.

On July 20, 2011, the United Nations responded to the drought and food crisis by declaring a famine in two regions of southern Somalia—southern Bakool and Lower Shabelle. UN Secretary General Ban Ki-moon reported that 3.7 million in the area were in crisis. "The United Nations has been sounding the alert for months," Ban said, calling for $1.6 billion in aid. Mark Bowden, UN humanitarian coordinator for Somalia, said, "If we don't act now, famine will spread to all eight regions of southern Somalia." He continued, "Every day of delay in assistance is literally a matter of life or death." At the time of the two-region famine declaration, tens of thousands had already died from malnutrition, and in some areas up to six children per 10,000 under age five were dying per day. Across the two regions, half of the children were acutely malnourished. A U.S. estimate claimed that between June and August, 29,000 children under the age of five had been killed by malnutrition in southern Somalia.

By September, the United Nations declared six famine regions in Somalia, and reported that millions were near starvation and 750,000 were at risk of death by the end of the year. "In total, four million people are in crisis in Somalia, with 750,000 people at risk of death in the coming four months in the absence of adequate response," according to the UN Food Security and Nutrition Analysis Unit. Half of those killed by malnutrition-related problems were children.

The 2011 Somali crisis went beyond the food shortage to include an increase in the risk of cholera, malaria, typhoid, and measles, because malnourishment suppresses the immune system, making those who survive the famine more susceptible to acquiring these and other diseases. Al Shabab, the Islamic militant group that controls many portions of the country, banned immunizations a few years before the 2011 famine, calling it a Western plot to kill Somali children.

AL SHABAB CONTROL

In 2010, the militant Islamic group forced Western aid organizations from Somalia, but by the time famine struck in 2011, it was pleading with them to return. Aid organizations were wary of doing so because of the dangerous situation in the country and the dozens of aid workers that had been killed in the nation over the years. In August 2011, al Shabab decided to leave most of Mogadishu in control of the transitional government, but this didn't mean immediate peace in the capital or easier aid deliveries. "An absence of conflict does not mean that there is security here," said Bowden. "It's too early to tell whether it is a good and lasting sign, but it does offer the possibility of getting more assistance in through Mogadishu," said Gayle Smith, a White House official. However, Valerie Amos, director of the UN Office for the Coordination of Humanitarian Affairs, reported, "We've had food deliveries in Mogadishu . . . But I do think it is important that we all remember that there are still 2.2 million people in the south and center who require aid and support."

As the famine wore on, questions were raised about how al Shabab and the Transitional Federal Government (TFG) would emerge from the crisis. TFG could capitalize on the crisis by providing aid to Somalis. "It could be a face-lift for them, an opportunity to deliver services and show they are committed," said militia leader Sheik Abdulkadir. "But if a lot of people die here, people will say it's the government's fault," he continued.

INTERNATIONAL RESPONSE

Because al Shabab control of the first two famine regions impacted the willingness and ability of international organizations to provide necessary food and other supplies, aid deliveries throughout the spring and summer of 2011 were insufficient. "Somalia is one of the most complicated places in the world to deliver aid, more complicated than Afghanistan," said Stefano Porretti, head of the World Food Programme effort in Somalia. The UN effort to deliver food aid was hampered by reports of contractors stealing the aid and sparked investigations and reductions in assistance. In August, Bowden reported that aid was only reaching 20 percent of those who needed it. The situation was better in the capital city of Mogadishu, where 50 percent of the needy were receiving aid, which was mainly geared toward children. Because of the lessons from the 1991–1992 effort, aid in 2011 focused more on food vouchers and cash than actual food stocks to prevent organized crime gangs from stealing food and wielding power when doling it out. The new method, according to aid organizations, encouraged Somalis to support local businesses and purchase what they needed most.

Regardless of international aid efforts, the world remained heavily critical of U.S. intervention, or lack thereof. In 2008, the United States declared al Shabab a terrorist organization, and government regulations prevent any material aid from being directed to terrorist groups. Because of the terrorist label, aid to Somalia had been declining for years, from $237 million in 2008 to $29 million in 2010, and aid organizations felt discouraged by the regulations, concerned that sending aid to Somalia might mean they would face prosecution because they had no way to ensure that al Shabab would not steal some or all of the aid sent into the country.

The United States was quick to deny that its own rules were complicating aid efforts. "The issue and the problem is Al Shabab," said Johnnie Carson, the assistant secretary for African affairs at the State Department. In July, the United States committed an additional $28 million to Somalia, on top of the $431 million it had already given to the Horn of Africa in 2011, and agreed that the aid would not be hindered by the material support to terrorists regulation. In August, Dr. Jill Biden, wife of Vice President Joe Biden, traveled to East Africa to highlight the growing crisis and U.S. commitment to aid. "One of the reasons to be here is just to ask Americans and people worldwide, the global community, the human family, if they could just reach a little deeper into their pockets and give money to help these poor people, these poor mothers and children," Dr. Biden said. At the time of Biden's trip, the United States announced another $100 million in aid to Somalia. In addition, the government provided $650 million in cash and kind to stock warehouses in refugee camps with necessary staples through 2012.

Refugee Impact

Thousands of Somali refugees fled across the borders into Ethiopia and Kenya every day, while others fled to Mogadishu where the food situation was less dire. The United Nations reported the arrival of 100,000 refugees in the capital by August. Refugees were forced to walk many miles, sometimes having to leave dying children behind or arriving at refugee camps too far emaciated to be saved. Others were robbed or assaulted on their way to safety. The refugee camps, even the world's largest located in northeastern Kenya, faced significant overcrowding and a lack of vital supplies. "Kenya is already going through a moment when there is not sufficient food in the country," said James Karanja, an outreach worker with the UN refugee agency in Nairobi, further indicating that additional declarations of famine would lead to an increase in the number of refugees. "Then we are having more and more people fleeing in— not because they are insecure because of war—but they are looking for food," said Karanja.

In an effort to stop Somalis from fleeing the country, al Shabab set up imprisonment camps twenty-five miles outside of Mogadishu, filling them with those caught trying to leave the country. Thousands of Somalis ended up in these camps, where there was little food. Al Shabab threatened to kill anyone caught leaving these areas, forcing Somalis to make dangerous escapes in the middle of the night. Sheik Yoonis, a spokesperson for Al Shabab, denied that the camps were set up for imprisonment, saying instead that the camps were attractive to Somalis for their "sense of serenity and security." The organization further denied the existence of famine, calling the UN declaration "an exaggeration."

By November, al Shabab had succeeded in closing virtually all routes to Kenya, and coupled with increased fighting along the border as Kenyan military forces entered Somalia to look for al Shabab insurgents, a growing number of refugees sought assistance in Ethiopia. By November, Ethiopia reported 135,000 Somali refugees, with numbers increasing each day. Like those in Kenya, Ethiopian refugee camps reported a lack of shelter, food, water, and medical supplies. Doubling their difficulties was fighting in nearby Sudan, which meant Ethiopia was also receiving an influx of Sudanese refugees. The United Nations estimated that 50,000 Sudanese refugees would enter Ethiopia by the end of 2011.

—Heather Kerrigan

Following is a statement on a July 20, 2011, United Nations press conference declaring famine in two regions of southern Somalia; a United Nations press release from August 3, 2011, declaring famine in three additional areas of Somalia; a press release on humanitarian aid in Somalia released on August 17, 2011; and an update given by United Nations Humanitarian Coordinator for Somalia Mark Bowden on September 8, 2011, on the famine and drought in Somalia.

UN Declares Famine in Southern Somalia

July 20, 2011

The United Nations today confirmed the existence of famine in two regions of southern Somalia: southern Bakool and Lower Shabelle, and made an urgent appeal for "exceptional efforts" to support Somalis in overcoming that humanitarian crisis, the United Nations Humanitarian Coordinator for Somalia, Mark Bowden, told correspondents today at a Headquarters press conference.

Speaking via video conference, Mr. Bowden reported that, across the country where malnutrition rates were currently the highest in the world and peaking at 50 percent in certain areas in the south, nearly half of the Somali population, or 3.7 million people, were now in crisis, with some 2.8 million in the south.

To expedite the delivery of supplies into the worst-affected areas, he said, the United Nations had begun airlifting urgently needed medical, nutrition and water supplies.

In southern Bakool and Lower Shabelle, acute malnutrition rates exceeded 30 percent, with deaths among children under 5 years old topping 6 per 10,000 a day in some areas. In the last few months, tens of thousands of Somalis had died—the majority, children—from malnutrition and related causes.

Consecutive droughts had affected the country in the last few years, while the ongoing conflict had made it difficult for agencies to operate and access communities in the south of the country, he explained. "If we don't act now, famine will spread to all eight regions of southern Somalia within two months, due to poor harvests and infectious disease outbreaks," he declared. "We still do not have all the resources for food, clean water, shelter and health services to save the lives of hundreds of thousands of Somalis in desperate need."

He estimated that $300 million was needed in the next two months to face the famine, and said that, meanwhile, the lack of resources was alarming. "Every day of delay in assistance is literally a matter of life or death for children and their families in the famine-affected areas," he warned.

While United Nations humanitarian agencies had welcomed the recent request by Al-Shabaab for international assistance in southern Somalia, he said, the inability of food agencies to work in the region since early 2010 had prevented the United Nations from reaching those who needed food—particularly children. That, of course, had contributed to the current crisis.

However, despite those challenges, he said, humanitarian agencies were working hard to respond, and in an effort to reach more children with life-saving interventions, the United Nations and its partners had scaled up emergency nutrition, water and sanitation, and immunization efforts to combat malnutrition and reduce disease.

He provided additional details about the most affected areas of Somalia in the south, in particular the region of Lower Shabelle, Middle and Lower Juba, Bay, Bakool, Benadir, Gedo and Hiraan, which hosted an estimated 310,000 acutely malnourished children. The number of people in crisis throughout the country had increased by over 1 million in the last six months. "More than ever, Somali people need and deserve our full attention. At this time of crisis, we must make exceptional efforts to support Somalis wherever they are in need and expect that all parties will do the same," he urged.

To a question about African support for humanitarian needs in the Horn of Africa, he said the countries affected were providing assistance to their own people but outside of that, African countries had not provided assistance to the United Nations appeal.

Responding to another question on whether it was possible to get the $300 million he felt was needed in the two months, he said it was possible if there was a willingness to provide it. He cited the strong lead taken by both the United Kingdom and the European Commission in that regard; they had accepted the risks that went with providing that support, based on the urgency of the need. He added, however, that their support was not enough; it was up to Member States to "step up to the plate at this time."

SOURCE: United Nations. Department of Public Information. "Press Conference on Somalia Famine by United Nations Humanitarian Coordinator." July 20, 2011. http://www.un.org/News/briefings/docs/2011/110720_Somalia.doc.htm.

UN Declares Famine in Three Somali Regions

August 3, 2011

The United Nations today declared a famine in three more areas in drought-ravaged Somalia, bringing to five the number of regions in the Horn of Africa country where acute malnutrition and starvation have already claimed the lives of tens of thousands of people.

The UN Humanitarian Coordinator for Somalia, Mark Bowden, said the Afgoye corridor outside Mogadishu, the capital itself, and the Middle Shabelle region are now in a state of famine. On 20 July the UN declared outright famine in Lower Shabelle and in southern Bakool region.

A famine can be declared only when certain measures of mortality, malnutrition and hunger are met. They are: at least 20 per cent of households in an area face extreme food shortages with a limited ability to cope; acute malnutrition rates exceed 30 per cent; and the death rate exceeds two persons per day per 10,000 persons.

The spread of the famine conditions highlights the seriousness of the food crisis facing internally displaced persons (IDPs) in Mogadishu. The declaration of famine in the capital follows the massive influx of starving adults and children into the city in the past two months.

The UN Office for the Coordination of Humanitarian Affairs (OCHA), meanwhile, said that the appeal for funds to respond the hunger crisis in the Horn of Africa region, including Ethiopia, Somalia, Kenya and Djibouti, is still only 44 per cent funded, with an additional $1.4 billion still required to cover unmet needs. An estimated 12.4 million people in the entire region are in need of assistance, according to OCHA.

In the Dadaab complex of refugee camps in Kenya—whose population has swelled to nearly 380,000 in recent months, including 40,000 arrivals from Somalia last month alone—the UN High Commissioner for Refugees (UNHCR) reported that mass screening for malnutrition conducted in two of the camps in July revealed alarmingly high rates of acute malnutrition.

The agency has transferred more than 10,500 recent Somali arrivals to Dadaab's Ifo camp extension in an ongoing relocation operation. UNHCR has airlifted thousands of tents to Kenya to accommodate the refugee population, but an additional 45,000 tents are still needed as the influx continues. The agency also voiced concern that Dadaab's water resources could soon be overstretched.

In a related development, the Special Representative of the Secretary-General for Somalia, Augustine Mahiga, appealed to all Somalis, both inside and outside the country, to work together to support the ongoing peace process and alleviate the plight of those suffering from famine.

"This is a time of great crisis, but also of rare opportunity. It is a time for everyone to pull together to help those suffering and to work towards a better future for all," said Mr. Mahiga in a letter to the Somali diaspora.

"I appeal to all those who are able—Somalis and the international community alike— to give as much as they can during this Holy Month to feed the hungry, heal the sick and prevent the famine spreading further," he stated, referring to the Islamic fasting month of Ramadan that began on Monday.

Mr. Mahiga noted that despite recent progress on the political front, one of the contributing factors to the famine has been the ongoing fighting in the country. Some of the extremists are continuing their efforts to intimidate the population by preventing the movement of people from the worst-hit areas, he said.

"We call for the humanitarian agencies to be given unhindered access to all areas to provide desperately needed help," he wrote, adding that the insecurity in many areas means that aid workers take huge risks to make their life-saving deliveries.

SOURCE: United Nations. News Centre. "UN Declares Famine in Another Three Areas of Somalia." August 3, 2011. http://www.un.org/apps/news/story.asp?NewsID=39225.

UN Press Conference on Humanitarian Aid to Somalia

August 17, 2011

Thank you very much. If I may I will make a brief statement on my recent visit to Somalia and Kenya and then of course open up for questions.

In Mogadishu, I was struck by the destruction in the city caused by years of war, but also by how people are nonetheless out in the streets and getting on with their lives. Our aid effort is doing a tremendous amount to help in Mogadishu. Hot meals are being given every day to almost 100,000 people. Half a million people are getting clean water, which is crucial as we seek to prevent the spread of cholera and other diseases. An emergency measles vaccination campaign to reach 88,000 children—80 per cent of the under 15 population in the city and 46,000 women is already happening.

Nonetheless it was clear that even in Mogadishu the famine has already claimed the lives of tens of thousands of people, and it will kill many more if we do not further scale up our efforts. I visited Banadir Hospital where children with the worst levels of malnutrition are given life-saving treatment. It was heartbreaking to see children so weak they couldn't lift their heads, their mothers in despair. Many children don't survive as they get there too late and their situation is too desperate. The medical staff are exhausted, working around the clock, and doing everything they can but they do not have enough medicines and supplies, even though they are getting support—for example, from UNICEF. We need to get more food and nutritional supplies, water, sanitation and hygiene equipment and medical care to those who are in desperate need.

Aid operations are reaching new areas of Somalia all the time. We have been able to provide safe drinking water to 50 per cent of the people in the Afgooye corridor, which hosts thousands of IDPs who have fled the ongoing violence in Mogadishu. Throughout the south of Somalia, in Al-Shabaab controlled areas, more than 500 nutrition centres are operating. These are major accomplishments, and I am optimistic that the work being done on the ground to improve access will continue to shrink the areas of the country that are still off-limits.

We have to remember that the needs are not limited to Somalia. Millions of people are also struggling in Ethiopia, Kenya, and Djibouti. And even as Kenyans and Ethiopians confront the impact of the drought on their own communities, they are hosting hundreds of thousands of Somali refugees, who have fled conflict and famine, and now live in vast, overcrowded camps.

I am grateful to the donors who have provided more than $1.3 billion to make our work possible.

While the situation in these countries has not reached famine proportions, and is not expected to, in part because of longer-term planning which has taken place, for example, safety net programmes, and the national and international aid efforts which are underway, I am very mindful of the need to keep the momentum going. In Ethiopia we have provided food aid to some 3.5 million Ethiopians, and 226,000 refugees. In Djibouti, we have assisted almost all the food affected people; and in Kenya, 1.3 million drought affected people have received food aid, out of the 2.7 million who have been targeted.

I visited Dadaab camp in Kenya which as you all know is the largest refugee camp in the world. It is really more a city than a camp. New arrivals from Somalia are still being registered every day. And despite a fall in the numbers of daily arrivals, the number of children with severe acute malnutrition has risen, and many lose their lives en route. I met one woman who had lost all four of her children on the journey from Somalia to Kenya. There's a tremendous amount of work going on in Dadaab to keep the camp and refugees in supplies. In the weeks ahead we also need to step up our efforts to ensure the host communities in areas accepting refugees are being helped as well.

We have demonstrated, I think, how much can be accomplished when aid agencies are given the resources they need and can get to where they need to. But we're faced with a stillspreading [*sic*] famine in Somalia, and with such scale of suffering, every effort needs to be expanded and sustained in the months ahead. That is why we are still appealing for another just under $1.2 billion. There are still many lives that need to be saved in the Horn of Africa.

Thank you.

SOURCE: United Nations. Office for the Coordination of Humanitarian Affairs. "United Nations Under-Secretary-General for Humanitarian Affairs and Emergency Relief Coordinator, Valerie Amos: Statement to Press on Visit to Somalia and Kenya." August 17, 2011. http://reliefweb.int/node/441463.

UN Update on Famine and Drought in Somalia

September 8, 2011

Thank you for joining us here today for the latest information on the drought and famine situation in Somalia. When I last spoke to you in this forum two months ago, it was to share the news that the drought impacting the Horn of Africa had pushed parts of Somalia into a famine. In the past 10 weeks, the Food Security and Nutrition Analysis Unit and FEWSNET teams have been conducting assessments in the field and investigating more in depth, conducting another 8 surveys that have confirmed the following developments:

- Somalia has suffered its worst 'Gu' harvest in 17 years. The production of crops was 25% of the normal average. The harvest failure serves to emphasize that the agricultural producing areas of southern Somalia are the most affected.
- Combined with the soaring food prices,poor households in southern Somalia can get only 40% to 50% of the food they need to survive. They are facing massive food deficits.
- Somalia's 'Dehr' rains are about to start. These short secondary rains are foreseen to be near normal. We must capitalize on these rains in order to alleviate the current food crisis by the end of the year. The rains also bring increased risks of disease. Cholera, Malaria and Measles could dramatically increase death rates in an already weakened population. Additional support will be required to ensure that we control these risks.

The latest round of surveys shows a continuing deterioration in Somalia. More people are in need of assistance and in some areas there has been a deepening of the crisis. We also know that people will have major needs for assistance well past the end of this year.

So what are we looking at in terms of the current humanitarian situation?

- There are now 4 million Somalis in crisis, more than 50% of the entire Somali population; this is an increase from the figure 3.7 million in July; 3 million of these people are located in the south, which is two-thirds of the entire population of southern Somalia.
- The entire Bay region has now been declared a famine area, so there are now six famine areas in Somalia, up from five. In these areas, there are some 750,000 people who are affected by famine conditions. This is an increase from the July figure of 350,000 people.

I am joined by Grainne Moloney, the Chief Technical Officer for the FSNAU. In the two months since the declaration of the famine, the FSNAU has been collecting data on the numbers of people in crisis, the malnutrition data. I turn the floor over to her to give you a brief explanation of the latest developments and then I will deliver a short statement and take questions. . . .

We cannot underestimate the scale of this crisis and we cannot afford to let our guard down. Somalia, particularly southern Somalia, is the epicenter—it's the famine area, it's the source of most refugees and we must focus our attention and to ensure that we assist those who are there, reduce excess mortality and do our utmost to stabilize and improve access to food.

The increase in humanitarian funds that have come in since July has allowed us to immediately and significantly scale up our response, but this external support will need to be sustained. These funds have only just begun to flow in now and we can expect our activities to continue to scale-up.

Some examples of scale up:

- Over one million people throughout Somalia received general food assistance in August compared to750,000 in July;
- Aid Agencies have provided over half a million beneficiaries with agriculture and livelihood assistance in August, up from 55,000 beneficiaries in July;
- Around 500,000 children are receiving nutritional support; an increase of 200,000 from the past months.
- More than 300,000 displaced people received Emergency Assistance Packages of plastic sheeting, sleeping mats, blankets and other emergency items in 2011;
- Some 465,000 in crisis received water and sanitation support in August, up from 131,000 in July.

International and local humanitarian organisations are now better placed to deliver aid to famine-affected populations. We have scaled up in the regions of Bay, Gedo, south Bakool and Hiraan, particularly in areas along the Kenyan and Ethiopian borders. We will continue to expand our coverage by ramping up the intensity of our coverage. We know we are not yet fully meeting the enormous needs the Somali people are facing. The next four months are critical; in which we must stabilize the situation. However, this is not a short-term crisis, we still need funds to continue to scale up our work and sustain the desperately needed support to the Somali people.

Thank you.

SOURCE: United Nations. Office for the Coordination of Humanitarian Affairs. "Press Statement, UN Humanitarian Coordinator for Somalia, Mr. Mark Bowden." September 8, 2011. http://reliefweb.int/node/445554.

OTHER HISTORIC DOCUMENTS OF INTEREST

FROM PREVIOUS *HISTORIC DOCUMENTS*

European Union Leaders Reach Deal to Save Greece From Financial Collapse

JULY 21, 2011

In a frantic bid to prevent a total financial collapse of one of their member countries, European Union leaders meeting in Brussels on July 21, 2011, agreed on a series of measures that they hoped would steady the Greek—and European—economy and calm the nerves of feverish financial markets. The agreement restructured the massive debt owed by the Greek government by lowering interest rates on the debt and extending the time Greece was allowed to pay back the money it had borrowed. In forging the agreement, the European Union showed its determination to prevent Greece from sinking into a disorderly default—a scenario they feared would damage the wider EU economy given that Greece, along with sixteen other EU states, uses the EU currency, the euro. The agreement gave short-term relief and markets responded positively. But the situation worsened in the following months as the Greek government fell, debt continued to mount, and ordinary Greeks protested—some violently—against painful austerity measures that were being imposed.

THE EURO'S WEAKEST LINK

Greece's financial problems are nothing new. Since being founded as a modern state in 1829, Greece has been in a state of default for the majority of its existence. What makes the current financial crisis different is that the Greek economy is now linked to other European countries more tightly than before because since 2001 it has been part of the EU single currency area, the eurozone. The EU's political decision to let Greece join the eurozone was controversial from the outset as there was evidence even then that Greece did not, in fact, fulfill the strict criteria the European Union devised in the early 1990s to ensure the stability of the new currency, the euro. Nevertheless, EU officials signed off on figures presented by the Greek government that indicated Greece was meeting the so-called convergence criteria, which included having a current account deficit that did not exceed 3 percent of gross domestic product (GDP) and having a public debt level that was no more than 60 percent of GDP.

In the early 2000s, as the European economy rolled along at a steady pace and the euro became integrated into the global economy, the decision to allow Greece to join the EU appeared to have been the correct one. But trouble was silently simmering—caused in large part by the monetary union itself. Under the rules governing the eurozone, member countries are bound to apply the interest rate set by the European Central Bank in Frankfurt. Throughout the early 2000s, those interest rates remained low. That encouraged

Greece to borrow heavily and sink itself deeper in debt, which it might not have done to the same extent had the cost of borrowing been higher.

Matters came to a head with the financial crisis that began in the United States in autumn 2008, when a lack of regulatory oversight of financial institutions contributed to a near collapse of the American banking system. Because the European and American banking sectors were so interconnected, EU governments found themselves scurrying to shore up their own crumbling banks by pumping hundreds of billions of euros into them. Consequently, sovereign debt levels across Europe soared in 2009, including in Greece, which found itself in the weakest of all positions, fiscally speaking, given its troubled history of debt compounded by a deeply ingrained culture of tax evasion.

Greece's Woes Become Europe's Crisis

The situation revealed itself to be even more serious than initially thought when there was a change of government in Greece in October 2009. The new prime minister, George Papandreou, discovered that the previous government had been disguising the degree of financial trouble the country was in and that Greece's deficit and debt levels were higher than previously disclosed. The markets lost all faith in Greece and interest rates on Greek government bonds skyrocketed. The Greek economy began to contract sharply, with unemployment levels increasing from 11.6 percent to 16.2 percent.

European leaders watched this worsening situation with growing alarm. In the initial weeks, German Chancellor Angela Merkel, a key figure given that Germany is Europe's largest and wealthiest economy, insisted that Greece should solve its own problems and that German taxpayers were not going to bail it out. Back in the early 1990s, Germany had been a reluctant convert to the proposal to create a single EU currency precisely because it feared other more profligate European countries—Greece being the classic example—would get into financial trouble and jeopardize the whole currency. Germans' worst nightmares, fomented in post–World War I chaos when hyperinflation got to a point where Germans were collecting their wages in wheelbarrows, seemed to be coming true. Realizing the euro's entire existence was at stake, Merkel changed her tune and in April 2010 the European Union approved its first bailout package for Greece, which totaled $163 billion in loans from national governments and the International Monetary Fund (IMF). Release of those funds was conditional upon Greece making severe cuts in public spending, raising taxes, and introducing structural reforms to make the economy more competitive. A troika consisting of the European Commission, the European Central Bank, and the IMF helped devise Greece's austerity and structural reform program and oversaw its implementation.

When the Greek government then started to roll out the requisite austerity measures in spring 2010, the Greek public became increasingly resistant, taking to the streets in protest and organizing crippling strikes. As the months passed, EU and IMF officials began to doubt the resolve of the Greek government to implement the reforms, which included painful measures like privatizing national assets, cutting public sector jobs and wages, and raising the retirement age. By summer 2011, it was apparent that further measures would need to be taken at the EU level to prevent a total meltdown of the Greek economy. The European Union, throughout this time, was in the process of establishing a $680 billion EU bailout fund that highly indebted EU nations would be able to draw from in times of crisis. Leaders felt that until this EU fund was in place, it was vital to prevent a disorderly default in Greece as that could trigger contagion, leading other EU countries to exit the eurozone and potentially threatening the euro itself. The most vulnerable states were Ireland and Portugal, which had been forced to accept EU-IMF bailouts comparable to Greece's in November 2010 and May 2011, respectively. Spain and Italy were at risk, too, and many doubted that the European Union was financially capable of bailing out economies of their size.

EU Redoubles Its Commitment to Save Greece

At a summit in Brussels on July 21, 2011, the leaders of the seventeen eurozone countries agreed on a range of measures that went beyond the initial April 2010 Greek bailout. While the leaders throughout the crisis were accused of doing too little too late, it was clear from their statement that they understood how high the stakes were. "We reaffirm our commitment to the euro and to do whatever is needed to ensure the financial stability of the euro area as a whole and its Member States," they said. Concretely, the leaders lowered interest rates on Greek debt to 3.5 percent and extended the maturities from 7.5 years to 15 to 30 years. One major innovation in the new package—insisted upon by Chancellor Merkel—was to commandeer the private sector to shoulder some of the burden of rescuing Greece. The statement noted that the private sector had shown itself willing to contribute roughly $139 billion between 2011 and 2019 to help Greece. In case anyone might worry that they were setting a dangerous precedent, the leaders underscored that "Greece requires an exceptional and unique solution." They went on, "All other euro countries solemnly reaffirm their inflexible determination to honour fully their own individual sovereign signature and all their commitments to sustain fiscal conditions and structural reforms."

Referendum Crisis and Government Change

The markets responded well to the summit accord, but as time passed their nervousness returned once more as uncertainty festered over the willingness and ability of the Greek government to implement what it had agreed to in the face of popular protests that became increasingly violent. The government started to fracture, with some party colleagues criticizing Prime Minister Papandreou for not being more forceful in pushing through reforms, while others opposed the severity of the austerity package. Having narrowly survived votes of confidence in the Greek parliament, in early November 2011 Prime Minister Papandreou sent waves of stunned consternation through EU corridors by suddenly announcing he would hold a referendum to consult the Greek people on the EU-IMF program. Key EU leaders like Chancellor Merkel and French President Nicolas Sarkozy, deeply dismayed by Papandreou's move, made their views known. Days later Papandreou resigned as prime minister and with his departure, all talk of a referendum evaporated. Lucas Papademos, an economist who had been vice president of the European Central Bank from 2002 to 2010, formed a new government on November 11. Papademos cobbled together a technocratic government of national unity made up of representatives from Greece's three main political parties.

By early 2012, Papademos was trying to implement the EU-IMF program as Greek law enforcement officers were contending with violent street protests against the austerity measures. Opinion polls showed that while Greeks were deeply unhappy with the measures, they also strongly wished to remain in both the European Union and the eurozone. As for the banks owed money by Greece, after initially grumbling about accepting debt write-offs of 20 percent, it now looked unlikely that they would be paid back even half of what they originally loaned. The long-term goal set for Greece was to reduce its debt to 120 percent of GDP by 2020. With a shrinking economy and years of shock-therapy structural reforms lying ahead, the picture looked bleak. Given the gravity of the situation, some predicted that Greece would soon sink into default and that would force it to abandon the euro. Meanwhile, EU leaders began to voice growing confidence that regardless of what happened to Greece, the euro itself would survive given the steps they had taken to buttress it, notably the creation of the EU bailout fund and the conclusion of the new fiscal compact.

—Brian Beary

Following is a joint statement by the heads of the European Union Euro Area governments, released on July 21, 2011, regarding agreements to stabilize Greece and the European Union monetary zone.

DOCUMENT

EU Statement on Euro Area and Greek Financial Measures

July 21, 2011

[Footnotes have been omitted.]

We reaffirm our commitment to the euro and to do whatever is needed to ensure the financial stability of the euro area as a whole and its Member States. We also reaffirm our determination to reinforce convergence, competitiveness and governance in the euro area. Since the beginning of the sovereign debt crisis, important measures have been taken to stabilize the euro area, reform the rules and develop new stabilization tools. The recovery in the euro area is well on track and the euro is based on sound economic fundamentals. But the challenges at hand have shown the need for more far reaching measures.

Today, we agreed on the following measures:

Greece:

1. We welcome the measures undertaken by the Greek government to stabilize public finances and reform the economy as well as the new package of measures including privatization recently adopted by the Greek Parliament. These are unprecedented, but necessary, efforts to bring the Greek economy back on a sustainable growth path. We are conscious of the efforts that the adjustment measures entail for the Greek citizens, and are convinced that these sacrifices are indispensable for economic recovery and will contribute to the future stability and welfare of the country.

2. We agree to support a new programme for Greece and, together with the IMF and the voluntary contribution of the private sector, to fully cover the financing gap. The total official financing will amount to an estimated 109 billion euro. This programme will be designed, notably through lower interest rates and extended maturities, to decisively improve the debt sustainability and refinancing profile of Greece. We call on the IMF to continue to contribute to the financing of the new

Greek programme. We intend to use the EFSF as the financing vehicle for the next disbursement. We will monitor very closely the strict implementation of the programme based on the regular assessment by the Commission in liaison with the ECB and the IMF.

3. We have decided to lengthen the maturity of future EFSF loans to Greece to the maximum extent possible from the current 7.5 years to a minimum of 15 years and up to 30 years with a grace period of 10 years. In this context, we will ensure adequate post programme monitoring. We will provide EFSF loans at lending rates equivalent to those of the Balance of Payments facility (currently approx. 3.5%), close to, without going below, the EFSF funding cost. We also decided to extend substantially the maturities of the existing Greek facility. This will be accompanied by a mechanism which ensures appropriate incentives to implement the programme.

4. We call for a comprehensive strategy for growth and investment in Greece. We welcome the Commission's decision to create a Task Force which will work with the Greek authorities to target the structural funds on competitiveness and growth, job creation and training. We will mobilise EU funds and institutions such as the EIB towards this goal and relaunch the Greek economy. Member States and the Commission will immediately mobilize all resources necessary in order to provide exceptional technical assistance to help Greece implement its reforms. The Commission will report on progress in this respect in October.

5. The financial sector has indicated its willingness to support Greece on a voluntary basis through a menu of options further strengthening overall sustainability. The net contribution of the private sector is estimated at 37 billion euro. Credit enhancement will be provided to underpin the quality of collateral so as to allow its continued use for access to Eurosystem liquidity operations by Greek banks. We will provide adequate resources to recapitalise Greek banks if needed.

Private sector involvement:

6. As far as our general approach to private sector involvement in the euro area is concerned, we would like to make it clear that Greece requires an exceptional and unique solution.

7. All other euro countries solemnly reaffirm their inflexible determination to honour fully their own individual sovereign signature and all their commitments to sustainable fiscal conditions and structural reforms. The euro area Heads of State or Government fully support this determination as the credibility of all their sovereign signatures is a decisive element for ensuring financial stability in the euro area as a whole.

Stabilization tools:

8. To improve the effectiveness of the EFSF and of the ESM and address contagion, we agree to increase their flexibility linked to appropriate conditionality, allowing them to:

   – act on the basis of a precautionary programme;
   – finance recapitalisation of financial institutions through loans to governments including in non programme countries;

    – intervene in the secondary markets on the basis of an ECB analysis recognizing the existence of exceptional financial market circumstances and risks to financial stability and on the basis of a decision by mutual agreement of the EFSF/ESM Member States, to avoid contagion.

We will initiate the necessary procedures for the implementation of these decisions as soon as possible.

   9. Where appropriate, a collateral arrangement will be put in place so as to cover the risk arising to euro area Member States from their guarantees to the EFSF.

Fiscal consolidation and growth in the euro area:

  10. We are determined to continue to provide support to countries under programmes until they have regained market access, provided they successfully implement those programmes. We welcome Ireland and Portugal's resolve to strictly implement their programmes and reiterate our strong commitment to the success of these programmes. The EFSF lending rates and maturities we agreed upon for Greece will be applied also for Portugal and Ireland. In this context, we note Ireland's willingness to participate constructively in the discussions on the Common Consolidated Corporate Tax Base draft directive (CCCTB) and in the structured discussions on tax policy issues in the framework of the Euro+ Pact framework.

  11. All euro area Member States will adhere strictly to the agreed fiscal targets, improve competitiveness and address macro-economic imbalances. Public deficits in all countries except those under a programme will be brought below 3% by 2013 at the latest. In this context, we welcome the budgetary package recently presented by the Italian government which will enable it to bring the deficit below 3% in 2012 and to achieve balance budget in 2014. We also welcome the ambitious reforms undertaken by Spain in the fiscal, financial and structural area. As a follow up to the results of bank stress tests, Member States will provide backstops to banks as appropriate.

  12. We will implement the recommendations adopted in June for reforms that will enhance our growth. We invite the Commission and the EIB to enhance the synergies between loan programmes and EU funds in all countries under EU/IMF assistance. We support all efforts to improve their capacity to absorb EU funds in order to stimulate growth and employment, including through a temporary increase in co-financing rates.

Economic governance:

  13. We call for the rapid finalization of the legislative package on the strengthening of the Stability and Growth Pact and the new macro economic surveillance. Euro area members will fully support the Polish Presidency in order to reach agreement with the European Parliament on voting rules in the preventive arm of the Pact.

  14. We commit to introduce by the end of 2012 national fiscal frameworks as foreseen in the fiscal frameworks directive.

15. We agree that reliance on external credit ratings in the EU regulatory framework should be reduced, taking into account the Commission's recent proposals in that direction, and we look forward to the Commission proposals on credit ratings agencies.

16. We invite the President of the European Council, in close consultation with the President of the Commission and the President of the Eurogroup, to make concrete proposals by October on how to improve working methods and enhance crisis management in the euro area.

Source: Council of the European Union. "Statement by the Heads of State or Government of the Euro Area and EU Institutions." July 21, 2011. http://www.consilium.europa.eu/uedocs/cms_data/docs/pressdata/en/ec/123978.pdf.

Other Historic Documents of Interest

From this volume

■ European Union Agrees to Fiscal Compact, p. 656

From previous *Historic Documents*

■ EU and IMF Help Stabilize Ireland's Banking System, *2010*, p. 583
■ Europeans Protest Austerity Measures and EU Monetary Policy, *2010*, p. 522
■ Greek Financial Crisis, *2010*, p. 201
■ Report on European Union Draft Constitution, *2003*, p. 492
■ European Commission President on the "Euro," *1998*, p. 271

Federal Officials on Certification of "Don't Ask, Don't Tell" Repeal

JULY 22 AND SEPTEMBER 20, 2011

In 2011, President Barack Obama and officials from the U.S. Department of Defense continued their efforts to implement the repeal of the "Don't Ask, Don't Tell" policy that prevented homosexuals from serving openly in the armed services. Congress passed legislation in December 2010 permitting the repeal under the condition that military leaders certify that such action would not hamper military readiness. After a months-long process of planning, policy revisions, and personnel training, officials certified the repeal in July 2011, enabling gay and lesbian service members to serve openly by late September.

A Controversial Policy

During his 2008 presidential campaign, then-Senator Barack Obama promised to make the repeal of "Don't Ask, Don't Tell" a priority for his administration. The controversial policy had been in place since 1993, when President Bill Clinton issued Defense Directive 1304.26. The directive was intended as a compromise measure that would loosen existing military policy that had expressly banned gays from serving since 1982. Under "Don't Ask, Don't Tell," military officials were prohibited from asking soldiers about their sexual orientation, and openly gay, lesbian, or bisexual Americans were prevented from serving because it was believed their presence would negatively impact morale and overall military readiness. The law further held that any service member who revealed his or her sexual orientation or engaged in homosexual acts could be dismissed.

While lawmakers made several attempts to repeal "Don't Ask, Don't Tell," none were successful until 2010, the second year of Obama's presidency. In February of that year, Chair of the Joint Chiefs of Staff Admiral Mike Mullen and then-Defense Secretary Robert Gates both voiced support for repealing the policy during a Senate Armed Services Committee hearing. Gates assured lawmakers that repeal would not happen anytime soon and that, in compliance with an order issued by Obama during his State of the Union address a month earlier, the Pentagon would conduct a full review of the policy and how its reversal might impact military readiness.

Lawmakers did their part to move forward with repeal. Rep. Patrick Murphy, D-Penn., and Sen. Joe Lieberman, I-Conn., proposed amendments to the National Defense Authorization Act that would allow the Defense Department and military commanders to repeal the ban. The amendments stipulated the ban could only be lifted once the Pentagon had completed its review of the repeal's anticipated impact and military leaders certified that it would not be disruptive. However, Senate Republicans refused to consider the full bill while it included Lieberman's amendment, and debate stalled on September 21, 2010.

While Congress debated the repeal amendments, a lawsuit first filed in 2004 challenging the constitutionality of "Don't Ask, Don't Tell" made its way to federal court. On September 9, 2010, U.S. District Court Judge Virginia Phillips ruled the ban unconstitutional. The U.S. government moved to appeal the ruling, and Phillips issued an injunction to prevent the government from enforcing the law during the appeal process. The Department of Defense then appealed Phillips's injunction to the Ninth Circuit Court of Appeals, which granted a stay on November 1, 2010, allowing the law to stay in place.

Meanwhile, the Pentagon's Comprehensive Review Working Group prepared to release its report on the expected impact of repealing "Don't Ask, Don't Tell." Issued on November 30, 2010, the report concluded that allowing gays and lesbians to serve openly would present a low risk to the military's effectiveness, even at a time of war. The report also stated that approximately 70 percent of active-duty personnel believed the impact of repeal on their units would be positive, mixed, or that there would be no impact at all. In announcing the report's findings, Secretary Gates described obtaining congressional approval of repeal as "a matter of some urgency," lest the courts decide it instead.

Sens. Lieberman and Susan Collins, R-Maine, introduced a separate, stand-alone bill in December 2010 that contained language similar to Lieberman's original amendment. The bill included a new requirement, proposed by Sen. Robert Byrd, R-W.Va., that repeal would not take place until sixty days after military leaders' certification that it could occur. Sen. Harry Reid, D-Nev., used his authority as majority leader to bring the bill directly to the Senate floor, where it passed on December 18. Three days earlier, the House of Representatives approved a similar stand-alone measure, sponsored by Rep. Murphy. President Obama signed the bill into law on December 22, and the process for certifying the repeal began.

PREPARING AND TRAINING THE TROOPS

On January 28, 2011, the Defense Department distributed two memos to its personnel related to the planning and implementation of the repeal. The first established a deadline of February 4 for developing plans and policies to facilitate repeal, while the second detailed policy changes that would occur when the repeal took place. This second memo also called on each branch of the military to immediately identify its specific regulations that would be affected by the law's repeal and to prepare draft changes to those policies based on the memo's guidance.

Two weeks later, on February 11, defense officials sent a repeal implementation plan consisting of several phases to the military branch secretaries. The first phase of the plan, pre-repeal, would focus on training all forces on related policy changes and establishing channels for the services to report every two weeks to the Pentagon and White House on the number of units and people trained and regulations updated. Trainings began later that month, and also involved a multistep approach.

The first phase focused on training service members who would be responsible for the administration of the new policy, such as chaplains, lawyers, and recruiters. In the second phase, senior leaders, including the highest-ranked officers and enlisted men and women, would be trained. The third and final phase would involve training rank-and-file troops. All uniformed military personnel and civilians in a position in which they supervised troops were required to complete the training. Trainings relied on PowerPoint presentations, but also included discussions of hypothetical situations, such as what a commander should do if he saw two male junior officers in civilian clothes at a shopping mall kissing and hugging. Certification of the "Don't Ask, Don't Tell" repeal could not begin until all policies were updated and the first two tiers of training had been completed. By late July, 1.9 million of 2.2 million service members had been trained.

These preparations were complicated somewhat by the Ninth Circuit Court of Appeals decision on July 6 to vacate its stay and order the government to stop enforcing "Don't Ask, Don't Tell" while it appealed the district court's September 2010 decision. However, on July 16, the court temporarily reinstated "Don't Ask, Don't Tell," but prohibited any investigation, penalties, or discharges to be carried out under the rule, following an emergency request by the Obama administration to let the Defense Department continue its repeal process in an orderly fashion.

On July 22, President Obama announced that all requirements had been met, and that he, Admiral Mullen, and newly sworn in Defense Secretary Leon Panetta had certified the "Don't Ask, Don't Tell" repeal. "Today, we have taken the final major step toward ending the discriminatory 'Don't Ask, Don't Tell' law that undermines our military readiness and violates American principles of fairness and equality," Obama said in a statement. "'Don't Ask, Don't Tell' will end, once and for all, in 60 days—on September 20, 2011."

The sixty-day implementation lag was intended to give Congress a second chance to review the measure, and, in fact, House Armed Services Committee Chair Howard McKeon, R-Calif., called for the administration to provide lawmakers with the assessments performed by each branch on the impact of repeal on their forces as well as all policy documents demonstrating that questions about implementation had been resolved. Officials at the Pentagon said they would use the intervening time period to examine whether, following repeal, they could extend certain benefits to same-sex married couples in the military, such as health insurance and base housing. In the end, officials determined several laws, including the Defense of Marriage Act, prevented the military from doing so. Military officials also began accepting applications from openly gay recruits in anticipation of repeal, but waited to process them.

On September 20, the formal repeal of "Don't Ask, Don't Tell" occurred at 12:01 a.m. Undersecretary of Defense for Personnel and Readiness Clifford Stanley distributed a memo to military and Defense Department officials, declaring that "effective today, statements about sexual orientation or lawful acts of homosexual conduct will not be considered as a bar to military service or admission to Service academies, ROTC or any other accession program." The memo further affirmed that "all Service members are to treat one another with dignity and respect regardless of sexual orientation," and noted that harassment or abuse based on an individual's sexuality would have consequences.

The repeal meant that any pending investigations, discharges, and other administrative proceedings initiated against personnel under "Don't Ask, Don't Tell" came to a halt, and any personnel who had been discharged under the law were allowed to re-enlist. Some military policies did not change with repeal, including personal standards of conduct, policies concerning the exercise of religious beliefs, or duty assignment. There were also no immediate changes to eligibility standards for benefits, although service members were granted the ability to designate a partner as a life insurance beneficiary or as a designated caregiver in the Wounded Warrior program. New policies also prohibited officials from creating separate bathroom facilities or living quarters based on sexual orientation, but did preserve commanders's discretion to alter "berthing or billeting" assignments in accordance with service policy. The military did not create a new policy to allow for the release of service members from their service commitments if they were opposed to the "Don't Ask, Don't Tell" repeal or to serving with gays, emphasizing that all troops were expected to fulfill their enlistment requirements.

Lawmakers applauded the repeal, describing it as a reaffirmation of American values. "[O]ur nation will finally close the door on a fundamental unfairness for gays and lesbians, and indeed affirm equality for all Americans," said House Minority Leader Nancy Pelosi, D-Calif. Former service members also praised the repeal. "Now, gays and lesbians can serve honestly and openly in the military with full integrity and have this 50-pound weight off their back," said former Air Force Major Mike Almy, who was discharged under "Don't Ask, Don't Tell."

Some, however, did not support the repeal. "This is not a legitimate victory for anyone," said the Center for Military Readiness in a statement. "The high-powered campaign for gays in the military was fueled by sophistry, administration-coordinated deception, faux 'research' from LGBT activists, and misuse of the military's own culture of obedience."

Ongoing Challenges

The repeal did not result in the resolution of all issues related to gay rights in the military and "Don't Ask, Don't Tell." Two days after the formal repeal, the U.S. government was in court to oppose a lawsuit filed by the American Civil Liberties Union (ACLU) seeking full severance pay for personnel dismissed under the policy. The ACLU sought class action status for 142 people who had only received half their expected severance pay upon being discharged. While the military grants severance pay to all personnel who serve at least six years but are involuntarily discharged, certain conditions, including homosexuality, resulted in automatic severance pay reduction prior to the "Don't Ask, Don't Tell" repeal. The Justice Department asked the U.S. Court of Federal Claims to dismiss the suit, arguing that the court cannot rewrite military regulations, but the presiding judge said she was unlikely to grant the government's request.

The military also continues to grapple with the issue of gay marriage and civil unions, particularly in states where such practices are legal. The Navy tried earlier in 2011 to train chaplains about same-sex civil unions but put an end to it after more than sixty lawmakers objected. The Pentagon is currently reviewing the issue and continues to examine opportunities to extend military benefits to nonmarried same-sex partners.

—Linda Fecteau

Following is a statement by President Barack Obama on July 22, 2011, on the certification of the "Don't Ask, Don't Tell" repeal; a memorandum from the under secretary of defense on September 20, 2011, on the formal "Don't Ask, Don't Tell" repeal; a statement by President Obama on September 20, 2011, on the formal "Don't Ask, Don't Tell" repeal; and a news briefing with Defense Secretary Leon Panetta and Joint Chiefs of Staff Chairman Admiral Mike Mullen on September 20, 2011, on "Don't Ask, Don't Tell."

President Obama on Certification of "Don't Ask, Don't Tell" Repeal

July 22, 2011

Today we have taken the final major step toward ending the discriminatory "don't ask, don't tell" law that undermines our military readiness and violates American principles of fairness and equality. In accordance with the legislation that I signed into law last December, I have certified and notified Congress that the requirements for repeal have been met. "Don't ask, don't tell" will end, once and for all, in 60 days—on September 20, 2011.

As Commander in Chief, I have always been confident that our dedicated men and women in uniform would transition to a new policy in an orderly manner that preserves unit cohesion, recruitment, retention, and military effectiveness. Today's action follows extensive training of our military personnel and certification by Secretary Panetta and Admiral Mullen that our military is ready for repeal. As of September 20th, servicemembers will no longer be forced to hide who they are in order to serve our country. Our military will no longer be deprived of the talents and skills of patriotic Americans just because they happen to be gay or lesbian.

I want to commend our civilian and military leadership for moving forward in the careful and deliberate manner that this change requires, especially with our Nation at war. I want to thank all our men and women in uniform, including those who are gay or lesbian, for their professionalism and patriotism during this transition. Every American can be proud that our extraordinary troops and their families, like earlier generations that have adapted to other changes, will only grow stronger and remain the best fighting force in the world and a reflection of the values of justice and equality that the define us as Americans.

SOURCE: U.S. Executive Office of the President. "Statement on Certification of Repeal of the Department of Defense's 'Don't Ask, Don't Tell' Policy." July 22, 2011. *Daily Compilation of Presidential Documents* 2011, no. 00517 (July 22, 2011). http://www.gpo.gov/fdsys/pkg/DCPD-201100517/pdf/DCPD-201100517.pdf.

Department of Defense on Official "Don't Ask, Don't Tell" Repeal

September 20, 2011

Under Secretary of Defense

4000 Defense Pentagon

Washington, D.C. 20301-4000

September 20, 2011

MEMORANDUM FOR SEE DISTRIBUTION

SUBJECT: Repeal of "Don't Ask, Don't Tell"

The purpose of this memorandum is to inform you that the law commonly known as "Don't Ask, Don't Tell" (DADT), 10 U.S.C. Sec 654, is repealed and no longer in effect in the Department of Defense.

This repeal today follows the certification to Congress by the President, Secretary of Defense, and Chairman of the Joint Chiefs of Staff on July 22, 2011 that the Armed Forces were prepared to implement repeal in a manner consistent with the standards of military readiness, military effectiveness, unit cohesion, and recruiting and retention.

Effective today, statements about sexual orientation or lawful acts of homosexual conduct will not be considered as a bar to military service or admission to Service academies, ROTC or any other accession program. It remains the policy of the Department of Defense that sexual orientation is a personal and private matter. Applicants for enlistment or appointment may not be asked, or required to reveal, their sexual orientation. Sexual orientation may not be a factor in accession, promotion, separation, or other personnel decision-making.

All Service members are to treat one another with dignity and respect regardless of sexual orientation. Harassment or abuse based on sexual orientation is unacceptable and will be dealt with through command or inspector general channels. The Department of Defense is committed to promoting an environment free from personal, social, or institutional barriers that prevent Service members from rising to the highest level of responsibility possible regardless of sexual orientation. Gay and lesbian Service members, like all Service members, shall be evaluated only on individual merit, fitness, and capability.

Effective today, the Department of Defense and Services will implement their respective pre-approved policy and regulatory revisions effected by repeal. Additional policy guidance can be found in the attached memorandum dated January 28, 2011, "Repeal of Don't Ask, Don't Tell and Future Impact on Policy," and the September 20, 2011, "Repeal Implementation Quick Reference Guide."

Clifford L. Stanley

[Attachments and a distribution list have been omitted.]

SOURCE: U.S. Department of Defense. "Memorandum: Repeal of Don't Ask, Don't Tell." September 20, 2011. http://www.defense.gov/home/features/2010/0610_dadt/USD-PR-DADT_Repeal_Day_Memo_20Sep.pdf.

President Obama on the Repeal of "Don't Ask, Don't Tell"

DOCUMENT

September 20, 2011

Today, the discriminatory law known as "Don't Ask, Don't Tell" is finally and formally repealed. As of today, patriotic Americans in uniform will no longer have to lie about who they are in order to serve the country they love. As of today, our armed forces will no longer lose the extraordinary skills and combat experience of so many gay and lesbian servicemembers. And today, as Commander in Chief, I want those who were discharged under this law to know that your country deeply values your service.

I was proud to sign the Repeal Act into law last December because I knew that it would enhance our national security, increase our military readiness, and bring us closer to the principles of equality and fairness that define us as Americans. Today's achievement is a tribute to all the patriots who fought and marched for change: to Members of Congress from both parties who voted for repeal, to our civilian and military leaders who ensured a smooth transition, and to the professionalism of our men and women in uniform who showed that they were ready to move forward together, as one team, to meet the missions we ask of them.

For more than two centuries, we have worked to extend America's promise to all our citizens. Our armed forces have been both a mirror and a catalyst of that progress, and our troops, including gays and lesbians, have given their lives to defend the freedoms and liberties that we cherish as Americans. Today every American can be proud that we have taken another great step toward keeping our military the finest in the world and toward fulfilling our nation's founding ideals.

SOURCE: U.S. Executive Office of the President. "Statement on the Repeal of the Department of Defense's 'Don't Ask, Don't Tell' Policy." September 20, 2011. *Compilation of Presidential Documents 2011*, no. 00653 (September 20, 2011). http://www.gpo.gov/fdsys/pkg/DCPD-201100653/pdf/DCPD-201100653.pdf.

Department of Defense Press Conference on "Don't Ask, Don't Tell" Repeal

DOCUMENT

September 20, 2011

SECRETARY LEON PANETTA: Good afternoon. It's good to see everyone again.

First of all, let me acknowledge that this is an historic day for the Pentagon and for the nation. As of 12:01 a.m. this morning, we have the repeal of "Don't Ask, Don't Tell," pursuant to the law that was passed by the Congress last December. Thanks to this change, I believe we move closer to achieving the goal at the foundation of the values that America's all about—equality, equal opportunity and dignity for all Americans.

As Secretary of Defense, I am committed to removing all of the barriers that would prevent Americans from serving their country and from rising to the highest level of responsibility that their talents and capabilities warrant. These are men and women who put their lives on the line in the defense of this country, and that's what should matter the most.

I want to thank the repeal implementation team and the service secretaries along with the service chiefs for all of their efforts to ensure that DOD is ready to make this change, consistent with standards of military readiness, with military effectiveness, with unit cohesion and with the recruiting and retention of the armed forces.

All of the service chiefs have stated very clearly that all of these elements have been met in the review that they conducted. Over 97 percent of our 2.3 million men and women in uniform have now received education and training on repeal as as result of these efforts.

I also want to thank the Comprehensive Review Working Group for the work they did on the report that laid the groundwork for the change in this policy, and above all, I'd like to single out the person who's next to me at this table, Admiral Mike Mullen.

His courageous testimony and leadership on this issue, I think, were major factors in bringing us to this day. And he deserves a great deal of credit for what has occurred. . . .

[The following three pages have been omitted and contain praise for Admiral Mullen and a discussion of defense budget negotiations.]

ADM. MULLEN: A word or two on today's implementation of the repeal of "don't ask, don't tell." As you all know, I testified in early 2010 that it was time to end this law and this policy. I believed then, and I still believe, that it was first and foremost a matter of integrity; that it was fundamentally against everything we stand for as an institution to force people to lie about who they are just to wear a uniform. We are better than that. We should be better than that. And today, with implementation of the new law fully in place, we are a stronger joint force, a more tolerant joint force, a force of more character and more honor, more in keeping with our own values.

I am convinced we did the work necessary to prepare for this change, that we adequately trained and educated our people, and that we took into proper consideration all the regulatory and policy modifications that needed to be made.

I appreciate the secretary's confidence in me and his kind praise, but today is really about every man and woman who serves this country, and every man and woman in uniform, regardless of how they define themselves. And tomorrow, they'll all get up, they'll all go to work, and they will all be able to do that work honestly, and their fellow citizens will be safe from harm. And that's all that really matters.

Thank you.

Q: Mr. Secretary, Admiral Mullen mentioned that men and women in uniform are more tolerant today than when the "Don't Ask, Don't Tell" policy was done 18 years ago. I'm wondering how do you guard against the possibility that some will try to undermine it or even reverse it by committing acts of harassment or violence against gays.

And also in your opening remarks you mentioned that you're committed to removing all barriers to equal opportunity and service in the military. Does that include allowing women to serve in any position in the military, combat?

If I may ask a quick question to the admiral, a follow-up, if you don't—

ADM./SEC.: A third one?

Q: Could you—would you comment on also—could you also elaborate on the remarks you made this morning about the timetable for the withdrawal in Iraq, which you've said, I believe, that the U.S. would be down to 30,000 troops [*sic*] (the estimated figure is approximately 40,000 troops) by the end of this month. I'm wondering, is that an acceleration of what the plan was recently? Because it's quite a large drop. And also, does this compress the time frame in which the Iraqis have to make a decision?

ADM. MULLEN: I'll just take the last one.

SEC. PANETTA: I'm going to let him go first.

ADM. MULLEN: No, this is—this is the time—this is the draw-down plan that General Austin has had in place, specifically. And it's really a plan that gets us to—under the current agreement to all the troops out by the end of December, so there's no change.

SEC. PANETTA: With regards to, you know, the possibility of harassment, look, we have a zero tolerance with regards to harassment. And my hope is that the command structure operating with the—you know, the standard disciplines that are in place will implement those disciplines and will ensure that harassment doesn't take place and that all behavior is consistent with the discipline and the best interests of our military.

With regards to other areas and other barriers, I mean, I think—I think that we always have to continue to look at those issues and not just simply, you know, shove—put them off the table.

I think—I think as we progress, particularly having taken this step, I think the opportunity to look at those other opportunities is something we ought to continue to pay attention to.

Q: Is it a high priority for you?

SEC. PANETTA: Right now I've got the budget, which is my highest priority.

Q: Mr. Chairman, you mentioned that you really did come out early and publicly in calling "Don't Ask, Don't Tell" an unfair law. As you prepare now to leave office and you look back on your career, where does that stand—taking that stand rank in your career. And are you comfortable leaving a military in which the partners of lot—of a lot of these gay and lesbian service members still won't have access to health care, to pensions, even spousal support networks, when the service members deploy?

ADM. MULLEN: I mean, one of the reasons that I've been in the military for over four decades is because I care immensely about the people and their families and that they are—they have been extraordinary to work with and depend on my whole career. From the point of view of this particular law, I mean, some of it was just actually timing. I—you know, I happened to be the chairman when this thing came into, obviously, very intense focus. I expressed very specifically my personal views at a time when I knew that that was going to be asked of me. And then obviously the process for change has evolved from there.

I'm not one that—I don't think about, you know, top 10, top 5, whatever. Obviously this is a—this is a huge change. It hits at—the heart of the issue for me is the integrity of the institution. It is a value for us. It serves us well.

And in that regard, seeing this change is a huge step in the right direction, to be consistent with those people that I—with all our people that I care so much about and to be consistent with that value. So, I mean, that's how I would describe it as I would look back on it.

And I think I said then, said today, it's the right thing to do. It's done. We need to move on.

Q: And to the second part as well, about leaving a military in which a lot of the partners still won't have equal treatment as some of their—some of the other service members?

ADM. MULLEN: Well, as you know, and we've talked about this, I mean, we follow the law here. And, you know, DOMA, that law restricts some of the issues that you talk about. And we're going to follow that law as long as it exists. Certainly we're aware there are—there are benefits which do accrue to this change very specifically and directly that are—that went into effect last night at midnight, and there are others, some of the ones that you talk about, which will—certainly in compliance with the law, there will not be any change. . . .

[The following two pages have been omitted and contain questions and answers about recent developments in Afghanistan.]

Q: Admiral Mullen?

ADM. MULLEN: Yes, sir?

Q: General James Amos made a recommendation against repealing "don't ask, don't tell" while testifying before Congress in early December. He said he couldn't turn his back on the Pentagon's "don't ask, don't tell" survey, showing that the majority of his combat units were concerned that repealing the ban would have a negative effect on the mission in Afghanistan. Was the general wrong in opposing "Don't Ask, Don't Tell" based on concerns among his combat troops, and what is the Pentagon doing to mitigate those concerns?

ADM. MULLEN: I'm—General Amos made his position very clear back then. The second part of his sentence was: If the law changes, the Marines will be the first ones to do the training and to comply with the law. And that's happened.

So the secretary spoke to the—both of us spoke to the training and quite frankly over the last several months, as we've conducted the training, we have in—not found, you know, any significant issues either—obviously the training was not to change one's view; it was to make sure everybody understood what the rules were. And the Marines do that better than anybody else. So I have great confidence, you know, the Marine Corps is going to march off and do this, as General Amos said they would and actually tells us they are.

SEC. PANETTA: I talked to—I talked to General Amos directly about that, and he said that, you know, after doing the review and finding that there was no impact in terms of recruitment or morale or unit cohesion, that he was committed to putting this in place and that it was now important to move on. . . .

[The following four pages have been omitted and contain questions and answers about U.S. relations in Afghanistan, Iraq, and Libya, and defense budget negotiations.]

SOURCE: U.S. Department of Defense. "DOD News Briefing With Secretary Panetta and Admiral Mullen From the Pentagon." September 20, 2011. http://www.defense.gov/transcripts/transcript.aspx?transcriptid=4886.

OTHER HISTORIC DOCUMENTS OF INTEREST

FROM PREVIOUS *HISTORIC DOCUMENTS*

Norwegian Government on Oslo and Utøya Terrorist Attacks

JULY 24, JULY 26, AND AUGUST 1, 2011

On July 22, 2011, 77 people were killed and more than 150 were wounded in an attack on Norway's government buildings in the capital city of Oslo and a shooting at a youth camp sponsored by the Liberal Party. Both the bombing and the shootings had been meticulously planned and were clearly targeted at the nation's ruling party. The man accused of both attacks, Anders Behring Breivik, admitted that he committed the terrorist acts to make clear the effect of the Liberal Party's immigration policies on Norway.

TWIN TERRORIST ATTACKS

On the afternoon of July 22, 2011, a car bomb exploded in Oslo, Norway, damaging the prime minister's offices and the finance and oil ministries. The bomb killed eight people. Shortly after the bombing, police received reports that a man dressed as a police officer was shooting campers on the island of Utøya, nineteen miles away from the capital. The twin attacks were the worst in Europe since 2004 when more than 350 were killed at a Russian school.

Police were slow to respond to Utøya and suspect that Anders Behring Breivik, the man who claimed responsibility for the attacks, used the Oslo bombing to draw the attention of police away from the island. At 4:57 p.m. local time, approximately an hour and a half after the Oslo explosion, Breivik asked for a boat to take him to Utøya, disguised as a police officer and telling the ferry driver that he was going to the island to do research related to the Oslo bombing. When he arrived on the island, Breivik gathered campers around him, claiming that he was there to check on their security. He then opened fire, shooting those around him and those who tried to escape by running or jumping into the water. Breivik used dum-dum bullets, which disintegrate in the victim's body and cause maximum internal damage.

Police faced a number of difficulties in reaching the island, which is accessible only by boat. Police first learned of the Utøya attack at 5:27 p.m., and a SWAT team was dispatched to the island at 5:40 p.m. At approximately 5:52 p.m., police arrived at the pier across the lake from the island, and an antiterrorism force joined them at 6:09 p.m. Both groups were forced to wait for suitable transportation to take them across the lake. Police arrived at the island at 6:25 p.m. using commercial boats, and it took an additional forty-five minutes for police to reach Breivik. Haarvard Gaasbakk led the first police squad that arrived on the island and was directed by campers to the location of the shooter. "The shots were coming thick and fast," said Gaasbakk. When police reached Breivik, he was armed with an automatic rifle and pistol, and still had a significant amount of ammunition. Breivik immediately surrendered.

During the time it took police to reach Breivik, he called the police emergency number twice and hung up both times. The first call was made twenty-six minutes before his arrest. "I am on Utøya. I want to hand myself in," Breivik told the dispatcher. The next call was made one minute before his arrest, and Breivik asked to be transferred to the commander of the antiterror police force. "I am a commander in the Norwegian resistance movement," he said. "I have fulfilled my operation, so I want to . . . surrender."

Police were criticized for their response to the shooting, specifically for driving to the lake rather than using a helicopter. Media helicopters had arrived on the scene before police and were recording footage of the shooting. According to police, their helicopter team was away on holiday, and the nearest available helicopter pilot was in the southern part of the country. They also argued that helicopter surveillance of the scene was unavailable because of the public holiday, and that the armed police units were tied up dealing with the bombing in Oslo.

ANDERS BEHRING BREIVIK

Breivik was born on February 13, 1979, in London, England, where his father, Jens Breivik, was stationed as a diplomat. "When he was young, he was a very ordinary boy. He was not interested in politics at the time," said Jens Breivik of his son. Breivik grew up in a middle-class town and his mother, a nurse, and father divorced when he was one. Breivik described his childhood as happy. He attended an elite high school and was regarded by his teachers as intelligent. Former classmates said the tall, blonde boy was easy to forget, and that he spent most of his time with a Muslim friend. It was in his 20s that Breivik's demeanor began to change and he started viewing immigration into Norway as a threat to society. "Around year 2000, I realized that the democratic struggle against the Islamization of Europe, European multiculturalism was lost," Breivik wrote in his manifesto. "I decided to explore alternative forms of opposition. Protesting is saying that you disagree. Resistance is saying you will put a stop to this. I decided I wanted to join the resistance movement." Breivik joined the Progressive Party, one of the leading Norwegian right-wing groups, in 1999, but left the group in 2006, frustrated by the party's move toward the center of the political spectrum.

Breivik became obsessed with immigration, specifically Muslim immigration and multiculturalism, which he saw as a threat to Norwegian culture. Immigration had been increasing since the 1970s, and by 2011, 10 percent of the population was foreign born. Most recently, many immigrants were asylum seekers from Afghanistan, Iraq, Somalia, and Eritrea. In 2007, seeking a group that shared his passion for a pure Norway, Breivik joined the Norwegian Order of Freemasons. He also claimed to be a member of the Knights Templar, a group that existed from the 12th to 14th centuries and took part in the Crusades. A number of white supremacist groups have taken inspiration from the Knights Templar. While preparing for the Oslo and Utøya attacks, Breivik spent most of his time participating in Internet debates and playing online video games. Prior to July 22, 2011, Breivik had no criminal record.

MANIFESTO AND VIDEO

In preparation for the attacks, Breivik rented a farm in eastern Norway, near Oslo. There, he created a front company, Geofarm, that would allow him to purchase six tons of ammonium nitrate fertilizer for his bomb while evading police detection. Breivik also joined a firearms club in 2005 to help him obtain weapons for the Utøya attack. Beginning in 2006, Breivik started researching and writing his manifesto, which he posted online a few hours before the attacks and which included details on his planning and preparation strategy and his views on multiculturalism and Muslim immigration in Norway. The manifesto, which took three years to write, derived entire sections word-for-word from Unabomber Ted Kaczynski's manifesto, only replacing the word "leftism" with the word "multiculturalism."

The 1,500-page manifesto was titled "2083: A European Declaration of Independence," and was published under the name Andrew Berwick, an Anglicized version of Breivik's name. Breivik selected 2083 as the year he believed a new Europe would emerge from the current state of multiculturalism. In his early entries, Breivik described preparing for his attacks. "I'm creating two different and 'professional looking' prospectuses for 'business ventures.' A mining company and a small farm operation. The reasoning for this decision is to create a credible cover in case I am arrested in regards to the purchase and smuggling of explosives or components of explosives," Breivik wrote. In July 2010, Breivik noted that he had finished his "armour acquisition phase" and by September of the same year he wrote that he had applied for a semiautomatic rifle. "On the application form I stated: 'hunting deer,'" Breivik wrote. "It would have been tempting to just write the truth: 'executing category A and B cultural Marxists/multicultural traitors' just to see their reaction." Between November 2010 and January 2011, Breivik devoted pages to describing his pistol and rifle training. In his last post only a few hours before the Oslo bombing, he wrote, "I believe this will be my last entry. It is now Fri July 22nd 12.51."

Forensic clinical psychologist Ian Stephen said the manifesto was "written by a man who is absolutely meticulous in his development of his philosophy and he has researched everything, obviously shut away for a long period of time reading, researching, digging into the internet, reading books." Stephen continued, Breivik "formulated this absolute policy of hatred of anything that is non-Nordic in a sense, and looking at planning how to take over the world [in a] rather insane, over-complicated deluded manner."

In addition to his manifesto, Breivik posted a twelve-minute anti-Muslim video on YouTube shortly before the attacks that featured pictures of him in a wetsuit and carrying automatic weapons. The video was titled "Knights Templar 2083," and consisted of four parts: "The Rise of Cultural Marxism," "Islamic Colonization," "Hope," and "New Beginning." The video advocated for a Norwegian uprising against Islam.

Arrest and Trial

Upon his arrest, Breivik quickly admitted to both the bombing and shooting rampage. Breivik was said to be calm during his first trial on July 25, and expressed his opinion that he anticipated spending the rest of his life in prison. Judge Kim Heger, citing Breivik, said his reason for the twin attacks was "not . . . to kill as many people as possible, but to give a 'sharp signal.' . . . As long as the Labor Party follows its ideological line and continues to deconstruct Norwegian culture and import Muslims en masse so they must take responsibility for this treason." Heger continued, "According to what the court understands, the accused believes that he needed to carry out these acts in order to save Norway and Western Europe from, among other things, cultural Marxism and Muslim takeover." Breivik's lawyer, Geir Lippestad, said his client admitted to long-term planning of the attacks, which Breivik called "gruesome but necessary." Breivik refused to accept criminal responsibility for the crimes because he believed the attacks were necessary to preserve Norway.

During his July 25 trial, the court argued for a media blackout to prevent giving Breivik a platform to share his extremist views. At this trial, the court ruled that Breivik could be held for eight weeks, and that four of those weeks would be in complete isolation, which was deemed necessary by the court because they wanted to stop Breivik from contacting anyone who may have acted as an accomplice during the planning, from hearing news from other prisoners, or from tampering with evidence. Given the "seriousness, the extent and character of this case, the court considers the arguments for isolation are immense," said Heger. On August 19, Breivik's isolation was extended for an additional four weeks.

Ultimately, Breivik was charged with acts of terrorism, which carries a maximum penalty of twenty-one years in prison. Prosecutors can request that Breivik be held longer if they determine that releasing him would be dangerous to society. If a judge ruled to keep Breivik in prison for longer than twenty-one years, he would need to appear in court for a new trial every five years.

In November, a psychiatric evaluation determined that Breivik was insane. The report produced by the psychiatrists who interviewed him found that he developed paranoid schizophrenia and created his "own delusional universe where all his thoughts and acts are guided by his delusions." The public expressed shock at the declaration, because Breivik's acts did not match their view of a paranoid schizophrenic. "How can someone who has planned this for such a long time . . . be considered insane," said Per Sandberg, deputy leader of the Progress Party. The report will still need to be reviewed by the Norwegian Board of Forensic Medicine before a determination of legal insanity is made. Even if Breivik is declared legally insane, he will still be tried in April 2012, but prosecutors will no longer be able to ask for the maximum prison sentence. Instead, they will have to ask for mental health treatment.

—Heather Kerrigan

Following is an address by Norwegian Prime Minister Jens Stoltenberg on July 24, 2011, on the Oslo and Utøya terrorist attacks; a statement by Norwegian Minister of Foreign Affairs Jonas Gahr Støre on July 26, 2011, at a memorial service for victims of the terrorist attacks; and an address delivered by the Norwegian prime minister on August 1, 2011, also in commemoration of the victims of the attacks.

Norwegian Prime Minister on Terrorist Attacks

DOCUMENT

July 24, 2011

Your Majesties,

Dear Eskil,

Dear all of you,

It is nearly two days since Norway was hit by the worst atrocity it has seen since the Second World War. On Utøya, and in Oslo.

It seems like an eternity.

These have been hours, days and nights filled with shock, despair, anger and weeping.

Today is a day for mourning. Today, we will allow ourselves to pause. Remember the dead. Mourn those who are no longer with us.

92 lives have been lost. Several people are still missing. Every single death is a tragedy. Together they add up to a national tragedy. We are still struggling to take in the scale of this tragedy. Many of us know someone who has been lost. Even more know of someone.

I knew several. One of them was Monica. She worked on Utøya for 20 years or so. For many of us she was Utøya. Now she is dead. Shot and killed while providing care and security for young people from all over the country. Her husband John and daughters Victoria and Helene are in Drammen Church today. It is so unfair. I want you to know that we are weeping with you.

Another is Tore Eikeland. Leader of the Labour Youth League in Hordaland and one of our most talented young politicians. I remember him being met with acclaim by the whole Labour national congress when he gave a stirring speech against the EU Postal Directive, and won the debate. Now he is dead. Gone for ever. It is incomprehensible.

These are two of those we have lost. We have lost many more on Utøya and in the government offices. We will soon have their names and pictures. Then the full extent of this evil act will become apparent in all its horror. This will be a new ordeal. But we will get through this too. Amidst all this tragedy, I am proud to live in a country that has managed to hold its head up high at a critical time. I have been impressed by the dignity, compassion and resolve I have met.

We are a small country, but a proud people. We are still shocked by what has happened, but we will never give up our values. Our response is more democracy, more openness, and more humanity. But never naivity. No one has said it better than the Labour Youth League girl who was interviewed by CNN:

"If one man can create that much hate, you can only imagine how much love we as a togetherness can create."

Finally, I would like to say to the families all over the country who have lost one of their loved ones:

You have my and the whole of Norway's deepest sympathy for your loss. Not only that. The whole world shares your sorrow. I have promised to pass on the condolences of Barack Obama, Vladimir Putin, Frederik Reinfeldt, Angela Merkel, David Cameron, Dimitry Medvedev and many other heads of state and government.

This cannot make good your loss. Nothing can bring your loved ones back. But we all need support and comfort when life is at its darkest. Now life is at its darkest for you. I want you to know that we are there for you.

Source: Office of the Prime Minister of Norway. Speeches and Articles. "Address by Prime Minister in Oslo Cathedral." July 24, 2011. http://www.regjeringen.no/en/dep/smk/aktuelt/taler_og_artikler/statsminist eren/statsminister_jens_stoltenberg/2011/tale-ved-statsminister-jens-stoltenberg.html?id=651789.

Norwegian Minister of Foreign Affairs on Terrorist Attacks

July 26, 2011

Consolation, peace, reconciliation, community—these are some of the things we come to mosques, churches and synagogues in search of. In our despair, in our vulnerability.

Not to find all the answers, but to find consolation. I quote from Sura 113 of the Quran: "I seek refuge in the Lord of the Daybreak (. . .) from the evil of darkness when it is intense". We find similar words in other holy texts, words that comfort people in this time of darkness. One minute's silence. Days of intense pain.

I have come straight from the University Hospital at Ulleval where I met survivors, the seriously injured, young people who will be marked for life. I have also met devastated parents, who will not see their children again.

We will need to stand together for a long time. We are going to need each other for a long time. We are a deeply affected nation—but we have not been stopped. Norway is up and running. Norway is taking responsibility. Norway is recognisable.

If there was one thing the employees in the ministries hit by the bomb and the young people on Utøya stood for, it was values such as democracy, the rule of law, justice and order. Values that are shared by all good people in this country.

We are standing together across all dividing lines. At the memorial service in Oslo Cathedral on Sunday, the Prime Minister quoted a Labour Youth League girl from Utøya— words that have been relayed all around the world: "If one man can create that much hate, you can only imagine how much love we can create together."

This is what the nation is doing now. This is what we are doing here this evening. We are showing love together; we are looking after one another.

We remember—and we look ahead. For this we know: we will move forward and life will go on. As a nation, we will always be marked by 22 July 2011. At the same time, we will not allow time to stand still.

We will go on, take care of each other, and protect our democracy, our open society, human rights and the hopes of young people for a better world.

The most important thing today and in the days ahead is that we take care of those who have the greatest pain—physical and psychological—to bear: those who have lost their loved ones, the injured who are fighting for their lives.

Dear friends,

Twenty or thirty years ago, we did not have congregations such as this. Norway is a country that is changing.

Historians tell us that the only thing that is constant is change. How are we to meet these challenges together? How are we to respond to those who are anxious, those who are afraid, those who express hatred?

I believe that hope is to be found in meeting change together from a secure common starting point.

Norway is a democracy. Norway is a state governed by the rule of law. Norway adheres to and respects universal human rights. But with this as a common platform, we can be different.

In the time ahead, this country is going to see a huge debate on how this tragedy could have happened.

The atrocities that took place in Oslo and on Utøya on 22 July 2011 do not originate from outside Norway. They were carried out by someone who has lived in the midst of us.

We must not be too hasty in looking for all the answers. But we will take the debate and the questions that are raised with us as we seek to understand.

The way we do this will be a test of the democracy and the values we share. This is why I find great consolation in the fact that we are gathering in our various houses of God. This is not my house of God—but I feel at home here.

Yesterday, I met a boy from Arendal, who had swum for his life away from Utøya. I told him that I would be visiting a mosque today, and he said this: "We who were swimming away from Utøya were not swimming for any god, we were swimming for life. We were Muslims, Christians, atheists and people with other beliefs. Afterwards we came together and focused on what was most important: life, togetherness and the future that we have together."

I have drawn strength these days from the Utøya I met on Thursday (21 July). Then the sun was shining on the island: young people were having fun, but were at the same time serious as they looked ahead with a resolve to help shape society.

Utøya was a fine example of Norway in all its diversity. A strong community of values and respect for differences.

Both the Prime Minister and I are able to pass on to all who are grieving a huge wave of warmth from all over the world. I receive telephone calls all day long from colleagues from every corner of the world who weep with me over the phone.

The response to what happened in Norway on 22 July 2011 has moved the whole world. We should take this sympathy and support into our hearts.

This is what we take with us as we meet the debates on Norwegian democracy that we have ahead of us. We will do this together, from a common value base, with deep respect for those we have lost.

SOURCE: Norwegian Ministry of Foreign Affairs. Speeches and Articles. "Memorial Following the Terrorist Attacks on 22 July 2011." July 26, 2011. http://www.regjeringen.no/en/dep/ud/aktuelt/taler_artikler/utenriksministeren/2011/minnemarkering-i-moskeen-tale.html?id=651888.

DOCUMENT

Prime Minister Stoltenberg Delivers Commemorative Address

August 1, 2011

Your Majesty,

Your Royal Highness,

Mr President,

The Norwegian people were put to the ultimate test on 22 July. The map was torn apart. The compass shot to pieces. Each and every one of us had to find our way through a landscape of shock, fear and devastation.

It could have gone very badly. We could have got lost.

But the Norwegian people found their way. Out of darkness and uncertainty, home to Norway.

Today I want to express my appreciation for this.

We are still a country in mourning. We are burying our dead from Utøya and the government offices.

Parents are sitting by hospital beds. Many are weeping. Hearts are bleeding. We will continue to comfort those who mourn. Take care of those who are struggling. Honour the dead.

But now it is also time to say thank you.

I would like to thank His Majesty The King, His Royal Highness The Crown Prince and the whole of the Royal Family for the warmth and compassion they have shown.

I would like to thank the Storting for its willingness and ability to stand together at a time when the nation needed unity.

There are many more who deserve our thanks.

The police.

The fire and rescue services.

Health personnel.

The armed forces.

The civil defence.

The Norwegian Church and other religious and belief communities.

Voluntary organisations.

Volunteers who provided invaluable help in the government office complex and on Utøya

Employees in the affected ministries.

The staff of Sundvolden Hotel.

All those around the Tyrifjorden lake who took resolute action.

Many of them put their own lives at risk.

On Sunday 21 August, we will pay tribute to their courage at a national memorial for all those who were directly affected and all those who have helped.

I would also like to express my gratitude for kind words and condolences from all over the world. For letters, flowers, messages of support on Facebook and other social media. We have felt that we are not alone. This has given us strength.

But my warmest thanks go to the Norwegian people.

Who took responsibility when it was most needed.

Who retained their human dignity.

Who chose democracy.

And the foremost amongst them are the young people.

The Labour Youth League came under fire.

But a whole generation has mobilised in sorrowful protest.

The 22 July generation are our heroes, our hope. This means that we can look to the future with renewed confidence in our fundamental values.

And with the hope that the commitment to decent dialogue and greater tolerance will continue to grow.

This time of mourning has made many of us stop and think about our own standpoints. Reflect on our thoughts and words.

In hindsight – after the tragedy of 22 July—we may well realise that we should sometimes have expressed ourselves differently.

And we will choose our words more carefully in the future. But I would ask people not to start a witch hunt, not to go looking for things that should not have been said.

We have shown extraordinary solidarity during this surreal period. Now we must continue to meet each other with good will. We can all learn something from this tragedy. We may all need to say, "I was wrong", and we should all be met with respect.

This is equally true in everyday conversations and in the public debate.

It applies to politicians and editors. It applies in the canteen at work and on the Internet. It applies to us all.

As politicians, we promise that we will take the spirit of 22 July with us when we start up normal political activities once again.

We will show the same wisdom and respect as the Norwegian people have done.

With freedom of speech as our weapon, and in the best traditions of this chamber, we will ensure that human dignity and security win over fear and hatred.

We owe this to the Norwegian people.

SOURCE: Office of the Prime Minister of Norway. Speeches and Articles. "Commemorative Address by the Prime Minister." August 1, 2011. http://www.regjeringen.no/en/dep/smk/aktuelt/taler_og_artikler/ statsministeren/statsminister_jens_stoltenberg/2011/tale1.html?id=651974.

OTHER HISTORIC DOCUMENTS OF INTEREST

FROM PREVIOUS HISTORIC DOCUMENTS

President Obama Remarks on the Debt Ceiling and Credit Downgrade

JULY 25, AUGUST 2, AND AUGUST 8, 2011

On May 16, 2011, the United States officially reached its debt ceiling, a cap set by Congress that limits the amount the government can borrow. Timothy Geithner, the secretary of the Treasury, announced that he would be able to hold off a government default until at least August 2 by using "extraordinary measures" and stopping investments in federal retirement accounts, which would give the Treasury the necessary funds to continue borrowing. Geithner promised to make up for the investments once the debt ceiling was raised. "Federal retirees and employees will be unaffected by these actions," Geithner wrote in a letter to Congress, further urging members to raise the debt ceiling "to protect the full faith and credit of the United States and avoid catastrophic economic consequences for citizens."

History of the U.S. Debt Ceiling

The debt ceiling was first set in 1917 at $11.5 billion in an effort to help fund the war effort and allow for the issuance of Treasury bonds. Before 1917, every time the government issued debt, Congressional approval was required. In 2011, the debt ceiling was set at $14.294 trillion. Debt has risen in the United States under every president during the past thirty years, after remaining relatively stable for the twenty-five years following World War II.

Congress has voted to raise the debt ceiling every time it has been necessary, amounting to seventy-eight increases since 1960. The debt ceiling has been raised forty-nine times under Republican presidents and twenty-nine times under Democratic presidents. Typically, when a Republican holds the executive office, Democrats in Congress vote to oppose a debt ceiling increase and vice versa.

The money the government is allowed to borrow under the debt ceiling is used to cover debt that the government has already incurred, including spending allocated in budget bills, Social Security payments, payments to contractors, and interest on bonds. This is because the government does not undertake budget and appropriations debates at the same time as it increases the debt ceiling. According to the Government Accountability Office (GAO), it would be better if "decisions about the debt level occur in conjunction with spending and revenue decisions as opposed to the after-the-fact approach now used," which "would help avoid the uncertainty and disruptions that occur during debates on the debt limit today."

If Congress were to decide not to increase the debt ceiling when necessary, the government would default on its payments. In the 1980s, then-President Ronald Reagan called on Congress to raise the debt ceiling, writing, "The full consequences of a default—or even the serious prospect of a default—by the United States are impossible to predict and awesome to contemplate." Potential impact of a default could be anything from a stop on payments to Social Security recipients and military families to a loss of confidence in U.S.

debt instruments. The United States has technically defaulted only once before, in 1979, when negotiations in Congress came right down to the wire. The default, however, was due to a glitch at the Treasury that amounted to some Treasury notes not being paid in full. This is generally not considered a true default because those Treasury notes were paid in full once the mistake was caught.

CONGRESSIONAL DEBATE

The White House was closely involved with Congressional debt ceiling negotiations throughout the spring and summer of 2011. In April, President Obama called on Congress to pass a clean debt ceiling bill that would not include any additional spending cut provisions. The president later admitted that it was unlikely that a clean bill would pass both houses without some spending cuts. Speaker of the House John Boehner, R-Ohio, made clear that under his leadership, the House would not pass a clean bill. "There will be no debt-limit increase unless it's accompanied by serious spending cuts and real budget reforms," Boehner said. In May, Republicans called a symbolic vote on the president's clean bill, which would have raised the debt ceiling to $16.7 trillion, and it failed 318 to 97. Rep. Dave Camp, R-Mich., said that the vote proved "to the American people, the financial markets, and the administration that we are serious about tackling our debt and deficit problems."

To stave off a default, Vice President Joe Biden opened discussions with congressional leaders from both parties to reach a debt ceiling agreement. In late May, Biden announced that progress was being made; however, the talks collapsed in June when Democrats demanded a debt ceiling increase unaccompanied by spending cuts and Republicans demanded that any increase in the debt ceiling be coupled with revenue increases and spending cuts.

In July, the White House tried again to compromise with Republicans to pass a bill. The plan proposed by the Obama administration would include a $4 trillion deficit reduction plan that would reduce spending on programs such as Medicare, Social Security, and Medicaid and close tax loopholes. Boehner expressed initial support, which he was forced to withdraw because of conservative Tea Party opposition to any tax increases. Democrats in the House were not necessarily on board with the president's plan either. House Minority Leader Nancy Pelosi, D-Calif., said, "Democrats stand ready to help with that grand bargain, but we want to do so without hurting our seniors and people with disabilities." Democrats in the House, she said, would not support a debt-ceiling bill that contained any cuts to Social Security and Medicare.

The president called a White House summit with Republican leadership in mid-July. The summit was fraught with tension, and Republicans accused the president of walking out of the meeting after a confrontation with Majority Whip Eric Cantor, R-Va., a representation the Democrats disputed. During the meetings, Obama made clear that he would veto any short-term extension of the debt ceiling, wishing instead for a longer-term measure that would help the nation avoid reaching the debt ceiling again for the next few years. Despite the tension, both Cantor and Sen. Mitch McConnell, R-Ky., called on Republicans to find common ground with their Democratic counterparts. McConnell made clear to his party that Obama could easily use a default to make Republicans look responsible for the economic crisis during the 2012 presidential election. "It is an argument that he could have a good chance of winning, and all of a sudden we have co-ownership of the economy. That is a very bad position going into the election," said McConnell.

REID AND BOEHNER BILLS

While the White House talks produced few results, a number of bills were introduced in Congress to ensure that the United States would not default on its obligations. On July 25, Sen. Harry Reid, D-Nev., and Boehner put forth competing plans in the House and Senate. The Reid plan would cut the deficit by $2.7 trillion during the next decade, which would include $1 trillion in savings from ending the wars in Iraq and Afghanistan. The bill would also raise the debt ceiling until 2013. The White House supported Reid's bill. According to Jay Carney, White House spokesperson, "Senator Reid's plan is a reasonable approach that should receive the support of both parties, and we hope the House Republicans will agree to this plan."

The Boehner plan was vastly different. It called for $3 trillion in deficit reduction to come in two parts—the first would involve a debt ceiling increase of $900 billion coupled with spending cuts; the second part would involve another vote in 2012 to raise the debt ceiling by up to $1.6 trillion after a twelve-member Congressional "super committee" found an additional $1.8 trillion in savings and presented the cuts to the House. Both the House and Senate would also have to vote on, but not necessarily pass, a balanced budget amendment and put a limit on discretionary spending. Boehner admitted that his plan was "less than perfect" but expected that it could pass both Houses. Tea Party conservatives rejected Boehner's plan, calling for mandatory passage of a balanced budget amendment, which quickly drew criticism from Sen. John McCain, R-Ariz. "It's unfair, it's bizzaro," he said.

On July 29, the House voted on the Boehner bill, passing it 218 to 210 with no Democratic support. The bill was slightly amended from his July 25 proposal, making passage of a balanced budget amendment required for a second debt ceiling increase. President Obama promised to veto the bill if it reached his desk. "Now that yet another political exercise is behind us, with time dwindling, leaders need to start working together immediately to reach a compromise that avoids default and lays the basis for balanced deficit reduction," said Carney. The Senate voted to table the bill. "To the American people, I'd say: We tried our level best," said Boehner. "We've tried to do the right thing by our country, but some people continue to say no." In response to the Senate action that tabled the Boehner bill, the House voted down the Reid plan 246 to 173 after it passed the Senate.

With the clock ticking toward the August 2 deadline, Republicans and Democrats came together at the White House again, optimistic that an agreement would be reached. On July 31, a bipartisan agreement was announced, modeled after the Boehner bill, that would raise the debt ceiling alongside $2.4 trillion in spending cuts over the next decade, thus protecting the debt ceiling until 2013. Upon passage, the debt ceiling would instantly be raised by $900 billion. A congressional super committee would be tasked with finding additional spending cuts. If the super committee failed to recommend, or Congress failed to enact, additional cuts, automatic reductions would be made to military spending, education, transportation, and Medicare payments.

The House voted to pass the compromise bill 269 to 161. The Senate passed the bill 74 to 26, and Obama immediately signed it, stating, "Voters may have chosen divided government, but they sure didn't vote for dysfunctional government." Both sides agreed that the bill was not perfect, but rather a must-pass. Proponents said the bill would place a new focus on restraint in federal spending and get the debt and deficit under control, while opponents said the nation would risk higher unemployment and another recession. A number of members expressed concern about how much power the twelve-member Joint

Select Committee on Deficit Reduction would have. "It's just a convoluted maze to do things in Washington the usual Washington way," said Sen. Ben Nelson, D-Neb.

DOWNGRADE

While Republicans and Democrats argued over the actual impact of a default, one point was clear—if Congress had not voted to increase the debt ceiling by August 2, the Treasury would be left with two options: raise taxes by hundreds of billions of dollars to cover payments through the end of the fiscal year or default, both of which would have significant repercussions. "Not only the default but efforts to resolve it would arguably have negative repercussions on both domestic and international financial markets and economies," the Congressional Research Service reported, stating that a default could effectively crash the bond and stock markets.

Throughout the Congressional debate, members of both parties were well aware that default could have a significant impact on the U.S. AAA credit rating. On July 29, after stating that neither the Reid nor the Boehner plans would keep the nation safe from a downgrade, Moody's stated that it would not immediately lower the AAA credit rating, but said it would consider a future downgrade if more was not done to control the deficit in the future. Fitch, the second of three credit rating agencies, also decided against a downgrade. Standard & Poor's was not as forgiving, and on August 5, it downgraded the credit rating to AA+, one notch below the highest possible rating. The downgrade had few immediate implications and was mostly symbolic. Standard & Poor's announced that the United States would need to take additional action to avoid another future downgrade. "The outlook on the long-term rating is negative. We could lower the long-term rating to 'AA' within the next two years if we see . . . less reduction in spending than agreed to," Standard & Poor's announced.

—Heather Kerrigan

Following are three statements by President Barack Obama. The first, delivered on July 25, 2011, is an update regarding the ongoing Congressional debt ceiling debate; the second, delivered on August 2, 2011, marks the debt ceiling compromise; and a third, delivered on August 8, 2011, explains the potential impact of the U.S. credit rating downgrade by Standard & Poor's.

President Obama on Congressional
Debt Ceiling Negotiations

DOCUMENT

July 25, 2011

Good evening. Tonight I want to talk about the debate we've been having in Washington over the national debt, a debate that directly affects the lives of all Americans.

For the last decade, we've spent more money than we take in. In the year 2000, the Government had a budget surplus. But instead of using it to pay off our debt, the money was spent on trillions of dollars in new tax cuts, while two wars and an expensive prescription drug program were simply added to our Nation's credit card.

As a result, the deficit was on track to top $1 trillion the year I took office. To make matters worse, the recession meant that there was less money coming in, and it required us to spend even more: on tax cuts for middle class families to spur the economy, on unemployment insurance, on aid to States so we could prevent more teachers and firefighters and police officers from being laid off. These emergency steps also added to the deficit.

Now, every family knows a little credit card debt is manageable. But if we stay on the current path, our growing debt could cost us jobs and do serious damage to the economy. More of our tax dollars will go toward paying off the interest on our loans. Businesses will be less likely to open up shop and hire workers in a country that can't balance its books. Interest rates could climb for everyone who borrows money: the homeowner with a mortgage, the student with a college loan, the corner store that wants to expand. And we won't have enough money to make job-creating investments in things like education and infrastructure or pay for vital programs like Medicare and Medicaid.

Because neither party is blameless for the decisions that led to this problem, both parties have a responsibility to solve it. And over the last several months, that's what we've been trying to do. I won't bore you with the details of every plan or proposal, but basically, the debate has centered around two different approaches.

The first approach says, let's live within our means by making serious, historic cuts in Government spending. Let's cut domestic spending to the lowest level it's been since Dwight Eisenhower was President. Let's cut defense spending at the Pentagon by hundreds of billions of dollars. Let's cut out waste and fraud in health care programs like Medicare, and at the same time, let's make modest adjustments so that Medicare is still there for future generations. Finally, let's ask the wealthiest Americans and biggest corporations to give up some of their breaks in the Tax Code and special deductions.

This balanced approach asks everyone to give a little without requiring anyone to sacrifice too much. It would reduce the deficit by around $4 trillion and put us on a path to pay down our debt. And the cuts wouldn't happen so abruptly that they'd be a drag on our economy or prevent us from helping small businesses and middle class families get back on their feet right now.

This approach is also bipartisan. While many in my own party aren't happy with the painful cuts it makes, enough will be willing to accept them if the burden is fairly shared. While Republicans might like to see deeper cuts and no revenue at all, there are many in the Senate who have said, "Yes, I'm willing to put politics aside and consider this approach because I care about solving the problem." And to his credit, this is the kind of approach the Republican Speaker of the House, John Boehner, was working on with me over the last several weeks.

The only reason this balanced approach isn't on its way to becoming law right now is because a significant number of Republicans in Congress are insisting on a different approach, a cuts-only approach, an approach that doesn't ask the wealthiest Americans or biggest corporations to contribute anything at all. And because nothing is asked of those at the top of the income scale, such an approach would close the deficit only with more severe cuts to programs we all care about, cuts that place a greater burden on working families.

So the debate right now isn't about whether we need to make tough choices. Democrats and Republicans agree on the amount of deficit reduction we need. The debate is about how it should be done. . . .

And keep in mind that under a balanced approach, the 98 percent of Americans who make under $250,000 would see no tax increases at all. None . . . . What we're talking about under a balanced approach is asking Americans whose incomes have gone up the most over the last decade—millionaires and billionaires—to share in the sacrifice everyone else has to make. And I think these patriotic Americans are willing to pitch in.

In fact, over the last few decades, they've pitched in every time we passed a bipartisan deal to reduce the deficit . . . .

Understand, raising the debt ceiling does not allow Congress to spend more money. It simply gives our country the ability to pay the bills that Congress has already racked up. In the past, raising the debt ceiling was routine. Since the 1950s, Congress has always passed it, and every President has signed it. President Reagan did it 18 times. George W. Bush did it seven times. And we have to do it by next Tuesday, August 2, or else, we won't be able to pay all of our bills.

Unfortunately, for the past several weeks, Republican House Members have essentially said that the only way they'll vote to prevent America's first-ever default is if the rest of us agree to their deep, spending-cuts-only approach.

If that happens and we default, we would not have enough money to pay all of our bills, bills that include monthly Social Security checks, veterans' benefits, and the Government contracts we've signed with thousands of businesses.

For the first time in history, our country's AAA credit rating would be downgraded, leaving investors around the world to wonder whether the United States is still a good bet. Interest rates would skyrocket on credit cards, on mortgages, and on car loans, which amounts to a huge tax hike on the American people. We would risk sparking a deep economic crisis, this one caused almost entirely by Washington.

So defaulting on our obligations is a reckless and irresponsible outcome to this debate. And Republican leaders say that they agree we must avoid default. But the new approach that Speaker Boehner unveiled today, which would temporarily extend the debt ceiling in exchange for spending cuts, would force us to once again face the threat of default just 6 months from now. In other words, it doesn't solve the problem.

First of all, a 6-month extension of the debt ceiling might not be enough to avoid a credit downgrade and the higher interest rates that all Americans would have to pay as a result. We know what we have to do to reduce our deficits; there's no point in putting the economy at risk by kicking the can further down the road.

But there's an even greater danger to this approach. Based on what we've seen these past few weeks, we know what to expect 6 months from now. The House of Representatives will once again refuse to prevent default unless the rest of us accept their cuts-only approach. . . .

This is no way to run the greatest country on Earth. It's a dangerous game that we've never played before, and we can't afford to play it now. Not when the jobs and livelihoods of so many families are at stake. We can't allow the American people to become collateral damage to Washington's political warfare.

And Congress now has one week left to act, and there are still paths forward. The Senate has introduced a plan to avoid default, which makes a downpayment on deficit reduction and ensures that we don't have to go through this again in 6 months.

I think that's a much better approach, although serious deficit reduction would still require us to tackle the tough challenges of entitlement and tax reform. Either way, I've told leaders of both parties that they must come up with a fair compromise in the next few days that can pass both Houses of Congress and a compromise that I can sign. I'm confident we can reach this compromise. Despite our disagreements, Republican leaders and I have found common ground before. And I believe that enough members of both parties will ultimately put politics aside and help us make progress.

Now, I realize that a lot of the new Members of Congress and I don't see eye to eye on many issues. But we were each elected by some of the same Americans for some of the same reasons. Yes, many want Government to start living within its means. And many are fed up with a system in which the deck seems stacked against middle class Americans in favor of the wealthiest few.

But do you know what people are fed up with most of all? They're fed up with a town where compromise has become a dirty word. They work all day long, many of them scraping by, just to put food on the table. And when these Americans come home at night, bone tired, and turn on the news, all they see is the same partisan three-ring circus here in Washington. They see leaders who can't seem to come together and do what it takes to make life just a little bit better for ordinary Americans. They're offended by that. And they should be.

The American people may have voted for divided Government, but they didn't vote for a dysfunctional Government. . . .

SOURCE: U.S. Executive Office of the President. "Address to the Nation on the Federal Budget." July 25, 2011. *Daily Compilation of Presidential Documents* 2011, no. 00528 (July 25, 2011). http://www.gpo.gov/fdsys/pkg/DCPD-201100528/pdf/DCPD-201100528.pdf.

President Obama on Debt Ceiling Compromise

DOCUMENT

August 2, 2011

Good afternoon, everybody. Congress has now approved a compromise to reduce the deficit and avert a default that would have devastated our economy. It was a long and contentious debate. And I want to thank the American people for keeping up the pressure on their elected officials to put politics aside and work together for the good of the country.

This compromise guarantees more than $2 trillion in deficit reduction. It's an important first step to ensuring that as a nation we live within our means. Yet it also allows us to keep making key investments in things like education and research that lead to new jobs and assures that we're not cutting too abruptly while the economy is still fragile.

This is, however, just the first step. This compromise requires that both parties work together on a larger plan to cut the deficit, which is important for the long-term health of our economy. And since you can't close the deficit with just spending cuts, we'll need a balanced approach where everything's on the table. Yes, that means making some adjustments to protect health care programs like Medicare so they're there for future generations. It also means reforming our Tax Code so that the wealthiest Americans and biggest corporations pay their fair share. And it means getting rid of taxpayer subsidies to oil and gas companies and tax loopholes that help billionaires pay a lower tax rate than teachers and nurses.

I've said it before, I will say it again: We can't balance the budget on the backs of the very people who have borne the biggest brunt of this recession. We can't make it tougher for young people to go to college or ask seniors to pay more for health care or ask scientists to give up on promising medical research because we couldn't close a tax shelter for the most fortunate among us. Everyone is going to have to chip in. . . .

. . . Our economy didn't need Washington to come along with a manufactured crisis to make things worse. That was in our hands. It's pretty likely that the uncertainty surrounding the raising of the debt ceiling—for both businesses and consumers—has been unsettling and just one more impediment to the full recovery that we need. And it was something that we could have avoided entirely.

So voters may have chosen divided Government, but they sure didn't vote for dysfunctional Government. They want us to solve problems. They want us to get this economy growing and adding jobs. And while deficit reduction is part of that agenda, it is not the whole agenda. Growing the economy isn't just about cutting spending; it's not about rolling back regulations that protect our air and our water and keep our people safe. That's not how we're going to get past this recession. We're going to have to do more than that.

And that's why, when Congress gets back from recess, I will urge them to immediately take some steps—bipartisan, commonsense steps—that will make a difference, that will create a climate where businesses can hire, where folks have more money in their pockets to spend, where people who are out of work can find good jobs.

We need to begin by extending tax cuts for middle class families so that you have more money in your paychecks next year. If you've got more money in your paycheck, you're more likely to spend it. And that means small businesses and medium-sized businesses and large businesses will all have more customers. That means they'll be in a better position to hire.

And while we're at it, we need to make sure that millions of workers who are still pounding the pavement looking for jobs to support their families are not denied needed unemployment benefits . . . .

So these are some things that we could be doing right now. There's no reason for Congress not to send me those bills so I can sign them into law right away as soon as they get back from recess. Both parties share power in Washington, and both parties need to take responsibility for improving this economy. It's not a Democratic responsibility or a Republican responsibility, it is our collective responsibility as Americans. And I'll be discussing additional ideas in the weeks ahead to help companies hire, invest, and expand. . . .

SOURCE: U.S. Executive Office of the President. "Remarks on the Federal Budget." August 2, 2011. *Daily Compilation of Presidential Documents* 2011, no. 00542 (August 2, 2011). http://www.gpo.gov/fdsys/pkg/DCPD-201100542/pdf/DCPD-201100542.pdf.

President Obama on U.S. Credit Rating Downgrade

August 8, 2011

Good afternoon, everybody. On Friday, we learned that the United States received a downgrade by one of the credit rating agencies, not so much because they doubt our ability to pay our debt if we make good decisions, but because after witnessing a month of wrangling over raising the debt ceiling, they doubted our political system's ability to act. The markets, on the other hand, continue to believe our credit status is AAA. In fact, Warren Buffett, who knows a thing or two about good investments, said, "If there were a AAAA rating, I'd give the United States that." I and most of the world's investors agree.

That doesn't mean we don't have a problem. The fact is, we didn't need a rating agency to tell us that we need a balanced, long-term approach to deficit reduction. That was true last week. That was true last year. That was true the day I took office. And we didn't need a rating agency to tell us that the gridlock in Washington over the last several months has not been constructive, to say the least.

So all of this is a legitimate source of concern. But here's the good news: Our problems are eminently solvable, and we know what we have to do to solve them. With respect to debt, our problems is not confidence in our credit; the markets continue to reaffirm our credit as among the world's safest. Our challenge is the need to tackle our deficits over the long term.

Last week, we reached an agreement that will make historic cuts to defense and domestic spending. But there's not much further we can cut in either of those categories. What we need to do now is combine those spending cuts with two additional steps: tax reform that will ask those who can afford it to pay their fair share and modest adjustments to health care programs like Medicare.

Making these reforms doesn't require any radical steps. What it does require is common sense and compromise. . . .

So it's not a lack of plans or policies that's the problem here, it's a lack of political will in Washington. It's the insistence on drawing lines in the sand, a refusal to put what's best for the country ahead of self-interest or party or ideology. And that's what we need to change. . . .

Of course, as worrisome as the issues of debt and deficits may be, the most immediate concern of most Americans, and of concern to the marketplace as well, is the issue of jobs and the slow pace of recovery coming out of the worst recession in our lifetime.

And the good news here is that by coming together to deal with the long-term debt challenge, we would have more room to implement key proposals that can get the economy to grow faster. Specifically, we should extend the payroll tax cut as soon as possible, so that workers have more money in their paychecks next year and businesses have more customers next year.

We should continue to make sure that if you're one of the millions of Americans who's out there looking for a job, you can get the unemployment insurance that your tax dollars contributed to. That will also put money in people's pockets and more customers in stores.

In fact, if Congress fails to extend the payroll tax cut and the unemployment insurance benefits that I've called for, it could mean 1 million fewer jobs and half a percent less growth. This is something we can do immediately, something we can do as soon as Congress gets back.

We should also help companies that want to repair our roads and bridges and airports so that thousands of construction workers who've been without a job for the last few years can get a paycheck again. That will also help to spur economic growth.

These aren't Democratic proposals. These aren't big government proposals. These are all ideas that traditionally Republicans have agreed to, have agreed to countless times in the past. There's no reason we shouldn't act on them now, none. . . .

Markets will rise and fall, but this is the United States of America. No matter what some agency may say, we've always been and always will be a AAA country. For all of the challenges we face, we continue to have the best universities, some of the most productive workers, the most innovative companies, the most adventurous entrepreneurs on Earth. And what sets us apart is that we've always not just had the capacity, but also the will to act, the determination to shape our future, the willingness in our democracy to work out our differences in a sensible way and to move forward, not just for this generation, but for the next generation.

And we're going to need to summon that spirit today. The American people have been through so much over the last few years, dealing with the worst recession, the biggest financial crisis since the 1930s, and they've done it with grace. And they're working so hard to raise their families, and all they ask is that we work just as hard here in this town to make their lives a little bit easier. That's not too much to ask. And ultimately, the reason I am so hopeful about our future—the reason I have faith in these United States of America— is because of the American people. It's because of their perseverance and their courage and their willingness to shoulder the burdens we face together as one Nation. . . .

SOURCE: U.S. Executive Office of the President. "Remarks on the National Economy." August 8, 2011. *Daily Compilation of Presidential Documents* 2011, no. 00557 (August 8, 2011). http://www.gpo.gov/fdsys/pkg/DCPD-201100557/pdf/DCPD-201100557.pdf.

OTHER HISTORIC DOCUMENTS OF INTEREST

FROM THIS VOLUME

FROM PREVIOUS *HISTORIC DOCUMENTS*

August

Evolving U.S. Involvement
in Afghanistan

AUGUST 6, OCTOBER 7, AND DECEMBER 5, 2011

As the war in Iraq drew to a close in 2011, focus shifted to Afghanistan, where the United States had been fighting since 2001. Public opinion fell to its lowest level by late 2011, with a CNN poll taken October 14 to 16 finding that only 34 percent of Americans supported the war in Afghanistan. The United States and its coalition partners began making plans for an accelerated troop withdrawal beginning in 2011 and concluding by 2014, but as it did, the Taliban was making a slow comeback and shifting tactics from direct battle confrontations to targeted attacks, including a September 2011 twenty-hour siege of the U.S. embassy in Kabul. Throughout the year, international leaders struggled to determine the best way to leave Afghanistan responsibly while giving the maximum assistance to the Afghan government to ensure future success.

Deadliest Day for American Troops

On August 6, 2011, thirty American soldiers, seven Afghan troops, and an interpreter were killed in a Chinook helicopter crash fifty miles south of the capital city of Kabul. Twenty-two of the Americans killed in the crash, which was caused by a rocket-propelled grenade (RPG), were Navy SEAL commandoes, some from SEAL Team 6, although none were involved in the raid that killed Osama bin Laden in May. "Their deaths are a reminder of the extraordinary sacrifices made by the men and women of our military and their families, including all who have served in Afghanistan," said President Barack Obama. The Taliban immediately claimed responsibility for the RPG that caused the crash.

At the time of the crash, the SEAL team was en route to assist Army Rangers that had come under insurgent fire as they tried to capture a Taliban leader in the Tangi Valley, a corridor that runs through Wardak Province and into Kabul. It is an area that has not been a focus of recent U.S. troop activity, as the United States shifted its attention farther south near the Pakistan border, where the Taliban enjoys a stronghold. The SEAL mission was not out of the ordinary. The United States has approximately 10,000 special operations forces in Afghanistan whose purpose is to protect Army Rangers and other teams when they get into dire situations.

Ten-Year Anniversary

Less than two months after the helicopter crash, the United States marked an important milestone, having spent a decade in Afghanistan on October 7, 2011. The war, which Obama has dubbed "the longest-running war in the nation's history," began in 2001 with an air mission and quickly moved to a ground invasion. The campaigns undertaken by

American and coalition troops have seen the death of Osama bin Laden and have largely pushed the Taliban from its position of power in the country, although the insurgent group has not been completely disbanded. "We've pushed the Taliban out of its key strongholds, Afghan security forces are growing stronger, and the Afghan people have a new chance to forge their own future," Obama said.

These advances, however, have come at a great cost. The war in Afghanistan has cost hundreds of billions of dollars over ten years. Additionally, more than 1,700 Americans, countless Afghanis, and 1,000 coalition troops have been killed. Troop casualties improved in 2011 for the first time since 2001, with U.S. military deaths down from a peak of 499 in 2010 to 417. U.S. officials cite troop increases and a shift in strategy from direct combat to targeted missions as reasons for the decline. The Taliban announced that the reason was American unwillingness to conduct major offensives. "This year, NATO forces have maintained defensive positions. They are not coming out of their bases. They have reduced their mobility everywhere," said Taliban spokesperson Zabiullah Mujahid.

In Afghanistan, U.S. troops did not mark the importance of October 7, as they had with the tenth anniversary of September 11. "I think that to us it was a far more significant date than ten years of fighting in Afghanistan because, really, when you look at the ten years, you're looking at different levels of forces, different levels of attention given to Afghanistan," said Marine Corps Maj. Gen. John Toolan Jr.

AFGHANISTAN TODAY

As United States and coalition forces continue to fight in Afghanistan, they still face significant challenges, specifically as they relate to the stability of the Afghan government and security forces. Transparency International, a group that tracks worldwide corruption, rated Afghanistan tied with Myanmar as the second-most corrupt nation in the world. This distinction is lodged in the most recent presidential and parliamentary elections. President Hamid Karzai's 2009 reelection campaign was marred when he declared himself the victor without a runoff vote. However, fraudulent ballots and tampering that were found to be in his favor, coupled with pressure from the United States, led to a runoff election. Karzai's challenger dropped out before the election, however, leaving Karzai the winner by default.

A similar situation arose in 2010, when voters went to the polls to elect members of the Wolesi Jirga, or lower house of parliament, the Afghan government body that serves as a check on Karzai's authority. Twenty percent of the ballots cast in the election had to be thrown out because of fraud. The Independent Election Commission went ahead and confirmed the election results in November 2010 without a recount, but in mid-2011, the body declared that it was changing the results and taking seats away from nine candidates. Because of the disputed election, Karzai postponed seating the parliament, leaving it unable to conduct legislative business. Without a seated parliament, Karzai could not appoint his cabinet or the nation's supreme court justices.

Coalition forces also face a training challenge. Specifically, the Afghanis are unprepared to fully take over security. The United States has slowly returned control of various areas of the country to Afghan security forces, only to find out that they are unprepared for the task and easily overtaken by Taliban insurgents. The Afghan security force also faces high attrition and has had difficulties weeding out Afghanis with insurgent tendencies from those who will peacefully fight alongside coalition troops. Afghan military leaders have argued that they do not have enough sophisticated equipment to protect their country.

WITHDRAWAL PLANS

Recognizing that the nation had grown weary of the war, and facing a deep budget crisis, in June 2011, Obama announced that he would accelerate the troop drawdown in Afghanistan because the United States had achieved many of its goals set out during the initial invasion. Obama made it clear that he planned to end the war in Afghanistan responsibly, and that he would not overextend the military or keep them in harm's way. "We will not try to make Afghanistan a perfect place," Obama said. "We will not police its streets or patrol its mountains indefinitely. That is the responsibility of the Afghan government," he said. The Obama drawdown plan called for 10,000 troops to be withdrawn from Afghanistan in 2011. The first withdrawals would include mostly support forces, leaving special forces and gun-heavy units in Afghanistan. During the summer of 2012, 20,000 troops from the 2009 surge would be withdrawn. This drawdown would continue until 2014 when the United States was scheduled to hand over all security control to the Afghan authorities. President Obama refused to set a timetable for withdrawal of the remaining troops, stating only that it would occur "at a steady pace." As the drawdown continues, American forces will focus more on clandestine counterterrorism operations like the one that killed bin Laden.

Military commanders and Secretary of State Hillary Rodham Clinton expressed reservations about the drawdown plans and recommended a slower timetable, indicating that the withdrawal would limit what areas the United States would be able to focus on and fully restore to some sense of security before 2014. During his time as top commander in Afghanistan, Then-Defense Secretary David Patraeus recommended a 5,000-troop withdrawal in 2011, followed by another 5,000 in early 2012. Defense Secretary Robert Gates, who had previously spoken about slowing the drawdown, came out in support of Obama's plan after it was announced in June.

Following the president's announcement, many coalition countries quickly followed suit and announced that they would also speed up their withdrawal plans. "Given the progress we have seen, France will begin a gradual withdrawal of reinforcement troops sent to Afghanistan, in a proportional manner and in a calendar comparable to the withdrawal of American reinforcements," said French President Nicolas Sarkozy. In early 2012, following the death of French troops, allegedly at the hands of Afghan military forces, Sarkozy announced that France's combat troops would instead fully withdraw by 2013.

Afghanistan's response to the withdrawal plans was mixed. At first, the nation accused North Atlantic Treaty Organization (NATO) of fleeing, which the group quickly disputed. "We are not leaving because we have to. We are leaving because we can," said German Brig. Gen. Carsten Jacobson, a NATO spokesperson. An Afghan military defense spokesperson, Gen. Mohammad Zahir Azimi, declared that the Afghan National Army "has this capability and quantity to fill the gap of those places where the foreign troops withdraw and leave Afghanistan." He continued, "We are ready." Karzai adviser Muhammad Siddique Aziz, however, asked for the coalition troops to stay until the Afghan government was in complete control and strong enough to govern the country. "I think they have to concentrate more on the Afghan government so when they leave, the government can stand up on its own," he said.

2012 AND BEYOND

In December 2011, leaders from across the world met in Bonn, Germany, to discuss their commitment to Afghanistan, "to renew our mutual commitment to a stable, democratic and prosperous future for the Afghan people," and lay out plans for involvement in the nation in 2012 and beyond. During these transition talks, Karzai called for political and military support from the international community to last until 2024, and also called for financial support to continue through 2030.

Beginning in 2012, the focus of coalition troops will move from the south near the Pakistan border to the east, where the powerful Haqqani network, a group allied with the Taliban, has a stronghold. All NATO troops will also have a less direct combat role, focusing instead on continuing to equip and train Afghan units, with an overall goal of training 195,000 Afghan troops by October 2012.

The coming year will also be marked by negotiations and peace talks between the Afghan government, the United States, and the Taliban. On January 3, 2012, the Taliban announced that it was opening a peace mission in Doha, Qatar, reversing earlier declarations that it had no interest in ending its insurgency in Afghanistan. The peace mission will give Western nations involved in Afghanistan a place to work out agreements with Taliban leaders. The Afghan government is also seeking to open up a dialogue with the Taliban in 2012, using Saudi Arabia as an intermediary.

—Heather Kerrigan

Following is a statement by President Barack Obama on August 6, 2011, marking the deadliest day in Afghanistan for American troops; a statement by President Obama on October 7, 2011, commemorating the tenth anniversary of the Afghanistan invasion; and the conclusions of the Bonn conference on future international involvement in Afghanistan, released on December 5, 2011.

DOCUMENT

President Obama on Afghanistan Troop Casualties

August 6, 2011

My thoughts and prayers go out to the families and loved ones of the Americans who were lost earlier today in Afghanistan. Their deaths are a reminder of the extraordinary sacrifices made by the men and women of our military and their families, including all who have served in Afghanistan. We will draw inspiration from their lives and continue the work of securing our country and standing up for the values that they embodied. We also mourn the Afghans who died alongside our troops in pursuit of a more peaceful and hopeful future for their country. At this difficult hour, all Americans are united in support of our men and women in uniform, who serve so that we can live in freedom and security.

SOURCE: U.S. Executive Office of the President. "Statement on United States Military Casualties in Afghanistan." August 6, 2011. *Daily Compilation of Presidential Documents* 2011, no. 00555 (August 6, 2011). http://www.gpo.gov/fdsys/pkg/DCPD-201100555/pdf/DCPD-201100555.pdf.

President Obama Commemorates Tenth Anniversary of Afghanistan Invasion

October 7, 2011

Ten years ago today, in response to the 9/11 terrorist attacks, our Nation went to war against Al Qaida and its Taliban protectors in Afghanistan. As we mark a decade of sacrifice, Michelle and I join all Americans in saluting the more than half a million men and women who have served bravely in Afghanistan to keep our country safe, including our resilient wounded warriors who carry the scars of war, seen and unseen. We honor the memory of the nearly 1,800 American patriots and many coalition and Afghan partners, who have made the ultimate sacrifice in Afghanistan for our shared security and freedom. We pay tribute to our inspiring military families who have persevered at home with a loved one at war. And we are grateful to our tireless diplomats and intelligence, homeland security and law enforcement professionals who have worked these 10 years to protect our country and save American lives.

Thanks to the extraordinary service of these Americans, our citizens are safer and our Nation is more secure. In delivering justice to Usama bin Laden and many other Al Qaida leaders, we are closer than ever to defeating Al Qaida and its murderous network. Despite the enormous challenges that remain in Afghanistan, we've pushed the Taliban out of its key strongholds, Afghan security forces are growing stronger, and the Afghan people have a new chance to forge their own future. We've fought alongside Afghans and close friends and allies from dozens of nations who have joined us in common purpose. In Afghanistan and beyond, we have shown that the United States is not and never will be at war with Islam and that we are a partner with those who seek justice, dignity, and opportunity.

After a difficult decade, we are responsibly ending today's wars from a position of strength. As the rest of our troops come home from Iraq this year, we have begun to draw down our forces in Afghanistan and transition security to the Afghan people, with whom we will forge an enduring partnership. As our sons and daughters come home to their families, we will uphold our sacred trust with our 9/11 generation veterans and work to provide the care, benefits, and opportunities they deserve. And as we reflect on 10 years of war and look ahead to a future of peace, Michelle and I call upon all Americans to show our gratitude and support for our fellow citizens who risk their lives so that we can enjoy the blessings of freedom and security.

SOURCE: U.S. Executive Office of the President. "Statement on the 10th Anniversary of United States Personnel in Afghanistan." October 7, 2011. *Daily Compilation of Presidential Documents* 2011, no. 00733 (October 7, 2011). http://www.gpo.gov/fdsys/pkg/DCPD-201100733/pdf/DCPD-201100733.pdf.

Bonn Conference Conclusions

December 5, 2011

CONFERENCE CONCLUSIONS

1. We, the Islamic Republic of Afghanistan and the International Community, met today in Bonn to mark the 10th anniversary of the 2001 Bonn Conference, which laid

the foundation of the ongoing partnership between Afghanistan and the International Community, and to renew our mutual commitment to a stable, democratic and prosperous future for the Afghan people. We honour all those, from Afghanistan and abroad, who have lost their lives for this noble cause. Afghanistan expressed its sincere gratitude for the steadfast commitment, solidarity and the immense sacrifices of its international partners.

2. Afghanistan and the International Community expressed deep appreciation to the Federal Republic of Germany for hosting this Conference. Germany is a longstanding friend of Afghanistan and, in particular over the past ten years, alongside other members of the International Community, has been a steadfast partner in Afghanistan's stabilization and development.

3. Ten years ago today at the Petersberg, Afghanistan charted a new path towards a sovereign, peaceful, prosperous and democratic future, and the International Community accepted the responsibility to help Afghanistan along that path. Together we have achieved substantial progress over these ten years, more than in any other period in Afghanistan's history. Never before have the Afghan people, and especially Afghan women, enjoyed comparable access to services, including education and health, or seen greater development of infrastructure across the country. Al Qaida has been disrupted, and Afghanistan's national security institutions are increasingly able to assume responsibility for a secure and independent Afghanistan.

4. However, our work is not yet done. Shortcomings must be addressed, achievements must be upheld. Our shared goal remains an Afghanistan that is a peaceful and promising home for all Afghans, at the centre of a secure and thriving region; an Afghanistan in which international terrorism does not again find sanctuary and that can assume its rightful place among sovereign nations.

5. In today's conference, chaired by Afghanistan, hosted by Germany and attended by 85 countries and 15 International Organisations, the International Community and Afghanistan solemnly dedicated themselves to deepening and broadening their historic partnership from Transition to the Transformation Decade of 2015–2024. Reaffirming our commitments as set out in the 2010 London Communiqué and the Kabul Process, this renewed partnership between Afghanistan and the International Community entails firm mutual commitments in the areas of governance, security, the peace process, economic and social development, and regional cooperation.

Governance

6. Afghanistan reaffirms that the future of its political system will continue to reflect its pluralistic society and remain firmly founded on the Afghan Constitution. The Afghan people will continue to build a stable, democratic society, based on the rule of law, where the human rights and fundamental freedoms of its citizens, including the equality of men and women, are guaranteed under the Constitution. Afghanistan recommits to upholding all of its international human rights obligations. Acknowledging that on this path Afghanistan will have its own lessons to learn, the International Community fully endorses this vision and commits to supporting Afghanistan's progress in that direction.

7. We have taken note of statements by Afghan civil society organisations, including today's statements by two of their delegates at this meeting. We all reaffirm that the human rights and fundamental freedoms enshrined in the Afghan Constitution, including

the rights of women and children, as well as a thriving and free civil society are key for Afghanistan's future. Therefore, we underscore the further promotion of civil society participation, including both traditional civil society structures and modern manifestations of civic action, including the role of youth, in the country's democratic processes.

8. We recognise that building a democratic society above all entails enabling legitimate and effective civilian authority embodied in a democratically elected government and served by transparent and strong, functioning institutions. Despite significant achievements, Afghanistan needs to continue its work to strengthen state institutions and improve governance throughout the country, including through reforming the civil service and strengthening the linkage between justice reform and development of its security institutions, including an effective civilian police force. Strengthening and improving Afghanistan's electoral process will be a key step forward in the country's democratization. Afghan government institutions at all levels should increase their responsiveness to the civil and economic needs of the Afghan people and deliver key services to them. In this context, the protection of civilians, strengthening the rule of law and the fight against corruption in all its forms remain key priorities. We will move this agenda forward, in accordance with our commitments under the Kabul Process in line with the principle of mutual accountability.

9. Consistent with Transition, we reaffirm that the role of international actors will evolve further from direct service delivery to support and capacity-building for Afghan institutions, enabling the Government of Afghanistan to exercise its sovereign authority in all its functions. This process includes the phasing out of all Provincial Reconstruction Teams, as well as the dissolution of any structures duplicating the functions and authority of the Government of Afghanistan at the national and sub-national levels.

10. We support the crucial role of the United Nations in Afghanistan. . . .

Security

11. We welcome the determination of the Afghan people to combat terrorism and extremism and take responsibility for their own security and for protecting their homeland. We share Afghanistan's vision for its national security forces to be built to modern standards and adequate capacity, so that they can effectively and independently defend Afghanistan.

12. We welcome the successful start of the Transition process. Afghan authorities are assuming full security responsibility for their country and will complete this process by the end of 2014. Correspondingly, the International Security Assistance Force (ISAF), authorized by the UN Security Council, has begun a gradual, responsible draw-down to be completed by that time. With the conclusion of the Transition process, our common responsibility for Afghanistan's future does not come to a close. The International Community, therefore, commits to remain strongly engaged in support of Afghanistan beyond 2014.

13. We underscore that the international support for sustainable Afghan National Security Forces (ANSF) needs to continue after 2014. In assistance to the ANSF, the International Community strongly commits to support their training and equipping, financing and development of capabilities beyond the end of the Transition period. It declares its intent to continue to assist in their financing, with the understanding that over

the coming years this share will gradually be reduced, in a manner commensurate with Afghanistan's needs and its increasing domestic revenue generation capacity. In this context, we look forward to define a clear vision and appropriately funded plan for the ANSF, which should be developed before the forthcoming NATO summit in Chicago in May 2012.

14. We recognise that the main threat to Afghanistan's security and stability is terrorism, and that this threat also endangers regional and global peace and security. In this regard, we recognise the regional dimensions of terrorism and extremism, including terrorist safe havens, and emphasise the need for sincere and result-oriented regional cooperation towards a region free from terrorism in order to secure Afghanistan and safeguard our common security against the terrorist threat. We reiterate our common determination to never allow Afghanistan to once again become a haven for international terrorism.

15. The production, trafficking and consumption of narcotics equally pose a grave threat to Afghanistan's security and the growth of a legitimate economy as well as to international peace and stability. Recognizing their shared responsibility, Afghanistan and the International Community reiterate their determination to counter, in a comprehensive manner, including by crop eradication, interdiction and promoting alternative agriculture, the menace of illicit drugs, including drug precursors, which causes widespread harm and suffering. We recognise that the narcotics problem is a global challenge which also requires tackling the demand side.

Peace Process

16. We stress the need for a political solution in order to achieve peace and security in Afghanistan. To ensure enduring stability, in addition to building up Afghanistan's capacity to defend itself, a political process is necessary, of which negotiation and reconciliation are essential elements. In addition, the process of reintegration will pave the way for post-conflict rehabilitation of Afghan society through improvement of security, community development and local governance. . . .

18. Mindful of the relevant UN resolutions, the International Community concurs with Afghanistan that the peace and reconciliation process and its outcome must be based on the following principles:

(a) The process leading to reconciliation must be
  o truly Afghan-led and Afghan-owned; as well as
  o inclusive, representing the legitimate interests of all the people of Afghanistan,
  o regardless of gender or social status.

(b) Reconciliation must contain
  o the reaffirmation of a sovereign, stable and united Afghanistan;
  o the renunciation of violence;
  o the breaking of ties to international terrorism;
  o respect for the Afghan Constitution, including its human rights provisions, notably the
  o rights of women.

(c) The region must respect and support the peace process and its outcome.

An outcome of the peace process respecting the above principles will receive the full support of the International Community.

Economic and Social Development

19. The International Community shares Afghanistan's aim of achieving self-reliance and prosperity through developing its human and resource potential on its path towards sustainable and equitable growth and improved standards of living, and welcomes the Afghan Government's economic Transition strategy as elaborated in the document *Towards a Self-Sustaining Afghanistan*. Shifting the strategy from stabilisation to long-term development cooperation, the International Community will continue to support Afghanistan, including in the areas of rule of law, public administration, education, health, agriculture, energy, infrastructure development and job creation, in line with the Afghan Government's priorities as specified in the National Priority Programmes framework under the Kabul Process. . . .

21. As Transition gathers momentum, we recognise the economic risks identified by the World Bank and the International Monetary Fund, including the economic impact tied to the reduction of the international military presence. We intend to mitigate this effect, including by increasing aid effectiveness, consistent with the Kabul Process. The International Community shares Afghanistan's concern that a strategy to address the near-term effects of Transition must also facilitate the goal of attaining a sustainable market economy in line with the social needs of the population.

22. The intensive international effort in Afghanistan over the last decade represents a unique engagement. The International Community's commitment, both to Afghanistan and to its role in international security, lasts beyond Transition. Transition will reduce the international presence and the financial requirements associated with it. We recognize that the Government of Afghanistan will have special, significant and continuing fiscal requirements that cannot be met by domestic revenues in the years following Transition. Therefore, during the Transformation Decade, the International Community commits to directing financial support, consistent with the Kabul Process, towards Afghanistan's economic development and security-related costs, helping Afghanistan address its continuing budget shortfall to secure the gains of the last decade, make Transition irreversible, and become self-sustaining.

23. Afghanistan's long-term economic growth will, above all, depend on the development of its productive sectors, notably agriculture and mining. The International Community commits to supporting the development of an export-oriented agriculture-based economy, which is crucial for Afghanistan to achieve food security, poverty reduction, widespread farm-based job creation, and expanding the Government's revenue generation capacity. Concerning mining, we welcome the growing interest of international investors in Afghanistan's mineral wealth but emphasise the need for a regulatory framework to guarantee that this mineral wealth directly benefits the Afghan people. The International Community supports Afghanistan's efforts to develop a transparent and accountable regulatory regime, consistent with international best practices, for collecting and managing public resources and preserving the environment.

24. We recognise that a vibrant, private sector-led economy in Afghanistan will require the development of a competitive service industry and a stable financial system, and achieving regional integration through expanding Afghanistan's trade and transit networks, as well as its regional connectivity. The International Community commits to support Afghanistan's efforts to put in place and enhance the infrastructure and the relevant regulatory frameworks for the development of trade and transit.

25. We emphasize that attracting private investment, including from international sources, are key priorities for activating Afghanistan's economic potential. The Afghan Government commits to improving conditions conducive to international investments, inter alia, by implementing the recommendations of the EUROMINES International Investors Forum in Brussels on 26 October 2011.

Regional Cooperation

26. We believe that a stable and prosperous Afghanistan can only be envisioned in a stable and prosperous region. For the entire region, the rewards of peace and cooperation outweigh those of rivalry and isolation by far. We endorse Afghanistan's vision for building strong, sustainable bilateral and multilateral relationships with its near and extended neighbours. Such relationships should end external interference, reinforce the principles of good neighbourly relations, non-interference and sovereignty, and further Afghanistan's economic integration into the region. . . .

28. With a view to the long-term prospects for Afghanistan's development, we share Afghanistan's vision of a well-connected, economically integrated region, where Afghanistan can serve as a land-bridge connecting South Asia, Central Asia, Eurasia and the Middle East. We support enhanced trade connectivity along historical trade routes to utilize Afghanistan's economic potential at the regional level. In this context, we recognize the importance of early implementation of sustainable projects to promote regional connectivity, such as the TAPI gas pipeline, CASA-1000, railways and other projects. In this context, we look forward to the 5th RECCA conference to be hosted by the Republic of Tajikistan in Dushanbe in March 2012.

29. We acknowledge the burden of Afghanistan's neighbours, in particular Pakistan and Iran, in providing temporary refuge to millions of Afghans in difficult times and are committed to further work towards their voluntary, safe and orderly return.

The Way Forward

30. With a view to the future, we underscore that the process of Transition, which is currently underway and is to be completed by the end of 2014, should be followed by a decade of Transformation, in which Afghanistan consolidates its sovereignty through strengthening a fully functioning, sustainable state in the service of its people. This Transformation Decade will see the emergence of a new paradigm of partnership between Afghanistan and the International Community, whereby a sovereign Afghanistan engages with the International Community to secure its own future and continues to be a positive factor for peace and stability in the region.

31. At today's meeting, Afghanistan laid out its vision of the future: a country that is a stable and functioning democracy, a strong and sustainable state in the service of its people, and a prospering economy. Embedded in a region that is conducive to prosperity and peace, and enjoying friendly relations with all of its near and extended neighbours, Afghanistan aspires to becoming a contributor to international peace and security.

32. With a view to realizing the above vision, the International Community and Afghanistan make firm mutual commitments to continue to working together in a spirit of partnership. Afghanistan reiterates its commitment to continue to improve governance,

while the International Community commits to an enduring engagement with Afghanistan through and beyond 2014.

33.   Today in Bonn, we solemnly declare a strategic consensus on deepening and broadening the partnership between Afghanistan and the International Community founded at the Petersberg ten years ago. Building on the shared achievements of the past ten years, and recognising that the security and well-being of Afghanistan continue to affect the security of the entire region and beyond, Afghanistan and the International Community strongly commit to this renewed partnership for the Transformation Decade. . . .

[The list of signatory nations has been omitted.]

SOURCE: Federal Foreign Office of Germany. "Afghanistan and the International Community: From Transition to the Transformation Decade." December 5, 2011. http://www.auswaertiges-amt.de/cae/servlet/contentblob/603686/publicationFile/162760/Conference_Conclusions_-_International_Afghanistan_Conference_Bonn_2011_engl.pdf;jsessionid=C439922ACF3B709206B8F9F6EA088407.

OTHER HISTORIC DOCUMENTS OF INTEREST

FROM THIS VOLUME

FROM PREVIOUS *HISTORIC DOCUMENTS*

President of South Sudan on Nation's Independence

AUGUST 8, 2011

South Sudan, an oil-rich area the size of Texas, became Africa's newest state on July 9, 2011. The independence ceremony took place at the mausoleum of the venerated former leader of the Sudanese People's Liberation Movement (SPLM), John Garang. President Salva Kiir is now the leader of the governing SPLM in South Sudan. Independence for South Sudan followed fifty-six years of armed struggle after the whole of Sudan gained its independence from joint British-Egyptian rule in 1955. The ensuing civil war claimed between 1.5 million and 2 million lives, with an Arab Muslim central government in the north pitted against an Animist and Christian African south.

In 2005, the Comprehensive Peace Agreement (CPA) promoted by former U.S. President George W. Bush prepared the southern third of Sudan for secession by allowing for a referendum on separation in January 2011. Independence was approved overwhelmingly by 98.83 percent of voters. President Barack Obama lobbied for peace between the new country and its erstwhile governing authority, Sudan, and pledged additional security support for South Sudan in January 2012.

International observers lauded the newfound opportunities for investors provided by South Sudanese independence. South Sudan straddles the White Nile and boasts abundant arable land that analysts believe could deliver between 200 and 300 percent higher crop yields with more efficient cultivation. More important, South Sudan also claims 75 percent of the former Sudan's oil reserves, although this advantage is offset somewhat by the north's enduring desire to control access to these reserves.

CURRENT ISSUES

Despite the euphoria surrounding South Sudan's independence, the terms of the CPA did not resolve the most contentious issues: the distribution of oil revenues and border demarcation, particularly the status of Abyei State. Violence continued to plague the border, which was expected to be only partially demarcated by March 2012. Blue Nile, a state just north of the border, faced air raids by the Sudanese government in early 2012. The contested border regions of South Kordofan and Abyei, both of which possess significant oil reserves, have withstood brutal attacks that have displaced thousands and prompted a wave of refugees into South Sudan. These attacks have included aerial campaigns, abductions, beatings, ethnic and sexual violence, and murder. Remote, mountainous South Kordofan is fraught with tension between the pro–South Sudan Nuba people and forces loyal to the northern Sudanese government. Abyei, to which both north and south claim historic ties, is considered a particularly intractable issue, with external observers referring to it as "Sudan's Jerusalem." Abyei is also internally divided between pro–South Sudan African Dinka farmers and Arab cattle herders who support the northern government. A 2009 ruling that equally divided Abyei between north and south has been ignored.

The northern Sudanese government, for its part, accused the southern SPLM-led government of supporting unrest in these regions by sponsoring rebel groups such as the Sudanese People's Liberation Movement–North (SPLM-N), the northern counterpart of the SPLM. Human rights abuses in these regions persisted into 2012, despite the establishment of a Joint Political and Security Mechanism in June 2011, just prior to southern independence. The mechanism was conceived to allow both countries to maintain a "safe demilitarized border zone" (SDBZ) with assistance from the United Nations. Little progress toward this aim had been made by early 2012.

Notwithstanding geographic disputes and human rights concerns, oil is possibly the greatest provocation of continued disagreement. South Sudan controls 75 percent of the former Sudan's national reserves but does not own any pipelines. It is dependent upon its northern neighbor to process oil and deliver it to external markets. In January 2012, South Sudan cut off its production of 350,000 barrels a day in response to the seizure by Sudan of some six million barrels of oil valued at $815 million as compensation in kind for what it viewed as delinquent oil processing fees that South Sudan did not recognize. Sudan had suggested a $36 charge per barrel, in a bid to recover lost revenues from southern oil fields, which previously had made up 36 percent of its budget. South Sudan countered with an offer of $1 per barrel, which was closer to the global rate for processing, but granted no recognition of Sudan's lost income following southern independence. The halt in production was damaging to both economies, as oil accounts for 98 percent of South Sudan's income.

The African Union (AU) sought to mediate the dispute for a second time in February 2012. An earlier treaty supported by the AU was rejected in late 2011 as it mandated that some southern oil fields supply northern export facilities. In the midst of the oil supply crisis, Sudanese president Omar al-Bashir stated that the two countries were "closer to war than peace." Nevertheless, negotiators hoped that the parties could reach an agreement on oil that also addressed border violence and resolved the status of Abyei. Separately, South Sudan began investigations of Chinese companies it viewed as complicit in oil smuggling. China is Sudan's most important investor and a major consumer of Sudanese and South Sudanese oil, which accounts for 5 percent of China's total supply.

While negotiations continued in early 2012, South Sudan remained determined to end north-south interdependence. The South Sudanese government announced in January 2012 that it had agreed to construct a new pipeline to Lamu, on Kenya's coast, within eleven months. Industry experts posited that three years was a more realistic timeframe.

Apart from outstanding differences with Sudan regarding natural resources and borders, the South Sudanese government must also deal with the internal issue of vicious tribal conflicts. The mutual desire for independence has been formally secured, removing the common cause that previously provided a bond between different ethnic groups. Although disturbances have affected the Warrop, Unity, and Lakes states, Jonglei, South Sudan's biggest state, has been the site of the worst violence, dominated by the rival militias from the Nuer and Murle tribes. The tribes's status as cattle herders necessitates competition for pasture and resources. Cattle raids have also increased in response to dowry inflation, which has seen a rise in the number of cows required as a bride price. Tribal raids have included savage attacks and reprisals, as well as the destruction of health clinics, water sources, and other essential infrastructure to deny essential support to any survivors if they emerge from hiding. In February 2012 an estimated 120,000 people had been rendered homeless by raids, with thousands more in hiding in the surrounding bush.

These attacks are becoming more organized, with a Nuer-supported White Army joining forces with the Dinka tribe against the Murle tribe in response to alleged abuses. The government has proven ineffective at stemming the violence, despite advance warning of some of the attacks. Critics have alleged that apparent government inaction is due to the presence of Nuer members in the government and military, although many affected areas are remote from major roads and other transportation infrastructure that would allow faster relief in a crisis. Turmoil has been deepened by the formation of rebel groups, such as the South Sudan Liberation Army (SSLA), that are opposed to the south's SPLM government. South Sudan believes the groups are sponsored by Sudan, a charge Sudan denies.

GOVERNMENT AGENDA

In addition to regional violence, the entire country faces urgent development needs. South Sudan has one of the world's highest maternal mortality rates and external aid groups provide 80 percent of its health care. Education is also inadequate: 75 percent of South Sudanese are illiterate and many communities do not have schools. Weak security conditions further inhibit human capital. Limited resources will likely be strained by the needs of returnees, who in some cases lost everything before arriving in South Sudan. These returnees include refugees from South Kordofan and Blue Nile, as well as South Sudanese previously residing in the north before their eviction by the Sudanese government.

As noted in the agenda given in President Salva Kiir's address to the legislature, the South Sudanese government has placed infrastructure development at the center of its strategy to raise living standards. Efficiency in public services will be evaluated by progress toward an ambitious agenda for the current term of government. Many objectives were set for the first 100 days alone, including expanded vaccination programs and the construction of 30 new schools and 100 new health clinics. Improved public services will be facilitated in part by greater transparency and accountability in government spending. The president has suggested that any officials who indulge in self-enrichment via public funds will be considered "enemies of the people." Security and independence will motivate the government's external policies.

SOUTH SUDAN'S FUTURE

Despite optimistic notes regarding development, anticorruption measures, and investment opportunities, the government will likely struggle to secure these objectives within the stated timeframe. Its management and sale of oil reserves will also continue to be difficult. Strategic security concerns, such as the risk of an attack by Sudan and the loss of oil revenue for an indefinite period of time, are in conflict with South Sudan's desire for permanent independence from Sudanese oil infrastructure and influence. In addition to its internal challenges, the country continues to face a credible prospect of renewed war.

—Anastazia Clouting

Following is a statement by the president of the Republic of South Sudan, on August 8, 2011, on the nation's independence and governing principles.

Remarks on South Sudan's *Independence*

August 8, 2011

... This day is yet another momentous occasion for our nation. The convening of this First Joint Sitting of our two houses: the Council of States and the National Assembly is a historical episode in our life time. These two houses constitute the National Legislature, which is the supreme authority in the land. The interests of the people are fully represented in this noble institution. Thus, allow me the opportunity to congratulate you and welcome you to the first sitting of this august house. ...

Rt. Honourable Speaker,

Honourable members of this august House,

Ladies and Gentlemen,

On July 9th, 2011, we ended a long period of misfortunes by the formal declaration of our independence. We have been occupied, colonized, marginalized and denied our dignity and humanity. This sitting clearly demonstrates the result of our long struggle and the beginning of a new journey for peace, democracy and prosperity. The independence we celebrated a few weeks ago is a great achievement for our people. ...

The freedom we have just achieved endows us with power and mandate. In return we must manage what is given to us with utmost care and responsibility. Moreover, as a sovereign body representing the sovereign will of the people of the Republic of South Sudan (RSS), it is incumbent upon this august House to manage the affairs of this land in order to deliver on what we promised to our people. While debating matters of national interest, it is important that we put the well being of our people and nation first. Our people have waited patiently for so long. It is time we act and we do so without delay. ...

Rt. Honourable Speaker,

Honourable members of this august House,

Ladies and Gentlemen,

Our dreams and hopes can only be met through hard work so that they can become a reality. A democratic and stable South Sudan will contribute to regional and international peace and prosperity. Remember, our independence also has its burdens and we must be ready to face them headlong. As I have pointed out in my past appeals, the worst experiences of the past and those of other nations must be considered in order for us as a new nation not to repeat them. We should not defend ourselves by using the failures of others as a threshold. Let us build our country by striving towards what others have achieved successfully.

As we move forward, the most serious challenge and responsibility we face is what we can deliver for future generations? What would be the best way to honour our heroes and heroines? I said it during Martyrs Day and I will repeat it here that there is nothing material to offer worth the sacrifices of our martyrs. What is worth the ultimate sacrifice they made is for us to build this nation. Nation-building requires cohesion, hard work, honesty and altruism. While I will continue to urge you to work harder, I am already at work. My next government will do the best it can to enhance the welfare of its citizens. Building a nation is not an easy enterprise. It takes time and in most cases those who build hardly reap the fruits of their own labour. Thus, let us keep in mind that we are here to serve our people and not to enrich ourselves. It is our duty to ensure that future generations must not experience the sufferings we have endured. In other words, let us end the promises and deliver the basic services to our people. Misfortunes of the past should end with us and let us set a brighter future for our people.

Rt. Honurable Speaker,

Honourable members of this august House,

Ladies and Gentlemen,

Together with the honourable members of this august Assembly, we must now focus on delivery of basic services to meet the great expectations of our people. This is only possible if we have a government whose first, second and final priorities are public interest, public interest, public interest! Let me make it clear once again that those individuals who are not willing and ready to make the sacrifices necessary to help our people will not be part of this government. Most important, the people of South Sudan will not sit ideally and allow corruption and abuses of public resources to continue unabated. You will agree with me that the people of South Sudan have not only suffered for far too long but they have also waited for basic services for too long. They cannot wait much longer. It is time for delivery and it is also time to put the public interest as the number one priority. . . .

Firstly, for South Sudan as a new nation to develop, we need education. No country has ever achieved development without educating its population. It remains a major challenge that only a minority of our children in South Sudan have access to education. When it comes to girl's education, it is even worse. All children in our independent country must have the opportunity to go to school. To do this there is a need to scale up education enrolment quickly all over the country. Together with our development partners we can achieve this. We will also encourage our communities to help build schools. To demonstrate our seriousness, within the first 100 days of the new government 30 new primary schools and four new secondary schools will be under construction. Together with our development partners, we will also launch a Teachers Training Development Program aiming at training 7000 teachers in the next three to five years. We are also going to build higher education institutions in the coming years. We cannot afford to lose our next generation leaders because of the absence of higher education institutions.

Secondly, the lack of good health care system in South Sudan has made our nation the most difficult place to live, especially for children and senior citizens. Many people still die because of preventable diseases. Let us be honest, you and I, and indeed our family members can afford to go out of the country to get treatment. But this is not the case for the millions of our people. And it is not because of war, rather because of the absence of health services. It is time to change that by providing basic health services for all our people in the villages, Bomas, Payams and Counties. Through community health programmes we can distribute anti-malarial bed nets to more people and save the lives of our children and their mothers. And we will start now.

Similarly, within the first 100 days of the government and together with development partners, we will make sure that 600,000 children are vaccinated against deadly diseases, including measles, particularly in the four states of Unity, Northern Bahr El Ghazal, Warrap and Upper Nile. And the good news is that 30 community midwives will finalize their training and be ready to be deployed to the rural areas. I also intend, with the support of this august House, to construct 100 small health care centers within the first year of this Administration.

Thirdly, South Sudan cannot develop without infrastructure. Our country is vast, and our communications are limited. Only through the use of roads and rivers can communities connect, agricultural production takes off, businesses flourish, the economy grows, and services are delivered. Infrastructure is at the heart of our development plan. Together with our development partners, we will invest in roads and bridges, and in river transport. But also here, we need our people to give a hand. They can help rehabilitate and construct feeder-roads. With the focus of this august Assembly, together, we can make it happen.

Within the first 100 days of the new government two roads and two airstrips will be opened in Unity and Warrap states. The repairs of Juba Bridge and the construction of a new bridge on the Nile donated by the Government of Japan will get underway. The rehabilitation of four roads will be in process, three in Eastern Equatoria State, Warrap and the Pagak-Mathiang road in Upper Nile.

Fourthly, no country can develop without abiding with basic principles of justice and rule of law. South Sudanese have been at the receiving end of aggression, injustices, arbitrary detention and absence of law and order during decades of war. Now similar incidences have occurred among our own police and security institutions. As I said on Martyrs' Day, this has to end. Criminality should cease or else those who perpetrate suffering to others will be subjected to the strong arm of the law. It is time to put our own house in order. We need to strengthen law and order, both within our own institutions and among citizens.

Within the first 100 days of our new government, 50 new police stations located throughout the country, will be opened. Two prisons will also be completed. Again together with our development partners the Government will do more.

Fifthly, no country can ensure peace and security and protect its citizens without a modern and professional Army. As a new and independent country, we will complete the transformation of the SPLA into a national army. For this to happen successfully, the Government must put in place programs that would provide new opportunities for former SPLA soldiers.

Within the first 100 days, we will launch our new programme for Disarmament, Demobilization and Reintegration (DDR). We will provide tailored programmes to give them a new start.

These are just but few caveats for the beginning. We have got more daunting tasks in front of us—development, development and development! And development does not only come with the donors or with oil money. As I said earlier it requires hard work and discipline. For example, the Republic of South Sudan should never depend on imports of food or handouts. We are endowed with fertile land. I said it and I will repeat it now; we must till the land to produce food. This is a moral responsibility for citizens—work, work, work and work! I want to reiterate again, a prosperous nation is not made up of indolent citizens, because laziness is useless. As pioneer members of this joint august Parliament, I call upon you all to help mobilize our communities to service in order to help develop our nation. We can only achieve our ambitious development goals if all of us dedicate ourselves to develop our country and pull together with unity of purpose.

On Independence Day I made it clear that from now onward we do not have any excuses or scapegoats. It is our responsibility to protect our land, our resources and ourselves and to develop our country. Moreover, the goat is dead therefore there is no one to blame!

Rt. Honourable Speaker,

Honourable members of this joint august sitting,

Ladies and Gentlemen,

For South Sudan to succeed, we need to abide with the principles of transparency and accountability. Only then can we build a strong foundation for our new nation. Another word for corruption is stealing and it is called 'stealing' because money which should have gone to build our country is stolen by selfish persons. Those who engage in corruption are undermining our country and the sovereignty of the Republic of South Sudan. To borrow from our liberation laws, join me in defining corrupt persons as the enemies of the people. We must therefore fight corruption with dedication, rigour and commitment. And that is why, on Independence Day, I pledged to the people, the nation and the heads of state and government present that I would do all that I could to remove this cancer.

Most important, let me put a human face on what corruption does to our people and country. With the amount of funds stolen over the past six years and half; we could have saved thousands of our citizens from unnecessary deaths and suffering, building more than a dozen of schools and hospitals, and feed many of our citizens.

At this juncture, allow me to take permission from this august Assembly to outline key priority expectations of your business in the first 100 days. This requires us to change the way we have been doing things and become more disciplined. For example, timekeeping has been one of the worst vices of the old Sudan. This honourable legislative body has loads of work to deliver to this nation, critical amongst which is legislation itself. We must pass crucial laws to cement our sovereignty and independence. There is need to work even extra harder in order to expedite the process of legislation and achieve the following:

One, in the first 100 days I will make sure that the new Government of the Republic of South Sudan passes 5 essential laws to establish full transparency and accountability in the management of our financial resources, natural resources and oil. Thus, we will send to Parliament a Public Financial Management and Accountability Act, a Procurement Act, an Internal Audit Act, a Petroleum Act for regulating the management of oil resources, and an Oil Revenue Management Law for sustainable and transparent management of the oil income.

Several of these laws are already prepared, and all of them will hold international standards. This is an essential part of putting our new Republic on a solid foundation cemented by the blood of our martyrs. I call upon you, the National Legislature of the new Republic of South Sudan, to process and pass these laws without delay. We need them to take effect as soon as possible.

Two, implementation of these Acts is essential. Within the first 100 days, the Republic of South Sudan will develop an implementation plan to put these policies into practice. This includes rules of procedures for our public service and large-scale training of staff. Here, we will have to ask for external assistance and support. We need to be ready to implement expeditiously as soon as Parliament passes these laws.

In the first 100 days, the Audit Chamber and the Anti Corruption Commission will also be strengthened. We will have audits underway in three of the most significant spending government ministries and agencies. We will take action on their findings and as I have pointed out before there will be no loopholes for people who are addicted to mishandling public resources. There will be no sacred cows this time round. Moreover the Anti-Corruption Commission has already been granted the right to independent investigations but the institution itself also requires restructuring. I will urge the Commission to make use of this right within the first 100 days. The Commission and its members will have my full support as President of the Republic.

Three, implementation always starts at home with us as political leaders. In all South Sudanese communities stealing is seen as deeply shameful! We all know what happens in our cultures and communities, particularly, if one is caught stealing? The community will start composing songs against you, and the whole family will be disgraced. Your children will have difficulties getting married respectably, and you cannot even become a chief or be in any position of authority.

I always wonder what has happened to these core values of our communities. It seems that people have forgotten them. This has to change and with determination it will change. We must set new standards to be eligible for public office. When the government is appointed I will make these standards clear to the public, and I will expect every Minister and civil servant to abide by these standards. The Republic of South Sudan will expect nothing less from those who serve our newly independent country.

With these actions, I hope we will have taken the first critical steps to put our new country on a solid footing. Remember no government performs well without checks and balances. The primary role of Parliament is, therefore, essential in this process. I request you, our Parliamentarians and our international partners, to assist us and to hold us responsible in the implementation process of these pledges. I will report back to you on all these deliverables when our first 100 days have passed. I promise you that this time, we will deliver.

Rt. Honourable Speaker,

Honourable Members of this Joint Assembly,

Distinguished Ladies and Gentlemen,

I shall be remiss if I do not say something about the Comprehensive Peace Agreement (CPA), particularly about the issues that are still outstanding. I would like to reassure all that Abyei is not a forgotten cause because we will remain actively seized of the matter until a final resolution is found. We are all aware that the United Nations Security Council has authorized the deployment of the UN Interim Security Force for Abyei (UNISFA) in order to ensure resettlement of the people of Abyei back in their homes. I trust that a final solution will be found that will reflect the true will of the people of Abyei. I am equally committed to ensuring peace and security along our common borders and the spirit of good neighbourliness is one of the guiding principles of our foreign policy. The massive attendance of the world during our independence celebrations is testimony that we are a friendly people. We will continue to engage with all our neighbours, particularly with the leadership in the Republic of the Sudan to build strong relations because we share a long border.

Finally, I would like to repeat what I said during the declaration of independence. Let us continue to celebrate our hard won freedom but we must always be sober to wake up the following day and work. I reiterate my appeal to this august House that this new nation is yours and let us commit ourselves to build it with optimism. Hard work is a virtue and in just a matter of time, we will prosper. There is nothing impossible and as it is said: 'If there is a will there is a way'. The role of government is to provide a conducive atmosphere while citizens must join hands and work. We will issue comprehensive priorities for the next five to ten years as soon as the new cabinet is constituted.

Let me say this again we cannot prosper as a nation without the unity and harmony of our people. We must accept our diversity and use our difficult past experiences to grow. We must work harder and harder so that in five years change must be apparent. Government will ensure that there is no hindrance or obstacle and people should go about doing their businesses in safety and without any kind of fear.

As for you the honourable members of this joint august House, legislation is your first order of business and I wish you all well in this national duty. I am always available and my office is there to attend to urgent national needs and emergencies.

Let us start to work right away.

Thank you all and may God bless South Sudan!

SOURCE: Government of the Republic of South Sudan. "H. E. Gen Salva Kiir Mayardit, President of the Republic Address to the First Joint Sitting of the National Legislature and to the Nation." August 8, 2011. http://www.goss.org.

OTHER HISTORIC DOCUMENTS OF INTEREST

FROM PREVIOUS *HISTORIC DOCUMENTS*

Prime Minister Cameron on Riots in Great Britain

AUGUST 10 AND AUGUST 15, 2011

Over a four-day period in early August 2011, a wave of rioting swept through Great Britain, concentrated in poor areas of large cities like London, Birmingham, and Liverpool. They caused major damage to local businesses and buildings, left five people dead, and resulted in more than 4,000 arrests. In the initial hours, police struggled to regain control, creating a sense of chaos, which, when relayed via television screens and social networking websites, encouraged more rioters to take to the streets. After police finally restored order, the country embarked on some heavy soul-searching as to what caused the riots. Views were sharply divided between those who blamed unjust government economic policies and those who insisted it was the moral decay of society that was at fault.

DISCONTENT OVER AUSTERITY POLICIES

The origins of the violence can be traced to the sharp economic downturn experienced by the United Kingdom following the autumn 2008 financial crisis. The UK government, like its American and European counterparts, chose to pump enormous sums of public money into its tottering banks in a desperate effort to prevent a credit crunch and financial meltdown. More than $3 trillion of taxpayer money was injected into the financial system in total. In addition, in response to the deep economic recession that the country sank into in 2009, the government introduced austerity measures that were very unpopular.

In May 2010, thirteen years of Labour Party rule came to an end following parliamentary elections that led to the formation of a new coalition government made up of Tories and Liberal Democrats. The new Prime Minister David Cameron, a Tory, at 43 years old was the youngest person to ascend to the job since Lord Liverpool in 1812. With his government faced with a current account deficit of 10 percent of gross domestic product (GDP) and unemployment levels reaching 8 percent, the highest since 1994, Cameron struggled to get the country's public finances back in order. His government proceeded to implement harsh policies such as slashing public spending by $131 billion over four years, reducing public sector employment by 490,000, and increasing the retirement age from 65 to 66 years. On March 26, 2011, 250,000 people protested in London over these austerity measures, the biggest protest the country had seen since the start of the 2003 Iraq war.

THE RIOTS

The spark for the summer 2011 riots was a fatal police shooting that took place on August 4. The victim was Mark Duggan, a twenty-nine-year-old father of four of Afro-Caribbean origin whom police stopped while he was riding in a cab. Peaceful protests over Duggan's killing in Tottenham, a low-income neighborhood in London, degenerated into violent clashes on August 6 in which two police cars and a double-decker bus were set on fire, stores were looted, and several buildings were reduced to smoldering shells. News of the riots spread via television news reports, while youths coordinated more attacks using text messages, instant messaging on Blackberry smartphones, and social networking sites such as Facebook and Twitter. The dominant narrative that emerged in the first hours was one of anarchy and chaos as images were relayed of burning buildings, garbage dumps being set on fire, and police being pelted with bottles and fireworks.

The riots spread to other parts of London, including Hackney, Chalk Farm, Croydon, Clapham, and Peckham, and to other British cities, including Manchester, Birmingham, Bristol, Nottingham, Leicester, and Liverpool. There were calls on police to employ heavier-handed tactics to restore order, such as the use of water cannons. In the end, they did not resort to such methods and the rioting gradually subsided, with a semblance of order having been restored by August 10. More than 4,000 arrests were made in connection with the riots, 805 in London alone, and 654 people had been charged by August 12.

Right from the outset, interviews revealed a diversity of opinion as to what caused the riots. For example, Bry Phillips, a twenty-eight-year-old self-described anarchist, was cited as proclaiming, "This is the uprising of the working class. We're redistributing the wealth." Young people were indeed filmed emerging from shops carrying both high-value goods such as televisions and jewelry and inexpensive food items such as chocolate bars, sweets, and ice-cream cones. Marilyn Mosley, a forty-nine-year-old resident of the Brixton neighborhood in London, called the riots "just an excuse for the young ones to come and rob shops." However, Matthew Yeoland, a forty-three-year-old local teacher, said, "There's been tension for a long time. The kids aren't happy. They hate the police."

MORAL DECAY TO BLAME

Prime Minister Cameron cut short his holiday in Tuscany, Italy, in response to growing demand for his immediate return, while London Mayor Boris Johnson and UK Home Secretary Theresa May also returned from their vacations to deal with the crisis. In a statement made on August 10, as the riots were dying down, Cameron sought to dispel any notion that the violence was a venting of hostility toward government policies or police practices. Instead, he argued that the rioters were nothing more than common criminals, products of a society in steep moral decline. "There are pockets of our society that are not just broken but, frankly, sick. When we see children as young as 12 or 13 looting and laughing, when we see the disgusting sight of an injured young man with people pretending to help him while they are robbing him, it is clear there are things that are badly wrong in our society," he said. The prime minister insisted that the root cause of the riots was "mindless selfishness" and a "complete lack of responsibility in parts of our society" where people "feel that the world owes them something."

Cameron elaborated on this theme in a speech delivered on August 15 and expanded it to also take a swipe at policies of previous governments that he said had not merely failed but had even created the culture that led to the riots. He said that the riots were not about race, cuts in public spending, or poverty, but were rather perpetrated by "people with a twisted moral code . . . people with a complete absence of self-restraint." He railed against the "decay of society," which, he claimed, was manifested in "children without fathers, schools without discipline, reward without effort, crime without punishment, rights without responsibilities, communities without control." He said he had no doubt that many of the rioters came from homes without fathers. He accused the "big bossy bureaucratic state" of taking away communities' sense of responsibility and said that the country's social welfare system had encouraged laziness and bad behavior. Finally, he attacked human rights legislation the previous Labour government had enacted in 1998, claiming it had "exerted a chilling effect on public sector organizations." And he highlighted a new policy initiative aimed at introducing a non-military, national citizen service program for young people.

Debate on the Root Cause of the Riots

There was renewed debate about the underlying cause of the riots following the publication in December 2011 of a study by *The Guardian* newspaper and the London School of Economics for which 270 of the rioters were interviewed. Eighty-five percent of those interviewed said that anger at police practices was a key factor behind the violence. "When we came across a police car it felt like we hit the jackpot . . . we thought we'd just kind of violate just like they violate us," said one rioter. More than 70 percent said that they had been stopped and searched by the police within the previous year. While half of the interviewees were black, they nevertheless did not consider the violence to have been "race riots." The same month, the British parliament produced its own report, which tended more toward the narrative of delinquent youth profiting from the police having lost control. "Clearly a feeling existed that desirable consumer goods could be made available by looting. There was a substantial element of opportunistic criminality and copycat behaviour," the report concluded. It added that for the local residents who had lost their homes and businesses, "the state effectively ceased to exist [during the riots]—sometimes for hours at a time."

Opinion editorials in leading British publications voiced similarly divergent views. Columnist Gary Younge for *The Guardian*, a liberal newspaper, leaned more toward the riots being an expression of discontent over the spending cuts and over police oppression. "The government's narrative may have been ridiculous, but in the absence of a counter-narrative, many believed it plausible," he wrote. By contrast, an editorial in the *Economist* magazine, asserted, "The rioters interviewed come across as criminals with a faulty moral compass who ran amok and hate the police." Pointing out that 213 small shopkeepers had been looted and five people left dead, the reporter expressed doubt that the rioters had been motivated by issues such as increases in student tuition fees, noting instead how most of those arrested had prior criminal convictions. The debate continued to rumble on, with both sides finding evidence from various reports to support these competing narratives.

—Brian Beary

Following are two statements delivered by British Prime Minister David Cameron on August 10 and August 15, 2011, on the riots in Great Britain.

Prime Minister on Violence in Great Britain

August 10, 2011

Good morning. I've just come from chairing another meeting of the COBRA emergency committee and I'd like to update you on the latest situation and the actions that we're taking to get this despicable violence off our streets.

Since yesterday there are more police on the street, more people have been arrested and more people are being charged and prosecuted. Last night there were around 16,000 police on the streets of London and there is evidence that a more robust approach to policing in London resulted in a much quieter night across the capital and let me pay tribute to the bravery of those police officers and, indeed, everyone working for our emergency services. In total, there have been 750 arrests in London since Saturday with more than 160 people being charged. . . .

We needed a fight back and a fight back is underway. We have seen the worst of Britain, but I also believe we've seen some of the best of Britain: the million people who've signed up on Facebook to support the police, communities coming together in the cleanup operations. But there is absolutely no room for complacency and there is much more to be done. . . .

This continued violence is simply not acceptable and it will be stopped. We will not put up with this in our country. We will not allow a culture of fear to exist on our streets. Let me be clear. At COBRA this morning we agreed full contingency planning is going ahead. Whatever resources the police need they will get. Whatever tactics the police feel they need to employ they will have legal backing to do so. We will do whatever is necessary to restore law and order onto our streets. Every contingency is being looked at. Nothing is off the table. The police are already authorised to use baton rounds and we agreed at COBRA that while they're not currently needed we now have in place contingency plans for water cannon to be available at 24 hours' notice.

It is all too clear that we have a big problem with gangs in our country. For too long there's been a lack of focus on the complete lack of respect shown by these groups of thugs. I'm clear that they are in no way representative of the vast majority of young people in our country who despise them, frankly, as much as the rest of us do, but there are pockets of our society that are not just broken but, frankly, sick. When we see children as young as 12 and 13 looting and laughing, when we see the disgusting sight of an injured young man with people pretending to help him while they are robbing him, it is clear there are things that are badly wrong in our society.

For me, the root cause of this mindless selfishness is the same thing that I have spoken about for years. It is a complete lack of responsibility in parts of our society. People allowed to feel that the world owes them something, that their rights outweigh their responsibilities and that their actions do not have consequences. Well, they do have consequences. We need to have a clearer code of values and standards that we expect people to live by and stronger penalties if they cross the line. Restoring a stronger sense of responsibility across our society, in every town, in every street, in every estate is something I'm determined to do.

Tomorrow, COBRA will meet again, Cabinet will meet, I'll make a statement to Parliament, I'll set out in full the measures that we'll take to help businesses that have been affected, to help rebuild communities, to help rebuild the shops and buildings that have been damaged, to make sure the homeless are rehoused, to help local authorities in all the ways that are necessary. But today, right now, the priority is still clear: we will take every action necessary to bring order back to our streets. . . .

[The question-and-answer section has been omitted.]

SOURCE: Office of the British Prime Minister. "PM Statement on Violence in England." August 10, 2011. http://www.number10.gov.uk/news/pm-statement-on-violence-in-england/.

Prime Minister on Response to British Riots

August 15, 2011

It is time for our country to take stock.

Last week we saw some of the most sickening acts on our streets.

I'll never forget talking to Maurice Reeves, whose family had run the Reeves furniture store in Croydon for generations.

This was an 80 year old man who had seen the business he had loved, that his family had built up for generations, simply destroyed.

A hundred years of hard work, burned to the ground in a few hours.

But last week we didn't just see the worst of the British people; we saw the best of them too.

The ones who called themselves riot wombles and headed down to the hardware stores to pick up brooms and start the clean-up.

The people who linked arms together to stand and defend their homes, their businesses.

The policemen and women and fire officers who worked long, hard shifts, sleeping in corridors then going out again to put their life on the line.

Everywhere I've been this past week, in Salford, Manchester, Birmingham, Croydon, people of every background, colour and religion have shared the same moral outrage and hurt for our country.

Because this is Britain.

This is a great country of good people.

Those thugs we saw last week do not represent us, nor do they represent our young people—and they will not drag us down.

WHY THIS HAPPENED

But now that the fires have been put out and the smoke has cleared, the question hangs in the air: 'Why? How could this happen on our streets and in our country?'

Of course, we mustn't oversimplify.

There were different things going on in different parts of the country.

In Tottenham some of the anger was directed at the police.

In Salford there was some organised crime, a calculated attack on the forces of order.

But what we know for sure is that in large parts of the country this was just pure criminality.

So as we begin the necessary processes of inquiry, investigation, listening and learning: let's be clear.

These riots were not about race: the perpetrators and the victims were white, black and Asian.

These riots were not about government cuts: they were directed at high street stores, not Parliament.

And these riots were not about poverty: that insults the millions of people who, whatever the hardship, would never dream of making others suffer like this.

No, this was about behaviour . . .

. . . people showing indifference to right and wrong . . .

. . . people with a twisted moral code . . .

. . . people with a complete absence of self-restraint.

Politicians and behaviour

Now I know as soon as I use words like 'behaviour' and 'moral' people will say—what gives politicians the right to lecture us?

Of course we're not perfect.

But politicians shying away from speaking the truth about behaviour, about morality . . .

. . . this has actually helped to cause the social problems we see around us.

We have been too unwilling for too long to talk about what is right and what is wrong.

We have too often avoided saying what needs to be said—about everything from marriage to welfare to common courtesy.

Sometimes the reasons for that are noble—we don't want to insult or hurt people.

Sometimes they're ideological—we don't feel it's the job of the state to try and pass judgement on people's behaviour or engineer personal morality.

And sometimes they're just human—we're not perfect beings ourselves and we don't want to look like hypocrites. . . .

One of the biggest lessons of these riots is that we've got to talk honestly about behaviour and then act—because bad behaviour has literally arrived on people's doorsteps.

And we can't shy away from the truth anymore.

Broken society agenda

So this must be a wake-up call for our country.

Social problems that have been festering for decades have exploded in our face.

Now, just as people last week wanted criminals robustly confronted on our street, so they want to see these social problems taken on and defeated.

Our security fightback must be matched by a social fightback.

We must fight back against the attitudes and assumptions that have brought parts of our society to this shocking state.

We know what's gone wrong: the question is, do we have the determination to put it right?

Do we have the determination to confront the slow-motion moral collapse that has taken place in parts of our country these past few generations?

Irresponsibility. Selfishness. Behaving as if your choices have no consequences.

Children without fathers. Schools without discipline. Reward without effort.

Crime without punishment. Rights without responsibilities. Communities without control.

Some of the worst aspects of human nature tolerated, indulged—sometimes even incentivised—by a state and its agencies that in parts have become literally de-moralised.

So do we have the determination to confront all this and turn it around?

I have the very strong sense that the responsible majority of people in this country not only have that determination; they are crying out for their government to act upon it. . . .

So I can announce today that over the next few weeks, I and ministers from across the coalition government will review every aspect of our work to mend our broken society. . .

. . . on schools, welfare, families, parenting, addiction, communities . . .

. . . on the cultural, legal, bureaucratic problems in our society too:

. . . from the twisting and misrepresenting of human rights that has undermined personal responsibility . . .

. . . to the obsession with health and safety that has eroded people's willingness to act according to common sense.

We will review our work and consider whether our plans and programmes are big enough and bold enough to deliver the change that I feel this country now wants to see.

Government cannot legislate to change behaviour, but it is wrong to think the State is a bystander.

Because people's behaviour does not happen in a vacuum: it is affected by the rules government sets and how they are enforced . . .

. . . by the services government provides and how they are delivered . . .

. . . and perhaps above all by the signals government sends about the kinds of behaviour that are encouraged and rewarded.

So yes, the broken society is back at the top of my agenda.

And as we review our policies in the weeks ahead, today I want to set out the priority areas I will be looking at, and give you a sense of where I think we need to raise our ambitions.

Security fightback

First and foremost, we need a security fight-back.

We need to reclaim our streets from the thugs who didn't just spring out of nowhere last week, but who've been making lives a misery for years.

Now I know there have been questions in people's minds about my approach to law and order.

Well, I don't want there to be any doubt.

Nothing in this job is more important to me than keeping people safe.

And it is obvious to me that to do that we've got to be tough, we've got to be robust, we've got to score a clear line between right and wrong right through the heart of this country—in every street and in every community.

That starts with a stronger police presence—pounding the beat, deterring crime, ready to re-group and crack down at the first sign of trouble. . . .

Our reforms mean that the police are going to answer directly to the people.

You want more tough, no-nonsense policing?

You want to make sure the police spend more time confronting the thugs in your neighbourhood and less time meeting targets by stopping motorists?

You want the police out patrolling your streets instead of sitting behind their desks?

Elected police and crime commissioners are part of the answer: they will provide that direct accountability so you can finally get what you want when it comes to policing.

The point of our police reforms is not to save money, not to change things for the sake of it—but to fight crime. . . .

It's time for something else too.

A concerted, all-out war on gangs and gang culture.

This isn't some side issue.

It is a major criminal disease that has infected streets and estates across our country.

Stamping out these gangs is a new national priority.

Last week I set up a cross-government programme to look at every aspect of this problem.

We will fight back against gangs, crime and the thugs who make people's lives hell and we will fight back hard.

The last front in that fight is proper punishment. . . .

Yes, last week we saw the criminal justice system deal with an unprecedented challenge: the courts sat through the night and dispensed swift, firm justice.

We saw that the system was on the side of the law-abiding majority.

But confidence in the system is still too low. . . .

So no-one should doubt this government's determination to be tough on crime and to mount an effective security fight-back.

But we need much more than that.

We need a social fight-back too, with big changes right through our society.

Families and parenting

Let me start with families.

The question people asked over and over again last week was 'where are the parents? Why aren't they keeping the rioting kids indoors?'

Tragically that's been followed in some cases by judges rightly lamenting: "why don't the parents even turn up when their children are in court?"

Well, join the dots and you have a clear idea about why some of these young people were behaving so terribly.

Either there was no one at home, they didn't much care or they'd lost control.

Families matter. . . .

So if we want to have any hope of mending our broken society, family and parenting is where we've got to start.

I've been saying this for years, since before I was Prime Minister, since before I was leader of the Conservative Party.

So: from here on I want a family test applied to all domestic policy.

If it hurts families, if it undermines commitment, if it tramples over the values that keeps people together, or stops families from being together, then we shouldn't do it.

More than that, we've got to get out there and make a positive difference to the way families work, the way people bring up their children . . .

. . . and we've got to be less sensitive to the charge that this is about interfering or nannying.

We are working on ways to help improve parenting—well now I want that work accelerated, expanded and implemented as quickly as possible.

This has got to be right at the top of our priority list.

And we need more urgent action, too, on the families that some people call 'problem', others call 'troubled'.

The ones that everyone in their neighbourhood knows and often avoids. . . .

Schools

The next part of the social fight-back is what happens in schools.

We need an education system which reinforces the message that if you do the wrong thing you'll be disciplined . . .

. . . but if you work hard and play by the rules you will succeed. . . .

But with the failures in our education system so deep, we can't just say 'these are our plans and we believe in them, let's sit back while they take effect'.

I now want us to push further, faster.

Are we really doing enough to ensure that great new schools are set up in the poorest areas, to help the children who need them most?

And why are we putting up with the complete scandal of schools being allowed to fail, year after year?

If young people have left school without being able to read or write, why shouldn't that school be held more directly accountable?

Yes, these questions are already being asked across government but what happened last week gives them a new urgency—and we need to act on it.

RESPECT FOR COMMUNITY

Just as we want schools to be proud of we want everyone to feel proud of their communities.

We need a sense of social responsibility at the heart of every community.

Yet the truth is that for too long the big bossy bureaucratic state has drained it away. . . .

That's why we want executive Mayors in our twelve biggest cities . . .

. . . because strong civic leadership can make a real difference in creating that sense of belonging.

We're training an army of community organisers to work in our most deprived neighbourhoods . . .

. . . because we're serious about encouraging social action and giving people a real chance to improve the community in which they live. . . .

RESPONSIBILITY AND WELFARE

But one of the biggest parts of this social fight-back is fixing the welfare system.

For years we've had a system that encourages the worst in people—that incites laziness, that excuses bad behaviour, that erodes self-discipline, that discourages hard work . . .

. . . above all that drains responsibility away from people.

We talk about moral hazard in our financial system—where banks think they can act recklessly because the state will always bail them out . . .

. . . well this is moral hazard in our welfare system—people thinking they can be as irresponsible as they like because the state will always bail them out.

We're already addressing this through the Welfare Reform Bill going through parliament. But I'm not satisfied that we're doing all we can.

I want us to look at toughening up the conditions for those who are out of work and receiving benefits . . .

. . . and speeding up our efforts to get all those who can work back to work

Work is at the heart of a responsible society.

So getting more of our young people into jobs, or up and running in their own businesses is a critical part of how we strengthen responsibility in our society. . . .

But there is more we need to do, to boost self-employment and enterprise . . .

. . . because it's only by getting our young people into work that we can build an ownership society in which everyone feels they have a stake.

Human rights and health and safety

As we consider these questions of attitude and behaviour, the signals that government sends, and the incentives it creates . . .

. . . we inevitably come to the question of the Human Rights Act and the culture associated with it.

Let me be clear: in this country we are proud to stand up for human rights, at home and abroad. It is part of the British tradition.

But what is alien to our tradition—and now exerting such a corrosive influence on behaviour and morality. . .

. . . is the twisting and misrepresenting of human rights in a way that has undermined personal responsibility.

We are attacking this problem from both sides.

We're working to develop a way through the morass by looking at creating our own British Bill of Rights. . . .

And as we urgently review the work we're doing on the broken society, judging whether it's ambitious enough—I want to make it clear that there will be no holds barred. . .

. . . and that most definitely includes the human rights and health and safety culture.

National Citizen Service

Many people have long thought that the answer to these questions of social behaviour is to bring back national service.

In many ways I agree . . .

. . . and that's why we are actually introducing something similar—National Citizen Service.

It's a non-military programme that captures the spirit of national service.

It takes sixteen year-olds from different backgrounds and gets them to work together.

They work in their communities, whether that's coaching children to play football, visiting old people at the hospital or offering a bike repair service to the community.

It shows young people that doing good can feel good.

The real thrill is from building things up, not tearing them down.

Team-work, discipline, duty, decency: these might sound old-fashioned words but they are part of the solution to this very modern problem of alienated, angry young people.

Restoring those values is what National Citizen Service is all about.

I passionately believe in this idea.

It's something we've been developing for years.

Thousands of teenagers are taking part this summer.

The plan is for thirty thousand to take part next year.

But in response to the riots I will say this.

This should become a great national effort.

Let's make National Citizen Service available to all sixteen year olds as a rite of passage.

We can do that if we work together: businesses, charities, schools and social enterprises . . .

. . . and in the months ahead I will put renewed effort into making it happen.

CONCLUSION

Today I've talked a lot about what the government is going to do.

But let me be clear:

This social fight-back is not a job for government on its own.

Government doesn't run the businesses that create jobs and turn lives around.

Government doesn't make the video games or print the magazines or produce the music that tells young people what's important in life.

Government can't be on every street and in every estate, instilling the values that matter.

This is a problem that has deep roots in our society, and it's a job for all of our society to help fix it.

In the highest offices, the plushest boardrooms, the most influential jobs, we need to think about the example we are setting.

Moral decline and bad behaviour is not limited to a few of the poorest parts of our society.

The restoration of responsibility has to cut right across our society.

Because whatever the arguments, we all belong to the same society, and we all have a stake in making it better.

There is no 'them' and 'us'—there is us.

We are all in this together, and we will mend our broken society—together.

SOURCE: Office of the British Prime Minister. "PM's Speech on the Fightback After the Riots." August 15, 2011. http://www.number10.gov.uk/news/pms-speech-on-the-fightback-after-the-riots/.

OTHER HISTORIC DOCUMENTS OF INTEREST

FROM PREVIOUS *HISTORIC DOCUMENTS*

September

U.S. Postal Service
Financial Crisis

SEPTEMBER 6, NOVEMBER 21, AND DECEMBER 13, 2011

The United States Postal Service (USPS), a quasi-government agency, is the nation's second-largest civilian employer with 574,000 employees, and subsists off of postage and mail service sales, rather than tax dollars. From fiscal year 2007 to 2011, the USPS posted multibillion-dollar deficits, largely brought on by a decrease in mail volume. Volume peaked in 2006 at more than 213 billion pieces of mail, but by 2010, it had dropped to 171 billion pieces, with volume expected to fall another 2 percent in 2011. Since 2001, stamped mail volume has dropped 47 percent, largely being overtaken by electronic means of communication and bill pay. "Electronic diversion continues to cause reductions in first-class mail," said Patrick Donahoe, the postmaster general. During the past four fiscal years, the postal service has worked to cut $12 billion from its costs, but even coupled with a 110,000-person labor force reduction, the USPS cannot make cuts fast enough to keep pace with falling revenue. "As impressive as these reductions have been," said Donahoe, "we must significantly accelerate the pace of cost reduction in the next four years." To return to profitability, the postal service estimates that it must reduce its annual costs by $20 billion by 2015. In 2011, the fiscal crisis facing the USPS reached a boiling point, and in August, the organization announced that it would be insolvent by September. To shore up its finances, the postal service, White House, and Congress made various recommendations for saving the ailing organization.

Postal Service Proposals

In August, the USPS announced that it would face insolvency in September "due to significant declines in first-class mail volume, the effects of a congressional mandate to prefund retiree health benefits, and increases in network costs, wages and benefits." To prevent financial meltdown, the USPS appealed to Congress to take quick action on legislation that would keep the organization financially stable. "The postal service is on the brink of default," Postmaster General Patrick Donahoe said during September testimony before the Committee on Homeland Security and Government Affairs. "The Postal Service requires radical change to its business model if it is to remain viable in the future," he continued, noting that "Failure to act could be catastrophic."

In submitting proposals to Congress for consideration, the postal service made clear that it believed it cannot escape its financial crisis if it is unable to operate like a business and have greater flexibility to amend its business plans as necessary. "To do so, the Postal Service requires the enactment of comprehensive, long-term legislation to provide it with needed flexibility," said Donahoe.

One proposal made by the postal service involved closing 3,700 postal locations and 120,000 layoffs. Employee costs total 80 percent of postal service expenses; however, current union contracts contain a no-layoff provision that bars the postal service from dismissing any employees that have been on the job for more than six continuous years. To be able to complete the needed layoffs, Congress would have to use Reduction in Force provisions currently available for federal competitive service employees for positions held by union employees. In total, the postal service estimates that it needs to eliminate 220,000 positions by 2015, only 100,000 of which will come through attrition. "To restore the Postal Service to financial viability, it is imperative that we have the ability to reduce our workforce rapidly," Donahoe said. Postal unions denounced the recommendation. "These proposals are outrageous, illegal and despicable," said Cliff Guffey, president of the American Postal Workers Union (APWU), also noting that the number of employees had already declined by 130,000 during the past four years. Sen. Orrin Hatch, R-Utah, defended the postal services's proposal. "If the postal union is standing in the way of efforts to guarantee the long-term solvency of the U.S. Postal Service, this would be a serious outrage," Hatch said.

A second proposal made by the postal service was to eliminate Saturday delivery and move to a five-day per week schedule. The proposal sparked concern from representatives of rural districts and the publication industry. "We are concerned that rural America is being thrown overboard by a postal system too eager to lavish its assets onto highly competitive urban areas," said Tonda Rush, director of public policy at the National Newspaper Association. "Within this context, the loss of Saturday residential delivery would be a major blow."

Additionally, the USPS recommended that it be able to remove its employees from federal health care and retirement plans to instead create internal health care and defined-contribution retirement plans. The USPS also asked Congress to return some of its pension overpayment. A 2006 Congressional mandate requires the postal service to pay approximately $5.5 billion per year for ten years for health coverage for future retirees. The postal service claimed this payment was what caused them to lose $20 billion during the past four years, and also estimated that it overpaid approximately $50 billion to $75 billion.

"We have advanced these and other proposals to provide Congress with a range of legislative options while we aggressively do what we can within our current business model," Donahoe told members of the committee. "We need the flexibility to operate more as a business would, in order to return to sound financial footing so we can meet America's evolving mailing and shipping needs for generations to come."

WHITE HOUSE PLAN

On September 6, the White House announced that it supported giving the USPS an extra three months to make its required $5.5 billion retiree health care payment due on September 30. The move was instantly criticized in Congress. Sen. Joe Lieberman, I-Conn., said, "That's not going to solve the problem for the long run." John Berry, director of the Office of Personnel Management, announced that the administration would put together a larger plan to release later in the month.

Alongside his deficit reduction package released in mid-September, Obama announced his official plan to help reduce the financial burden on the postal service. "The administration recognizes the enormous value of the U.S. Postal Service to the nation's commerce and communications, as well as the urgent need for reform to ensure its future viability," the president's proposal said. The Obama plan would allow the agency to end Saturday delivery;

restructure retiree health benefit prefunding; refund more than $6.9 billion in prefunding overpayment; provide for the sale of non-postal products; and would give the USPS the ability to better align costs of postage with costs of delivery while still staying within its price cap. This final proposal would include a modest one-time increase of postal rates. The Obama plan did not support postal employee layoffs, and also made no mention of allowing the USPS to move employees into a cheaper health insurance plan.

Although it would stop the postal service from running out of money by the end of 2011, Donahoe said the White House plan would still lead to a shutdown of the organization by the summer of 2012. Contrary to earlier criticism over delayed action on the part of the executive, Obama did receive some support for his mid-September proposal. "The president's proposal would help the Postal Service update its business model to reflect Americans' changing communications habits," said Sen. Tom Carper, D-Del.

CONGRESSIONAL PLANS

A flurry of activity took place in Congress as Democrats and Republicans drafted bills featuring competing plans on the best methods for keeping the organization afloat. But with an election year coming up in 2012, the prospects of passage for any of the plans were grim. In June, House Oversight Committee Chair Darrell Issa, R-Calif., and Subcommittee Chair Dennis Ross, R-Fla., introduced the Issa-Ross Postal Reform Act, aimed at helping the postal service achieve a mandatory minimum savings of $10.7 billion annually. The plan would eliminate Saturday delivery; allow the USPS to charge postal rates in line with delivery costs; create a panel to make recommendations about the elimination of redundant post offices; require employees to pay the same health and life insurance premiums as federal workers; look at new ways to raise revenues; create a payment plan for prefunded retiree health care benefits; use the surplus in the pension account toward reducing the size of the workforce; end the no-layoff clause; and implement a procedure that would result in a management takeover aimed at cutting costs while maintaining service after a default of more than thirty days.

The Issa-Ross plan refused to agree to the USPS proposal that it be able to stop annual prefunding payments. According to Issa, if the USPS did not make these payments, "unfunded liabilities will soar to around $100 billion by the end of the decade." He continued, "This huge unfunded liability would be a burden that the Postal Service could not afford to bear." If the postal service was unable to cover pension and retirement benefits, Issa said, taxpayers would be stuck with the bill. The Congressional Research Service agreed with Issa's assessment in a report that stated, "Prefunding is a prudent measure to protect employee's earned benefits and taxpayer money."

In the Senate, Sens. Susan Collins, R-Maine, Scott Brown, R-Mass., Lieberman, and Carper introduced the 21st Century Postal Service Act of 2011 on November 2. "Time and time again in the face of more red ink, the Postal Service puts forward ideas that could well accelerate its death spiral," said Collins. "Closing thousands of rural post offices, eliminating Saturday delivery, and slowing first-class mail delivery could harm many businesses and their customers," she said. The legislation, which as of November 9 is pending before the full Senate, would allow the postmaster general to access overpayment of pension funds and use this money to offer buyouts or retirement incentives to help reduce the workforce by 100,000 over the next few years. The plan would not allow for an end of Saturday delivery for at least two years, which Collins maintained would push more Americans to electronic bill pay and e-mail, thus accelerating additional decline in mail volume. Additionally, the legislation would create a prefunding payment schedule; reform the workers compensation system; allow the USPS to offer new products and services; and require evaluations of any processing center slated for closure, to include consideration of downsizing.

First-Class Mail Slows

In December, the USPS announced that it would cut $3 billion in costs by slowing first-class mail delivery. The slow-down would be caused by the closure of around 250 of 500 processing centers, increasing the distance mail has to travel. Approximately 100,000 jobs would be cut in the process, totaling an additional savings of $6.5 billion. Currently, first-class mail is delivered in one to three days. The USPS closures would change the delivery timeframe to two to three days, or two to nine days for periodicals. Following the change, 51 percent of first-class mail is expected to arrive within two days, compared to the current rate of 42 percent delivered the next day. Under the new system, there is still a possibility that some first-class mail will be delivered next day. "It's a potentially major change, but I don't think consumers are focused on it and it won't register until the service goes away," said Jim Corridore, an analyst with S&P Capital IQ. Pointing out that the slowed delivery would be a step toward financial solvency, Donahoe said, "We know our business, and we listen to our customers. Customers are looking for affordable and consistent mail service, and they do not want us to take tax money." Under pressure from Congress, on December 13, 2011, the USPS announced that it would hold off on any processing center closures until May 15, 2012, to allow for additional evaluation and public input.

—Heather Kerrigan

Following are excerpts from testimony given by Postmaster General Patrick Donahoe on the financial status of the postal service before the Committee on Homeland Security and Government Affairs on September 6, 2011; edited remarks delivered by Donahoe at the National Press Club on November 21, 2011, on proposed changes to the postal service; and a press release from the U.S. Postal Service on December 13, 2011, announcing a delay of processing center closures.

DOCUMENT

Postmaster General on Financial State of U.S. Postal Service

September 6, 2011

[All charts and graphs, and references to them, have been omitted.]

. . . The importance of a healthy and thriving Postal Service cannot be overstated. The mailing industry, of which the Postal Service is only one component, depends on the continued evolution, growth and development of our organization. Over 8 million Americans are employed by thousands of companies and businesses which are deeply invested in the mail. The mailing industry, with the Postal Service at its core, is a major driver of the nation's economic engine—generating over $1 trillion each year. Our collective actions—particularly those of the Postal Service and Congress—to secure the future of the nation's postal system will directly affect a significant portion of the American economy. The mailing industry makes up approximately seven percent of the country's Gross Domestic Product (GDP). Failure to act could be catastrophic.

The most recent financial results continue to be grim. The Postal Service ended Quarter III of fiscal year 2011 (April 1—June 30) with a net loss of $3.1 billion. Net losses for the nine months which ended June 30 amount to $5.7 billion and we are currently projecting a net loss of up to $10 billion by the end of this fiscal year, depending on interest rates. Total mail volume is expected to decline by 2.0 percent, to approximately 167 billion pieces, when compared to last year. This is being driven largely by continued and accelerated drops in First-Class Mail, historically the Postal Service's core product.

The growth in electronic communications continues to drive the diversion of First-Class Mail. Instead of buying stamps, many consumers pay bills online, send "e-vites" to friends and family, and simply press "Send" when they want to communicate. These shifting customer habits will continue to add to the migration away from traditional First-Class Mail.

In addition, the stagnant economy has held other mail classes to a flat or relatively modest growth pattern. . . .

Of even greater concern is the looming liquidity crisis that will come to a head in less than one month. By the end of this fiscal year, on September 30, the Postal Service will reach its statutory $15 billion borrowing limit. We are committed to paying our employees and our suppliers first, but without changes to the law, we will be unable to maintain the aggressive Retiree Health Benefits (RHB) pre-funding schedule set forth in the Postal Accountability and Enhancement Act (PAEA).

Without legislative change this year, the Postal Service faces default, as available liquidity at the end of this month will be insufficient to meet our financial obligations. Even our unavoidable default on the required $5.5 billion RHB pre-payment and the suspension of our employer contribution to the defined benefit portion of the Federal Employees' Retirement System (FERS) will not stave off financial disaster. After reimbursing the Department of Labor (DoL) $1.3 billion for workers' compensation payments in October 2011, we will have liquidity equal to approximately one week's operating expenses. Foregoing the RHB pre-payment this year, without fundamental changes in the funding schedule, will likely only forestall insolvency until this time next year. An adverse decision by the Department of Justice on our FERS funding suspension would likely accelerate this date. In the absence of legislation, and before savings from the planned network realignment, the Postal Service projects a $9 billion loss next year, as well as mounting losses which could reach an estimated $16 billion by 2015 and exceed $20 billion by 2020. . . .

. . . Our actions alone will not be enough, however. This must be a collaborative effort—one which includes legislative changes. Congress must act this year to address these core issues:

- Resolve the pre-funding of Retiree Health Benefits (RHB)
- Return the $6.9 billion overfunding of the Postal Service's obligations to the Federal Employees' Retirement System (FERS)
- Grant the Postal Service the authority to determine delivery frequency
- Allow the Postal Service the flexibility to restructure its healthcare and pension systems
- Permit the streamlining of pricing and product development

For its part, the Postal Service will continue to focus relentlessly on narrowing the future estimated $20 billion revenue and cost gap by responsibly employing a variety of strategies and plans. This includes optimizing the overall network by properly aligning mail processing, retail and delivery operations, in accordance with the realities of consumer habits in the 21st century; continuing to eliminate work hours and employee complement; and pursuing the flexibility to set wages, benefits and employee complement. As a self-supporting entity for more than 40 years, receiving no taxpayer appropriations for our operations, the Postal Service knows how to balance cost management and efficiency increases.

Our employee workforce continues to decline significantly. . . . Similarly, work hour reductions have produced additional savings. . . . Without these savings, our level of huge net losses would, today, be three times worse. . . .

Although we have achieved cost reductions totaling $12 billion over the last four fiscal years—results that any company would be proud to claim—we are not slowing down. The Postal Service has a well-supported strategy going forward to build on the successes of the past decade. As always, the focus remains on all areas under our direct control. . . . These actions, occurring simultaneously across the organization, will combine to bring the Postal Service to its goal of reducing costs by $20 billion to earn a profit in 2015, rather than losing $16 billion as forecast under the current cost and revenue base. . . .

In conjunction with our network optimization effort, the Postal Service continues to explore ways to reduce our greatest cost—that of labor and benefits. Compensation and benefits costs, including workers' compensation and the federally-mandated prefunding of RHB, represent approximately 80 percent of total operating costs. . . .

To further reduce costs, the Postal Service is continuing the implementation of its January 2011 plan to significantly realign administrative functions (employees not covered by collective bargaining agreements). We are in the process of reducing headquarters management positions, as well as reducing the number of Area and District Offices, and decreasing the number of administrative, supervisory, and Postmaster positions by approximately 7,500. . . .

Our plans and strategies for the future are not limited merely to cost cutting. We are rightfully proud of our achievements in making significant productivity gains while simultaneously reducing work hours. Our employees have worked hard to bring about incredible cost savings while at the same time achieving record levels of service. In fact, something that often gets lost in the discussions about record volume and revenue losses is the point that, even with monumental expense reductions, we continue to maintain excellent service performance. That is quite an achievement—one that belongs to every employee in the organization.

It isn't enough to simply cut costs. You also have to build your business, grow revenue and develop products and services customers need and want to use. We are doing that as well; continually pursuing new revenue by creating innovative products and building upon existing services. . . .

In addition to ongoing cost savings efforts and revenue generation activities, the Postal Service is putting a variety of new ideas on the table. Our stated goal is to reduce annual costs by $20 billion over the next three years, ultimately driving costs down to under $60 billion per year with a streamlined workforce of approximately 425,000 employees. This can only be achieved through a combination of initiatives, including operational changes, legislative changes, and changes in compensation and benefits. With all of these efforts working in concert, future cost/revenue gaps can be significantly narrowed and eliminated. With $20 billion of cost savings in 2015, the previously projected loss of $16 billion will become a $4 billion profit.

Recently, the Postal Service released two white papers which contained cutting-edge proposals. These proposals are in keeping with our desire to do all that we can to continue adapting to the changing world of communications by reducing the size of our workforce and addressing legacy benefits costs.

The first proposal, which addresses the issue of labor costs and the sheer size of our workforce, calls for the Postal Service to be provided with the ability to more rapidly reduce its workforce. . . .

Current labor agreements prevent the Postal Service from moving swiftly enough to achieve these workforce reductions. Our proposal would address existing collective bargaining prohibitions against layoffs and allow the Postal Service to make these difficult, but absolutely necessary, personnel moves, in order to remain viable. . . .

The second major idea recently presented by the Postal Service addresses an area of tremendous cost—health care benefits plans. Under this proposal, the Postal Service would withdraw from the Federal Employees' Health Benefits Plan (FEHBP) and sponsor its own health care plan. Currently, health care benefit costs for the Postal Service annually reach approximately $12.8 billion, consisting of $2.5 billion for health benefit premiums for current retirees; $4.8 billion for health benefit premiums for active employees; and $5.5 billion (the largest portion) for RHB pre-funding, as required by PAEA. In addition, some of the existing health care plan offerings for Postal employees do not reflect a good value to participants, relative to their costs. . . .

The proposal for the Postal Service to sponsor its own health care plan would reduce annual operating costs and provide a viable option to significantly **reduce or eliminate** RHB pre-funding. The requirement in the PAEA that the Postal Service pre-fund its RHB liability by $59 billion on an extremely aggressive ten-year schedule has had a significant impact on Postal Service finances. . . .

Allowing the Postal Service to gain control of its own health care program would save money annually, **reduce or eliminate** the current RHB unfunded liability, and allow for better management of health care costs going forward. We have laid out a solid structure for governance and oversight of such a plan, to ensure fairness, fiduciary responsibility, and 13 transparency. Providing a stable and dependable health care plan for all employees is a crucial part of our future strategic plans. Having an affordable arrangement, similar in size and scope to FEHBP and utilizing best practices found in the private sector, will serve Postal Service employees well.

For the past few months, the Postal Service has discussed another provision that would further our cost savings into the future. This is the ability of the Postal Service to implement a more cost-effective retirement system for new employees; one that would consist of only a defined contribution system similar to TSP, plus Social Security. The authority to permit the Postal Service to implement such a retirement system is within the purview of Congress. . . .

We are committed to working with every stakeholder group to find long-term solutions to our ongoing financial issues. But despite all our efforts, there remain areas that are not under our direct control. These areas must be addressed by the members of Congress. I cannot emphasize enough the importance of action *this year* to help the Postal Service avoid default and insolvency. . . .

. . . We continue to appeal to Congress for action on a wide array of issues. Specifically, action is needed to address the following areas:

RHB pre-funding: The Postal Service is required to pre-fund health benefits for future retirees on an extremely aggressive schedule, like no other business in America. In the last four fiscal years, the Postal Service contributed $21 billion to the trust fund for RHB, while incurring $20 billion of net losses. This pre-funding requirement has put a stranglehold on our finances and cannot be sustained.

FERS overpayment: Refunding the Postal Service's estimated $6.9 billion overpayment into the FERS would give the Postal Service needed liquidity and provide several options, including paying down its debt.

Delivery frequency: The authority to determine delivery frequency would result in sub-stantial annual savings of $3 billion. A recent Rasmussen Reports poll showed that 75 percent of Americans would prefer to see the Postal Service cut back mail delivery, rather than force the government to cover those losses. This is up considerably from 2009, when just 50 percent favored cutting back mail delivery.

Controlling legacy benefits costs: Allowing the Postal Service to restructure its existing healthcare and pension programs would yield significant long-term cost reductions. A separate Postal Service health care program would control rising fixed costs and provide a viable means to reduce or eliminate the unfunded RHB liability. Additionally, providing new employees with only a defined contribution pension plan (Thrift Savings Plan) and not a defined benefit pension (FERS) would provide an upper limit on future pension obligations.

Streamlining of pricing: The Postal Service should be permitted to price market dominant products based on demand and market conditions, rather than capping prices for each class at the rate of inflation. This would ensure that each class of mail covers its costs and would greatly enhance the ability of the Postal Service to compete for customers in a dynamic marketplace.

The world is changing. The way people work, interact, learn, communicate, do busi-ness, and live their daily lives is vastly different than it was for our parents and even for many of us. The Postal Service has a place in this new world, but getting there requires us to change and adapt in ways that might not have been thought of before.

We are at a critical juncture. Action from Congress is sorely needed by the close of this fiscal year. The Postal Service, as I have described in this testimony, has done and will con-tinue to do our utmost to address both cost savings and generation of new sources of revenue. Solving these complex issues will take a truly collective effort, involving the Postal Service, Congress, our mailing industry partners, employees, and union leaders. A healthy Postal Service equates to a healthy mailing industry and to a more robust and vital Amer-ican economy overall.

The American people have been well served by the Postal Service since the nation's beginning. We plan to continue serving them well into the future. Our future business model will undoubtedly look different from the Postal Service of today, but the core of what we do will not change. Our vast delivery network, reaching every home and business every day is something no one else 16 offers. We intend to build upon that by continuing our evolution to fit the changing needs of the American public. They deserve no less.

I look forward to working with each of you and all our other partners to keep the Postal Service a solid, stable and meaningful symbol of our country's greatness and possibility. Thank you and I will answer your questions at this time.

SOURCE: U.S. Postal Service. "Postmaster General/CEO Patrick R. Donahoe Before the Committee on Homeland Security and Government Affairs." September 6, 2011. http://about.usps.com/news/ speeches/2011/pr11_pmg0906.pdf.

Postmaster General Outlines Financial Solutions

November 21, 2011

. . . The Postal Service is fundamentally a business. Yes, it is a part of the government—but it operates as a business. . . .

That means the Postal Service must compete for customers. We must sell—not just offer, but actively sell and persuade people to buy our products and services in a competitive marketplace.

Unfortunately, while we have a mandate to operate like a business, the reality is that we do not have the flexibility under current law to function as a business. . . .

Will there always be a role for the traditional full service Post Office?

Absolutely.

There are a lot of other creative, more convenient options for providing access to our products and services. We just need the flexibility, like any other business, to provide them.

We are in a deep financial crisis today because we have a business model that is tied to the past. We are expected to operate like a business, but we do not have the flexibility to do so.

Our business model is fundamentally inflexible. It prevents the Postal Service from solving problems and being effective in the way a business would. . . .

Looking ahead, we are greatly accelerating the pace of cost reduction.

- We announced plans to reduce the total number of mail processing facilities from 460 today to less than 200 by the year 2013.
- We announced plans to study 3,500 low-activity post offices for potential closure or consolidation.
- We are streamlining our delivery operations with a goal of reducing another 20,000 delivery routes. . . .

But as significant as these cost reductions and revenue generating activities are, they don't come close to returning the Postal Service to profitability.

To turn a profit and to get on a sustainable financial track, we have advanced a plan to achieve a $20 billion cost reduction by 2015. Unfortunately, as things stand, we do not currently have the flexibility in our business model to achieve this goal.

For this reason, we have proposed important changes to the laws that govern the Postal Service. . . .

These and other proposals would enable the Postal Service to operate more as a business does, to provide better service, and be better able to compete for customers.

I am grateful that Congress is now working on postal reform legislation. The entire universe of postal stakeholders should be grateful as well. We've seen a strong commitment to our issues from Congress and the Administration.

However, there's a big question to be answered about whether the final package will treat the Postal Service as a business and give it the business model flexibility it needs.

There is a simple standard to apply, and it has to do with the concept of speed.

Speed is the answer. Speed is also the best way to judge whether Congress is truly interested in enabling the Postal Service to operate like a business.

Provisions that delay our ability to cut costs will result in sizable financial losses.

For example, if we are unable to implement a five-day delivery schedule now, we will needlessly carry a $3 billion annual cost. Multiply that by several years and you start getting a large number.

If, instead of consolidating 260 mail processing facilities in the next two years, legislation were to slow or delay that process, we might needlessly carry another $3 billion in annual costs.

The same goes for provisions that would impact our ability to modernize our retail networks, and to manage our workforce and our healthcare costs more effectively.

If Congress does not pass legislation that allows for more effective cost control, and does not make fundamental changes to our business model, the Postal Service could soon be running deficits in the range of $10 to $15 billion annually. . . .

We need provisions in the final legislation that provide us with the speed to reduce our costs by $20 billion by 2015.

Businesses don't decide to study operational issues for years on end, and create impediments to resolving issues. They make decisions quickly, and they act quickly.

Unfortunately, the legislation as currently drafted—in both houses of Congress—would not provide the Postal Service with the speed and flexibility it needs.

Both bills have elements that delay tough decisions and impose greater constraints on our business model. Taken as they are, they do not come close to enabling cost reductions of $20 billion by 2015—which they must do for the Postal Service to return to profitability.

If passed today, either bill would provide at best a couple of years of profitability, and at least a decade of steep losses.

However, by taking the best of the House, Senate and Administration approaches, Congress can provide the Postal Service with the legal framework and the business model it needs. . . .

It will only happen if Congress develops a simple, straightforward piece of legislation that provides key areas of flexibility:

- The ability to determine our own delivery frequency.
- The ability to develop and price products quickly.
- The ability to control our healthcare and retirement costs.
- The ability to quickly realign our mail processing, delivery and retail networks.
- A streamlined governance model.
- And, we need more flexibility in the way we leverage our workforce.

All of this needs to be done right now.

The Postal Service is far too integral to the economic health of the nation to be handcuffed to the past and to an inflexible business model. America needs a Postal Service that can evolve and operate with fewer restraints.

I have no doubt the Postal Service will remain as a great American institution. But to do so, we need to operate with a great business model.

Thank you.

SOURCE: U.S. Postal Service. "U.S. Postal Service Postmaster General Pat Donahoe—National Press Club Address, Washington, DC." November 21, 2011. http://about.usps.com/news/speeches/2011/pr11_pmg1121.pdf.

DOCUMENT

Postal Service Announces Closure Delay

December 13, 2011

The U.S. Postal Service, in response to a request made by multiple U.S. Senators, has agreed to delay the closing or consolidation of any Post Office or mail processing facility until May 15, 2012. The Postal Service will continue all necessary steps required for the review of these facilities during the interim period, including public input meetings.

The Postal Service hopes this period will help facilitate the enactment of comprehensive postal legislation. Given the Postal Service's financial situation and the loss of mail volume, the Postal Service must continue to take all steps necessary to reduce costs and increase revenue.

The Postal Service receives no tax dollars for operating expenses and relies on the sale of postage, products and services to fund its operations.

SOURCE: U.S. Postal Service. "Statement on Delay of Closing or Consolidation of Post Offices and Mail Processing Facilities." December 13, 2011. http://about.usps.com/news/national-releases/2011/pr11_1213closings.htm.

President Obama and Senate Republicans Release Jobs Plans

SEPTEMBER 8 AND OCTOBER 13, 2011

In late 2011, continuing high unemployment and voter discontent with the Washington establishment pushed Democrats and Republicans to find concrete solutions to solve the nation's job crisis. Led by President Barack Obama, Democrats supported plans that would invest additional federal funds in job creation at the public and private sector levels, all of which would be paid for mainly through a tax increase on the wealthiest Americans. Republicans in the House and Senate opposed any tax increases, and instead sought to support private sector innovation that they claimed would lead to job growth, while subsequently reducing the federal deficit. Heading into an election year, neither side wanted to make significant concessions, and by the close of 2011, no job growth legislation had passed both the House and Senate.

American Jobs Act of 2011

Before a joint session of Congress on September 8, 2011, President Barack Obama outlined his plan to "put more people back to work and put more money in the pockets of working Americans." The American Jobs Act of 2011, which was sent to Congress on September 12, featured key points of economic recovery, rebuilding, investment, competing in the global economy, and keeping business in the United States. In outlining his plan before Congress, "pass this bill" was the popular refrain. "Tell them that if you want to create jobs right now—pass this bill," Obama said. "If you want construction workers renovating schools . . . pass this bill. If you want to put teachers back in the classroom—pass this bill. If you want tax cuts for middle-class families and small-business owners, then what do you do? Pass this bill," Obama told Congress. The president encouraged Democrats and Republicans to "stop the political circus" and do something to help turn the economy around. He also noted that the bill should be easy to pass because, "Everything in here is the kind of proposal that's been supported by both Democrats and Republicans—including many who sit here tonight."

Under the American Jobs Act of 2011, small businesses would benefit by a reduction in business taxes on the first $5 million in payroll; an elimination of payroll taxes for those businesses that hire new employees or increase wages; a continuation of the 100 percent equipment expensing program; and a reduction in regulations that would increase access to capital. One-hundred-and-sixty-million Americans would receive tax relief under the act through a halving of payroll taxes in 2012. A greater number of homeowners would also be given the ability to refinance under new mortgage regulations.

The act would also place a focus on rebuilding America, through tax credits of up to $9,600 for businesses that hire unemployed veterans; stopping teacher layoffs and keeping police officers and firefighters on the job; modernizing schools; investing in infrastructure; putting people to work rehabilitating homes, businesses, and communities; and expanding access to high-speed wireless Internet. The president's plan also aimed to put people back to work by implementing reforms that prevent layoffs; developing a more flexible unemployment insurance system; promoting work sharing; giving wage insurance to older workers; aiding states with programs to make it easier for young entrepreneurs to start businesses; awarding a $4,000 tax credit for hiring the long-term unemployed; helping to end hiring discrimination against the unemployed; and increasing job opportunities and training for low-income adults and young people.

Obama told Congress that, at a cost of $447 billion, his bill would be fully paid for. To achieve this, the president called on the congressional super committee that had already been tasked with finding $1.2 trillion in deficit reduction, to look for additional cuts to help cover the cost of the act. Obama proposed that these cuts come from limiting to 28 percent the itemized deductions for families earning more than $250,000; increasing taxes on investment fund income; and repealing some oil and gas drilling subsidies.

DEMOCRAT AND REPUBLICAN RESPONSE

Although Democrats would likely support the president's plan if it came up for a vote on the floor, response from his traditional supporters was mixed. Some wondered whether a jobs bill like Obama's was the proper thing to focus on. "Every dollar that is spent on the jobs bill . . . is not going to be available to Congress to deal with the debt," said Sen. Joe Lieberman, I-Conn. "And to me, the top priority of ours should be long-term major debt reduction," Lieberman said. Others, like Sen. Tom Carper, D-Del., admitted that the Obama plan was unlikely to pass in its current form. "I think the best jobs bill that can be passed is a comprehensive long-term deficit reduction plan," he said, adding, "That's better than everything else the president is talking about—combined." To Carper's point, Obama promised to release a deficit-reduction plan on September 19 that would propose changes in the tax system along with entitlement program reforms.

Republicans in the House, led by Speaker John Boehner, R-Ohio, who said the president's proposals "merit consideration," were also unenthused. GOP leaders released a memo to House Republicans opposing almost all of Obama's proposals, even the payroll tax cuts that they contended would lead to a tax increase in 2013. "There may be significant unforeseen downsides to large temporary tax cuts immediately followed by large tax increases," the memo stated, continuing, "We are creating significant new uncertainty in an already uncertain economy."

Specifically, GOP leadership in the House disagreed with the president's proposals to cut payroll taxes in half for individuals and small businesses; raise taxes for upper-income earners to cover the cost of the plan; send $30 billion to the states for school repairs; spend $50 billion on transportation repairs; and give states $35 billion for teacher, police, and firefighter rehiring. On state payouts, the Republicans argued that states misused earlier American Recovery and Reinvestment Act (ARRA) funds and that any required school repairs should be left to the states to deal with themselves. On transportation repairs, Republicans noted that they were negotiable, but would prefer to amend the current federal highway bill and make cuts there. "To be clear, we don't agree with portions of President Obama's proposal, and Republicans have a different vision for the steps that need to be taken to help our economy get back to creating jobs," Republican leadership wrote. "We are, however, committed to passing legislation to implement the policies in the areas where agreement can be found to support job creation and long-term economic growth."

Jobs Plan Stalls

By October, Republican opposition put the brakes on Obama's jobs plan, with Senate Republicans unanimously voting to block it and House Republicans refusing to bring the act to a vote on the floor. Republicans cited one of their major disagreements as funding the plan by raising taxes on the wealthy, but also noted that they would be most open to considering a payroll tax cut that would include the first $106,800 in earnings, basically a partial extension of tax cuts passed under the administration of former President George W. Bush.

In response, Obama took action using "we can't wait" as his mantra, and promised to issue executive orders to shore up housing, education, and other economic challenges. White House aides said the president would release one proposal each week from November through the end of the year. Obama used the proposals to show that he would not be left inactive by Republicans, even though he knew his executive orders would not be as far-reaching as congressional legislation might allow. Dan Pfeiffer, Obama's communications director, said, "The president will continue to pressure Congressional Republicans to put country before party and pass the American Jobs Act, but he believes we cannot wait, so he will act where they won't."

Obama's first executive order toward this goal set up new rules for federally guaranteed mortgages to help those with little or no equity refinance their homes to avoid foreclosure, a change to the Home Affordable Refinance Program. The administration kept expectations for the program low, because a number of other housing programs had not produced the desired results.

Senate GOP Releases Jobs Plan

To compete with the president's jobs plan, and to present a Republican version of job creation legislation that to this point had been missing from the debate, in October, Sens. John McCain, R-Ariz., Rand Paul, R-Ky., and Rob Portman, R-Ohio, released the Jobs Through Growth Act. "I think we should have a Republican jobs plan," said Paul. "It's just unfair for [Obama] to say that there is no Republican jobs plan—there is one, and we're going to put [it] into legislation," Paul continued. The act contained few new proposals but rather outlined bills that had already been introduced. It was meant to represent the best ideas endorsed by the Senate Republican caucus, which thus far had failed to support a full set of policy proposals. The plan included five key sections—spending reform, tax reform, regulation reform, domestic energy production, and export promotion. The plan sought to create revenue neutral tax code changes; target labor and environmental regulations; expand free trade; encourage domestic energy production; reduce the individual income tax rate to a maximum of 25 percent; and reduce the top corporate tax rate to 25 percent. The Jobs Through Growth Act also called for a balanced budget amendment to the Constitution, a provision unlikely to pass the House and Senate. Upon announcing their plan, the Republican trio cited a claim by the conservative Heritage Foundation that the plan would create 1.6 million private sector jobs. McCain, Paul, and Portman offered no cost estimate for their proposals.

House Republicans released their own jobs plan, The House Republican Plan For America's Job Creators, in May. Their plan focused on reducing regulations on small businesses to encourage economic growth; amending the tax code to spur investment; passing pending free trade agreements to open more markets for American products; encouraging development of new products by individual entrepreneurs; promoting domestic energy production; and enacting spending cuts to bring the federal debt under control.

The competing plans released by Obama and House and Senate Republicans clearly showed the different opinions on the problem with the economy and how to fix it. Obama saw a lack of demand—consumers aren't buying, so businesses can't hire, and it's up to government to invest to help increase demand and hiring. Republicans said the problem is that businesses would be hiring if they didn't fear future taxes or additional government regulations, so reducing government is the answer. There are a few places in which the president and Republicans agree, including the need to simplify the tax code, boost exports, promote free trade, create a more educated workforce, and be more competitive in the global economy. However, the president and Republicans see different methods for reaching each of these goals.

After reviewing the proposals, Moody's Analytics and Macroeconomic Advisers reported that the Obama plan could create as many as 1.9 million jobs but that the House Republican plan would have little immediate impact on job creation. Boehner, however, released a list of 132 economists, many of them from conservative organizations including the American Enterprise Institute and Manhattan Institute, who supported the Republican plan. "This list underscores the need for immediate action on the now-22 bipartisan jobs bills passed by the Republican-led House that are awaiting a vote in the Democratic-controlled Senate," Boehner said. "To help support job creation in both the short-term and long-term, we need bipartisan action to halt unnecessary government regulations and fix the tax code to help private-sector job creators. Our plan does that," Boehner continued. At the close of 2011, the Senate had not voted on the House-passed jobs bills.

—Heather Kerrigan

Following is the edited text of a statement given by President Barack Obama on September 8, 2011, introducing his job growth plan before a joint session of Congress; and the text of a job growth plan introduced by Senate Republicans on October 13, 2011.

President Obama Announces Job Growth Plan

September 8, 2011

. . . Those of us here tonight can't solve all our Nation's woes. Ultimately, our recovery will be driven not by Washington, but by our businesses and our workers. But we can help. We can make a difference. There are steps we can take right now to improve people's lives.

I am sending this Congress a plan that you should pass right away. It's called the "American Jobs Act." There should be nothing controversial about this piece of legislation. Everything in here is the kind of proposal that's been supported by both Democrats and Republicans, including many who sit here tonight. And everything in this bill will be paid for—everything.

The purpose of the "American Jobs Act" is simple: to put more people back to work and more money in the pockets of those who are working. It will create more jobs for construction workers, more jobs for teachers, more jobs for veterans, and more jobs for long-term unemployed. It will provide a tax break for companies who hire new workers, and it will cut payroll taxes in half for every working American and every small business. It will provide a jolt to an economy that has stalled and give companies confidence that if they invest and if they hire, there will be customers for their products and services. You should pass this jobs plan right away.

Everyone here knows that small businesses are where most new jobs begin. And you know that while corporate profits have come roaring back, smaller companies haven't. So for everyone who speaks so passionately about making life easier for "job creators," this plan is for you.

Pass this jobs bill . . . and starting tomorrow, small businesses will get a tax cut if they hire new workers or if they raise workers' wages. Pass this jobs bill, and all small-business owners will also see their payroll taxes cut in half next year. If you have 50 employees making an average salary, that's an $80,000 tax cut. And all businesses will be able to continue writing off the investments they make in 2012.

It's not just Democrats who have supported this kind of proposal. Fifty House Republicans have proposed the same payroll tax cut that's in this plan. You should pass it right away.

Pass this jobs bill, and we can put people to work rebuilding America. Everyone here knows we have badly decaying roads and bridges all over the country. Our highways are clogged with traffic. Our skies are the most congested in the world. It's an outrage.

Building a world-class transportation system is part of what made us a [sic] economic superpower. And now we're going to sit back and watch China build newer airports and faster railroads, at a time when millions of unemployed construction workers could build them right here in America?

There are private construction companies all across America just waiting to get to work. . . .

The "American Jobs Act" will repair and modernize at least 35,000 schools . . . . It will rehabilitate homes and businesses in communities hit hardest by foreclosures. It will jump-start thousands of transportation projects all across the country. And to make sure the money is properly spent, we're building on reforms we've already put in place. No more earmarks. No more boondoggles. No more bridges to nowhere. We're cutting the redtape that prevents some of these projects from getting started as quickly as possible. And we'll set up an independent fund to attract private dollars and issue loans based on two criteria: how badly a construction project is needed and how much good it will do for the economy. . . .

Pass this jobs bill, and thousands of teachers in every State will go back to work. These are the men and women charged with preparing our children for a world where the competition has never been tougher. But while they're adding teachers in places like South Korea, we're laying them off in droves. It's unfair to our kids. It undermines their future and ours. And it has to stop. Pass this bill, and put our teachers back in the classroom where they belong.

Pass this jobs bill, and companies will get extra tax credits if they hire America's veterans. We ask these men and women to leave their careers, leave their families, risk their lives to fight for our country. The last thing they should have to do is fight for a job when they come home.

Pass this bill, and hundreds of thousands of disadvantaged young people will have the hope and the dignity of a summer job next year. And their parents, low-income Americans who desperately want to work, will have more ladders out of poverty.

Pass this jobs bill, and companies will get a $4,000 tax credit if they hire anyone who has spent more than 6 months looking for a job. We have to do more to help the long-term unemployed in their search for work. This jobs plan builds on a program in Georgia that several Republican leaders have highlighted, where people who collect unemployment insurance participate in temporary work as a way to build their skills while they look for a permanent job. The plan also extends unemployment insurance for another year. If the millions of unemployed Americans stopped getting this insurance and stopped using that money for basic necessities, it would be a devastating blow to this economy. Democrats and Republicans in this chamber have supported unemployment insurance plenty of times in the past. And in this time of prolonged hardship, you should pass it again right away.

Pass this jobs bill, and the typical working family will get a $1,500 tax cut next year. Fifteen hundred dollars that would have been taken out of your pocket will go into your pocket. This expands on the tax cut that Democrats and Republicans already passed for this year. . . .

And here's the other thing I want the American people to know: The "American Jobs Act" will not add to the deficit. It will be paid for. And here's how: The agreement we passed in July will cut Government spending by about $1 trillion over the next 10 years. It also charges this Congress to come up with an additional $1.5 trillion in savings by Christmas. Tonight I am asking you to increase that amount so that it covers the full cost of the "American Jobs Act." And a week from Monday, I'll be releasing a more ambitious deficit plan, a plan that will not only cover the cost of this jobs bill, but stabilize our debt in the long run. . . .

So we can reduce this deficit, pay down our debt, and pay for this jobs plan in the process. But in order to do this, we have to decide what our priorities are. We have to ask ourselves, "What's the best way to grow the economy and create jobs?" . . .

This isn't political grandstanding. This isn't class warfare. This is simple math. These are real choices.These are real choices that we've got to make. And I'm pretty sure I know what most Americans would choose. It's not even close. And it's time for us to do what's right for our future.

Now, the "American Jobs Act" answers the urgent need to create jobs right away. But we can't stop there. . . .

And this task of making America more competitive for the long haul, that's a job for all of us, for Government and for private companies, for States and for local communities, and for every American citizen. All of us will have to up our game. All of us will have to change the way we do business. . . .

But what we can't do—what I will not do—is let this economic crisis be used as an excuse to wipe out the basic protections that Americans have counted on for decades. I reject the idea that we need to ask people to choose between their jobs and their safety. I reject the argument that says for the economy to grow, we have to roll back protections that ban hidden fees by credit card companies, or rules that keep our kids from being exposed to mercury, or laws that prevent the health insurance industry from shortchanging patients. I reject the idea that we have to strip away collective bargaining rights to compete in a global economy. We shouldn't be in a race to the bottom, where we try to offer the cheapest labor and the worst pollution standards. America should be in a race to the top. And I believe we can win that race.

In fact, this larger notion that the only thing we can do to restore prosperity is just dismantle Government, refund everybody's money, and let everyone write their own rules, and tell everyone they're on their own, that's not who we are. That's not the story of America.

Yes, we are rugged individualists. Yes, we are strong and self-reliant. And it has been the drive and initiative of our workers and entrepreneurs that has made this economy the engine and the envy of the world. But there's always been another thread running throughout our history, a belief that we're all connected and that there are some things we can only do together as a nation. . . .

No single individual built America on their own. We built it together. We have been and always will be one Nation, under God, indivisible, with liberty and justice for all; a nation with responsibilities to ourselves and with responsibilities to one another. And Members of Congress, it is time for us to meet our responsibilities.

Every proposal I've laid out tonight is the kind that's been supported by Democrats and Republicans in the past. Every proposal I've laid out tonight will be paid for. And every proposal is designed to meet the urgent needs of our people and our communities. . . .

I don't pretend that this plan will solve all our problems. It should not be, nor will it be, the last plan of action we propose. What's guided us from the start of this crisis hasn't been the search for a silver bullet. It's been a commitment to stay at it—to be persistent—to keep trying every new idea that works and listen to every good proposal, no matter which party comes up with it.

Regardless of the arguments we've had in the past, regardless of the arguments we will have in the future, this plan is the right thing to do right now. You should pass it. And I intend to take that message to every corner of this country. And I ask every American who agrees to lift your voice: Tell the people who are gathered here tonight that you want action now. Tell Washington that doing nothing is not an option. Remind us that if we act as one Nation and one people, we have it within our power to meet this challenge. . . .

SOURCE: U.S. Executive Office of the President. "Address Before a Joint Session of the Congress on Job Growth." September 8, 2011. *Daily Compilation of Presidential Documents* 2011, no. 00614 (September 8, 2011). http://www.gpo.gov/fdsys/pkg/DCPD-201100614/pdf/DCPD-201100614.pdf.

DOCUMENT   *Senate Republicans Release Jobs Plan*

October 13, 2011

[The introductory press release has been omitted.]

SPENDING REFORM

Require a Balanced Budget Amendment to the Constitution—(S.J.Res.10, Sen. Hatch)

Limit the ability of Washington to raise taxes to pay for runaway spending and would enshrine firm tax and spending limitations in our Constitution. Job creators will have certainty that Washington will not continue to grow unchecked and consume more and more resources that would otherwise be available to fuel job creation.

Enact Enhanced Rescission Authority—(S.102, Sens. McCain & Carper)

This bipartisan proposal would give the President the statutory line-item veto authority to reduce wasteful spending. This is an important tool to ensure that tax dollars are spent wisely and efficiently. Congress would vote up-or-down on proposed spending cuts.

TAX REFORM

Reduce and Reform Individual, Small Business and Corporate Taxation

A simplified tax system will keep more money in the hands of consumers, small businesses and job-creators. Reduce individual income tax rates to a maximum of 25 percent with two marginal rates. Within 90 days, the Senate Finance Committee will report back on recommended changes in credits and deductions to make this revenue neutral.

Reduce the top corporate tax rate to no more than 25%. Within 90 days, the Senate Finance Committee will report changes in credits, deductions and subsidies, with priority given to eliminating all industry-specific provisions and revenue neutrality.

Repatriation and Territorial Reform

Our current corporate tax code is outdated and is a major reason why there is up to $1.4 trillion in foreign earnings trapped overseas in countries where U.S.-based multinational companies do business. Under a reformed territorial system of corporate taxation, this plan would create a permanent incentive for companies repatriating foreign earnings to the U.S. economy.

Withholding Tax Relief Act—(S. 164, Sens. Scott Brown, Olympia Snowe, David Vitter)

Removes the undue burden on businesses of all sizes by repealing the provision in the tax code requiring federal, state and local governmental entities to withhold 3% of payments due to private vendors who supply their goods and services.

REGULATION REFORM

Repeal the Job-Killing Health Care Law Act—(S.192, Sen. DeMint)

Repealing and replacing Obamacare will remove over $550 billion in new taxes, over $300 billion in higher health care costs, and $2,100 in increased family insurance premiums from employers and workers. . . .

Medical Malpractice Reform—(S. 197—The Medical Care Access Protection Act)

Medical malpractice abuse in the US health care system is out of control. Junk lawsuits drive up the cost of health care and the system must be reformed. Reform Medical Malpractice law based on Texas "stacked caps" to improve patient access to health care and provide improved medical care by reducing the excessive burden the liability system places on the health care delivery system.

Financial Takeover Repeal—(S.712, Sen. DeMint)

We need to lift the burdens the Dodd-Frank bill placed on community banks and the small businesses that depend on them for financing, from oppressive new regulations to the resulting uncertainty that prevents growth. Repealing Dodd-Frank will also significantly reduce financing costs for consumers and businesses, as well as reduce costs to manufacturers in hedging their risks in the financial markets. Research compiled by the Financial Services Roundtable indicates that the cumulative weight of new financial rules, from Dodd-Frank to similar efforts abroad, could cost the U.S. economy 4.6 million jobs by 2015.

Regulations from the Executive In Need of Scrutiny (REINS Act)—(S.299, Sen. Paul)

The REINS Act would require Congressional approval by joint resolution of any federal rule that would cost the economy $100 million or more.

Regulation Moratorium and Jobs Preservation Act—(S.1438, Sen. Ron Johnson)

Prohibits any federal agency from issuing new regulations until the unemployment rate is equal to or less than 7.7 percent (the unemployment rate in January 2009).

Freedom from Restrictive Excess Executive Demands and Onerous Mandates Act—(S.1030, Sens. Snowe and Coburn)

Streamlines and strengthens the Regulatory Flexibility Act by requiring regulators to include "indirect" economic impacts in small-business analyses, requiring periodic review and sunset of existing rules, and expanding small business review panels as a requirement for all federal agencies, instead of just the Environmental Protection Agency (EPA) and the Occupational Safety and Health Administration (OSHA).

Unfunded Mandates Accountability Act—(S. 1189, Sen. Portman)

Requires agencies specifically to assess the potential effect of new regulations on job creation and to consider market-based and non-governmental alternatives to regulation; broadens the scope of Unfunded Mandate Reform Act to include rules issued by independent agencies and rules that impose direct or indirect economic costs of $100 million or more; requires agencies to adopt the least burdensome regulatory option that achieves the goal of the statute authorizing the rule; creates a meaningful right to judicial review of an agency's compliance with the law.

The Government Litigation Savings Act—(S.1061, Sen. Barrasso)

Reforms the Equal Access to Justice Act (EAJA) by disallowing the reimbursement of attorney's fees and costs to well-funded special interest groups who repeatedly sue the federal government. The bill retains federal reimbursements for individuals, small businesses, veterans and others who must fight in court against a wrongful government action. By eliminating taxpayer-funded reimbursement of attorney's fees for wealthy special interest groups, the legislation helps eliminate repeated, procedural lawsuits that delay permitting, exploration and land management.

Employment Protection Act of 2011—(S.1292, Sen. Toomey)

Requires the EPA to analyze the impact on employment levels and economic activity before issuing any regulation, policy statement, guidance document, endangerment finding, or denying any permit. Each analysis is required to include a description of estimated job losses and decreased economic activity due to the denial of a permit, including any permit denied under the Federal Water Pollution Control Act.

Farm Dust Regulation Prevention Act—(S.1528, Sen. Johanns)

Prevents the EPA from regulating dust in rural America, while still maintaining protections to public health under the Clean Air Act. . . . Under this bill, the EPA would still be allowed to regulate dust, but only after demonstrating scientific evidence of substantial adverse health effects of farm dust.

National Labor Relations Board Reform—(S.1523, Sen. Graham)

From back-door card-check, to threatening jobs in South Carolina, the out-of-control National Labor Relations Board (NLRB) is paying back union officials at the expense of worker rights and jobs. To create more jobs, legislation prohibiting the NLRB from stopping new plants and legislation to prevent coercive, quick-snap union elections should be passed.

Government Neutrality in Contracting Act—(S.119, Sen. Vitter)

Repeals the President's order requiring government-funded construction projects to only use union labor. This would reduce costs of federal jobs projects by as much as 18 percent.

Financial Regulatory Responsibility Act—(S. 1615, Sen. Shelby)

Requires financial regulators to conduct consistent economic analysis on every new rule they propose, provide clear justification for the rules, and determine the economic impacts of proposed rulemakings, including their effects on growth and net job creation.

Regulatory Responsibility for our Economy Act—(S. 358, Sen. Roberts)

Codifies and strengthens President Obama's January 18th Executive Order that directs agencies within to review, modify, streamline, expand, or repeal those significant regulatory actions, that are duplicative, unnecessary, overly burdensome or would have significant economic impacts on Americans. It directs meaningful review and possible revocation of regulations counter to our nation's economic growth.

Reducing Regulatory Burdens Act—(H.R. 872, Rep. Bob Gibbs)

Eliminates a new duplicate EPA regulation that will cost millions of dollars to implement without providing additional environmental protection. The current rules for pesticides, which have been in place for decades, will remain in force.

Domestic Energy Job Promotion

The Domestic Jobs, Domestic Energy, and Deficit Reduction Act—(S.706, Sen. Vitter)

Will require the Interior Department to move forward with offshore energy exploration, and create a timeframe for environmental and judicial review.

The Jobs and Energy Permitting Act—(S.1226, Sen. Murkowski)

Eliminates confusion and uncertainty surrounding the EPA's decision-making process for air permits, which is delaying energy exploration in the Alaskan Outer-Continental Shelf (OCS). It will create over 50,000 jobs and produce one million barrels of oil a day.

The American Energy and Western Jobs Act—(S.1027, Sen. Barrasso)

This bill streamlines the preleasing, leasing and developmental process for drilling on public land and requires this Administration to create goals for American oil and gas production.

Mining Jobs Protection Act—(S.468, Sens. McConnell, Inhofe, Paul)

Requires the EPA to "use or lose" their 404 permitting review authority. Under this bill the EPA will have 60 days to voice concerns about a permit application, or the permit moves forward. Any concerns voiced by the EPA would need to be published in the Federal Register within 30 days.

Energy Tax Prevention Act—(S.482, Sen. Inhofe)

Prohibits the EPA from using the Clean Air Act to regulate greenhouse gases. It is estimated that greenhouse gas regulation could result in a loss to the economy of as much as $75 billion and 1.4 million jobs by 2014.

Repeal Restrictions on Government Use of Domestic Alternative Fuels

Repeal Section 526 of the Energy Independence and Security Act of 2007, which prohibits federal agencies from contracting for alternative fuels, such as coal-to-liquid fuel. This provision stifles the coal industry and puts our national security at risk by limiting the Pentagon's ability to get its fuels from domestic sources.

Public Lands Job Creation Act—(Sen. Heller)

Eliminates a burdensome and unnecessary delay in approval of projects on federal lands by allowing the permitting process to move forward unless the Department of the Interior objects within 45 days. This will streamline the permitting process for domestic energy and mineral production on BLM lands without compromising environmental analysis.

Export Promotion

Renew Trade Promotion Authority—(S. Amdt. 626, Sen. McConnell)

Provide the President with fast-track authority to negotiate trade agreements that will eliminate foreign trade barriers and open new markets for American goods.

Source: Office of Senator John McCain. "Republican Senators Introduce Alternative Jobs Bill, the Jobs Through Growth Act." October 13, 2011. http://mccain.senate.gov/public/index.cfm?FuseAction=PressOffice.Press Releases&ContentRecord_id=feb4d840-c3be-83b1-a1fb-b7f2a039e94d.

OTHER HISTORIC DOCUMENTS OF INTEREST

From this volume

From previous *Historic Documents*

Patent Reform Legislation Signed

SEPTEMBER 8 AND SEPTEMPER 16, 2011

On September 16, 2011, the United States moved from a first-to-invent to a first-to-file patent system that Republicans and Democrats agreed would help create jobs by aiding inventors in acquiring patents faster to in turn allow them to hire faster. "This bi-partisan legislation will transform our patent system, enhance our Nation's competitiveness and promote economic growth and job creation," said U.S. Patent Office Director David Kappos. A change to patent law had been in the works for six years, but in 2011 lawmakers recognized the need to move quickly because for the first time, China was expected to have the largest number of patents in the world, surpassing both the United States and Japan.

AMERICA INVENTS ACT

A work-in-progress for six years, the Leahy-Smith America Invents Act (AIA) signed by President Barack Obama on September 16, 2011, represented the first change to the patent system since 1952. "For years, low-quality patents have been a drain on our patent system, and in turn our economy, by undermining the value of what it means to hold a patent. Higher-quality patents will infuse greater certainty into the patent system, which will better incentivize investment in American businesses, create jobs and grow our economy," said Sen. Patrick Leahy, D-Vt., co-sponsor of the bill. The president agreed. "If we want startups here and if we want established companies . . . to continue to make products here and hire here, then we're going to have to be able to compete with any other country around the world. So this patent bill will encourage that innovation," Obama said.

As passed, the final bill made changes to patent filing and funding for the United States Patent and Trademark Office (USPTO). The most significant change involved patent filing. The United States, which had traditionally given patents to the first person to invent, under the AIA would now award patents to the first person to file. This change will bring the United States in line with a majority of other countries. Concerns have been raised about other Western experiences with the first-to-file system. A 2010 study on Canada's first-to-file system, which took effect in 1989, found that "long-term returns in the Canadian venture capital industry are such that capital has fled the market." Similarly, in May, the United Kingdom Small Medium-Sized Entity Innovation Alliance wrote to Prime Minister David Cameron to express their concern that they "know only too well the failure of the patent system and have given up."

The first-to-file system, which takes effect eighteen months after the president's signature, means that the first person to invent an item may not ultimately end up with the patent. The AIA does provide one exception to this rule. An inventor can file a disclosure with the patent office before filing an official patent application, as long as the application is filed within one year of the disclosure. This exception gives the inventor time to look further into the feasibility and commercial appeal of a product and secure financial resources for it before requesting a patent. The act provided no specific language on what would constitute a disclosure, but it did make clear that inventors should quickly contact the USPTO after a discovery is made.

The new law will also provide more funding to the USPTO. Funding for the office was a major point of contention during House and Senate negotiations of the bill. The Senate first passed a version of the AIA in March 2011, by a vote of 95 to 5, and the House passed a similar bill in June, 304 to 117. When the two bills went to the conference committee for changes to be reconciled and the final bill produced, the House and Senate realized that they had significantly different views of how the USPTO should be funded. Currently, the USPTO brings in more revenue from application and patent maintenance fees than what Congress appropriates for it. Congress was able to use this additional money for miscellaneous projects not necessarily related to the patent office. The Senate wanted to allow the patent office to roll over its extra funds and have access to that money without congressional approval. The House version wanted the extra money to go into a reserve fund held by the Treasury, called the Patent and Trademark Fee Reserve Fund, which the USPTO would need congressional approval to withdraw from. When the House version of the bill arrived back in the Senate, Sen. Tom Coburn, R-Okla., tried to add an amendment that would have reverted funding back to the original Senate method; however, the amendment did not pass. Ultimately, the final bill contained the House provision that extra money be kept in a reserve fund accessible only with congressional approval.

The AIA also mandated two studies. One would be completed by the Government Accountability Office (GAO) and would focus on the economic cost of lawsuits brought by non-practicing entities that buy up patents from companies, don't use them, and instead sue other companies for patent infringement. The GAO study will also look at any benefits to commerce brought about by the non-practicing entities. A second study will be conducted on the difficulties that smaller businesses face when trying to protect their patents both domestically and internationally.

Patent Challenges

Since its inception, the USPTO has been hampered by a number of shortcomings that have kept it from effectively fulfilling its duties. Today, the biggest problem for the office has been outdated technology that has contributed to a significant patent backlog. In 2008, for every one patent issued, there were 6.6 pending. Although the department processes 500,000 applications each year, it currently has a backlog of approximately 700,000 patent applications. It takes two years for a ruling on a patent application and one year for a final patent grant to be issued, meaning that inventors can expect to wait up to three years for an official patent. The USPTO has estimated that the AIA will bring in an extra $300 million that the office will use for new staff and technology with the hope of reducing its backlog to 350,000 over the next few years.

Academics have raised concerns that the AIA will have a negative impact on university discoveries and will make inventors more secretive. Prior to the AIA, a patent could be declared invalid if it failed to "set forth the best mode contemplated by the inventor of carrying out" the invention. The new law eliminated this stipulation, and may lead some inventors to withhold information that could be beneficial to society as a whole. Additionally, argued Carl Gulbrandsen, managing director of the Wisconsin Alumni Research Foundation, an organization that helps commercialize University of Wisconsin inventions, the AIA could "increase the costs of obtaining, maintaining, and enforcing patents for universities and individual inventors." These additional funds are not always available.

Universities did, however, support the first-to-file disclosure exemption and lobbied for its inclusion. On the academia side, this exemption will give academics a year to file for a patent after disclosing a discovery in a journal or another publication without fear that a competitor would capitalize on the invention and file first.

PATENT LAWSUITS

After passage of the AIA in the House and Senate, the number of multiple-defendant patent infringement lawsuits filed increased tenfold, most of them being brought by non-practicing entities. After the president's signature, the ability of multiple-defendant lawsuits to be filed would be limited and would require defendants to have commonality. Patent lawyers expect this will likely lead to more individual patent infringement trials.

The new law is, however, expected to make settling patent disputes easier. The AIA created a post-grant review process that allows a person who is not the patent owner to request cancellation as invalid any patent granted or reissued during the previous nine months. This provision is intended to help weed out bad patents, and mostly pertains to business method patents, such as those for electronic check imaging within the banking industry. The provision is also intended to keep patent cases out of the courtroom. The AIA established a new USPTO administrative body, the Patent Trial and Appeal Board, tasked specifically with post-grant review. In addition to the post-grant review, patent seekers will be able to call on the USPTO to use a supplemental examination procedure that requires the office to "consider, reconsider, or correct information believed to be relevant to a patent."

The new law also changes the prior-use provision as it relates to defense against infringement. The provision protects companies that use an invention under trade secret protection. AIA will prevent a patent holder from forcing the prior user to pay royalties.

SUPPORT AND OPPOSITION

Despite strong backing in Congress, outside of Washington, D.C., support for the new law lies mainly with large companies. Smaller firms and independent inventors argue that these larger companies have more funds for legal aid and research and development, making racing to file for a patent more difficult for smaller companies. This rush to file has also been cited as a hindrance to fixing USPTO's backlog. "It will create a rush to the patent office, with innovators seeking to file anything and everything. The applications will be less complete, less well written and it will create more of a backlog," said Valerie Gaydos, a Baltimore-based investor in early-stage companies.

Those who support the bill, however, dispute that only large companies support the AIA. "Many, many, many independent inventors support the bill, as well as universities, labor unions and a whole array, a vast array, a very diverse group of people support this bill," said Gary Griswold, chairman emeritus of the Coalition for 21st Century Patent Reform. Supporters also pointed to the fact that in the past five years, there has only been one instance in which the first person to invent an item was the second to file and that person managed to win the case with the patent office. This, supporters of the AIA say, is an indication that first-to-file will present no major changes to the way business is conducted, and will therefore have no significant impact on small businesses and individual inventors.

—Heather Kerrigan

Following is a press release from the House Judiciary Committee on September 8, 2011, upon Senate passage of the Leahy-Smith America Invents Act; a statement by Patent Office Director David Kappos upon final passage of the America Invents Act on September 8, 2011; and a press release from the House Judiciary Committee upon President Barack Obama's signing of the America Invents Act on September 16, 2011.

DOCUMENT   *Senate Passes America Invents Act*

September 8, 2011

The Senate today passed the *Leahy-Smith America Invents Act* (H.R. 1249), a bipartisan, bicameral bill that updates our patent system to encourage innovation, job creation and economic growth. The Senate passed the bill today by a vote of 89-9. The House overwhelmingly approved H.R. 1249 by a vote of 304-117 earlier this year.

Much-needed reforms to our patent system are long overdue. The last major patent reform was nearly 60 years ago. The House patent reform bill implements a first-inventor-to-file standard for patent approval, creates a post-grant review system to weed out bad patents, and helps the Patent and Trademark Office (PTO) address the backlog of patent applications.

Chairman Smith (R-Texas): "After more than six years of bipartisan efforts and negotiations, we have crossed the finish line on patent reform. Today's vote is a victory for America's innovators and job creators who rely on our patent system to develop new products and grow their businesses. These reforms constitute the most significant change to U.S. patent law in 175 years, since the Patent Act of 1836. And when President Obama signs the bill into law, H.R. 1249 will be one of the most significant jobs creation bills enacted by Congress this year.

"The *America Invents Act* creates a better patent system for inventors and innovative industries. I thank Chairman Leahy for working with me to improve and turn around the House patent reform bill. This is a true example of bipartisan success that will benefit the American people.

"Six years ago, industry leaders and American inventors came to Congress saying that the current patent system had become a barrier to the very innovation that drives our economy. The average wait time for patent approval in the U.S. is three years. The PTO has a backlog of 1.2 million patents pending approval. Time is money in America, and even more so for innovators who are forced to wait years before they can market and distribute their inventions. This puts American innovators at a competitive disadvantage in a global marketplace.

"H.R. 1249 brings our patent system into the 21st century, reducing frivolous litigation while creating a more efficient process for the approval of patents. These reforms will help the innovators and job creators of today launch the products and businesses of tomorrow."

Chairman Leahy (D-Vt.): "The *America Invents Act* is a true jobs bill at a time when we need it the most. After six long years of debate spanning three Congresses and two administrations, it is finally set to become law. This is bipartisan, commonsense legislation that will spur the innovation that drives the American economy.

"Chairman Smith has been a true partner in our joint effort to enact meaningful patent reform legislation. I have been grateful for his partnership and support, and commend his work in the House to move this bill forward. I commend Senator Hatch, Senator Grassley, and Senator Kyl for their commitment to this important bill. The *America Invents Act* shows what we can accomplish when we cast aside political ideology, and work together for the American people.

"The creativity that drives our economic engine has made America the global leader in invention and innovation. The *America Invents Act* will ensure that inventors large and small maintain the competitive edge that has put America at the pinnacle of global innovation. This is historic legislation. It is good policy. And it is long overdue to be signed into law."

IP Subcommittee Chairman Bob Goodlatte (R-Va.): "The last time our patent laws were significantly updated was in 1952. The nature of our economy has changed significantly since then, and it is only right that Congress review our patent laws and amend them as necessary to make sure they still work efficiently to promote progress and innovation as outlined in the U.S. Constitution.

"The *America Invents Act* creates more certainty about patent rights, which will attract investment in these ideas. This will unleash further innovation in America by ensuring that more products and services come to market which will help put Americans back to work."

SOURCE: U.S. House of Representatives Committee on the Judiciary. "Senate Sends Patent Reform to President's Desk." September 8, 2011. http://judiciary.house.gov/news/Patent%20Reform%20to%20President.html.

Patent Office Director on America Invents Act

DOCUMENT

September 8, 2011

"I want to congratulate the United States Senate for passing the Leahy-Smith America Invents Act (H.R. 1249) today, and again thank Senate and House Judiciary Chairmen Leahy and Smith, as well as House and Senate leadership and many other Members of Congress for their unwavering commitment to this critical job-creating legislation.

"Once signed into law by President Obama, this bill will give the United States Patent and Trademark Office the tools it needs to deliver cutting-edge technologies to the marketplace sooner, drive down the backlog of patent applications, and expedite the issuance of high-quality patents—all without adding a dime to the deficit.

"Significantly, as stated by leadership in both houses of Congress, this legislation enables us to access all of our fees. We intend to aggressively implement that mandate by immediately hiring new examiners, instituting new patent acceleration tools, and aggressively modernizing our IT infrastructure.

"The effort to reform our nation's patent system began more than a decade ago, and Senate passage today provides a substantial down payment on an American economic agenda aggressively committed to unleashing 21st century innovation. This bipartisan bill will modernize our intellectual property system, ensure the United States Patent and Trademark Office is sufficiently resourced to operate efficiently, and afford inventors the timely and consistent patent protections they need to spur business growth and hiring.

"We appreciate the strong support of the legislation's co-sponsors, as well as the continuing commitment of all Members of Congress and our stakeholders, to ensure that the USPTO retains the funding it needs to implement this legislation, perform its core mission, and fuel American ingenuity. I'd also like to thank the Commerce Department leadership, which has offered continued support under former Commerce Secretary Gary Locke and now Acting Secretary Rebecca Blank.

We look forward to the President signing the America Invents Act so the nation can unlock new technologies, new jobs and new industries."

SOURCE: U.S. Patent and Trademark Office. "Statement of USPTO Director David Kappos Following Final Senate Passage of Leahy-Smith America Invents Act." September 8, 2011. http://www.uspto.gov/news/pr/2011/statementaia.jsp.

DOCUMENT   *America Invents Act Becomes Law*

September 16, 2011

President Obama today signed into law the *Leahy-Smith America Invents Act* (H.R. 1249) a bipartisan, bicameral bill that updates our patent system to encourage innovation, job creation and economic growth. Both Houses of Congress overwhelmingly supported the proposal, which was sponsored by House Judiciary Committee Chairman Lamar Smith (R-Texas). The House of Representatives passed H.R. 1249 by a vote of 304-117 earlier this year. The Senate passed the bill by a vote of 89-9. Senator Patrick Leahy (D-Vermont) partnered with Chairman Smith on the legislation. Congressman Smith led the House efforts on patent reform for more than six years.

Much-needed reforms to our patent system are long overdue. The last major patent reform was nearly 60 years ago. The House patent reform bill implements a first-inventor-to-file standard for patent approval, creates a post-grant review system to weed out bad patents, and helps the Patent and Trademark Office (PTO) address the backlog of patent applications. This bill is supported by local companies as well as many national organizations and businesses. . . .

Chairman Smith (R-Texas): "The *America Invents Act* is one of the most significant job creation bills enacted by Congress this year. Our outdated patent system has been a barrier to innovation, unnecessarily delaying American inventors from marketing new products and creating jobs for American workers. It takes over three years to get a patent approved in the U.S. American innovators are forced to wait years before they can hire workers and market their inventions.

"The enactment of H.R. 1249 is a victory for America's innovators and job creators who rely on our patent system to develop new products and grow their businesses. The *America Invents Act* brings our patent system into the 21st century, reducing frivolous litigation while creating a more efficient process for the approval of patents. These reforms will help the innovators and job creators of today launch the products and businesses of tomorrow."

SOURCE: U.S. House of Representatives Committee on the Judiciary. "Smith Patent Reform Bill Becomes Law." September 16, 2011. http://judiciary.house.gov/news/Patent%20Reform%20Law.html.

Census Bureau Reports on Poverty in the United States

SEPTEMBER 13, 2011

In 2010, the poverty rate in the United States rose to its highest level in seventeen years, according to the U.S. Census Bureau's *Income, Poverty, and Health Insurance Coverage in the United States: 2010*, which was published on September 13, 2011. Given the continuing impact of the 2007 to 2009 recession, as expected, poverty rose across all sectors of the American population. The report and accompanying commentary also indicated that investments made in expanding the unemployment insurance, food stamp, and other welfare benefits programs had a significant impact on a number of Americans. Two months after releasing the *Income, Poverty, and Health Insurance* report, the Census Bureau released a supplemental report on poverty in the United States, a years-long effort to find a more comprehensive way to look at poverty, that took into account factors like government benefits and the cost of living in different parts of the United States. The supplemental report generated an even more negative view of the economic landscape.

POVERTY RISES ACROSS THE COUNTRY

In 2010, the first calendar year post-recession, rising poverty impacted every segment of the population by varying degrees. In that year, the poverty level was set at $11,139 for individuals and $22,314 for a family of four. The Census Bureau labeled 46.2 million Americans as impoverished, or 9.2 million families. While the poverty rate increased, median household income continued to fall, dropping 2.3 percent from 2009 to $49,445. The declines were worse than expected. "This is truly a lost decade," said Lawrence Katz, an economics professor at Harvard. "We think of America as a place where every generation is doing better, but we're looking at a period when the median family is in worse shape than it was in the late 1990s," Katz said. The decline in median household income continued to widen the rich-poor gap—since peaking in 1999, income for the bottom tenth of income earners fell 12 percent, while the top 10 percent only experienced a 1.5 percent decrease from 1999 to 2010. In 2010, the bottom 60 percent of households experienced a drop in income, while those making more than $100,000 per year experienced income growth. At this rate, a Brookings Institute analysis estimates that by the middle of the 2010 to 2020 decade, ten million more people will be considered impoverished.

By demographic group, the poverty rate for children under 18 rose from 20.7 percent in 2009, to 22 percent in 2010, meaning that more than one in five children were living in poverty in 2010. The poverty rate also increased for those aged 18 to 64 from 12.9 percent to 13.7 percent. Senior citizens did not experience a statistically significant increase in poverty rate from 2009 to 2010. Non-Hispanic whites had the lowest rate of poverty of any racial group, while African Americans had the highest rate at 27.4 percent followed by Hispanics at 26.6 percent.

Geographically, the South experienced the only statistically significant increase in the number of those living in poverty, rising from 17.6 million in 2009 to 19.1 million in 2010. The Northeast had the lowest poverty rate at 12.8 percent. Mississippi had the nation's poorest households with a median income of $37,985, while New Hampshire residents received the highest median income at $66,707.

IMPACT OF THE FINANCIAL CRISIS

Prior to the 2007 to 2009 recession, during each of the past three recessions—March to November 2001, January to July 1980, and December 1969 to November 1970—the poverty rate rose during the first full calendar year following the recession's end, and 2010 was no exception. In fact, from 2007 to 2010, the poverty rate grew faster than any three-year period since the early 1980s. More Americans also sunk into deep poverty, defined as less than half of the official poverty line, and in 2010 that number stood at 20.5 million, according to the official Census numbers. The worst, however, may be yet to come according to Bruce Meyer, a public policy professor at the University of Chicago. He draws his conclusion from evidence that food stamp demand continues to rise, as is the number of long-term unemployed Americans. Additionally, in 2010, 48 million Americans aged 18 to 64 did not work for even one week, an increase of three million from 2009. Coupled with this, median income decline was the highest among young workers aged 15 to 24. "We're risking a new underclass," said Timothy Smeeding, director of the Institute for Research on Poverty at the University of Wisconsin–Madison. "Young, less-educated adults, mainly men, can't support their children and form stable families because they are jobless."

Another result of the financial crisis was a rise in the number of doubled-up households, defined by the Census as homes with one additional adult, "a person 18 or older who is not enrolled in school and is not the householder, spouse or cohabitating partner of the householder." In the spring of 2007, before the recession hit, there were 19.7 million doubled-up households in the United States. By the spring of 2011, that number rose to 21.8 million, with 5.9 million people aged 25 to 34 living with their parents, as opposed to 4.7 million before the recession. The official household poverty rate of these young adults and their parents was 8.4 percent, however, if the status were determined based solely on the income of the young individual, the poverty rate would be 45.3 percent. "It's just another sign of what a difficult time this is for so many people," said Paul Osterman, a labor economist at the Massachusetts Institute of Technology.

SUPPLEMENTAL POVERTY MEASURE

In November, the Census Bureau released its supplemental poverty measure, a years-long effort to find a more comprehensive way to look at poverty. The supplemental measure found the number of those in poverty to be 49.1 million, making the economic landscape in the United States look worse than the official poverty measure had shown. "The big picture is that in this so-called recovery, there are more people in distress regardless of how you measure poverty," said Katz. According to the supplemental report, in 2010 one-third of Americans earned 100 to 200 percent of the poverty level, and families making more than $97,372 made up 17 percent of the population. The official poverty measure indicated that families making more than $97,372 accounted for 36 percent of the population. Kathleen Short, the Census Bureau economist who led the creation of the new report, cautioned that Americans are not ending up in poverty at greater rates. "Below 200 percent of the poverty threshold is the lower end of the distribution," Short said. "But we would not call it low-income per se."

The supplemental measure, which the Census Bureau said is still a work in progress, takes into consideration social services benefits, medical care expenses, and payroll taxes, and also accounts for the cost of living in different parts of the country and whether someone rents or owns a home, all factors the official measure does not include. The supplemental measure is not meant to replace the official estimate that the federal government uses to calculate various forms of spending, including assistance to states, but rather to help lawmakers see the impact of social welfare programs.

The November supplemental poverty measure showed a higher rate of poverty among those 65 and older, rising from 9 percent from the official measure to 15.9 percent, or one in six. One reason for the increase was out-of-pocket medical expenses not accounted for in the official measure. However, the supplemental measure did not take into account savings, earnings from stocks, and some other forms of wealth. "If you look at what they consume, you see that their living standard is much higher," said Meyer, who believed the supplemental report overestimated the poverty rate for those 65 and older. On the other hand, those 65 and older could be greatly impacted if cuts to Medicare currently being discussed in Congress are passed. A bright spot in the supplemental report was the decrease in the poverty rate for those under age 18, making it four percentage points lower than the official measure.

Government programs had a clear impact on the number of people in poverty. According to the Census Bureau, if not for the earned income tax credit, the poverty rate would be at 18 percent rather than 15.1 percent. And according to the Center on Budget and Policy Priorities, food stamps, coupled with tax credit expansions, helped keep millions of Americans above the poverty line. "This shows that the social safety net is helping but not as much as we'd like to see," said Dave Cooper with the Economic Policy Institute, a liberal think tank. "The programs we have right now are, if anything, inadequate."

Near-Poor

The supplemental poverty measure raised questions about the near-poor, an unofficial term used to describe those who have an income at less than 50 percent above the poverty threshold. The supplemental measure counted 51 million Americans in this category, 76 percent higher than the official Census count. "These numbers are higher than we anticipated," said Trudi Renwick, the Census chief poverty statistician. "There are more people struggling than the official numbers show," she said. And because 28 percent of the people in this category work full-time for the entire year, "These estimates defy stereotypes of low-income families," said Renwick. Only one-quarter of those in the near-poor category have health insurance.

Critics of the new Census supplemental poverty measure say the statistics on the near-poor might make the situation look worse than it is. In rural North Dakota, for example, a family of four falls below 50 percent of the poverty threshold with an income of up to $25,500, while a family in Silicon Valley is in this category if they make up to $51,000. The Heritage Foundation, a conservative think tank, agrees that these new figures, coupled with terms like "near-poor," paint a picture that might not necessarily exist. "The emotionally charged terms 'poor' or 'near poor' clearly suggest to most people a level of material hardship that doesn't exist. It is deliberately used to mislead people," said Robert Rector, a Heritage Foundation senior research fellow. Meyer agrees in part. "I do think this is a better measure, but I wouldn't say that 100 million people are on the edge of starvation or anything close to that," Meyer said. But Sheila Zedlewski, a researcher with the Urban Institute, says the supplemental measure of poverty is evidence of the impact of a long-term recession. "It's very consistent with everything we've been hearing in the last few years about families' struggle, earnings not keeping up for the bottom half," Zedlewski said. "There are a lot of low-income Americans struggling to make ends meet, and we don't pay enough attention to them."

—Heather Kerrigan

Following is the edited report released by the U.S. Census Bureau on September 13, 2011, on the state of poverty in the United States.

Census Bureau Report on Poverty in the United States

DOCUMENT

September 13, 2011

[All portions of the report not corresponding to poverty have been omitted.]

[Tables, graphs, and footnotes, and references to them, have been omitted.]

POVERTY IN THE UNITED STATES

Highlights

- The official poverty rate in 2010 was 15.1 percent—up from 14.3 percent in 2009. This was the third consecutive annual increase in the poverty rate. Since 2007, the poverty rate has increased by 2.6 percentage points, from 12.5 percent to 15.1 percent.
- In 2010, 46.2 million people were in poverty, up from 43.6 million in 2009—the fourth consecutive annual increase in the number of people in poverty.
- Between 2009 and 2010, the poverty rate increased for non-Hispanic Whites (from 9.4 percent to 9.9 percent), for Blacks (from 25.8 percent to 27.4 percent), and for Hispanics (from 25.3 percent to 26.6 percent). For Asians, the 2010 poverty rate (12.1 percent) was not statistically different from the 2009 poverty rate.
- The poverty rate in 2010 (15.1 percent) was the highest poverty rate since 1993 but was 7.3 percentage points lower than the poverty rate in 1959, the first year for which poverty estimates are available.
- The number of people in poverty in 2010 (46.2 million) is the largest number in the 52 years for which poverty estimates have been published.

- Between 2009 and 2010, the poverty rate increased for children under age 18 (from 20.7 percent to 22.0 percent) and people aged 18 to 64 (from 12.9 percent to 13.7 percent), but was not statistically different for people aged 65 and older (9.0 percent).

Poverty in the First Year After a Recession

Since 2010 represents the first full calendar year after the recession that ended in June 2009, it is interesting to compare changes in poverty between 2009 and 2010 with changes during the first year after the end of other recessions. The poverty rate and the number of people in poverty increased in the first calendar year following the end of the last three recessions. On the other hand, in the calendar year following the recessions that ended in 1961 and 1975, the poverty rate decreased.

Race and Hispanic Origin

For non-Hispanic Whites, the poverty rate increased to 9.9 percent in 2010 from 9.4 percent in 2009, while the number in poverty increased to 19.6 million from 18.5 million. The poverty rate for non-Hispanic Whites was lower than the poverty rates for other racial groups. Non-Hispanic Whites accounted for 42.4 percent of the people in poverty, but 64.5 percent of the total population.

For Blacks, the poverty rate increased to 27.4 percent in 2010, up from 25.8 percent in 2009, while the number in poverty increased to 10.7 million from 9.9 million. For Asians, the 2010 poverty rate and the number in poverty (12.1 percent and 1.7 million) were not statistically different from 2009. However, the poverty rate increased for Hispanics to 26.6 percent in 2010 from 25.3 in 2009, and the number of Hispanics in poverty increased to 13.2 million from 12.4 million.

Age

For people aged 18 to 64, the poverty rate increased to 13.7 percent in 2010 from 12.9 percent in 2009, while the number in poverty increased to 26.3 million from 24.7 million. For people aged 65 and older in 2010 neither the poverty rate (9.0 percent) nor the number in poverty (3.5 million) were statistically different from the 2009 estimates.

From 2009 to 2010, the poverty rate for children under age 18 increased to 22.0 percent from 20.7 percent, while the number of children under age 18 in poverty increased to 16.4 million from 15.5 million. The poverty rate for children was higher than the rates for people aged 18 to 64 and those aged 65 and older. Children accounted for 35.5 percent of people in poverty, but only 24.4 percent of the total population.

Related children are people under age 18 related to the householder by birth, marriage, or adoption who are not themselves householders or spouses of householders.32 The poverty rate for related children increased to 21.5 percent in 2010 from 20.1 percent in 2009, and the number of related children in poverty increased to 15.7 million from 14.8 million. For related children in families with a female householder, 46.9 percent were in poverty, compared with 11.6 percent of related children in married-couple families.

For related children under age 6, the poverty rate between 2009 and 2010 increased to 25.3 percent from 23.8 percent, while the number in poverty increased to 6.3 million from 6.0 million. For related children under age 6 in families with a female householder, 58.2 percent were in poverty, about four times the rate of their counterparts in married-couple families (13.4 percent).

Nativity

The poverty rate and the number in poverty for the native-born population increased to 14.4 percent in 2010 from 13.7 percent in 2009, while the number in poverty increased to 38.6 million from 36.4 million. Among the foreign-born population, 7.6 million people lived in poverty in 2010—up from 7.2 million in 2009. Their poverty rate (19.9 percent) was not statistically different in 2010.

Of the foreign-born population, 44.0 percent were naturalized U.S. citizens. For naturalized citizens, the 2010 poverty rate of 11.3 percent was not statistically different from 2009, while the number in poverty increased to 1.9 million in 2010 from 1.7 million in 2009. The poverty rate for those who were not citizens rose to 26.7 percent in 2010 from 25.1 percent in 2009, while the 2010 number in poverty (5.7 million) was not statistically different from 2009.

Region

The South was the only region to show increases in both the poverty rate and the number in poverty—16.9 percent and 19.1 million in 2010, up from 15.7 percent and 17.6 million in 2009. In 2010, the poverty rates and the number in poverty for the Northeast (12.8 percent and 7.0 million), the Midwest (13.9 percent and 9.1 million), and the West (15.3 percent and 11.0 million) were not statistically different from 2009. The South had the highest regional poverty rate.

Residence

Inside metropolitan statistical areas, the poverty rate and the number of people in poverty were 14.9 percent and 38.3 million in 2010—up from 13.9 percent and 35.7 million in 2009. Among those living outside metropolitan areas, the poverty rate and the number in poverty were 16.5 percent and 7.9 million in 2010, not statistically different from 2009.

Between 2009 and 2010, the poverty rate for people in principal cities increased to 19.7 percent from 18.7 percent, while the number in poverty increased to 19.5 million from 18.3 million. Within metropolitan areas, people in poverty were more likely to live in principal cities. While 38.2 percent of all people living in metropolitan areas in 2010 lived in principal cities, 50.8 percent of poor people in metropolitan areas lived in principal cities. For those inside metropolitan areas but not in principal cities, the poverty rate rose to 11.8 percent from 11.0 percent, while the number in poverty increased to 18.9 million from 17.4 million.

Work Experience

Among all workers aged 16 and older, neither the poverty rate (7.0 percent) nor the number in poverty (10.7 million) in 2010 were statistically different from 2009.

People aged 16 years and older who worked some or all of 2010 had a lower poverty rate than those who did not work at any time—7.0 percent compared to 23.9 percent. In 2010, the poverty rate among full-time, year-round workers (2.6 percent) was lower than the rate for those who worked less than full time, year round (15.0 percent).

Among those who did not work at least 1 week last year, the poverty rate and the number in poverty increased to 23.9 percent and 20.7 million in 2010 from 22.7 percent and 18.9 million in 2009. Those who did not work in 2010 represented 66.0 percent of people aged 16 and older in poverty, compared with 36.2 percent of all people aged 16 and older.

Disability Status

Between 2009 and 2010, the poverty rate and number in poverty for people aged 18 to 64 with a disability rose from 25.0 percent and 3.7 million to 27.9 percent and 4.2 million. Among people aged 18 to 64 without a disability, 12.5 percent and 22.0 million were in poverty in 2010—up from 12.0 percent and 21.0 million in 2009. People aged 18 to 64 with a disability represented 15.9 percent of people aged 18 to 64 in poverty compared to 7.8 percent of all people aged 18 to 64.

Families

The poverty rate and the number of families in poverty were 11.7 percent and 9.2 million in 2010, compared with 11.1 percent and 8.8 million in 2009.

The poverty rate and the number in poverty increased for both married-couple families (6.2 percent and 3.6 million in 2010 from 5.8 percent and 3.4 million in 2009) and families with a female householder (31.6 percent and 4.7 million in 2010 from 29.9 percent and 4.4 million in 2009). For families with a male householder, the poverty rate and the number in poverty (15.8 percent and 880,000 in 2010) were not statistically different from 2009.

Depth of Poverty

Categorizing people as "in poverty" or "not in poverty" is one way to describe their economic situation. The income-to-poverty ratio and the income deficit or surplus describe additional aspects of economic well-being. While the poverty rate shows the proportion of people with income below the appropriate poverty threshold, the income-to-poverty ratio gauges the depth of poverty and shows how close a family's income is to its poverty threshold. The income-to-poverty ratio is reported as a percentage that compares a family's or an unrelated person's income with their appropriate poverty threshold.

For example, a family with an income-to-poverty ratio of 125 percent has income that is 25 percent above its poverty threshold.

The income deficit or surplus shows how many dollars a family's or an unrelated person's income is below (or above) their poverty threshold. For those with an income deficit, the measure is an estimate of the dollar amount necessary to raise a family's or an unrelated person's income to their poverty threshold.

Ratio of Income to Poverty

. . . In 2010, 6.7 percent of all people, or 20.5 million, had income below one-half of their poverty threshold, up from 6.3 percent, or 19.0 million people, in 2009. This group represented 44.3 percent of the poverty population in 2010.

The percentage and number of people with income below 125 percent of their threshold were 19.8 percent and 60.4 million, up from 18.7 percent and 56.8 million in 2009. For children, 9.9 percent and 7.4 million in 2010 lived in families with income below 50 percent of their poverty threshold, up from 9.3 percent and 6.9 million in 2009. The percentage and number of children living in families with income below 125 percent of their poverty threshold in 2010 were 27.8 percent and 20.7 million, up from 26.3 percent and 19.6 million in 2009.

The percentage of the elderly with income below 50 percent of their poverty threshold was 2.5 percent, less than one-half the percent of the total population at this poverty level (6.7 percent). On the other hand, the percentage of the elderly with income below 200 percent of their poverty threshold was 34.6 percent, not statistically different from the percent of the total population with income below this level.

The demographic makeup of the population differs at varying degrees of poverty. Children represented 24.4 percent of the overall population, 31.3 percent of the people with income below 200 percent of their poverty threshold, but 36.0 percent of the people with income below 50 percent of their poverty threshold. The elderly represented 12.8 percent of the overall population, 13.1 percent of those with income below 200 percent of their poverty threshold, but 4.8 percent of the people with income below 50 percent of their poverty threshold.

Income Deficit

The income deficit for families in poverty (the difference in dollars between a family's income and its poverty threshold) averaged $9,244 in 2010, which was not statistically different from the 2009 estimate. The average income deficit was larger for families with a female householder ($9,742) than for married-couple families ($8,660).

The average income deficit per capita for families with a female householder ($2,908) was higher than for married-couple families ($2,179). The income deficit per capita is computed by dividing the average deficit by the average number of people in that type of family. Since families with a female householder were smaller on average than married-couple families, the larger per capita deficit for female-householder families reflects their smaller average family size as well as their lower average family income.

For unrelated individuals in poverty, the average income deficit was $6,225 in 2010. The $5,982 deficit for women was lower than the $6,504 deficit for men.

Doubled-Up Households

People may cope with challenging economic circumstances by combining households with other families or individuals. The number and percentage of doubled-up households and adults sharing households in the United States increased over the course of the recession that began in December 2007 and ended in June 2009. While poverty estimates are based on income in the previous calendar year, doubling-up estimates reflect household composition at the time of survey, which is conducted during the months of February, March, and April of each year. In spring 2007, doubled-up households totaled 19.7 million. By spring 2011, the number of doubled-up households had increased by 2.0 million to 21.8 million, and the percent of households doubled-up had increased by 1.3 percentage points from 17.0 percent to 18.3 percent. Among adults, 61.7 million (27.7 percent) were doubled-up in 2007, while 69.2 million (30.0 percent) lived in doubled-up households in 2011.

The adult population increased by 3.8 percent between 2007 and 2011, but the number of doubled-up adults increased by 12.2 percent.

An estimated 5.9 million young adults aged 25 to 34 resided in their parents' households in 2011, compared to 4.7 million before the recession. By spring 2011, 14.2 percent of young adults lived in their parents' households, representing an increase of 2.4 percentage points since spring 2007.

It is difficult to precisely assess the impact of doubling-up on overall poverty rates. Young adults aged 25 to 34 living with their parents had an official poverty rate of 8.4 percent (when the entire family's income is compared to the threshold that includes the young adult as an additional adult in the family), but if their poverty status were determined using their own income, 45.3 percent had income below the poverty threshold for a single person under age 65 ($11,344).

Alternative/Experimental Poverty Measures

The poverty estimates in this report compare the official poverty thresholds to money income before taxes, not including the value of noncash benefits. The money income measure does not completely capture the economic well-being of individuals and families, and there are many questions about the adequacy of the official poverty thresholds. Families and individuals also derive economic well-being from noncash benefits, such as food and housing subsidies, and their disposable income is determined by both taxes paid and tax credits received. The official poverty thresholds developed more than 40 years ago do not take into account rising standards of living or such issues as child care expenses, other work-related expenses, variations in medical costs across population groups, or geographic differences in the cost of living. Poverty estimates using the new Supplemental Poverty Measure, for which the Census Bureau expects to publish preliminary estimates in October 2011, will address many of these concerns. . . .

National Academy of Sciences (NAS)-Based Measures

The Census Bureau currently computes alternative poverty measures based on the 1995 recommendations of the National Academy of Sciences Panel on Poverty and Family Assistance. The NAS-based measures use both alternative poverty thresholds and an expanded income definition. In October 2011, the Census Bureau will release estimates for these alternative measures for 2010. Estimates for 2009 for the NAS-based measures can be found at <www.census.gov/hhes/povmeas /data/public-use.html>.

The Census Bureau also makes available a research file that provides microdata with variables used to construct the NAS-based alternative measures, available at <www.census .gov/hhes/www/povmeas/datafiles.html>, and an expanded version of the CPS ASEC public-use file that includes estimates of the value of taxes and noncash benefits, available at <www.bls.census.gov/cps_ftp.html#cpsmarch>. Both microdata files are currently available for 2009. Data for 2010 will be released before the end of the year.

CPS Table Creator II

CPS Table Creator II is a Web-based tool designed to help researchers explore alternative income and poverty measures. The tool is available from a link on the Census Bureau's poverty Web site, <www.census.gov /hhes/www/cpstc/apm/cpstc_altpov.html>. Table Creator II allows researchers to produce poverty and income estimates using their own combinations of threshold and resource definitions and to see the incremental impact of the addition or subtraction of a single resource element. For example:

- Taking into account the value of the federal earned income tax credit would reduce the number of children classified as poor in 2010 by 3.0 million.
- In 2010, the number of people aged 65 and older in poverty would be higher by almost 14 million if social security payments were excluded from money income, quintupling the number of elderly people in poverty.
- If unemployment insurance benefits were excluded from money income, 3.2 million more people would be counted as poor in 2010.

Researchers can also estimate poverty rates using alternative poverty thresholds. Many other countries use relative poverty measures with thresholds that are based on a percentage of median or mean income. Table Creator II allows researchers to estimate poverty rates using a relative poverty threshold calculated as any percentage of mean or median equivalence-adjusted income. For example, using poverty thresholds based on 50 percent of median income rather than the official poverty thresholds would increase the overall poverty rate in 2009 from 14.3 percent to 22.1 percent.

SOURCE: U.S. Census Bureau. "Income, Poverty, and Health Insurance Coverage in the United States: 2010." September 13, 2011. http://www.census.gov/prod/2011pubs/p60-239.pdf.

OTHER HISTORIC DOCUMENTS OF INTEREST

FROM PREVIOUS *HISTORIC DOCUMENTS*

FBI Report on Crime
in the United States

SEPTEMBER 19, 2011

The Federal Bureau of Investigation (FBI) released an annual statistical report, *Crime in the United States, 2010*, on September 19, 2011. The document lays out the number of crimes committed in the United States from January 1 through December 31, 2010. The report shows that the number of violent crimes declined for the fourth consecutive year. In 2007, the decline was 0.7 percent over the previous year; in 2008, the volume of violent crimes declined by 1.9 percent; in 2009, violent crimes declined by 5.3 percent; and in 2010, they declined by 6 percent. The volume of property crimes also decreased in 2010, by 2.7 percent, making 2010 the eighth straight year in which the volume of property crime had fallen. The volumes of the four types of violent crimes—murder and nonnegligent manslaughter, aggravated assault, robbery, and forcible rape, a category that includes assaults, attempt to commit rape, and forcing a female to have sex against her will, but does not include nonforcible rape (i.e., statutory)—all declined from 2009 to 2010. Murder and nonnegligent manslaughter declined by 4.2 percent; aggravated assault decreased by 4.1 percent; robbery declined by 10 percent; and forcible rape dropped by 5 percent.

This year's report was accompanied by a warning against using the crime statistics presented by the FBI to rank cities, counties, and states. "These rankings . . . are merely a quick choice made by the data user; they provide no insight into the many variables that mold the crime in a particular town, city, county, state, region, or other jurisdiction. Consequently, these rankings lead to simplistic and/or incomplete analyses that often create misleading perceptions adversely affecting cities and counties, along with their residents," according to the report. The FBI wrote that a clear analysis of any area is only possible after looking at a number of factors that impact law enforcement in each locality.

The FBI also cautioned that the Uniform Crime Report only includes crimes that are reported to law enforcement. In addition, if multiple crimes are committed during one incident, only the most serious offense is included in the FBI report; this practice obviously has an effect on the overall numbers associated with certain crimes. Each year, the U.S. Department of Justice conducts the National Crime Victimization Survey, which estimates unreported crimes. When the two studies are looked at together, they give the most accurate representation of the actual crime rate in the United States. The version of the National Crime Victimization Survey released on September 15, 2011, showed a decline in both violent crime and property crime victimization, of 13 percent and 6 percent, respectively, for U.S. residents aged 12 and older.

CRIME RATES

The FBI does not indicate reasons for the rise and fall of crime rates in its annual reports, but criminologists speculated that reasons for the continuing drops in violent and property crime might include an aging population, better community policing, and programs targeting youth and recent prison parolees. One fact they could all agree on was that high unemployment and housing issues have not had a noticeable effect on the crime rate. Attorney General Eric Holder linked the work of law enforcement agencies across the country to the decline. "Safe communities are the foundation of our nation's prosperity and I have made it a priority of this Department of Justice to protect the American public by aggressively fighting violent crime," Holder said.

The decline in crime was widespread in 2010, and when factoring in the year-to-year increase in population, an even larger decline in violent crime of 6.5 percent per 100,000 can be seen. Since 2001, the violent crime rate is down 13.4 percent. Despite these positive statistics, a murder still occurs in the United States every thirty-five minutes.

In each violent crime category—murder and nonnegligent manslaughter, forcible rape, robbery, and aggravated assault—the number of offenses declined from 2009 to 2010. The violent crime rate in 2010 was 403.6 offenses per 100,000 people, a decrease of 6 percent since 2009. Aggravated assaults made up the greatest portion of all violent crimes, at 62.5 percent, while robbery accounted for 29.5 percent, forcible rape for 6.8 percent, and murder for 1.2 percent. The FBI annual crime report also offers information on the type of weapon used during a murder. According to the report, firearms were used during 67.5 percent of murders in the United States in 2010, 41.4 percent of robberies, and 20.6 percent of aggravated assaults.

The rate of property crime, including burglary, larceny-theft, motor vehicle theft, and arson, fell 2.7 percent from 2009 to 2010 to a rate of 2,941.9 offenses committed per 100,000 people. The property crime rate in 2010 was 12.1 percent lower than in 2006. The FBI estimates that in 2010, $15.7 billion in losses were caused by property crime, of which larceny-theft accounted for 68.1 percent, burglary 23.8 percent, and motor vehicle theft 8.1 percent.

Nationwide, 56,825 arsons were reported in 2010, of which 45.5 percent involved structures including houses, storage units, and office buildings; 26 percent involved mobile property; and 28.5 percent involved other forms of property, such as crops and fences. Per event, the average dollar amount lost was estimated at $17,612. Arson decreased 7.6 percent from 2009 to 2010.

In 2010, the FBI reported 13,120,947 arrests for all offenses, excluding traffic violations. Of those, more than 552,000 were for violent crime while more than 1.6 million were for property crime. Most of the arrests were for drug abuse, driving under the influence, and larceny-theft. From 2009 to 2010, the number of violent-crime arrests declined 5.3 percent; arrests for property crime decreased 4.7 percent; arrests of juveniles decreased 9.7 percent; and arrests of adults decreased 3.7 percent. Males were more likely to be arrested than females, accounting for nearly 75 percent of those arrested in 2010. Arrests of white citizens accounted for 69.4 percent of all arrests, while the arrest of black citizens was 28 percent.

Robert Mueller III, director of the FBI, said the crime trends reported by the FBI are important for recognizing the work of law enforcement officers. "While the conventional activities of law enforcement officers do not always attract the media headlines created when terrorist threats are disrupted, the UCR Program's statistics are proof of the strength and courage routinely demonstrated to enforce law and order in our communities," Mueller said. "National security is as much about keeping our streets safe from crime as it is about protecting the United States from terrorists."

HATE CRIMES

In May, the Department of Justice won its first conviction under the Matthew Shepard and James Byrd, Jr., Hate Crimes Prevention Act. The act was passed in October 2009 to expand on an earlier hate crimes law. The act gave the federal government authority to prosecute hate crimes in states with inadequate hate crime laws, or where authorities are unwilling or unable to prosecute suspected offenders. It also granted the government greater authority to investigate and prosecute hate crimes based on actual or perceived sexual orientation, gender, gender identity, or disability.

On May 25, a federal jury convicted Frankie Maybee of crimes against five Hispanic men. The Justice Department's case stated that Maybee and his accomplice, Sean Popejoy, accosted the five victims subsequently pursued their vehicle in a truck yelling racial epithets, and forced the victims' vehicle across the road and into a tree. All five Hispanic men suffered injuries, with one experiencing life-threatening injuries. Popejoy plead guilty to one count of committing a federal hate crime and one count of conspiring to commit a federal hate crime. "The defendants targeted five men because they were Hispanic, and today's verdict shows that the Justice Department is committed to vigorously prosecuting individuals who perform acts of hate because of someone's race or national origin," said Thomas Perez, assistant attorney general for the Civil Rights Division.

On November 14, 2011, the FBI released its annual publication on hate crimes in the United States, which also looked at data collected in 2010. Unlike most other forms of crime, the number of hate crimes increased slightly from 2009 to 2010, from 6,604 to 6,628. The number of reported victims was 8,199. Reporting hate crimes statistics to the FBI is voluntary, but of the nearly 15,000 law enforcement agencies that participated in 2010, 87 percent reported no hate crimes.

The Anti-Defamation League (ADL) called on more law enforcement agencies to participate in the report. "It is necessary for all agencies to participate in this vital report, and to accurately and effectively communicate the reality of hate crimes in their jurisdiction," said Robert Sugarman, ADL National Chair and Abraham Foxman, ADL National Director in a statement. "The . . . report provides an opportunity to emphasize the importance of a swift and effective response to each and every bias crime. Behind the aggregated data are victims who have been intentionally subjected to violence or vandalism based solely on race, religion, sexual orientation, disability, or national origin."

As defined by the FBI, victims of hate crimes can be individuals, businesses, institutions, or even society as a whole. In 2010, 4,824 of hate crimes were carried out against people, while 2,861 were committed against property. More than 47 percent of the reported hate crimes were motivated by racial bias. Religion bias hate crimes accounted for 20 percent of reported hate crimes. More than 19 percent of hate crimes committed were motivated by sexual orientation, 12.8 percent dealt with ethnicity or national origin, and 0.6 percent were because of a person's disability. A significant rise in the number of anti-Islamic hate crimes occurred from 2009 to 2010.

A majority of hate crimes, 31.4 percent, took place in or near the victim's home, while another 17 percent took place on highways, roads, alleys, or streets. Nearly 11 percent happened at a school, 5.8 percent in a parking lot or garage, and 3.7 percent in a place of worship.

A majority of the more than 6,000 known hate crime offenders were white and 18.4 percent were black. Twelve percent of offenders were of unknown race. More than

4,800 hate crimes were committed against individuals, with 46.2 percent involving intimidation, 34.8 percent simple assaults, 18.4 percent aggravated assault, and seven murder and nonnegligent manslaughters.

Online Crime

While not accounted for in the annual *Crime in the United States* publication, the FBI, in cooperation with the National White Collar Crime Center, compiles statistics on online crimes and victims through its Internet Crime Complaint Center (IC3). In its tenth annual report, released on February 24, 2011, the IC3 reported 303,000 online crime complaints, the second highest in the report's history.

A majority of the online crimes reported to the IC3 in 2010 were for identity theft, non-delivery of payment or merchandise, and scammers impersonating the FBI. Auction fraud, while accounting for nearly three-quarters of all reported online crimes in 2004, had significantly decreased to 5.9 percent in 2010. Not all complaints were accompanied by a financial loss, and those that involve financial or another type of victimization are referred to local law enforcement. The number of referred cases in 2010 was 121,710.

A majority of online crime complaints were made by men aged 40 to 59, who reported a loss of $1.25 for every $1 reported by women. Nearly 75 percent of those who committed online crime were male, and more than half resided in California, Florida, New York, Texas, Washington, and Washington, D.C. Foreign criminals resided mainly in Canada, Nigeria, and the United Kingdom. "The 2010 Internet Crime Report demonstrates how pervasive online crime has become, affecting people in all demographic groups," the report states. "As this report demonstrates, cyber criminals have become more creative in devising ways to separate Internet users from their money."

—Heather Kerrigan

Following are excerpts from the FBI's annual report, Crime in the United States, 2010, *released on September 19, 2011.*

FBI Statistics on Crime in the United States

September 19, 2011

Violent Crime

Definition

In the FBI's Uniform Crime Reporting (UCR) Program, violent crime is composed of four offenses: murder and nonnegligent manslaughter, forcible rape, robbery, and aggravated assault. Violent crimes are defined in the UCR Program as those offenses which involve force or threat of force.

Data Collection

The data presented in *Crime in the United States* reflect the Hierarchy Rule, which requires that only the most serious offense in a multiple-offense criminal incident be counted. The descending order of UCR violent crimes are murder and nonnegligent manslaughter, forcible rape, robbery, and aggravated assault, followed by the property crimes of burglary, larceny-theft, and motor vehicle theft. Although arson is also a property crime, the Hierarchy Rule does not apply to the offense of arson. In cases in which an arson occurs in conjunction with another violent or property crime, both crimes are reported, the arson and the additional crime.

Overview

- In 2010, an estimated 1,246,248 violent crimes occurred nationwide, a decrease of 6.0 percent from the 2009 estimate.
- When considering 5- and 10-year trends, the 2010 estimated violent crime total was 13.2 percent below the 2006 level and 13.4 percent below the 2001 level.
- There were an estimated 403.6 violent crimes per 100,000 inhabitants in 2010.
- Aggravated assaults accounted for the highest number of violent crimes reported to law enforcement at 62.5 percent. Robbery comprised 29.5 percent of violent crimes, forcible rape accounted for 6.8 percent, and murder accounted for 1.2 percent of estimated violent crimes in 2010.
- Information collected regarding type of weapon showed that firearms were used in 67.5 percent of the Nation's murders, 41.4 percent of robberies, and 20.6 percent of aggravated assaults. (Weapons data are not collected for forcible rape.) . . .

MURDER

Definition

The FBI's Uniform Crime Reporting (UCR) Program defines murder and nonnegligent manslaughter as the willful (nonnegligent) killing of one human being by another. The classification of this offense is based solely on police investigation as opposed to the determination of a court, medical examiner, coroner, jury, or other judicial body. The UCR Program does not include the following situations in this offense classification: deaths caused by negligence, suicide, or accident; justifiable homicides; and attempts to murder or assaults to murder, which are scored as aggravated assaults. . . .

Overview

- An estimated 14,748 persons were murdered nationwide in 2010. This was a 4.2 percent decrease from the 2009 estimate, a 14.8 percent decrease from the 2006 figure, and an 8.0 percent decrease from the 2001 estimate.
- In 2010, there were 4.8 murders per 100,000 inhabitants, a 4.8 percent decrease from the 2009 rate. Compared with the 2006 rate, the murder rate decreased 17.4 percent, and compared with the 2001 rate, the murder rate decreased 15.0 percent.
- Nearly 44 percent (43.8) of murders were reported in the South, the most populous region, with 20.6 percent reported in the West, 19.9 percent reported in the Midwest, and 15.6 percent reported in the Northeast. . . .

Forcible Rape

Definition

Forcible rape, as defined in the FBI's Uniform Crime Reporting (UCR) Program, is the carnal knowledge of a female forcibly and against her will. Attempts or assaults to commit rape by force or threat of force are also included; however, statutory rape (without force) and other sex offenses are excluded. . . .

Overview

- There were an estimated at 84,767 forcible rapes reported to law enforcement in 2010. This estimate was 5.0 percent lower than the 2009 estimate and 10.3 percent and 6.7 percent lower than the 2006 and 2001 estimates, respectively.
- The rate of forcible rapes in 2010 was estimated at 54.2 per 100,000 female inhabitants.
- Rapes by force comprised 93.0 percent of reported rape offenses in 2010, and attempts or assaults to commit rape accounted for 7.0 percent of reported rapes. . . .

Robbery

Definition

The FBI's Uniform Crime Reporting (UCR) Program defines robbery as the taking or attempting to take anything of value from the care, custody, or control of a person or persons by force or threat of force or violence and/or by putting the victim in fear.

Overview

- Nationwide in 2010, there were an estimated 367,832 robberies.
- The estimated number of robberies decreased 10.0 percent from the 2009 estimate and 18.1 percent from the 2006 estimate.
- The 2010 estimated robbery rate of 119.1 per 100,000 inhabitants reflected a decrease of 10.5 percent when compared with the 2009 rate.
- An estimated $456 million in losses were attributed to robberies in 2010.
- The average dollar value of property stolen per reported robbery was $1,239. The highest average dollar loss was for banks, which lost $4,410 per offense.
- Firearms were used in 41.4 percent of the robberies for which the UCR Program received additional information in 2010. In a nearly equal percentage of robberies (42.0 percent), strong-arm tactics were used, followed by knives and cutting instruments used in 7.9 percent of robberies, and other dangerous weapons used in 8.8 percent of robberies in 2010. . . .

Aggravated Assault

Definition

The FBI's Uniform Crime Reporting (UCR) Program defines aggravated assault as an unlawful attack by one person upon another for the purpose of inflicting severe or aggravated bodily injury. The UCR Program further specifies that this type of assault is usually accompanied by the use of a weapon or by other means likely to produce death or great bodily harm. Attempted aggravated assault that involves the display of—or threat to use—a gun, knife, or other weapon is included in this crime category because serious personal injury would likely result if the assault were completed. When aggravated assault and larceny-theft occur together, the offense falls under the category of robbery.

Overview

- In 2010, there were an estimated 778,901 aggravated assaults in the Nation.
- The estimated number of aggravated assaults in 2010 declined 4.1 percent from 2009 and 14.3 percent when compared with the estimate for 2001.
- In 2010, the estimated rate of aggravated assaults was 252.3 offenses per 100,000 inhabitants.
- A comparison of data for 2001 and 2010 showed that the rate of aggravated assaults in 2010 dropped 20.8 percent.
- Of the aggravated assault offenses in 2010 for which law enforcement agencies provided expanded data, 27.4 percent were committed with personal weapons such as hands, fists, or feet. Slightly more than 20 percent (20.6) of aggravated assaults were committed with firearms, and 19.0 percent were committed with knives or cutting instruments. The remaining 33.1 percent of aggravated assaults were committed with other weapons. . . .

PROPERTY CRIME

Definition

In the FBI's Uniform Crime Reporting (UCR) Program, property crime includes the offenses of burglary, larceny-theft, motor vehicle theft, and arson. The object of the theft-type offenses is the taking of money or property, but there is no force or threat of force against the victims. The property crime category includes arson because the offense involves the destruction of property; however, arson victims may be subjected to force. Because of limited participation and varying collection procedures by local law enforcement agencies, only limited data are available for arson. Arson statistics are included in trend, clearance, and arrest tables throughout *Crime in the United States*, but they are not included in any estimated volume data. The arson section in this report provides more information on that offense.

Data Collection

The data presented in *Crime in the United States* reflect the Hierarchy Rule, which requires that only the most serious offense in a multiple-offense criminal incident be counted. In descending order of severity, the violent crimes are murder and nonnegligent manslaughter, forcible rape, robbery, and aggravated assault, followed by the property crimes of burglary, larceny-theft, and motor vehicle theft. Although arson is also a property crime, the Hierarchy Rule does not apply to the offense of arson. In cases in which an arson occurs in conjunction with another violent or property crime, both crimes are reported, the arson and the additional crime.

Overview

- In 2010, there were an estimated 9,082,887 property crime offenses in the Nation.
- The 2-year trend showed that property crime decreased 2.7 percent in 2010 compared with the 2009 estimate. The 5-year trend, comparing 2010 data with that of 2006, showed a 9.3 percent drop in property crime.
- In 2010, the rate of property crime was estimated at 2,941.9 per 100,000 inhabitants, a 3.3 percent decrease when compared with the rate in 2009. The 2010 property crime rate was 12.1 percent lower than the 2006 rate and 19.6 percent below the 2001 rate.
- Larceny-theft accounted for 68.1 percent of all property crimes in 2010. Burglary accounted for 23.8 percent and motor vehicle theft for 8.1 percent.
- Property crimes in 2010 resulted in losses estimated at 15.7 billion dollars. . . .

BURGLARY

Definition

The FBI's Uniform Crime Reporting (UCR) Program defines burglary as the unlawful entry of a structure to commit a felony or theft. To classify an offense as a burglary, the use of force to gain entry need not have occurred. The UCR Program has three subclassifications for burglary: forcible entry, unlawful entry where no force is used, and attempted forcible entry. The UCR definition of "structure" includes apartment, barn, house trailer or houseboat when used as a permanent dwelling, office, railroad car (but not automobile), stable, and vessel (i.e., ship).

Overview

- In 2010, there were an estimated 2,159,878 burglaries—a decrease of 2.0 percent when compared with 2009 data.
- Burglaries increased 2.0 percent in 2010 compared to the 2001 estimate.
- Burglary accounted for 23.8 percent of the estimated number of property crimes committed in 2010.
- Of all burglaries, 60.5 percent involved forcible entry, 33.2 percent were unlawful entries (without force), and the remainder (6.3 percent) were forcible entry attempts.
- Victims of burglary offenses suffered an estimated $4.6 billion in lost property in 2010; overall, the average dollar loss per burglary offense was $2,119.
- Burglaries of residential properties accounted for 73.9 percent of all burglary offenses. . . .

LARCENY-THEFT

Definition

The FBI's Uniform Crime Reporting (UCR) Program defines larceny-theft as the unlawful taking, carrying, leading, or riding away of property from the possession or constructive possession of another. Examples are thefts of bicycles, motor vehicle parts and accessories, shoplifting, pocket-picking, or the stealing of any property or article that is not taken by force and violence or by fraud. Attempted larcenies are included. Embezzlement, confidence games, forgery, check fraud, etc., are excluded.

Overview

- In 2010, there were an estimated 6,185,867 larceny-thefts nationwide.
- The number of estimated larceny-thefts dropped 2.4 percent in 2010 when compared with the 2009 estimate. The 2010 figure was a 6.6 percent decline from the 2006 estimate.
- The rate of estimated larceny-thefts in 2010 was 2,003.5 per 100,000 inhabitants.
- From 2009 to 2010, the rate of estimated larceny-thefts declined 3.0 percent, and from 2001 to 2010, the rate decreased 19.4 percent.
- Larceny-thefts accounted for an estimated 68.1 percent of property crimes in 2010.
- The average value of property taken during larceny-thefts was $988 per offense. Applying this average value to the estimated number of larceny-thefts shows that the loss to victims nationally was over $6.1 billion.
- Over 26 percent (26.4) of larceny-thefts were thefts from motor vehicles. . . .

MOTOR VEHICLE THEFT

Definition

In the FBI's Uniform Crime Reporting (UCR) Program, motor vehicle theft is defined as the theft or attempted theft of a motor vehicle. In the UCR Program, a motor vehicle is a self-propelled vehicle that runs on land surfaces and not on rails. Examples of motor vehicles include sport utility vehicles, automobiles, trucks, buses, motorcycles, motor scooters, all-terrain vehicles, and snowmobiles. Motor vehicle theft does not include farm equipment, bulldozers, airplanes, construction equipment, or water craft such as motorboats, sailboats, houseboats, or jet skis. The taking of a motor vehicle for temporary use by persons having lawful access is excluded from this definition.

Overview

- Nationwide in 2010, there were an estimated 737,142 thefts of motor vehicles. The estimated rate of motor vehicle thefts was 238.8 per 100,000 inhabitants.
- The estimated number of motor vehicle thefts declined 7.4 percent when compared with data from 2009, 38.5 percent when compared with 2006 figures, and 40.0 percent when compared with 2001 figures.
- More than $4.5 billion was lost nationwide to motor vehicle thefts in 2010. The average dollar loss per stolen vehicle was $6,152.
- Nearly 73 percent (72.9) of all motor vehicles reported stolen in 2010 were automobiles. . . .

ARSON

Definition

The FBI's Uniform Crime Reporting (UCR) Program defines arson as any willful or malicious burning or attempting to burn, with or without intent to defraud, a dwelling house, public building, motor vehicle or aircraft, personal property of another, etc.

Data collection

Only the fires that investigation determined to have been willfully set are included in this arson data collection. Fires labeled as suspicious or of unknown origin are excluded from these data. . . .

Overview

- In 2010, 15,475 law enforcement agencies provided 1–12 months of arson data and reported 56,825 arsons. Of the participating agencies, 14,747 provided expanded offense data regarding 48,619 arsons.
- Arsons involving structures (e.g., residential, storage, public, etc.) accounted for 45.5 percent of the total number of arson offenses. Mobile property was involved in 26.0 percent of arsons, and other types of property (such as crops, timber, fences, etc.) accounted for 28.5 percent of reported arsons.
- The average dollar loss due to arson was $17,612.
- Arsons of industrial/manufacturing structures resulted in the highest average dollar losses (an average of $133,717 per arson).
- Arson offenses decreased 7.6 percent in 2010 when compared with arson data reported in 2009.
- Nationwide, there were 19.6 arson offenses for every 100,000 inhabitants. . . .

Offenses Cleared

In the FBI's Uniform Crime Reporting (UCR) Program, law enforcement agencies can clear, or "close," offenses in one of two ways: by arrest or by exceptional means. Although an agency may administratively close a case, that does not necessarily mean that the agency can clear the offense for UCR purposes. To clear an offense within the UCR Program's guidelines, the reporting agency must adhere to certain criteria, which are outlined in the following text. (Note: The UCR Program does not distinguish between offenses cleared by arrest and those cleared by exceptional means in collecting or publishing data via the traditional Summary Reporting System.). . .

Clearances Involving Only Persons Under 18 Years of Age

When an offender under the age of 18 is cited to appear in juvenile court or before other juvenile authorities, the UCR Program considers the incident for which the juvenile is being held responsible to be cleared by arrest, even though a physical arrest may not have occurred. When clearances involve both juvenile and adult offenders, those incidents are classified as clearances for crimes committed by adults. Because the clearance percentages for crimes committed by juveniles include only those clearances in which no adults were involved, the figures in this publication should not be used to present a definitive picture of juvenile involvement in crime.

Overview

- In 2010, 47.2 percent of violent crimes and 18.3 percent of property crimes in the Nation were cleared by arrest or exceptional means.

- Among violent crimes, 64.8 percent of murder offenses were cleared, 40.3 percent of forcible rape offenses were cleared, 28.2 percent of robbery offenses were cleared, and 56.4 percent of aggravated assault offenses were cleared.
- Clearance data for property crimes revealed that 21.1 percent of larceny-theft offenses were cleared, 12.4 percent of burglary offenses were cleared, and 11.8 percent of motor vehicle theft offenses were cleared.
- Nineteen percent of arson offenses were cleared by arrest or exceptional means in 2010.
- 34.3 percent of arson offenses cleared involved juveniles (persons under age 18); this was the highest percentage of all offense clearances involving only juveniles. . . .

Arrests

Definition

The FBI's Uniform Crime Reporting (UCR) Program counts one arrest for each separate instance in which a person is arrested, cited, or summoned for an offense. The UCR Program collects arrest data on 28 offenses, as described in Offense Definitions. (Please note that, beginning in 2010, the UCR Program no longer collected data on runaways.) Because a person may be arrested multiple times during a year, the UCR arrest figures do not reflect the number of individuals who have been arrested; rather, the arrest data show the number of times that persons are arrested, as reported by law enforcement agencies to the UCR Program.

Data Collection—Juveniles

The UCR Program considers a juvenile to be an individual under 18 years of age regardless of state definition. The program does not collect data regarding police contact with a juvenile who has not committed an offense, nor does it collect data on situations in which police take a juvenile into custody for his or her protection, e.g., neglect cases.

Overview

- Nationwide, law enforcement made an estimated 13,120,947 arrests (except traffic violations) in 2010. Of these arrests, 552,077 were for violent crimes and 1,643,962 were for property crimes.
- The highest number of arrests were for drug abuse violations (estimated at 1,638,846 arrests), driving under the influence (estimated at 1,412,223), and larceny-theft (estimated at 1,271,410).
- The estimated arrest rate for the United States in 2010 was 4,257.6 arrests per 100,000 inhabitants. The arrest rate for violent crime (including murder and nonnegligent manslaughter, forcible rape, robbery, and aggravated assault) was 179.2 per 100,000 inhabitants, and the arrest rate for property crime (burglary, larceny-theft, motor vehicle theft, and arson) was 538.5 per 100,000 inhabitants.
- Two-year arrest trends show violent crime arrests declined 5.3 percent in 2010 when compared with 2009 arrests, and property crime arrests decreased 4.7 percent when compared with the 2009 arrests.

- Arrests of juveniles for all offenses decreased 9.7 percent in 2010 when compared with the 2009 number; arrests of adults declined 3.7 percent.
- Nearly three-quarters (74.5 percent) of the persons arrested in the Nation during 2010 were males. They accounted for 80.5 percent of persons arrested for violent crime and 62.4 percent of persons arrested for property crime.
- In 2010, 69.4 percent of all persons arrested were white, 28.0 percent were black, and the remaining 2.6 percent were of other races. . . .

SOURCE: U.S. Department of Justice. Federal Bureau of Investigation. "Crime in the United States, 2010." September 19, 2011. http://www.fbi.gov/about-us/cjis/ucr/crime-in-the-u.s/2010/crime-in-the-u.s.-2010.

OTHER HISTORIC DOCUMENTS OF INTEREST

FROM PREVIOUS *HISTORIC DOCUMENTS*

Saudi Arabia Extends Women's Political Participation Rights

SEPTEMBER 25, 2011

Amid calls for increased women's rights and greater political participation, Saudi Arabia's absolute monarch, King Abdullah, announced historic changes in September 2011 that would allow women to participate in elections and government in the coming years. While political and women's rights activists hailed the change, they also cautioned that the decree was a small step and its implementation could be slow. The country's religious establishment largely opposed the changes. A Saudi Arabian sociologist, Khalid al-Dakhil, stated that some ultraconservative clerics were likely "out of their minds" with anger at the announcement. The timing of the announcement in large part stemmed from the king's desire to defuse potential discontent in the country in the face of popular political uprisings in other Arab states. It was also a reflection of sustained pressure by political activists for a more representative form of government. Despite the changes, women's rights in the kingdom remain severely restricted, including a continued ban on female drivers.

HISTORICAL ANNOUNCEMENT

On September 25, 2011, King Abdullah, the 87-year-old Saudi Arabian monarch, announced that women would be allowed as members of the Majlis Al-Shura, a consultative body, beginning in the next session, and that women would also have the right to nominate candidates for Municipal Councils, as well as nominate themselves for membership on the councils. The king noted in his announcement that the decision had been taken after consultations with Saudi religious scholars and a review of Islamic guidelines. King Abdullah also stated that "balanced modernization" is an "important requirement" in the current era, and rejected marginalizing the role of women in Saudi society.

The changes are considered to be a step forward for women's rights in Saudi Arabia. The rights currently granted to women are based on traditional tribal customs and the conservative Wahhabi sect of Sunni Islam. The absolute monarchy relies on support from the ultraconservative clerics and religious establishment, and the king is unlikely to undertake reforms that undermine its support. Under Saudi law, most women are required to have a male chaperone or guardian. The chaperone or guardian can determine, among other things, whether or not a woman works, travels, or studies. Segregation of the sexes is enshrined in Saudi law and is meant to ensure that unrelated men and women do not mingle, which is a punishable crime. The constraints placed on women in the country are strictly enforced.

IMPACT ON THE GOVERNMENT

The Majlis Al-Shura, or Shura, is a consultative body tasked with advising the king on matters of importance to the Saudi state. The 150 current members serve a four-year renewable term and advise the monarch on regulations and issues of national and public interest, as well as propose legislation and amend existing laws. Nevertheless, the right to pass laws is reserved for the king, who is also responsible for appointing all of the members of the Shura. In 2006, six women were appointed as advisers to the Shura, although they were not allowed to vote. The number of female advisers has since risen to twelve. The current term, which began in 2009, will end in 2013.

Municipal Councils have long been a focal point of political reform in the kingdom. Until the 1960s, members of Municipal Councils were elected. But the early 1960s ushered in a conservative era for Saudi Arabia, and religious leaders deemed that elections were unlawful. The Municipal Councils were dissolved and replaced by district and provisional councils, members of which were appointed. In 1977, the decision was taken to reinstate Municipal Councils, but it was not implemented until 2005. There are 179 Municipal Councils in the Kingdom, each with between four and fourteen members—the size of the council is determined by the population of the municipality. Half of the members are elected, while the other half is appointed by the minister of municipal and rural affairs. The role of the councils is to draft the municipality's budget, manage urban planning, and determine tax and service charges, among other responsibilities.

At the time the Municipal Councils were reinstated in 2005, the government barred female candidates and women's right to vote, but stated that women would be allowed to participate in the upcoming elections, due in 2009. However, in 2009 women were once again barred from participation, with the government claiming that "technical difficulties" prevented women from voting or otherwise participating. In 2011, the government again announced that women would not be able to take part in the elections. The elections for the current councils took place just days after the king's announcement. Only men over the age of twenty-one are currently enfranchised.

The king's announcement that the changes would be implemented "from the next session" means that women will gain the right to vote in Municipal Council elections and seek membership in the councils starting in 2015. Participation in the Shura could happen as early as 2013. There are concerns that the implementation of the king's decree could be slow, given the history of stalled decrees in the face of strong opposition to change from conservatives and weak enactment on the part of the government.

REFLECTION OF UPRISING IN THE ARAB WORLD

King Abdullah is considered to be a cautious reformer, stating publicly around a decade ago that women should be central to the Saudi economy. Since then, change has come gradually. Observers cited a number of reasons for the significant policy change. First, the uprisings in Egypt, Libya, Tunisia, Yemen, Syria, and Bahrain since late 2010 did not go unnoticed in Saudi Arabia. In an effort to dampen potential discontent, the government announced major public spending initiatives—totaling $130 billion—in February and March 2011. The decision to increase women's political participation was thought to be motivated in part by the desire to prevent discontent from boiling over into popular unrest. Second, prior to the announcement, there had been sustained domestic pressure for a more representative form of government, as well as for increased women's rights. While political activists have hailed the decree as a major milestone for the kingdom, many are also cautious about the timeframe for implementation. Moreover, political activists have called for the membership of the Shura to be elected by popular vote, and there are concerns that the participation of women may come at the expense of further changes to the Shura in the short term.

Driving Ban for Women

While many welcomed the changes announced by King Abdullah, significant hurdles must be overcome if women are to participate in government. Indeed, after the announcement some political observers questioned how women in Saudi Arabia would campaign if they were not allowed to drive. The right of women to drive is a more contentious issue than even political participation by women. Saudi Arabia is the only country in the world that does not allow women to drive. The ban on women driving in the kingdom is a social convention and in fact is not codified in law. Islamic clerics have issued *fatwas*, or religious edicts, stating that women should not be allowed to drive. It is almost unheard of for a woman to drive in Saudi Arabia, particularly in major metropolitan areas. In some rural areas, however, women drive without a license and the social convention is less strictly enforced. In the cities, however, a male guardian or a chauffeur must drive women. There are reportedly hundreds of thousands of foreign chauffeurs in the kingdom. Women's rights activists argue that the social convention severely constrains women's right to movement.

In recent years, a small grassroots campaign to end the ban on women driving in Saudi Arabia has gained traction. In June 2011, around forty women drove in the nation's cities, defying the ban. No arrests or violence were reported, although some of the women received tickets for driving without a license. The relatively mild enforcement of the convention is likely a reflection of the monarchy's desire to avoid international condemnation and domestic outcry, particularly given the popular political uprisings in neighboring states. Nevertheless, change is unlikely to come quickly given the religious establishment's strong opposition to women drivers.

This opposition is largely based on the belief that allowing women to drive will increase opportunities for unmarried men and women to interact. A well-known conservative cleric, Kamal Subhi, submitted a report to the Shura in December 2011, with the aim of ensuring that the ban remains in place. The report stated that allowing women to drive would jeopardize the country's tradition of virgin brides, and warns that prostitution, homosexuality, and divorce would increase if women were granted the right to drive. Women's rights activists claimed that argument for the ban was nonsensical, as forcing women to hire a male driver increases contact with non-family members of the opposite sex. Activists also argued that the ban is impractical as it puts women at the mercy of male relatives or hired drivers to go to medical appointments, attend school, and go shopping.

Future Change

The changes announced by King Abdullah in September 2011 may usher in further changes in women's rights in the kingdom. But change is likely to be gradual, reflecting resistance from the ultraconservative and powerful clerics from which the absolute monarchy draws its support. Nevertheless, that women will have the right to vote and participate in government in Saudi Arabia in the coming years is a historic step forward.

—Hilary Ewing

Following is a statement by King Abdullah of Saudi Arabia on September 25, 2011, announcing the extension of political participation rights to women.

King Abdullah on Women's Political Participation

September 25, 2011

Dear Brothers:

I am pleased to meet you at the opening of the third year of the fifth term of Majlis Al-Shura, praying to Allah Almighty to crown your works with success.

The struggle of the father of all people, the late King Abdul-Aziz, with your grandfathers, mercy be upon their souls, has resulted in the unity of hearts, land, and one destiny. Today, this destiny imposes on us to preserve this legacy, and not to stop here, but to develop it further in line with Islamic and moral values.

Yes, it is a responsibility towards our religion, and the interest of our country and its citizens that we should not stop at the hurdles of the current time; but we should strengthen our determination by patience and works with dependence on Allah to address them. Balanced modernization in line with our Islamic values, which preserve rights, is an important requirement in an era with no room for the weak and undecided people.

All people know that Muslim women have had in the Islamic history, positions that cannot be marginalized, including correct opinions and advice since the era of Prophet Mohammed, as examples, we cite the advice of the Mother of Believers Umm Salamah on Al-Hudaybiyah Day, in addition to many examples during the era of the Prophet's companions and followers until today.

Since we reject to marginalize the role of women in the Saudi society, in every field of works, according to the (Islamic) Shariah guidelines, and after consultations with many of our scholars, especially those in the senior scholars council, and others, who have expressed the preference for this orientation, and supported this trend, we have decided the following:

First, the participation of women in the Majlis Al-Shura as members from next session in accordance with the Shariah guidelines.

Second, as of the next session, women will have the right to nominate themselves for membership of Municipal Councils, and also have the right to participate in the nomination of candidates with the Islamic guidelines.

You, my brothers and sisters, have rights that we strive to achieve all matters that are for your pride, your dignity and your interests. It is our right to seek your opinions and advices, according to Shariah guidelines, and the fundamentals of religion, and those who keep away from these guidelines, they are arrogant persons and they have to bear the responsibility of these actions. I pray Allah Almighty for help and glory.

May peace and Allah's mercy and blessings be upon you.

SOURCE: Royal Embassy of Saudi Arabia in Washington, D.C. "King Abdullah Address to Majlis Al-Shura." September 25, 2011. http://www.saudiembassy.net/announcement/announcement09251101.aspx.

OTHER HISTORIC DOCUMENTS OF INTEREST

October

Senate Passes Currency Misalignment Act

OCTOBER 11, 2011

The complicated relationship between the United States and China hit another speed bump in October 2011 when the U.S. Senate voted to give the Treasury new powers to deal with nations suspected of manipulating or devaluing their currencies. Although the bill did not make specific mention of China, floor debate made clear that it was aimed at the Asian nation, which is estimated to devalue its currency between 15 and 40 percent. The House refused to take up the bill, and President Barack Obama made lukewarm comments on the measure, but even without becoming law, the Currency Exchange Rate Oversight Reform Act of 2011 incensed Chinese leaders.

Hu Jintao Visits Washington

During the first year of his presidency, Barack Obama visited Beijing seeking closer ties with the Chinese government. In 2011, with the relationship still on rocky footing, China's president, Hu Jintao, came to Washington. Prior to Hu's arrival, the Obama administration was out in force, calling for closer ties with China and indicating that the United States would be taking a tougher stance on the actions of the Asian nation. In Beijing, then-Secretary of Defense Robert Gates told reporters that China's military buildup in the Pacific would lead the United States to expand its investments in weapons, fighter jets, and other military technology. Secretary of State Hillary Rodham Clinton criticized the Asian state's human rights record, while Treasury Secretary Timothy Geithner encouraged the Chinese government to allow its currency to appreciate in value, while also calling on the nation to open its domestic market to the United States. If it did so, Geithner said, the United States would give China greater access to high-tech products and expand trade opportunities.

Each nation approached the 2011 talks with different issues at the top of its agenda. President Obama was hoping to make progress on revaluing Chinese currency, have a serious discussion on Chinese and U.S. militaries and military interventions, and create a more level playing field for American investors in China. On the other hand, Hu wanted to focus on American arms sales to Taiwan, the United States's continued support of the Dalai Lama, fear that the United States was seeking to suppress China's rise, and continuing U.S. debt, of which China owns a large portion, and has been highly critical of, especially since the U.S. credit downgrade.

During his meetings with Hu, President Obama appeared to take a harder line on China after earlier criticism that he was too soft on the country. In late 2010, during the Group of 20 meeting in Seoul, the U.S. sought action on China's currency devaluation, but China convinced Europe to reject principle pieces of the U.S. strategy. Some nations at the meeting even accused the Federal Reserve of devaluing the U.S. dollar to avoid putting tough spending measures in place. Seeking to reverse this image, during public sessions, Obama pressed Hu on currency, pirating software and intellectual property, the Chinese government's refusal to speak to the Dalai Lama, and China's human rights record. On the latter point, Hu admitted that "a lot still needs to be done in China in terms of human rights." His comments came just one month after the Chinese government was highly critical of the awarding of the Nobel Peace Prize to Chinese dissident Liu Xiaobo.

The two nations also addressed the ongoing tension on the Korean peninsula. The United States, an ally of South Korea, had been working to press North Korea to scale back its nuclear program without any success. Hu, an ally of North Korea, admitted that he was concerned about North Korea's uranium-enrichment plans.

CURRENCY DEVALUATION

The United States has long accused China of manipulating its currency to make U.S. goods in China more expensive and Chinese exports to the United States cheaper. This devaluation is thought to hurt American manufacturers and kill American jobs. Economists believe the Chinese currency is undervalued somewhere between 15 and 40 percent. According to the Peter G. Peterson Institute for International Economics, a non-partisan organization devoted to studying international economic policy, China devalues its currency by pumping $1 billion to $2 billion in government funds per day into the Chinese economy. "What they are doing is the definition of currency manipulation," said Alan Greenspan, former Federal Reserve Board chair, in June 2011.

According to the *Wall Street Journal*, the impact of this devaluation is significant. A September 2011 article reported that an economic study of every U.S. county found that those where manufacturers are more exposed to China lose more manufacturing jobs; experience a rise in unemployment; and have a greater number of workers receiving food stamps, unemployment insurance, and disability payments. Consequently, the newspaper reported, there is an overall indication that any benefit from Chinese trade is wiped out. If China allowed a 20 percent appreciation in its currency, it could create up to 500,000 American jobs and reduce the trade deficit by up to $120 billion, according to the Peterson Institute. During a Congressional Joint Economic Committee hearing in June, Mark Zandi, chief economist of Moody's Analytics, said, "Nothing is more important from a macroeconomic perspective for manufacturing, than to get these currencies better aligned. They are not aligned and that's a significant competitive disadvantage for all manufacturers, [and] increasingly other businesses as well."

China has consistently denied that it purposefully devalues its currency and that the exchange rate between the two nations has any impact on the trade deficit. According to China, if the United States wanted to improve the trade deficit that exists between the two nations, it should lift the ban on high-tech sales to China. China, however, has taken some steps in response to U.S. criticism. In 2010, it implemented policies to allow more flexibility in its exchange rate, but since then the yuan, or renminbi, has only risen a few percentage points. In 2011, following the change, one U.S. dollar could buy 6.4 yuan. In June 2008, $1 could buy 6.8 yuan. Since 2005, the Chinese yuan has appreciated against the dollar by 20 percent. There is some indication that the yuan is growing closer to its proper market value because the trade surplus has been declining in China since 2007.

Senate Currency Misalignment Act

For the past six years, the Senate has been floating versions of bills that would allow the U.S. Treasury to take action against nations that devalue their currencies. In October 2011, a bill with bipartisan support finally made it to a vote on the Senate floor. The bill, which made no specific mention of China, had two major parts. The first would require the Treasury to determine that another nation's currency is misaligned, and then give that nation's government ninety days to make changes before additional tariffs are imposed on imports. Currently, the Treasury has to declare that a nation is willfully manipulating its currency before action can be taken, something it has been unlikely to do. The second part of the bill makes the process for industry petitions to the Commerce Department easier for those that believe they are being impacted by another country's currency manipulation. A similar provision passed the House in September 2010 by a vote of 348 to 79, but the Senate failed to vote on the bill before the end of its session.

Sens. Charles Schumer, D-N.Y., and Lindsey Graham, R-S.C., reached across the aisle to support the currency bill in the Senate, where debate revolved around China. "They get away with economic murder and thus far our country has just said, 'Oh, we don't care,'" said Schumer. "This legislation will send a huge shot across China's bow." According to Schumer, millions of U.S. jobs have been lost because of Chinese currency devaluation, and it is also the primary reason why the nation's trade deficit with China reached a record $273 billion in 2010.

Opposition to the bill was wide ranging, coming from multinational companies based in the United States and their related trade organizations, the Obama administration, the U.S. Chamber of Commerce, the Business Roundtable, and the Club for Growth, a conservative anti-tax group. Neither Obama nor anyone in his administration made a public statement in opposition to the Senate bill, but they did make it clear that they prefer other diplomatic efforts to influence Chinese policies, fearing that forcing the Treasury to act could create a trade war and might have additional impact on other administration goals in China like those related to intellectual property rights or cooperation on North Korea. "[W]hatever tools we put in place, let's make sure that these are tools that can actually work, that they're consistent with our international treaties and obligations," said Obama. The Chamber of Commerce, Business Roundtable, and Club for Growth reflected the White House sentiment, expressing concern that passage of the bill would lead to Chinese action against U.S. exports. Fifty groups submitted a letter to Senate leaders expressing additional concern that the action might violate World Trade Organization (WTO) rules and would have no impact on domestic jobs. If Chinese goods became more expensive in the United States, the letter stated, another country would be prepared to step in and manufacture cheaper products to make up the gap.

Senate Votes

On October 6, the Senate held a procedural vote that would advance the legislation and allow it to come up for a final vote. Sen. Mitch McConnell, R-Ky., tried to hold up the procedural vote because Sen. Harry Reid, D-Nev., was using a tactic to stop Republicans from attaching unrelated amendments to the bill. One of the amendments would have forced a vote on Obama's jobs bill, which would almost certainly have failed. It was Graham who stepped forward to secure the final Republican votes to advance the bill. "Enough is enough," Graham said. "I am sorry the amendment process around this place is so screwed up . . . I try to be a team player where I can be, because I believe Senator McConnell is doing a very good job, Senator Reid has got his agenda [but] it is not about Harry Reid or Mitch McConnell. It is about people in my state who will lose their job if we don't do something." Graham continued, "The institution I need to be protecting is the American workforce, who is having their clock cleaned by a communist dictatorship who cheats." The procedural vote passed 62 to 38.

When the currency misalignment bill came to a vote on the Senate floor, it passed 63 to 35, and marked the first time ever that the Senate passed a bill that would allow for currency sanctions against nations like China. The bill went to the House, where Speaker John Boehner, R-Ohio, refused to bring the bill to a vote on the floor. Admitting that he shared concern about the Chinese currency situation, Boehner said, "It's pretty dangerous to be moving legislation through the U.S. Congress forcing someone to deal with the value of their currency." He continued, "This is well beyond, I think, what the Congress ought to be doing." Members of the House supporting the bill circulated a petition to bring it to a vote, and claimed that they had the support to pass it. According to Rep. Sander Levin, D-Mich., the lead sponsor of the bill in the House, Republican leaders "don't want this bill on the floor for one reason: it would pass." The House version of the bill had 225 sponsors, of which 61 were Republican.

Regardless of whether the House took up the bill, supporters of the measure said it sent a message to China even if it was never signed into law. China was not shy about expressing its dissatisfaction with the bill, claiming that it violated the rules of the WTO. While not indicating any specific steps it would take if the bill became law, Vice Foreign Minister Cui Tiankai said, "Should the proposed legislation be made into law, the result would be a trade war and that would be a lose-lose situation for both sides." He continued, "It would be detrimental to the development of economic ties and might have an adverse impact on bilateral relations."

—Heather Kerrigan

Following is the edited text of the Currency Exchange Rate Oversight Reform Act of 2011, engrossed in the Senate on October 11, 2011.

Currency Exchange Rate Oversight Reform Act

October 11, 2011

S. 1619

AN ACT

To provide for identification of misaligned currency, require action to correct the misalignment, and for other purposes. Be it enacted by the Senate and House of Representatives of the United States of America in Congress assembled,

Section 1. Short Title.

This Act may be cited as the "Currency Exchange Rate Oversight Reform Act of 2011". . . .

[Section 2, containing definitions, has been omitted.]

Sec. 3. Report on International Monetary Policy and Currency Exchange Rates.

(a) REPORTS REQUIRED.—

(1) IN GENERAL.—Not later than March 15 and September 15 of each calendar year, the Secretary, after consulting with the Chairman of the Board of Governors of the Federal Reserve System and the Advisory Committee on International Exchange Rate Policy, shall submit to Congress and make public, a written report on international monetary policy and currency exchange rates.

(2) CONSULTATIONS.—On or before March 30 and September 30 of each calendar year, the Secretary shall appear, if requested, before the Committee on Banking, Housing, and Urban Affairs and the Committee on Finance of the Senate and the Committee on Financial Services and the Committee on Ways and Means of the House of Representatives to provide testimony on the reports submitted pursuant to paragraph (1).

(b) CONTENT OF REPORTS.—Each report submitted under subsection (a) shall contain the following:

(1) An analysis of currency market developments and the relationship between the United States dollar and the currencies of major economies and trading partners of the United States.

(2) A review of the economic and monetary policies of major economies and trading partners of the United States, and an evaluation of how such policies impact currency exchange rates.

(3) A description of any currency intervention by the United States or other major economies or trading partners of the United States, or other actions undertaken to adjust the actual exchange rate relative to the United States dollar.

(4) An evaluation of the domestic and global factors that underlie the conditions in the currency markets, including—

(A) monetary and financial conditions;
(B) accumulation of foreign assets;
(C) macroeconomic trends;
(D) trends in current and financial account balances;
(E) the size, composition, and growth of international capital flows;
(F) the impact of the external sector on economic growth;
(G) the size and growth of external indebtedness;
(H) trends in the net level of international investment; and
(I) capital controls, trade, and exchange restrictions.

(5) A list of currencies designated as fundamentally misaligned currencies pursuant to section 4(a)(2), and a description of any economic models or methodologies used to establish the list.

(6) A list of currencies designated for priority action pursuant to section 4(a)(3).

(7) An identification of the nominal value associated with the medium-term equilibrium exchange rate, relative to the United States dollar, for each currency listed under paragraph (6).

(8) A description of any consultations conducted or other steps taken pursuant to section 5, 6, or 7, including any actions taken to eliminate the fundamental misalignment.

(9) A description of any determination made pursuant to section 9(a).

(c) CONSULATIONS.—The Secretary shall consult with the Chairman of the Board of Governors of the Federal Reserve System and the Advisory Committee on International Exchange Rate Policy with respect to the preparation of each report required under subsection (a). Any comments provided by the Chairman of the Board of Governors of the Federal Reserve System or the Advisory Committee on International Exchange Rate Policy shall be submitted to the Secretary not later than the date that is 15 days before the date each report is due under subsection (a). The Secretary shall submit the report to Congress after taking into account all comments received from the Chairman and the Advisory Committee.

Sec. 4. Identification of Fundamentally Misaligned Currencies.

(a) IDENTIFICATION.—

(1) IN GENERAL.—The Secretary shall analyze on a semiannual basis the prevailing real effective exchange rates of foreign currencies.

(2) DESIGNATION OF FUNDAMENTALLY MISALIGNED CURRENCIES.— With respect to the currencies of countries that have significant bilateral trade flows with the United States, and currencies that are otherwise significant to the operation, stability, or orderly development of regional or global capital markets, the Secretary shall determine whether any such currency is in fundamental misalignment and shall designate such currency as a fundamentally misaligned currency.

(3) DESIGNATION OF CURRENCIES FOR PRIORITY ACTION.—The Secretary shall designate a currency identified under paragraph (2) for priority action if the country that issues such currency is—

(A) engaging in protracted large-scale intervention in the currency exchange market, particularly if accompanied by partial or full sterilization;

(B) engaging in excessive and prolonged official or quasi-official accumulation of foreign exchange reserves and other foreign assets, for balance of payments purposes;

(C) introducing or substantially modifying for balance of payments purposes a restriction on, or incentive for, the inflow or outflow of capital, that is inconsistent with the goal of achieving full currency convertibility; or

(D) pursuing any other policy or action that, in the view of the Secretary, warrants designation for priority action.

(b) REPORTS.—The Secretary shall include a list of any foreign currency designated under paragraph (2) or (3) of subsection (a) and the data and reasoning underlying such designations in each report required by section 3.

Sec. 5. Negotiations and Consultations.

(a) IN GENERAL.—Upon designation of a currency pursuant to section 4(a)(2), the Secretary shall seek to consult bilaterally with the country that issues such currency in order to facilitate the adoption of appropriate policies to address the fundamental misalignment.

(b) CONSULTATIONS INVOLVING CURRENCEIS DESIGNATED FOR PRIORITY Action.—With respect to each currency designated for priority action pursuant to section 4(a)(3), the Secretary shall, in addition to seeking to consult with a country pursuant to subsection (a)—

(1) seek the advice of the International Monetary Fund with respect to the Secretary's findings in the report submitted to Congress pursuant to section 3(a); and

(2) encourage other governments, whether bilaterally or in appropriate multinational fora, to join the United States in seeking the adoption of appropriate policies by the country described in subsection (a) to eliminate the fundamental misalignment.

Sec. 6. Failure to Adopt Appropriate Policies.

(a) IN GENERAL.—Not later than 90 days after the date on which a currency is designated for priority action pursuant to section 4(a)(3), the Secretary shall determine whether the country that issues such currency has adopted appropriate policies, and taken identifiable action, to eliminate the fundamental misalignment. The Secretary shall promptly notify Congress of such determination and publish notice of the determination in the Federal Register. If the Secretary determines that the country that issues such currency has failed to adopt appropriate policies, or take identifiable action, to eliminate the fundamental misalignment, the following shall apply with respect to the country until a notification described in section 7(b) is published in the Federal Register:

(1) ADJUSTMENT UNDER ANTIDUMPING LAW.—For purposes of an antidumping investigation under subtitle B of title VII of the Tariff Act of 1930 (19 U.S.C. 1673 et seq.), or a review under subtitle C of such Act (19 U.S.C. 1675 et seq.), the following shall apply:

(A) IN GENERAL.—The administering authority shall ensure a fair comparison between the export price and the normal value by adjusting the price used to establish export price or constructed export price to reflect the fundamental misalignment of the currency of the exporting country.

(B) SALES SUBJECT TO ADJUSTMENT.—The adjustment described in subparagraph (A) shall apply with respect to subject merchandise sold on or after the date that is 30 days after the date the currency of the exporting country is designated for priority action pursuant to section 4(a)(3).

(2) FEDERAL PROCUREMENT.—

    (A) IN GENERAL.—The President shall prohibit the procurement by the Federal Government of products or services from the country.

    (B) EXCEPTION.—The prohibition provided for in subparagraph (A) shall not apply with respect to a country that is a party to the Agreement on Government Procurement.

(3) REQUEST FOR IMF ACTION.—The United States shall inform the Managing Director of the International Monetary Fund of the failure of the country to adopt appropriate policies, or to take identifiable action, to eliminate the fundamental misalignment, and the actions the country is engaging in that are identified in section 4(a)(3), and shall request that the Managing Director of the International Monetary Fund—

    (A) consult with such country regarding the observance of the country's obligations under article IV of the International Monetary Fund Articles of Agreement, including through special consultations, if necessary; and

    (B) formally report the results of such consultations to the Executive Board of the International Monetary Fund within 180 days of the date of such request.

(4) OPIC FINANCING.—The Overseas Private Investment Corporation shall not approve any new financing (including insurance, reinsurance, or guarantee) with respect to a project located within the country.

(5) MULTILATERAL BANK FINANCING.—(A) IN GENERAL.—The Secretary shall instruct the United States Executive Director at each multilateral bank to oppose the approval of any new financing (including loans, other credits, insurance, reinsurance, or guarantee) to the government of the country or for a project located within the country.

    (B) MULTILATERAL BANK.—The term "multilateral Bank" includes each of the international financial institutions described in section 1701(c)(2) of the International Financial Institutions Act (22 U.S.C. 262r).

(b) WAIVER.—(1) IN GENERAL.—The President may waive any action provided for under subsection (a) if the President determines that—

    (A) taking such action would cause serious harm to the national security of the United States; or

    (B) it is in the vital economic interest of the United States to do so and taking such action would have an adverse impact on the United States economy greater than the benefits of such action.

(2) NOTIFICATION.—The President shall promptly notify Congress of a determination under paragraph (1) (and the reasons for the determination, if made under paragraph (1)(B)) and shall publish notice of the determination (and the reasons or the determination, if made under paragraph (1)(B)) in the Federal Register.

(c) REPORTS.—The Secretary shall describe any action or determination pursuant to subsection (a) or (b) in the first semiannual report required by section 3 after the date of such action or determination.

Sec. 7. Persistent Failure to Adopt Appropriate Policies.

(a) PERSISTENT FAILURE TO ADOPT APPROPRIATE POLICIES.—Not later than 360 days after the date on which a currency is designated for priority action pursuant to section 4(a)(3), the Secretary shall determine whether the country that issues such currency has adopted appropriate policies, and taken identifiable action, to eliminate the fundamental misalignment. The Secretary shall promptly notify Congress of such determination and shall publish notice of the determination in the Federal Register. If the Secretary determines that the country that issues such currency has failed to adopt appropriate policies, or take identifiable action, to eliminate the fundamental misalignment, in addition to the actions described in section 6(a), the following shall apply with respect to the country until a notification described in subsection (b) is published in the Federal Register:

    (1) ACTION AT THE WTO.—The United States Trade Representative shall request consultations in the World Trade Organization with the country regarding the consistency of the country's actions with its obligations under the WTO Agreement.(2) REMEDIAL INTERVENTION.—

        (A) IN GENERAL.—The Secretary shall consult with the Board of Governors of the Federal Reserve System to consider undertaking remedial intervention in international currency markets in response to the fundamental misalignment of the currency designated for priority action, and coordinating such intervention with other monetary authorities and the International Monetary Fund. In doing so, the Secretary shall consider the impact of such intervention on domestic economic growth and stability, including the impact on interest rates.

        (B) NOTICE TO COUNTRY.—At the same time the Secretary takes action under subparagraph (A), the Secretary shall notify the country that issues such currency of the consultations under subparagraph (A).

(b) NOTIFICATION.—The Secretary shall promptly notify Congress when a country that issues a currency designated for priority action pursuant to section 4(a)(3) adopts appropriate policies, or takes identifiable action, to eliminate the fundamental misalignment, and publish notice of the action of that country in the Federal Register.

(c) Waiver.—(1) IN GENERAL.—The President may waive any action provided for under this section, or extend any waiver provided for under section 6(b), if the President determines that—

        (A) taking such action would cause serious harm to the national security of the United States; or

        (B) it is in the vital economic interest of the United States to do so, and that taking such action would have an adverse impact on the United States economy substantially out of proportion to the benefits of such action.

    (2) NOTIFICATION.—The President shall promptly notify Congress of a determination under paragraph (1) (and the reasons for the determination, if made under paragraph (1)(B)) and shall publish notice of the determination (and the reasons for the determination, if made under paragraph (1)(B)) in the Federal Register.

(d) DISAPPROVAL OF WAIVER.—If the President waives an action pursuant to subsection (c)(1)(B), or extends a waiver provided for under section 6(b)(1)(B), the waiver shall cease to have effect upon the enactment of a resolution of disapproval described in section 8(a)(2).

(e) REPORTS.—The Secretary shall describe any action or determination pursuant to subsection (a), (b), or (c) in the first semiannual report required by section 3 after the date of such action or determination.

Sec. 8. Congressional Disapproval of Waiver.

(a) RESOLUTION OF DISAPPROVAL.—

(1) INTRODUCTION.—If a resolution of disapproval is introduced in the House of Representatives or the Senate during the 90-day period (not counting any day which is excluded under section 154(b)(1) of the Trade Act of 1974 (19 U.S.C. 2194(b)(1))), beginning on the date on which the President first notifies Congress of a determination to waive action with espect to a country pursuant to section 7(c)(1)(B), that resolution of disapproval shall be considered in accordance with this subsection.

(2) RESOLUTION OF DISAPPROVAL.—In this subsection, the term "resolution of disapproval'" means only a joint resolution of the two Houses of the Congress, the sole matter after the resolving clause of which is as follows: "That Congress does not approve the determination of the President under _____ of the Currency Exchange Rate Oversight Reform Act of 2011 with respect to _____, of which Congress was notified on _____.", with the first blank space being filled section 7(c)(1)(B) or section 6(b)(1)(B), whichever is applicable, the second blank space being filled with the name of the appropriate country, and the third blank space being filled with the appropriate date.

(3) PROCEDURES FOR CONSIDERING RESOLUTIONS.—

(A) INTRODUCTION AND REFERRAL.—Resolutions of disapproval—

(i) in the House of Representatives—

(I) may be introduced by any Member of the House;

(II) shall be referred to the Committee on Financial Services and, in addition, to the Committee on Rules; and

(III) may not be amended by either Committee; and

(ii) in the Senate—

(I) may be introduced by any Member of the Senate;

(II) shall be referred to the Committee on Banking, Housing, and Urban Affairs; and

(III) may not be amended.

(B) COMMITTEE DISCHARGE AND FLOOR CONSIDERATION.—The provisions of subsections (c) through (f) of section 152 of the Trade Act of 1974 (other than paragraph (3) of such subsection (f)) (19 U.S.C. 2192)

(c) through (f)) (relating to committee discharge and floor consideration of certain resolutions in the House and Senate) apply to a resolution of disapproval under this section to the same extent as such subsections apply to joint resolutions under such section 152. . . .

[Sections 9–13, containing information on international financial institution governance arrangements, the adjustment for fundamentally misaligned currency designated for priority action, currency undervaluation under countervailing duty law, nonmarket economy status, and the application of the law to Canada and Mexico, have been omitted.]

SEC. 14. ADVISORY COMMITTEE ON INTERNATIONAL EXCHANGE RATE POLICY.

(a)   ESTABLISHMENT.—

   (1)   IN GENERAL.—There is established an Advisory Committee on International Exchange Rate Policy (in this section referred to as the "Committee"). The Committee shall be responsible for—

      (A)   advising the Secretary in the preparation of each report to Congress on international monetary policy and currency exchange rates, provided for in section 3; and

      (B)   advising Congress and the President with respect to—

         (i)   international exchange rates and financial policies; and

         (ii)   the impact of such policies on the economy of the United States. . . .

[Terms of membership on the committee have been omitted.]

   (b)   DURATION OF COMMITTEE.—Notwithstanding section 14(c) of the Federal Advisory Committee Act (5 U.S.C. App.), the Committee shall terminate on the date that is 4 years after the date of the enactment of this Act unless renewed by the President pursuant to section 14 of the Federal Advisory Committee Act (5 U.S.C. App.) for a subsequent 4-year period. The President may continue to renew the Committee for successive 4-year periods by taking appropriate action prior to the date on which the Committee would otherwise terminate.

   (c)   PUBLIC MEETINGS.—The Committee shall hold at least 2 public meetings each year for the purpose of accepting public comments, including comments from small business owners. The Committee shall also meet as needed at the call of the Secretary or at the call of two-thirds of the members of the Committee.

   (d)   CHAIRPERSON.—The Committee shall elect from among its members . . .

   (e)   STAFF.—The Secretary shall make available to the Committee such staff, information, personnel, administrative services, and assistance as the Committee may reasonably require to carry out its activities. . . .

[Section 15, repealing the Exchange Rates and Economic Policy Coordination Act of 1988, has been omitted.]

Passed the Senate October 11, 2011.

SOURCE: U.S. Senate. "Currency Exchange Rate Oversight Reform Act of 2011." *Congressional Bills*, 112th Congress (2011–2012), S. 1619. http://www.gpo.gov/fdsys/pkg/BILLS-112s1619es/pdf/BILLS-112s1619es.pdf.

OTHER HISTORIC DOCUMENTS OF INTEREST

Congress Passes Colombia, Panama, and South Korea Trade Agreements

OCTOBER 11 AND 12, 2011

Negotiations that spanned two presidencies came to a quick conclusion in mid-October, when both houses of Congress passed free trade agreements with Colombia, Panama, and South Korea. The agreements were originally negotiated under former President George W. Bush, and after critical changes were made under President Barack Obama, they passed less than two weeks after being sent to Congress.

Economists believed that the agreements would benefit all four nations by creating a larger market for goods and services, increasing sales, and reducing prices by eliminating tariffs. The House Ways and Means Committee said the agreements would create 250,000 new jobs without increasing government spending and increase exports by at least $13 billion per year. Small and medium-sized businesses, which in 2008 accounted for 80 percent of all U.S. exports to Colombia, Panama, and South Korea, were expected to see the greatest benefit.

Despite the benefits touted by economists and supporters in Washington, there was still some concern that Panama, Colombia, and South Korea would experience far greater benefit than the United States. In 2007, the U.S. International Trade Commission said the three agreements would have little economic impact because the three countries presented a small market for American goods and services. And according to Lori Wallach, director of Public Citizen's Global Trade Watch, jobs were another concern. "It is true that our exports will increase. The problem is our imports from Korea are going to increase a lot more," said Wallach. "If you subtract the jobs that will be wiped out by imports from the jobs that will be created by exports, you come up with a deficit."

SUPPORT AND OPPOSITION

When he submitted the Colombia, Panama, and South Korea free trade agreements to Congress, President Barack Obama made clear his belief that they would create jobs and help boost the economy, and would be critical in reaching his goal of doubling exports by 2015. "The series of trade agreements I am submitting to Congress today will make it easier for American companies to sell their products in South Korea, Colombia, and Panama and provide a major boost to our exports," the president said. "These agreements will support tens of thousands of jobs across the country for workers making products stamped with three proud words: Made in America."

Democrats in Congress were not quick to support the agreements, arguing that they would likely mimic the results of the North American Free Trade Agreement

(NAFTA), which some claimed never delivered on its economic promises. The most vocal Democratic opposition came from Rep. Mike Michaud, D-Maine, leader of the House Trade Working Group, a coalition of mostly Democrats who are skeptical of free trade agreements. Of the trio of agreements before the House and Senate in 2011, Michaud said, "What I am seeing firsthand is devastation that these free trade agreements can do to our communities." Gaining Democratic support hinged on reworking the agreements to increase protection for unions and other industry groups.

For Republicans, the benefits of the trade agreements were clear. Speaker of the House John Boehner, R-Ohio, said, "American job creators will have new opportunities to expand and hire as they access new markets abroad." And according to House Majority Leader Eric Cantor, R-Va., the agreements were a "no-cost jobs plan." Support from Republicans in the Senate was equally strong. "At long last, we are going to do something important for the country on a bipartisan basis," said Senate Minority Leader Mitch McConnell, R-Ky.

All three agreements were set to be made with quickly growing economies—Colombia's gross domestic product (GDP) rose 5.2 percent from January to June 2011 and South Korea's increased 3.4 percent. Supporters said that by targeting these growing markets, prices for American consumers would be reduced at home, and foreign sales of American goods and services would increase, both factors that could benefit the still struggling U.S. economy. And with 95 percent of the world's consumers living outside of the United States, failure to continue competing in growing markets would put the United States behind. "If we do not seize the opportunity to lead, others will, and the accompanying economic benefits will accrue to their nations rather than ours," said Jim McNerney, chief executive of Boeing and a member of the President's Council on Jobs and Competitiveness.

The response from U.S. trade unions was mixed. Some, like the American Federation of Labor and Congress of Industrial Organizations (AFL-CIO), feared that the free trade agreements would result in a loss of jobs. AFL-CIO President Richard Trumka claimed that by passing the three agreements, 159,000 American jobs would be lost. "These flawed trade deals are the wrong medicine at the wrong time," Trumka said. "Working people know what too many politicians apparently do not: These deals will be bad for jobs, workers' rights and our economy," he added. The United Steelworkers Union, made up primarily of auto-parts workers, echoed these remarks. "With 9.1% unemployment and 13000 manufacturing jobs lost last month, this is not the time for a big new trade deal," said Linda Andros, legislative counsel for the union. The United Auto Workers (UAW), however, supported passage of the agreements, but only after auto tariffs and additional protections for autoworkers were added.

Panama

The free trade agreement (FTA) with Panama, one of the fastest-growing economies in Latin America, passed the House 300 to 129 and the Senate 77 to 22 on October 12. Michaud led the opposition, stating, "Panama simply isn't a significant market opportunity for U.S. exports, and this FTA won't do anything to reduce our 9 percent unemployment."

Before passage of the agreement with Panama, U.S. industrial goods imported into the country faced an average tariff of 7 percent, with some as high as 81 percent. Agricultural goods saw an average 15 percent tariff, which on some products went up to

260 percent. Once the agreement received the president's signature, 87 percent of consumer and industrial products became duty free immediately. The remaining import tariffs will be phased out over the next ten years.

The agreement will allow the United States to maintain its market share in Panama, an increasingly important goal after Canada signed a free trade agreement with Panama in 2010, which is not yet in force. U.S. goods compete with Canadian goods in Panama, specifically in the areas of pork and frozen French fries. The European Union signed a free trade agreement with Panama in March 2011, and although not yet in force, the United States and European Union compete in the Latin American nation on machinery, transportation equipment, chemicals, and metals.

The agreement also presents a significant infrastructure opportunity for the United States. Panama is currently boosting its infrastructure spending, including the $5.25 billion Panama Canal expansion project and $10 billion in other infrastructure projects, and the United States expects to benefit from demand for construction equipment. According to Bill Lane, the Washington director for heavy equipment manufacturer Caterpillar, "Once these agreements go in effect, Caterpillar products produced in Illinois and Mississippi and the Carolinas will be able to be exported . . . duty-free." Lane said the ability to work on these infrastructure projects would increase job security for Caterpillar at home. "That's a big deal," he said.

SOUTH KOREA

The South Korean free trade agreement, the largest trade deal for the United States since NAFTA in 1994, easily passed both houses of Congress 278 to 151 and 83 to 15. To gain support for passage, the Obama administration worked with Congress to amend the deal put together by former President George W. Bush to include new terms on auto tariffs—South Korea will lower its import tariffs faster than the United States lowers them for Korean car imports. Additionally, the Obama version of the agreement meant South Korea would agree to allow imports of cars from the United States that do not meet its environmental and safety standards. The new auto tariffs and additional protections for American automakers were instrumental in helping to gain the support of some Midwestern Democrats and the UAW. "We have to be able to compete, and our auto industry can now compete," said House Ways and Means Ranking Member Sander Levin, D-Mich.

An agreement with South Korea, the world's fifteenth-largest economy and seventh-largest U.S. trading partner, was expected to result in a number of economic benefits for both countries. Shortly after Obama signed the trade agreement, South Korean President Lee Myung-bak visited Washington and called it a "win-win agreement" that "will create more jobs, generate more trade, and stimulate our economies." The biggest beneficiaries of the South Korea agreement are expected to be machinery and equipment manufacturers, pork and beef producers, and chemical and plastic product makers.

Under the agreement, the United States expects to increase exports of goods by $10 billion to $11 billion and create more than 70,000 jobs. Exports of machinery and equipment will increase by more than one-third, and once the agreement is fully implemented, agriculture exports are anticipated to increase by up to $3.8 billion, mostly through exports of major grain, oilseed, fiber, fruits, vegetables, and livestock products. Motor vehicle exports are expected to increase 54 percent, or $194 million, for the United States, while South Korea will benefit from $907 million in additional exports to the United States.

Colombia

The U.S.-Colombia Trade Promotion Agreement was the most controversial of the three, mainly because of Colombia's treatment of labor unions and their members. "Colombia remains the most dangerous place in the world to be a trade unionist," said Sen. Sherrod Brown, D-Ohio. In the past decade, 1,700 union members have been killed in Colombia, representing 63 percent of the global total, according to the country's National Union School, a labor-rights organization. To ensure passage, the Obama administration amended the original Bush trade agreement proposal to include a stipulation that Colombia must follow through on the Colombian Action Plan Related to Labor Rights, agreed to in April 2011. Prior to the free trade agreement, Colombia had already passed legislation to criminalize interference with labor rights, secured legislation to form a labor ministry, imposed severe fines for employment and relationships that undermine worker rights, expanded protection programs for union members, and began reforming procedures to prosecute union homicides. However, disagreement remains over whether additional labor-rights agreements negotiated by the Obama administration will actually be enforceable, because they were not written into the bill. "[W]e believe in workers' rights and we believe in human rights . . . But when we write a trade agreement for Colombia, we're unwilling to write in the demands for the Colombian workers, that's what's wrong with this and that's why most of us will vote against it," said Rep. Jim McDermott, D-Wash.

Even without the support of those pushing for stronger labor union rights, the agreement with the third-largest economy in Central and South America passed the House 262 to 167 and the Senate 66 to 33. With the president's signature, more than 80 percent of consumer and industrial products will become duty free immediately, with the remaining tariffs phased out over the next decade.

The agreement is expected to expand exports by more than $1.1 billion, thus increasing U.S. GDP by $2.5 billion. Small to medium-sized businesses will experience the greatest impact. These businesses made up nearly 35 percent of all U.S. merchandise exports to Colombia in 2009. The agreement has been touted for its significance in maintaining U.S. market share in Colombia, which already had trade agreements with Canada, Brazil, Argentina, Paraguay, and Uruguay; one with the European Union was expected to follow.

Trade Adjustment Assistance Renewal

The Democratic support that the president did garner for the three trade agreements was based largely on renewal of the Trade Adjustment Assistance program, which offers benefits to American workers who lose their jobs because of overseas competition. The renewal passed the House 307 to 122 with heavy Democratic support, and passed the Senate 70 to 27. The renewal expanded the benefits programs for workers whose jobs are displaced by foreign competition, and included $1.2 billion in spending over the next five years for health insurance, unemployment compensation, and other benefits for these workers.

—Heather Kerrigan

Following is a floor statement by Representative Henry Cuellar, D-Texas, on October 11, 2011, in support of the free trade agreements; a floor statement delivered on October 12, 2011, by Representative Mike Michaud, D-Maine, in opposition to the Panama, Colombia, and South Korea free trade agreements; and a statement released on October 12, 2011, by U.S. Trade Representative Ron Kirk on the passage and signing of the three free trade agreements.

Rep. Cuellar in Support of the Free Trade Agreements

October 11, 2011

Mr. CUELLAR. By leveling the playing field with 21st century trade deals with Panama, Colombia, and South Korea, we will increase American exports abroad and spur domestic job creation. Now, more than ever, the U.S. needs trade to fuel growth, create jobs, and preserve America's position as a leader of the greater economy.

I represent a border region of Texas where trade is part of daily life. I understand the importance of trade to my hometown's value in supporting the local economy. As the chairman of the Pro-Trade Caucus and representing a trade-centric district, I support all three pending trade agreements.

Today, trade supports over 50 million American jobs, according to the U.S. Department of the Treasury. These pending FTAs would create an additional quarter of a million new jobs in industries like manufacturing, agriculture, and service sectors, according to the U.S. Chamber of Commerce. Last week, The Wall Street Journal reported the FTAs could boost U.S. exports by $13 billion annually. To grow, we must be an export powerhouse.

The U.S.-Panama FTA would remove barriers to American goods entering into Panama. According to the U.S. Trade Representative, over 87 percent of U.S. exports of consumer and industrial products to Panama will become duty-free immediately, with the remaining tariffs phased out over the following 10 years.

The U.S. International Trade Commission estimates passage of the U.S.-Korea Free Trade Agreement would increase U.S. exports by over $10 billion and create 70,000 jobs. According to the National Association of Manufacturers, the U.S. exports to Korea would grow by more than one-third. The U.S.-Colombia FTA would expand exports by more than $1.1 billion with the tariff reductions, according to the International Trade Commission. Without the U.S.-Colombia FTA, the U.S. cotton exporters to Colombia will have unnecessarily paid over $14 million in tariffs.

Lawmakers have a choice. Pass the deals or allow America to lose the opportunity to emerge in the constantly growing global market. Pass the deals or miss the chance to create 250,000 jobs. Pass the deals or allow American businesses to sit on the sidelines while foreign countries forge ahead.

America must pass the Colombia, Korea, and Panama trade deals, or we will fall behind.

SOURCE: Rep. Henry Cuellar. "United States-Panama Trade Promotion Agreement Implementation Act." *Congressional Record* 2011, pt. 157, H6757. http://www.gpo.gov/fdsys/pkg/CREC-2011-10-11/pdf/CREC-2011-10-11-pt1-PgH6745.pdf.

Rep. Michaud in Opposition to the Free Trade Agreements

October 12, 2011

Mr. MICHAUD. Madam Speaker, I yield myself such time as I may consume.

I rise today as a former mill worker who punched a time clock for over 29 years at the Great Northern Paper Company in East Millinocket, Maine. What I've seen firsthand is the devastation that these free trade agreements can do to our communities.

This agreement is the most economically significant since NAFTA, and its consequences for America's middle class will be enormous. Since NAFTA, we have lost more than 5 million manufacturing jobs. We've seen more than 50,000 factories close in the last 10 years alone. The Korea FTA will bring more of the same. It will cost us more manufacturing jobs, it will shut down more factories, and it will ship more jobs overseas, all at a time of 9 percent unemployment when the American middle class can least afford it.

My colleagues have already highlighted the many reasons to oppose the Korea FTA, but I want to highlight two of those issues again. First, it does nothing to protect the U.S. in the face of Korea's currency manipulation. Second, this agreement isn't just a giveaway to Korea; it's also a giveaway to China.

Korea has a history of manipulating its currency to boost its exports. Once in 1988 and twice in 1989, the U.S. Treasury Department officially labeled Korea a currency manipulator. Even though the Treasury stopped officially identifying currency manipulators, in their February and May report of 2011 they stated explicitly, "Korea should adopt a greater degree of exchange rate flexibility and less intervention."

The International Monetary Fund agrees. In August of this year, the IMF stated that the won was undervalued by 5 to 20 percent. The fact is, Korea manipulates its currency. Our own Treasury Department recognizes it. But the FTA does nothing to protect American businesses and workers from it.

You only have to look at Mexico's 1994 devaluation of the peso to see how effectively an undervalued currency can wipe out an FTA's benefits. Our trade balance with Mexico has never been positive since.

Without a provision to protect us from the won undervaluation, Korea's exports will continue to be cheaper than our own exports. This Korean advantage will wipe out the FTA's tariff benefits for American companies and cost American workers their jobs.

Candidate Barack Obama recognized this threat, claiming that as President he would "insist that our trade deals include prohibition against illegal subsidies and currency manipulation." But this FTA includes no such prohibition at all.

And, second, this agreement is not just good for Korea; it's great for China too. Today, we're actually voting on an FTA that will be an outright boon for China's auto parts sector. The agreement's rules of origin require that only 35 percent of the car's content value come from Korea or the U.S.

We have two FTAs with car-producing countries: NAFTA and the Australia FTA. In the Australia FTA, the content requirements are 50 percent. And in the NAFTA, the content requirements are 62.5 percent. Korea's car production in 2010 was almost equal to that of Canada's and Mexico's combined; yet the Korea FTA content requirements are much lower than NAFTA's. By allowing 65 percent of a car's content value to come from a third country, we're opening the door for that 65 percent to come from—guess who—China. As a result, these rules of origin will be devastating to the American auto parts industry.

The U.S. auto supply chain is already facing challenges from China. According to the Commerce Department 2010 report titled, "On the Road," China auto parts exports to the U.S. have increased 43 percent from 2004 to 2009, and they're expected to account for an increased share of U.S. automotive parts in the future. In fact, Commerce predicts that many auto parts companies will continue to move production to China in an effort to reduce costs and remain competitive. If this FTA passes, that's not a prediction; that's a guarantee.

I've already mentioned the fact that we have lost more than 50,000 factories since 2001. Before voting today, I urge you to imagine how many more factories will close if we are to pass this agreement, and to think about the devastation that will be brought to those towns when that happens.

I oppose it because it will devastate our manufacturing sector at a time when we need to rebuild it. I oppose it because this President promised hope and change, not more of the same. I oppose it because in my home town, unemployment is more than 28 percent. I oppose it because I want to create jobs in the United States, not South Korea, and definitely not in China.

As a former mill worker from East Millinocket and on behalf of America's middle class, I urge my colleagues to oppose the Korea FTA agreement.

I would like to insert into the Record a letter from the AFL-CIO in opposition to all three free trade agreements.

American Federation of Labor and Congress of Industrial Organizations,

Washington, DC, July 7, 2011.

Dear Representative: On behalf of the AFL-CIO, I write to urge you to oppose the proposed trade agreements with Colombia, Korea and Panama. Working people, in the U.S. and around the world, are bearing the brunt of decades of flawed trade policy. We need Congress and the White House to focus on creating the millions of good jobs at home that we so desperately need—not passing more flawed trade deals. These trade agreements, negotiated by the Bush Administration, incorporate too many of the disastrous policies of the past, rather than laying out a new and progressive vision for the future.

Instead of using valuable time and effort advancing these flawed agreements, Congress should instead focus on effective job creation measures, including currency rebalancing and enforcing existing trade laws. We need to invest in a modern, functional infrastructure; in a high-tech, high-skilled workforce; and in clean renewable energy. It is time to update our trade model for the 21st century so that it strengthens labor rights protections for all workers, safeguards domestic laws and regulations, and promotes the export of U.S. goods rather than jobs.

Colombia Free Trade Agreement

Violence: Colombia is the most dangerous place in the world for trade unionists. In 2010, 51 labor leaders were killed in Colombia, an increase over 2009 and more than in the rest of the world combined. So far in 2011, another 17 have been killed. The government of Colombia—despite renewed efforts—has been unable to effectively guarantee the rule of law allowing workers to exercise their legal rights without fear of violence.

Impunity: Impunity in cases of violence against trade unionists remains high, with more than 95% of cases unsolved.

No Opportunity to Exercise Fundamental Rights: As a result of this campaign of violence, as well as weak labor laws and inconsistent enforcement, only four percent of Colombian workers are unionized today, and only one percent of workers are covered by a collective bargaining agreement. Most workers lack freedom of association, the ability to engage in collective bargaining, and the right to strike effectively.

Labor Action Plan Inadequate: In April 2011, the Obama Administration negotiated a Labor Action Plan with the Colombian government to address long-standing concerns about violence, impunity, and weak and unenforced labor laws. Unfortunately, the Labor Action Plan does not go nearly far enough in addressing these issues. It fails to require sustained, meaningful, and measurable results with respect to reductions in violence and improvements in impunity prior to ratification or implementation of the agreement, and it does not address the need for broad labor law reform. In addition, the Action Plan is not enforceable under the trade agreement itself.

Need to Wait for Results: Once the agreement is in force, the United States will have lost its most important leverage to improve the human rights situation in Colombia. The Labor Action Plan will not fix Colombia's problems overnight. Congress should wait to see if it is implemented as promised, and if conditions for working families in Colombia actually improve as a result.

KOREA-US FREE TRADE AGREEMENT

Job Loss: The Korea FTA is the largest trade deal of its kind since NAFTA. If enacted, the Economic Policy Institute estimates the Korea FTA would displace 159,000 U.S. jobs—mostly in manufacturing.

Kaesong: The Korea FTA does not adequately protect against goods from the Kaesong Industrial Complex, a sweatshop zone in North Korea where workers have few rights and earn an average wage of $61 a month. Kaesong provides $20 million a year to a dangerous North Korean regime.

Weak Rules of Origin: In order to qualify for reduced tariff under the Korea FTA, automobiles need only have 35% U.S. or South Korean Content—meaning up to 65% of the content of autos traded under the deal could be from other any other country, including China.

Transshipment: South Korea has already reported an increase in transshipped goods (primarily from China) illegally and improperly labeled "made in South Korea." This illegal transshipment is likely to increase further as unscrupulous businesses try to take advantage of reduced U.S. tariff rates specified in the Korea FTA.

PANAMA FREE TRADE AGREEMENT

Investment, Financial Services, and Procurement Problems: The Panama FTA contains similar flaws as other past trade agreements, including: Investment provisions that give foreign investors the right to bypass U.S. courts while they challenge our domestic health, safety, labor, and environmental laws.

Provisions that reduce our ability to re-regulate the financial sector; prevent banks from becoming "too big to fail"; and even use taxpayer money to "buy American" and create local jobs.

Labor Rights: Panama has a history of failing to protect workers and enforce labor rights.

Tax Haven: Panama is known as a "tax haven," with a history of attracting money launderers and tax dodgers. The Tax Information Exchange Treaty that Panama recently signed does not go into effect for another year and may be too weak to fix the problems. Only time will tell if Panama will live up to its promises.

American families need a new way forward on trade, not more of the same. So long as these agreements fall short of protecting the broad interests of American workers and their counterparts around the world in these uncertain economic times, we will oppose them.

Sincerely,

William Samuel,

Director,

Government Affairs Department.

SOURCE: Representative Mike Michaud. "United States-Korea Free Trade Agreement Implementation Act." *Congressional Record* 2011, pt. 157, H6820-6822. http://www.gpo.gov/fdsys/pkg/CREC-2011-10-12/pdf/CREC-2011-10-12-pt1-PgH6812.pdf.

U.S. Trade Representative on Signing of Free Trade Agreements

October 12, 2011

United States Trade Representative Ron Kirk today released a statement following President Barack Obama's signature into law of legislation implementing the U.S.-Korea, U.S.-Colombia, and U.S.-Panama trade agreements, as well as Trade Adjustment Assistance (TAA) reforms, the Generalized System of Preferences (GSP), and the Andean Trade Preference Act.

In 2010 and 2011, the Obama Administration successfully worked with Korea, Colombia, and Panama to address outstanding issues related to each of the three agreements. In particular, the Administration secured: greater U.S. access to the Korean auto market; significantly increased labor rights and worker protections in Colombia; and enhanced tax transparency and labor rights in Panama. The Administration has been clear that once approved by Congress, agreements will enter into force only if trading partners are meeting their commitments.

"USTR has already started the work necessary to bring these agreements into force as soon as possible," said Ambassador Kirk. "We're eager for American businesses and workers to begin reaping the benefits of these hard-won agreements. We know that more exports of Made-in-America goods and services flowing to consumers in Korea, Colombia, and Panama can support tens of thousands more jobs here at home. Supporting more American jobs with responsible trade policy has always been our goal."

TAA provides training and support for American workers who are negatively affected by trade and is traditionally in place as trade agreements pass. It is designed to help workers, firms, farmers and fishermen transition to alternative employment. The legislation approved today is consistent with the goals of the 2009 law that improved the scope and effectiveness of the program—for instance, covering Americans employed in the services sector in addition to U.S. manufacturing workers. TAA is an essential component of President Obama's balanced trade agenda.

"Typically, TAA recipients are the breadwinners of American families, older, with fewer transferable skills or credentials than other laid-off workers. These TAA reforms make smart investments in American workers negatively affected by trade, including services workers," said Ambassador Kirk. "The TAA program offers not just benefits to help workers stay afloat financially, but also services to upgrade their skills and help them re-enter the workforce in viable growth industries."

GSP promotes economic growth in the developing world by providing preferential duty-free entry for products from designated beneficiary countries and territories; it also supports American jobs and improves American competitiveness since many American businesses use imports under this program as inputs to manufacture goods in the United States. The Andean Trade Preference Act was enacted in December 1991 to help Andean countries in their fight against drug production and trafficking by expanding their economic alternatives.

"America's preference programs support both international economic development and U.S. jobs," said Ambassador Kirk. "For over 35 years, the GSP program has been helping developing countries across the world use trade to grow their economies and alleviate poverty. GSP and ATPA support tens of thousands of American jobs involved in moving goods from the docks to businesses and consumers. Preference programs also improve U.S. competitiveness by reducing costs of inputs for U.S. manufacturers and helps American families on a budget by lowering prices for many consumer goods."

SOURCE: Office of the United States Trade Representative. Press Releases. "Statement by U.S. Trade Representative Ron Kirk on Presidential Signature of Trade Legislation." October 12, 2011. http://www.ustr.gov/about-us/press-office/press-releases/2011/october/statement-us-trade-representative-ron-kirk-preside.

OTHER HISTORIC DOCUMENTS OF INTEREST

FROM PREVIOUS *HISTORIC DOCUMENTS*

Israel and Palestine Remark on Prisoner Swap

OCTOBER 18, 2011

Following five years of negotiations, on October 18, 2011, Israeli soldier Gilad Shalit, who had been captured in 2006 by Palestinian forces, was reunited with his family. In return, the Israeli government agreed to release more than 1,000 Palestinian prisoners, many of them leaders in Hamas, the Palestinian militant extremist group, or responsible for terrorist acts against Israel. The swap raised questions about whether the freed terrorists would return to violence, and whether Hamas would be encouraged to capture other Israeli soldiers in an effort to gain the release of 5,000 Palestinian prisoners who remain in Israeli jails.

GILAD SHALIT CAPTURE AND EARLY NEGOTIATIONS FOR RELEASE

Israeli soldier Gilad Shalit was captured at age nineteen on June 25, 2006, by Palestinian forces that had tunneled under the Gaza-Israeli border. During the capture, two Israeli soldiers and two Palestinian militants were killed; a number of others were wounded. At the time of his capture, Shalit was a corporal and a tank gunner in the Israeli military. The military arm of Hamas claimed responsibility for the militant raid that led to Shalit's capture, and Israel demanded that Hamas immediately release the soldier. When their demand was not met, Israeli forces invaded Gaza by ground; airstrikes soon followed. Members of the Hamas political wing, including members of the Palestinian parliament, were arrested in the West Bank, but the Israeli military response had no impact on Shalit's captors. The young soldier was kept in a secret location and denied any visits from the outside, including Red Cross aid. There was no indication that Shalit was still alive until late 2009, when Hamas released a video of the prisoner holding the day's newspaper and asking for his freedom.

Following their ground and air invasion, Israel refused any other negotiations for Shalit's release. However, the nation did eventually enter talks brokered by German and Egyptian mediators. The ongoing negotiations did not end when Egyptian President Hosni Mubarak was deposed; in fact, the interim military council that took over Egypt's government improved its relationship with Hamas, a group Mubarak had been hostile toward. The deal being worked out between Israel and Palestine would involve swapping prisoners, an idea Israeli Prime Minister Benjamin Netanyahu was initially opposed to, noting that a swap would free dangerous terrorists and put Israel at risk.

In early negotiations, it became clear that Palestine would release only Shalit in return for hundreds of its own countrymen being held by Israel. Such lopsided agreements are not uncommon for Israel. In 1985, then–Prime Minister Shimon Peres signed on to the Jibril Deal, in which Israel released 1,150 prisoners in return for three Israeli soldiers captured in Lebanon by the Palestinian Militant Front. Only one cabinet member, Yitzhak Navon, voted against the 1985 deal, stating, "I thought this was a terrible example, for us to show all our enemies that for them the best deal is to kidnap soldiers and citizens. We must have the strength to tell the families of the captive soldiers—there is a line that the nation cannot cross."

Netanyahu, who at the time was serving as Israeli ambassador to the United Nations, was opposed to the Jibril Deal as well, in 1988 telling Larry King, "We wanted to get our POWs back, and the government, in my judgment, made a big mistake and traded terrorists." In his 1995 book *A Place in the Sun*, Netanyahu wrote about the deal, saying, "The release of thousands of terrorists . . . will inevitably lead to a terrible escalation of violence, because these terrorists will be accepted as heroes." According to the Almagor Terror Victims Association, a group that works for the welfare of terror victims and their families, of the 238 terrorists freed in the Jibril Deal who were sent to the West Bank, 48 percent returned to terrorism and were captured and arrested by Israel for a second time.

2011 Prisoner Swap

Even given his resistance to the earlier Jibril Deal, Netanyahu eventually gave in to a similar swap to release Shalit, realizing that he might lose the chance at ever freeing the soldier under his watch. After five years of negotiations, on October 11, 2011, Hamas and Israel announced that they had reached an agreement. Hamas would release only Shalit. In return, Israel would immediately release 477 Palestinian prisoners, with an additional 550 to be released after Shalit returned home to Israel. No time frame was given for the release of the 550, but it was thought to be about two months after Shalit was released. The initial group of 477 included those who had bombed Israeli hotels and cafes, a founder of the Hamas militant wing, a leader of an elite Hamas unit, a senior Hamas leader, and others who carried out terrorist attacks against Israelis. Notable prisoners not being released by Israel included Marwan Bargouti, a Palestinian leader who was thought to be a possible successor to Palestinian President Mahmoud Abbas; Abdullah Barghouti, a Hamas bomb maker; and Ahmed Saadat, who was jailed for his role in the assassination of an Israeli tourism minister in 2001. Of the total number of Palestinian prisoners being freed, 315 were serving life sentences.

Following the announcement of the agreement, the families of terror victims were given time to review the prisoner list and petition the Israeli Supreme Court. "As we have done in the past, we intend to give the public a period of at least 48 hours from the moment of the publication of the list of prisoners to submit reservations or opposition to this or that release," the Israeli Justice Ministry said.

The official prisoner swap was set for October 18, 2011, and prior to its start, the Israeli Supreme Court ruled against all petitions made by the families of terror victims. Netanyahu wrote to these families to defend his position. "I know the price is very heavy for you," he wrote. "I understand the difficulty to countenance that the evil people who perpetrated the appalling crimes against your loved ones will not pay the full price that they deserve. During these moments I hope that you will find solace that I and the entire nation of Israel embrace you and share your pain."

On October 18, Shalit was taken from his prison to Rafah Crossing on the Gaza-Egypt border where he was given to Egyptian mediators in the presence of Israeli representatives. Before being sent to Israel, Shalit was unexpectedly interviewed on Egyptian television, during which he said he "would be happy" to see more Palestinians freed "on the condition that they stop fighting against Israel." Following the interview, Shalit was sent to Israel via the Kerem Shalom crossing where he phoned his parents and received a short medical exam. He then flew by helicopter to Tel Nof airbase near Tel Aviv, and after a second medical exam he met with his family, the prime minister, and the army chief of staff before being flown to his home village of Mitzpe Hila. "Today we are all united in joy and in pain," Netanyahu told his citizens. "We will continue to fight terror and every released terrorist who returns to terror will be held accountable."

While Shalit was making his journey home, the release of the 477 Palestinian prisoners began. When Shalit reached Egyptian mediators, the first group of prisoners, twenty-seven women, was released. The remaining prisoners followed shortly after. Prisoners from Israel were sent to various locations upon their release. Some were sent to the Gaza Strip, others went into exile. Some of those that were deported were sent to Turkey, Syria, and Egypt. As Palestinians gathered in the streets awaiting the return of their compatriots, loudspeakers broadcast the phrases "God is great!" and "Victory to God!" President Abbas told the prisoners, "We thank God that you returned safe and sound to your families, your brothers, and your homeland after this forced disappearance because you struggled for your homeland. . . . Your sacrifices, and efforts and work were not in vain. You worked and struggled and sacrificed. You will see the results of your sacrifices in the independent Palestinian state."

REACTION AND IMPACT

Although they received only one prisoner in the deal, Israelis were highly supportive of the swap. A poll published shortly before the prisoner exchange showed that four out of five Israelis supported it. Support was high in Israel's cabinet as well where only three votes were cast against the deal and twenty-six in favor. But the opinions of those families impacted by terrorist acts of the released prisoners were mixed. Arnold Roth, whose daughter was killed in a bombing, said, "It's extraordinary to me that people can call this a celebration, a happy day, on our side. This is absolutely beyond me. This is a terrible day." Other family members supported the swap. Robi Damelin, whose son was killed by a Palestinian sniper at a West Bank checkpoint, said, "I'm more convinced now than ever that if we don't release prisoners there can be no end to this conflict." Damelin, who set up a support network for parents, continued, "If you look at Ireland or you look at South Africa, some of the most violent murderers, who had blood on their hands exactly like many people here, are today the greatest peace workers that ever were."

The Almagor Terror Victims Association expressed concern that the prisoners released to Palestine would return to violence, indicating that this fear of future attacks by those released was well founded in statistics—since 2000, agreements to release suspected Palestinian terrorists have resulted in 180 Israelis being killed. "I recommend that the public wear flak jackets," said Meir Indor, head of Almagor. Yehya Sinwar, a cofounder of the early security wing of Hamas promised "to work hard to free all prisoners, especially those who serve high sentences, whatever the price was," while Wafa al-Bass, who was arrested for bringing a suicide belt through an Israeli checkpoint, called on Palestinians to "take another Shalit" every year until all 5,000 remaining prisoners were freed.

Hamas is expected to get an immediate boost from the deal, especially after being recently overshadowed by rival Fatah, which was leading a bid at the United Nations for Palestinian statehood. Efraim Inbar, an analyst at the Begin-Sadat Center for Strategic Studies, worried how Hamas and Palestine might respond to the agreement. "First of all, it's quite clear that the Palestinian terrorists have additional incentives to try to kidnap additional Israeli soldiers, because they get a huge price," he said. "The second repercussion is there are clear statistics which show that 60 percent of the released terrorists from previous exchanges have returned to terror."

Even though the agreement gives Hamas a temporary upper hand, it is unlikely to lead to any greater peace talks between Hamas and Israel or Palestine and Israel. UN Secretary General Ban Ki-moon, however, expressed hope that what he called a "significant humanitarian breakthrough" would lead to additional measures in the Middle East peace process that might help Israel and Palestine realize the global vision of living together in peace.

—Heather Kerrigan

Following is a statement by Israeli Prime Minister Benjamin Netanyahu on October 18, 2011, on the release of Gilad Shalit by Palestine; and a press release from Palestine's Ministry of Information, also on October 18, 2011, on the release of Palestinian prisoners from Israel.

DOCUMENT

Prime Minister Netanyahu on Release of Gilad Shalit

October 18, 2011

Citizens of Israel, today we are all united in joy and in pain. Two-and-a-half years ago, I returned to the Prime Minister's Office. One of the principal and most complicated missions that I found on my desk, and which I set my heart to, was to bring our abducted soldier Gilad Shalit back home, alive and well. Today, that mission has been completed.

It entailed a very difficult decision. I saw the need to return home someone whom the State of Israel had sent to the battlefield. As an IDF soldier and commander, I went out on dangerous missions many times. But I always knew that if I or one of my comrades fell captive, the Government of Israel would do its utmost to return us home, and as Prime Minister, I have now carried this out. As a leader who daily sends out soldiers to defend Israeli citizens, I believe that mutual responsibility is no mere slogan—it is a cornerstone of our existence here.

But I also see an additional need, that of minimizing the danger to the security of Israel's citizens. To this end, I enunciated two clear demands. First, that senior Hamas leaders, including arch-murderers, remain in prison. Second, that the overwhelming majority of those designated for release either be expelled or remain outside Judea and Samaria, in order to impede their ability to attack our citizens.

For years, Hamas strongly opposed these demands. But several months ago, we received clear signs that it was prepared to back down from this opposition. Tough negotiations were carried out, night and day, in Cairo, with the mediation of the Egyptian government. We stood our ground, and when our main demands were met—I had to make a decision.

I know very well that the pain of the families of the victims of terrorism is too heavy to bear. It is difficult to see the miscreants who murdered their loved ones being released before serving out their full sentences. But I also knew that in the current diplomatic circumstances, this was the best agreement we could achieve, and there was no guarantee that the conditions which enabled it to be achieved would hold in the future. It could be that Gilad would disappear; to my regret, such things have already happened.

I thought of Gilad and the five years that he spent rotting away in a Hamas cell. I did not want his fate to be that of Ron Arad. Ron fell captive exactly 25 years ago and has yet to return. I remembered the noble Batya Arad. I remembered her concern for her son Ron, right up until her passing. At such moments, a leader finds himself alone and must make a decision. I considered—and I decided. Government ministers supported me by a large majority.

And today, now Gilad has returned home, to his family, his people and his country. This is a very moving moment. A short time ago, I embraced him as he came off the helicopter and escorted him to his parents, Aviva and Noam, and I said, 'I have brought your son back home.' But this is also a hard day; even if the price had been smaller, it would still have been heavy.

I would like to make it clear: We will continue to fight terrorism. Any released terrorist who returns to terrorism—his blood is upon his head. The State of Israel is different from its enemies: Here, we do not celebrate the release of murderers. Here, we do not applaud those who took life. On the contrary, we believe in the sanctity of life. We sanctify life. This is the ancient tradition of the Jewish People.

Citizens of Israel, in recent days, we have all seen national unity such as we have not seen in a long time. Unity is the source of Israel's strength, now and in the future. Today, we all rejoice in Gilad Shalit's return home to our free country, the State of Israel. Tomorrow evening, we will celebrate Simchat Torah. This coming Sabbath, we will read in synagogues, as the weekly portion from the prophets, the words of the prophet Isaiah (42:7): 'To bring out the prisoners from the dungeon, and them that sit in darkness out of the prison-house.' Today, I can say, on behalf of all Israelis, in the spirit of the eternal values of the Jewish People: 'Your children shall return to their own border [Jeremiah 31:17].' Am Yisrael Chai! [The People of Israel live!]

SOURCE: Office of the Prime Minister of Israel. "PM Netanyahu's Remarks Following the Release of Gilad Shalit." October 18, 2011. http://www.pmo.gov.il/PMOEng/Communication/PMSpeaks/speechshalit 181011.htm.

DOCUMENT

Palestinian Ministry of Information on Prisoner Release

October 18, 2011

Tuesday Oct. 18, 2011 marks an appointment with freedom for both Palestinian war prisoners and families. For the first time since decades, few Palestinian war prisoners will breathe things other than the humidity of cells and enjoy a space they never had. Families, on the other hand, will be freed from the torturing heart attacking fears to poisoned sons and daughters for mere Israeli claims. They will swap worries, humiliating scheduled visits to the Negev desert where some hero Palestinians were poisoned under the burning sun and subject to the moody Israeli administration of the prisons and the underground prisons elsewhere.

Cameras will capture tears and hugging. Pens will record touchy stories. But the story begins now. The story of heroes and heroines who spent decades in Israeli prisons as a result of the war it launched against the Palestinian land and history.

Israel proves by all means that it is not ready for making the desired peace. Israel proves all the time that peace shall be attained through violence and does not care for the life of its own citizens: young Israeli men and women are thrown to the furnace of a battle than can be avoided if Israel succumbs to the Palestinians calls for peace. The Israeli public has to face the claims and carelessness of its government and wasting of lives, time and resources. Political and social must play a role in forming the Israeli political map. They must push Benjamin Netanyahu and the Likud Party to move from the extremist Israeli right wing and their peace impeding dogmas to advanced positions on the political map to allow for making peace between the Israelis and the Palestinians.

SOURCE: Palestinian Ministry of Information. "October 18, 2011 Marks an Appointment With the Freedom of Palestinian War Prisoners." October 18, 2011. http://www.minfo.ps/English/index.php?pagess= main&id=888&butt=5.

OTHER HISTORIC DOCUMENTS OF INTEREST

FROM THIS VOLUME

FROM PREVIOUS *HISTORIC DOCUMENTS*

Arab Spring: NATO and President Obama on the Death of Muammar Qaddafi

---

OCTOBER 20 AND 21, 2011

The Arab Spring movement sweeping across Africa and the Middle East in 2011 reached Libya in February, as protesters took to the streets calling for the end of Col. Muammar el-Qaddafi's four-decade regime. Qaddafi defiantly remained in his position throughout the spring and summer and authorized his security forces to use any force necessary to stop the demonstrations. The anti-government protesters fought back, forming rebel groups and clashing with Qaddafi forces for control of major cities in the oil-rich nation. United Nations and North Atlantic Treaty Organization (NATO) member nations provided air-strikes in support of the rebel movement in an attempt to protect civilians from Qaddafi's ruthless campaign. The combined effort led to the overthrow of Qaddafi and his government in August and the leader's subsequent death at the hands of his people in October.

Muammar el-Qaddafi

For more than four decades, Libya was ruled by Col. Muammar el-Qaddafi, who first took power in 1969 in a bloodless coup. Qaddafi maintained his stranglehold on power through tribal alliances and control of the profits from Libyan oil resources. Qaddafi also kept the nation's military poorly trained and divided in the hope that they would not be able to topple his regime. This ensured that factions of the military remained loyal to their own tribes, so no one commander could gain the loyalty of all the troops. For additional protection, Qaddafi surrounded himself with a 3,000-member revolutionary guard corps.

During his rule, Qaddafi's relationship with the international community was mixed. In 1988, Libya accepted responsibility for the bombing of Pan Am Flight 103 over Scotland that killed 270, and the government ultimately agreed to compensate the families of the victims. By 2003, Qaddafi's government renounced terrorism and sought to establish dip-lomatic and economic ties with European and African nations. Qaddafi founded a pan-African confederation and was named chair of the African Union in 2009. International goodwill came to an end in 2009, however, when Pan Am bomber Abdel Basset Ali al-Megrahi received a hero's welcome in Libya after being released from Scotland on compas-sionate grounds. However, it has been reported that Qaddafi shared his files on al Qaeda with the United States after September 11 to aid the coalition invasion of Afghanistan.

Before the 2011 Arab Spring rebellion that shook Libya and dismantled Qaddafi's government, forcing him from power, there had been some talk of change in the nation, but it was led by Qaddafi's son, Seif al-Islam el-Qaddafi, who sought to open up the nation to better economic ties by creating tax-free investment zones, a tax haven for foreigners, and more luxury hotels. His ideas never came to fruition.

Protests and Rebel Movement

In February 2011, the arrest of a Libyan human rights supporter sparked demonstrations against Qaddafi's government that began in Benghazi on February 17, 2011, during what was called a Day of Rage. The protests quickly spread to the capital of Tripoli and out into other parts of the coastal nation. The long-suffering population that faced an unemployment rate estimated at 30 percent, and was mostly uneducated and untrained, was quick to join armed rebel groups calling for the overthrow of the Qaddafi regime. Qaddafi's government responded to the early movement with violence. Air power was the government's biggest strength, allowing equipment and troops to quickly be moved, and airstrikes to be used against rebels. On February 22, Qaddafi made a televised appearance aimed at cementing his control over the nation, and also maintained his stance that, contrary to reports from rebel groups, his forces had killed no civilians.

When Qaddafi first responded to the rebellion, it seemed that the hundreds of rebel groups that had formed had little chance of toppling the government, especially given their internal division and lack of proper equipment and training. But undeterred by Qaddafi's promise to "fight until the last man," the rebels gained control of Benghazi, which served as the center of the rebellion. Oil reserve towns along the nation's eastern coast quickly followed, falling to the rebels. In late February and early March, fighting took place along the northern coast in Brega, Ras Lanuf, Bin Jawad, Zawiya, and Misrata, with rebels gaining control of Ras Lanuf. By mid-March, Qaddafi's forces recaptured the city and took control of Bin Jawad and Brega, pushing the rebels back. Fighting in Misrata and Zawiya led to Zawiya being taken by the government. Amid international pressure to stop the government campaign against the protesters, on March 18, Qaddafi declared a unilateral ceasefire. However, his military forces continued to attack the rebels.

UN and NATO Intervention

Concerned about the security of civilians in Libya, the international community took action through the United Nations. On March 17, the Security Council voted to allow for military action in Libya with the aim of protecting civilians, approving "all necessary measures" for this goal. On March 19, the United States, the United Kingdom, and France began airstrikes in Benghazi, targeting Qaddafi strongholds. The French forces took the first shots, and French President Nicolas Sarkozy called for "all necessary means" to be used to prevent the killing of civilians. The three nations used the airstrikes to destroy communications and missile centers, and succeeded in establishing a no-fly zone over Libya, thus taking away a key Qaddafi advantage. While President Barack Obama defended U.S. involvement in a March 28 televised address, noting that the campaign would be limited and that the United States could not stand by and allow possible genocide to take place, Qaddafi maintained his defiance. "We promise you a long, drawn-out war with no limits," Qaddafi said. "We will fight inch by inch."

From late March through mid-April, nearly all Qaddafi forces withdrew from Benghazi, and rebels were able to capture Ajdabiya, Brega, Uqayla, Ras Lanuf, and Bin Jawad, key cities on the nation's northern coast. However, the rebels soon retreated east of Brega, forced back by Qaddafi forces. During the battle for Brega, a coalition airstrike accidentally hit a rebel base and forced the rebels to retreat beyond Ajdabiya, into the eastern part of Libya. Fighting continued throughout March and April in Zintan, Yafran, and Misrata in the northwest, where, according to aid agencies, the humanitarian situation deteriorated significantly.

The week of April 16 brought about the battle for Misrata, Libya's third-largest city. As intense fighting began, international organizations worked to rescue trapped migrant workers and other foreigners, while the United Nations sent in food supplies and the North Atlantic Treaty Organization (NATO) sent equipment to the rebel forces. On March 25, NATO assumed command over the international mission in Libya, and by late May, the NATO-led campaign helped give the rebels momentum to gain control of Misrata and a number of other eastern and western cities. But by summer, as NATO airstrikes continued, targeting the capital and other Qaddafi-held cities, the battle between the pro-government and rebel forces reached a stalemate.

A breakthrough came on August 21 when rebels, after taking control of some surrounding strategic locations, overran Tripoli and were met with little resistance from Qaddafi forces. By August 23, Qaddafi's power was called into question when the rebels took control of his compound in the capital. Shortly after that, the rebels gained control of Qaddafi's hometown of Surt, the last Qaddafi stronghold. Despite these losses, Qaddafi remained defiant, but the anti-government forces that had established the Transitional National Council in February 2011 released a constitutional declaration, creating a path that would allow the interim body to eventually establish a permanent government to replace Qaddafi. A number of nations, led by the West, recognized the Transitional National Council as the rightful government of Libya. With the Qaddafi government overthrown, rebels continued to take control of Libyan cities into the fall.

On October 20 the Transitional National Council, announced that Qaddafi had been killed. "This is a momentous day in the history of Libya," said President Obama. "The dark shadow of tyranny has been lifted. And with this enormous promise, the Libyan people now have a great responsibility: to build an inclusive and tolerant and democratic Libya that stands as the ultimate rebuke to Qaddafi's dictatorship." Cell phone video showed Qaddafi in a crowd, wounded and begging for mercy, with the crowd shouting, "God is great!" Photographs released after Qaddafi's death revealed bullet holes in his head thought to have been fired at close range. This contrasted with the government's initial report that Qaddafi had been killed during crossfire with rebel forces.

LIBYA'S FUTURE AFTER QADDAFI

Libya was officially declared liberated by the Transitional National Council on October 23. This announcement paved the way for the creation of a new constitution and the election of a new government. Abdel Rahim el-Keeb was named interim prime minister by the council, but there was significant division over how the government would be set up. It was not until November 22 that the prime minister named a new cabinet, which would be in charge until an election in 2012. After briefly remaining in Libya to ensure the continued security of civilians under the interim government, NATO forces ended Operation Unified Protector on October 31. "We did what we said we would do, and now is the time for the Libyan people to take their destiny fully into their own hands, to build a new, inclusive Libya based on democracy and reconciliation, human rights, and the rule of law," said NATO Secretary General Anders Fogh Rasmussen.

Significant questions of legitimacy faced the interim government, which lacks transparency, and in which ministries are unable to make decisions without deferring directly to the top, as the government had under Qaddafi. It is hoped that the 2012 election will allow the government to gain the trust of the people to be able to effectively rule.

The government also faces the challenge of encouraging the rebel militias to give up their arms. There are estimated to be 250 separate rebel groups just in Misrata, and citizens have come to despise their existence despite their role in toppling Qaddafi's government. The interim government made one attempt at ending rebel tension by appointing a local militia leader to the position of defense minister.

The Transitional National Council is also hampered by an inability to manage the economy in a way that brings relief to citizens. In the coming months and years, the government is expected to rely heavily on the country's oil reserves. In November, Libya's government worked to restore production in oilfields that had been closed during the violence, repaired damaged oil tanks and generators, and reopened pipelines. Luckily, critical oil reserves were not destroyed during the fighting, but at the end of 2011, oil production was only at about 40 percent of its pre-rebellion capacity.

—Heather Kerrigan

Following is a statement by President Barack Obama following the death of Libyan leader Muammar Qaddafi, delivered on October 20, 2011; and the text of a press conference held on October 21, 2011, by North Atlantic Treaty Organization (NATO) Secretary General Anders Fogh Rasmussen on developments in Libya.

President Obama on the Death of Muammar Qaddafi

October 20, 2011

Good afternoon, everybody. Today the Government of Libya announced the death of Muammar Qadhafi. This marks the end of a long and painful chapter for the people of Libya, who now have the opportunity to determine their own destiny in a new and democratic Libya.

For four decades, the Qadhafi regime ruled the Libyan people with an iron fist. Basic human rights were denied. Innocent civilians were detained, beaten, and killed, and Libya's wealth was squandered. The enormous potential of the Libyan people was held back, and terror was used as a political weapon.

Today we can definitively say that the Qadhafi regime has come to an end. The last major regime strongholds have fallen. The new Government is consolidating the control over the country. And one of the world's longest serving dictators is no more.

One year ago, the notion of a free Libya seemed impossible. But then the Libyan people rose up and demanded their rights, and when Qadhafi and his forces started going city to city, town by town, to brutalize men, women, and children, the world refused to stand idly by.

Faced with the potential of mass atrocities and a call for help from the Libyan people, the United States and our friends and allies stopped Qadhafi's forces in their tracks. A coalition that included the United States, NATO, and Arab nations persevered through the summer to protect Libyan civilians. And meanwhile, the courageous Libyan people fought for their own future and broke the back of the regime.

So this is a momentous day in the history of Libya. The dark shadow of tyranny has been lifted. And with this enormous promise, the Libyan people now have a great responsibility: to build an inclusive and tolerant and democratic Libya that stands as the ultimate rebuke to Qadhafi's dictatorship. We look forward to the announcement of the country's liberation, the quick formation of an interim Government, and a stable transition to Libya's first free and fair elections. And we call on our Libyan friends to continue to work with the international community to secure dangerous materials and to respect the human rights of all Libyans, including those who have been detained.

Now, we're under no illusions. Libya will travel a long and winding road to full democracy. There will be difficult days ahead. But the United States, together with the international community, is committed to the Libyan people. You have won your revolution. And now we will be a partner as you forge a future that provides dignity, freedom, and opportunity.

For the region, today's events prove once more that the rule of an iron fist inevitably comes to an end. Across the Arab world, citizens have stood up to claim their rights. Youth are delivering a powerful rebuke to dictatorship, and those leaders who try to deny their human dignity will not succeed.

For us here in the United States, we are reminded today of all those Americans that we lost at the hands of Qadhafi's terror. Their families and friends are in our thoughts and in our prayers. We recall their bright smiles, their extraordinary lives, and their tragic deaths. We know that nothing can close the wound of their loss, but we stand together as one nation by their side.

For nearly 8 months, many Americans have provided extraordinary service in support of our efforts to protect the Libyan people and to provide them with a chance to determine their own destiny. Our skilled diplomats have helped to lead an unprecedented global response. Our brave pilots have flown in Libya's skies, our sailors have provided support off Libya's shores, and our leadership at NATO has helped guide our coalition. Without putting a single U.S. servicemember on the ground, we achieved our objectives, and our NATO mission will soon come to an end.

This comes at a time when we see the strength of American leadership across the world. We've taken out Al Qaida leaders, and we've put them on the path to defeat. We're winding down the war in Iraq and have begun a transition in Afghanistan. And now, working in Libya with friends and allies, we've demonstrated what collective action can achieve in the 21st century.

Of course, above all, today's [sic] belongs to the people of Libya. This is a moment for them to remember all those who suffered and were lost under Qadhafi and look forward to the promise of a new day. And I know the American people wish the people of Libya the very best in what will be a challenging but hopeful days, weeks, months, and years ahead.

Thank you very much.

SOURCE: U.S. Executive Office of the President. "Remarks on the Death of Former Leader Muammar Abu Minyar al-Qadhafi of Libya." October 20, 2011. Daily Compilation of Presidential Documents 2011, no. 00773 (October 20, 2011). http://www.gpo.gov/fdsys/pkg/DCPD-201100773/pdf/DCPD-201100773.pdf.

NATO Press Conference on Developments in Libya

October 21, 2011

ANDERS FOGH RASMUSSEN (Secretary General of NATO): Good evening. We have met today with our operational partners to assess the situation in Libya. We agreed that our operations are very close to completion, and we have taken a preliminary decision to end Operation Unified Protector on the 31st of October.

We will take a formal decision early next week. In the meantime, I will consult closely with the United Nations and the National Transitional Council.

We agreed that NATO will wind down the operation, during which period—and that means until the 31st of October—during which period NATO will monitor the situation and retain the capacity to respond to threats to civilians if needed.

I am very proud of what we have achieved together with our partners, including many from the region. Our military forces prevented a massacre and saved countless lives. We created the conditions for the people of Libya to determine their own future. Their courage and determination in the cause of freedom is an inspiration to the world.

NATO launched Operation Unified Protector on the basis of an historic mandate from the United Nations to protect the people of Libya against attacks and to enforce the no-fly zone and the arms embargo. Together with our partners, we have carried out that mandate with remarkable success.

We mounted a complex operation with unprecedented speed, and conducted it with the greatest of care. We worked closely with a wide range of international and regional partners. We were fast, flexible, effective, and precise.

We did what we said we would do, and now is the time for the Libyan people to take their destiny fully into their own hands, to build a new, inclusive Libya based on democracy and reconciliation, human rights, and the rule of law.

Let me say once again how proud I am of what we have achieved together. This is a special moment in history, not only for the people of Libya and the wider region, but also for the NATO Alliance. It shows that freedom is the strongest force in the world.

Now I'm happy to take a few questions.

OANA LUNGESCU: And we'll start with Europa Press.

UNIDENTIFIED (Europa Press): Thank you, Secretary General. I would like to ask if you don't have a bit of a bad taste in the mouth, seeing how the operation has ended with Qadhafi. Because I know that he was never an objective of the mission; that's very clear. And we now know that the attack that the NATO participated in, that halted the convoy, didn't actually kill Qadhafi.

Would you have preferred him to have been taken to The Hague? I don't know if you have, because yesterday as well, in your statement, you made it very clear to the CNT that they had to show restraint now with how they deal with the rest of the Qadhafi—pro-Qadhafi forces. Thank you.

ANDERS FOGH RASMUSSEN: Let me stress once again, and I've done that on several occasions, neither Colonel Qadhafi nor any other individual have been targets of our operations.

We have conducted our operations with the aim to protect civilians against attacks. And as part of that, we have also targeted armed convoys that might constitute a threat to civilians. Such convoys were legitimate military targets.

As regards Colonel Qadhafi and his death, I would expect the new authorities in Libya to live up fully to the basic principles of the rule of law, respect for human rights, including full transparency.

OANA LUNGESCU: Egyptian TV.

MAC DUSA (ph) (Nile News, Egyptian TV): Thank you very much. I'm Mac Dusa (ph) from Nile News, Egyptian Television.

Secretary General, starting from the first of November, once the operation is over, are you keeping some army pieces close to the Libya? I'm talking here about ships or something like this belonging to NATO.

And my second question, since the beginning of the operation till the day, today, we didn't see any resistant . . . resistance from Qadhafi troops. Does it mean that the technology of NATO was very strong, or the Libyan didn't have any missiles or any resistant to . . . to have . . . I mean, to shoot some of that (inaudible) of NATO? Was the regime of Qadhafi empty of any weapon to have any resistant?

ANDERS FOGH RASMUSSEN: First of all, let me stress that it's our intention to wind down the operation during a period, and during that period we will closely monitor the situation in Libya, and of course also take action if necessary, because we take full implementation of the United Nations' mandate to protect civilians very seriously.

So we will of course make sure that there are no attacks against civilians during that transitional period.

As regards the first part of your question, no, we have no intention to keep armed forces in . . . in the neighbourhood of Libya. It's our intention to close the operation. It will be a clear-cut termination of our operation.

OANA LUNGESCU: Kuwaiti News Agency.

UNIDENTIFIED (Kuwaiti News Agency): Mr. Secretary General, you had the press conference, a delay of about four hours. Was there a differences among the member states on the time of withdrawal? Thank you.

ANDERS FOGH RASMUSSEN: No. As . . . as you know, we take all decisions by consensus. So per definition, the message I have delivered today is based on a unanimous decision in the Council.

But this is serious business. It was serious business to take on the responsibility of this operation in Libya. It is also serious business to take the decision to terminate such an operation because we take full implementation of the United Nations' mandate very seriously.

So of course we have discussed many aspects of this. But this is a decision taken by consensus in the Council and with support of our operational partners.

OANA LUNGESCU: One last question, NPR.

TERI SHULTZ (National Public Radio and Global Post): Teri Shultz with the National Public Radio and Global Post.

Sir, when you say that you expect the NTC to follow the rule of law, does that mean that you would . . . would join calls for an investigation into the death of . . . of Colonel Qadhafi? Do you have concerns that the Geneva Convention on Treatment of Prisoners may have been violated here, since we did see pictures of him alive and then . . . and then killed?

And also, I realize once again that you . . . you . . . NATO doesn't target individuals, but do you have any information on the whereabouts of Seif al-Islam? Thank you.

ANDERS FOGH RASMUSSEN: No, we have no knowledge of his whereabouts. And I think it's very important to stress that now it is the responsibility of the Libyan authorities to deal with the internal Libyan affairs.

We have conducted our operation with the aim to protect civilians against attacks, according to United Nations' mandate. We have conducted these operations from air and at sea. We have no troops . . . NATO troops on . . . on the ground. So it is for the Libyan authorities to deal with such issues.

The National Transitional Council has called for freedom and democracy, and this is the reason why I take it for granted that the new authorities in Libya will live up to their international responsibility, will live up to the basic principles of democracy, including the respect for the rule of law and . . . and human rights.

And then it's for the Libyan authorities to decide whether a special investigation is needed or not. But I would expect them to live up to the spirit the National Transitional Council itself has called for, namely democracy and transparency.

OANA LUNGESCU: Thank you very much.

SOURCE: North Atlantic Treaty Organization. Newsroom. "Press Conference by NATO Secretary General on the Latest Developments in Libya and Operation Unified Protector." October 21, 2011. http://www.nato.int/cps/en/natolive/opinions_79807.htm.

OTHER HISTORIC DOCUMENTS OF INTEREST

FROM THIS VOLUME

FROM PREVIOUS *HISTORIC DOCUMENTS*

Remarks by President Obama
and Defense Secretary Gates
on Iraq Troop Withdrawal

OCTOBER 21, DECEMBER 12, AND DECEMBER 15, 2011

The first American troops slipped into Iraq under the cover of early morning darkness on March 20, 2003. Nearly nine years later, shortly before Christmas 2011, the last of a contingent of 50,000 soldiers departed in convoys of trucks loaded with hundreds of millions of dollars of military gear. One of the longest wars in American history, and among the most controversial, had come to an end. "It's harder to end a war than begin one," President Barack Obama told a group of returning soldiers at Fort Bragg, North Carolina, on December 14, 2011, thanking them for their service and saying, "Welcome home."

A Long War

As an Illinois state senator running for the U.S. Senate in 2003, Barack Obama had spoken out against the impending war, and one of his promises as a candidate for president five years later was to end American involvement in the conflict. On October 21, 2011, Obama said, "today I can report that, as promised, the rest of our troops in Iraq will come home by the end of the year. After nearly nine years, America's war in Iraq will be over." Secretary of Defense Leon Panetta said that although the U.S. military mission was ending, the nation still planned to forge a relationship with Iraq. "Our goal will be to establish a normal relationship similar to others in the region that focuses on meeting security and training needs. . . . Going forward, we will work closely with the Iraqi government and their armed forces to help them continue to build a stronger and more prosperous country," said Panetta.

By the time the last U.S. troops returned home in December 2011, nearly one million men and women in uniform had been deployed to Iraq, many for multiple tours of duty. At its highest point, during the surge of U.S. forces in 2007, nearly 170,000 U.S. troops were stationed at 505 bases throughout the country. The conflict took nearly 4,500 U.S. military lives and left more than 32,000 wounded. Panetta promised that the lives lost would not be forgotten and that "they gave birth to an independent, free, and sovereign Iraq." Those two numbers reflected major advances in battlefield medicine since the Vietnam War, when the dead to wounded ratio was one-third higher. The war cost between one and three trillion dollars, depending on how government statisticians calculate the ongoing expense of treating physically and psychologically traumatized veterans over the coming decades. Iraqi deaths, by the conservative calculations of Iraq Body Count, a public database that records the number of Iraqi civilian deaths, have been estimated at between 105,000 and 115,000.

The war already has produced dozens of histories and memoirs. One of the most definitive histories, *Cobra II* by *New York Times* journalist Michael Gordon and retired

Marine Lt. Gen. and analyst Bernard Trainor, offered this conclusion: "The Iraq War is a story of hubris and heroism, of high technology wizardry and cultural ignorance."

PLANNING A WITHDRAWAL

The process of the U.S. withdrawal was as political and diplomatic as it was military. As Defense Secretary Panetta noted in a change of command ceremony in Baghdad, the war had reached a low point for the United States in 2006, as terrorist assaults from al Qaeda in Iraq and other groups inflicted increasing casualties on U.S. troops. Coincidentally, both Panetta and his Pentagon predecessor Robert Gates had served in 2006 on the Baker-Hamilton Commission, which had advocated a U.S. drawdown and diplomatic effort to wind down the war. Instead, then-President George W. Bush gambled on the advice of his Iraq commander, General David Petraeus, for a temporary increase in U.S. troop strength and a plan to use force and money to woo tribal leaders in provinces dominated by the minority Sunni sect away from terrorist groups.

The plan, known as the "surge," bought enough calm and time for the Bush administration to negotiate a Status of Forces agreement with the Iraqi government of Prime Minister Nouri al-Maliki. The agreement called for a two-stage withdrawal: U.S. combat forces would leave Iraq by July 2010 and all troops would be gone within another eighteen months. But the expectation among the outgoing administration was that a side deal could be reached with the Iraqis to keep a smaller U.S. presence of about 20,000 special forces and trainers. The Obama and Maliki governments never could come to terms on such an agreement, even though several Iraqi political groups wanted some U.S. troops to remain. The sticking point was immunity for U.S. troops from the Iraqi criminal justice system. The U.S. insisted on the immunity; Maliki's Shiite political partners refused to go along.

Some Republican politicians and conservative commentators criticized the total withdrawal. Republican presidential candidate Mitt Romney said, "President Obama's astonishing failure to secure an orderly transition in Iraq has unnecessarily put at risk the victories that were won through the blood and sacrifice of thousands of American men and women." As a partial compromise while still maintaining Obama's goal of full withdrawal, a contingent of 200 U.S. Marines and other service members remained in Iraq after December 31 to protect the U.S. Embassy complex in Baghdad's Green Zone. It is often described as the largest U.S. diplomatic mission in the world, once expected to house as many as 16,000 State Department and other civilian agency employees as well as private contractors. But in recent months, especially as pressure from Congress mounts to cut federal spending, some of those estimates are being scaled back.

ONGOING CHALLENGES

Without the presence of thousands of troops, the American role in the nation of nearly 30 million people remains to be seen. On the political front, well before the Arab Spring revolts of 2011, Iraq was the first Arab dictatorship to hold genuine elections. But after the voting in early 2010, it took a full nine months before the political and sectarian factions could agree on a government.

On the economic front, Iraq sits on the world's third-largest oil reserves, and by some estimates has the potential to be the largest oil producer in the world. But production still remains below pre-invasion levels. The Baghdad government has been cautious in apportioning exploration contracts, with far more going to European and Asian companies than to American oil companies.

Despite its potential wealth and Iraq's pre-war image as a cosmopolitan and sophisticated society, the country struggles to provide basic services to its citizens. The average Iraqi household receives 14.6 hours of electricity daily, in a country where the summer temperatures can exceed 120 degrees Fahrenheit. Iraqis rate the lack of reliable electric service as the country's worst failing. The water situation is barely more encouraging. Some 41 percent of the population has reliable safe water; 21 percent has no access at all to clean water.

These gaps in basic services persist despite a multibillion-dollar reconstruction effort, much of which went to projects that were never finished or looted as soon as they came on line, according to reports from the Special Inspector General for Afghanistan Reconstruction, a U.S. military organization that promotes U.S.-led reconstruction in Afghanistan. Aside from those projects, which were partly funded by Iraqi oil revenues, the United States is expected to spend $1.6 billion in military and security assistance and hundreds of millions in economic aid in 2012.

Despite these difficulties, when President Obama welcomed Prime Minister Maliki to the White House in December 2011, he spoke of the country's "impressive progress"; its democratically elected, inclusive, and transparent government; and its increasing oil production. He hailed "a new Iraq that's determining its own destiny—a country in which people from different religious sects and ethnicities can resolve their differences peacefully through the democratic process." And Obama promised, "You have a strong and enduring partner in the United States of America." Maliki noted Iraq's appreciation for the support, stating the country "remains in need of cooperation . . . in security issues and information and combating terrorism, and in the area of training and the area of equipping."

Political Warnings

The combination of economic and political stalemate in Iraq has led to some dire warnings from American analysts and commentators. Former *Los Angeles Times* correspondent Ned Parker warned in an article in *Foreign Affairs* that Iraq "has become something close to a failed state" with Prime Minister Maliki presiding over a system rife with corruption and brutality. Another analyst, Kimberly Kagan of the Institute for the Study of War, told a congressional committee in March 2012 that Iraq "is poised on the knife's-edge of a civil war. The United States has not achieved its core national security objectives in Iraq."

The U.S. and Iraqi opposition did accomplish the mission of ridding the country of the murderous dictatorship of Saddam Hussein, even if they never found the weapons of mass destruction that were the primary rationale for invading the country. For the first time since British colonial rule, majority Shiite rather than minority Sunnis dominate politics. But the country retains geographic, political, and sectarian cleavages among those groups and Kurdish populations in the north. Terrorist attacks have been on the upswing since early 2012. And Iraq sits between Iran and Turkey—two militarily powerful and politically influential and ambitious neighbors who both seek to play a major or dominating role in the region.

The American role in Iraq, however controversial in both nations, was relatively brief in the time frames of either Mideast or American history. For Iraq, it was but one more chapter in an often-violent legacy since the country was cobbled together by British colonialists in the early 20th century. For the first time, as a genuinely self-governing and independent nation, Iraq is really on its own.

—Michael D. Mosettig

Following is a statement by President Barack Obama on October 21, 2011, on the end of American troop involvement in Iraq; a statement by Defense Secretary Leon Panetta on October 21, 2011, affirming the commitment to withdraw U.S. troops from Iraq by the end of 2011; a joint statement by President Obama and Iraqi Prime Minister Nouri al-Maliki on December 12, 2011, on the continuing troop withdrawal; and a speech given by Secretary Panetta on December 15, 2011, at the Iraq End of Mission ceremony.

DOCUMENT

President Obama on U.S. Troop Withdrawal From Iraq

October 21, 2011

Good afternoon, everybody. As a candidate for President, I pledged to bring the war in Iraq to a responsible end, for the sake of our national security and to strengthen American leadership around the world. After taking office, I announced a new strategy that would end our combat mission in Iraq and remove all of our troops by the end of 2011.

As Commander in Chief, ensuring the success of this strategy has been one of my highest national security priorities. Last year, I announced the end to our combat mission in Iraq. And to date, we've removed more than 100,000 troops. Iraqis have taken full responsibility for their country's security.

A few hours ago, I spoke with Iraqi Prime Minister Maliki. I reaffirmed that the United States keeps its commitments. He spoke of the determination of the Iraqi people to forge their own future. We are in full agreement about how to move forward.

So today I can report that, as promised, the rest of our troops in Iraq will come home by the end of the year. After nearly 9 years, America's war in Iraq will be over.

Over the next 2 months, our troops in Iraq—tens of thousands of them—will pack up their gear and board convoys for the journey home. The last American soldier [soldiers; White House correction] will cross the border out of Iraq with their held—heads held high, proud of their success, and knowing that the American people stand united in our support for our troops. That is how America's military efforts in Iraq will end.

But even as we mark this important milestone, we're also moving into a new phase in the relationship between the United States and Iraq. As of January 1 and in keeping with our strategic framework agreement with Iraq, it will be a normal relationship between sovereign nations, an equal partnership based on mutual interests and mutual respect.

In today's conversation, Prime Minister Maliki and I agreed that a meeting of the higher coordinating committee of the strategic framework agreement will convene in the coming weeks. And I invited the Prime Minister to come to the White House in December, as we plan for all the important work that we have to do together. This will be a strong and enduring partnership. With our diplomats and civilian advisers in the lead, we'll help Iraqis strengthen institutions that are just, representative, and accountable. We'll build new ties of trade and of commerce, culture and education that unleash the potential of the Iraqi people. We'll partner with an Iraq that contributes to regional security and peace, just as we insist that other nations respect Iraq's sovereignty.

As I told Prime Minister Maliki, we will continue discussions on how we might help Iraq train and equip its forces, again, just as we offer training and assistance to countries around the world. After all, there will be some difficult days ahead for Iraq, and the United States will continue to have an interest in an Iraq that is stable, secure, and self-reliant. Just as Iraqis have persevered through war, I'm confident that they can build a future worthy of their history as a cradle of civilization. . . .

And finally, I would note that the end of war in Iraq reflects a larger transition. The tide of war is receding. The drawdown in Iraq allowed us to refocus our fight against Al Qaida and achieve major victories against its leadership, including Usama bin Laden. Now, even as we remove our last troops from Iraq, we're beginning to bring our troops home from Afghanistan, where we've begun a transition to Afghan security in [and; White House correction] leadership. When I took office, roughly 180,000 troops were deployed in both these wars. And by the end of this year that number will be cut in half. And make no mistake: It will continue to go down. . . .

Source: U.S. Executive Office of the President. "Remarks on the Withdrawal of United States Military Personnel From Iraq." October 21, 2011. *Compilation of Presidential Documents* 2011, no. 00778 (October 21, 2011). http://www.gpo.gov/fdsys/pkg/DCPD-201100778/pdf/DCPD-201100778.pdf.

Defense Secretary on Troop Withdrawal Commitment

October 21, 2011

The United States and Iraq affirmed today that the U.S. will fulfill its commitments under the current U.S.-Iraq Security Agreement and withdraw all of our military forces by the end of 2011.

Today's announcement means that at the end of this year, there will be a clear end to the U.S. combat presence in Iraq. I wanted to take this opportunity to express my profound gratitude and appreciation to our men and women in uniform who have served in Iraq since 2003. Our troops and their families have borne a heavy burden during more than eight years of war, and paid a great price. Yet it is a testament to their strength and resilience that we are now able to bring this war to a responsible end. Thanks to their service and sacrifice, Iraq is ready to govern and defend itself and to contribute to security and stability in a vital part of the world.

We will now turn our full attention to pursuing a long-term strategic partnership with Iraq based on mutual interests and mutual respect. Our goal will be to establish a normal relationship similar to others in the region that focuses on meeting security and training needs. Iraq is a sovereign nation that must determine how to secure its own future. Going forward, we will work closely with the Iraqi government and their armed forces to help them continue to build a stronger and more prosperous country.

Source: U.S. Department of Defense. Office of the Assistant Secretary of Defense (Public Affairs). "Statement by Secretary Panetta on Iraq." October 21, 2011. http://www.defense.gov/releases/release.aspx?releaseid=14876.

President Obama and Prime Minister al-Maliki Joint Statement on Iraq Troop Withdrawal

DOCUMENT

December 12, 2011

President Obama.

Please have a seat. Good afternoon, everyone.

When I took office, nearly 150,000 American troops were deployed in Iraq, and I pledged to end this war, responsibly. Today, only several thousand troops remain there, and more are coming home every day.

This is a season of homecomings, and military families across America are being reunited for the holidays. In the coming days, the last American soldiers will cross the border out of Iraq with honor and with their heads held high. After nearly 9 years, our war in Iraq ends this month.

Today I'm proud to welcome Prime Minister Maliki, the elected leader of a sovereign, self-reliant, and democratic Iraq. We're here to mark the end of this war, to honor the sacrifices of all those who made this day possible, and to turn the page, begin a new chapter in the history between our countries, a normal relationship between sovereign nations, an equal partnership based on mutual interests and mutual respect.

Iraq faces great challenges, but today reflects the impressive progress that Iraqis have made. Millions have cast their ballots—some risking or giving their lives—to vote in free elections. The Prime Minister leads Iraq's most inclusive government yet. Iraqis are working to build institutions that are efficient and independent and transparent.

Economically, Iraqis continue to invest in their infrastructure and development. And I think it's worth considering some remarkable statistics. In the coming years, it's estimated that Iraq's economy will grow even faster than China's or India's. With oil production rising, Iraq is on track to once again be one of the region's leading oil producers.

With respect to security, Iraqi forces have been in the lead for the better part of 3 years, patrolling the streets, dismantling militias, conducting counterterrorism operations. Today, despite continued attacks by those who seek to derail Iraq's progress, violence remains at record lows.

And, Mr. Prime Minister, that's a tribute to your leadership and to the skill and the sacrifices of Iraqi forces.

Across the region, Iraq is forging new ties of trade and commerce with its neighbors, and Iraq is assuming its rightful place among the community of nations. For the first time in two decades, Iraq is scheduled to host the next Arab League Summit, and what a powerful message that will send throughout the Arab world. People throughout the region will see a new Iraq that's determining its own destiny, a country in which people from different religious sects and ethnicities can resolve their differences peacefully through the democratic process.

Mr. Prime Minister, as we end this war and as Iraq faces its future, the Iraqi people must know that you will not stand alone. You have a strong and enduring partner in the United States of America.

And so today the Prime Minister and I are reaffirming our common vision of a long-term partnership between our nations. This is in keeping with our strategic framework agreement, and it will be like the close relationships we have with other sovereign nations. Simply put, we are building a comprehensive partnership.

Mr. Prime Minister, you've said that Iraqis seek democracy, "a state of citizens and not sects." So we're partnering to strengthen the institutions upon which Iraq's democracy depends: free elections, a vibrant press, a strong civil society, professional police and law enforcement that uphold the rule of law, an independent judiciary that delivers justice fairly, and transparent institutions that serve all Iraqis.

We're partnering to expand our trade and commerce. We'll make it easier for our businesses to export and innovate together. We'll share our experiences in agriculture and in health care. We'll work together to develop Iraq's energy sector even as the Iraqi economy diversifies, and we'll deepen Iraq's integration into the global economy.

We're partnering to expand the ties between our citizens, especially our young people. Through efforts like the Fulbright Program, we're welcoming more Iraqi students and future leaders to America to study and form friendships that will bind our nations together for generations to come. And we'll forge more collaborations in areas like science and technology.

We'll partner for our shared security. Mr. Prime Minister, we discussed how the United States could help Iraq train and equip its forces, not by stationing American troops there or with U.S. bases in Iraq—those days are over—but rather, the kind of training and assistance we offer to other countries. Given the challenges we face together in a rapidly changing region, we also agreed to establish a new, formal channel of communication between our national security advisers.

And finally, we're partnering for regional security. For just as Iraq has pledged not to interfere in other nations, other nations must not interfere in Iraq. Iraq's sovereignty must be respected. And meanwhile, there should be no doubt, the drawdown in Iraq has allowed us to refocus our resources, achieve progress in Afghanistan, put Al Qaida on the path to defeat, and to better prepare for the full range of challenges that lie ahead.

So make no mistake, our strong presence in the Middle East endures, and the United States will never waver in defense of our allies, our partners, or our interests. This is the shared vision that Prime Minister Maliki and I reaffirm today: an equal partnership, a broad relationship that advances the security, the prosperity, and the aspirations of both our people.

Mr. Prime Minister, you've said it yourself: Building a strong and durable relationship between our two countries is vital. And I could not agree more. So this is a historic moment. A war is ending. A new day is upon us. And let us never forget those who gave us this chance, the untold number of Iraqis who've given their lives; more than 1 million Americans, military and civilian, who have served in Iraq; nearly 4,500 fallen Americans who gave their last full measure of devotion; tens of thousands of wounded warriors; and so many inspiring military families. They are the reason that we can stand here today. And we owe it to every single one of them—we have a moral obligation to all of them—to build a future worthy of their sacrifice.

Mr. Prime Minister.

[At this point, Prime Minister Maliki spoke in Arabic, and his remarks were translated by an interpreter and joined in progress.]

Prime Minister Maliki. —positive atmosphere that prevailed among us, and for the obligations, the common obligations, of ending the war, and the commitment to which the American forces will withdraw from Iraq, which is a withdrawal that affects—that indicates success, and not like others have said, that it was negative, but the goals that we established were achieved.

Iraq had a political process established, a democratic process, and adoption of the principles of elections and the transfer—peaceful transfer of authority. Iraq is following a policy, a foreign policy, which does not intervene in the affairs of others and does not allow the others to intervene in its own affairs. Iraq is looking for common grounds with the others and establishes its interest at the forefront and the interest of the others, which it is concerned about, like from any confusion.

Your Excellency, today we meet in Washington after we have completed the first page of a constructive cooperation in which we also thank you and appreciate you for your commitment to everything that you have committed yourself to. And anyone who observes the nature of the relationship between the two countries will say that the relationship will not end with the departure of the last American soldier. . . .

Iraq now has become reliant completely on its own security apparatus and internal security as a result of the expertise that it gained during the confrontations and the training and the equipping. But it remains in need of cooperation with the United States of America in security issues and information and combating terrorism and in the area of training and the area of equipping, which is needed by the Iraqi army. And we have started that. And we want to complete the process of equipping the Iraqi army in order to protect our sovereignty and does not violate the rights of anybody—or do not take any missions that violate the sovereignty of others. . . .

The common vision that we used as a point of departure we have confirmed today. And I am very happy. Every time we meet with the American side, I find determination and a strong will to activate the strategic framework agreement. And I will say frankly, this is necessary, and it serves the interests of Iraq, as it is necessary and serves the interests of the United States of America.

This makes us feel that we will succeed with the same commitment, common commitment that we had in combating terrorism and accomplishing the missions, the basis of which Iraq was independent. Iraq today has a lot of wealth, and it needs experience and expertise, and American and foreign expertise, to help Iraq exploiting its own wealth in an ideal way. Iraq is still suffering from a shortage of resources, and we have established a strategy to increase the Iraqi wealth. And we hope that the American companies will have the largest role in increasing our wealth in the area of oil and other aspects as well.

Iraq wants to rebuild all these sectors that were harmed because of the war and because of the adventurous policies that were used by the former regime, and we need a wide range of reform in the area of education.

We have succeeded in signing several agreements through the educational initiative, which put hundreds of our college graduates to continue their graduate studies and specialized subject in American universities. And I am putting it before everyone who is watching the relationship between the U.S. and Iraq. It is a very—it has very high aspirations.

And I would like to renew my thanks for His Excellency the President for giving me this opportunity, and I wish him more success, God willing. Thank you very much. . . .

[The question-and-answer section has been omitted.]

Source: U.S. Executive Office of the President. "The President's News Conference With Prime Minister Nuri al-Maliki of Iraq." December 12, 2011. *Compilation of Presidential Documents* 2011, no. 00942 (December 12, 2011). http://www.gpo.gov/fdsys/pkg/DCPD-201100942/pdf/DCPD-201100942.pdf.

Secretary Panetta Remarks at End of Mission Ceremony in Iraq

December 15, 2011

Mr. Ambassador, thank you very much. Sergeant Major, General Austin, General Mattis, General Dempsey, honored guests: it is a profound honor to be here in Baghdad, and to have the opportunity to participate in this moving ceremony, on this very historic occasion for both the Iraqi people and the American people.

No words, no ceremony, can provide full tribute to the sacrifices that have brought this day to pass. I'm reminded of what President Lincoln said at Gettysburg, about a different war, in a different time. As he paid tribute to the fallen in that war, his words echo through the years as we pay tribute to the fallen of this war: "the world will little note, nor long remember, what we say here, but it can never forget what they did here."

Today we are honored by the presence of so many distinguished guests from the Iraqi and American governments.

And to the distinguished members of the Iraqi government, and the Iraqi military, thank you for your courage, for your leadership, for your friendship over these many years. More importantly, thank you for your loyalty to the future of Iraq. Your dream of an independent and sovereign Iraq is now a reality.

We are deeply fortunate that in addition to all the great commanders who led our troops here, there are two great Americans who stepped forward to lead this mission through this final transition. Today we honor these two national treasures: Ambassador Jeffrey and General Austin. . . .

[The following paragraphs, containing thank-you messages to U.S. commanders, have been omitted.]

Nor will we ever forget the sacrifices of the more than one million men and women of the United States armed forces who served in Iraq, and the sacrifices of their families. Through deployment after deployment after deployment, families somehow withstood the strain, the sacrifice, and the heartbreak of watching their loved ones go off to war. The loved ones fought in places like Fallujah, Ramadi, Sadr City and elsewhere. And today, in particular, we remember the nearly 4,500 brave Americans who made the ultimate sacrifice for their country, as well as the more than 30,000 wounded warriors many of whom still struggle with serious, life-altering injuries.

To all of the men and women in uniform today: your nation is deeply indebted to you. You have done everything your nation asked you to do and more. Your dedication, your commitment to this mission has been the driving force behind the remarkable progress that we've seen here in Baghdad and across this country.

You came to this "Land between the Rivers" again and again and again. You did not know whether you'd return to your loved ones. You will leave with great pride—lasting pride—secure in knowing that your sacrifice has helped the Iraqi people begin a new chapter in history, free from tyranny and full of hope for prosperity and peace, particularly for this country's future generations.

This outcome was never certain, especially during the war's darkest days. In 2006, as a member of President Bush's Iraq Study Group, I traveled here at a time when sectarian violence was skyrocketing and it seemed as if nothing was working. Iraq was struggling with turmoil, with violence, with uncertainty.

Today, some five years later, and after a great deal of blood was spilled by Iraqis and Americans, the mission of an Iraq that could govern and secure itself has become real: the Iraqi army and police have been rebuilt and they are capable of responding to threats; violence levels are down; al Qaeda has been weakened; the rule of law has been strengthened; educational opportunities have been expanded; and economic growth is expanding, as well. And this progress has been sustained even as we have withdrawn nearly 150,000 U.S. combat forces from this country.

With the departure of the remaining U.S. forces within these last few days to the end of the year, we salute the fact that Iraq is now fully responsible for directing its own path to future security and future prosperity.

To be sure, the cost was high—the blood and treasure of the United States and also of the Iraqi people. But those lives have not been lost in vain—they gave birth to an independent, free, and sovereign Iraq. And because of the sacrifices made, these years of war have now yielded to a new era of opportunity. Together with the Iraqi people, the United States welcomes the next stage in U.S.-Iraq relations, one that will be rooted in mutual interest and mutual respect.

Let me be clear: Iraq will be tested in the days ahead—by terrorism, by those who would seek to divide, by economic and social issues, by the demands of democracy itself. Challenges remain, but the United States will be there to stand with the Iraqi people as they navigate those challenges to build a stronger and more prosperous nation.

To that end, the U.S. is deepening our relationship through our Office of Security Cooperation, and Iraq Security Forces will continue to partner with U.S. Central Command, led by General Jim Mattis. The U.S. will maintain a significant diplomatic presence here in Iraq. We will continue to help Iraq address violent extremism and defend against external threats. We will continue to have a robust and enduring military presence across the Middle East. We are not about to turn our backs on all that has been sacrificed and accomplished, and we will not allow those who would seek to undermine success to have their way.

But in the end, this is not about the United States. Rather, today is about Iraq. This is a time for Iraq to look forward. This is an opportunity for Iraq to forge ahead on the path to security and prosperity. And we undertake this transition today reminding Iraq that it has in the United States a committed friend and a committed partner. We owe it to all of the lives that have been sacrificed in this war not to fail.

I believe that the fundamental dream of all humanity is to be able to give our children a better life. Today, the Iraqi people move closer to realizing that dream, and Iraqis can take pride in knowing that through the service and sacrifice of so many brave warriors, your children will have that better future. That is the reward that we all cherish on this historic day. This is not the end, this is truly the beginning.

May God bless our troops, may God bless America, and may God bless Iraq, its people, and its future.

Source: U.S. Department of Defense. Office of the Assistant Secretary of Defense (Public Affairs). "U.S. Forces-Iraq End of Mission Ceremony." December 15, 2011. http://www.defense.gov/speeches/speech .aspx?speechid=1641.

OTHER HISTORIC DOCUMENTS OF INTEREST

Congressional Hearing on
U.S. Troops in Uganda

OCTOBER 25, 2011

In October 2011, President Barack Obama announced that he had authorized the deployment of 100 troops to central Africa to assist in rooting out and stopping the Lord's Resistance Army (LRA), a militant group that had held a twenty-four-year reign of terror over the region, and its ruthless leader, Joseph Kony. The 2011 troop deployment was counter to past U.S. strategy in Africa. Over time, the United States has been less willing to send troops to get involved in regional and tribal disputes. The troops were not intended to have a direct combat role, but would instead assist regional governments in forming plans to combat the LRA and protect civilians. The deployment, which was not given a definitive end date, stirred emotions in Congress, pitting human rights advocates against those who felt the nation could not afford to take up another region's fight on the U.S. dime.

Joseph Kony and the LRA

The Lord's Resistance Army (LRA) is a militant group responsible for committing atrocities including rape, murder, and kidnapping in central Africa for more than two decades. The group's reach extends through the Central African Republic (CAR), Democratic Republic of the Congo (DRC), Uganda, and South Sudan and has a significant impact on regional security. The twenty-four-year LRA reign of terror is considered to be one of the worst human rights crises in the world today. In the time the LRA has operated in central Africa, it is estimated that 300,000 have fled their homes while thousands have been killed. Since 2008, more than 3,400 people have been kidnapped. The group's ranks have dropped significantly over the years, with an estimated 12,000 defections, but there are still thought to be at least 200 core fighters. The LRA has been able to continue operating because countries affected by its presence have not made much retaliatory effort. In addition, its small size makes it extremely mobile in an area with difficult terrain.

To bolster its forces, the LRA kidnaps children—the boys are forced to fight and the girls are used as sex slaves. "A large portion of the LRA itself are children who have been abducted from their homes," said Erin Baines, assistant professor at Liu Institute for Global Issues at the University of British Columbia. "So they are the front line of many of these battles and they are the first to be killed because they have the least knowledge of how to hide and protect themselves," Baines said. It is estimated that 80 percent of the LRA non-core fighters are children.

Since its inception, the LRA has been led by Joseph Kony who since 2005 has been wanted by the International Criminal Court for crimes against humanity. The whereabouts of Kony have rarely been known, but he is believed to be hiding along the Sudan-Congo border. In October 2011, Ugandan troops claimed that they nearly caught the ruthless LRA leader.

The CAR appealed many times for international support to combat the LRA. Beginning in November 2010, the CAR received aid from France that supported the deployment of 300 CAR troops into east Uganda. The French Foreign Ministry called the support "important and permanent" and it includes fuel, air transportation, telecommunications systems, and other necessary equipment. In September 2011, the UN General Assembly came under fire from the CAR Foreign Minister Antoine Gambi, who expressed discontent with the withdrawal of the UN mission to his country even as the LRA continued to attack civilians.

Past attempts have been made at peace agreements with the LRA but without much success. In 2006, negotiations began in South Sudan between the government of Uganda and the LRA in hopes of reaching a cease-fire and eventual peace treaty. A cease-fire was negotiated in September 2006, but in April 2008, Kony refused to sign on. In both 2009 and 2010, the LRA called for the renewal of peace talks with Uganda and a potential cease-fire, but neither instance produced an end to the violence.

U.S. INVOLVEMENT IN UGANDA

In the past, the United States has helped the CAR, the DRC, Uganda, and South Sudan train and equip local troops to combat the LRA by providing funding to the nations, but has not participated in direct combat. In 2008–2009, under the administration of President George W. Bush, the United States sent a team of seventeen counterterrorism advisers to train Ugandan troops. In addition to the Pentagon's manpower, the United States also provided monetary support, fuel trucks, satellite phones, and military equipment to Ugandan troops. The operation was largely considered a failure because it only succeeded in dispersing the LRA into regional groups, which led to additional attacks that killed as many as 900 civilians.

The U.S. Congress got involved in May 2010, passing the Lord's Resistance Army Disarmament and Northern Uganda Recovery Act of 2009 with bipartisan support. The bill, which was signed into law on May 24, 2010, promised to provide "political, economic, military, and intelligence support for viable multilateral efforts to protect civilians from the Lord's Resistance Army." The law made clear U.S. support for a comprehensive effort to end the threat posed by the LRA to citizens of the region and regional security. President Barack Obama said the law "crystallizes the commitment of the United States to help bring an end to the brutality and destruction that have been a hallmark of the LRA across several countries for two decades, and to pursue a future of greater security and hope for the people of Central Africa."

On October 14, 2011, President Obama sent a letter to Congress stating that, as part of a larger U.S. strategy against the LRA authorized by the Lord's Resistance Army Disarmament and Northern Uganda Recovery Act of 2009, approximately 100 troops were being deployed from the United States to Uganda, South Sudan, and the DRC to remove Kony and LRA leaders from the battlefield. "I believe that deploying these US Armed Forces furthers US national security interests and foreign policy and will be a significant contribution toward counter-LRA efforts in Central Africa," Obama wrote. The troops would be mostly Green Beret Special Forces and were given the authorization to capture or kill Kony and his LRA leaders; however, they would have no direct combat role. "Although the U.S. forces are combat-equipped, they will only be providing information, advice, and assistance to partner nation forces, and they will not themselves engage LRA forces unless necessary for self-defense," Obama wrote.

2011 Troop Deployment

According to those involved with the plan, the deployment aimed at encouraging those nations affected by the LRA to take action and pursue the group, and had nothing to do with oil or Islamic extremists operating in the area. In their advisory and assistance role, the U.S. troops will work with national forces and the local governments in Uganda, South Sudan, and the DRC on protecting citizens and forming plans to combat the LRA. The troops will also provide real-time information on LRA whereabouts, numbers, equipment, and other factors and will use this information to help craft and reform current efforts against the LRA. Most of the troops will be stationed in Uganda's capital, but some will be sent on missions to jungle areas in the CAR, the DRC, and South Sudan, where the LRA has been known to operate.

Officials in the Ugandan capital of Kampala were supportive of the U.S. troop deployment. "We welcome this gesture, it has been well overdue," said Ugandan Acting Foreign Minister Henry Okello Oryem. "We are aware that they are coming. We are happy about it. We look forward to working with them and eliminating Kony and his fighters," said Uganda's military spokesperson Col. Felix Kulayigye. In the northern part of the nation, however, there was concern that U.S. involvement would spark more LRA attacks.

A "peace team" established by the LRA called the U.S. mission "not only misconceived, but unacceptable," according to Justice Nyeko Labeja, the leader of the team. The U.S. mission was called an attempt to back a dictatorial regime in Uganda and contravene the African Union's role in the region. While asserting that it maintained a commitment to peaceful resolution of conflict, the LRA peace team said in a written statement for the *Sudan Tribune*, "Our peoples' struggle is principally against this evil system of slavery, degradation and dehumanization and not merely against the individual authors and perpetrators of the gross suffering of our people under the satellite military regime."

No timeline was given for U.S. involvement in central Africa, but it is expected to last for many months. The Pentagon was clear that the mission "will not be an open-ended commitment," but, according to the spokesperson for U.S. Africa Command, "our forces are prepared to stay as long as necessary to enable regional security forces to carry on independently."

Congressional Hearing

The 100-troop commitment garnered mixed support on Capitol Hill. "I have witnessed firsthand the devastation caused by the LRA, and this will help end Kony's heinous acts that have created a human rights crisis in Africa," said Sen. James Inhofe, R-Okla. Other senators and representatives took issue with the president's failure to consult Congress before deploying troops and failure to make a strong case for U.S. involvement in the region. "When it comes to sending our brave young men and women into foreign nations, we have to first demonstrate a vital American national interest," said Rep. Michele Bachmann, R-Minn. "Once you send your troops in, it's very difficult to get them out."

In October, the House Foreign Affairs Committee convened a hearing on the troop deployment. Committee chair Rep. Ileana Ros-Lehtinen, R-Fla., opened the hearing, noting, "The LRA makes no attempt to hold territories, but murders, mutilates, tortures, rapes and loots with impunity." Pentagon officials were on hand to answer questions from committee members that ranged from how the mission fit into U.S. security goals, what the overall cost might be, and how U.S. troops would avoid direct combat. On the latter point,

Pentagon officials at the hearing admitted that they could not give Congress any guarantee that U.S. troops would remain out of direct fighting because some will be close to the front lines. However, said Donald Yamamoto, the principal deputy assistant secretary of state for African affairs, their main role will be to advise and attempt to get LRA forces to defect.

The importance of the mission, and its relation to overall U.S. security goals, was also reviewed. "While weakened, LRA leader Joseph Kony and other top commanders remain at large, and they continue to direct the group's members to commit unspeakable atrocities," said Alexander Vershbow, assistant secretary of defense for international security affairs at the Department of Defense. Vershbow went on to note that "everything is interconnected" and that without support, terrorist networks like the LRA and others that the United States has hunted for years can use nations like those in central Africa as a place to plan and train for attacks.

In relation to cost, the Pentagon was unable to provide an official projection at the time of the hearing, but noted that the operation was being paid for by U.S. Africa Command operations and maintenance funds. Still, some committee members bristled at the thought that the United States was committing more money to a deployment without a specified end date. Rep. Dana Rohrabacher, R-Calif., made clear that "The United States cannot afford to pay the price to win everyone's freedom across the world."

—Heather Kerrigan

Following is the opening statement and testimony delivered on October 25, 2011, during the House Foreign Affairs Committee hearing on the U.S. troop deployment to Uganda.

House Foreign Affairs Committee Holds Hearing on Troop Deployment

October 25, 2011

Chairman ROS-LEHTINEN. The committee will come to order.

That was my gavel. We improvise. But before we begin, I'd like to acknowledge the presence of Ms. Evelyn Apoko.

Evelyn, is that you right there? Thank you, Evelyn. Evelyn, if you could stand a second? Thank you. Evelyn is an LRA survivor who has traveled to Washington to witness this important hearing firsthand. We thank her for coming and for her continued efforts on behalf of children impacted by this horrific conflict.

After recognizing myself and the ranking member, Mr. Berman, for 7 minutes each for our opening statements, I will recognize the chair and ranking member of the Africa Global Health and Human Rights Subcommittee for 3 minutes and the chair and ranking member of the Terrorism, Nonproliferation, and Trade Subcommittee also for 3 minutes each for their opening remarks.

We will then hear from our witnesses and without objection the witnesses' prepared statements will be made a part of the record. And members may have 5 legislative days to insert statements and questions for the record subject to the length limitations in the rules.

The Chair now recognizes herself for 7 minutes. The Department of State has included the Lord's Resistance Army, LRA, on the "Terrorist Exclusion List" since 2001. In 2008, its leader, Joseph Kony, was designated as a "Specially Designated Global Terrorist" (SDGT). The LRA is responsible for one of the longest, most violent, yet most under reported conflicts in Africa—a conflict which has spread from Northern Uganda to South Sudan, the Democratic Republic of the Congo, and Central African Republic—and threatens costly U.S. investments in peace and stability in the region. It is a predatory, guerilla force which has perpetrated some of the most deplorable human rights atrocities known to man.

The LRA makes no attempt to hold territories but murders, mutilates, tortures, rapes and loots with impunity. They move in small groups with limited communication, striking remote villages, slaughtering civilians, abducting woman and children to serve as fighters, porters, and sex slaves. It has been estimated that more than 80 percent of the LRA is comprised of abducted children.

These children are forced to commit atrocities in front of their families and participate in bizarre indoctrination rituals before being forced to fight. Those who manage to escape find it difficult, if not impossible, to return home.

But we are not here today to determine whether Joseph Kony is evil. We know that he is. We are here because in May 2010, the President signed into law the Lord's Resistance Army Disarmament and Northern Uganda Recovery Act. With the backing of thousands of committed advocates, including from my own District, and with over 200 co-sponsors in the House and some 64 co-sponsors in the Senate, the act enjoyed overwhelming support. It required the President to develop a comprehensive strategy to deal with the LRA and established that it shall be the policy of the United States to: "Provide political, economic, military, and intelligence support for viable multilateral efforts to protect civilians, apprehend or eliminate top LRA commanders, and disarm and demobilize remaining LRA fighters."

The President's strategy was released in November 2010. It set four strategic objectives: (1) increased protection of civilians; (2) apprehension to or "removal" of Kony and other senior LRA commanders; (3) promotion of defections from the LRA and the disarmament, demobilization, and reintegration of remaining LRA combatants; and lastly, provision of humanitarian relief to affected communities.

The strategy emphasized that the U.S. will "work with national government and regional organizations" to accomplish these goals. What steps did the U.S. undertake in the last year to achieve the objectives outlined in this strategy? That is what we will be focusing on with our witnesses.

Further, I would to ask our distinguished witnesses to summarize for the committee, what progress had been achieved toward meeting the strategic objectives before the President's recent announcement that U.S. troops were being deployed to central Africa?

On October 14, 2011, the President transmitted a report, consistent with the War Powers Resolution, informing the Congress that: "In furtherance of the Congress' stated policy, I have authorized a small number of combat-equipped U.S. forces to deploy to central Africa to provide assistance to regional forces that are working toward the removal of Joseph Kony from the battlefield." He further stated: "Although the U.S. forces are combat equipped, they will only be providing information, advice, and assistance to partner nation forces, and they will not themselves engage LRA forces unless necessary for self-defense."

As the sole House committee of jurisdiction for the LRA Act and the primary committee of jurisdiction over the War Powers Act, it is incumbent upon us to ensure that this action complies with both the letter and the spirit of the law and further U.S. national security interests. Pertinent information related to this mission, such as the anticipated cost, the scope the duration of this deployment, was omitted from the report to Congress. We need clarity on the rules of engagement, the mission parameters, and the definition of success, as well as how U.S. military presence in central Africa furthers U.S. national security interests and the objectives outlined in the President's November 2010 strategy. What is the precise nature of the assistance that will be provided to our partners, and how will these partners be vetted? Does the submission of the October 14th report to Congress start the clock on reporting and authorization requirements, consistent with the War Powers Resolution?

If not, why? Does the administration interpret the LRA Act as an authorization of use of force?

We intend to address these issues and more throughout the course of the hearing.

Thank you to the Assistant Secretary Vershbow for attending and the Ambassador, for making yourselves available to testify on this very important issue today. We thank both of you, gentlemen. I now am pleased to recognize my good friend, Mr. Berman, the ranking member for his opening remarks....

[Committee member opening remarks have been omitted.]

STATEMENT OF THE HONORABLE DONALD YAMAMOTO, PRINCIPAL DEPUTY ASSISTANT SECRETARY OF STATE FOR AFRICAN AFFAIRS, U.S. DEPARTMENT OF STATE

Mr. YAMAMOTO. Thank you so very much, Madam Chairwoman, Congressman Berman, and the honored members of this committee. Thank you so very much for having this hearing here today on a very important and very difficult topic and for the opportunity to brief this committee on the implementation of the on-going U.S. strategy to help our regional partners mitigate, eliminate the threat posed by the Lord's Resistance Army.

We are deeply grateful for Congress' widespread bipartisan support for the LRA Disarmament in Northern Uganda Recovery Act that was signed last year. The legislation sent a very strong message, not only the support of Congress, but of the American people that we will help to protect civilians and bring an end to the LRA threat.

We also want to express our deep appreciation to the hundreds of thousands of Americans who have sent and mobilized and expressed their concern for the communities under siege by the LRA and also the people who are here today and those who have the courage to stand up to the atrocities of the LRA.

For two decades the LRA has terrorized innocent people across central Africa. The LRA has filled its ranks with abducting tens of thousands of children and forcing them to become child soldiers and sex slaves. From 2005 to 2006, the LRA moved from Uganda into the more remote border regions of Central Africa Republic, the Democratic Republic of the Congo, and what is now known as the Republic of Southern Sudan. In that region, the LRA has continued to commit atrocities. The United Nations estimates that over 385,000 people are currently displaced in this region as a result of the LRA activities and according to the U.N., there have been over 250 attacks attributed to the LRA this year alone.

Over the recent years, regional militaries have worked together to pursue the LRA across a vast area of densely forested and difficult jungle terrain. They have had some success in reducing the LRA's numbers and keeping them from regrouping. However, as long as the LRA's leader, Joseph Kony, and other top commanders remain at large, the LRA will continue to pose its serious regional threat which undermines stability and development.

In its report to Congress in November 2010, our strategy centers on four areas: The increased protection of civilians, apprehension and removal of Joseph Kony and his senior LRA commanders from the battlefield, the promotion of defections from the LRA and support of disarmament, demobilization, and reintegration of remaining LRA fighters, and finally, the provision of continued humanitarian relief to afflicted areas.

Over the past year, the United States has continued to work with the United Nations, the African Union, and the regional governments to sustain and increase diplomatic and military pressure on the LRA. We have provided logistical support, training to the regional militaries pursuing the LRA. The United States has a strong interest in supporting our partners in the region to develop their capacity and to address the threats to peace and security posed by the LRA.

The United States is now deploying U.S. military advisors to improve our support to the regional coalition, to increase the likelihood of successful military operations against the LRA. And I would defer to my colleague, Ambassador Vershbow in the Department of Defense to describe the details of those operations.

We continue to consult with all the regional leaders and they have all said, granted their consent for the deployment of these advisors to the field. Remember, this is a short-term deployment with specific goals and objectives. We believe the U.S. advisors can provide critical capabilities to help regional forces succeed. We will regularly review and assess whether the advisors' effort is sufficient to enhance the regional effort to justify continued deployment.

Our Ambassadors and Embassy staff will work closely with these advisors and make sure that they are sensitive to civilian protection consideration and local regional political dynamics. The State Department has also deployed an officer to the region to help coordinate all of our efforts in the field to counter the LRA with the work of the advisors.

The administration is funding projects to help communities in the DRC that involve protection plans and join an early warning network. This includes setting up high frequency radios and cell phone towers. The same kind of early warning and basic telecommunication capacity does not yet exist across the border in the CAR. We recognize this gap and we hope to work with our partners over the coming year to help address this.

We will continue to call on the LRA fighters to peacefully disarm and leave the organization ranks and to come home. And currently, there are about 12,000 who have done so. Over the coming months, we will continue to work with the regional governments to ensure that the rank-and-file fighters and abductees who escape the LRA have the necessary support to be reunited with their families and reintegrated into normal society.

Madam Chairwoman, again, we appreciate and we are grateful to you and the members of both the House and the Senate for this bipartisan support in countering the LRA. Thank you. . . .

[Yamamoto's prepared testimony has been omitted.]

STATEMENT OF THE HONORABLE ALEXANDER VERSHBOW, ASSISTANT SECRETARY OF DEFENSE FOR INTERNATIONAL SECURITY AFFAIRS, U.S. DEPARTMENT OF DEFENSE

Mr. VERSHBOW. Thank you, Madam Chairman, Congressman Berman, and distinguished members of the committee. I want thank you all for inviting me today to discuss with you our efforts to assist the central African militaries encountering the Lord's Resistance Army.

As has already been mentioned, there are four pillars to the administration's comprehension strategy to help our regional partners end the threat posed by the LRA. The second of these is the apprehension or removal of Joseph Kony and other top LRA commanders from the battlefield. That's the focus of DoD's efforts and will be the focus of my remarks this morning.

The Ugandan military in cooperation with other regional militaries has been pursuing the LRA for several years. They've reduced the LRA's strength significantly. The LRA has moved out of northern Uganda completely. It's now operating in small groups across the Democratic Republic of the Congo and Central African Republic and South Sudan. While weakened, LRA leader Joseph Kony and other top commanders remain at large and they continue to direct the group's members to commit unspeakable atrocities. So consistent with the LRA Act and with the consent of the regional governments, we have deployed a small number of U.S. military personnel to the LRA-affected area to advise and assist the regional forces who are pursuing the LRA.

The personnel deploying under this mission will travel out to field locations with the regional forces where they will work in an advisory and liaison role. These U.S. personnel, which are primarily U.S. Army Special Forces, will collaborate with the regional militaries engaged in the counter LRA effort to strengthen information sharing, operational cooperation and overall effectiveness.

While the Department of Defense isn't in the lead with regard to the other pillars of the President's strategy, our advisors working alongside regional forces will be sensitive to the challenges of civilian protection and they'll work to ensure that protection considerations are incorporated into operational planning by our partners.

They'll also seek to encourage defections and to strengthen the relationships in sharing of information between regional militaries and local populations, officials, and humanitarian actors.

The approach we're undertaking reflects lessons learned from prior regional operations in pursuit of the LRA and it is designed to fill key capabilities gaps by enhancing regional forces' ability to fuse intelligence with operational planning. This approach will deliver maximum operational impact while exposing U.S. forces to minimum risk. Although roughly 100 personnel will ultimately deploy for this mission, we expect that only a portion of the personnel will directly advise and assist forces in the field pursuing the LRA. Most of the U.S. personnel will carry out logistical and other functions to support the advisors.

To be clear, U.S. forces deploying to this mission will not themselves engage LRA forces, but given the potential need to defend themselves, they will be equipped for combat. That's why consistent with the War Powers Resolution, the administration provided a formal report to Congress on their deployment.

We appreciate the strong congressional interest in and support for this effort and we are committed to continuing to engage with the Congress to keep you informed about the progress of our effort as it moves forward. I would say that this is a great example of a joint initiative between the Executive and Legislative branches. Despite the strong bipartisan support, we know that there are still many questions. Many of them were posed by you, Madam Chairman, and by Mr. Berman at the outset. I'd like to address several of these questions in the remainder of my remarks.

First regarding the purpose and timing of the deployment, we're providing advisors to the regional forces because Joseph Kony and the other senior leaders have proven unwilling to end the conflict peacefully and have continued to commit atrocities against innocent civilians. As you know, there was an opportunity for a negotiated peace agreement during the Juba talks in 2006, 2008, but they ended when Kony refused to sign and conducted new attacks and abductions. So regional governments have had to continue to pursue a military approach to end the LRA threat.

As for our regional partners, we have provided significant assistance to the region's militaries in recent years, training the 391st Battalion of the Democratic Republic of the Congo's armed forces, assisting in professionalization of the Sudan People's Liberation Army, providing equipment to the armed forces of the Central African Republic and supporting the Ugandan People's Defense Force, so it can both counter the LRA and maintain its critical presence in Somalia. But we think despite the assistance to date, the Ugandan and other regional militaries would benefit from increased capacity to acquire and process actionable information on the locations of LRA leaders and to convert that information quickly into operational plans.

The U.S. advisors deploying for the operation have the right skill sets to help address these capability shortfalls and the specific timing of the deployment was predicated in part upon the availability of the approach U.S. forces. . . .

[Questions, prepared statements, and the appendix have been omitted.]

Source: U.S. House of Representatives. Foreign Affairs Committee. "Deployment of U.S. Forces in Central Africa and Implementation of the Lord's Resistance Army Disarmament and Northern Uganda Recovery Act." October 25, 2011. http://foreignaffairs.house.gov/112/70947.pdf.

OTHER HISTORIC DOCUMENTS OF INTEREST

FROM PREVIOUS *HISTORIC DOCUMENTS*

November

New York City Responds to Occupy Wall Street Movement

NOVEMBER 2 AND NOVEMBER 15, 2011

With the global economy failing to grow, unemployment remaining high, and perceptions that the wealthy held an undue influence over lawmakers growing, Americans' dissatisfaction with the performance of the U.S. government continued to rise. In the early fall of 2011, this sentiment manifested itself in New York City in the Occupy Wall Street protests. By the end of the year, these protests would grow to become a full-fledged Occupy Movement, spreading to cities across the country and around the world, and bringing the demands of "the 99 percent" to the forefront of public consciousness.

A Movement Is Born

The first Occupy Wall Street protest began in New York City on September 17, 2011. The protest was motivated by a call to action from *Adbusters*, a Canadian anti-consumerist magazine. In a blog post dated July 13, magazine staff wrote, "On September 17, we want to see 20,000 people flood into lower Manhattan, set up tents, kitchens, peaceful barricades and occupy Wall Street for a few months." The post went on to describe Wall Street as "the financial Gomorrah of America" and the "greatest corrupter of our democracy." It also suggested that the protesters' demand should be for President Barack Obama to establish a presidential commission tasked with ending the influence of moneyed interests on Washington. Inspiration for the protests also came from a series of earlier international demonstrations, such as the Spanish Indignants Movement, which called for radical changes to Spain's political system in protests throughout the spring and summer, as well as the demonstrations in countries such as Tunisia and Egypt during the Arab Spring.

Adbusters subscribers and other supporters began organizing themselves in the months that followed, relying heavily on social media to spread word of their plans. New York City officials were able to determine that the protesters planned to march to 1 Chase Plaza by the famous "Charging Bull" sculpture, and fenced off the area. Protesters instead gathered peacefully in plazas and public spaces across Lower Manhattan, but eventually settled into Zuccotti Park, a privately owned park located near the city's financial district, and began setting up camps.

The overall goal of Occupy Wall Street was to protest corporate greed and social inequality, as well as the power major banks and multinational corporations held over the democratic process and their role in the financial crisis. Yet those involved in the protest also gave voice to an array of other causes and concerns. Some participants wanted the wealthy to pay a fairer share of their income in taxes, banks to be held accountable for their reckless practices, and more to be done to help the unemployed find jobs.

Others demonstrated against globalization, war, and government in general. Critics of what would become the Occupy Movement often pointed to its lack of a clear, central message and singular leader as evidence that it would ultimately be unable to effect change.

The protesters did, however, have a slogan that eventually wound its way into the political and cultural lexicon of the United States—"We are the 99 percent." The phrase referred to the findings of a Congressional Budget Office (CBO) report that concluded that the country's wealth was concentrated among the top 1 percent of income earners, and that those individuals had nearly tripled their after-tax income during the past thirty years.

As September wore on, the size of the Occupy Wall Street camp in Zuccotti Park continued to grow, and protesters organized a series of marches to different points in the city, including the Brooklyn Bridge, Times Square, Police Plaza, and Washington Square Park. To help govern the movement, the camp organized itself into various committees or working groups. These groups would present various proposals to their peers during a weekly general assembly, which were operated by discussion facilitators. The camp also set up a makeshift kitchen in the park and posted requests for food donations through Facebook and Twitter. Nearby restaurants reported that they had received an influx of take-out orders from distant parts of the country, with Occupy Wall Street supporters requesting the deliveries be sent to Zuccotti Park. In October, the protesters launched their own newspaper, *The Occupied Wall Street Journal*, with an initial print run of 50,000.

The New York Police Department (NYPD) initially made efforts to accommodate the protests to a certain extent, and established special rules. This included allowing protesters to march on any street without a permit as long as they were with an NYPD escort and stayed on the sidewalk. Protesters were not allowed to occupy a public place after it closed, but Zuccotti Park was an exception as it was open twenty-four hours a day. Yet the cooperation between police and protesters did not last.

On September 24, NYPD broke a protest march from the city's financial district to Union Square, claiming the protesters were breaking the law by not having a permit and obstructing the street. The confrontation escalated, and the police put up orange mesh netting to corral protesters, forcibly, arresting some. One deputy used pepper spray on several protesters who had already been detained by the netting—an incident that quickly became controversial and focused public attention on law enforcement's handling of the protests.

Police and protesters clashed again on October 1, when police arrested more than 700 protesters as they attempted to cross the Brooklyn Bridge. The police claimed they only arrested protesters who had blocked the road and prevented vehicles from crossing, in violation of city law, but some protesters argued they had been tricked by the officers, who initially allowed them onto the bridge. They claimed police had offered no warning before beginning to deploy orange netting to catch protesters and arrest them, but video later showed that several officers had issued warnings through bullhorns.

Occupy Wall Street Grows

Within weeks of the initial protest, Occupy Wall Street spread across the country to cities including Los Angeles, Oakland, Washington, D.C., Chicago, Boston, Baltimore, and even Hilo, Hawaii. Occupy Oakland would go on to become known as one of the most resistant and longest-running groups, due in part to violent acts on the part of some protesters and the group's success in shutting down the Port of Oakland on November 2. The Occupy DC movement began on October 1 with a smaller group of protesters gathering in downtown Washington's McPherson Square, located several blocks from the White House, and held its first significant demonstration in the city's Freedom Plaza on October 6. The Occupy DC movement became one of the longest-running offshoots of the Occupy Movement, due in part to their compliance with National Park Service rules. The "occupiers" continued to rely on social media to spread movement-related news and share demonstration methods. Several websites also helped protesters to connect, engage, and learn about upcoming protests.

On October 15, the same day as a meeting in Paris, France, of finance ministers and central bankers from the Group of 20 nations, Occupy Wall Street went global. Protests were coordinated in part through a website called 15October.net, which called on supporters to "meet on the streets to initiate the global change we want." Protests occurred in Japan, China, Canada, Australia, Mexico, and across Europe, with participants demonstrating against austerity measures, corporate greed, and the global economy's continued lack of growth. Demonstrations in Rome drew public attention in particular, as protesters set cars and trash bins on fire, smashed ATMs and shop windows, and threw rocks and bottles at police. Officials attempted to regain control by using tear-gas grenades and water cannons, injuring dozens of protesters in the process.

Throughout the movement's growth, a number of policymakers expressed support for the protesters and acknowledged their concerns. During a news conference on October 6, President Obama noted, "I think it expresses the frustrations the American people feel, that we had the biggest financial crisis since the Great Depression, huge collateral damage all throughout the country . . . and yet you're still seeing some of the same folks who acted irresponsibly trying to fight efforts to crack down on the abusive practices that got us into this in the first place." Democrats were initially cautiously supportive of the movement, but would later go on to use its 99 percent slogan in calling for passage of certain legislation, including President Obama's jobs bill. Republicans, however, including presidential candidates, were generally critical of the movement and accused protesters of waging class warfare.

Yet a number of other organizations and officials lent their support. On October 5, thousands of union members marched with New York protesters from Foley Square to the encampment at Zuccotti Park. On November 2, Manhattan Community Board No. 2, representing the Washington Square Park neighborhood, sent a letter to New York City Mayor Michael Bloomberg and Police Chief Raymond Kelly acknowledging NYPD's efforts to accommodate protests, and calling on them to continue working with Occupy Wall Street and "to show restraint and respect for the practice of the 1st Amendment freedoms." In Los Angeles, the city council unanimously approved a joint resolution on October 12 supporting the Occupy L.A. demonstration and calling for "accountability and results from the banks we invest taxpayer dollars in."

City Governments Lose Patience

Despite these showings of support, concerns about crime, sanitation, and homelessness among the various encampments began to grow. Occupy Movement organizers argued that those causing problems within the camps were not truly a part of the movement but were anarchists or otherwise seeking trouble.

But between late October and the end of the year, mayors in cities including New York, Los Angeles, Philadelphia, and Boston took steps to clear the camps out, with authorities in some cities using force to dispel protesters. On October 25, Oakland police used tear gas and arrested 100 people in an effort to prevent protesters from re-entering a City Hall plaza after they had been cleared out of the area. The following day, Atlanta Mayor Kasim Reed ordered the police to arrest more than 50 protesters and remove their tents from a downtown park.

In New York City, officials decided to take action in the early morning hours of November 15. NYPD and Brookfield Properties, the owner of Zuccotti Park, told protesters they had to remove their belongings and follow park rules if they wanted to continue using the space. The protesters were told they were free to return to the park once it was cleaned, but they would no longer be able to camp overnight. Most protesters left, but those that did not were forced out by the New York Sanitation Department at 1 a.m.

In a statement, Mayor Bloomberg explained the need for emptying the park. "The park had become covered in tents and tarps, making it next to impossible to safely navigate for the public, and for first responders who are responsible for guaranteeing public safety." Bloomberg also noted the park "was becoming a place where people came not to protest, but rather to break laws," and that while the majority of protesters had acted responsibly, those that had not had created "an intolerable situation."

That same day, *Adbusters*, which had little involvement in the movement since its initial blog posts, issued a new "tactical briefing" suggesting it might be time for protesters to "declare victory" and scale back their camps before winter set in. Magazine cofounder Kalle Lasn also acknowledged that the narrative surrounding the movement had become more focused on criminal activity and drug use within the camps, and less about what the protesters were trying to achieve.

An Unclear Future

While these developments made it appear as though the Occupy Movement may be coming to an end, protesters continue to inhabit public spaces around the world, and the movement continues to evolve. In November, a series of campus-based Occupy Wall Street groups began to spring up across the United States, with a focus on protesting tuition hikes at colleges and universities. In addition, an offshoot of the Occupy Movement called Occupy Our Homes began, protesting the current housing crisis, with participants re-occupying foreclosed homes, disrupting bank auctions of foreclosed properties, and blocking homeowner evictions. The movement will at least continue to live on in the judicial system, as a number of protesters have filed lawsuits in state and federal courts claiming their First Amendment rights to free speech and peaceful assembly had been violated by law enforcement officials' arrests and use of force to dismantle camps.

—Linda Fecteau

Following is the resolution regarding the Occupy Wall Street protests adopted on November 2, 2011, by Community Board No. 2; and a statement by New York City Mayor Michael Bloomberg on November 15, 2011, on the clearing of protesters from Zuccotti Park.

Community Board Adopts Occupy Wall Street Resolution

November 2, 2011

Hon. Michael Bloomberg

Mayor of the City of New York

City Hall

New York, New York 10007

Raymond Kelly, Commissioner

NYC Police Department

One Police Plaza

New York, New York 10038

Dear Mayor Bloomberg and Commissioner Kelly

At it's [*sic*] Full Board meeting October 20, 2011, Community Board #2, Manhattan, adopted the following resolution:

Resolution Regarding the Occupy Wall Street Protests

Whereas, a group calling themselves "Occupy Wall Street" ("OWS") have been engaged in peaceful, non-violent protests around different areas of New York City since September 17, 2011; and

Whereas, OWS has been originating their protests from Zuccotti Park in the Financial District, and sometimes spreading out to other areas of the City including, Washington Square Park, 1 Police Plaza, Brooklyn Bridge, Times Square; and

Whereas, the NYPD has worked to accommodate OWS as much as possible within reasonable limits, these include such rules as: no amplified sound; marching is permitted on any street without a permit if the protesters are with an NYPD escort and as long as they stay on the sidewalk; they must leave and may not occupy a public place after closing (e.g. Washington Square Park, that closes at midnight); and

Whereas, as of October 17, 2011, the NYPD 6th Precinct arrested 14 people, all of whom were occupying Washington Square Park after closing time; and

Whereas, many members of OWS and other protesters, residents of the downtown community and the public appeared at the NYPD 1st Precinct Council Meeting on September 29th to discuss issues of the OWS occupation of Zuccotti Park and other protest activities, including possible inappropriate behavior on the part of both some members of the NYPD and some protesters and adverse impacts of the demonstrations on the local businesses and residents; and the officers of the 1st Precinct, including the Commanding Officer,

Captain Winski, the leadership of the Precinct Council, appeared to be actively encouraging more open, cooperative and constructive communication between the NYPD, the community, and the OWS protesters;

Therefore Be It Resolved, Manhattan Community Board 2 calls on the NYPD to show restraint and respect for the practice of the 1st Amendment freedoms, and that they continue to work with OWS as they exercise these rights; and

Therefore Be It Further Resolved, we appreciate that the Mayor's office and the NYPD have allowed the protests to proceed in an organic fashion, without requiring OWS to file a permit before every march; and

Therefore Be It Further Resolved, that the NYPD, the Precinct Councils, OWS protesters, and the local communities must keep the lines of communication open and productive, and they must all continue to work with each other to find the appropriate balance that respects the rights of all stakeholders as the peaceful, non-violent protests continue.

Vote: Unanimous, with 41 Board members in favor.

Please advise us of any decision or action taken in response to this resolution.

Sincerely,

Brad Hoylman, Chair

Community Board #2, Manhattan

Jason Mansfield, Chair

Environment Public Safety & Public Health Committee

Community Board #2, Manhattan

JH/gh

c: Hon. Jerrold L. Nadler, Congressman

Hon. Thomas K. Duane, NY State Senator

Hon. Daniel L. Squadron, NY State Senator

Hon. Sheldon Silver, Assembly Speaker

Hon. Deborah J. Glick, Assembly Member

Hon. Scott M. Stringer, Man. Borough President

Hon. Christine C. Quinn, Council Speaker

Hon. Margaret Chin, Council Member

Hon. Rosie Mendez, Council Member

Sandy Myers, CB2 liaison, Man. Borough President's Office

Pauline Yu, Community Assistance Unit

Edward J. Winski, 1st Precinct, Commanding Officer

Brandon del Pozo, 6th Precinct, Commanding Officer

SOURCE: City of New York. Community Board No. 2. "Resolution Regarding the Occupy Wall Street Protests." November 2, 2011. http://home2.nyc.gov/html/mancb2/downloads/pdf/monthly_cb2_resolutions/october_2011/10october2011_environment.pdf.

Mayor Bloomberg on Zuccotti Park Clearing

November 15, 2011

At one o'clock this morning, the New York City Police Department and the owners of Zuccotti Park notified protestors in the park that they had to immediately remove tents, sleeping bags and other belongings, and must follow the park rules if they wished to continue to use it to protest. Many protestors peacefully complied and left. At Brookfield's request, members of the NYPD and Sanitation Department assisted in removing any remaining tents and sleeping bags. This action was taken at this time of day to reduce the risk of confrontation in the park, and to minimize disruption to the surrounding neighborhood.

Protestors were asked to temporarily leave the park while this occurred, and have been told that they will be free to return to the park once Brookfield finishes cleaning it later morning. Protestors—and the general public—are welcome there to exercise their First Amendment rights, and otherwise enjoy the park, but will not be allowed to use tents, sleeping bags, or tarps and, going forward, must follow all park rules.

The law that created Zuccotti Park required that it be open for the public to enjoy for passive recreation 24 hours a day. Ever since the occupation began, that law has not been complied with, as the park has been taken over by protestors, making it unavailable to anyone else.

From the beginning, I have said that the City had two principal goals: guaranteeing public health and safety, and guaranteeing the protestors' First Amendment rights.

But when those two goals clash, the health and safety of the public and our first responders must be the priority.

That is why, several weeks ago the City acted to remove generators and fuel that posed a fire hazard from the park.

I have become increasingly concerned—as had the park's owner, Brookfield Properties—that the occupation was coming to pose a health and fire safety hazard to the protestors and to the surrounding community. We have been in constant contact with Brookfield and yesterday they requested that the City assist it in enforcing the no sleeping and camping rules in the park. But make no mistake—the final decision to act was mine.

The park had become covered in tents and tarps, making it next to impossible to safely navigate for the public, and for first responders who are responsible for guaranteeing public safety. The dangers posed were evident last week when an EMT was injured as protestors attempted to prevent him and several police officers from helping a mentally ill man who was menacing others. As an increasing number of large tents and other structures have been erected, these dangers have increased. It has become increasingly difficult even to monitor activity in the park to protect the protestors and the public, and the proliferation of tents and other obstructions has created an increasing fire hazard that had to be addressed.

Some have argued to allow the protestors to stay in the park indefinitely—others have suggested we just wait for winter and hope the cold weather drove the protestors away— but inaction was not an option. I could not wait for someone in the park to get killed or to injure another first responder before acting. Others have cautioned against action because enforcing our laws might be used by some protestors as a pretext for violence— but we must never be afraid to insist on compliance with our laws.

Unfortunately, the park was becoming a place where people came not to protest, but rather to break laws, and in some cases, to harm others. There have been reports of businesses being threatened and complaints about noise and unsanitary conditions that have seriously impacted the quality of life for residents and businesses in this now-thriving neighborhood. The majority of protestors have been peaceful and responsible. But an unfortunate minority have not been—and as the number of protestors has grown, this has created an intolerable situation.

No right is absolute and with every right comes responsibilities. The First Amendment gives every New Yorker the right to speak out—but it does not give anyone the right to sleep in a park or otherwise take it over to the exclusion of others—nor does it permit anyone in our society to live outside the law. There is no ambiguity in the law here—the First Amendment protects speech—it does not protect the use of tents and sleeping bags to take over a public space.

Protestors have had two months to occupy the park with tents and sleeping bags. Now they will have to occupy the space with the power of their arguments.

Let me conclude by thanking the NYPD, FDNY, and the Department of Sanitation for their professionalism earlier this morning. Thank you.

Source: Office of the Mayor of New York City. News and Press Releases. "Statement of Mayor Michael R. Bloomberg on Clearing and Re-Opening of Zuccotti Park." November 15, 2011. http://www.nyc.gov/ portal/site/nycgov/menuitem.c0935b9a57bb4ef3daf2f1c701c789a0/index.jsp?pageID=mayor_press_ release&catID=1194&doc_name=http%3A%2F%2Fwww.nyc.gov%2Fhtml%2Fom%2Fhtml%2F2011b %2Fpr410-11.html&cc=unused1978&rc=1194&ndi=1.

Attorney General Remarks on Fast and Furious Gun-Walking Program

NOVEMBER 8, 2011

The Bureau of Alcohol, Tobacco, Firearms and Explosives (ATF) has a history of controversy and scandal. Located within the Department of Justice, the bureau works mainly to enforce gun laws and regulate the gun industry, something that has often put it at odds with Congress and the National Rifle Association, a powerful lobbying group. The ATF and its supporters argue that congressional policies make it ineffective. For example, the Firearm Owners Protection Act of 1986 banned the ATF from inspecting gun dealers unannounced more than once per year. Opponents argue that the bureau, which has 2,500 agents and runs a $1 billion annual budget, should merge with the Federal Bureau of Investigation (FBI) because both bodies work toward similar goals, thus reducing the ATF's enforcement power.

The last high-profile case gone wrong for the ATF was the 1993 raid on the Waco, Texas, compound of the Branch Davidian cult, a fifty-one-day standoff that resulted in eighty-six deaths between a gun battle and fire that destroyed the Waco compound. ATF was also embroiled in scandal in 2006, when questions circled about spending by its director. In response, Congress decided that all future ATF directors would need to be confirmed by the Senate. Since 2006, no director has been confirmed, and everyone serving in the post has been considered an acting director.

In 2011, ATF experienced another setback when its use of a controversial program, known as gun-walking, came to light. In what it titled the Fast and Furious program, ATF agents along the Mexico border allowed guns to be purchased legally and then transferred to members of Mexican drug cartels and crime rings. Instead of apprehending the suspects and weapons, ATF agents allowed the guns to enter Mexico in hopes that they would lead them to larger targets. However, the program resulted in thousands of lost weapons and a murdered U.S. Border Patrol agent.

FAST AND FURIOUS

In response to increasing violence along the U.S.-Mexico border and the increasing use of assault weapons in drug trafficking transactions, in the fall of 2009, the ATF unit stationed in Phoenix, Arizona, opened its Fast and Furious program. The program used a controversial technique known as gun-walking, which involved tracking so-called straw purchasers, those who can legally buy firearms for themselves, but who subsequently transferred the weapons to criminals or drug trafficking organizations. The Fast and Furious program sought to link these straw purchasers who bought assault weapons in the United States to drug traffickers and crime bosses in both the United States and Mexico. Weapons bought by the straw purchasers included AK-47 weapons and variants, AR-15s, Barrett .50 caliber sniper rifles, .38 caliber revolvers, and the FN Five-seveN, all of which are high-power guns.

To track these straw purchasers, the ATF worked with gun shop owners to obtain the serial numbers off of the guns that were sold. These serial numbers were entered into the Suspect Gun Database, which notified agents if the guns were recovered at a crime scene on either side of the border. Sometimes, ATF agents, with the assistance of local law enforcement, would track the movement of the weapons by following the straw purchasers to their stash houses or to the third party weapons handoffs. Outside of the gun-walking program, law enforcement agents would typically stop straw purchasers and question them to establish reasonable suspicion for an arrest, but Fast and Furious sought to allow the weapons to continue changing hands to find out where the guns ended up.

QUESTIONS RAISED AND WHISTLES BLOWN

The Fast and Furious program was led by the ATF Phoenix Field Office, and more specifically by Group VII, a gun trafficking group that focused on the gun-walking strategy. Throughout the program's existence, ATF agents and gun dealers expressed unease. In one instance in November 2009, Group VII tracked a suspected gun trafficker who had purchased 34 firearms in twenty-four days, and in the following month bought another 212 weapons with the help of his associates. In each instance, ATF agents were told to stand down and not apprehend the suspected trafficker. Those leading the operation attempted to calm the gun dealers and agents by ensuring them that the weapons were being carefully tracked and would not end up in the wrong hands.

In late 2009, ATF agents stationed in Mexico, who had not been told about the gun-walking program, began to notice a large number of weapons showing up on their side of the border that could be traced to the Phoenix Field Office. Darren Gil, attaché to Mexico, and Carlos Canino, deputy attaché, expressed concern to leaders in Washington and Phoenix about the increase in the number of weapons, but ATF leaders did not investigate their claims. In November and December 2009, two large weapons recoveries in Mexico provided the definitive evidence for Gil and Canino that Fast and Furious was a gun-walking program with the intent to send guns into Mexico.

ATF leaders in Phoenix refused to back down. In a March 2010 e-mail, group supervisor David Voth wrote, "I will be damned if this case is going to suffer due to petty arguing, rumors, or other adolescent behavior." He continued, "I don't know what all the issues are but we are all adults, we are all professionals, and we have an exciting opportunity to use the biggest tool in our law enforcement tool box. If you don't think this is fun you are in the wrong line of work—period!"

Although a strategy to end the program was called for by ATF Deputy Director William Hoover in March 2010, the continued existence of the gun-walking program became clear on December 14, 2010, when U.S. Border Patrol Agent Brian Terry was killed during a patrol in the Arizona desert after a shootout with suspected illegal immigrants. Two of the weapons found at the scene were AK-47s linked to the gun-walking program.

Following Terry's murder, Group VII agents blew the whistle on the program, alerting Department of Justice and ATF headquarters and Congress. Once it was public, the gun-walking program was quickly brought to an end. It resulted only in the indictment of twenty straw purchasers, with charges filed on January 19, 2011. The indictments were mostly for lying on the forms used to obtain a weapon. Over the course of the program, 2,020 firearms were purchased, and 227 were recovered in Mexico while 363 were recovered in the United States. The whereabouts of the remaining weapons are unknown.

Reports and Investigations

On February 4, 2011, Sen. Charles Grassley, R-Iowa, received a letter from the DOJ responding to his questions about the Fast and Furious program. In its response, the DOJ wrote, "ATF makes every effort to interdict weapons that have been purchased illegally and prevent their transportation to Mexico." Grassley and his colleague Rep. Darrell Issa, R-Calif., subsequently opened an investigation into the Fast and Furious program, trying to find out if those at the highest levels of the Justice Department were aware of the program and whether the department knowingly put guns in the hands of criminals and allowed them to disappear. ATF and DOJ leaders denied that gun-walking was used as a technique in the Fast and Furious program, stating that the term *gun-walking* only refers to programs in which ATF or DOJ directly supply the weapons to traffickers. In June, Grassley and Issa released a report on the Fast and Furious program, which found what many already suspected—agents used gun-walking techniques to allow 2,000 weapons purchased legally by straw purchasers to be handed over to third parties. Grassley and Issa called the program "ill-conceived" and "abhorrent," indicating that agents should have known that most gun recoveries would have involved a death, something that should have been avoided.

Democrats on the House Oversight and Government Reform Committee released their own report on the Fast and Furious program on January 31, 2012, that placed blame on Arizona ATF agents and not Justice Department officials. In the cover letter of the report, titled "Fatally Flawed: Five Years of Gun-Walking in Arizona," Rep. Elijah Cummings, D-Md., wrote, "Contrary to repeated claims by some, the committee obtained no evidence that Operation Fast and Furious was a politically motivated operation conceived and directed by high-level Obama administration political appointees at the Department of Justice."

Holder Testimony

Attorney General Eric Holder was called before Senate and House committees on four separate occasions to testify on his knowledge of the gun-walking program. During his November testimony before the Senate Judiciary Committee, Holder admitted that the operation was flawed, and praised ATF whistleblowers for alerting the highest levels of DOJ, ATF, and Congress that the agency needed help. Holder also expressed concern that although Fast and Furious had ended, it would continue to have an impact. "Unfortunately, we will feel its effects for years to come as guns that were lost during this operation continue to show up at crime scenes both here and in Mexico," Holder said.

Committee members asked Holder when he first learned about the Fast and Furious program's use of gun-walking, citing memos and emails sent between March and November 2010, proving that leaders at the Justice Department were at least partly briefed on the program's existence. The memos, however, contained no details on the gun-walking tactics. Holder denied seeing these documents and claimed that he and other DOJ leaders did not know about the program until after Terry's death. In previous testimony, Holder had said that he did not know about the Fast and Furious program until a few weeks before his first May 3 hearing, but during the November hearing he backtracked and admitted that he heard the name Fast and Furious in early 2011. "I did say a few weeks," Holder admitted. "I probably could have said a couple of months." Holder also admitted that the information sent to Rep. Grassley in February was flawed. "There was information that was inaccurate. The letter could have been better crafted. I regret that." But, Holder said, the letter was written with "information they thought was accurate."

During the November hearing, Holder asked Congress to provide more resources to combat gun trafficking and noted that it was necessary to maintain awareness that "We are losing the battle to stop the flow of illegal guns to Mexico." Holder said he would not take action against any officials suspected of being involved in the gun-walking program until a separate DOJ inspector general's investigation was complete.

In December, Holder was called before the House Judiciary Committee and battered by Republican members who accused him of having knowledge of gun-walking as well as accusing the Justice Department of lying to Congress in an effort to cover up the program. Some members called on Holder to resign, which he refused. The charged meeting, during which Issa said Holder was in "contempt of Congress" and Rep. Ted Poe, R-Texas, said officials at DOJ who knew about the gun-walking program should be charged with manslaughter, produced little new evidence.

—Heather Kerrigan

Following is the testimony given by Attorney General Eric Holder before the Senate Judiciary Committee on November 8, 2011, in regard to the Bureau of Alcohol, Tobacco, Firearms and Explosives' Fast and Furious program.

Attorney General Testifies on Fast and Furious Program

November 8, 2011

Chairman Leahy, Ranking Member Grassley, and distinguished members of the Committee. I appreciate the opportunity to appear before you today.

Over the last three years, I have been privileged to address this Committee on numerous occasions—and to partner with many of you—in advancing the goals and priorities that we share. I am extremely proud of the Department's historic achievements over the last two years. Despite significant financial constraints, we have effectively confronted a range of national security threats and public safety challenges.

I'm especially pleased to report that our efforts to combat global terrorism have never been stronger. Since I last appeared before this Committee in May—just three days after the decade-long manhunt for Osama bin Laden came to a successful end—the Department has achieved several additional milestones. For example, last month, we secured a conviction against Umar Farouk Abdulmutallab for his role in the attempted bombing of an airplane traveling from Amsterdam to Detroit on Christmas Day 2009. We also worked closely with our domestic and international partners to thwart an attempted plot—allegedly involving elements of the Iranian government—to assassinate the Saudi Arabian Ambassador to the United States on American soil. We have also disrupted numerous alleged plots by homegrown violent extremists—including one targeting a military recruiting center in Washington State and another targeting U.S. soldiers in Texas. Meanwhile, in one of the most complex counter-intelligence operations in history, we brought down a ring involving 10 Russian spies. And just last week, a federal jury in Manhattan convicted

Viktor Bout, one of the world's most prolific arms dealers, for his efforts to sell millions of dollars-worth of weapons—including 800 surface-to air-missiles and 30,000 AK-47s—for use in killing Americans.

On other fronts, the Department has made extraordinary progress in protecting civil rights, combating financial fraud, safeguarding our environment, and advancing our fight against violent crime. We have filed a record number of criminal civil rights cases. And, in the last fiscal year, our Civil Rights Division's Voting Section opened more investigations, participated in more cases, and resolved more matters than in any other similar time period in the last dozen years. This section is also immersed in reviewing over 4,500 submissions for review under Section 5, including redistricting plans and other proposed state and local election-law changes that would impact the access some Americans would have to the ballot box.

We've also worked to ensure that states do not institute an unconstitutional patchwork of immigration laws. In recent months, the Department has challenged immigration-related laws in several states that directly conflict with the enforcement of federal immigration policies. Not only would these laws divert critical law enforcement resources from the most serious public safety threats, they can lead to potentially discriminatory practices and undermine the vital trust between local jurisdictions and the communities they serve.

The Department also has focused its efforts on the fight against financial fraud over the last two years—by spearheading the interagency Financial Fraud Enforcement Task Force and successfully executing the largest financial and health-care fraud takedowns in history. In addition, we secured a conviction in the biggest bank fraud prosecution in a generation, taking down a nearly $3 billion fraud scheme. And, through our aggressive enforcement of the False Claims Act, a law significantly strengthened in recent years by this Committee, we've secured record-setting recoveries that have exceeded $8 billion since January 2009.

I am proud of these—and our many other—achievements. And, I am committed to building on this progress. Although I hope to spend much of our time together discussing the work that's ongoing throughout the Department, I'd like to take a moment to address the public safety crisis of guns flowing across our border into Mexico—and the local law enforcement operation known as "Fast and Furious" that has brought renewed public attention to this shared national security threat.

I want to be clear: any instance of so-called "gun walking" is unacceptable. Regrettably, this tactic was used as part of Fast and Furious, which was launched to combat gun trafficking and violence on our Southwest Border. This operation was flawed in concept, as well as in execution. And, unfortunately, we will feel its effects for years to come as guns that were lost during this operation continue to show up at crimes scenes both here and in Mexico. This should never have happened. And it must never happen again.

To ensure that it will not, after learning about the allegations raised by ATF agents involved with Fast and Furious, I took action. I asked the Department's Inspector General to investigate the matter, and I ordered that a directive be sent to the Department's law enforcement agents and prosecutors stating that such tactics violate Department policy and will not be tolerated. More recently, the new leadership at ATF has implemented reforms to prevent such tactics from being used in the future, including stricter oversight procedures for all significant investigations.

Today, I would like to correct some of the inaccurate—and irresponsible—accusations surrounding Fast and Furious. Some of the overheated rhetoric might lead you to believe that this local, Arizona-based operation was somehow the cause of the epidemic of gun violence in Mexico. In fact, Fast and Furious was a flawed *response* to, not the *cause* of, the flow of illegal guns from the United States into Mexico.

As you all know, the trafficking of firearms across our Southwest Border has long been a serious problem—one that has contributed to approximately 40,000 deaths in the last five years. As Senator Feinstein highlighted just last week, of the nearly 94,000 guns that have been recovered and traced in Mexico in recent years, over 64,000 were sourced to the United States.

The mistakes of Operation Fast and Furious, serious though they were, should not deter or distract us from our critical mission to disrupt the dangerous flow of firearms along our Southwest Border. I have supported a number of aggressive, innovative steps to do so and our work has yielded significant successes. We've built crime-fighting capacity on both sides of the border by developing new procedures for using evidence gathered in Mexico to prosecute gun traffickers in U.S. courts; by training thousands of Mexican prosecutors and investigators; by successfully fighting to enhance sentencing guidelines for convicted traffickers and straw purchasers; and by pursuing coordinated, multi-district investigations of gun-trafficking rings.

This year alone, we have led successful investigations into the murders of U.S. citizens in Mexico, created new cartel-targeting prosecutorial units, and secured the extradition of 104 defendants wanted by U.S. law enforcement—including the former head of the Tijuana Cartel. This work has undoubtedly saved and improved lives in the United States as well as Mexico. I am personally committed to combating gun trafficking and reducing the alarming rate of violence along the Southwest Border by using effective—and appropriate—tools.

Like each of you, I want to know why and how firearms that should have been under surveillance could wind up in the hands of Mexican drug cartels. But beyond identifying where errors occurred and ensuring that they never occur again, we must be careful not to lose sight of the critical problem that this flawed investigation has highlighted: we are losing the battle to stop the flow of illegal guns to Mexico. That means we have a responsibility to act. And, we can start by listening to the agents who serve on the front lines of this battle. Not only did they bring the inappropriate and misguided tactics of Operation Fast and Furious to light, they also sounded the alarm to Congress that they need our help.

ATF agents who testified before a House committee this summer explained that the agency's ability to stem the flow of guns from the United States into Mexico suffers from a lack of effective enforcement tools. One critical first step should be for Congressional leaders to work with us to provide ATF with the resources and statutory tools it needs to be effective. Another would be for Congress to fully fund our request for teams of agents to fight gun trafficking. Unfortunately, earlier this year the House of Representatives actually voted to keep law enforcement in the dark when individuals purchase multiple semi-automatic rifles and shotguns in Southwest border gun shops. Providing law enforcement with the tools to detect and disrupt illegal gun trafficking is entirely consistent with the constitutional rights of law-abiding citizens and it is critical to addressing the public safety crisis on the Southwest border.

As someone who has seen the consequences of gun violence firsthand—and who has promised far too many grieving families that I would do everything in my power not only to seek justice on behalf of their loved ones, but also to prevent other families from experiencing similar tragedies—I am determined to ensure that our shared concerns about Operation Fast and Furious lead to more than headline-grabbing Washington "gotcha" games and cynical political point scoring.

We have serious problems to address—and sacred responsibilities to fulfill. We must not lose sight of what's really at stake here: lives, futures, families, and communities. When it comes to protecting our fellow citizens—and stopping illegal gun trafficking across our Southwest Border—I hope we can engage in a responsible dialogue and work toward common solutions. And, I hope we can begin that discussion today.

I welcome any questions that you have for me.

SOURCE: U.S. Senate. Committee on the Judiciary. "Oversight of the U.S. Department of Justice." November 8, 2011. http://www.judiciary.senate.gov/pdf/11-11-8HolderTestimony.pdf.

OTHER HISTORIC DOCUMENTS OF INTEREST

FROM PREVIOUS *HISTORIC DOCUMENTS*

IAEA Releases Report on Iranian Nuclear Activities

NOVEMBER 8, 2011

While many Western countries have long had a tenuous relationship with Iran, a series of developments in the fall of 2011 further strained these relations. In November, the United Nations' International Atomic Energy Agency (IAEA) released a report on Iran's nuclear activities that provided the strongest evidence to date that the country was engaging in a bomb-making program in violation of the Nuclear Non-Proliferation Treaty (NPT). The storming of two British diplomatic compounds in Tehran, Iranian claims that they had shot down an unmanned U.S. drone, and the continued detention of two American hikers on espionage charges created additional tension between Iran and the international community.

FOMENTING NUCLEAR SUSPICIONS

Iran has long sought to develop technology that would enable it to build a nuclear bomb but has a history of attempting to conceal these activities and their possible military applications from the international community. The country's nuclear program first began in 1957. It was abandoned by Ayatollah Ruhollah Khomeini following the 1979 Iranian Revolution but re-started in the mid-1980s—a decision motivated in part by the Iran-Iraq War. In 2003, Iran's then-President Mohammad Khatami agreed to suspend uranium enrichment activities, key to developing fuel for its nuclear program, and to allow the IAEA to conduct increased inspections of its nuclear facilities. Yet three years later, President Mahmoud Ahmadinejad announced Iran would resume its enrichment activities and significantly restricted the IAEA's access to information on the country's nuclear activities.

Iran insisted throughout this period that it remained true to its obligations under the NPT, which it signed in 1968. The treaty was designed to prevent the spread of nuclear weapons and promote peaceful uses of nuclear energy. Further, Iran entered into an NPT Safeguards Agreement with the IAEA in May 1974 that provided for the implementation of various safeguards included in the NPT. Iran has traditionally claimed its nuclear program is intended to generate electricity for its citizens. Officials have also claimed that the IAEA's allegations that some of Iran's nuclear activities have militaristic purposes are fabricated and influenced by the West.

Since 2006, the United Nations has imposed four rounds of sanctions on the country, including travel bans and asset freezes applied to individuals and Iranian entities, in response to Iran's unwillingness to cooperate. The United States and the European Union have also taken separate steps to penalize Iran through additional sanctions. Russia, China, Great Britain, France, Germany, and the United States have attempted to find a diplomatic solution to the nuclear dispute with Iran and encourage greater cooperation with the IAEA, but those efforts have since stalled.

The IAEA Reports

In September 2011, Iranian Vice President Dr. Fereydoun Abbasi and IAEA Director General Yukiya Amano met in Vienna to discuss issues surrounding implementation of the NPT Safeguards Agreement. Then, on October 30, Abbasi stated Iran was willing "to remove ambiguities, if any" about its nuclear program and invited the IAEA's deputy director general for safeguards to visit Iran for discussions, an invitation the agency accepted.

On November 8, 2011, Amano issued the IAEA's report on the findings of this visit, which confirmed that Iran had not fully implemented its obligations under the NPT Safeguards Agreement. Most notably, the report laid out the IAEA's concerns that there are military dimensions to Iran's nuclear activities, stating that "Iran has carried out activities relevant to the development of a nuclear device" and that the project may still be ongoing. While the report did not provide evidence of a fully constructed nuclear weapon, it cited activities such as high explosives testing and the development of atomic bomb triggers as indicators of possible ongoing weapons research. The report also cited documents indicating Iran was working to secure a source of uranium suitable for use in an undisclosed fuel-making program; evidence that Iran had acquired nuclear weapons development information from a clandestine nuclear supply network; intelligence that officials affiliated with Iran's military had attempted to procure nuclear-related and dual-use equipment and materials; documentation of at least fourteen draft designs for a missile that could deliver a nuclear warhead to distant targets; and information that Iran conducted experiments on possible detonation systems and other components. The report acknowledged that several of Iran's activities did have both civilian and military applications, but that others were specific to developing nuclear weapons. The IAEA was particularly concerned about computer modeling studies of explosions that Iran had conducted in 2008 and 2009.

In an unusual move, the IAEA also included an annex at the end of the report to help establish the credibility of the information used to assess Iran's program. According to the annex, the agency had gathered information from more than ten countries and other independent sources, some of which was corroborated by foreigners who had helped Iran conduct its nuclear activities. Some of the IAEA's information also reportedly came from a laptop that had been smuggled out of the country by an Iranian scientist.

The report concluded that "as Iran is not providing the necessary cooperation . . . the Agency is unable to provide credible assurance about the absence of undeclared nuclear material and activities in Iran, and therefore to conclude that all nuclear material in Iran is in peaceful activities." It also requested that Iran immediately engage with the IAEA to provide clarifications about the possible military dimensions of its nuclear program, and urged Iran to fully implement its obligations under the NPT.

International Reaction

Iran's ambassador to the IAEA decried the report as "unbalanced, unprofessional and prepared with political motivation and under political pressure by mostly the United States" and claimed the agency was "playing a very dangerous game." Iranian officials also claimed the report was intended to bolster Israel's case for a preemptive military strike on the country to disable its nuclear capabilities.

International reaction to the report was mixed. The United States immediately called for tougher sanctions on Iran, and was joined in this effort by France, Great Britain, and Germany. Russia, however, expressed opposition to any new sanctions, and Chinese officials were noncommittal. Some nations were concerned the report would spur Israel to attempt a unilateral military effort against Iran, but Prime Minister Benjamin Netanyahu made no mention of such a strike in his reaction to the report. Instead, he only said it confirmed Israeli suspicions that Iran was working on a nuclear weapon.

On November 21, the United States, Great Britain, and Canada announced new coordinated measures against Iran, aimed at cutting the country off from the international financial system and disabling its central and commercial banks. The United States labeled Iran's banking system as a "primary money laundering concern" to discourage foreign banks from extending credit to the country, and also imposed sanctions on companies involved in Iran's nuclear, petrochemical, and oil industries in an effort to hinder their ability to refine gasoline. That same day, Iranian officials boycotted a November 21 meeting of ninety-seven countries at the IAEA headquarters in Vienna that had been called to discuss nuclear issues in the Middle East.

STORMING OF THE BRITISH EMBASSY

On November 29, several hundred Iranians gathered outside of the British Embassy compound in downtown Tehran to protest the new Western sanctions, which included a ban on British financial institutions dealing with their Iranian counterparts. Local police had managed to clear the protesters away once, but they later returned and managed to break through security to storm the compound. Several dozen protesters scaled the compound gates and entered the inner buildings, pulling down and burning the British flag, smashing windows, and setting a car on fire. The group reportedly stole a number of items from the compound, though British officials later said they did not take any sensitive material. That same day, a second group of protesters broke into a British diplomatic compound at Qolhak in north Tehran. Six embassy staff were held briefly by the protesters, but later freed by police. All embassy staff from both compounds were accounted for.

British Prime Minister David Cameron called the attacks "outrageous and indefensible" and in a statement declared, "The failure of the Iranian government to defend British staff and property was a disgrace." He added, "The Iranian government must recognize that there will be serious consequences for failing to protect our staff." One British diplomat raised the possibility that the Iranian government may have incited the demonstrations, as the incidents followed the Iranian parliament's passage of a measure demanding that the government expel the British ambassador in retaliation for the latest round of sanctions. Great Britain ultimately pulled its diplomats from Iran and expelled Iranian envoys from London.

FREEING U.S. HIKERS

While news surrounding Iran's nuclear program and the IAEA report unfolded, the United States also focused on the plight of two Americans who had been detained in Iran since 2009. Shane Bauer and Josh Fattal had been arrested along with Sarah Shourd in July 2009 after accidentally crossing the Iraq border into Iran while on a hiking trip. In what they called a "humanitarian gesture," Iranian officials released Shourd on $500,000 bail in September 2010 after she found a lump in her breast, but continued to hold Bauer and Fattal. The two men were convicted on charges of espionage and entering the country illegally in August 2011, and were sentenced to eight years in Iran's famous Evin Prison.

On September 14, 2011, while in the United States for a UN General Assembly meeting, President Ahmadinejad told NBC News that Bauer and Fattal would be released "in a couple of days." The hikers' defense lawyer later said the Iranian court would free the men after they had each paid $500,000 bail. Yet the following day, Iran's judiciary said the president did not have the authority to free the prisoners, and that their release was not imminent. To many, the disagreement was another sign of the growing split between the conservative-led government and the president.

Bauer and Fattal were finally released on September 21, and taken by a diplomatic envoy to a plane that flew them to Oman. The case against all three hikers remains open, but none plan to return to Iran, and Iran never publicly provided evidence to support the charges against the hikers.

A Lost Drone

On December 4, Iran claimed it had captured an unmanned U.S. drone. Iranian officials said the military brought the drone down by means of electronic warfare, and warned the United States of possible retaliation for violating Iran's airspace. The U.S.-led North Atlantic Treaty Organization (NATO) coalition in Afghanistan issued a statement saying the aircraft may have been a missing drone that operators lost contact with a week before while it was flying a mission over western Afghanistan. However, U.S. officials disputed Iran's claim that it had brought the drone down, in part because of the aircraft's stealth features, its ability to operate at relatively high altitudes, and the encryption of its flight controls, but also because it was programmed to fly back to its home base if it lost its data link to the pilots who were flying it remotely. Given these capabilities and the fact that the drone did not return to its base, U.S. officials said it was far more likely that the aircraft had experienced a technical malfunction that caused it to crash.

Several days after the incident, Iranian television aired the first video footage of the drone, which showed Iranian officials inspecting the aircraft. The U.S. Defense Department did not confirm whether the drone in the video was an American aircraft, but some lawmakers expressed concerns that Iran may be able to glean important technical information from studying the drone, despite the encryption of the craft's systems. Meanwhile, Iran's Ministry of Foreign Affairs summoned the Swiss envoy to express to the United States its "strongest protest over the invasion of a U.S. spy drone deep into its airspace" and said the United States owed Iran an apology. President Barack Obama asked Iran to return the drone, but the country has not yet obliged.

—Linda Fecteau

Following is the edited text of the report on Iranian nuclear activities released by the International Atomic Energy Agency (IAEA) on November 8, 2011. The report was declassified on November 18, 2011.

IAEA Releases Iranian Nuclear Report

November 8, 2011

[All footnotes have been omitted.]

A. Introduction

1. This report of the Director General to the Board of Governors and, in parallel, to the Security Council, is on the implementation of the NPT Safeguards Agreement and relevant provisions of Security Council resolutions in the Islamic Republic of Iran (Iran).

2. The Security Council has affirmed that the steps required by the Board of Governors in its resolutions are binding on Iran. The relevant provisions of the aforementioned Security Council resolutions were adopted under Chapter VII of the United Nations Charter, and are mandatory, in accordance with the terms of those resolutions.

3. By virtue of its Relationship Agreement with the United Nations, the Agency is required to cooperate with the Security Council in the exercise of the Council's responsibility for the maintenance or restoration of international peace and security. All Members of the United Nations agree to accept and carry out the decisions of the Security Council, and in this respect, to take actions which are consistent with their obligations under the United Nations Charter.

4. In a letter dated 26 May 2011, H.E. Dr Fereydoun Abbasi, Vice President of Iran and Head of the Atomic Energy Organization of Iran (AEOI), informed the Director General that Iran would be prepared to receive relevant questions from the Agency on its nuclear activities after a declaration by the Agency that the work plan (INFCIRC/711) had been fully implemented and that the Agency would thereafter implement safeguards in Iran in a routine manner. In his reply of 3 June 2011, the Director General informed Dr Abbasi that the Agency was neither in a position to make such a declaration, nor to conduct safeguards in Iran in a routine manner, in light of concerns about the existence in Iran of possible military dimensions to Iran's nuclear programme. On 19 September 2011, the Director General met Dr Abbasi in Vienna, and discussed issues related to the implementation of Iran's Safeguards Agreement and other relevant obligations. In a letter dated 30 September 2011, the Agency reiterated its invitation to Iran to reengage with the Agency on the outstanding issues related to possible military dimensions to Iran's nuclear programme and the actions required of Iran to resolve those issues. In a letter dated 30 October 2011, Dr Abbasi referred to his previous discussions with the Director General and expressed the will of Iran "to remove ambiguities, if any", suggesting that the Deputy Director General for Safeguards (DDG-SG), should visit Iran for

discussions. In his reply, dated 2 November 2011, the Director General indicated his preparedness to send the DDG-SG to "discuss the issues identified" in his forthcoming report to the Board of Governors.

5. This report addresses developments since the last report (GOV/2011/54, 2 September 2011), as well as issues of longer standing, and, in line with the Director General's opening remarks to the Board of Governors on 12 September 2011, contains an Annex setting out in more detail the basis for the Agency's concerns about possible military dimensions to Iran's nuclear programme. The report focuses on those areas where Iran has not fully implemented its binding obligations, as the full implementation of these obligations is needed to establish international confidence in the exclusively peaceful nature of Iran's nuclear programme. . . .

[Section B has been omitted and enumerates the facilities declared under Iran's Safeguards Agreement.]

C. Enrichment Related Activities

7. Contrary to the relevant resolutions of the Board of Governors and the Security Council, Iran has not suspended its enrichment related activities in the following declared facilities, all of which are nevertheless under Agency safeguards.

C.1. Natanz: Fuel Enrichment Plant and Pilot Fuel Enrichment Plant

8. **Fuel Enrichment Plant (FEP):** There are two cascade halls at FEP: Production Hall A and Production Hall B. According to the design information submitted by Iran, eight units are planned for Production Hall A, with 18 cascades in each unit. No detailed design information has yet been provided for Production Hall B.

9. As of 2 November 2011, 54 cascades were installed in three of the eight units in Production Hall A, 37 of which were declared by Iran as being fed with UF6. Whereas initially each installed cascade comprised 164 centrifuges, Iran has subsequently modified 15 of the cascades to contain 174 centrifuges each. To date, all the centrifuges installed are IR-1 machines. As of 2 November 2011, installation work in the remaining five units was ongoing, but no centrifuges had been installed, and there had been no installation work in Production Hall B.

10. Between 15 October and 8 November 2011, the Agency conducted a physical inventory verification (PIV) at FEP, the results of which the Agency is currently evaluating.

11. Iran has estimated that, between 18 October 2010 and 1 November 2011, it produced 1787 kg of low enriched UF6, which would result in a total production of 4922 kg of low enriched UF6 since production began in February 2007. The nuclear material at FEP (including the feed, product and tails), as well as all installed cascades and the feed and withdrawal stations, are subject to Agency containment and surveillance. The consequences for safeguards of the seal

breakage in the feed and withdrawal area will be evaluated by the Agency upon completion of its assessment of the PIV.

12. Based on the results of the analysis of environmental samples taken at FEP since February 2007 and other verification activities, the Agency has concluded that the facility has operated as declared by Iran in the Design Information Questionnaire (DIQ)....

[The remainder of Section C.1 has been omitted and contains information about activities at Iran's Pilot Fuel Enrichment Plant.]

C.2. Fordow Fuel Enrichment Plant

20. In September 2009, Iran informed the Agency that it was constructing the Fordow Fuel Enrichment Plant (FFEP), located near the city of Qom. In its DIQ of 10 October 2009, Iran stated that the purpose of the facility was the production of UF6 enriched up to 5% U-235, and that the facility was being built to contain 16 cascades, with a total of approximately 3000 centrifuges.

21. In September 2010, Iran provided the Agency with a revised DIQ in which it stated that the purpose of FFEP was to include R&D as well as the production of UF6 enriched up to 5% U-235.

22. As previously reported, Iran provided the Agency with another revised DIQ in June 2011 in which the stated purpose of FFEP was the production of UF6 enriched up to 20% U-235, as well as R&D. Iran informed the Agency that initially this production would take place within two sets of two interconnected cascades, and that each of these cascades would consist of 174 centrifuges. Iran was reported to have decided to "triple its (production) capacity", after which Iran would stop the "20% fuel production" at Natanz....

[The remainder of Section C has been omitted. It provides further detail about construction and enrichment activities at the Fordow plant and Iran's miscellaneous enrichment-related activities, as well as a statement that Iran continues to conduct reprocessing activities and heavy water–related projects.]

G. Possible Military Dimensions

38. Previous reports by the Director General have identified outstanding issues related to possible military dimensions to Iran's nuclear programme and actions required of Iran to resolve these. Since 2002, the Agency has become increasingly concerned about the possible existence in Iran of undisclosed nuclear related activities involving military related organizations, including activities related to the development of a nuclear payload for a missile, about which the Agency has regularly received new information.

39. The Board of Governors has called on Iran on a number of occasions to engage with the Agency on the resolution of all outstanding issues in order to exclude the existence of possible military dimensions to Iran's nuclear programme. In

resolution 1929 (2010), the Security Council reaffirmed Iran's obligations to take the steps required by the Board of Governors in its resolutions GOV/2006/14 and GOV/2009/82, and to cooperate fully with the Agency on all outstanding issues, particularly those which give rise to concerns about the possible military dimensions to Iran's nuclear programme, including by providing access without delay to all sites, equipment, persons and documents requested by the Agency. Since August 2008, Iran has not engaged with the Agency in any substantive way on this matter.

40. The Director General, in his opening remarks to the Board of Governors on 12 September 2011, stated that in the near future he hoped to set out in greater detail the basis for the Agency's concerns so that all Member States would be kept fully informed. In line with that statement, the Annex to this report provides a detailed analysis of the information available to the Agency to date which has given rise to concerns about possible military dimensions to Iran's nuclear programme.

41. The analysis itself is based on a structured and systematic approach to information analysis which the Agency uses in its evaluation of safeguards implementation in all States with comprehensive safeguards agreements in force. This approach involves, inter alia, the identification of indicators of the existence or development of the processes associated with nuclear-related activities, including weaponization.

42. The information which serves as the basis for the Agency's analysis and concerns, as identified in the Annex, is assessed by the Agency to be, overall, credible. The information comes from a wide variety of independent sources, including from a number of Member States, from the Agency's own efforts and from information provided by Iran itself. It is consistent in terms of technical content, individuals and organizations involved, and time frames.

43. The information indicates that Iran has carried out the following activities that are relevant to the development of a nuclear explosive device:

- Efforts, some successful, to procure nuclear related and dual use equipment and materials by military related individuals and entities (Annex, Sections C.1 and C.2);
- Efforts to develop undeclared pathways for the production of nuclear material (Annex, Section C.3);
- The acquisition of nuclear weapons development information and documentation from a clandestine nuclear supply network (Annex, Section C.4); and
- Work on the development of an indigenous design of a nuclear weapon including the testing of components (Annex, Sections C.5–C.12).

44. While some of the activities identified in the Annex have civilian as well as military applications, others are specific to nuclear weapons.

45. The information indicates that prior to the end of 2003 the above activities took place under a structured programme. There are also indications that some activities relevant to the development of a nuclear explosive device continued after 2003, and that some may still be ongoing. . . .

[Sections H, I, and J have been omitted and explain that the IAEA is still waiting for Iran to supply it with design information for new nuclear facilities, that Iran is not implementing its Additional Protocol, and that the IAEA is working to resolve several miscellaneous issues.]

K. SUMMARY

52. While the Agency continues to verify the non-diversion of declared nuclear material at the nuclear facilities and LOFs declared by Iran under its Safeguards Agreement, as Iran is not providing the necessary cooperation, including by not implementing its Additional Protocol, the Agency is unable to provide credible assurance about the absence of undeclared nuclear material and activities in Iran, and therefore to conclude that all nuclear material in Iran is in peaceful activities.

53. The Agency has serious concerns regarding possible military dimensions to Iran's nuclear programme. After assessing carefully and critically the extensive information available to it, the Agency finds the information to be, overall, credible. The information indicates that Iran has carried out activities relevant to the development of a nuclear explosive device. The information also indicates that prior to the end of 2003, these activities took place under a structured programme, and that some activities may still be ongoing.

54. Given the concerns identified above, Iran is requested to engage substantively with the Agency without delay for the purpose of providing clarifications regarding possible military dimensions to Iran's nuclear programme as identified in the Annex to this report.

55. The Agency is working with Iran with a view to resolving the discrepancy identified during the recent PIV at JHL.

56. The Director General urges Iran, as required in the binding resolutions of the Board of Governors and mandatory Security Council resolutions, to take steps towards the full implementation of its Safeguards Agreement and its other obligations, including: implementation of the provisions of its Additional Protocol; implementation of the modified Code 3.1 of the Subsidiary Arrangements General Part to its Safeguards Agreement; suspension of enrichment related activities; suspension of heavy water related activities; and, as referred to above, addressing the Agency's serious concerns about possible military dimensions to Iran's nuclear programme, in order to establish international confidence in the exclusively peaceful nature of Iran's nuclear programme.

57. The Director General will continue to report as appropriate. . . .

[The report's annex and attachments have been omitted.]

SOURCE: International Atomic Energy Agency. Board of Governors. "Implementation of the NPT Safeguards Agreement and Relevant Provisions of the Security Council Resolutions in the Islamic Republic of Iran." November 8, 2011. http://www.iaea.org/Publications/Documents/Board/2011/gov2011-65.pdf.

OTHER HISTORIC DOCUMENTS OF INTEREST

FROM PREVIOUS *HISTORIC DOCUMENTS*

Secretary Chu Remarks on Solyndra Loan Controversy

NOVEMBER 17, 2011

A 2005 Energy Department loan program meant to help the United States encourage the development of more renewable sources of energy met significant criticism in 2011 when Solyndra, the first company to receive a loan guarantee under the program, went bankrupt after spending millions in federal dollars. Both the George W. Bush and Barack Obama administrations had been keen to approve the Solyndra application to prove that the loan guarantee program was working as intended. Since taking office, President Obama highlighted the project as shovel-ready, and in May 2010, addressing Solyndra employees, said, "It's here that companies like Solyndra are leading the way toward a brighter and more prosperous future." After Solyndra's failure, a flurry of hearings took place on Capitol Hill as lawmakers tried to pin down what went wrong, who in the federal government could be held responsible for the loss of $535 million in taxpayer dollars, and how to avoid a future failure of this magnitude. Republicans, seeking to pin the failure on the Obama administration, took direct aim at Secretary of Energy Steven Chu, who refused to take the blame for the loan failure when he testified on Capitol Hill in November.

Department of Energy Loan Guarantee Program

In 2005, then-President George W. Bush signed the Energy Policy Act into law. The law gave the Department of Energy (DOE) permission to give loan guarantees to companies focused on clean energy technology and renewable energy. Under the Energy Policy Act, any company receiving a loan through the program was required to pay a credit subsidy. This subsidy was equal to the amount of the loan financed by taxpayers and protected the taxpayers if the company defaulted. Critics argued that this stipulation slowed the guarantee process, and by the time President Barack Obama took office in January 2009, no loan guarantees had been made, although a number were under review.

The American Recovery and Reinvestment Act of 2009 included an appropriation for the DOE loan guarantee program. The appropriation of approximately $6 billion would pay the credit subsidy for some of the companies applying for loan guarantees. This appropriation was seen as integral to making the loan guarantee program a success because many clean energy companies seeking a loan could not pay the credit subsidy up front. From the 2009 appropriation to September 2011, the DOE has made seventeen loan guarantees, totaling nearly $8 billion.

Solyndra Loan

Chris Gronet founded Gronet Technologies, a solar panel company in Fremont, California, in 2005. He later changed the company's name to Solyndra. In December 2006, Solyndra applied for a loan guarantee after being solicited to do so by the DOE. The Solyndra proposal included building solar panels that the company claimed were more advantageous than those of its competitors because they were cylindrical in design, making them easier and cheaper to install. Because of the shape, the solar panels were also potentially more efficient. According to Solyndra, it would use the loan guarantee to build a full-scale manufacturing plant, but admitted that the panels would not be cost-competitive until the plant was fully operational.

In August 2007, the DOE completed the technical review of Solyndra's application, and the company was invited to submit a full application, which it did in May 2008. By August 2008, the DOE determined that the application was complete based on its internal criteria. Following this declaration, the loan was submitted for an independent engineering review. The Credit Review Committee at the DOE expected to receive the application on January 15, 2009, but the DOE staff did not believe their independent market analysis would be complete by that time. To make up the market analysis gap, the staff used what it termed an "off the shelf" analysis of Solyndra's finances to look at the viability of the company and its solar panels.

In January 2009, the DOE made a presentation on the Solyndra loan to the Office of Management and Budget (OMB) to highlight the components of the Solyndra business plan. During the presentation, DOE officials said the total project cost would be more than $722 million, of which $535 million would come from the loan guarantee program. This money would be used to build a solar facility and run three production lines. At full capacity, in the second stage of Solyndra's plan, a total of six production lines would be operational. The DOE expressed concern that the technology being used by Solyndra was still in its infancy and that the company had not yet presented significant evidence that it could achieve its desired results.

On January 9, 2009, the DOE Credit Review Committee reviewed the Solyndra loan application, and found that while "the project appears to have merit, there are several areas where the information presented did not thoroughly support a finding that the project is ready to be approved at this time." Their reasoning behind this decision was that there was no independent market analysis looking at the long-term viability of the company and there was no guarantee on when the Solyndra factory would be completed or in production. A "number of issues unresolved makes a recommendation for approval premature at this time," the committee concluded.

Seeking to reverse the Credit Review Committee decision, the DOE called on an outside consultant to provide a market analysis. The first draft of the analysis was submitted to the Credit Review Committee on March 6, 2009. The committee met one week later and voted unanimously to grant a loan to the program if eleven questions were answered to address Solyndra's risks and additional information provided on Solyndra's revenue sources. The committee met again on March 17 to review the conditional loan commitment, and on March 20, 2009, announced that it had conditionally approved the loan. "This investment is part of President Obama's aggressive strategy to put Americans back to work and reduce our dependence on foreign oil by developing clean, renewable sources of energy," said Secretary of Energy Steven Chu at the time. "We can create millions of new, good paying jobs that can't be outsourced. Instead of relying on imports from other countries to meet our energy needs, we'll rely on America's innovation, America's resources, and America's workers."

On September 2, 2009, Solyndra became the first company to receive a loan guarantee. The loan required Solyndra to meet specific milestones to receive installments of its

$535 million guarantee. At the time of the finalization of the loan, it was estimated that the Solyndra project would create 3,000 construction jobs and 1,000 additional jobs once the manufacturing plant was operational. "These are the jobs that won't be exported. These are the jobs that are going to define the 21st century and the jobs that are going to allow America to compete and to lead like we did in the 20th century," said Vice President Joe Biden at Solyndra's September groundbreaking.

FINANCIAL PROBLEMS AND FALLOUT

In 2010, the fledgling company's financial problems began to come to light. In March, company auditor PricewaterhouseCoopers said the "company has suffered recurring losses from operations, negative cash flows since inception and has a net stockholder's deficit that, among other concerns, raise substantial doubt about its ability to continue as a going concern." In fact, since first applying for a DOE loan guarantee, the market price for solar panels was quickly falling as Chinese manufacturers, bolstered by government subsidies, flooded the market. In June 2010, Solyndra canceled its plans to sell public stock, and on November 3, the company announced that it was closing its older facility, laying off 175 full- and part-time employees.

By fall, the DOE refused to make a loan disbursement until Solyndra raised more capital. In response, Solyndra began working with two of its investors to restructure its loan guarantee. On February 23, 2011, the DOE agreed to the loan restructure, under which Solyndra investors would pay a $75 million credit subsidy, with the option that another $75 million could be paid if necessary. At the same time, the DOE extended the loan guarantee from seven to ten years and postponed Solyndra's first loan payment from 2012 to 2013. Because of the financial problems the company was experiencing, the DOE increased its financial monitoring, requiring Solyndra to submit weekly information about its cash flow and monthly financial reports and statements. A spokesperson for Secretary Chu, Damien LaVera, said the restructure gave Solyndra "the best possible chance to succeed in a very competitive marketplace and put the company in a better position to repay the loan."

In August 2011, the DOE called on the second $75 million credit payment to be made by Solyndra's investors, but they refused, saying they would not make another payment unless the loan guarantee was restructured for a second time. The DOE worked with Solyndra on another restructure, but on August 30, determined that a second revised loan guarantee could not be made. One day later, Solyndra announced that it was bankrupt and on September 6 officially filed for Chapter 11 bankruptcy protection. In its announcement, the company cited "dramatically reduced solar panel pricing world-wide" as the reason for its financial woes. By the time Solyndra went bankrupt, it had received $527.8 million in DOE loan guarantees.

INVESTIGATION AND HEARINGS

A number of investigations were opened both before and after Solyndra went bankrupt. On September 8, the Federal Bureau of Investigation (FBI) working in conjunction with DOE Office of the Inspector General (OIG) agents searched Solyndra headquarters and the homes of Solyndra executives. Details of this criminal investigation remain sealed. The Department of Justice opened its own investigation, as did the Department of the

Treasury OIG, which was intended to look at everything the Federal Financing Bank (FFB), an organization with power to buy government-issued loans to ensure they are run efficiently, had to do with the loan.

The House Energy and Commerce Committee Oversight and Investigations Subcommittee opened its own investigation on February 17, 2011, focused on the overall DOE loan guarantee program. By summer, the investigation turned its focus primarily to Solyndra. On July 15, Solyndra executives were called to testify before the subcommittee. At the time, Solyndra leadership claimed that the financial condition of the company and its revenue were improving. However, at a later hearing, the DOE stated that in mid-July, Solyndra was planning to revise its projected financial statements because of market pressures that would lead to a decrease in revenue.

In September, the subcommittee called the chief executive officer and chief financial officer of Solyndra to testify. Rep. Cliff Stearns, R-Fla., the subcommittee chair, opened the meeting, asking, "Why was the leadership at DOE so stubborn, ignoring every warning sign that Solyndra was a bad bet, continuing to throw good money after bad right up until Solyndra's fate was sealed and taxpayers were left holding the bag on DOE's $535 million bust?" The Solyndra executives invoked their Fifth Amendment right against self-incrimination.

In October, the subcommittee turned its attention to DOE and FFB failings. "It's clear to me the Department of Energy violated the law when they agreed to subordinate taxpayers' money to private investors," said Rep. Joe Barton, R-Texas. Gary Grippo, who oversees the FFB, testified that the DOE consulted with his department about the loan, but that Treasury cannot approve or deny loans and cannot tell the DOE how to follow energy law. The only thing his department did was to make suggestions about the loan guarantee restructure.

On November 17, 2011, Rep. Stearns convened another hearing on Solyndra, specifically targeted at the loss of taxpayer dollars and who should be responsible for this loss. "No one has admitted any fault whatsoever, and the president and our Democrat colleagues just shrug and say, 'Hey, sometimes things don't work out,'" Stearns said. Secretary Chu was called to testify and called Solyndra's bankruptcy "extremely unfortunate" but refused to apologize. Companies fail when "the bottom of the market falls out," Chu said. "This company and several others got caught in a very, very bad tsunami." During the hearing, Republicans argued that Solyndra's failure, and the subsequent loss of government funds, was caused by overt political influence and ignoring key facts. Republicans indicated that their belief was that the approval was pushed through without enough review in an effort to allow Biden to announce the loan at the plant's groundbreaking. Chu said the loan was guaranteed based not on politics but "on the analysis of experienced professionals and on the strength of the information they had available to them at the time." Democrats didn't defend Solyndra during the hearing, but did defend the DOE loan guarantee program, pointing to its necessity in allowing the United States to continue competing globally, especially with nations like China.

—Heather Kerrigan

Following is the opening statement by Chairman Cliff Stearns R-Fla. and testimony delivered by Secretary of Energy Steven Chu before the House Energy and Commerce Committee on November 17, 2011, regarding the loan given to former solar panel company Solyndra.

Rep. Stearns Opens Solyndra Hearing

DOCUMENT

November 17, 2011

We convene this hearing of the Subcommittee on Oversight and Investigations to further examine the Department of Energy's review and approval of the $535 million loan guarantee to Solyndra, as well as its repeated efforts to keep this company atop President Obama's green jobs pedestal. While our investigation continues, it is readily apparent that senior officials in the Administration put politics before the stewardship of taxpayer dollars.

We have been methodically investigating the circumstances surrounding Solyndra's failure for nine months now and have followed the facts every step of the way. Our goal is to determine why DOE and the administration tied themselves so closely to Solyndra, and why they were so desperate to repeatedly prop this company up. Why did DOE make these bad decisions, and what can we do to prevent such a waste of taxpayer dollars in the future? But as our investigation has unfolded, many more questions have emerged about the loan guarantee to Solyndra, the subsequent restructuring and subordination of the taxpayer's money, and the extent of the White House's involvement. Today we are focused on the loss of $535 million in taxpayer dollars.

When DOE was reviewing the Solyndra application at the end of the Bush Administration, too many issues with the parent company's cash flow and liquidity remained unresolved, leading them to end discussions with Solyndra and remand the application. Later that month, President Obama was inaugurated and Secretary Chu took over the reins at DOE. He implemented an acceleration policy for the loan guarantee reviews and, despite the deal posing significant financial problems, Solyndra was labeled a litmus test for the program's ability to fund good projects quickly. Secretary Chu and Vice President Biden's ribbon cutting ceremony was scheduled before DOE even presented the final deal to OMB. OMB staff did not feel as though they had sufficient time to conduct adequate due diligence and their concerns about models showing Solyndra running out of cash in September 2011 were apparently ignored. Only six months after the loan closed, Solyndra's financial troubles became increasingly severe. Nonetheless, President Obama visited Solyndra in May 2010 and proclaimed, "the true engine of economic growth will always be companies like Solyndra."

It is important to understand how Secretary Chu addressed these concerns and the extent of authority he was granted to make sure this company—so closely connected with the fate of President Obama's green jobs agenda—ultimately succeeded. In the fall of 2010, just one year after the loan closed, Solyndra had basically flat-lined and started to default on the terms of the loan. Documents show DOE granting the company several waivers, including waivers from Davis-Bacon requirements, and desperately trying to figure out ways to keep it afloat. In early December, after several lengthy negotiating sessions with Solyndra's primary investors and, despite clear language in the statute barring them from doing so, DOE made a last minute offer that would subordinate taxpayers with regard to the first $75 million recovered in the event of liquidation. We have since uncovered serious disagreements within the administration about not only the legality of this arrangement but whether it was a good deal for anyone involved but the rich hedge fund investors.

As I've said before, if Solyndra really is the litmus test, we have a much bigger problem on our hands. Two of the first three deals approved under Secretary Chu's acceleration policy have now blown up and filed for bankruptcy. GAO has serious concerns with DOE's ability to monitor the loans, the White House has now initiated a review of the portfolio, no one has admitted any fault whatsoever, and the president and our Democrat colleagues just shrug and say, "Hey, sometimes things don't work out." The Administration is still refusing to allow DOE and OMB witnesses to testify under oath, and OMB refuses to make some important witnesses available at all. Will no one from this Administration take responsibility?

SOURCE: U.S. House of Representatives. Energy and Commerce Committee. "Opening Statement of the Honorable Cliff Stearns Chairman, Subcommittee on Oversight and Investigations 'The Solyndra Failure: Views From DOE Secretary Chu.'" November 17, 2011. http://republicans.energycommerce.house.gov/Media/file/Hearings/Oversight/111711_solyndra/Stearns.pdf.

Energy Secretary Chu Testifies Before Congress

DOCUMENT

November 17, 2011

Thank you Chairman Stearns, Ranking Member DeGette, and members of the Subcommittee for the opportunity to speak with you today.

Investments in clean energy reached a record $243 billion last year. Solar photovoltaic systems alone represent a global market worth more than $80 billion today. In the coming decades, the clean energy sector is expected to grow by hundreds of billions of dollars. We are in a fierce global race to capture this market.

In the past year and a half, the China Development Bank has offered more than $34 billion in credit lines to China's solar companies. China is not alone: To strengthen their countries' competitiveness, governments around the world are providing strong support to their clean energy industries. Germany and Canada operate government-backed clean energy lending programs, and more than 50 countries offer some type of public financing for clean energy projects.

In the United States, Congress established the Section 1703 and 1705 loan guarantee programs as well as the Advanced Technology Vehicles Manufacturing Program—all of which provide support to cutting-edge clean energy industries that involve technology and market risks. In doing so, Congress appropriated nearly $10 billion to cover potential losses in our total loan portfolio, thereby acknowledging and ensuring that the inherent risks of funding new and innovative technologies were recognized and accounted for in the budget. We appreciate the support the loan programs have received from many members of Congress—including nearly 500 letters to the Department—who have urged us to accelerate our efforts and to fund worthy projects in their states.

Through the loan programs, the Energy Department is supporting 38 clean energy projects that are expected to employ more than 60,000 Americans, generate enough clean electricity to power nearly 3 million homes and displace more than 300 million gallons of gasoline annually. These important investments are helping to make America more competitive in the global clean energy economy.

Today, we are here to specifically discuss the Solyndra loan guarantee. The Department takes our obligation to the taxpayer seriously, and welcomes the opportunity to discuss this matter.

As you know, the Department has consistently cooperated with the Committee's investigation, providing more than 186,000 pages of documents, appearing at hearings, and briefing or being interviewed by Committee staff eight times.

As this extensive record has made clear, the loan guarantee to Solyndra was subject to proper, rigorous scrutiny and healthy debate during every phase of the process.

As the Secretary of Energy, the final decisions on Solyndra were mine, and I made them with the best interest of the taxpayer in mind. I want to be clear: over the course of Solyndra's loan guarantee, I did not make any decision based on political considerations.

My decision to guarantee a loan to Solyndra was based on the analysis of experienced professionals and on the strength of the information they had available to them at the time.

The Solyndra transaction went through more than two years of rigorous technical, financial and legal due diligence, spanning two Administrations, before a loan guarantee was issued. Based on thorough internal and external analysis of both the market and the technology, and extensive review of information provided by Solyndra and others, the Department concluded that Solyndra was poised to compete in the marketplace and had a good prospect of repaying the government's loan.

Solyndra's potential was widely recognized outside the Department. Highly sophisticated, professional private investors, after conducting their own reviews, had collectively invested nearly a billion dollars in the company, which was named as one of the world's "50 Most Innovative Companies" by MIT's Technology Review in February of 2010.

It is common for it to take some time for start-up companies, especially manufacturing companies, to turn a profit. And in the two years since the Department issued the loan guarantee, Solyndra faced deteriorating market conditions.

Solar PV production has expanded at the same time that demand has softened due to the global economic downturn and a decline in subsidies in countries including Spain, Italy and Germany. The result has been an acute drop in the price of solar cells, which has taken a toll on many solar companies in Europe, Asia and the United States. Meanwhile, countries like China are playing to win in the solar industry. China has invested aggressively to support its companies, and in recent years, China has seen its market share in solar cell and solar module production grow significantly, to roughly half the market today.

Facing a liquidity crisis near the end of 2010, Solyndra informed us that it needed emergency financing from its existing investors to complete scale-up of its operations and reach profitability.

The Department faced a difficult decision: force the company into immediate bankruptcy or restructure the loan guarantee to allow the company to accept emergency financing that would be paid back first if the company was still unable to recover.

Immediate bankruptcy meant a 100 percent certainty of default, with an unfinished plant as collateral. Restructuring improved the chance of recovering taxpayer money by giving the company a fighting chance at success, with a completed plant as collateral. Although both options involved significant uncertainty for the value of the company, our judgment was that restructuring was the better option to recover the maximum amount of the government's loan. It also meant continued employment for the company's approximately 1,000 workers. I approved restructuring of the loan guarantee to give the taxpayers the best chance at recovery. It is worth noting that the nearly $1 billion of original equity investment from Solyndra's investors remains subordinate to the debt owed to the government.

In August of 2011, Solyndra faced another liquidity crisis and the Department again faced a tough choice. We asked some of the smartest financial analysts to look at the health of the company. We reviewed a number of options, and ultimately, we concluded that providing additional support to this company was not in the taxpayer's best interests.

While we are disappointed in the outcome of this particular loan, we support Congress' mandate to finance the deployment of innovative technologies, and believe that our portfolio of loans does so responsibly. The President has asked for a review of the Department's loan portfolio. We support that review, and I look forward to the results. The Energy Department is committed to continually improving and applying lessons learned in everything we do, because the stakes could not be higher for our country.

When it comes to the clean energy race, America faces a simple choice: compete or accept defeat. I believe we can and must compete.

Thank you, and I welcome your questions.

SOURCE: U.S. House of Representatives. Energy and Commerce Committee. "Statement of Secretary Steven Chu U.S. Department of Energy Before the Subcommittee on Oversight and Investigations Committee on Energy and Commerce U.S. House of Representatives." November 17, 2011. http://republicans .energycommerce.house.gov/Media/file/Hearings/Oversight/111711_solyndra/Chu.pdf.

OTHER HISTORIC DOCUMENTS OF INTEREST

FROM THIS VOLUME

FROM PREVIOUS *HISTORIC DOCUMENTS*

Federal Deficit Reduction Committee Folds Without Conclusion

NOVEMBER 21, 2011

In the August 2011 agreement forged to allow the United States to raise its debt ceiling and avoid default, both Houses of Congress agreed to $2 trillion in deficit reductions. The first $900 billion in reduction was written into the debt ceiling law, and a congressional deficit reduction committee would make the remaining $1.2 trillion in cuts. If the committee failed to reach an agreement on deficit reduction, $1.2 trillion in spending cuts would automatically be made in January 2013—half of the automatic cut would come from the Pentagon's budget. The bipartisan super committee, as it became known, was not the first congressional attempt at using a committee to look at the nation's fiscal problems. There have been more than a dozen established over the past six decades, the most recent of which was the 2010 National Commission on Fiscal Responsibility and Reform, or Simpson-Bowles commission, created by President Barack Obama with the purpose of improving the nation's fiscal stability and sustainability. Congress failed to pass the commission's recommendations. "Most of these deficit commissions have ended up exactly the way Simpson-Bowles did: with lots of talk, lots of congratulations and no actual changes," said Bruce Bartlett, an economic adviser to former presidents Ronald Reagan and George H. W. Bush. The 2011 super committee met a similar fate, and on November 21 announced that it had failed to reach a consensus after nearly three months of work, thus triggering an automatic $1.2 trillion in spending cuts.

JOINT SELECT COMMITTEE ON DEFICIT REDUCTION

The Joint Select Committee on Deficit Reduction was created by the deal struck to raise the debt ceiling before a U.S. default on August 2, 2011. This debt ceiling agreement mandated up to $2.5 trillion in deficit reduction during the next decade to offset the $2.1 trillion debt-ceiling rise. The twelve-member, bipartisan Deficit Reduction Committee, which became known as the "super committee," would be in charge of determining how to reach $1.2 trillion of the total cuts. Under the agreement, the committee was given until November 23, 2011, to make recommendations to the House and Senate on how to reduce the deficit. The House and Senate, in turn, were required to immediately vote on the recommendations, with no amendments or filibusters allowed, and pass the recommendations by December 23. If the committee failed, or if Congress failed to pass the committee's recommendations, $1.2 trillion would automatically be cut beginning in January 2013. Half of the automatic cuts would come from the Pentagon; Medicaid and Medicare benefits were exempt from cuts, but provider payments would be reduced.

From the outset, both Democrats and Republicans were critical of the committee. Democrats complained that they would lose either way—Republicans could refuse tax increases, which would mean automatic spending cuts, a win for the Republican Party.

"I do not see how the committee will be successful in making a presentation to Congress," said Sen. Robert Menendez, D-N.J., calling the committee "a stacked deck." On the other hand, Republicans expressed concern that entitlement programs would not be cut deep enough because Democrats would refuse any such proposal. Both parties agreed that the committee concentrated too much power in the hands of twelve people. "I hate it with a passion," said Rep. Michael Burges, R-Texas. "In this new twelve-member committee, a seven-person vote can change the world," he said.

The bipartisan committee was made up of six Republicans and six Democrats, split evenly between the House and Senate. Senate Majority Leader Harry Reid, D-Nev.; Senate Minority Leader Mitch McConnell, R-Ky.; Speaker of the House John Boehner, R-Ohio; and House Minority Leader Nancy Pelosi, D-Calif., chose the members of the committee. As co-chair, Boehner chose Rep. Jeb Hensarling, R-Texas, the chair of the House Republican Conference, who served on the failed 2010 Simpson-Bowles panel, and voted against its recommendations. Hensarling is a stark opponent of tax increases. Reid chose Sen. Patty Murray, D-Wash., as the other co-chair. Murray chairs the Democratic Senatorial Campaign Committee, is a member of the powerful Budget and Appropriations committees, and is viewed by the Republican Party as being too political. The ten other members were Rep. Chris Van Hollen, D-Md., the ranking Democrat on the Budget Committee who played a key role in debt ceiling discussions with the White House; Sen. Jon Kyl, R-Ariz., the number two Republican in the Senate who is a strong military advocate; Sen. John Kerry, D-Mass., the 2004 presidential candidate who is a member of the Finance Committee and best known for his foreign policy experience; Sen. Pat Toomey, R-Penn., the most junior member of the committee who was first elected in 2010 and who before coming to Congress was president of the anti-tax group Club for Growth; Sen. Max Baucus, D-Mont., the chair of the Senate Finance Committee who served on the Simpson-Bowles panel but voted against the final recommendations because of deep farm subsidy cuts and changes to Medicare, Medicaid, and Social Security; Sen. Rob Portman, R-Ohio, a former White House budget director who is considered a more moderate Republican; Rep. Xavier Becerra, D-Calif., a senior member of the House Ways and Means Committee and member of the Simpson-Bowles commission who voted against the plan because it did not raise revenue enough and made too many discretionary spending cuts; Rep. Dave Camp, R-Mich., the House Ways and Means Committee chair, who served on the Simpson-Bowles commission and voted against the recommendations because of tax hikes and a failure to find a solution to rising health care costs; Rep. James Clyburn, D-S.C., the third-ranking Democrat in the House who is a member of the Appropriations Committee; and Rep. Fred Upton, R-Mich., the chair of the House Energy and Commerce Committee.

REPUBLICAN AND DEMOCRATIC PLANS

Republicans were highly organized from the outset of the committee and met in person or by phone every day; Democrats did not have this type of cohesion although they were confident early in negotiations that they could have the upper hand because Republicans did not want to see the automatic defense spending cuts. The first committee meeting was held on September 8, and the work was mainly congenial in the beginning with cupcakes brought in for birthday celebrations and lawmakers bringing in lunch for their co-workers. Committee negotiations were kicked off by a deficit reduction plan from President Barack Obama that called for $1.5 trillion in tax increases and the expiration of the Bush-era tax cuts on high-income earners. Obama also sought to close tax loopholes, limit high-income deductions, and make $580 billion in health and entitlement program adjustments.

Negotiations began in earnest on October 25, when Democrats made the first committee proposal. The Democratic plan called for reducing the deficit by $3 trillion over the next decade. These savings would be made up of a combination of spending cuts and $1.3 trillion in new revenue, mainly from tax increases, specifically for high-income earners. Additionally, $500 billion would come from health care savings, higher Medicare premiums for high-income earners, and a reduction of cost-of-living adjustments in Social Security benefits.

One day later, Republicans rejected the Democrats' plan and countered with their own. The October 26 Republican plan called for a $2.2 trillion deficit reduction, including $640 billion in nontax revenue. Democrats were quick to criticize the plan, saying that it did not cut the deficit far enough.

On November 7, Sen. Toomey proposed a $1.2 trillion package that included $300 billion in new tax revenue during the next decade and a rewrite of the tax code. The Toomey plan would permanently reduce tax revenue for all taxpayers including high-income earners. Democrats immediately rejected the plan because it made the Bush-era tax cuts permanent. Toomey's plan earned heavy support from Republicans on the committee and in both Houses.

Committee Breaks Down

After the first Democratic and Republican plans were rejected, it became apparent that the committee would likely not reach a conclusion by its November 23 deadline. On November 1, Democratic leadership suggested that the committee might be able to ask for a deadline extension, but on November 2, McConnell denied that this would be a possibility. One day later, thirty-three Republican senators sent a letter to the committee stating that any plan should include "no net tax increase" and should "balance our budget within 10 years, place entitlements on a path to fiscal solvency," and include "comprehensive tax reform that lowers rates and promotes economic growth."

On November 4, sensing the impending committee failure, members of Congress began drafting legislation that would halt the $1.2 trillion in automatic cuts. Senators John McCain, R-Ariz., and Lindsey Graham, R-S.C., drafted and proposed a bill that would replace the automatic cuts with across-the-board reductions on all government spending. Howard McKeon, R-Calif., the chair of the House Armed Services Committee, promised to introduce a bill to prevent the $500 billion in defense cuts. The president, however, announced that any legislation that reached his desk seeking to stop the automatic cuts would be vetoed.

By November 20, the committee knew it was bound for failure and began finger pointing. Reid criticized Republicans who, he said, "never found the courage to ignore tea party extremists" and "never came close to meeting us half way." Toomey blamed Democrats. "Unfortunately, our Democratic colleagues refused to agree to any meaningful deficit reduction without $1 trillion in job-crushing tax increases."

On November 21, Hensarling and Murray announced that the committee had failed to reach an agreement and would miss its November 23 deadline. "After months of hard work and intense deliberations, we have come to the conclusion today that it will not be possible to make any bipartisan agreement available to the public before the committee's deadline," the co-chairs said in a statement. "Despite our inability to bridge the committee's significant differences, we end this process united in our belief that the nation's fiscal crisis must be addressed and that we cannot leave it for the next generation to solve."

Following the announcement, Boehner promised to allow the automatic cuts to be made. "Doing otherwise is not an option," he said. Other Republicans renewed their calls to continue working to reduce the size of government and reform the tax and entitlement systems, while Democrats committed themselves to finding a deficit reduction solution that both parties could agree to. In a *Wall Street Journal* op-ed, Hensarling outlined the reasons for the committee failure, pinning it on Democratic unwillingness to compromise. "Ultimately, the committee did not succeed because we could not bridge the gap between two dramatically competing visions of the role government should play in a free society, the proper purpose and design of the social safety net, and the fundamentals of job creation and economic growth," Hensarling wrote. Conversely, Obama blamed Republicans. "There's still too many Republicans in Congress that have refused to listen to the voices of reason and compromise."

IMPACT OF THE COMMITTEE FAILURE

The failure of the committee was announced after the stock market closed, but even so, the rumor of a failure caused the Dow, Nasdaq, S&P 500, oil prices, gold, and ten-year Treasury yields to fall. The three credit ratings agencies, Standard & Poor's, Moody's Investors Service, and Fitch all agreed to maintain the U.S. credit rating but took differing outlooks on long-term credit. Moody's adjusted its long-term outlook to negative, and Fitch followed suit. Fitch's decision to move the long-term outlook from Stable to Negative "indicates a slightly greater than 50% chance of a downgrade over a two-year horizon," the credit agency stated. "The Negative Outlook reflects Fitch's declining confidence that timely fiscal measures necessary to place U.S. public finances on a sustainable path and secure the U.S. 'AAA' sovereign rating will be forthcoming."

—Heather Kerrigan

Following is a joint statement by Joint Select Committee on Deficit Reduction co-chairs Representative Jeb Hensarling, R-Texas, and Senator Patty Murray, D-Wash., on the failure of the committee to reach an agreement, released on November 21, 2011; and a statement by President Barack Obama on November 21, 2011, on the failure of the committee.

Deficit Reduction Committee Co-Chairs on Inability to Reach Consensus

DOCUMENT

November 21, 2011

After months of hard work and intense deliberations, we have come to the conclusion today that it will not be possible to make any bipartisan agreement available to the public before the committee's deadline.

Despite our inability to bridge the committee's significant differences, we end this process united in our belief that the nation's fiscal crisis must be addressed and that we cannot leave it for the next generation to solve. We remain hopeful that Congress can build on this committee's work and can find a way to tackle this issue in a way that works for the American people and our economy.

We are deeply disappointed that we have been unable to come to a bipartisan deficit reduction agreement, but as we approach the uniquely American holiday of Thanksgiving, we want to express our appreciation to every member of this committee, each of whom came into the process committed to achieving a solution that has eluded many groups before us. Most importantly, we want to thank the American people for sharing thoughts and ideas and for providing support and good will as we worked to accomplish this difficult task.

We would also like to thank our committee staff, in particular Staff Director Mark Prater and Deputy Staff Director Sarah Kuehl, as well as each committee member's staff for the tremendous work they contributed to this effort. We would also like to express our sincere gratitude to Dr. Douglas Elmendorf and Mr. Thomas Barthold and their teams at the Congressional Budget Office and Joint Committee on Taxation, respectively, for the technical support they provided to the committee and its members.

SOURCE: Office of Rep. Jeb Hensarling. "Statement from Co-Chairs of the Joint Select Committee on Deficit Reduction." November 21, 2011. http://hensarling.house.gov/news/press-releases/2011/11/statement-from-co-chairs-of-the-joint-select-committee-on-deficit-reduction.shtml.

President Obama on Deficit Reduction Committee Failure

November 21, 2011

Good afternoon. As you all know, last summer I signed a law that will cut nearly $1 trillion of spending over the next 10 years. Part of that law also required Congress to reduce the deficit by an additional $1.2 trillion by the end of this year.

In September, I sent them a detailed plan that would have gone above and beyond that goal. It's a plan that would reduce the deficit by an additional $3 trillion by cutting spending, slowing the growth in Medicare and Medicaid, and asking the wealthiest Americans to pay their fair share.

In addition to my plan, there were a number of other bipartisan plans for them to consider from both Democrats and Republicans, all of which promoted a balanced approach. This kind of balanced approach to reducing our deficit—an approach where everybody gives a little bit and everyone does their fair share—is supported by an overwhelming majority of Americans: Democrats, Independents, and Republicans. It's supported by experts and economists from all across the political spectrum. And to their credit, many Democrats in Congress were willing to put politics aside and commit to reasonable adjustments that would have reduced the costs of Medicare, as long as they were part of a balanced approach.

But despite the broad agreement that exists for such an approach, there are still too many Republicans in Congress who have refused to listen to the voices of reason and compromise that are coming from outside of Washington. They continue to insist on protecting $100 billion worth of tax cuts for the wealthiest 2 percent of Americans at any cost, even if it means reducing the deficit with deep cuts to things like education and medical research, even if it means deep cuts in Medicare.

So at this point at least, they simply will not budge from that negotiating position. And so far, that refusal continues to be the main stumbling block that has prevented Congress from reaching an agreement to further reduce our deficit.

Now, we are not in the same situation that we were in August. There is no imminent threat to us defaulting on the debt that we owe. There are already $1 trillion worth of spending cuts that are locked in. And part of the law that I signed this summer stated that if Congress could not reach an agreement on the deficit, there would be another $1.2 trillion of automatic cuts in 2013, divided equally between domestic spending and defense spending.

One way or another, we will be trimming the deficit by a total of at least $2.2 trillion over the next 10 years. That's going to happen, one way or another. We've got $1 trillion locked in, and either Congress comes up with $1.2 trillion, which so far they've failed to do, or the sequester kicks in, and these automatic spending cuts will occur that bring in an additional $1.2 trillion in deficit reduction.

Now, the question right now is whether we can reduce the deficit in a way that helps the economy grow—that operates with a scalpel, not with a hatchet—and if not, whether Congress is willing to stick to the painful deal that we made in August for the automatic cuts. Already, some in Congress are trying to undo these automatic spending cuts.

My message to them is simple: No. I will veto any effort to get rid of those automatic spending cuts to domestic and defense spending. There will be no easy off-ramps on this one.

We need to keep the pressure up to compromise, not turn off the pressure. The only way these spending cuts will not take place is if Congress gets back to work and agrees on a balanced plan to reduce the deficit by at least $1.2 trillion. That's exactly what they need to do. That's the job they promised to do. And they've still got a year to figure it out.

Although Congress has not come to an agreement yet, nothing prevents them from coming up with an agreement in the days ahead. They can still come together around a balanced plan. I believe Democrats are prepared to do so. My expectation is, is that there will be some Republicans who are still interested in preventing the automatic cuts from taking place. And as I have from the beginning, I stand ready and willing to work with anybody that's ready to engage in that effort to create a balanced plan for deficit reduction.

Now, in the meantime, we've got a lot of work left to do this year. Before Congress leaves next month, we have to work together to cut taxes for workers and small-business owners all across America. If we don't act, taxes will go up for every single American, starting next year. And I'm not about to let that happen. Middle class Americans can't afford to lose $1,000 next year because Congress won't act. And I can only hope that Members of Congress who've been fighting so hard to protect tax breaks for the wealthy will fight just as hard to protect tax breaks for small-business owners and middle class families.

We still need to put construction workers back on the job rebuilding our roads and our bridges. We still need to put our teachers back in the classroom educating our kids.

So when everybody gets back from Thanksgiving, it's time to get some work done for the American people. All around the country, Americans are working hard to live within their means and meet their responsibilities. And I know they expect Washington to do the same.

Thanks.

SOURCE: U.S. Executive Office of the President. "Remarks on the Joint Select Committee on Deficit Reduction." November 21, 2011. *Compilation of Presidential Documents* 2011, no. 00893 (November 21, 2011). http://www.gpo.gov/fdsys/pkg/DCPD-201100893/pdf/DCPD-201100893.pdf.

OTHER HISTORIC DOCUMENTS OF INTEREST

FROM THIS VOLUME

FROM PREVIOUS *HISTORIC DOCUMENTS*

December

Secretary of State Clinton's Visit to Burma

DECEMBER 1 AND 2, 2011

After two decades of strained relations, the United States and Burma (Myanmar) took an important step toward improving relations in December 2011 when Secretary of State Hillary Rodham Clinton met with the Burmese president, U Thein Sein, and other senior officials. The visit by Secretary Clinton came after approximately twenty visits by senior U.S. diplomats in recent years, and was the first visit by a U.S. secretary of state in more than five decades. The top U.S. diplomat expressed ongoing concerns over nuclear non-proliferation and Burma's military relations with North Korea; political reform and democratization; reconciliation with ethnic minorities; the release of political prisoners; and the rule of law and human liberties. President Thein Sein outlined the government's planned reform agenda and noted that the country welcomed support from the United States and international community. During her visit, Secretary Clinton also met with the leader of the main opposition, Aung San Suu Kyi, who as recently as November 2010 had been held under house arrest. Secretary Clinton said that the United States would take "measured steps" to encourage continued reform in the reclusive nation.

BILATERAL RELATIONS DETERIORATE

In November 2011, President Barack Obama announced that Secretary of State Hillary Rodham Clinton would visit Burma the following month. Since 1989, Burma has been officially known as the Republic of the Union of Myanmar, but the U.S. government, as a matter of policy, does not recognize the name. Secretary Clinton was the first U.S. Secretary of State to visit the isolated nation since 1955, when John Foster Dulles made an official visit with the intention of convincing the Burmese government to sign a defense alliance against China.

The political relationship between the United States and Burma has been strained in recent decades. A military junta took power in Burma in a coup d'état on March 2, 1962. By 1988, public dissatisfaction over the government's economic management and political status quo resulted in widespread pro-democracy protests, known as the 8888 Uprising. Security forces killed thousands of protestors, and the uprising spurred another military coup. Ongoing demonstrations by pro-democracy protestors resulted in the government imposing martial law in 1989. The country's military leadership determined that elections would be held, and in May 1990 Burma's first free elections in almost thirty years took place. The opposition National League for Democracy, led by Aung San Suu Kyi, won 392 out of the 489 seats in the parliament. However, the military junta refused to recognize the results of the election.

The bilateral relationship between the United States and Burma was severely strained by these events. Indeed, in the aftermath of the government's violent suppression of protesters and failure to recognize the outcome of the election, the U.S. government downgraded its level of representation in the country from Ambassador to Charge d'Affaires. Since 1990, the United States had maintained broad sanctions against Burma and criticized the Southeast Asian nation for failing to meet numerous international obligations, including those for religious freedom and the prevention of human and drug trafficking. Nevertheless, in early 2009 Secretary Clinton launched a policy review of U.S.-Burma relations. The outcome of the review, which was announced in September 2009 by President Obama, reaffirmed the position that the United States supports a "unified, peaceful, prosperous, and democratic Burma that respects the human rights of its citizens." The president also spoke of "flickers" of progress in the reclusive country. Importantly, the policy review concluded that the United States would provide humanitarian assistance to Burma and engage in senior-level dialogue. That same month, and in the months that followed, the first such meetings between senior Obama administration and Burmese officials took place. Early the following year, Obama announced the nomination of Derek Mitchell to the post of U.S. special representative and policy coordinator for Burma. Mitchell was confirmed to the role in August 2011.

Meanwhile, in November 2010 Burma held parliamentary elections for the first time in two decades. The polls, which were marred by voting irregularities, resulted in the military-aligned political party, the Union Solidarity and Development Party, securing the majority of contested seats. Although the opposition parties did pick up a small number of seats, the military's cement-like grip on power remained in place.

GOVERNMENT'S REFORM AGENDA

On December 1, 2011, Secretary Clinton met with Burma's new president, U Thein Sein, and other senior Burmese officials. A senior U.S. official described the meeting as "relatively formal," with both President Thein Sein and Secretary Clinton giving lengthy presentations. The president addressed three key areas of reform: economic, political, and minority relations. During the presentation, the president acknowledged the leadership's lack of experience with reform and stated that they were receptive to outside help. In regard to economic reform, the president addressed his desire to continue efforts to alleviate poverty and spur economic development. In addition, he noted that the government needed to do more in terms of education.

The president also spoke to political and minority relations reforms. Just a month prior to Secretary Clinton's visit, the Burmese leader had denied that the country had political prisoners. Yet during his presentation, President Thein Sein noted the recent release of 200 political prisoners and stated that the government was considering additional releases in an effort to create a more inclusive political environment. Importantly, the presentation also touched upon Burma's support for nuclear non-proliferation, and the president provided reassurances that the government would uphold its international commitments in this area. In regard to minority relations, the president indicated that discussions with ten minority groups were underway. The ultimate goal, he stated, was ceasefire, reconciliation, and for minority groups to come into the political fold. Relations between the government and ethnic minorities have been fraught since the country's independence in 1948. Many ethnic groups fought for secession for their regions, and while most of the country is now under the control of the central government, some armed groups remain in active opposition.

CLINTON ENCOURAGES REFORM

Following President Thein Sein's presentation, Secretary Clinton addressed the audience, touching upon five key areas of concern for the U.S. government. These areas were nuclear non-proliferation and Burma's military relations with North Korea, political reform and democratization, reconciliation with ethnic minorities, the release of political prisoners, and the rule of law and human liberties. In particular, Secretary Clinton called for Burma to end its military relations with North Korea and expressed concern over nuclear pro-liferation. U.S. officials have voiced concerns about possible ballistic missile development and even the sharing of nuclear technology between the two countries.

Clinton also called for the continuation of domestic political reform, including allowing any interested opposition parties to register and participate in elections, and for by-elections to be held in a timely manner. According to a senior U.S. official, Secretary Clinton spoke extensively about ongoing conflicts with ethnic minority groups, and U.S. concern over human rights abuses and the use of rape as a weapon. Moreover, Clinton noted that the United States would support efforts for reconciliation and encourage international assistance in this area.

Secretary Clinton repeated to journalists at a press conference what she said privately during the meeting regarding political reform. She told the Burmese leadership that while the United States encouraged efforts in political reform, and applauded the release of 200 political prisoners, "no person in any country should be detained for exercising universal freedoms of expression, assembly, and conscience." Clinton also called on the Burmese government to implement UN Security Council resolutions related to nuclear non-proliferation.

While Secretary Clinton spoke to each of the areas in which Burma needed to make further progress, she offered a carrot for continued reforms—"measured steps to lessen the isolation and to help improve the lives" of the Burmese people. The secretary of state outlined those measured steps, which included an invitation to join the Lower Mekong Initiative and an agreement to allow International Monetary Fund (IMF) and World Bank assessment teams to review the country's needs in the areas of development and poverty reduction. The United States had previously blocked efforts by the IMF and World Bank to operate in Burma. Moreover, Secretary Clinton discussed loosening restrictions on United Nations Development Programme (UNDP) health and microfinance programs. Notably, a joint effort to recover the remains of U.S. service members who were killed in Burma during World War II was also tabled. Secretary Clinton said that "these are beginning steps, and we are prepared to go even further if reforms maintain momentum."

CLINTON MEETS WITH AUNG SAN SUU KYI

In addition to meeting with the president and senior-level Burmese officials, Secretary Clinton also met with the opposition leader and Nobel peace laureate Aung San Suu Kyi. The first meeting was a private dinner, at the beginning of which the two women reportedly greeted each other warmly and Clinton said later that, "it was like seeing a friend you hadn't seen for a very long time even though it was our first meeting." Clinton and Suu Kyi also held a morning of formal talks at Suu Kyi's home in Rangoon, Burma's largest city, where the opposition leader was held under house arrest for a number of years. During the meeting, Clinton and Suu Kyi agreed to work together toward a democratic Burma.

At a press conference following the meeting, Suu Kyi said, "I am very confident that if Burma and the United States work together . . . there will be no turning back from the road to democracy," although she added that the country was not yet on that road.

The Obama administration did not develop a timetable for action by either country. But Secretary Clinton did refer to President Obama's reference to "flickers" of progress in Burma and stated that, "It will be up to the leaders and the people to fan those flickers of progress into flames of freedom that light the path toward a better future. That and nothing less is what it will take for us to turn a solitary visit into a lasting partnership." It is likely that the next step, "if reforms maintain momentum," would be for the United States to appoint an ambassador to Burma, upgrading its current diplomatic status. Economic sanctions, however, are likely to remain in place until substantial reforms have been implemented.

—Hilary Ewing

Following are edited remarks from a press conference with Secretary of State Hillary Rodham Clinton on December 1, 2011, regarding her trip to Burma; and a joint statement by Secretary Clinton and Aung San Suu Kyi on December 2, 2011.

Secretary Clinton Remarks on Her Trip to Burma

December 1, 2011

SECRETARY CLINTON: Good afternoon, and—*mingalaba*, is that how you say it? Yeah? How?

QUESTION: *Mingalaba.*

SECRETARY CLINTON: *Mingalaba.* Thank you.

Let me start by saying that I want to emphasize that while I may be the first United States Secretary of State to visit in over a half century, our two nations are far from strangers. We've had a long history together, from the earliest American missionaries to generations of traders and merchants to the shared sacrifices of World War Two. The United States was among the first to recognize this country's independence, and we have welcomed the many contributions of Burmese Americans to our own culture and prosperity. And Americans from all walks of life are following closely the events here.

So I come with a great deal of interest and awareness of what is happening. And on behalf of my country and President Obama, I came to assess whether the time is right for a new chapter in our shared history. Today, I met with President Thein Sein, his foreign minister, other senior ministers, and the speakers and members of parliament in both houses. We had candid, productive conversations about the steps taken so far, and the path ahead for reform.

Tomorrow, I will be meeting with ethnic minority groups and civil society. I will be meeting tonight and tomorrow with Aung San Suu Kyi and other members of the political opposition.

President Thein Sein has taken the first steps toward a long-awaited opening. His government has eased some restrictions on the media and civil society, opened a dialogue with Aung San Suu Kyi, rewritten election and labor laws, and released 200 prisoners of conscience. The president told me he seeks to build on these steps, and I assured him that these reforms have our support. I also told him that while the measures already taken may be unprecedented and certainly welcome, they are just a beginning. It is encouraging that political prisoners have been released, but over a thousand are still not free. Let me say publicly what I said privately earlier today. No person in any country should be detained for exercising universal freedoms of expression, assembly, and conscience.

It is also encouraging that Aung San Suu Kyi is now free to take part in the political process. But that, too, will not be sufficient unless all political parties can open offices throughout the country and compete in free, fair, and credible elections. We welcome initial steps from the government to reduce ethnic tensions and hostilities. But as long as terrible violence continues in some of the world's longest-running internal conflicts, it will be difficult to begin a new chapter.

This country's diversity, its dozens of ethnic groups and languages, its shrines, pagodas, mosques, and churches should be a source of strength in the 21st century. And I urged the president to allow international humanitarian groups, human rights monitors and journalists access to conflict zones.

National reconciliation remains a defining challenge, and more needs to be done to address the root causes of conflict and to advance an inclusive dialogue that will finally bring peace to all of the people. We discussed these and many other challenges ahead, including the need to combat illegal trafficking in persons, weapons, and drugs. And I was very frank in stating that better relations with the United States will only be possible if the entire government respects the international consensus against the spread of nuclear weapons. We look to the government to fully implement UN Security Council Resolutions 1718 and 1874, and we support the government's stated determination to sever military ties with North Korea.

In each of my meetings, leaders assured me that progress would continue and broaden. And as it does, the United States will actively support those, both inside and outside of government, who genuinely seek reform. For decades, the choices of this country's leaders kept it apart from the global economy and the community of nations. Today, the United States is prepared to respond to reforms with measured steps to lessen the isolation and to help improve the lives of its citizens. That includes an invitation to join neighboring countries as an observer in the Lower Mekong Initiative. We have agreed to IMF and World Bank assessment missions to begin studying the needs on the ground for development, particularly in rural areas, and poverty reduction.

We discussed loosening restrictions on UNDP health and microfinance programs, pursuing education and training efforts, and resuming joint counter-narcotics missions. And just as the search for missing Americans once helped us repair relations with Vietnam, today we spoke about a new joint effort to recover the remains of hundreds of Americans lost here during World War II during the building of the Burma Road.

These are beginning steps, and we are prepared to go even further if reforms maintain momentum. In that spirit, we are discussing what it will take to upgrade diplomatic relations and exchange ambassadors. Over time, this could become an important channel to air concerns, monitor and support progress, and build trust on both sides.

The last time an American Secretary of State came to Burma, it was John Foster Dulles, and this country was considered the jewel of Asia, a center of higher learning and the rice bowl of the region. In the last half century, other countries have raced ahead and turned East Asia into one of the world's great centers of dynamic growth and opportunity. So the most consequential question facing this country, both leaders and citizens, is not your relationship with the United States or with any other nation. It is whether leaders will let their people live up to their God-given potential and claim their place at the heart of the 21st century, a Pacific century.

There is no guarantee how that question will be answered. If the question is not answered in a positive way, then once again, the people could be left behind. But if it is answered in a positive way, I think the potential is unlimited.

I'm told there is an old Burmese proverb which says, "When it rains, collect water." Well, we don't know yet if the path to democracy is irreversible, as one of the leaders told me today, if the opening of the economy will be considered a positive and moved quickly to achieve. So the question is not for me to answer. The question is for all of you, particularly leaders, to answer. But we owe it to nearly 60 million people who seek freedom, dignity, and opportunity to do all we can to make sure that question is answered positively.

President Obama spoke of flickers of progress. Well, we know from history that flickers can die out. They can even be stamped out. Or they can be ignited. It will be up to the leaders and the people to fan those flickers of progress into flames of freedom that light the path toward a better future. That and nothing less is what it will take for us to turn a solitary visit into a lasting partnership. As I told President Thein Sein earlier today, the United States is prepared to walk the path of reform with you if you choose to keep moving in that direction. And there's no doubt that direction is the right one for the people.

I'll be happy to take some questions.

MS. NULAND: We have time for four questions today. I guess the first one is *The New York Times*, Steve Myers.

QUESTION: Thanks, Toria. Madam Secretary, thank you. Sorry. Thank you, Madam Secretary. The—Aung San Suu Kyi yesterday said that she personally trusted the president but wasn't sure about the views of others in the government. After your meetings today, do you share that view?

And in your discussions today, did you talk about a timetable for some of the reciprocal steps from both countries that you would like to see? Is this a matter of months or years? Thank you.

SECRETARY CLINTON: Well, Steve, we had a very substantive, serious, and candid, long discussion, both in the formal setting and then over lunch, between myself and President Thein Sein. He laid out a comprehensive vision of reform, reconciliation, and economic development for his country, including specifics such as the release of political prisoners, an inclusive political process, and free, fair, and credible bi-elections, a rigorous peace and reconciliation process to bring to an end some of the longest-standing conflicts anywhere in the world, and strong assurances regarding his country's compliance with United Nations Security Council Resolutions 1718 and 1874, and their nonproliferation commitments with respect to North Korea.

I made it clear that he and those who support that vision which he laid out for me, both inside and outside of government, will have our support as they continue to make progress, and that the United States is willing to match actions with actions. We want to be a partner in this reform process, starting with the steps that I laid out today. I also told him that, based on my experience and my observation, I am well aware that he has people in his government who are very supportive of this reform agenda, and he has people who are worried about it or opposed to it, and he has people in the middle who are sitting on the fence, trying to make up their minds. . . .

[Additional questions on the meeting with Burma's president, the Chinese response to the U.S. visit to Burma, and the release of political prisoners have been omitted.]

SOURCE: U.S. Department of State. Media Center. "Press Availability in Nay Pyi Taw, Burma." December 1, 2011. http://www.state.gov/secretary/rm/2011/12/177994.htm.

DOCUMENT

Remarks by Secretary Clinton and Aung San Suu Kyi

December 2, 2011

MS. KYI: Are we all settled? I'd like to say that it's a great pleasure and a privilege for us—can you hear me—

QUESTION: Yes.

MS. KYI: —to welcome Secretary Clinton to my country and to my home. It's, I think, a historical moment for both our countries because we hope that from this meeting, we will be able to proceed to us renewing the ties of friendship and understanding that bound our countries together since independence. There has been times when that tie has weakened, but I don't think it was ever really broken. And we hope that from now on, not only will the understanding and friendship between our two countries be reestablished and strengthened, but we will bring in also other members of the international community who share our commitment to human dignity, to peace, to democratic institutions, and to sustainable development.

We are so happy that Secretary Clinton had very good meetings at Nay Pyi Taw, and we are happy with the way in which the United States is engaging with us. It is through engagement that we hope to promote the process of democratization. Because of this engagement, I think our way ahead will be clearer, and we will be able to trust that the process of democratization will go forward. For this, we do need the help not just of the United States, but of other members of the international community. We need capacity-building in Burma, we need technical assistance, we are very eager that the time will come soon when the World Bank can send in an assessment team to find out what it is that our country really needs.

Before we decide what steps to take, we have to find out what our greatest needs are. And of course, two of the greatest needs of this country are rule of law and a cessation to civil war. All hostilities must cease within this country as soon as possible. That will really build up ethnic harmony and peace and a union that is prosperous and stable.

Now, when I say rule of law, I must mention that rule of law is essential to prevent more prisoner—political prisoners from appearing in Burma. First of all, we need all those who are still in prison to be released, and we need to ensure that no more are arrested in future for their beliefs. This is why we put so much emphasis on rule of law, and I am confident that the United States and our other friends will help us in our endeavors to bring rule of law to this country, and also in our endeavors to help our country to develop its educational and health facilities, which are the basic needs of all our peoples.

Whatever we do in the predominantly Burmese areas, we hope to be matched by similar programs and projects in the ethnic nationality areas, because we are a union of many peoples. And in a union of many peoples, there must be equality, there must be consideration for those who are in gracious need. And to that end, we look to our friends from all over the world to help us to meet the needs of the people of our country.

I am very confident that if we all work together—and by "we," I mean the Government of Burma, the opposition in Burma, our friends from the United States and all over the world who are committed to the same values—if we go forward together, I am confident that there will be no turning back from the road towards democracy. We are not on that road yet, but we hope to get there as soon as possible with the help and understanding of our friends.

I was very pleased to read today that the Chinese foreign ministry said—put out a statement welcoming the engagement of the United States and Burma. This shows that we have the support of the whole world. And I'm particularly pleased because we hope to maintain good, friendly relations with China, our very close neighbor—and not just with China, but with the rest of the world.

Now I think I must give time to Secretary Clinton, who you're all wishing to hear, because we are rather behind schedule.

SECRETARY CLINTON: Well, I want to begin by not only thanking you for your hospitality and welcoming us all here to your home today, but for your steadfast and very clear leadership of the opposition and of many here in Burma whose voices would not otherwise be heard, including ethnic nationalities.

About the way forward, democracy is the goal. That has been the goal from the very beginning. And yet we know that it has been a long, very difficult path that has been followed. We do see openings today that, as Aung San Suu Kyi just said, give us some grounds for encouragement. My visit, both here with members of the opposition as well as representatives of civil society and the ethnic nationalities, in concert with my visit with government officials yesterday, is intended to explore the path forward.

The United States wants to be a partner with Burma. We want to work with you as you further democratization, as you release all political prisoners, as you begin the difficult but necessary process of ending the ethnic conflicts that have gone on far too long, as you hold elections that are free, fair, and credible. But we also, because of our close work with you, know that there's much work to be done to build the capacity of the government. This is going to be an area that we will continue to consult closely with you to see what kind, as you said, technical assistance might be offered. The rule of law is essential in any democracy, and we will also look for ways we can work to further that.

But let me conclude by underscoring that you have been an inspiration, but I know you feel that you are standing for all the people of your country who deserve the same rights and freedoms of people everywhere. The people have been courageous and strong in the face of great difficulty over too many years. We want to see this country take its rightful place in the world. We want to see every child here given the chance for a good education, for the healthcare that he or she needs, for a job that will support a family, for development not only in the cities, but in the rural areas as well.

So we hold the dream that you have so long represented to many of us around the world, and we want to be a partner with you, with the new government, and with all people of goodwill who want finally to see the future that is right there waiting realized for every single citizen.

So thank you again for your gracious hospitality, but thank you even more for your leadership and your strong partnership with the United States.

MS. KYI: I would like to thank—end with a last note of thanks, a word of thanks to President Obama and to the United States of America for working so closely with us throughout, consulting us along each step of the way, and for the careful and collaborated way in which they are approaching engagement in this country. This will be the beginning of a new future for all of us, provided we can maintain it, and we hope to be able to do so.

Thank you.

SECRETARY CLINTON: Thank you so much.

SOURCE: U.S. Department of State. Media Center. "Remarks With Aung San Suu Kyi." December 2, 2011. http://www.state.gov/secretary/rm/2011/12/178106.htm.

OTHER HISTORIC DOCUMENTS OF INTEREST

FROM PREVIOUS *HISTORIC DOCUMENTS*

Russian Voters Elect State Duma Amid Fraud Allegations

DECEMBER 5, 6, 13, AND 22, 2011

Vladimir Putin has dominated the Russian political landscape since 1999, when then-President Boris Yeltsin named him acting prime minister. Putin was subsequently elected president in 2000, a position he held until 2008, when Russian law prevented him from seeking a third consecutive term. Putin, who was widely popular despite his consolidation of government control, guided his handpicked successor, Dmitry Medvedev, from the position of prime minister to the presidency. Medvedev appointed Putin prime minister after his victory. Throughout 2010 and into 2011, Putin's popularity remained near 80 percent, but discontent about the weakened economy and public perception of widespread corruption within the highest ranks of government was spreading. Although it did not have a significant impact on Putin, the party he leads, United Russia, bore the brunt of this discontent. Once as widely popular as Putin, the party held a more than two-thirds majority in the lower house of parliament, the State Duma, allowing it to pass any law and make any constitutional change without opposition support. But in early December 2011, Russian voters went to the polls and dealt United Russia a significant blow, taking away its opposition-proof majority. Putin would go on to be reelected to a non-consecutive third term in March 2012.

State Duma Election

When the date of the State Duma election was announced in August, United Russia was expected to easily achieve another large victory over the three main opposition parties, the Communists, Liberal Democrats, and A Just Russia. Although anticipating a victory in the 450-member body, President Dmitry Medvedev said he "would very much like our next Duma to reflect the political preferences of the largest possible number of citizens."

But when the votes were counted after the December 4 vote, United Russia suffered an embarrassing loss and was unable to garner 50 percent of the votes. In the previous Duma election in 2007, the party received more than 64 percent of the vote. In 2011, United Russia lost 77 seats and would hold a total of 238 in the next session. "This is a bad climate for Putin. He has got used to the fact that he controls everything, but now how can he go into a presidential campaign when United Russia has embittered people against their leader," asked Dmitry Oreshkin, an independent political analyst. All three Russian opposition groups made significant gains. The Communist party made the largest gain, receiving nearly 20 percent of the vote and ninety-two seats. "Russia has a new political reality," said Communist member of the Duma Sergei Obukhov. A Just Russia won sixty-four Duma seats, while the Liberal Democrats won fifty-six.

In response to the election outcome, Putin expressed his willingness to work with the opposition parties. "This is an optimal result which reflects the real situation in the country,"

Vladmir Putin said. "Yes there were losses. . . . They are inevitable for any political force, particularly for the one which has been carrying the burden of responsibility for the situation in the country." Medvedev agreed. "A tragedy has not taken place," he said. "On the contrary, in my view, everything is quite decent and respectable. I for one am glad that we shall have a merrier parliament because we understand that truth can emerge only from a debate."

The vote, which was seen as a referendum on Putin, was considered by his Russian opponents and international observers to be fraudulent. International observers noted that a limited number of political parties were allowed to participate—only seven were allowed to run in the election, with no vocal opposition groups allowed to participate. In the 2007 election, eleven parties had been allowed to participate. They also noted that United Russia received an abundance of positive coverage heading into the election from state-run media. Inside Russia, there were claims that United Russia used government funds for its campaigns and reports of ballot stuffing. According to Golos, the only independent Russian election monitor, which is funded mainly by the United States and European Union, the liberal media outlets of Ekho Moskvy and Slon.ru were taken offline at 8 a.m. on Election Day.

In the run-up to Election Day, the Russian government attempted to discredit Golos, running television programs indicating that the group supported opposition parties and was trying to overthrow the elections with the backing of the United States. The group was fined $1,000 for violating an election law that disallows publishing any opinion research conducted on an election five days before the vote is scheduled to take place. "The campaign against Golos provides additional reason for doubt about the legitimacy of the parliamentary election that will take place in Russia . . . and the broader state of democracy there," the Helsinki Commission, a board that advises the United States on issues related to security, human rights, and other policies in Europe, said in a statement.

After the election, Golos reported receiving 5,300 complaints about election law violations, approximately one-third of which were from students and government employees who said they were pressured to support United Russia. Golos director Liliya Shibanova was detained at a Moscow airport for carrying a laptop that officials said contained illegal software. She was released after agreeing to give her laptop to airport security.

Despite reports of fraud, Russia's Central Election Commission verified the results. "The elections are declared valid, and there is no reason for any other assessment," said Stanislav Vavilov, the deputy chair of the commission. "There is no reason to revise the results of the elections."

PROTESTS

Widespread, public displays of discontent with the government have been rare since Putin first took office, but following the Duma election, tens of thousands protested in Russian cities, moved by alleged vote fraud. Many of the protesters were middle-class Russian citizens expressing dissatisfaction with the growing gap between the rich and poor and United Russia's inability to raise equality. The protesters demanded the release of prisoners arrested for taking part in demonstrations, new Duma elections, the replacement of the head of the Central Election Commission, investigations into suspected election fraud, and the opening up of the political system to allow more parties to participate.

Both Putin and Medvedev dismissed the protests, with Putin blaming them on the United States and its secretary of state, Hillary Rodham Clinton. "She set the tone for some actors in our country and gave them a signal," Putin said. "They heard the signal and with the support of the U.S. State Department began active work." In an attempt to dissuade

Russians from joining the protests, Putin claimed they could lead to another collapse like the one seen after the fall of the Soviet Union because the demonstrators were dedicated to a violent overthrow of the government.

The first major protest took place on December 5, when 5,000 gathered in Moscow for a demonstration organized by Solidarity, a Russian opposition group. Police, who were out in force in riot gear, put the number of protesters closer to 2,000 and made 300 arrests, including protest leaders Alexei Navalny, a blogger, and Solidarity activist Ilya Yashin, who were both jailed for obstructing police and given fifteen-day sentences. On the next day, December 6, protests were reported in fifty cities across Russia, with the largest taking place in Moscow. Police broke up the Moscow protest, while subsequently allowing a pro-government rally to continue. More than 500 arrests were reported in Moscow on December 6, with another 230 taking place in St. Petersburg.

On December 10, protesters again gathered in Moscow chanting "Russia Without Putin" and carrying signs that read, "These elections are a farce." Police estimated the number of protesters reached 25,000 but protest organizers said the total number was at least double. Unable to stop the demonstration, the government gave the protesters a license, but sent in helicopters, troop carriers, dump trucks, and bulldozers to contain the crowd. Russian opposition leaders hoped the protests would draw national and international attention to the idea that Russians would no longer accept one-man rule. "Today we just proved that civil society does exist in Russia, that the middle class does exist and that this country is not lost," said Yevgeniya Albats, the editor of *New Times*, a magazine critical of Putin's government.

IMPACT OF SOCIAL MEDIA

Social media played an important role both before and during the Duma vote and during the protests. During the Duma campaign, smartphones were used to film alleged fraud and instances of officials bribing voters to back United Russia. On Election Day, the same method was used and young Russians staked out positions at polling locations to act as independent monitors, uploading their videos to YouTube. In one video, Yegor Duda filmed an election official filling in ballots. "This is a violation of the criminal code. The chairman of the electoral commission is filling out ballots. Everything has been captured on the video camera," Duda said while filming. The Moscow City Elections Commission confirmed the content of the video, and an investigation was opened into ballot tampering at that polling location. After the substance of the video was confirmed, Duda commented, "I now understand better what goes on there. And as long as I think it will be useful, I will continue to tell people about what is happening."

In one of the most popular videos, a group at a polling location had ballots hidden in bags under their clothes marked for United Russia, which they tried to put into ballot boxes. Police at first did nothing to stop those with the fraudulent ballots, but once they saw the cameras, they apprehended the group. Most of the clips uploaded to YouTube on Election Day showed violations committed by United Russia, but party leaders denied any wrongdoing. "I've seen these clips people are uploading to the Internet," Medvedev said. "Nothing can be seen in them."

After the vote, the videos, coupled with popular blogs, were used to rally protesters. Navalny, who used his blog to encourage Russians to take to the streets, said in a statement from prison, "It's impossible to beat and arrest hundreds of thousands, millions. We have not even been intimidated. For some time, we were simply convinced that the life of toads and rats, the life of mute cattle, was the only way to win the reward of stability and economic growth. . . . We have voices and votes and we have the power to uphold them."

INTERNATIONAL RESPONSE AND CONTINUING CHALLENGES

Following the election, the Organization for Security and Co-operation in Europe (OSCE) announced that the election was "well organized" but that its monitors had witnessed ballot box stuffing and other election fraud. "The contest was also slanted in favour of the ruling party, the election administration lacked independence, most media were partial and state authorities interfered unduly at different levels," said Petros Efthymiou, an official with OSCE. Mikhail Gorbachev, the former head of the Soviet Union, called for the election results to be thrown out and a revote held. "In my opinion, disregard for public opinion is discrediting the authorities and destabilizing the situation," Gorbachev said. In the United States—the nation blamed by Putin for backing the demonstrators—the response was equally critical. Sen. John McCain, R-Ariz., wrote on Twitter, "Dear Vlad, the Arab Spring is coming to a neighborhood near you."

The Duma election raised questions about Putin's ability to regain the presidency in 2012. "These elections are unprecedented because they were carried out against the background of a collapse in trust in Putin, Medvedev, and the ruling party," said Vladimir Ryzhkov, a liberal opposition leader who had been prohibited from running in the December Duma election. "I think that the March [presidential] election will turn into an even bigger political crisis; disappointment, frustration, with even more dirt and disenchantment, and an even bigger protest vote." Despite the anti-establishment environment, Putin went on to win his third term as president in March 2012.

—Heather Kerrigan

> *Following are the preliminary conclusions of the international election observation mission of the Organization for Security and Co-operation in Europe (OSCE) on the Russian Duma elections, released on December 5, 2011; a statement by Russian President Dmitry Medvedev on December 6, 2011, on the election outcomes; a statement by Medvedev before parliamentary leaders on December 13, 2011, regarding improving the political system; and an address by Medvedev on December 22, 2011, before the Russian federal assembly on initiatives to improve the Russian political system.*

OSCE Preliminary Findings on Russian State Duma Elections

December 5, 2011

[The introduction and all footnotes have been omitted.]

PRELIMINARY CONCLUSIONS

The preparations for the 4 December State Duma elections were technically well-administered across a vast territory, but the elections were marked by the convergence of the State and the governing party. Despite the lack of a level playing field during the electoral process, voters took advantage of their right to express their choice. Although seven parties ran, the prior denial of registration to certain political parties narrowed political competition. The contest was also slanted in favour of the ruling party as evidenced by the lack of independence of the election administration, the partiality of most media, and the undue interference of state authorities at different levels. This all did not provide the necessary conditions for fair electoral competition. The legal framework, however, was improved in some respects and televised debates provided one level platform for contestants.

The legal framework is comprehensive and provides an adequate basis for the conduct of elections. However, structurally, the legal framework is overly complex and open to interpretation, which led to its inconsistent application by various stakeholders, often in favour of one party over the others. Laws guaranteeing the right of assembly were in some cases applied restrictively, undermining contestants' rights. Numerous amendments to the legal framework were adopted since the last elections. A number of changes improved certain elements of the electoral process, although the recent reduction of the parliamentary threshold to five per cent did not apply in these elections.

The Central Election Commission (CEC) adopted detailed instructions to facilitate preparations for the elections. It held regular sessions and took most decisions unanimously, without debate. The manner in which the CEC dealt with complaints undermined contestants' rights to effective and timely redress. Representatives of most political parties expressed a high degree of distrust in the impartiality of election commissions at all levels and questioned their independence from various state administration bodies.

The denial by the Ministry of Justice of registration to a number of political parties reduced the choices available to voters. In one case, the European Court of Human Rights recently ruled that the state's disbanding of one party was disproportionate and constituted an unlawful interference in the party's internal functioning.

The campaign lacked vibrancy. OSCE/ODIHR observers noted unequal treatment of contestants by the election administration, local authorities and service providers in favour of the governing party. Political parties in some regions filed formal complaints about seizure of campaign materials, unequal access to billboard space, and undue restrictions on the right to hold rallies. Thus, the playing field was slanted in favour of United Russia.

In the campaign, the distinction between the state and the governing party was frequently blurred by taking advantage of an office or official position, contrary to paragraph 5.4 of the 1990 OSCE Copenhagen Document. Campaign materials for United Russia and voter information materials in Moscow bore a clear resemblance to one another. Observers received numerous credible allegations of attempts by local state structures to influence voter choice and to pressure them into voting for the governing party.

Most broadcast media covered the election campaign to only a limited extent. From 5 November to 2 December, state media were required by law to provide equal opportunities to all candidates. In line with these requirements, all parties contesting the elections could participate in national televised debates, which provided them with one level platform for reaching out to voters. The majority of television newscasts monitored were dominated by reports of state officials' activities. The coverage of all monitored broadcasters except one channel favored the governing party.

Observation of elections by international and political party observers is provided for by the electoral law. However, it is of concern that the legislation and the manner in which it was applied limited the quantity of international observers and their activities in several aspects. An undefined complaint by the CEC about the pre-electoral mission of PACE put PACE's participation in the observation of the elections at risk. In addition, the law does not allow observation of parliamentary elections by domestic civil society groups. Nevertheless, certain groups actively monitored the preparation for the elections and the campaign. Last minute pressure and intimidation of a key domestic observer group, however, aimed to obstruct and discredit its work. It was noteworthy that so many websites were down during election day.

During voting, election officials were observed to be dedicated and experienced and procedures were followed overall. However, the quality of the process deteriorated considerably during the count, which was characterized by frequent procedural violations and instances of apparent manipulation, including several serious indications of ballot box stuffing. Result protocols were not publically displayed in more than one-third of polling stations observed. Throughout election day, observers also reported a number of instances of obstruction to their activities, in particular during count and tabulation. . . .

[The remaining sections, including background on the elections, legal system, registration, campaigns, media, complaint and appeals processes, participation of women and minorities, election observers, and election day, have been omitted.]

Source: Organization for Security and Co-operation in Europe. Parliamentary Assembly. "Statement of Preliminary Findings and Conclusions." December 5, 2011. Used with permission of OSCE. http://www.osce.org/odihr/85757.

Russian President Medvedev on Duma Elections

December 6, 2011

As far as the outcomes of the State Duma elections are concerned, I will be meeting with the heads of all our parties, both parliamentary and non-parliamentary. I think that they will also have some suggestions on improving our legislation. Naturally, we will discuss all this, because our democracy is still developing and is not ideal—this is something I have said many times. And after every election, we have always made adjustments to election legislation. Naturally, certain proposals are more drastic. Yesterday, I once again received the suggestion of returning to the mixed system for electing deputies to the State Duma, i.e., via party lists and majority constituencies. But that is a topic for a separate discussion. I think that we should discuss it in order to have the full palette on the table, so to speak. We will certainly meet to discuss this issue later.

Source: Office of the President of Russia. Speeches and Transcripts. "Meeting with Central Election Commission Chairman Vladimir Churov." December 6, 2011. http://eng.kremlin.ru/transcripts/3182.

Russian President Speaks With Parliamentary Leaders

December 13, 2011

Colleagues,

This is our first meeting after the State Duma elections and the results are finalised. I congratulate all of you on your victory.

United Russia received a majority. The opposition strengthened its influence in the State Duma significantly. This is a new situation. I must also mention that not everyone is satisfied with the election results. But the fact is, this is normal. People also have complaints concerning voting at certain polling stations. The election commissions and corresponding judicial authorities will have to thoroughly examine all complaints and relevant claims. And in places where real violations of the law are detected, we will need to make just decisions. There were 117 such complaints on the elections day.

Furthermore, the State Duma must begin its work. Members of parliament always have a great deal to do. Today, I signed the Executive Order on the first session of the State Duma of the sixth convocation, proposed to be held on December 21.

Clearly, we must urgently continue working on our legislation, since that is the whole point of creating a parliament. Modernising the economy and public life, resolving pressing social problems, improving citizens' living standards, strengthening our defence capacity—all these issues remain at the centre of attention for every party present here, and naturally, must be resolved jointly, taking into account all parties' points of view.

In order to guarantee the rights of all the parties present in the new convocation of the State Duma, we need a significant proportion of the committees to be controlled not just by the majority party, but the opposition as well. As the head of the United Russia party list, I'd like to ask you to keep this in mind.

I also feel it is imperative to continue all our efforts not just on the economic front, but in reforming our political system as well. I have worked on this in recent years—in some cases, it went more slowly, in other cases, more quickly, but what's certain is that nobody can blame me of failing to create laws aimed at improving the political system. We must therefore make new decisions and truly take more decisive steps toward removing the accumulated restrictions concerning political activity—this, too, is an obvious fact, and is particularly important for our nation, to ensure we don't allow a social rupture or a divide between particular social groups, or between particular institutions. We will talk about this today.

These are our common goals, regardless of what position you hold or what party you represent today. And I am certain that these positions are dictated by one thing: our common desire to ensure that our nation develops, that it will be prosperous, and that its citizens will have good lives.

In conclusion, I also want to let you know that on December 22, I plan to make my Presidential Address to the Federal Assembly.

Let's discuss all these issues, as well as others. And then, the heads of the different parties can express their views to the media, as they always do.

Source: Office of the President of Russia. Speeches and Transcripts. "Meeting With Leaders of Parliamentary Parties." December 13, 2011. http://eng.kremlin.ru/transcripts/3216.

Medvedev Addresses Federal Assembly

December 22, 2011

Citizens of Russia, State Duma deputies and members of the Council of Federation,

Yesterday, the State Duma of the sixth convocation held its first meeting. I congratulate all the deputies on the start of their work. I wish you every success and would like to assure you of my openness to dialogue on all issues.

Following the parliamentary elections in Russia, various statements were made regarding their results, both in Russia and abroad. Some people were pleased with the elections' results, others were not entirely satisfied, and still others were not happy at all. It was the same after the previous elections. This always happens.

I would therefore like to stress that we treat any criticism of state institutions and individual officials with the utmost attention and respect. We draw relevant conclusions where criticism is valid, restore justice where laws had been broken, take the necessary decisions in consultation with the main political forces, openly state our position and justify it if the criticism is unfounded.

People have a guaranteed right to express their opinions using all legitimate means but attempts to manipulate Russian citizens, to mislead them and incite social discord are unacceptable. We will not let instigators and extremists involve society in their reckless activities, and we will not allow foreign interference in our internal affairs.

Russia needs democracy, not chaos; it needs faith in the future and justice. The fact that society is changing and people are increasingly expressing their views and making legitimate demands on the authorities are a positive sign, a sign of a maturing democracy. In my view, this is a positive trend that will benefit our country, just as increased political competition, which forces us to work more efficiently and to respond more promptly to the problems of millions of Russian families.

Today I will state my proposals for the near future aimed at expanding people's opportunities to influence Russian state policy and the decisions on matters that involve their rights and interests. But first, if I may, I would like to talk about the results of our efforts.

I am sincerely grateful to those who have given their support to my work as President of Russia in the past four years. Bear in mind that the start of my term in office coincided with a very difficult period. Everyone remembers the events in South Ossetia in August 2008. Just a month later we faced the most severe global financial crisis. This has left a serious mark on all of our work. The problems generated by the crisis have remained unresolved to this day in many countries. I would like to name our most important achievements of this challenging period and the main results. . . .

[Results of Medvedev's term as president have been omitted.]

Colleagues, now let us move on to the practical aspects of our country's modernisation. I would like to start by telling you what I, as President of the Russian Federation, intend to achieve in the coming months.

First. Today, at the new stage of the nation's development and in support of the new initiative put forward by Prime Minister Vladimir Putin, I propose a comprehensive reform of our political system.

I would like to say that I hear all those who talk about the need for change, and I understand them. We must give all active citizens a legitimate opportunity to participate in the country's political life. To achieve that, I believe the following measures are necessary.

To return to direct regional elections for the heads of Russian constituent entities.

To introduce a simplified procedure for the registration of political parties. My suggestion is that it should require an application signed by at least 500 people representing no less than 50% of the regions.

Next. To abolish the requirement to collect signatures for the elections to the State Duma and regional legislatures.

Finally, to reduce the number of voter signatures needed to participate in the presidential elections to 300,000, and for candidates from non-parliamentary parties to 100,000.

In addition, I propose to change the State Duma election system. I consider it expedient for strengthening the links between the deputies and the electorate to introduce proportional representation of 225 districts. This measure will allow each region to have a direct representative in parliament. Now, unfortunately, as everybody knows, some constituent entities of the Russian Federation do not have a single deputy elected by local residents.

I also suggest changing the procedure for forming the Central and regional election commissions. We should have broader representation by political parties in the election commissions. The parties must have the right to recall their representatives in the commissions before term, if necessary. I will soon submit the corresponding draft laws to the State Duma.

Colleagues, this is not the final list of initiatives. But let's be patient. Ancient Chinese philosopher Lao Tzu once said that governance must be consistent, business must spring from opportunities, and all actions must take time into account. Nevertheless, we will take additional necessary steps in the future.

I suppose that the measures already proposed will make our nation's political system more efficient, better able to meet the needs of our citizens. These changes are particularly relevant ahead of a very important political event: Russia's presidential elections. The elections must be just, transparent, and meet modern standards for lawfulness and fairness . . . .

[The remainder of Medvedev's plans for Russian modernization, as well as the challenges facing the nation in the coming years, have been omitted.]

SOURCE: Office of the President of Russia. Speeches and Transcripts. "Address to the Federal Assembly." December 22, 2011. http://eng.kremlin.ru/transcripts/3268.

OTHER HISTORIC DOCUMENTS OF INTEREST

FROM PREVIOUS *HISTORIC DOCUMENTS*

- Medvedev on His Inauguration as President of Russia, *2008,* p. 169
- Russian President Putin on World Affairs and Russian Politics, *2007,* p. 62
- Putin on His Inauguration as President of Russia, *2000,* p. 171

Department of Justice Announces Settlement in Coal Mine Disaster

DECEMBER 6, 2011

On December 6, 2011, the Justice Department announced that it had reached a settlement with Alpha Natural Resources, the company that purchased Massey Energy Company after the Upper Big Branch Mine explosion on April 5, 2010. Alpha agreed to pay a total of $209 million in restitution, civil, and criminal penalties. Eighteen wrongful death lawsuits filed against Massey were still outstanding. Just hours after the settlement was announced, the federal Mine Safety and Health Administration (MSHA) released its long-awaited report into the cause of the mine disaster that killed twenty-nine men. Contrary to the Alpha and Massey opinion that the West Virginia explosion was caused by a methane gas bubble, MSHA cited a buildup of coal dust as the cause of the explosion, which it concluded could have easily been prevented.

UPPER BIG BRANCH MINE

The Upper Big Branch (UBB) mine had long been on the federal Mine Safety and Health Administration's (MSHA) radar for a number of safety violations. In December 2007, the MSHA warned that the mine had a "potential pattern of violations." At that time, the mine had been cited for 204 violations over two years the MSHA called serious and significant. In 2008, the MSHA announced that UBB management was working to fix the violations, and that the agency planned to pursue no further enforcement action. Even if it was working toward amending its problems, between April 2009 and April 2010, the mine was cited eight additional times for substantial methane control violations.

On April 5, 2010, a spark set off a fire and explosion in the mine, which was at the time being operated by Massey subsidiary Performance Coal Company. The fire quickly traveled through the mine's tunnels, killing twenty-nine of the thirty-one miners at UBB that day. It was the most lethal mining disaster in the United States in forty years.

In 2011, Massey Energy Company was purchased by Alpha Natural Resources for $7.1 million, making Alpha the owner of the second-largest coal reserves in the country. In the sale, Alpha accepted responsibility for any lawsuits filed by the families of the mine disaster victims. A number of shareholders requested that the sale be blocked, fearing that Massey executives were only trying to protect themselves from prosecution.

FEDERAL AND STATE INVESTIGATIONS

Three reports were released in 2011 that looked at the cause of the UBB explosion. One, released by the United Mine Workers of America in October 2011, called the disaster "industrial homicide" that "constituted a massive slaughter" at a nonunion mine. Another study, which had been commissioned by former West Virginia Governor Joe Manchin III, was released in May 2011 and concluded that Massey "operated its mines in a profoundly reckless manner." Although Massey had long claimed that the explosion was caused by a large amount of methane gas that bubbled up from the ground under the mine that the company had no way of predicting or containing, the Manchin investigation reported that the damage and evidence from the mine, including the bodies of the miners, did not match this theory. Only two of the twenty-nine miners killed had methane in their lungs.

MSHA investigators released preliminary results of their own investigation in June 2011, and the final 1,000-page report on December 6, 2011. The report concluded that a buildup of coal dust, coupled with a methane buildup, and broken and old cutting tools caused a spark that ignited the fire and subsequent explosion. A broken water sprayer system in the mine allowed the fire to move quickly through the mine's tunnels, killing miners instantly. "The physical conditions that led to the explosion were the result of a series of basic safety violations at UBB and were entirely preventable," according to the report.

The MSHA report did partly confirm the Massey methane gas explanation for the disaster. The report found that UBB had a methane pocket below it that helped to fuel the explosion. "Based on physical evidence, the investigation concluded that methane was likely liberated from floor fractures into the mine atmosphere on April 5, the day of the explosion," the report stated.

Of the 369 violations for which UBB had been cited, the final report said that twelve contributed directly to the explosion, and that nine of those were designated as flagrant, the highest violation rating. These flagrant violations included providing advance notification of the arrival of mine inspectors to employees, failure to measure air quality before entering the mine, failure to examine the mine for safety hazards, failure to amend coal dust hazards identified by federal investigators, failure to take weekly air readings, hazardous levels of coal dust build up, failure to apply rock dust as an explosion preventative, failure to maintain cutting machine water sprays, and failure to adequately train miners. "Every time Massey sent miners into the UBB mine, Massey put those miners' lives at risk," said Joe Main, the assistant secretary of labor and head of the MSHA. "This was a coal-mine dust explosion that never should have happened."

The federal report also took note of the culture cultivated by Massey management. "Massey management created a culture of fear and intimidation in their miners to hide their reckless practices. Today's report brings to light the tragic consequences of a corporate culture that values production over people," said Main. Mine management threatened those miners who tried to report or fix violations, and employees were expected to hide any violations they saw. In one instance, a section foreman was suspended for delaying production to make a safety correction. Massey management premeditated how to circumvent federal inspectors not just by encouraging employees to cover up violations when inspectors came to the mine, but also by keeping two official records books to mislead federal inspectors into believing that Massey was working to improve safety conditions at UBB.

There are still two outstanding investigations. One is an ongoing federal criminal investigation, and the other is an internal investigation of MSHA to learn if it could have dealt with UBB violations in a different manner to prevent the explosion. Two questions that have been raised about the MSHA's handling of UBB include why it was not added to a "pattern of violations" list that would have subjected the mine to increased investigations by MSHA and why UBB and Massey were never taken to court before the explosion for the violations it had incurred. Kevin Stricklin, the MSHA administrator for coal, defended the agency's actions, stating, "We did shut the mine down 48 times in the year leading up to the explosion"; however, it is outside of MSHA ability to shut a mine down permanently. Tony Oppegard, a former MSHA official, was not as sympathetic. "When you read the report [Upper Big Branch] sounds like one of the worst mines in the history of mining," he said. "You have an enforcement agency that had to know this was an outlaw operation and they did not use the stringent enforcement tools they had which possibly could have prevented the disaster."

While Main said he expected the internal investigation to "identify shortcomings we need to address," Oppegard said, "It's hard to imagine that MSHA is going to do a real thorough job, a real critical analysis of itself given the magnitude of this disaster."

DEPARTMENT OF JUSTICE SETTLEMENT

On December 6, 2011, the MSHA imposed a $10.8 million fine on Massey, the largest in MSHA history, for the 369 UBB citations. On the same day, the Department of Justice (DOJ) announced the largest settlement ever in a criminal investigation of a mine accident. "While we continue to investigate individuals associated with this tragedy, this historic agreement—one of the largest payments ever for workplace safety crimes of any type—will help to create safer work environments for miners in West Virginia and across the country," said Attorney General Eric Holder. Under the agreement, Alpha agreed to pay $209 million, $46.5 million of which would go toward the two injured in the blast and the families of the victims; $128 million to safety improvements, research, and training; and $35 million to pay for safety violation fines incurred at UBB and other Massey mines. The settlement ensured that Alpha would have no further action taken against it, but the agreement did not protect Massey executives from being prosecuted for their roles in the disaster.

Alpha accepted the 2011 settlement, and chief executive Kevin Crutchfield stated, "We believe the agreements we've reached represent the best path forward for everyone." The families of the victims were not satisfied. "$200 million for the lives of 29 men certainly doesn't bring justice to the families of those dead miners," said Mark Moreland, an attorney for two families of UBB victims. Booth Goodwin, the U.S. attorney in Charleston, West Virginia, who announced the settlement with Holder, said its purpose was to make sure mining disasters like that at UBB do not happen in the future. "We can never place a value on the lives of these victims," said Booth, but we can make "a commitment to making the lives of miners safe every day."

CHARGES AGAINST MASSEY EXECUTIVES

In 2011, federal charges were filed against a Massey security chief and foreman for their roles in the mine disaster. Hughie Elbert Stover, the security chief, was convicted in October 2011 for lying to federal investigators and attempting to destroy records. At the end of 2011, he was still awaiting sentencing.

A third federal case was filed on February 22, 2012, against Gary May, a superintendent with Massey who was at the mine at the time of the disaster. Charges filed against May included conspiracy to defraud the United States by hampering a federal investigation and falsifying record books. According to the charges, May would use secret phrases to alert mine employees that federal investigators were on their way to the mine. The employees would subsequently conceal known violations to help Massey avoid citations and fines. These concealments included moving around a ventilation system to make overall mine ventilation appear better than it was. May entered a guilty plea in response to the charges in March 2012, and faces up to five years in prison and a $250,000 fine. So far, May is the most senior Massey employee to be charged in federal court.

The families of some of the men killed in the mine disaster have indicated their desire to see individual Massey executives held accountable. "I want to see someone actually go to jail," said Gene Jones, who lost his twin brother in the explosion. Action against individuals, he said, would "show these other coal companies, 'Listen. If you do wrong, you're going to go to jail.'"

—Heather Kerrigan

Following is a news release from the Department of Justice announcing the $209 million settlement related to the Upper Big Branch mine explosion, issued on December 6, 2011; and excerpts from the executive summary of the Mine Safety and Health Administration (MSHA) report on the Upper Big Branch mine explosion, also released on December 6, 2011.

Department of Justice Announces Mine Explosion Settlement

December 6, 2011

Alpha Natural Resources Inc. has agreed to make payments and safety investments totaling $209 million in connection with the criminal investigation of the April 5, 2010, explosion at the Upper Big Branch mine (UBB) in Montcoal, W.Va., announced Attorney General Eric Holder, U.S. Attorney R. Booth Goodwin II for the District of West Virginia and officials with the FBI and Department of Labor's Office of Inspector General.

The explosion at the UBB mine claimed the lives of 29 coal miners and injured two others. At the time of the explosion, the mine was owned by Massey Energy Company, whose operations came under Alpha's control in a June 1, 2011, merger.

"The tragedy at Upper Big Branch will never be forgotten, and the families affected by it will never be made completely whole again. Today's agreement represents the largest-ever resolution in a criminal investigation of a mine disaster and will ensure appropriate steps are taken to improve mine safety now and will fund research to enhance mine safety in the future," said Attorney General Holder. "While we continue to investigate individuals associated with this tragedy, this historic agreement—one of the largest payments ever for workplace safety crimes of any type—will help to create safer work environments for miners in West Virginia and across the country."

"There should never be another UBB, and this announcement is aimed squarely at that goal. For far too long, we've accepted the idea that catastrophic accidents are an inherent risk of being a coal miner. That mindset is unacceptable," said U.S. Attorney Goodwin. "Collectively, these requirements will set a new standard for what can and should be done to protect miners. We look forward to a future in which coal mining is as safe as any other occupation."

As part of the non-prosecution agreement, Alpha will invest at least $80 million in mine safety improvements at all of its underground mines, including those formerly owned by Massey. Alpha will also place $48 million in a mine health and safety research trust, to be used to fund academic and non-profit research that will advance efforts to enhance mine safety. In addition, the company will pay restitution of $1.5 million to each of the families of the 29 miners who died at UBB and to the two individuals who were injured, for a total restitution payment of $46.5 million.   Alpha also will pay a total of up to $34.8 million in penalties owed to the Mine Safety and Health Administration (MSHA), including all penalties that arise from the UBB accident investigation.

The remedial safety measures included in the agreement include the following:

- Installation of digital monitoring systems in all its underground mines to continuously monitor compliance with ventilation requirements and to ensure mines are free of potentially explosive methane gas;
- Implementation of a plan to ensure that each of its underground mines has the personnel and resources necessary to meet all legal requirements concerning incombustible material and accumulations of coal dust and loose coal;
- Purchase state-of-the-art equipment to monitor its mines for explosive concentrations of coal dust and use that equipment in all its underground mines;
- Purchase next-generation rock dusting equipment (pending MSHA approval), further enhancing its ability to combat explosion hazards;
- Installation of oxygen cascading systems to help miners make their way to safety if a serious accident should occur; and
- Building of a state-of-the-art training facility and implementation of a full training curriculum to train Alpha miners, which will be available to other mining companies.

The agreement announced today is the largest-ever resolution in a criminal investigation of a mine disaster. It addresses only the corporate criminal liability of the former Massey, not potential criminal charges for any individual. The criminal investigation of individuals associated with Massey remains ongoing.

SOURCE: U.S. Department of Justice. Office of Public Affairs. "Alpha Natural Resources Inc. and Department of Justice Reach $209 Million Agreement Related to Upper Big Branch Mine Explosion." December 6, 2011. http://www.justice.gov/opa/pr/2011/December/11-ag-1577.html.

MSHA Report on Upper Big Branch Mine Explosion

December 6, 2011

Executive Summary . . .

[The introduction to the report has been omitted.]

OVERVIEW OF THE UBB ACCIDENT INVESTIGATION REPORT'S FINDINGS

The 29 miners who perished at UBB died in a massive coal dust explosion that started as a methane ignition. The physical conditions that led to the explosion were the result of a series of basic safety violations at UBB and were entirely preventable. PCC/Massey disregarded the resulting hazards. While violations of particular safety standards led to the conditions that caused the explosion, the unlawful policies and practices implemented by PCC/Massey were the root cause of this tragedy. The evidence accumulated during the investigation demonstrates that PCC/Massey promoted and enforced a workplace culture that valued production over safety, including practices calculated to allow it to conduct mining operations in violation of the law.

The investigation also revealed multiple examples of systematic, intentional, and aggressive efforts by PCC/Massey to avoid compliance with safety and health standards, and to thwart detection of that non-compliance by federal and state regulators.

Witness testimony revealed that miners were intimidated by UBB management and were told that raising safety concerns would jeopardize their jobs. As a result, no safety or health complaints and no whistleblower disclosures were made to MSHA from miners working in the UBB mine in the approximately four years preceding the explosion. This is despite an extensive record of PCC/Massey safety and health violations at the UBB mine during this period.

PCC/Massey established a practice of using staff to relay advance notice of health and safety inspections to mine personnel when federal and state inspectors arrived at the mine. The advance notice allowed PCC/Massey employees to conceal violations from enforcement personnel. PCC's chief of security was convicted in federal court for lying to MSHA about whether advance notice was a practice at UBB; the evidence at the trial showed that it indeed was a practice and he had directed UBB personnel to provide advance notice of inspectors' arrival on the mine property. His conviction underscores the extent to which practices designed to hide PCC/Massey safety and health violations were engrained at UBB.

PCC/Massey kept two sets of books with respect to safety and health hazards in the UBB mine. The first set was the required examination book mandated by the Mine Act, which was open for review by MSHA and miners and was required to include in it a complete record of all hazards identified by PCC examiners and other company officials. PCC/Massey also maintained a second set of books that reported on production and maintenance, as well as hazards and violations of law. PCC/Massey noted some hazards in this second set of books that it did not record in the required examination books. PCC/Massey did not make this second set of books available to mine employees or inspectors.

PCC/Massey allowed conditions in the UBB mine to exist that set the stage for a catastrophic mine explosion. The tragedy at UBB began with a methane ignition that transitioned into a small methane explosion that then set off a massive coal dust explosion. If basic safety measures had been in place that prevented any of these three events, there would have been no loss of life at UBB.

PCC/Massey could have prevented the methane ignition and explosion had it maintained its longwall shearer in safe operating condition. A longwall shearer is part of a longwall mining machine and has large rotating cutting drums equipped with bits that cut coal as it moves on a track across the working face. A system of water sprays suppresses dust as well as "hot streaks," which are smears of metal found on rock when metal is heated to near its melting point from friction caused by the shearer's bits hitting into layers of rock above or below the coal seam. PCC/Massey operated the shearer at UBB with worn bits and missing water sprays, creating an ignition source for methane on the longwall.

Had PCC/Massey followed basic safety practices, the small methane explosion that set off the dust explosion would have been contained or prevented. PCC/Massey did not take proper measures to detect methane concentrations throughout the mine. PCC/Massey's failure to comply with UBB's approved ventilation and roof control plans exacerbated the risk of methane accumulation. The law requires adequate ventilation of underground coal mines to prevent unsafe levels of methane and other dangerous gasses, and provide miners with breathable air. PCC/Massey ventilation practices led to erratic changes in air flow and direction. Its failure to install supplemental roof supports as required by UBB's plan led to a roof fall in an airway that limited airflow, contributing to the accumulation of methane in the area where the explosion originated.

Finally, PCC/Massey violated fundamental safety standards by permitting significant amounts of float coal dust, coal dust, and loose coal to accumulate in the mine. This became the fuel for the explosion. Sufficient rock dust, used to make coal dust inert and prevent it from catching fire or fueling an explosion, would have prevented a coal dust explosion from occurring. PCC/Massey did not follow the fundamental safety practice of applying rock dust adequately to eliminate this hazard.

PCC/Massey knew or should have known about all of these hazards but failed to take corrective action to prevent a catastrophic accident. For example, UBB's required examination books showed records of hazards that PCC/Massey did not correct. The examination books also showed that PCC/Massey failed to perform required pre-shift, on-shift, and weekly examinations to find and correct hazards. When the books indicated PCC/Massey examiners did conduct exams, they failed to identify obvious hazards, such as accumulations of loose coal, coal dust, and float coal dust in the area where the explosion occurred.

Specific Accident Investigation Conclusions—PCC/Massey's Management Practices that Led to the Explosion

PCC/Massey failed to perform required mine examinations adequately and remedy known hazards and violations of law

MSHA regulations require mine operators to examine certain areas of the mine on a weekly basis, as well as before and during each shift, to identify hazardous conditions. MSHA's accident investigation found that PCC/Massey regularly failed to examine the mine properly for hazards putting miners at risk and directly contributing to the April 5 explosion. At UBB, PCC/Massey examiners often did not travel to areas they were required to inspect or, in some cases, travelled to the areas but did not perform the required inspections and measurements. For example, PCC/Massey conducted no methane examinations on the longwall tailgate, the area of the longwall where the explosion began, in the weeks prior to the explosion. Even when PCC/Massey performed inspections and identified hazards, it frequently did not correct them. Because of these practices, loose coal, coal dust, and float coal dust accumulated to dangerous levels over days, weeks, and months and provided the fuel for the April 5 explosion.

PCC/Massey kept two sets of books, thus concealing hazardous conditions

During the course of the investigation, MSHA discovered that PCC/Massey kept two sets of books at UBB: one set of production and maintenance books for internal use only, and the required examination books that, under the Mine Act, are open to review by MSHA and miners. MSHA regulations mandate that the required examination books contain a record of all hazards. Enforcement personnel must rely on their accuracy and completeness to guide them in conducting their physical inspections.

PCC/Massey often recorded hazards in its internal production and maintenance books, but failed to record the same hazards in the required examination book provided to enforcement personnel to review. Some of the hazards described in the hidden "second set of books" were consistent with conditions that existed at the time of the explosion, including the practice of removing sprays on the longwall shearer. Testimony from miners at UBB revealed they felt pressured by management not to record hazards in the required examination books. Furthermore, even when PCC/Massey recorded hazards in the required examination books—such as belts that needed to be cleaned or rock dusted—it often failed to correct the identified hazards.

In addition to undocumented hazards in the required examination books, PCC/Massey failed to report accident data accurately. MSHA's post-accident audit revealed that, in 2009, UBB had twice as many accidents as the operator reported to MSHA.

PCC/Massey intimidated miners to prevent MSHA from receiving evidence of safety and health violations and hazards

The Mine Act protects miners if they are fired or subjected to other adverse employment actions because they reported a safety or health hazard. These whistleblower protections give miners a voice in the workplace and allow them to protect themselves when mine operators engage in illegal and dangerous practices. Testimony revealed that UBB's miners were intimidated to prevent them from exercising their whistleblower rights. Production delays to resolve safety-related issues often were met by UBB officials with threats of retaliation and disciplinary actions. On one occasion when a foreman stopped production to fix ventilation problems, Chris Blanchard, PCC's president, was overheard saying: "If you don't start running coal up there, I'm going to bring the whole crew outside and get rid of every one of you." Witness interviews also revealed that a top company official suspended a section foreman who delayed production for one or two hours to make needed safety corrections.

MSHA did not receive a single safety or health complaint relating to underground conditions at UBB for approximately four years preceding the explosion even though MSHA offers a toll-free hotline for miners to make anonymous safety and health complaints. PCC/Massey also had a toll-free number for safety and health complaints, but miners testified that they were reluctant to use it for fear of retaliation.

PCC/Massey failed to provide adequate training for workers

Records and testimony indicate that PCC/Massey inadequately trained their examiners, foremen and miners in mine health and safety. It failed to provide experienced miner training, especially in the area of hazard recognition; failed to provide task training to those performing new job tasks; and failed to provide required annual refresher training. This lack of training left miners unequipped to identify and correct hazards at UBB.

PCC/Massey established a regular practice of giving advance notice of inspections to hide violations and hazards from enforcement personnel

Under the Mine Act, it is illegal for mine operators' employees to give advance notice of an inspection by MSHA enforcement personnel. Despite this statutory prohibition, UBB miners testified that PCC/Massey mine personnel on the surface routinely notified them prior to the arrival of enforcement personnel. Miners and others testified they were instructed by upper management to alert miners underground of the arrival of enforcement personnel so hazardous conditions could be concealed. UBB dispatchers testified they were told to notify miners underground when MSHA inspectors arrived on the property, and if they did not, there would be consequences.

Advance notice gave those underground the opportunity to alter conditions and fix or hide hazards immediately prior to enforcement personnel's arrival on the working section. PCC/Massey also made ventilation changes in the areas where MSHA inspectors planned to travel, concealing actual production conditions from enforcement personnel.

On October 26, 2011, Hughie Elbert Stover, PCC's former head of security for UBB, was found guilty in the United States District Court for the Southern District of West Virginia of a felony count of making false, fictitious and fraudulent statements to MSHA regarding company policy on advance notice. In an interview with the MSHA accident investigation team, Stover testified that Massey had a policy prohibiting security guards from providing advance notice of MSHA inspections; however, the evidence indicated that he had personally directed guards to provide advance notice.

Specific Accident Investigation Conclusions—Physical Causes of the Explosion

A small amount of methane, likely liberated from the mine floor, accumulated in the longwall area due to poor ventilation and roof control practices

Based on physical evidence, the investigation concluded that methane was likely liberated from floor fractures into the mine atmosphere on April 5, the day of the explosion. The investigation team subsequently identified floor fractures with methane liberation at longwall shields (a system of hydraulic jacks that supports the roof as coal is being mined) near the tailgate, the end of the longwall where the explosion began. This methane liberation occurred because PCC/Massey mined into a fault zone that was a reservoir and conduit for methane. MSHA believes that this is the same fault zone associated with methane inundations at UBB in 2003 and 2004, and a 1997 methane explosion.

PCC/Massey's failure to comply with its roof control plan allowed methane to accumulate in the tailgate area. UBB's roof control plan required placement of supplemental supports, in the form of two rows of 8-foot cable bolts or posts, between the primary supports in the longwall tailgate. PCC/Massey installed only one row of these supplemental supports. This lack of roof support contributed to the fall of the tailgate roof, which in turn restricted the airflow leaving the longwall face. The reduced air flow allowed methane to accumulate in the tailgate without being diluted or ventilated from the mine. As a result, an explosive mixture of methane was present in this area.

PCC/Massey failed to maintain the UBB longwall shearer, creating an ignition source for accumulated methane

MSHA has identified the longwall shearer as the likely source of the ignition of the methane accumulated in the tailgate area. PCC/Massey was using the longwall shearer to mine in the area near the tailgate. Evidence showed that methane likely migrated from behind the longwall shields to the longwall shearer, and that an accumulation of methane developed near the tailgate. Evidence also revealed that the longwall shearer was not properly maintained by PCC/Massey. Two of the cutting bits on the tail drum were worn flat and lost their carbide tips. The dull, worn shearer bits likely created an ignition source by creating hot streaks while cutting sandstone.

Well-maintained longwall shearers, which include sharp bits and effective water spray systems, protect against these kinds of ignitions and also control the dust during the mining process. The water sprays create air pressure to move methane away from the area where the shearer is cutting and prevents ignitions by spraying water to suppress hot streaks on the longwall face. At the time of the accident, PCC/Massey's longwall shearer was cutting through both coal and sandstone with seven water-spray nozzles missing. As a result, the shearer did not have the minimum required water pressure. The ineffective sprays failed to move the methane away from the shearer bits and cool the hot streaks created during the mining process. As a result, methane ignited.

The evidence indicated that the flame from the initial methane ignition then ignited a larger accumulation of methane. . . .

PCC/Massey allowed coal dust to accumulate throughout UBB, providing a fuel source for a massive explosion

The small methane explosion near the tailgate immediately encountered fuel in the form of dangerous accumulations of float coal dust and coal dust, which propagated the explosion beginning in the tailgate entry. The resulting coal dust explosion killed the 29 miners. PCC/Massey records demonstrate that examiners allowed these and other accumulations in the mine to build up over days, weeks, and months. Loose coal, coal dust and float coal dust were abundant in all areas of the mine, including the area affected by the explosion. Many of these accumulations were left from the initial development of this area of the mine, indicating a long-established policy of ignoring basic safety practices.

PCC/Massey failed to rock dust the mine adequately to prevent a coal dust explosion and its propagation through the mine

If the mine had been rock dusted so that the coal dust had contained sufficient quantities of incombustible content, the localized methane explosion would not have propagated, or expanded, any further. According to testimony and other evidence, PCC/Massey applied grossly inadequate quantities of rock dust. Miners stated that areas were not well dusted, that the walls, roof and floor in areas of the mine were dark-colored—which indicates a lack of rock dust. . . .

[Details on the rescue and recovery efforts at UBB have been omitted.]

SPECIFIC ACCIDENT INVESTIGATION CONCLUSIONS—ALTERNATE THEORIES TESTED AND FOUND INSUFFICIENT

The MSHA accident investigation team carefully considered other possible scenarios to explain the events of April 5, 2010, but a lack of supporting evidence disproved these alternative explanations. One theory tested was that a massive inundation of methane caused the explosion. However, the flame path, pressures generated by the explosion, and the limited quantity of methane detected prior to and after the explosion were inconsistent with that theory. In addition, previous methane inundations at UBB in 2003 and 2004 were localized at the point of gas discharging from fractures in the mine floor and gas release would dissipate within a few days. The volume and pressure of gas and the size of the floor fractures were relatively small. Thus, the volume of gas released from the floor was also small. Similarly, the team could find no evidence to support the theory that the explosion was caused by cutting into a gas well or by a seismic event.

SPECIFIC ACCIDENT INVESTIGATION
CONCLUSIONS—CITATIONS AND ORDERS ISSUED

Associated with the issuance of this accident investigation report, MSHA issued 12 citations and orders to PCC/Massey for violations of the Mine Act and its implementing regulations that contributed to the April 5 explosion. MSHA also issued 357 violations of the Mine Act and regulations to PCC/Massey for conditions and practices discovered at UBB that did not directly contribute to the explosion.

MSHA designated 9 of these contributory violations as "flagrant." Flagrant violations, the most serious violations MSHA can issue, are eligible for the highest penalty possible under the Mine Act. . . .

[The list of flagrant violations and notes on the MSHA's internal review have been omitted.]

SOURCE: U.S. Department of Labor. Mine Safety and Health Administration. "Executive Summary." December 6, 2011. http://www.msha.gov/Fatals/2010/UBB/ExecutiveSummary.pdf.

OTHER HISTORIC DOCUMENTS OF INTEREST

FROM PREVIOUS *HISTORIC DOCUMENTS*

European Union Agrees
to Fiscal Compact

DECEMBER 9, 2011

Two years of ever-deepening concern over the mounting debts of European Union governments culminated in a historic agreement by political leaders on December 9, 2011, to tighten budgetary rules to avoid such a crisis from recurring. The new "Fiscal Compact" Treaty, agreed after a long and fractious EU leaders's summit in Brussels, was mainly the brainchild of Germany's chancellor, Angela Merkel, and France's president, Nicolas Sarkozy. One of the treaty's key innovations was the creation of a "golden rule" requiring national governments to keep their structural deficits below 0.5 percent of gross domestic product (GDP). The United Kingdom, worried that the treaty would further infringe on its sovereignty and undermine London's supremacy as a financial services center, opted out of the pact, triggering speculation about how the UK's relationship with the European Union would evolve.

Recession Precipitates Sovereign Debt Crisis

The first stirrings of an impending debt crisis in Europe came in October 2009, when a new government in Greece revealed that its predecessor had concealed the severity of the country's debt level. As economists began to crunch the revised numbers, it soon became apparent that unless drastic steps were taken, Greece was heading down the path of a default. This sent shockwaves through the European Union because Greece was part of the eurozone, the EU's single currency area that became fully operational on January 1, 2002, when the euro coins and notes were introduced. Originally a club of twelve, by late 2009 use of the euro had expanded to seventeen member countries, with most of the remaining ten EU countries intending to eventually join. A political consensus gradually developed that Greece should not be allowed to default as that could have devastating, perhaps fatal, consequences for the euro.

As the economic situation in Greece worsened in early 2010, EU leaders, after initially hesitating, moved in May to give Greece a $146 billion bailout loan, with the International Monetary Fund (IMF) agreeing to provide additional financial support. In return for the loan, the Greek government agreed to introduce an EU/IMF-supervised austerity program to reduce its debt level to 120 percent of GDP by 2020. But the problem was far from resolved with the Greek deal. Europe had been hit by a major recession in 2009 as a result of the United States' banking crisis, which was precipitated by the bankruptcy in September 2008 of investment bank Lehman Brothers. Europe's debt soared to dangerously high levels in 2009 and 2010 due to a combination of declining tax revenues, government spending packages aimed at stimulating sputtering economies, and government bailouts for failing banks.

The countries with the most serious deficit and debt problems were Greece, Ireland, Italy, Portugal, and Spain. In response, in November 2010 EU leaders adopted a $113 billion bailout-austerity package for Ireland and one for $103 billion for Portugal in May 2011. In addition, in May 2010 they set up a temporary $584 billion EU-wide bailout fund, which they later turned into an even bigger permanent fund, called the European Stability Mechanism (ESM), by amending the EU treaties that previously had prohibited bailouts. One step the leaders refused to take, however, was to allow "euro-bonds" through which national governments could raise funds on the markets by selling bonds that all other eurozone states would guarantee. The consensus was that EU controls over national budgets were not yet sufficiently robust to give the green light for euro-bonds. However, the Frankfurt-based European Central Bank did intervene significantly by buying up from the markets large quantities of bonds that troubled euro-zone countries had issued.

PUSH FOR A NEW ECONOMIC GOVERNANCE MODEL

As 2011 progressed, leaders realized that their bailouts and austerity programs only addressed the symptoms of the problem and that action was also needed to address the cause, namely the EU's failure to prevent governments from running up debt levels in breach of EU treaty rules. Those rules were first laid out in February 1992 when the seeds of the euro were first sown with the signing of the EU's Maastricht Treaty. Germany had insisted on strict rules because it did not want to give up the Deutschmark for a less stable currency. Thus, the so-called Maastricht Criteria were agreed, requiring all countries that wanted to join the euro to maintain a debt level of no more than 60 percent of GDP and a deficit level that did not exceed 3 percent of GDP. As the 1990s progressed and the necessary steps were taken to make the single currency a reality, aspiring eurozone governments mostly succeeded in meeting the criteria so that when the euro was rolled out in 2002, of the then-fifteen EU members, twelve joined. The three that did not—Denmark, Sweden, and the UK—opted out not because they failed to meet the entry criteria, but because they were reluctant to cede control of fiscal and monetary policy to the European Union.

In the early 2000s the euro's introduction seemed to encourage bad behavior, fiscally speaking, among euro members. With interest rates uniformly low, economies growing steadily and buoyed by a heightened sense of confidence born out of being part of a large single currency area, some countries spent excessively, with property booms, for instance, in Ireland and Spain. In 2003, when Germany and France breached the euro's rules on excessive deficits, their EU colleagues balked at penalizing them, despite EU treaty rules clearly stipulating they should have been penalized. The failure to reprimand Germany and France undermined the credibility of the Stability and Growth Pact, the EU's mechanism for correcting excessive deficits.

By 2011, the political climate had completely changed, however, the sovereign debt crisis having firmly impressed on political leaders the imperative of budgetary responsibility if they wanted to preserve the euro. They came to understand that should one euro member default, even a relatively small economy like Greece, financial markets could, through speculation, bring another one down, then another and a domino effect could ensue, causing the whole currency to collapse. This was all the more plausible given that the European Union simply did not have the financial means to bail out larger economies like Spain and Italy should they edge toward a default.

FISCAL PACT FORGED

Dubbed "Merkozy" in the media because of their close collaboration in adopting policy solutions for Europe's economic and fiscal problems, by autumn 2011, Chancellor Angela Merkel and President Nicolas Sarkozy had agreed that the European Union needed a new treaty to promote greater fiscal prudence. With the financial markets increasingly jittery over the debt crisis, the twenty-seven EU leaders were called to a summit in Brussels on December 9, which was billed as the make-or-break moment for their treaty plan. In advance, Merkel and Sarkozy traveled to the French city of Marseilles for a "pre-summit-summit" consisting of leaders of center-right European governments in an effort to shore up support for their proposals. The Brussels EU summit was an all-night affair, with leaders emerging at 5 a.m. having agreed on a new treaty.

The treaty's core elements were annual structural deficits were not to exceed 0.5 percent of GDP, a rule that was to be enshrined in national constitutions; any member with an excessive deficit was to submit a plan to the EU Commission to correct the problem; and countries exceeding the 3 percent deficit limit were to be automatically fined unless a qualified majority of states opposed such action. The latter provision reversed the existing procedure under which members had to take an active decision to fine a country, something that was difficult to do politically and accounted for why France and Germany escaped a fine back in 2003. The new treaty also stipulated that summits on the euro were to be held at least twice yearly, and that the timetable for entry into force of the $663 billion ESM bailout fund be brought forward to July 2012. "For the longer term, we will continue to work on how to further deepen fiscal integration so as to better reflect our degree of interdependence," the euro leaders's statement added. In March 2012, EU leaders agreed to raise the ESM bailout fund to $930 billion to reassure markets in case a bailout of Spain or Italy was necessary.

REFUSAL TO SIGN

Much of the media coverage of the summit focused on the refusal by Great Britain's prime minister, David Cameron, to sign onto the pact, making the United Kingdom, at that particular moment, the only one of the EU-27 to categorically rule out being part of this new framework. Cameron's decision was to a large extent expected, because he faced enormous pressure back home from a euro-skeptic British press and public to not give up any further sovereignty to the European Union. The reason his government gave for opting out on this occasion was that the treaty could jeopardize the City of London's dominant position as a financial services hub by forcing the United Kingdom to give up its veto over EU financial services regulation. Many commentators concluded that the opt-out marked a defining moment in Britain's long and often strained relationship with the European Union and had marginalized it from EU decision-making on economic and fiscal matters. As the weeks passed, it transpired that the United Kingdom was not entirely alone as the Czech Republic, for similar reasons, also opted out. Thus, when the Fiscal Treaty was signed on March 1, 2012, the signatory count was 25 of the EU-27.

The British and Czech opt-outs meant that, legally speaking, the fiscal pact was not an "EU Treaty" but an intergovernmental one, again marking a break from precedent as previous agreements—like those in Maastricht, Nice, and Lisbon—were signed by all members. A new ratification procedure was introduced to enable the treaty to enter into force once twelve of the seventeen euro members had ratified it. Previously, all signatories had to complete ratification for treaties to take effect, which meant any country could delay or block its entry into force. This had happened on numerous occasions in the past when treaties were rejected in popular referenda. Thus, while Ireland plans to hold a referendum on the Fiscal Treaty, even if the Irish people vote "no," it can enter into force. However, any country that fails to ratify will not be eligible to receive bailout funds from the ESM, which provides a powerful incentive to approve the pact.

—Brian Beary

Following is a statement released on December 9, 2011, by the Council of the European Union, announcing the fiscal compact agreed to by European Union member states.

EU Heads of State Announce Fiscal Compact

December 9, 2011

The European Union and the euro area have done much over the past 18 months to improve economic governance and adopt new measures in response to the sovereign debt crisis. However, market tensions in the euro area have increased, and we need to step up our efforts to address the current challenges. Today we agreed to move towards a stronger economic union. This implies action in two directions:

> *- a new fiscal compact and strengthened economic policy coordination;*

> *- the development of our stabilisation tools to face short term challenges.*

A REINFORCED ARCHITECTURE FOR ECONOMIC AND MONETARY UNION

1. The stability and integrity of the Economic and Monetary Union and of the European Union as a whole require the swift and vigorous implementation of the measures already agreed as well as further qualitative moves towards a genuine "fiscal stability union" in the euro area. Alongside the single currency, a strong economic pillar is indispensable. It will rest on an enhanced governance to foster fiscal discipline and deeper integration in the internal market as well as stronger growth, enhanced competitiveness and social cohesion. To achieve this objective, we will build on and enhance what has been achieved in the past 18 months: the enhanced Stability and Growth Pact, the implementation of the European Semester starting this month, the new macro-economic imbalances procedure, and the Euro Plus Pact.

2. With this overriding objective in mind, and fully determined to overcome together the current difficulties, we agreed today on a new "fiscal compact" and on significantly stronger coordination of economic policies in areas of common interest.

3. This will require a new deal between euro area Member States to be enshrined in common, ambitious rules that translate their strong political commitment into a new legal framework.

A new fiscal compact

4. We commit to establishing a new *fiscal rule*, containing the following elements:

- General government budgets shall be balanced or in surplus; this principle shall be deemed respected if, as a rule, the annual structural deficit does not exceed 0.5% of nominal GDP.
- Such a rule will also be introduced in Member States' national legal systems at constitutional or equivalent level. The rule will contain an automatic correction mechanism that shall be triggered in the event of deviation. It will be defined by each Member State on the basis of principles proposed by the Commission. We recognise the jurisdiction of the Court of Justice to verify the transposition of this rule at national level.
- Member States shall converge towards their specific reference level, according to a calendar proposed by the Commission.
- Member States in Excessive Deficit Procedure shall submit to the Commission and the Council for endorsement, an economic partnership programme detailing the necessary structural reforms to ensure an effectively durable correction of excessive deficits. The implementation of the programme, and the yearly budgetary plans consistent with it, will be monitored by the Commission and the Council.
- A mechanism will be put in place for the *ex ante* reporting by Member States of their national debt issuance plans.

5. The **rules governing the Excessive Deficit Procedure (Article 126 of the TFEU) will be reinforced for euro area Member States**. As soon as a Member State is recognised to be in breach of the 3% ceiling by the Commission, there will be automatic consequences unless a qualified majority of euro area Member States is opposed. Steps and sanctions proposed or recommended by the Commission will be adopted unless a qualified majority of the euro area Member States is opposed. The specification of the debt criterion in terms of a numerical benchmark for debt reduction (1/20 rule) for Member States with a government debt in excess of 60% needs to be enshrined in the new provisions.

6. We **will examine swiftly the new rules proposed by the Commission on 23 November 2011** on (i) the monitoring and assessment of draft budgetary plans and the correction of excessive deficit in euro area Member States and (ii) the strengthening of economic and budgetary surveillance of Member States experiencing or threatened with serious difficulties with respect to their financial stability in the euro area. We call on the Council and the European Parliament to rapidly examine these regulations so that they will be in force for the next budget cycle. Under this new legal framework, the Commission will in particular examine the key parameters of the fiscal stance in the draft budgetary plans and will, if needed, adopt an opinion on these plans. If the Commission identifies particularly serious non-compliance with the Stability and Growth Pact, it will request a revised draft budgetary plan.

7. For the longer term, we will continue to work on how to further deepen fiscal integration so as to better reflect our degree of interdependence. These issues will be part of the report of the President of the European Council in cooperation with the President of the Commission and the President of the Eurogroup in March 2012. They will also report on the relations between the EU and the euro area.

Stronger policy coordination and governance

8. We agree to make more active use of enhanced cooperation on matters which are essential for the smooth functioning of the euro area, without undermining the internal market.

9. We are committed to working towards a common economic policy. A procedure will be established to ensure that all major economic policy reforms planned by euro area Member States will be discussed and coordinated at the level of the euro area, with a view to benchmarking best practices.

10. Euro area governance will be reinforced as agreed at the Euro Summit of 26 October. In particular, regular Euro Summits will be held at least twice a year.

Strengthening the stabilisation tools

11. Longer term reforms such as the ones set out above must be combined with immediate action to forcefully address current market tensions.

12. The European Financial Stability Facility (EFSF) leveraging will be rapidly deployed, through the two concrete options agreed upon by the Eurogroup on 29 November. We welcome the readiness of the ECB to act as an agent for the EFSF in its market operations.

13. We agree on an acceleration of the entry into force of the European Stability Mechanism (ESM) treaty. The Treaty will enter into force as soon as Member States representing 90 % of the capital commitments have ratified it. Our common objective is for the ESM to enter into force in July 2012.

14. Concerning financial resources, we agree on the following:

    - the EFSF will remain active in financing programmes that have started until mid-2013 as provided for in the Framework Agreement; it will continue to ensure the financing of the ongoing programmes as needed;
    - we will reassess the adequacy of the overall ceiling of the EFSF/ESM of EUR 500 billion (USD 670 billion) in March 2012;
    - during the phasing in of the paid-in capital, we stand ready to accelerate payments of capital in order to maintain a minimum 15% ratio between paid-in capital and the outstanding amount of ESM issuances and to ensure a combined effective lending capacity of EUR 500 billion;
    - euro area and other Member States will consider, and confirm within 10 days, the provision of additional resources for the IMF of up to EUR 200 billion (USD 270 billion), in the form of bilateral loans, to ensure that the IMF has adequate resources to deal with the crisis. We are looking forward to parallel contributions from the international community.

15. We agree on the **following adjustments to the ESM Treaty to make it more effective**:

    - Concerning the **involvement of the private sector**, we will strictly adhere to the well established IMF principles and practices. This will be unambiguously reflected in the preamble of the treaty. We clearly reaffirm that the decisions taken on 21 July and 26/27 October concerning Greek debt are unique and exceptional; standardised and identical Collective Action Clauses will be included, in such a way as to preserve market liquidity, in the terms and conditions of all new euro government bonds.

- In order to ensure that the ESM is in a position to take the necessary decisions in all circumstances, **voting rules in the ESM will be changed to include an emergency procedure**. The mutual agreement rule will be replaced by a qualified majority of 85 % in case the Commission and the ECB conclude that an urgent decision related to financial assistance is needed when the financial and economic sustainability of the euro area is threatened.[1]

16. We welcome the measures taken by Italy; we also welcome the commitment of the new Greek government, and of the parties supporting it, to fully implement its programme, as well as the significant progress achieved by Ireland and Portugal in implementing their programmes.

* * *

Some of the measures described above can be decided through secondary legislation. The euro area Heads of State or Government consider that the other measures should be contained in primary legislation. Considering the absence of unanimity among the EU Member States, they decided to adopt them through an international agreement to be signed in March or at an earlier date. The objective remains to incorporate these provisions into the treaties of the Union as soon as possible. The Heads of State or Government of Bulgaria, Czech Republic, Denmark, Hungary, Latvia, Lithuania, Poland, Romania and Sweden indicated the possibility to take part in this process after consulting their Parliaments where appropriate.

SOURCE: European Council. "Statement by the Euro Area Heads of State or Government." December 9, 2011. http://www.consilium.europa.eu/uedocs/cms_data/docs/pressdata/en/ec/126658.pdf.

OTHER HISTORIC DOCUMENTS OF INTEREST

FROM THIS VOLUME

FROM PREVIOUS *HISTORIC DOCUMENTS*

---

[1] subject to confirmation by Finnish Parliament.

Three Women Awarded
Nobel Peace Prize

DECEMBER 10, 2011

On the heels of two controversial Nobel Peace Prize awards in 2009 and 2010, given to President Barack Obama and Chinese dissident Liu Xiaobo, respectively, in 2011, speculation suggested that the Nobel Committee would make a more conventional choice. The committee received more than 250 nominations for the 2011 award, and in a year that saw the toppling of Middle Eastern dictators, there was some belief that a blogger or social media activist would be awarded for his or her work during the Arab Spring. In the end, the award committee chose three women—two from Liberia and one from Yemen—to jointly receive the award for their work to peacefully fight for the rights of women to fully participate in all aspects of life, in their respective countries.

Award Announcement

On October 7, 2011, Thorbjørn Jagland, the Nobel Committee chair, announced the three winners. "The Norwegian Nobel Committee has decided that the Nobel Peace Prize for 2011 is to be divided in three equal parts between Ellen Johnson Sirleaf, Leymah Gbowee and Tawakkol Karman for their non-violent struggle for the safety of women and for women's rights to full participation in peace-building work." Reading the committee statement, Jagland continued, "It is the Norwegian Nobel Committee's hope that the prize . . . will help to bring an end to the suppression of women that still occurs in many countries, and to realise the great potential for democracy and peace that women can represent." Including the 2011 award, of the 101 individuals who have won a Nobel Peace Prize, only 15 were women. U.S. Secretary of State Hillary Rodham Clinton, who is considered to be one of the most powerful women in the world, commented on the award that "The unflinching courage, strength and leadership of these women to build peace, advance reconciliation and defend the rights of fellow citizens in their own countries provide inspiration for women's rights and human progress everywhere."

Ellen Johnson Sirleaf

The award for Johnson Sirleaf was announced during her reelection campaign for president of Liberia. Johnson Sirleaf was the first female president democratically elected in modern African history, and first took office in January 2006. The seventy-two-year-old Harvard-educated economist served as Liberian finance minister in 1979 but fled the country in 1980 during a military coup. Johnson Sirleaf was sent to prison in the 1980s for voicing criticism of the military government led by Samuel Doe, and subsequently backed the rebellion of Charles Taylor, a move she now says she regrets. Johnson Sirleaf also served as a United Nations and World Bank executive, in the former role serving as Africa director for the United Nations Development Programme in 1992.

Johnson Sirleaf first ran for president in 1997 against Taylor and lost. She was subsequently charged with treason and fled the country. In 2003, she returned to Liberia to serve as head of the nation's Government Reform Commission, a committee established to help end the country's civil war that stretched from 1989 to 2003. During her 2005 campaign, Johnson Sirleaf ran against former Liberian football star George Weah and called for greater transparency in government to help fight corruption. Johnson Sirleaf said she wanted to be president "to bring motherly sensitivity and emotion to the presidency" that she thought would help heal the nation after fourteen years of war. Johnson Sirleaf defeated Weah in a runoff vote.

Johnson Sirleaf has many critics in Liberia. Even though she improved the nation since taking office by negotiating debt forgiveness and new, large oil ore contracts, unemployment remains high and many residents are impoverished. In 2009, Liberia's Truth and Reconciliation Commission called for Johnson Sirleaf to be prohibited from continuing her term or from holding office for thirty years because of her initial backing of the Taylor rebellion. To her critics, Johnson Sirleaf has responded, "You cannot rebuild a broken country in six years. This country was totally destroyed—dysfunctional institutions, destroyed infrastructure, no laws." So, she said, "it took us time to rebuild, and we've made a lot of progress." In the end, Johnson Sirleaf won her 2011 reelection during a runoff.

Upon learning that she had won the Nobel Peace Prize, Johnson Sirleaf said she accepted "this honor on behalf of the Liberian people, and the credit goes to them." Most of this credit is due, she said, "to Liberian women, who have consistently led the struggle for peace, even under conditions of neglect. It sends a message to the Liberian people that peace must prevail as Liberia goes through this critical event; that we must demonstrate to the world that we can be peaceful, that we can be politically mature and that we can all work together for a better Liberia." Her presidential opponent, Winston Tubman, called the award "undeserved," noting, "She has brought war here. She is a war-monger. She didn't stop the war at all. . . . Now that the war has stopped, she wants to stay on top of the country as if she's some liberator—she's not."

Leymah Gbowee

Gbowee is a thirty-nine-year-old Liberian peace activist who worked during Liberia's civil war as a trauma counselor, helping women and girls who were raped by members of Liberia's military. She worked to bring these women together to stop the violence. In 2003, Gbowee staged a protest with thousands of women against Taylor's government in the nation's capital of Monrovia. "In 2003, it was very difficult," said Gbowee. "We had lived with 14 years of conflict. A group of us, women, decided to take action for peace—including picketing, fasting and praying." During the protest, Gbowee proposed a sex strike, encouraging women to withhold sex from their spouses in an effort to stop the leaders of various factions from killing and fighting each other.

Currently, Gbowee serves as the head of the Women Peace and Security Network—Africa, a non-governmental organization dedicated to the participation of women in leadership, peace, and security. According to the Nobel Committee, Gbowee was awarded for her work bringing together Christian and Muslim women to fight against a tyrannical government. "I am confused. I am humbled. This is the first time in 39 years that I am out of words," Gbowee said of the award. "This whole process of three women receiving the Nobel Peace Prize is really overwhelming," said Gbowee. "It's finally a recognition that we can't ignore the other half of the world's population. We cannot ignore their unique skills."

TAWAKKOL KARMAN

Karman is the youngest Nobel Peace Prize recipient at age thirty-two, and the first female Arab winner. The Yemeni pro-democracy campaigner struggled to unite women to fight for their rights in a male-dominated society. She has been jailed many times, and during her various campaigns, her rivals sent threats to her male friends and relatives, including one that said she and her children would be killed. These threats did not stop Karman from working to unite women to speak out against the Yemeni government, encouraging reform in line with the principles of Islam. In 2005, Karman founded Women Journalists Without Chains and since then has worked to lead protests and sit-ins for human rights and the release of political prisoners.

In January 2011, Karman began protesting in the capital of Yemen, calling on President Ali Abdullah Saleh to resign. She helped to organize women to join her mission, in April 2011 commenting, "In Yemen, women are not allowed out of the house after 7pm, now they are sleeping [in the streets]. This goes beyond the wildest dream I have ever dreamt." She continued, "I am so proud of our women."

According to the Nobel Committee, Karman received the award for playing an integral part, both before and during the Arab Spring, "in the struggle for women's rights and for democracy and peace in Yemen." Expressing shock at learning that she had been awarded, Karman called her award "a victory for Arab women." She continued, "I am so happy, and I give this award to all of the youth and all of the women across the Arab world, in Egypt, in Tunisia." Without peace, Karman said, "We cannot build our country or any country in the world."

Some thought the prize had gone to Karman to encourage a reevaluation of what Islam, a religion that has typically been associated with terrorism, really means. According to Nadia Mostafa, a professor of international relations at Cairo University, Karman's award "means Islam is not against peace, it's not against women, and Islamists can be women activists, and they can fight for human rights, freedom and democracy."

NOBEL PEACE PRIZE CEREMONY

At the time of the Nobel Peace Prize ceremony on December 10, 2011, three Middle Eastern leaders had been deposed—in Tunisia, Egypt, and Libya—and a fourth, Saleh, was close behind. The significance of this was not lost on Jagland, who said, "The promising Arab Spring will become a new winter if women are again left out." Speaking directly to Saleh, who had signed an agreement one month earlier to cede power, and Syria's President Bashar al-Assad, he said, "No dictator can in the long run find shelter from this wind of history. . . . The leaders in Yemen and Syria who murder their people to retain their own power should take note of the following: mankind's fight for freedom and human rights never stops."

In her acceptance speech, Johnson Sirleaf reflected on the committee's decision to award three women who struggle to promote democracy in nations that have long been torn apart by corrupt governments and armed conflict. "On behalf of all the women of Liberia, the women of Africa, and the women everywhere in the world who have struggled for peace, justice and equality, I accept with great humility the 2011 Nobel Prize for Peace," said Johnson Sirleaf. Similarly, Gbowee credited the democratic struggle around the world for the honor. "I believe that the prize this year not only recognizes our struggle in Liberia and Yemen. It is in recognition and honor of the struggles of grass roots women in Egypt, the Democratic Republic of Congo, Cote d'Ivoire, Tunisia, in Palestine and Israel, and in every troubled corner of the world," she said.

Karman, whose nation was still facing uncertainty over the continuation of Saleh's regime, used her acceptance speech to call on the global community to continue pressing the dictator to resign. The ongoing struggles in the Middle East, she said, "should haunt the world's conscience because it challenges the very idea of fairness and justice." She called on the dictators to "be brought to justice before the International Criminal Court; there should be no immunity for killers who rob the food of the people." Speaking in Arabic and citing commandments in the Torah, Bible, and Koran, Karman said she accepted the prize "on my behalf and on behalf of the Yemeni and Arab revolutionary youth, who are leading today's peaceful struggle against tyranny and corruption with moral courage and political wisdom."

—Heather Kerrigan

Following is the speech given by Nobel Committee chair Thorbjørn Jagland on December 10, 2011, upon awarding the Nobel Peace Prize to Ellen Johnson Sirleaf, Leymah Gbowee, and Tawakkol Karman.

DOCUMENT   *Nobel Peace Prize Presentation Speech*

December 10, 2011

Your Majesties, Your Royal Highnesses, Laureates, Excellencies, ladies and gentlemen Ellen Johnson Sirleaf, Leymah Gbowee, and Tawakkol Karman:

Ever since the Norwegian Nobel Committee made this year's decision known, the people of Norway have looked forward to seeing you on this stage. All those with empathy for children and women who are ill-treated and killed, all those who believe in a future free from violence and war, will acclaim you today out of respect for the will to act that you represent.

You give concrete meaning to the Chinese proverb which says that "women hold up half the sky". That was why, when giving its reasons for this year's award, the Nobel Committee stated that "We cannot achieve democracy and lasting peace in the world unless women acquire the same opportunities as men to influence developments at all levels of society".

We thank you for the hope you awaken in us all.

And we congratulate you on this year's Peace Prize.

Men and women have at all times experienced war in different ways. Although women, too, have fought in wars through the centuries, and today even engage in terrorism, it is the men who to a far greater extent have engaged in the actual warfare. In modern wars the majority of the victims are often civilian, and very many of them are women and children.

Rape has always been one of the horrors of war. But in recent years, in Bosnia-Herzegovina, in Darfur, in Rwanda, and in Congo, among many other places, we have seen rape working not just as a massive violation in itself. Rape has become part of the tactics of war. The aim is to break down the enemy's morale, to force populations to move, and to punish opponents also after the war is over.

This was defined as a crime against humanity and as war crimes by the International Criminal Tribunal for the former Yugoslavia. The International Criminal Court (ICC) has since reached the same conclusion.

Popular opinion in favour of this view must be strengthened, and that is what we are doing here today.

We are doing so by attracting renewed attention to the resolution adopted in October 2000 by the UN Security Council, Resolution 1325. The resolution for the first time made violence against women in wartime an international security issue. It underlined the need to have women become participants on an equal footing with men in peace processes and in peace work in general. Women had to break out of their roles as victims; they must themselves become players who will contribute to creating peace. These goals were then hammered out further in four new Security Council resolutions, 1820, 1888, 1889 and 1960. These resolutions must be given prominent and visible places on the desks of all heads of state.

For there is still a long way to go before the goals of these resolutions are reached. In recent peace negotiations in various parts of the world which are surveyed, fewer than 8 percent of the participants in the negotiations and fewer than 3 percent of the peace agreement signatories were women. No woman has ever been appointed chief negotiator in any peace negotiations led by the UN.

Meanwhile the rapes continue, thousands of them, day after day.

The situation of women is difficult in many parts of the world. When a little progress is made, it is often men who benefit most.

A brief illustration: Bicycles have in recent years made their entry in rural districts in many poor countries. The women, who often both till the soil, carry goods to market, and see that the children get to school, rarely get to use the bicycle. It is for the male member of the family. Far too often, he uses it to visit the local bar, and now he can also get to the bars in the neighbouring villages. As so many have pointed out, help for women is help for the family; help for men is unfortunately far too often only help to them alone. Investment in girls' education is probably the best investment any developing country can make.

But luckily women are not only victims. Some take action.

Three of them are today receiving the Nobel Peace Prize for 2011.

Ellen Johnson Sirleaf's whole life can be seen as a realization of the intentions of Resolution 1325. In 1980 she went into exile after having been imprisoned and threatened with rape. For several years she served as Director of the UNDP's Regional Bureau for Africa. She was one of seven eminent persons who investigated the genocide in Rwanda on behalf of the Organization of African Unity (OAU). When the civil war broke out in Liberia in 1989, Johnson Sirleaf first supported Charles Taylor in the hope that he might represent a solution, but gradually dissociated herself from him, and ran against Taylor, unsuccessfully, in the presidential election in 1997. In the election in 2005, however, Johnson Sirleaf won a convincing victory, which made her the first democratically elected female head of state on the African continent.

Liberia remains one of the poorest countries in the world, and faces huge problems, but much progress has nevertheless been made since Johnson Sirleaf was installed as President in 2006. The civil war is over; democracy is working; there has been considerable economic growth; the very widespread corruption has been somewhat reduced; women's education and participation in social life has been significantly strengthened; the monstrous number of rapes has diminished.

Few other persons better satisfy the criteria for receiving the Peace Prize mentioned in Alfred Nobel's will.

Congratulations!

The same applies to Leymah Gbowee. She is the trauma specialist who switched from treating war victims to working for peace. In 2002, she mobilized a network of over 2,000 women in 15 provinces in Liberia to protest against the war and the violence. They dressed in white and took their stand near Monrovia's fish market. It was very important that Gbowee managed to unite women with quite different religious and ethnic backgrounds in this struggle. During the peace negotiations in Ghana, the women in frustration shut the male negotiators in and threatened to strip themselves naked, something which in that country would have brought utter disgrace on the men.

As we know, they were able to keep their clothes on. A peace agreement was reached.

Gbowee's work inspired many women to engage in a non-violent struggle against war and violence and for women's rights. As a network-builder, she took the initiative in forming the Women in Peacebuilding Network (WIPNET), which focused not only on Liberia but also on other parts of West Africa.

Gbowee currently heads the Women Peace and Security Network Africa (WIPSEN), headquartered in Accra in Ghana. We hope this year's prize will help to strengthen this network.

Congratulations!

Yemen is the country in the world which has made the least progress where women's rights are concerned. In her home, Peace Prize Laureate Tawakkol Karman keeps pictures of her heroes, Mahatma Gandhi, Martin Luther King, Nelson Mandela and Hillary Clinton. Many years before the Arab Spring in 2011, she was a youth and female activist. She became a journalist and founded the organization Women Journalists Without Chains. She organized peaceful sit-ins and information campaigns; she trained other women to take part in this struggle.

In a country where the vast majority of women wear niqabs, Tawakkol Karman changed to the hijab. She is at the same time a member of an Islamic party.

In 2011 she was one of the leaders of the demonstrations on Change Square in Sana. She was imprisoned and exposed to serious threats, but nothing stopped her. Day in and day out, she has campaigned against President Ali Abdullah Saleh and for democracy, women's rights, and tolerance. She advocates understanding between Shias and Sunnis and between Islam and other religions.

The promising Arab Spring will become a new winter if women are again left out. The visible as well as the invisible and indirect violence to them must cease. Women must be fully accepted in all sectors of community life. In her own way of life and struggle, Karman has shown that Islam presents no obstacle to this. On the contrary, Islam must be part of the solution. Only then will there be democracy and peaceful development in this part of the world. That will mean greater security for all of us.

What Karman has achieved in a short space of time is incredible. As a 32-year-old, she is the youngest laureate in the history of the Peace Prize.

Her struggle is our struggle. Congratulations and good luck for the future!

The leaders in Yemen and Syria who murder their people to retain their own power should take note of the following: mankind's fight for freedom and human rights never stops. No dictator can in the long run find shelter from this wind of history. It was this wind which led people to crawl up onto the Berlin Wall and tear it down. It is the wind that is now blowing in the Arab world. Not even President Saleh was able and President Assad in Syria will not be able to resist the people's demand for freedom and human rights.

As we have with us today two strong women from Liberia—the country that was built by slaves who had the opportunity to return to Africa, and since we have an equally strong woman from a country, Yemen, where the women are at present demanding freedom, I shall conclude with a quotation from the American author and civil rights advocate James Baldwin, who wrote:

"The people that once walked in darkness are no longer prepared to do so."

Make a note of that!—all those who wish to be on the right side of history.

We congratulate this year's winners of the Nobel Peace Prize. You represent one of the most important motive forces for change in today's world, the struggle for human rights in general and the struggle of women for equality and peace in particular.

Thank you for your attention.

SOURCE: Nobel Foundation. "Presentation Speech by Thorbjørn Jagland, Chairman of the Norwegian Nobel Committee." December 10, 2011. Copyright © 2011 The Nobel Foundation. Used with permission. http://www.nobelprize.org/nobel_prizes/peace/laureates/2011/presentation-speech.html.

OTHER HISTORIC DOCUMENTS OF INTEREST

FROM THIS VOLUME

FROM PREVIOUS *HISTORIC DOCUMENTS*

2011 Durban Climate Change Conference; Canada Leaves Kyoto

DECEMBER 11, 2011

Delegates meeting in Durban, South Africa, at the seventeenth annual United Nations climate change summit in late 2011 had an insurmountable challenge in front of them—the 2012 expiration of the Kyoto Protocol that previous summits had thus far failed to renew or replace. Many nations and climate change scientists see Kyoto as ineffective because it does not place greenhouse gas emissions caps on developing nations, nor does it have many sanction powers if a signatory nation does not reach its emissions targets. Putting in place a stronger, more enforceable agreement was seen as a necessity to help avoid the damaging effects of global warming.

KYOTO CHALLENGE

In 1997, nations gathered at the United Nations Framework Convention on Climate Change established an agreement on greenhouse gas emissions. The agreement would require industrialized nations to reduce their carbon emissions. No caps were placed on developing nations. Kyoto set up commitment periods during which signatory nations would be required to meet emissions targets. The first commitment period ends in 2012. Any nation exceeding their emissions target would have stricter requirements placed on it; might not be able to participate in emissions trading; or might simply be declared "non-compliant," an embarrassing distinction in the global community, but one that came with few sanctions.

Since its inception, the potential impact of Kyoto has been hotly debated. The United States never signed on to Kyoto because it disagreed with the imbalance between industrialized and developing nations, some of which, like China, contribute a major portion of greenhouse gas emissions. The agreement was set to expire in 2012 and some signatories, including Japan and Russia, have refused to agree to an extension of the agreement unless the gap between developing and industrialized nations was addressed. At subsequent UN climate change conferences, delegates have worked to determine how to make Kyoto fairer for all nations involved, with heavy resistance on both the industrialized and developing sides to any proposed solution.

It has been argued that a global initiative for climate change, while a worthy goal, is unlikely to have any impact if each individual signatory does not have its own climate change regulations in place. "In reality, the most effective thing we can do to address climate change is for all relevant countries to act vigorously at home," said Todd Stern, the lead climate change negotiator for the United States. "You can't rationally address this problem at the international level unless you get all the major economies, developed and developing, acting in a common system." Each nation wants to see that the other is doing its part before agreeing to more stringent global controls. As such, a number of countries have emissions caps in place. But others, like the United States, a major player in climate change politics, have failed at this aim. When he came to office, President Barack Obama proposed that emissions be reduced to 17 percent below 2005 levels by 2020, but Congress failed to approve his cap-and-trade approach. The United States still has no official plan in place for reducing carbon emissions. However, due to a drop in manufacturing during the recession, U.S. levels have fallen 6 percent during the past five years. The Canadian government is currently working toward a domestic plan with a similar 17 percent emissions cut.

Durban Summit

Nearly 200 nations came together in Durban, South Africa, from November 28 to December 9, 2011, for the seventeenth meeting of the United Nations Framework Convention on Climate Change. Officially referred to as COP17, the delegates at the conference discussed issues related to climate change and how to work together to combat this global issue. Heading into the conference, any talk of outcomes and agreements was downplayed because of failure to live up to expectations at earlier conferences. In 2009, for example, the conference held in Copenhagen failed to renew the Kyoto Protocol or any agreement to replace it. Instead, the conference only resulted in a two-page accord in which governments recognized, but did not adopt through the formal UN process, that temperature rise should be capped at 2° Celsius. Similarly in 2010, in Cancún, Mexico, the summit delegates reached agreements to create a fund for helping impoverished nations move toward clean energy and adapt to climate change, provide compensation for preserving tropical forests, develop clean energy technology transfer mechanisms, and reaffirm support for greenhouse gas emission reductions discussed in Copenhagen. The 2010 meeting again failed to deal with the issue of Kyoto.

In the buildup to the 2011 meeting, climate change scientists pushed for fast action on climate change because, according to the Intergovernmental Panel on Climate Change (IPCC), an international group of scientists and statisticians that provide technical assistance to the UN talks, extreme weather events like drought, floods, and tornadoes are occurring at greater rates. "All of these indicate that inaction in dealing with climate change and delays would only expose human society and all living species to risk that could become serious," said Rajendra Pachauri, director of the organization. The World Meteorological Organization (WMO), a specialty organization of the United Nations, agreed, citing 2011 as the tenth warmest year on record since measurements began in 1850, with Arctic sea ice reaching record thinness. "Our science is solid and it proves unequivocally that the world is warming and that this warming is due to human activities," said WMO Secretary General Michel Jarraud. "Concentrations of greenhouse gases in the atmosphere have reached new highs and are very rapidly approaching levels consistent with a 2 to 2.4° Celsius rise in average global temperatures." At this level, irreversible climate impact is anticipated. Scientists were keen to remind those gathering in Durban that climate change skeptics, especially those that exist in the U.S. Congress, are still a small, but vocal group and could prove to be a roadblock in getting the largest nations to sign on to any new climate change accord.

European Union Roadmap

Throughout the meeting, delegates debated whether to extend Kyoto beyond 2012 or whether to work toward replacing it. The European Union pushed for developing an action plan that would move the participating nations to a legally binding agreement on reducing greenhouse gas emissions that would replace Kyoto. This roadmap would try to keep global temperatures from rising more than 2° Celsius above current temperatures. The European Union received support from major developing nations for its roadmap proposal, including many African countries and Pacific islands, specifically those threatened by rising sea levels. China and India, on the other hand, resisted. Under Kyoto, the two nations were considered to be "developing," meaning that they did not have to adhere to the strict greenhouse gas emission reductions that industrialized nations signed on for. Under the EU roadmap, the two nations would be required to meet strict caps and cuts that they claimed would slow development. "What qualifies you to tell us what to do," asked Xie Zhenhua, who headed China's delegation. India and China also took issue with the short timeframe proposed by the European Union—negotiations on the roadmap were expected to be completed by 2015, and the roadmap would enter into force by 2020.

Debate on the EU roadmap caused the Durban meeting to run more than a day past its close because India and the European Union could not reach an agreement on the wording of the roadmap. EU delegates wanted the agreement to be legally binding, while India resisted any binding language. A Brazilian negotiator ended the stalemate, and both countries agreed that the roadmap could instead have "legal force." By agreeing to work toward a new treaty, the nations at the conference also agreed to leave Kyoto as the global climate change doctrine until something replaced it. Instead of expiring in 2012, Kyoto is now expected to expire sometime between 2017 and 2020. The terms of the roadmap and ultimate agreement will be worked out at future climate change conferences. Japan, Canada, and Russia did not agree to the EU roadmap or the extension of Kyoto.

Other agreements at the Durban meeting included reaffirmation of support for the development of clean energy technology, tropical forest preservation, and the Green Climate Fund for assisting impoverished nations with capping greenhouse gas emissions. The delegates agreed that this fund would provide $100 billion per year in public and private funds by 2020, but sources of the funds were not determined in Durban.

Those leading the Durban conference celebrated its outcomes. "We came here with plan A, and we have concluded this meeting with plan A to save one planet for the future of our children and our grandchildren to come," said Maite Nkoana-Mashabane, South Africa's international relations minister. "We have made history." Christiana Figueres, the UN Framework Convention on Climate Change executive secretary, said, "I salute the countries who made this agreement. They have all laid aside some cherished objectives of their own to meet a common purpose—a long-term solution." The delegates at the conference made clear that there was still work to be done. "It's a middle ground. . . . Of course we are not completely happy about the outcome, it lacks balance, but we believe it is starting to go into the right direction," said the head of the Africa Group, Tosi Mpanu-Mpanu.

Climate change scientists were less enthusiastic about the outcomes. While recognizing that important steps had been taken, Alden Meyer, director of strategy and policy at the Union of Concerned Scientists, said, "While governments avoided disaster in Durban, they by no means responded adequately to the mounting threat of climate change." He continued, "The decisions adopted here fall well short of what is needed." Andy Atkins, executive director of Friends of the Earth, concurred. "This empty shell of a plan leaves the planet hurtling towards catastrophic climate change. If Durban is to be a historic stepping stone towards success the world must urgently agree ambitious targets to slash emissions," he said.

Canada Leaves Kyoto

After the Durban conference, Canada, one of the first Kyoto signatories, announced its intent to withdraw from the protocol. "Kyoto, for Canada, is in the past," said Peter Kent, Canada's environmental minister. "As such, we are invoking our legal right to formally withdraw." Canada cited its reason for leaving as a necessity to avoid billions of dollars in fines for not complying with its emissions targets. Under Kyoto, Canada was expected to cut 5 percent of its emissions from its 1990 levels by 2012. However, the nation's emissions have actually risen, partly due to the growing Alberta oil sands industry. To reach its target by 2012, Kent said Canada would have to take all vehicles off the roads or purchase $14 billion in carbon emission permits from other nations. "While our government has taken action since 2006 to make real reductions in greenhouse gas emissions, under Kyoto Canada is facing radical and irresponsible choices if we are to avoid punishing, multibillion-dollar payments," said Kent. Canada made clear that it will continue to support a new climate change agreement, but noted that Kyoto, as written, cannot work because it does not cover the United States, a non-signatory, and China, a developing nation. According to Kent, the agreement only accounts for 13 percent of greenhouse gas emissions around the world. "It is now clear that Kyoto is not the path forward for a global solution to climate change; instead, it is an impediment," said Kent.

Opponents of Canada's decision called the move irresponsible and an abdication of moral obligation to the global community. Many blamed the withdrawal on the United States' unwillingness to sign on to Kyoto. "If the Americans move we'll move in lock-step with them because of the integrated nature of the economies," said Fen Osler Hampson, director of the Norman Paterson School of International Affairs at Carleton University in Ottawa. Canada is the United States' largest oil and gas supplier.

It is not yet known how Canada will be affected by its decision because many nations view Kyoto as ineffective. However, there is an expectation that Canada's withdrawal and non-compliance will make it more difficult to demand nations like China and India limit their own emissions in future climate change agreements.

—Heather Kerrigan

Following is a press release from December 11, 2011, from the United Nations Framework Convention on Climate Change on the agreements reached during the seventeenth annual summit.

DOCUMENT

Agreements Reached at Annual UNFCCC Meeting

December 11, 2011

Countries meeting in Durban, South Africa, have delivered a breakthrough on the future of the international community's response to climate change, whilst recognizing the urgent need to raise their collective level of ambition to reduce greenhouse gas emissions to keep the average global temperature rise below two degrees Celsius.

"We have taken crucial steps forward for the common good and the global citizenry today. I believe that what we have achieved in Durban will play a central role in saving tomorrow, today," said Maite Nkoana-Mashabane, South African Minister of International Relations and Cooperation and President of the Durban UN Climate Change Conference (COP17/CMP7).

"I salute the countries who made this agreement. They have all laid aside some cherished objectives of their own to meet a common purpose—a long-term solution to climate change. I sincerely thank the South African Presidency who steered through a long and intense conference to a historic agreement that has met all major issues," said Christiana Figueres, Executive Secretary of the United Nations Framework Convention on Climate Change (UNFCCC).

In Durban, governments decided to adopt a universal legal agreement on climate change as soon as possible, but not later than 2015. Work will begin on this immediately under a new group called the Ad Hoc Working Group on the Durban Platform for Enhanced Action.

Governments, including 38 industrialised countries, agreed to a second commitment period of the Kyoto Protocol from January 1, 2013. To achieve rapid clarity, Parties to this second period will turn their economy-wide targets into quantified emission limitation or reduction objectives and submit them for review by May 1, 2012.

"This is highly significant because the Kyoto Protocol's accounting rules, mechanisms and markets all remain in action as effective tools to leverage global climate action and as models to inform future agreements," Ms. Figueres said.

A significantly advanced framework for the reporting of emission reductions for both developed and developing countries was also agreed, taking into consideration the common but differentiated responsibilities of different countries.

In addition to charting the way forward on reducing greenhouse gases in the global context, governments meeting in South Africa agreed the full implementation of the package to support developing nations, agreed last year in Cancun, Mexico.

"This means that urgent support for the developing world, especially for the poorest and most vulnerable to adapt to climate change, will also be launched on time," said Ms. Figueres.

The package includes the Green Climate Fund, an Adaptation Committee designed to improve the coordination of adaptation actions on a global scale, and a Technology Mechanism, which are to become fully operational in 2012 (see below for details).

Whilst pledging to make progress in a number of areas, governments acknowledged the urgent concern that the current sum of pledges to cut emissions both from developed and developing countries is not high enough to keep the global average temperature rise below two degrees Celsius.

They therefore decided that the UN Climate Change process shall increase ambition to act and will be led by the climate science in the IPCC's Fifth Assessment Report and the global Review from 2013–2015.

"While it is clear that these deadlines must be met, countries, citizens and businesses who have been behind the rising global wave of climate action can now push ahead confidently, knowing that Durban has lit up a broader highway to a low-emission, climate resilient future," said the UNFCCC Executive Secretary.

The next major UNFCCC Climate Change Conference, COP 18/ CMP 8, is to take place 26 November to 7 December 2012 in Qatar, in close cooperation with the Republic of Korea.

Details of key decisions that emerged from COP17 in Durban

Green Climate Fund

- Countries have already started to pledge to contribute to start-up costs of the fund, meaning it can be made ready in 2012, and at the same time can help developing countries get ready to access the fund, boosting their efforts to establish their own clean energy futures and adapt to existing climate change.
- A Standing Committee is to keep an overview of climate finance in the context of the UNFCCC and to assist the Conference of the Parties. It will comprise 20 members, represented equally between the developed and developing world.
- A focused work programme on long-term finance was agreed, which will contribute to the scaling up of climate change finance going forward and will analyse options for the mobilisation of resources from a variety of sources.

Adaptation

- The Adaptation Committee, composed of 16 members, will report to the COP on its efforts to improve the coordination of adaptation actions at a global scale.
- The adaptive capacities above all of the poorest and most vulnerable countries are to be strengthened. National Adaptation Plans will allow developing countries to assess and reduce their vulnerability to climate change.
- The most vulnerable are to receive better protection against loss and damage caused by extreme weather events related to climate change.

Technology

- The Technology Mechanism will become fully operational in 2012.
- The full terms of reference for the operational arm of the Mechanism—the Climate Technology Centre and Network—are agreed, along with a clear procedure to select the host. The UNFCCC secretariat will issue a call for proposals for hosts on 16 January 2012.

Support of developing country action

- Governments agreed a registry to record developing country mitigation actions that seek financial support and to match these with support. The registry will be a flexible, dynamic, web-based platform.

Other key decisions

- A forum and work programme on unintended consequences of climate change actions and policies were established.
- Under the Kyoto Protocol's Clean Development Mechanism, governments adopted procedures to allow carbon-capture and storage projects. These guidelines will be reviewed every five years to ensure environmental integrity.
- Governments agreed to develop a new market-based mechanism to assist developed countries in meeting part of their targets or commitments under the Convention. Details of this will be taken forward in 2012. . . .

[Background information on the UN Framework Convention on Climate Change has been omitted.]

SOURCE: United Nations Framework Convention on Climate Change. "Durban Conference Delivers Breakthrough in International Community's Response to Climate Change." December 11, 2011. http://unfccc.int/files/press/press_releases_advisories/application/pdf/pr20111112cop17final.pdf.

OTHER HISTORIC DOCUMENTS OF INTEREST

FROM THIS VOLUME

FROM PREVIOUS *HISTORIC DOCUMENTS*

Election Outcome and Governance in the Democratic Republic of the Congo

DECEMBER 15, 2011

On December 9, 2011, Joseph Kabila, president of the Democratic Republic of the Congo (DRC), was reelected to a second term. His election came on the heels of a constitutional change he made to elect the president in one round rather than through a runoff system. Kabila's election was fraught with violence and allegations that his security forces were detaining and shooting at voters and those protesting his regime. Kabila's election raised questions about his administration's ability to effectively govern a nation so starkly divided.

Kabila and the DRC

In 2006, the Democratic Republic of the Congo (DRC) held its first democratic presidential election in four decades under the auspices of the United Nations. The election, which was held in two rounds, sparked violence in the capital between supporters of Joseph Kabila and supporters of his opponent, Jean-Pierre Bemba, a former rebel leader. Kabila defeated Bemba in the second round of voting, but hundreds were killed during and after the two election rounds.

Kabila first came to power in the DRC in 2001 after his father Laurent was assassinated. Before becoming president, Kabila received military training in China and assumed the role of DRC army chief of staff. During his ten years in power, Kabila's government has been accused of profiting from the DRC's natural resources, including copper, cobalt, diamonds, and gold, and his military forces have been accused of human rights abuses. Kabila, who keeps a low profile and avoids public speaking, enjoys most of his support in the east where citizens give him credit for ending the 1998–2003 war that killed four million. Those in the west, where the capital is located, believe Kabila is too closely tied to foreign governments.

The United Nations considers the DRC the least-developed country in the world. The population is largely impoverished and still plagued by armed conflict between local militias that has continued since the close of the 2003 war. The Kabila government has been criticized for not aiding social development or providing adequate health care and education. The average annual income in the DRC is $300 per year and less than 10 percent of households have access to electricity, according to the United Nations and World Bank. More than 19,000 UN peacekeepers remain in the DRC since the end of the war, attempting to maintain security.

Election Changes and Polling

In January 2011, Kabila announced the intention of his government to change election law to elect the president in one round of first-past-the-post voting, rather than in an election that requires one person to get at least 50 percent of the vote during the initial election or a runoff. The president claimed that the change would help avoid the same violence experienced during the 2006 election. Shortly after his announcement, Kabila revised the constitution to reflect the new election format. Opponents of the Kabila government saw the move as an attempt to keep Kabila in power after the 2011 election. According to Francois Mwamba of the Movement for the Liberation of the Congo, the decision "has the sole aim of organizing fraud on a grand scale and of allowing a single individual to confiscate all state powers."

Campaigning for the November 28, 2011, presidential and parliamentary election began on October 28. Thirty million registered voters were able to choose from 18,000 candidates vying for 500 seats in parliament and eleven candidates for president. In the capital of Kinshasa, the overwhelming number of candidates meant the ballot would run for fifty-six pages. Prior to the election, the UN peacekeeping mission announced that it would not have a formal role in the election, but that it would help the Congolese improve their own security forces before the vote. Roger Meece, the head of the UN peacekeeping mission, said, "I've reassured the president of the electoral commission of the willingness and commitment of the United Nations to fulfill our role providing logistical support and technical assistance."

In the presidential race, Kabila campaigned on what he called "five building sites of the republic" defined as infrastructure, health and education, water and electricity, housing, and employment. Kabila had two main challengers, Etienne Tshisekedi and Vital Kamerhe. Kamerhe was a former parliament speaker who enjoyed strong support in the east, typically a Kabila stronghold. Kamerhe was once a Kabila ally but fell out of favor with the president over a 2009 agreement to allow Rwandan troops into eastern DRC to find rebels. At age fifty-two, Kamerhe was considered an experienced politician, but his major shortfall was that many voters still saw him as too closely linked to Kabila.

Tshisekedi represented Kabila's most significant challenge. A member of the Union for Democracy and Social Programs, Tshisekedi was seventy-eight years old heading into the election and had been active in DRC politics since the 1960s but never ran for office. Tshisekedi helped to organize peaceful protests in the 1990s against the ruling dictator and helped in the assassination of Patrice Lumumba, the first DRC independence leader. Tshisekedi served as prime minister twice in the early 1990s, but left office both times over disputes with dictator Mobutu Sese Seko. He boycotted the 2006 election claiming the Kabila government would rig the vote. In announcing his campaign on November 11, Tshisekedi, who considers himself a Moses to his people, said "The Congolese people are sovereign in this country and has proclaimed me president a long time ago."

As voters went to the polls on November 28, the election was not as peaceful as had been hoped. The vote had to take place over multiple days because of long lines and delays in getting voting materials to polling locations. Reports surfaced that some polling locations did not receive enough ballots and that voters were turned away because of administrative errors. There were also reports of election officials casting multiple ballots. Shootings and violent clashes took place at a number of polling locations.

Human Rights Watch (HRW) reported that Kabila forces killed a number of voters, a claim the government dismissed with the information minister stating that an internal investigation showed that guards had only fired into the air to disperse unruly crowds, but that three were killed during clashes between pro- and anti-government groups. HRW said witnesses and victims' families corroborated its information. The group also reported that an election official in North Kivu held all ballots until everyone agreed to vote for

Kabila. African election observers had called the vote successful, but an election observation mission from the European Union noted "numerous irregularities," some of which it considered serious.

After the vote, businesses closed and police began patrolling the streets in an attempt to stop the violence that had killed dozens since the polls opened. Text messaging was blocked by all five phone servicers in the DRC, a move Free Fair DRC and Falling Whistles called in a joint statement an attempt "to further hinder the efforts of Congolese poll-watchers to monitor an election that has been marked by well-documented voting irregularities." Kabila's government claimed the text message blackout was meant to calm the violence. In the West Kasai province, where the opposition enjoyed strong support, television and radio stations were shut down, and tear gas was fired at opposition supporters in the capital where thousands fled their homes. Daniel Ngoy Mulunda, head of the election commission and a supporter of Kabila, threatened to throw out tens of thousands of ballots where opposition groups had attacked government poll watchers and other government agents. The supposed violence reported by Mulunda was centered in opposition strongholds.

Election Results

Initial results released at polling locations during the vote made it look like the opposition would win. According to some vote tallies, Tshisekedi was leading three-to-one. On December 1, five days before preliminary results were due to be released, Tshisekedi declared himself the winner of the presidential race and said he would reject the outcome if Kabila was named president. The preliminary results were delayed for what Mulunda said was to "assure the credibility" of the count.

On December 9, Kabila was declared the winner of the election with 49 percent of the vote to Tshisekedi's 32 percent. "The Independent National Electoral Commission certifies that candidate Kabila Kabange Joseph has obtained the simple majority of votes," said Mulunda. Tshisekedi declared himself the winner, and said that he would not trust the supreme court, the body required to verify the results, to fairly confirm the vote totals. "I consider myself from this day on as the elected president of the Democratic Republic of Congo," said Tshisekedi, calling the vote an "outright provocation to our people" and encouraging supporters "to stick together as one man behind me to face the events that will follow." Riot police remained in the capital in anticipation of another outbreak of violence, and national police confirmed killing at least four people—three looters and one person hit by a stray bullet.

On December 16, the supreme court verified the vote. "The credibility of these elections cannot be put in doubt," said Kabila, arguing that he had been elected legally. "Am I uncomfortable with the results? No, not at all," he said. Kabila called on Tshisekedi to accept the outcome of the vote and recognize Kabila as the rightful president of the DRC. Kabila was sworn in on December 20. Tshisekedi's supporters held a swearing-in ceremony for their candidate as well during a rally in the capital.

According to the Carter Center, a non-governmental organization focused on human rights that had been on hand to monitor the vote, a number of voting irregularities were apparent. Tens of thousands of ballots were missing after the vote; in the capital, 2,000 polling locations reported losing ballots. And in some areas, the vote percentages for Kabila were too high. "Based on the detailed results released by [the Independent National Election Commission], it is also evident that multiple locations, notably several Katanga province constituencies, reported impossibly high rates of 99 to 100 percent voter turnout with all, or nearly all, votes going to incumbent President Joseph Kabila." In his home-town, Kabila received more than 100 percent of the vote. The Carter Center admitted that it could not verify the election results because it was not given adequate access to polling centers. Kinshasa archbishop Cardinal Laurent Monsengwo Pasinya agreed with the Carter Center report, stating the results "do not conform either to truth or to justice."

Ongoing Challenges

According to HRW, from December 9 through Kabila's inauguration, the president's secu-rity forces detained dozens and killed more than twenty-four people. "Those killed include opposition activists and supporters as well as people gathered on the street or even in their homes," the organization said. "The government had instructed hospitals and morgues not to provide information about the number of dead or any details about individuals with bullet wounds to family members, human rights groups, or United Nations person-nel, among others."

In addition to these suspected human rights violations, following his reelection Kabila's government faced more challenges to its legitimacy than it had in the past. So far, it is unknown how the president plans to proceed. Of perhaps greater importance in the short term for Kabila is gaining full control of the Congolese Armed forces (FARDC), the nation's military, which includes multiple rebel groups. According to Johnnie Carson, Assistant Secretary of the Bureau of African Affairs at the U.S. Department of State, FARDC is "oversized, unprofessional, and lacking training on almost all levels. The DRC Government has no real command and control over many of these forces." Although the UN mission remains in the DRC and can assist the government in better integrating these forces, it cannot stay in the DRC forever to ensure stability and peace.

—Heather Kerrigan

Following is a transcript of testimony delivered by Johnnie Carson, assistant secre-tary, Bureau of African Affairs, U.S. Department of State, before the Senate Foreign Relations Committee on December 15, 2011, on the 2011 Democratic Republic of the Congo elections and continuing work toward improved governance.

U.S. Official on Governance Improvements in DRC

December 15, 2011

Good afternoon, Chairman Coons, Ranking Member Isakson, honorable Members of the Committee: Thank you for the opportunity to testify before you on the United States' policy toward the Democratic Republic of the Congo, the DRC.

The DRC is the largest country in Sub-Saharan Africa. With a population of over 71 million, it lies at the core of Central Africa and is bordered by nine other countries. It is also a country of enormous economic potential, with vast natural resources and large min-eral deposits. This economic wealth has contributed to the DRC's turbulent history and the current complex political situation. This is the site of what has been dubbed Africa's World War—a series of conflicts that devastated the country for some seven years and led to continued violence in the eastern provinces even after a peace agreement concluded in 2003. Rebuilding the DRC, establishing security, and helping its people to improve governance are some of our highest priorities on the continent. It is critical for us to stay engaged in the DRC, because the DRC's trajectory is pivotal to security and stability in the region.

The United States is the DRC's largest donor, having committed over $900 million this past fiscal year bilaterally and through multilateral organizations for peacekeeping, humanitarian and development assistance. We have supported the DRC's efforts to emerge from conflict and realize a just and lasting peace that is based on democratic principles, the rule of law, and respect for human rights. The top priorities for the United States in the DRC are promoting credible elections, strengthening capacity to govern and protect, improving economic governance and reducing violence and conflict in the eastern DRC. My statement will focus on our immediate concern in the DRC—the stability of the country and the current election cycle.

ELECTIONS

On November 28, the DRC held its second democratic election since the end of the Mobutu era. Eleven candidates vied for the presidency, and almost 19,000 candidates competed for 500 seats in Parliament. The Independent National Electoral Commission (known by its French acronym—CENI) announced the provisional election results on December 9 declaring the incumbent, President Joseph Kabila, the winner with approximately 49 percent of the vote. Second place went to leading opposition candidate Etienne Tshisekedi with 32 percent of the vote. In a distant third place, per the CENI's provisional results, was Vital Kamerhe with 7.7 percent of the vote. Both national and international observer missions (including the U.S.-funded Carter Center observer mission) identified flaws with the vote tabulation process as well as other problems that occurred ahead of the actual vote. Mr. Tshisekedi responded to the announced results by calling them a "provocation of the Congolese people" and declaring himself president. He has also called on the international community to help address the problems in the electoral process.

On December 10, the Carter Center released a public statement on its assessment that the CENI's provisional results "lack credibility," noting that "the vote tabulation process has varied across the country, ranging from the proper application of procedure to serious irregularities." The statement goes on to say, however, that "this assessment does not propose the final order of candidates is necessarily different than announced by the CENI, only that the results process is not credible." Other observer groups, including the EU, have since issued similar assessments.

We share the deep concerns expressed in the assessments of the Carter Center and others over the execution of the election and the vote tallying process. It is clear that the elections were deficient in many ways. The CENI did not meet internationally-accepted standards in the vote counting process. The U.S. government along with some of our international partners has found the management and technical aspect of these elections to be seriously flawed, the vote tabulation to be lacking in transparency, and not on par with positive gains in the democratic process that we have seen in other recent African elections. However, it is important to note that we do not know—and it might not be possible to determine with any certainty whether the final order of candidates would have been different from the provisional results had the management of the process been better. Further assessments by elections experts could determine whether the numerous shortcomings identified were due to incompetence, mismanagement, willful manipulation, or a combination of all three.

President Kabila has publicly acknowledged that there were "mistakes" in the process but has reportedly rejected any assessment that the results were not credible. An opposition candidate has formally filed a petition with the DRC Supreme Court which is presently reviewing the results and has until December 19 to issue its ruling, which is just one day before the inauguration planned for December 20.

We have been watching the electoral process for months. I have met and spoken with all of the major candidates numerous times. Last week, I spoke with Mr. Tshisekedi and CENI Chair Pastor Mulunda. We continue to advocate that all Congolese political leaders and their supporters act responsibly, renounce violence, and resolve any disagreements through peaceful constructive dialogue and existing legal remedies. We believe that a rapid technical review of the electoral process by the Congolese authorities may shed light on the cause of the irregularities, suggest ways in which governance could be structured to give better effect to the will of the Congolese people, and provide guidance for future elections. The United States stands ready to provide technical assistance for such a review and will encourage other countries to contribute as well.

It is important that the relevant Congolese authorities complete the remaining steps in the electoral process with maximum openness and transparency. We are urging them to put forward greater efforts for an improved tabulation process throughout the rest of the Congolese election cycle. This is especially important as the tabulation process is ongoing for 500 National Assembly seats where, unlike with the presidential election, a small number of votes could determine the winners.

We are also engaging with other governments at the highest levels, particularly in the region, asking them to reach out to President Kabila and Etienne Tshisekedi and other relevant actors to embrace a peaceful solution to this potential impasse. We have called on all Congolese political leaders to renounce violence and resolve any disagreements through peaceful dialogue and existing legal mechanisms.

Although there are major challenges with these elections, I want to emphasize that these elections demonstrated important and positive attributes of a democracy—the election was competitive, and the voters who turned out in large numbers were committed to selecting their government through peaceful, democratic means. Unlike in 2006, the Government of the DRC was principally responsible for the organization and, conduct for much of the financing of these elections. This was an important step forward. The CENI was able to register over 32 million Congolese voters, and over 18 million voters endured admittedly difficult conditions to cast their votes.

The United States played an active role in assisting in the elections process. We committed approximately $15 million from multi-year bilateral and multilateral funding in election assistance through USAID. The funding supported The Carter Center ($4 million) and the International Foundation for Electoral Systems (IFES) ($11 million) projects on civic and voter education, national election observer training, and capacity-building of human rights organizations. In addition, we deployed Mission observer teams in each of the ten provinces and Kinshasa enabling wide coverage and observance of the elections.

On the Public Diplomacy side, VOA and Embassy Kinshasa conducted a program to strengthen democratic and social institutions. VOA spear-headed a "citizen journalist" training of key opinion-makers (non-journalists) in local communities to report on important domestic issues, including elections. By using inexpensive mobile phones, the citizen journalists posted texts, videos, photographs and audio directly to the "100 Journalistes" Facebook page.

CONTINUING INSECURITY

Both in the context of the elections, and more broadly across many of our key objectives, the United States strongly supports the United Nations Stabilization Mission in the Democratic Republic of the Congo (MONUSCO) and its efforts to help the Congolese government bring peace and stability to the DRC. The Mission is essential to the international community's efforts to promote the protection of civilians, which remains its number-one objective, as outlined in UN Security Council Resolution 1991 (2011). It has undertaken new initiatives in the last few years—including the deployment of Joint Protection Teams, Community Liaison Assistants, and Community Alert Networks—that have made it more responsive to the vast needs of the eastern provinces. We continue to believe MONUSCO must remain in the DRC until the government can effectively take over protecting civilians and legitimately take over the security function. Any decision on the Mission's drawdown or eventual withdrawal must be conditions-based to avoid triggering a relapse into broader insecurity.

At the same time, MONUSCO cannot be in the Congo forever. Sustainable peace and stability in eastern Congo will require professional and accountable Congolese security forces and a strong and independent judicial system. The Congolese Armed forces (FARDC) is faced with numerous challenges partly due to integrated former armed groups who continue to maintain parallel command structures. The FARDC remains a force that is continuously trying to integrate former rebels into a force structure that is itself oversized, unprofessional, and lacking training on almost all levels. The DRC government has no real command and control over many of these forces, particularly the ex-CNDP forces that remain under the command of the ICC-indicted Jean Bosco Ntaganda, whose forces continue to commit human rights abuses and engage in illegal minerals trafficking and whose arrest we continue to call for. In many cases, the Government of the DRC is unable to properly provide its forces with the necessary logistical support. Helping the DRC develop professional forces that are able and disciplined enough to protect civilians is essential to ending sexual and gender-based violence and other serious human rights abuses.

U.S. government assistance attempts to address some of these underlying problems by providing military and police professionalization training with an emphasis on rule of law, respect for human rights and developing leadership skills that set a high moral bar for subordinates to emulate. For FY2011, the State Department funded approximately $30 million in bilateral security assistance to support peace and security in the DRC. One critical component of this support is our training and assistance to the Congolese military justice sector. Effective and independent military judges and prosecutors helped prosecute and convict the officers accused of responsibility for the January 1 mass rapes in the town of Fizi. We continue to urge the DRC government to take vigorous and effective actions in investigating and prosecuting security force officials accused of rape or other crimes.

Helping the governments of the region, including the DRC government, to counter the threat of rebel armed groups is another key element of our approach to help the DRC establish sustainable security. As this Committee knows, countering the Lord's Resistance Army (LRA) continues to be a particular priority for us. The LRA's continued atrocities are an affront to human dignity and a threat to regional stability. In line with the legislation passed by Congress last year, we are pursuing a comprehensive, multi-year strategy to help our partners in the region to better mitigate and ultimately the threat posed by the LRA.

As part of developing that strategy, we reviewed how we could improve our support to national militaries in the region to increase the likelihood of apprehending or eliminating the LRA's leaders. In October, President Obama reported to Congress that he had authorized a small number of U.S. forces to deploy to the LRA-affected region, in consultation with the region's national governments, to act as advisors to the militaries that are pursuing the LRA. Starting this month, advisor teams are beginning to deploy forward to certain LRA-affected areas, subject to the consent of the host governments. Let me also stress that although these advisors are equipped to defend themselves if the need arises, the U.S. forces in this operation are there to play only an advising role to the militaries pursuing the LRA.

We continue to work closely with the people and government of the DRC on countering the LRA and enhancing the protection of civilians. With our encouragement, earlier this year, the government of DRC deployed a U.S.-trained and -equipped battalion to participate in counter-LRA efforts in the LRA's areas of operations in the DRC. We continue to work with this battalion. We are also working to help MONUSCO augment its protection efforts in LRA-affected areas. At MONUSCO's request, the United States has embedded two U.S. military personnel into MONUSCO's Joint Intelligence and Operations Center in Dungu. These personnel are working with MONUSCO, FARDC, and UPDF representatives there to enhance information-sharing, analysis, and planning with regard to the LRA threat. Finally, we are also funding projects to expand existing early warning networks and to increase telecommunications in the LRA-affected areas of the DRC. In addition to the LRA, we are also working with the DRC government to address other violent armed groups that continue to destabilize the country's eastern region.

ILLICIT MINERALS TRADE

We are also concerned about the illicit trade in the DRC's natural resources. Unregulated exploitation and illicit trade in minerals have exacerbated the climate of insecurity in the eastern DRC as armed groups have used profits from such trade to fund their activities. It has also denied the Congolese population opportunities for livelihoods in the mineral trade market. Consistent with the provisions of the Dodd-Frank Act, the Department has updated its strategy to break the links between the illicit minerals trade and abusive soldiers and armed groups. Using a variety of tools and programs, our strategy aims to help end the commercial role of DRC security forces in the minerals trade; enhance civilian regulation of the DRC minerals trade; protect mining communities; promote corporate due diligence; support regional and international efforts to develop credible due diligence mechanisms, particularly the certification scheme of the International Conference on the Great Lakes Region; and, contribute to establishing secure trade routes for legal mining.

We currently have approximately $11 million in funds specifically aimed at increasing the transparency and regulation of the illegal trade in key minerals in the eastern DRC.

These efforts, as well as the Public-Private Alliance (PPA) that we recently launched with our private and civil society partners, are aimed at supporting the creation of pilot conflict-free supply chains. These are intended to demonstrate that minerals can be "cleanly" sourced from the DRC and that the legitimate, conflict-free trade in minerals can continue even as companies begin to apply internationally-agreed principles of due diligence. The PPA has already received commitment from more than 20 companies, trade associations, and NGOs prepared to contribute their funds or expertise to these efforts. More notably, the Secretariat of the International Conference on the Great Lakes Region (ICGLR), a group comprised of representatives of each of the Great Lakes countries, is a participant demonstrating that the initiative has regional buy-in to support the intended pilot supply chain efforts.

We recognize that there are great challenges in the DRC. However, the DRC and the United States have a solid and positive relationship, and our governments continue to engage at the highest levels on all of these issues.

Thank you, Mr. Chairman. I welcome your questions.

SOURCE: Embassy of the United States of America, Brussels, Belgium. U.S. Policy. "Improving Governance in the Democratic Republic of the Congo." December 15, 2011. http://www.uspolicy.be/headline/state%E2%80%99s-carson-improving-governance-drc.

OTHER HISTORIC DOCUMENTS OF INTEREST

FROM PREVIOUS *HISTORIC DOCUMENTS*

House and Senate Debate Temporary Payroll Tax Extension

DECEMBER 17 AND DECEMBER 20, 2011

A heated debate played out in the House and Senate in late 2011 over the extension of payroll tax cuts first established in 2010 that were set to expire in March 2012. Both parties recognized the difficulty of opposing a tax cut that would impact millions heading into an election year, but neither party could agree on how to pay for the extension. Democrats proposed a tax increase on the wealthy, which Republicans strongly opposed, saying it would have a detrimental impact on the economy that relied on high-income earners and businesses to create jobs and infuse money into the growing economy. It was not until early 2012 that the two parties reached an agreement to maintain the payroll tax cut, but neither side got everything it wanted.

Payroll Tax Debate

In December 2010, Congress passed a tax cut on Social Security payroll taxes paid by employees and the self-employed, reducing the tax rate from 6.2 percent to 4.2 percent of wages. Without an extension, that cut was set to expire on March 1, 2012, and would instantly increase payroll taxes for approximately 160 million Americans, most of whom were middle class. As written, the expiration of the 2010 tax cut would also impact benefits for 2.2 million long-term unemployed Americans. At the passage of the 2010 bill, the unemployed were given the opportunity to receive a maximum of ninety-nine weeks of benefits. The expiration would reduce the maximum to twenty-six weeks.

The two sides had differing opinions on the advantages of the payroll tax cut. Democrats argued that failure to pass the extension would stunt economic growth by preventing millions of Americans from purchasing goods and services necessary for continued economic recovery. Early in the debate, Democrats sensed that they had the upper hand, with an October CBS/*New York Times* poll showing that nearly 70 percent of Americans believed Republicans in Congress favor the rich. Using this information, Democrats worked to paint Republicans as those willing to harm 160 million mostly middle-class Americans to protect 350,000 people with a taxable income over $1 million. "There is very broad support in the electorate for having millionaires pay more in taxes to help address the country's needs," Democratic Party pollster Geoff Garin told Senate Democrats. "The bottom line is, Republicans are on the wrong side of public opinion."

Republicans recognized that it would be difficult to offer significant resistance given the upcoming 2012 election. "Even those members who question its value come to the conclusion that voting against it is a political loser," said Brian Gardner, a senior vice president at research group KBW Inc. The argument raised by Republicans was how to pay for an extension of these tax cuts. Republicans in Congress disagreed with the Democratic proposal that the extension should be paid for by raising taxes on high-income earners, which House Speaker John Boehner, R-Ohio, called a "job-crushing tax hike on small businesses." Boehner's argument was based on information that a number of small-business owners report their business income on personal income tax returns. Other Republicans in Congress disagreed with the overall purpose of the tax cut, believing it would do nothing to grow the economy. "Unless we are willing to have a commensurate change in benefits, then we shouldn't do it. It certainly isn't a supply-side or simulative tax cut. I'm for ending it," said Rep. Jeff Flake, R-Ariz.

Varying Proposals

In late 2011, both parties put forward proposals on how to extend and pay for the tax cut. In late November, Senate Republicans introduced a bill that would keep the payroll tax rate at 4.2 percent. The cost of maintaining the tax cut, they said, would be approximately $120 billion, which they proposed offsetting by freezing federal employee salaries through 2015 and reducing the federal workforce by 10 percent in the coming years. Under their bill, the highest-income earners would become ineligible for unemployment and food stamps, and would be required to pay higher Medicare premiums. The non-partisan Congressional Budget Office (CBO) said the bill would reduce the federal deficit by $111 billion. Democrats immediately attacked the plan, saying that it did not make a deep enough cut in payroll taxes and also noted that the wealthy are already prohibited from collecting food stamps. The bill came to a vote on the Senate floor on December 1 and was rejected 78 to 20, with more than half of Republicans voting in opposition. Some opposition Republicans supported the source of funding for the measure but did not want to see the tax cut extended. Others preferred that Congress work on long-term changes to the tax code rather than short-term tax fixes. "Our economy and American taxpayers need more permanency to the tax code, not less. This is another example of why comprehensive tax reform that simplifies and lowers the tax burden on American families and job creators is so desperately needed," said Sen. James Inhofe, R-Okla.

Senate Democrats released their own plan in late November. The Democratic bill would reduce the Social Security payroll tax to 3.1 percent of wages. It would also reduce the Social Security payroll tax for employers on the first $5 million in payroll to 3.1 percent. Democrats also included a tax cut for small businesses that hire new workers. They proposed paying for their bill, which would cost approximately $265 billion, with a 3.25 percent tax on gross income over $1 million for single filers or married couples filing joint taxes, which they said would raise $267.5 billion in revenue during the next decade. According to Moody's Analytics, the Democratic proposal would create 750,000 new jobs, if the cost was offset by higher taxes on millionaires starting in 2013.

Sen. Harry Reid, D-Nev., announced that the bill would give most working families an additional $1,500 per year, to which he added that it "seems to me the most important thing we can do is to make sure they have money to keep their bills paid to the best of their ability." Republicans criticized the bill, stating that it would not stimulate the economy and disagreeing with the way it was paid for. "There's no reason folks should suffer even more than they already are from the president's failure to turn this jobs crisis around," said Sen. Mitch McConnell, R-Ky. Republicans claimed that the tax on high-income earners would hurt small businesses that create jobs, citing an analysis from the nonpartisan Joint Committee on Taxation that said that 34 percent of business income reported on personal income taxes would be subject to the surtax. Treasury Secretary Timothy Geithner said his agency's study found that less than 1 percent of those who would be paying the surtax are small businesses. When it came to a vote on the floor on December 1, the bill passed the Senate 51 to 49, with one Republican, Susan Collins of Maine, supporting it.

TEMPORARY EXTENSION

In December, the House passed its own bill to extend the tax cut 234 to 193, but attached a controversial provision that would speed up completion of the Keystone XL pipeline to transport oil from Canada to the United States. With Senate Democrats promising to kill the House bill, and House Republicans refusing to vote on the Senate measure, the Senate proposed and passed a two-month extension of the tax cut on December 17, 2011. The extension would keep the payroll tax cut intact until the House and Senate reconvened in 2012. The temporary extension passed the Senate with 89 votes—all but seven Republicans supported the measure. Senators recognized that it was not the optimal solution but would prevent the tax hike in the near term. "This bill is deeply flawed," said Sen. Jack Reed, D-R.I., "but I could not in good conscience vote against providing a tax cut to the middle class."

The House refused to accept the bill, and voted instead to set up a conference committee to work out the differences between the House and Senate on the full-year extension. Of the Republican-backed conference bill, Boehner said, "Let's extend the payroll tax credit for a year. And all we're asking for is to get the Senate members over here to work with us to resolve our differences so we can do what everybody wants us to do: extend the payroll tax credit for the next year." Democrats in the House and Senate refused to send any members to the conference committee and continued to press Boehner to bring the Senate two-month extension to a vote.

The debate cast a shadow over the Republican Party according to the *Wall Street Journal* editorial board, which wrote, "The GOP leaders have somehow managed the remarkable feat of being blamed for opposing a one-year extension of a tax holiday that they are surely going to pass. This is no easy double play." The White House stepped into the debate, sending an e-mail to supporters saying that failure to extend the payroll tax cut would mean that a family making $50,000 per year would lose $40 per paycheck. The e-mail asked recipients to tell the White House how that $40 would impact their family, and received 10,000 responses. "Opponents of the payroll tax cut dismiss its impact by insisting $40 isn't a lot of money, but that's not the case for many families who are already working hard to make ends meet," the White House said. "Forty dollars buys a tank of gas or a fridge and pantry full of groceries. It covers a water bill or the cost of a prescription."

Republicans criticized Democrats for their refusal to send members to the conference committee, but were even more vocally opposed to the Senate's two-month tax cut extension, which Rep. Dave Camp, R-Mich., called a ploy to allow the body to leave for its winter vacation. "America is not on vacation; nor should the Senate be," said Camp. "We have two weeks to find a solution and send something to the President for his signature." On December 23, Republicans dropped their objections to a two-month extension after forging an agreement with Sen. Reid that would add a provision to call on President Obama to speed up approval of the Keystone XL pipeline. But as they left Washington for the holiday season, Republicans and Democrats both knew they were facing a long tax-cut fight upon their January return.

PASSAGE

It was not until February 17, 2012, when the House and Senate voted to keep payroll taxes at the 2010 level and extend unemployment benefits. The House passed the measure 293 to 132 and the Senate 60 to 36. In the bill, Republicans were able to get cuts to federal health care programs and government pensions to help cover spending increases; new limits on unemployment compensation; and cuts in preventative health care spending mandated by the Affordable Care Act of 2010. Democrats were forced to give in on a tax hike on the wealthy and large corporations and were unable to close some tax loopholes. According to the CBO, the bill will increase the federal deficit by $119.5 million over five years.

—Heather Kerrigan

Following is the text of a floor statement by Senator Jack Reed, D-R.I., in support of a two-month temporary payroll tax extension, delivered on December 17, 2011; and a floor statement from Representative Dave Camp, R-Mich., delivered on December 20, 2011, in opposition to the two-month extension.

DOCUMENT

Sen. Reed in Support of Temporary Payroll Tax Extension

December 17, 2011

Mr. REED. Mr. President, today I voted to prevent a tax increase on the middle class and to continue jobless benefits for millions of Americans and thousands of Rhode Islanders. Unfortunately, despite my and many of my colleagues' best efforts, this bill is deeply flawed. It doesn't provide needed certainty to Americans or to our economy because it does not provide a year-long extension of the payroll tax cut and jobless benefits, nor does it include needed reforms, like work sharing, which will help prevent layoffs in our still fragile economy. By insisting that jobless benefits be paid for, we are undermining the countercyclical nature of the program and blunting its purpose to stabilize our economy. But worst of all, it fails to address a provision of the unemployment insurance law that is absolutely necessary given our current employment crisis.

As a result, this bill effectively cuts 20 weeks of unemployment benefits. This means Rhode Islanders who have exhausted their normal UI benefits and extended—EUC08—benefits in February will not be eligible to receive the same help that was given to an unemployed person in the same situation back in the middle of 2011.

There is no reason to cut back on jobless benefits now. Over 13 million Americans are out of work, and our Nation is still grappling with the worst case of chronic long-term unemployment since the Great Depression. Unemployment benefits are a lifeline to millions of families and are our most effective tool in battling economic decline. Without these benefits unemployed Americans who are looking for a job wouldn't be able to pay for absolute necessities—their rent, mortgage, groceries, or for transportation as they hit the streets looking for work.

This reduction in coverage that my Republican colleagues have insisted upon is deeply damaging to American households and the broad economy. We should not be engaged in these short-term extensions of the payroll tax cut and jobless benefits—and then cut those jobless benefits as we go along.

In addition to cutting jobless benefits that help a broad swath of Americans, Republicans refuse to ask the wealthiest Americans to contribute to offsetting these policies. The payroll tax and jobless benefits could have been paid for by asking the wealthiest one-tenth of 1 percent to share in the sacrifice that middle-class America has made, but Republicans have voted time and again in favor of millionaire and billionaires and against tax cuts for the middle class.

I will continue to fight for maintaining jobless benefits and extending the payroll tax cut through 2012. I will continue to oppose efforts that would cut benefits and that would pay for continuing benefits by hurting the middle class.

As today's bill shows, though, my Republican colleagues are not interested in helping middle-class Americans and instead insist on tacking on controversial environmental riders and including offsets that hit the middle class.

Indeed, this bill includes a provision that would require the President to make a decision on the Keystone XL Pipeline within 60 days. This timeframe would dramatically shorten the important environmental review of the project, which includes assessing its potential impacts on critical water resources in the Ogallala aquifer, as well as increased carbon pollution.

I have been working to support and urge serious steps to reduce our dependence on oil, such as increasing the fuel efficiency of our vehicles and developing advanced biofuels. Even if Canadian oil displaces the importation of oil from other countries, the price of oil is determined by the global market, and the best way to decrease our exposure to the rising price of oil is to decrease our demand.

In addition, since America has recently become a net exporter of petroleum products, I am concerned that the proposed pipeline would merely allow big oil companies to import the oil from Canada, transport it by a pipeline—and with it, the risks of leaking into a critical aquifer—down to Texas refineries, where it would be refined into petroleum products that, in part, would be exported to foreign markets.

It is for those reasons that I have opposed the proposed Keystone XL Pipeline and urge the President to reject it.

As I have stated previously, I would have preferred to pay for this legislation by asking the wealthiest one-tenth of 1 percent of Americans to share in the sacrifices that all other Americans have made in working to right our economic ship. However, in the search for pay-fors, the House of Representatives added language that would increase the guarantee-fees—g-fees—the government-sponsored enterprises charge over the next 10 years, diverting funds away from shoring up the GSEs to fund a benefit that is unrelated to our housing markets. If there is any capacity to increase the g-fees, those resources should be directed to our housing markets, which still remain too fragile.

I find it incredibly ironic that my Republican colleagues, many of whom say they believe the mortgage securitization market should be completely privatized, have suggested an offset that uses a 10-year revenue stream from the enterprises' business operations as a piggy bank for governmental purposes. This seems like inconsistent policy at best.

This bill is deeply flawed, but I could not in good conscience vote against providing a tax cut to the middle class and providing desperately needed relief to nearly 10,000 Rhode Islanders who would have lost jobless benefits through the month of January.

I will not stop fighting for the middle class, to continue jobless benefits and working to improve our economy and create jobs. I will work tirelessly to continue the payroll tax cut and jobless benefits through the rest of the year and to fix this egregious reduction in benefits.

SOURCE: Sen. Jack Reed. "Middle Class Tax Relief and Job Creation Act of 2011." *Congressional Record* 2010, pt. 157, S8752-8753. http://www.gpo.gov/fdsys/pkg/CREC-2011-12-17/pdf/CREC-2011-12-17-pt1-PgS8748.pdf.

Rep. Camp in Opposition to Temporary Payroll Tax Extension

December 20, 2011

Mr. CAMP. Mr. Speaker, I yield myself such time as I may consume.

The differences between the bipartisan, House-passed Middle Class Tax Relief and Job Creation Act and what the Senate did so it could go on vacation could not be clearer. The House bill puts the American people first. It provided certainty for middle class families struggling to make ends meet by extending the middle class holiday; it provided certainty for those left behind in this economy by extending not only unemployment benefits for 1 year but also the Nation's welfare program; it provided certainty to seniors by ensuring their doctors would not see reimbursement rates slashed by nearly 30 percent; and it provided incentives for job creators looking for ways to hire more workers by extending tax relief.

The Senate decided not to do any of this. Worse yet, in a rush to get home for the holidays, the Senate passed something that is totally unworkable. Yesterday, the Congress received a letter from the National Payroll Reporting Consortium, a nonprofit trading association whose members cover more than one-third of the private-sector workforce. Their letter says the Senate bill "could create substantial problems, confusion, and costs affecting a significant percentage of U.S. employers and employees."

The National Federation of Independent Business, the largest small business advocacy group in the Nation, representing 350,000 small business owners nationwide and in every State, has issued a statement on the Senate bill. They say:

"The 2-month payroll tax holiday would present a number of complications and costs that would disproportionately affect small businesses. In addition, many small employers do payroll processing in-house by hand, and this would require them to spend time to make these changes."

With more than 5 million people working in the construction industry, this is what the Associated General Contractors have said about the Senate bill:

"This legislation will extend the payroll tax holiday in the most complex way possible, at the busiest time possible, provide little benefit to taxpayers and unfairly hit the small member companies of the Associated General Contractors of America the hardest."

As the Associated General Contractors say, this legislation will provide little benefit to taxpayers and unfairly hit the small member companies of the organization the hardest. This legislation will add more uncertainty, more confusion for employers and employees, and more complexity, especially for small employers.

"Any economic benefit derived from the law would likely be eaten up by the inefficiency and confusion surrounding the bill's implementation."

Mr. Speaker, I ask unanimous consent that these letters, along with letters in opposition to the Senate bill from the National Roofing Contractors Association, which has over 4,000 members and is represented in every State; the Associated Builders and Contractors, which represent over 2 million American workers; and the Small Business Entrepreneurship Council, with over 100,000 members, be entered into the RECORD. . . .

[The text of the letters has been omitted.]

Mr. CAMP. These letters, many of them were written to both parties, both leaders. I think Mr. LEVIN and I both received these letters. They were written to the Congress. It's routine that we do these. And on his own time the gentleman may do as he wishes.

I would say, Mr. Speaker, our economy is too weak and the American people have been struggling for far too long for Congress not to work out our differences. America is not on vacation, nor should the Senate be. We have 2 weeks to find a solution and send something to the President for his signature. That is what House Republicans are proposing today.

Let's look at the differences between the House and the Senate.

The House extended unemployment for 13 months. The Senate bill extended unemployment benefits for only 2 months, meaning an estimated 4 million Americans could lose the extended unemployment benefits next year they would get under the House bill.

The House reformed the unemployment program to focus it more on getting people the training and education they need to get back to work, not just handing out checks. The Senate did not.

The House protected seniors' health care for the next 2 years by ensuring doctors in the Medicare program don't have their reimbursements cut by more than 27 percent. The Senate did this for only 2 months.

The House provided a 1-year extension of the payroll tax holiday, ensuring a worker earning $50,000 next year has $1,000 more in their pocket. The Senate did this for only 2 months, meaning that same worker would have less than $200 in their pocket, or $800 less in take-home pay than under the House-passed bill.

The House included a pay freeze for Members of Congress and civilian Federal workers. The Senate did not.

The House put an end to welfare benefits being accessed at ATMs located in casinos, liquor stores, and strip clubs. The Senate did not.

The House protected Social Security by reducing overpayments. The Senate did not.

The House included a provision that saves taxpayers $9 billion by cracking down on fraud and abuse that is known to exist in a refundable tax credit program. The Senate did not.

The House provided for economic growth and job creation in the high-tech industry through spectrum auctions. The Senate did not.

The House cut taxes to promote business investment and hiring. The Senate did not.

Mr. Speaker, while it may sound like there are great differences between the House and Senate bill, it's not a difference over policy. It's simply a difference between the House deciding to act and the Senate deciding not to act on so many items.

The House bill includes commonsense reforms the American people want, and it adopts a number of the President's legislative initiatives which represent the bipartisan cooperation the American people are demanding. All told, 90 percent of the House bill is paid for with policies the President has endorsed in one form or another.

So what's really standing in our way? I've heard the President's people say that this breaks the agreement over the discretionary caps in the Budget Control Act, but look at that talking point. Those caps are adjusted only because we are proposing, as the President has before, to freeze the pay of Members of Congress and other Federal workers. Do the President and the Senate really want to risk unemployment benefits, a middle class tax cut, and reimbursement to doctors treating seniors and those with disabilities because they don't want to freeze the pay for Members of Congress and Federal workers?

Mr. Speaker, it's not too late. I urge all of my colleagues to support a 1-year extension of the payroll tax holiday, 1 year of unemployment benefits with critical reforms, and a 2-year extension of reimbursements for Medicare doctors.

I urge my Democrat colleagues to name conference committee members to resolve the differences between the two bills. Conference committees are a Jeffersonian concept, and we would be wise to follow the model laid out by our Founding Fathers. If the Senate agrees to work together, we will help get the American people back to work and get those struggling in this economy the help they need.

Source: Representative Dave Camp. "Motion to Go to Conference on H.R. 3630, Middle Class Tax Relief and Job Creation Act of 2011." *Congressional Record* 2011, pt. 157, H9963-9964. http://www.gpo.gov/fdsys/pkg/CREC-2011-12-20/pdf/CREC-2011-12-20-pt1-PgH9960.pdf.

OTHER HISTORIC DOCUMENTS OF INTEREST

FROM PREVIOUS *HISTORIC DOCUMENTS*

- President Obama Establishes the National Commission on Fiscal Responsibility and Reform, *2010,* p. 53

Power Transfer in North Korea

DECEMBER 19, 2011

On December 19, 2011, it was announced that the leader of North Korea, the world's most-secretive, isolated country, had died of a heart attack. The death of the sixty-nine-year-old leader put surrounding nations on high alert, fearful of what a power transition might mean. The world watched as images poured out of North Korea's tightly controlled state-run media, featuring citizens crying, screaming, and pounding the ground in reaction to their Dear Leader's death. The subsequent ascension to power by Kim Jong-il's youngest son, Kim Jong-un, a relatively unknown and untested figure, left open many questions for both the North Korean population and world leaders determined to continue talks to disarm the nuclear nation.

Kim Jong-il

According to his official life story, Kim Jong-il was born on the highest mountain in the Korean peninsula in 1942. At the time of his birth, the story claims, the stars brightened and a double rainbow appeared. In reality, Kim was born in 1941 in the Soviet Union where his father, Kim Il-sung, was stationed at an army base as the commander of a Korean battalion. Seven years later, Kim Il-sung, then known as the "eternal president," took control of the newly created Democratic People's Republic of Korea (DPRK), where he ruled, alongside his Workers' Party, as a communist dictator until his death in 1994.

During his early years, Kim Jong-il was considered a playboy. He avoided the spotlight and raised questions about whether he could lead the nation upon his father's death. But when the time came, Kim stepped in and quickly took control of the nation, continuing to rule with an iron fist. Kim, known as "Dear Leader" in North Korea, never frequented the world outside of his own country, but was known by those close to him to be highly intelligent about outside events. In foreign media, Kim has been portrayed as an eccentric leader, sporting elevator shoes, bouffant hair, and large sunglasses.

Under Kim's rule, many of North Korea's twenty-three million citizens were kept close to starvation while the government pursued a military-first ideology, under which money was directed toward the million-man army, thought to be the fifth largest in the world, rather than toward social programs. Millions are estimated to have died from malnutrition, but no official reports on the number are available. During the time the two Kims led North Korea, they helped to establish a significant dichotomy on the Korean peninsula—since the end of the Korean War in 1953, South Korea rose as a regional leader and gained significant influence on the global economic stage. The North, in contrast, has undergone significant de-industrialization.

Kim's relationship with the outside world wavered between cooperation and stubborn rebelliousness. The most significant source of tension has been North Korea's decision to become a nuclear nation. The country set off its first atomic device in 2006, followed by another test in 2009. It faced significant criticism from the international community and was repeatedly sanctioned by the United Nations. Seeking to encourage

North Korea to back away from its nuclear program, the United States, South Korea, China, Russia, and Japan have worked over the years on so-called six-party talks to encourage the nation to give up its nuclear weapons ambition in return for easing of economic sanctions and additional aid. The on-off talks produced little and there are questions about whether North Korea wants to work with the international community out of actual interest in reducing its nuclear program or simply to win additional economic aid by claiming that it will stand down.

The North has also had a strained relationship with South Korea. The two nations remain technically at war since the end of the 1950–1953 Korean War and sometimes exchange fire at the demilitarized zone, the 38th parallel that separated the two nations following the war. The relationship has wavered over time—North Korea has sometimes looked for closer ties only to quickly back away from its promises. Recently, any relationship between the two nations fell apart. In March 2010, a North Korean torpedo sunk the *Cheonan,* a South Korean warship, an event the North refused to claim responsibility for. Following the incident, South Korea declared the North its "principal enemy," and the North ended all remaining ties with its neighbor. The sinking also led other nations, including the United States, to announce additional sanctions against the communist state. Eight months later, in November 2010, the North, claiming that it had been provoked, shelled the South Korean island of Yeonpyeong during South Korea's annual offensive drill training. The South Koreans fired back. In the end, two South Korean soldiers and two civilians were killed.

DEATH AND FUNERAL

Kim Jong-il died on December 17, 2011, but his death was kept secret for two days until December 19. It is believed that Kim's death was concealed to keep North Koreans and outside observers from believing the nation would be in crisis. When announcing his death, the female broadcaster on state-run Korean Central News Agency (KCNA), dressed all in black and choking back tears, announced that Kim had died of physical and mental overwork. The network later amended its statement to indicate that Kim died of a "severe myocardial infarction along with a heart attack." According to state-run media, following Kim's death, a series of natural phenomenon took place, including a giant lake of ice cracking in half "so loud it seemed to shake the Heavens and the Earth"; a glowing red message in the mountain where Kim was said to be born that read "Mount Paektu, holy mountain of revolution. Kim Jong-il"; a Manchurian crane standing at Kim Il-sung's statue in a posture of grief; and magpies gathering in a single tree in a display of grief. On the latter occurrence, a Workers' Party official declared, "It shows that not only the people of the world, but the animals too, cannot forget our Dear Leader."

The North Korean public responded to Kim's death with what appeared to be a large outpouring of grief. Images from state-run media showed citizens sobbing and beating their fists against the pavement. "How can he go like this? What are we supposed to do?" asked Workers' Party member Kang Tae-Ho. Hong Sun-Ok, another mourner, said, "He tried so hard to make our lives much better and he just left like this." Many psychologists agreed, following Kim's death, that it would be difficult for the outside world to ever know if the grief was authentic. "You have to remember this is a regime where everything that isn't forbidden is compulsory, so it's difficult to know what their state of mind really is," said Anthony Daniels, a psychiatrist and writer. Brian Myers, a professor of international relations at Dongseo University in South Korea, linked the public outpouring of grief to the guilt felt by North Koreans. "Kim Jong-il's official image in the propaganda was always a man with no time for himself, and a large part of the propaganda was aimed at making the public feel guilty about the overwork that he was subjecting himself to," said Myers.

A state of mourning was declared from December 17 to December 29, and Kim's funeral was held on December 28. Kim's youngest son and successor, Kim Jong-un, walked with the hearse, but his two elder brothers were not seen at the funeral. Kim Jong Nam, the oldest of Kim's three children, who was once expected to succeed Kim after his death, fell out of favor with his father after being arrested at Narita airport in Tokyo for using a false passport in an attempt to take his son to Disneyland. The whereabouts of Kim's middle son, Kim Jong Chol, are unknown.

WORLD RESPONDS

Upon learning of Kim's death, the United States said that it would continue to closely monitor the security situation on the Korean peninsula and the power transfer. The White House renewed its plan to work in cooperation with South Korea to ensure security in the region and remained "committed to stability on the Korean peninsula, and to the freedom and security of our allies." China, one of the North's closest and few allies, expressed shock at Kim's death and said it would continue "active contributions to peace and stability on the Korean peninsula and in this region."

In South Korea, the military was put on high alert, but the public was urged to "go about their usual economic activities." President Lee Myung-bak sent representatives to Beijing to discuss the issue of North Korean power transfer, specifically as it related to the North's nuclear power. Lee also offered his sympathies, but with an aim toward reopening peace talks between the two nations. "The measures we have taken so far are basically aimed at showing North Korea we are not hostile toward the North," said Lee. "An early stabilization of North Korea's system is in the interests of neighboring countries." He continued, "On future relations with North Korea, there is room for exercising as much flexibility as possible. We will discuss the matter with all political parties."

UNLIKELY SUCCESSOR

Shortly after the December 19 announcement of Kim's death, the Workers' Party declared that Kim Jong-un would be the nation's new leader. The statement released by the party called him "the great successor to the revolution" and "eminent leader of the military and the people." KCNA encouraged, "All party members, military men and the public should faithfully follow the leadership of comrade Kim Jong-un and protect and further strengthen the unified front of the party, military and the public." A full transition of power is expected to take months or years but international analysts expect that once in full control, the youngest Kim will rule North Korea much like his father.

Little is known about the successor, who is thought to be in his late twenties and looks similar to his grandfather, the eternal president. Kim Jong-un was born to Kim's now-deceased wife, Ko Yong-hui, the Dear Leader's favorite wife, and spent much of his childhood in Switzerland, where he was educated. Kim Jong-un was not politically active until September 2010 when his father named him a four-star general and vice chair of the Central Military Commission of the Workers' Party. In contrast to his son, Kim Jong-il was already leading the military at the time of his father's death in 1994 and was a powerful force in North Korea. While no such training seemed to be offered to Kim Jong-un, newspaper reports indicate that he received a key position on the powerful National Defense Commission in February 2011.

FUTURE CHALLENGES AND EXPECTATIONS

The political situation in North Korea and its relationship with the world is unlikely to be well established under the new leader for months or years. "Kim Jong-il was the glue that held the system together. We don't know how the system will respond in his absence," said Scott Snyder, a Korea expert with the Council on Foreign Relations. "The only person who had the experience and who held the exclusive power is gone," said Shi Yinhong, an international relations professor at Renmin University in Beijing, noting that everything could change for the nation. But there is hope that Kim's death might mark North Korea's return to nuclear negotiations and a more open relationship with the global community.

In the near term, global leaders will be watching the successor and his uncle, Jan Song-taek, the vice chair of the National Defense Council, who some believe might make an attempt to gain more power. Tension between the North and South is likely to rise, at least temporarily, and there is some expectation that the North might do something to provoke the South to allow the new leader to show that he is in full control of the nation. "We have to be very worried because whenever there is domestic instability North Korea likes to find an external situation to divert the attention away from that—including indulging in provocation," said professor Lee Jung-hoon, who specializes in international relations at Yonsei University in Seoul.

—Heather Kerrigan

Following is a news release from the Korean Central News Agency (KCNA) announcing the death of Kim Jong-il on December 19, 2011; and an announcement from the Central Committee, Central Military Commission of the Workers' Party of Korea, the National Defense Commission of the DPRK, the Presidium of the Supreme People's Assembly, and the Cabinet of the DPRK, in regard to Kim's death and the appointment of his successor, released on December 19, 2011, by KCNA.

North Korea Announces
Kim Jong-il's Death

December 19, 2011

Kim Jong Il, general secretary of the Workers' Party of Korea, chairman of the DPRK National Defence Commission and supreme commander of the Korean People's Army, passed away from a great mental and physical strain at 08:30 December 17, 2011, on train during a field guidance tour.

The WPK Central Committee and Central Military Commission, DPRK National Defence Commission, Presidium of the Supreme People's Assembly and Cabinet released a notice on Saturday informing the WPK members, servicepersons and all other people of his passing away.

SOURCE: Korean Central News Agency of DPRK. "Kim Jong Il Passes Away (Urgent)." December 19, 2011. http://www.kcna.co.jp/item/2011/201112/news19/20111219-02ee.html.

Workers' Party Message on North Korean Succession

December 19, 2011

The Central Committee and the Central Military Commission of the Workers' Party of Korea, the National Defence Commission of the DPRK, the Presidium of the Supreme People's Assembly and the Cabinet of the DPRK on Saturday announced the following notice to all party members, servicepersons and people:

The Central Committee and the Central Military Commission of the Workers' Party of Korea, the National Defence Commission of the DPRK, the Presidium of the Supreme People's Assembly and the Cabinet of the DPRK notify with bitterest grief to all the party members, servicepersons and people of the DPRK that Kim Jong Il, general secretary of the Workers' Party of Korea, chairman of the National Defence Commission of the DPRK and supreme commander of the Korean People's Army, passed away of a sudden illness at 08: 30 on December 17, Juche 100 (2011) on his way to field guidance.

He dedicated all his life to the inheritance and accomplishment of the revolutionary cause of Juche and energetically worked day and night for the prosperity of the socialist homeland, happiness of people, reunification of the country and global independence. He passed away too suddenly to our profound regret.

His sudden demise at a historic time when an epochal phase is being opened for accomplishing the cause of building a powerful and prosperous socialist state and the Korean revolution is making steady victorious progress despite manifold difficulties and trials is the greatest loss to the WPK and the Korean revolution and the bitterest grief to all the Koreans at home and abroad.

Kim Jong Il, who was born as a son of guerillas on Mt. Paektu, the holy mountain of the revolution, and grew up to be a great revolutionary, wisely led the party, the army and people for a long period, performing undying revolutionary feats on behalf of the country, the people, the times and history.

Kim Jong Il possessed of personality and qualifications as a great man on the highest and perfect level was an outstanding thinker and theoretician who led the revolution and construction along the path of steady victories with his profound ideologies and theories and remarkable leadership. He was also peerlessly political elder and outstanding and illustrious commander of Songun and peerless patriot and tender-hearted father of the people who recorded the whole history of the revolutionary struggle with ardent love for the country and its people and noble dedication.

Considering it as his lifelong mission to carry to completion generation after generation the revolutionary cause of Juche started by President Kim Il Sung, Kim Jong Il pushed forward the revolution and construction in line with the idea and intention of the President as the dearest comrade and the most loyal comrade-in-arms of the President.

Kim Jong Il comprehensively developed in depth the immortal Juche idea, Songun idea, fathered by the President and glorified it as the idea guiding the era of independence with his clairvoyant wisdom and energetic ideological and theoretical activities. He firmly defended and carried forward the revolutionary traditions of Mt. Paektu with pure mind, thereby giving a steady continuity to the Korean revolution.

Kim Jong Il, genius of the revolution and construction, developed the party, army and state to be the party, army and state of Kim Il Sung, put the dignity and power of the nation on the highest level and ushered in the golden days of prosperity unprecedented in the nation's history spanning 5,000 years under the uplifted banner of modeling the whole society on the Juche idea.

Kim Jong Il, supreme incarnation of the revolutionary moral obligation, set a great example in perpetuating the memory of President Kim Il Sung unknown in human political history, thus making sure that the august name of the President, his undying revolutionary career and exploits always shine along with the eternal history of Juche Korea.

Kim Jong Il, great master of politics and illustrious commander born of Heaven, honorably defended the socialist gains, noble heritage bequeathed by the President, by dint of Songun politics despite the collapse of the world socialist system, the demise of the President which was the greatest loss to the nation, the vicious offensive of the imperialist allied forces to stifle the DPRK and severe natural disasters. He turned the DPRK into an invincible political and ideological power in which single-minded unity has been achieved and made it emerge a nuclear weapons state and an invincible military power which no enemy can ever provoke.

True to President Kim Il Sung's behest, Kim Jong Il set a gigantic goal to build a prosperous and powerful country and led an all-people general advance for attaining it, thus making the drive for a great revolutionary surge rage throughout the country and bringing about great innovations and leap forward on all fronts of socialist construction.

Kim Jong Il, father of the nation and lodestar of national reunification, led all the fellow countrymen to the road of independence and great national unity with his rock-firm will to implement the instructions of the President for national reunification and ushered in the June 15 era of reunification in which the noble idea of "By our nation itself" is materialized.

As a great guardian of socialism and justice, he conducted energetic external activities for the victory of the socialist cause, global peace and stability and friendship and solidarity among peoples under the uplifted banner of independence against imperialism, thus remarkably raising the international position and prestige of the DPRK and making immortal contributions to the human cause of independence.

In the whole period of his protracted revolutionary guidance, he valued and loved the people very much and always shared weal and woe with them. He continued to make difficult forced march for field guidance, making unremitting efforts and working heart and soul to build a thriving country and improve the standard of people's living. He died from repeated mental and physical fatigue on a train in that course.

The whole life of Kim Jong Il was the most brilliant life of a great revolutionary who covered an untrodden thorny path with his iron will and superhuman energy, holding aloft the red flag of revolution. It was the life of the peerless patriot who dedicated his all to the country and its people.

He passed away to our regret before seeing the victory of the cause of building a thriving nation, the national reunification and the accomplishment of the revolutionary cause of Juche so ardently desired by him, but laid a strong political and military base for ensuring the steady advance of the Korean revolution through generations and provided a solid foundation for the eternal prosperity of the country and the nation.

Standing in the van of the Korean revolution at present is Kim Jong Un, great successor to the revolutionary cause of Juche and outstanding leader of our party, army and people.

Kim Jong Un's leadership provides a sure guarantee for creditably carrying to completion the revolutionary cause of Juche through generations, the cause started by Kim Il Sung and led by Kim Jong Il to victory.

We have the invincible revolutionary army of Mt. Paektu faithful to the cause of the Workers' Party of Korea, the great unity of the army and people closely rallied around the Party, the best Korean-style socialist system centered on the popular masses and the solid foundation of the independent national economy.

Under the leadership of Kim Jong Un we should turn our sorrow into strength and courage and overcome the present difficulties and work harder for fresh great victory of the Juche revolution.

Our army and people will hold leader Kim Jong Il in high esteem forever with unshakable faith and noble sense of moral obligation. True to his behests, they will make neither slightest concession nor delay on the road of the Juche revolution, the Songun revolution but resolutely defend his undying feats and glorify them for all ages.

All the party members, servicepersons and people should remain loyal to the guidance of respected Kim Jong Un and firmly protect and further cement the single-minded unity of the party, the army and the people.

Under the uplifted banner of Songun, we should increase the country's military capability in every way to reliably safeguard the Korean socialist system and the gains of revolution and make the torch lit in South Hamgyong Province, the drive for the industrial revolution in the new century, rage throughout the country and thus bring about a decisive turn in building an economic power and improving the standard of people's living.

We will surely achieve the independent reunification of the country by concerted efforts of all Koreans by thoroughly implementing the Three Charters for National Reunification and the north-south joint declarations.

Our party and people will strive hard to boost friendship and solidarity with the peoples of different countries, guided by the idea of independence, peace and friendship, and build an independent and peaceful, new world free from domination, subjugation, aggression and war.

Arduous is the road for our revolution to follow and grim is the present situation. But no force on earth can check the revolutionary advance of our party, army and people under the wise leadership of Kim Jong Un.

The heart of Kim Jong Il stopped beating, but his noble and august name and benevolent image will always be remembered by our army and people and his glorious history of revolutionary activities and undying feats will remain shining in the history of the country forever.

SOURCE: Korean Central News Agency of DPRK. "Notice to All Party Members, Servicepersons and People." December 19, 2011. http://www.kcna.co.jp/item/2011/201112/news19/20111219-04ee.html.

OTHER HISTORIC DOCUMENTS OF INTEREST

FROM PREVIOUS *HISTORIC DOCUMENTS*

Cumulative Index 2007–2011

*The years in **boldface type** in the entries indicate which volume is being cited. Names starting with al- are alphabetized by the subsequent part of the name.*